ELEMENTARY STATISTICAL METHODS
in Psychology and Education

SECOND EDITION

ELEMENTARY STATISTICAL METHODS

in Psychology and Education

SECOND EDITION

Paul J. Blommers
The University of Iowa

Robert A. Forsyth
The University of Iowa

Houghton Mifflin Company   Boston
Atlanta   Dallas   Geneva, Illinois
Hopewell, New Jersey   Palo Alto   London

TO E. F. LINDQUIST

As an expression of our gratitude
for his contributions to psychological
and educational statistics in general,
and to the development of this book in particular.

Printed in the U.S.A.
Library of Congress Catalogue Card Number: 76-11983
ISBN: 0-395-24340-8

Contents

* *Optional Section*

10 The Normal Probability Distribution 180

11 Introduction to Sampling Theory 207

* *Optional Section*

* Optional Section

INDEX 561

Preface to the Second Edition

The second edition of *Elementary Statistical Methods in Psychology and Education* is a fairly substantial revision of the first edition. The modifications are more of a substantive nature than of a philosophical nature, however. While we have included several new topics and eliminated others, the basic philosophy of the text and accompanying study manual remains the same. Pages xix–xx of the Preface to the First Edition and Chapter 1 of this text outline this philosophy in great detail. We feel that it is extremely important for students to understand the orientation and philosophy of this text and strongly urge all students to read the prefaces to both editions and Chapter 1 carefully.

There are three entirely new chapters in this edition: (1) Chapter 2, "Some Remarks About the Nature of Behavior Science Data"; (2) Chapter 9, "Introduction to Some Probability Concepts"; (3) Chapter 16, "Introduction to Bayesian Inference." Chapter 2 emphasizes the critical importance of good measurements to any research study in psychology and education. The fundamental probability concepts which serve as a foundation for the inferential procedures are presented in Chapter 9. Additional probability ideas also are developed in Chapter 16. Chapter 16 provides students with the basic concepts of Bayesian inference. This chapter discusses fundamental differences between the classical approach and the Bayesian approach to data analysis and presents one relatively elementary Bayesian procedure in some detail.

In addition to these new chapters, the following major changes have been made:

1 Computational procedures for grouped data are deemphasized.
2 Sections related more to educational and psychological measurement than to data analysis have been omitted. E.g., Chapter 7 in the first edition was entitled "Standard Scores." The last several sections of this chapter were concerned with interpreting standard scores from several reference groups, interpreting standard scores derived from different raw score scales, and forming test battery composite scores. In the new edition standard scores are presented merely as an example of the more general and useful concept of linear transformations, and the sections indicated above have been eliminated.

3 Some topics, such as plotting histograms when unequal intervals are used, have been removed from the text and included as supplementary problems in the study manual.

4 Analytical procedures for estimating percentiles and percentile ranks are not presented, except for the estimation of the median.

5 Optional sections (including all proofs) are specifically identified.

6 A discussion of the binomial probability distribution and its applications is included. Also, the use of the normal probability model to approximate the binomial distribution is described.

7 In the first edition, the basic concepts of statistical inference and the sampling error theory (large sample) for means, medians, proportions, differences between means and differences between proportions were treated in Chapter 9 and the use of this theory in hypothesis testing was discussed in Chapter 10. In this second edition, these topics are broken into smaller segments. Chapter 11 presents the basic concepts of statistical inference and the sampling error theory for means, medians, and proportions. Then, Chapter 12 develops the application of this theory in classical hypothesis testing. Chapter 13 then presents the sampling error theory for differences between means and between proportions. Also, the application of this theory in hypothesis testing is included as the second part of Chapter 13. This breakdown into smaller units has proven advantageous in preliminary try-outs of the text.

8 The sampling error theory for the Pearson product moment correlation coefficient is now included immediately after the basic correlation concepts are discussed.

9 One major notational change has been made. For reasons presented on page xxi of the preface to the first edition, the German final ess (s) was used to represent the standard deviation of a set of observed scores. In this second edition we use S to represent the standard deviation.

We have kept the correlation and regression topics at the end of the text. This is contrary to most introductory statistics books which usually include these topics immediately after a discussion of indexes of central tendency and variability. However, we feel very strongly that it is necessary for the student to have encountered the basic inferential concepts before encountering some of the more important topics in correlation and regression. Two of the most fundamental concepts of correlation and regression are (1) "linearity," and (2) "best fitting straight line." In our opinion these concepts are more easily presented and learned if the student has been exposed to the concepts of sampling error and accuracy of estimates.

As with the first edition, our goal of a full detailed presentation has led to a long book in spite of the restrictions placed on topical coverage. We do not believe it to be too long for a one semester course, meeting three or four times per week, since its length derives from the detail of presentation rather than from the multiplicity of concepts treated. For a strictly minimal course it may contain more than can be properly covered. Teachers responsible for such minimal courses will, if they desire to use these materials, find it necessary to either omit certain sections of the book and manual or to make them optional with the student. Such teachers will, of course, wish to decide for themselves precisely which topics should be so treated. However, we suggest for consideration the following sections and/or chapters (sections bear the same numbers in both book and study manual): 9.7, 9.8, 9.9, 10.7, 12.15, 15.11, Chapter 16, 18.12, and, of course, parts or all of the last chapter.

Sections 9.7, 9.8, 9.9, 10.7, and 15.11 involve the binomial probability distribution. While references in other parts of the text may be made to these sections, we doubt that any serious problems will develop if the sections are omitted. Likewise, the Bayesian inference chapter is basically a self-contained unit and can be excluded without difficulty.

A special word of explanation is needed regarding Chapter 5. In this chapter we have defined the various schemes for the symbolic representation of numerical data which are used throughout the book. We had some slight preference for organizing this material into a unit so that if desired it could be assigned or presented as such. We recognize that many teachers may prefer not to present material of this type as a unit. Where this is the case we simply suggest the omission of the chapter as a chapter and the subsequent individual assignment of the sections which comprise it as the need for them first arises.

It is impossible in a book of this type to make proper acknowledgment of the multitude of sources out of which it developed. What former teachers, what writers, what books or articles, what former students led us to adopt this or that mode of presentation is no longer possible for us to say, but to all of them we owe a debt of gratitude. Specifically, we wish to express our appreciation to Dr. E. F. Lindquist, one of the authors of the original book, for the encouragement he has given us to proceed with this revision. We also feel particularly fortunate that Professor Melvin R. Novick consented to write a short elementary exposition of the Bayesian approach to data analysis and to allow us to publish it as a chapter of this book. We are deeply indebted to Professor Anthony Nitko of the University of Pittsburgh who read most of the manuscript and whose criticisms were of great assistance in the final version. In addition, Professors Leonard S. Feldt, H. D. Hoover, and E. James Maxey of the University of Iowa provided many valuable suggestions as the revision developed.

Finally, we are indebted to Professor Egon Pearson (and the Biometrika Trustees) for permission to reprint Tables 1 and 12 from E. S. Pearson and H. O. Hartley, eds. *Biometrika Tables for Statisticians* (3rd edition); to Iowa State University Press to reprint the table of random numbers from G. W. Snedecor and W. Cochran, *Statistical Methods*; to John Wiley and Sons for permission to reprint Table 6.4 from R. L. Thorndike and E. Hagen, *Measurement and Evaluation in Psychology and Education*; and to the University of Iowa to adapt materials from Tables 28 and 29 of G. L. Issacs, D. E. Christ, M. R. Novick, and P. H. Jackson, *Tables for Bayesian Statisticians*.

Paul J. Blommers
Robert A. Forsyth

Preface to the First Edition

This book and the accompanying study manual were designed strictly as *teaching instruments* or *learning aids* for use in a first course in statistical methods. The orientation is toward psychology and education. A fairly adequate notion of the topical coverage can be acquired by skimming the detailed table of contents. The general nature of this book and study manual is described in the introductory chapter (see particularly the first three sections) where it is most likely to be read by the student.

Courses in statistical methods have been regarded as exceedingly difficult by a substantial number of students—even by many who have achieved a high level of success in other aspects of their professional work. This is probably due not so much to an inadequate mathematical background as to lack of practice in close and rigorous thinking. Such students have never learned to pay close attention to precise meanings in their reading, or to strive for high precision in the expression of their own ideas. In an effort to make their courses more palatable to the student, many teachers of statistics have eliminated almost entirely any discussion of mathematical bases, have "simplified" the treatment by glossing over underlying assumptions and important qualifications, have provided rule-of-thumb procedures in the selection techniques and the interpretation of results, and have emphasized the more easily mastered computational procedures rather than the interpretive aspects of the course. In the opinion of the writers, these instructional practices serve only to defeat their very purpose. They not only make it impossible for the student to acquire any real understanding of the techniques and concepts involved, but also deny him the satisfaction which accompanies such understanding and deepen his mystification and frustration by requiring him to memorize and to use stereotyped procedures which he fully realizes that he does not really understand. The result is that in his subsequent use of statistics the student is incapable of reasoning out for himself what procedures are appropriate in novel situations or of exercising critical judgment in the interpretation of results in such situations. These instructional practices evade the real issue, which is that training in the use of precise and rigorous logic is precisely what the student most needs, not just a set of half-understood "recipes" for use in model situations whose counterparts are rarely found in practice—with the discrepancy more often than not going unrecognized.

This book represents an effort to make a relatively few basic statistical concepts and techniques *genuinely meaningful* to the student, through a reasonably rigorous developmental treatment that may be readily understood by the student and which will hold his interest. It is not intended as a general reference book, nor does it include materials for advanced courses. Instead, a relatively small number of basic statistical techniques and concepts have been developed much more thoroughly and systematically than is customary in texts with a wider topical coverage. Recognizing that many students have poor mathematical backgrounds and are unaccustomed to the use of precise and rigorous logic, this book attempts to provide the needed experience in such reasoning, and to develop all necessary concepts from "scratch," taking no more for granted in the student's previous mathematical training than some facility with first-year high school algebra or general mathematics. The result is a much longer book in relation to the topics covered than typifies elementary texts in this field, but it is hoped that the expanded treatment will enable the student to master the concepts in less rather than in more time.

Many students in a first course in statistics are prone to take a passive attitude in the learning process. Upon meeting concepts they do not readily understand, they often resort to the memorization of stereotyped interpretations rather than to a persistent and aggressive effort to discover underlying meanings. The primary purpose of the study manual accompanying this text is to induce the student to assume a more active and aggressive role in learning. The manual is designed to lead the student to discover—or rediscover—for himself many of the important properties of the techniques considered in the text. In it an effort has been made to apply the Socratic method to reinforce the textbook presentations by using a series of leading questions or exercises which will educe many important conclusions from the student himself. To a certain extent the manual is a second presentation of the same concepts in another context—in more of a work-type setting—than is provided in the text. It also provides the student with a means of checking on his understanding and mastery of the textbook materials. An effort has been made in these exercises to reduce computational difficulties to a minimum, and to emphasize interpretational aspects as much as possible.

The question may occur to some readers whether this book and manual are to be regarded as a revision of an earlier set of teaching materials prepared by one of the present authors.* The decision to

*E. F. Lindquist, *A First Course in Statistics* and *Study Manual for A First Course in Statistics* (Boston: Houghton Mifflin Company, 1938; rev. ed., 1942).

prepare this book and manual did grow out of the need for a revision of these earlier materials. It was decided at the outset, however, to provide a new and different treatment in the text, rather than simply revise the earlier book. The study manual, on the other hand, may fairly be regarded as a revision of its predecessor. Many of the exercises used are based upon those appearing in the old manual.

In a perhaps rather stubborn resistance to trend in statistical methods books, we have defined the variance of a sample as the sum of squares divided by N rather than by $N - 1$. The only justification of which we are aware for the latter practice is that certain formulas assume a slightly simpler form. It seems important to us that as early as possible the student be introduced to the distinction between a sample fact (statistic), a population fact (parameter), and a sample estimate of the latter. These concepts are basic in sampling theory, there being no practical way in which the latter (sample estimate) can in all situations be eliminated by the device of defining the statistic as the estimator. Not only does the "best" estimate vary with definition of "best," but, in the case of some parameters, with the form of the population distribution as well. The gain in the simplicity with which certain formulas may be stated seems to us to be too great a price to pay for the loss of one of the best elementary examples of the very distinction we feel it important to make, not to mention the problem of confronting the student with a definition of variance, the logic of which he is at the time unprepared to appreciate. The many writers who have defined sample variance as the unbiased population estimate have, for the most part, used the symbol s^2 to represent this value. In keeping with the practice of using Greek letters to represent parameters and Roman letters to represent statistics, we should have liked to use this symbol to represent the sample variance as we defined it and the symbol $\tilde{\sigma}^2$ to represent the unbiased estimate. However, in deference to the student who, upon turning to another book might misinterpret the meaning of the s^2 he reads there, we requested our publisher to use some distinctive ess, not Greek, in representing sample variance as defined in this book. The character selected was the German final ess (ſ). It is suggested that instructors in presenting material at the blackboard use either the more easily written lower-case script ess or the conventional Roman ess in the sense in which we have used the German ess throughout the text.

Our goal of a full detailed presentation has led to a long book in spite of the restriction placed on topical coverage. We do not believe it to be too long for a beginning one-semester course, meeting three or four times per week, since its length derives from the detail of presentation rather than from the multiplicity of concepts treated. For a strictly minimal course it may contain more than can be properly covered. Teachers responsible for such minimal courses will, if they desire to use these materials, find it necessary to either omit certain sections of the book and manual or to make them optional with the student. Such teachers will, of course, wish to decide for themselves precisely which topics should be so treated. However, we suggest for consideration the following sections (sections bear the same numbers in both book and manual): 3.9, 3.10, 3.11, 3.12, 5.17, 7.10, 8.9, 8.10, 8.12, 8.13, 10.15, 10.22, 13.9, 14.10, 15.6, 15.7, 15.8, and 15.9. In addition, we suggest for the minimal course the possibility of omitting some or even all of the formal proofs or derivations provided in the text.

A special word of explanation is needed regarding Chapter 3. In this chapter we have defined the various schemes for the symbolic representation of numerical data which are used throughout the book. We had some slight preference for organizing this material into a unit so that if desired it could be assigned or presented as such. We recognize that many teachers may prefer not to present material of this type as a unit. Where this is the case we simply suggest the omission of the chapter as a chapter and the subsequent individual assignment of the sections which comprise it as the need for them first arises.

It is impossible in a book of this type to make proper acknowledgment of the multitude of sources out of which it developed. What former teachers, what writers, what books or articles, what former students led us to adopt this or that mode of presentation is no longer possible for us to say, but to all of them we owe a debt of gratitude. Specifically, we are deeply indebted to Professor David A. Grant, of the University of Wisconsin, who read the entire manuscript and whose criticisms were of great assistance in the final revision. We are also deeply indebted to Professor Leonard S. Feldt of the State University of Iowa, who used his classes to try out much of the material and whose valuable suggestions were of great assistance.

Finally, we are indebted to Professor Sir Ronald A. Fisher, Cambridge, to Dr. Frank Yates, Rothamsted, and to Messrs. Oliver and Boyd Ltd., Edinburgh, for permission to reprint parts of Table III from their book, *Statistical Tables for Biological, Agricultural, and Medical Research*; to Cambridge University Press for their permission to reprint Tables 1 and 12 from E. S. Pearson and H. O. Hartley, eds., *Biometrika Tables for Statisticians*; and to the Iowa State College Press for their permission to reprint the table of random numbers from George W. Snedecor, *Statistical Methods*.

Paul J. Blommers
E. F. Lindquist

1

Introduction

1.1 The General Nature of Statistical Methods

Statistical methods are the techniques used to facilitate the interpretation of collections of quantitative or numerical data. The variety of things that people can measure or count and thereby use to generate collections of numerical data is virtually unlimited. These measured or counted things (characteristics, traits, attributes) usually involve groups of individuals or objects, although they may also apply to repeated measurements obtained for a single individual or object. Consider a few examples. The individuals or objects may be the rats in a psychologist's laboratory, the influenza patients in a certain hospital during a given period of time, the pupils in an elementary school classroom, the workers in a particular manufacturing plant, television tubes of a given size and make, the various types of containers in which orange juice is distributed, and so on almost without end. For the groups of individuals and objects just enumerated, there are a number of different counts or measurements in which we might be interested. In the case of the rats, for example, we might want to know the number of times after a period of conditioning that each animal follows a particular path in a Y-maze; in the case of the influenza patients, we might be concerned with periodic measurements of body temperature; with the elementary school pupils, measurements of reading rate might be our chief interest; perhaps we would want to know the workers' gross annual incomes, or the length of life of the television tubes; and in the case of the containers, we might wish to gauge consumer preference as indicated by numbers sold during a given period.

To be of value, such collections of numbers require interpretation. Do the numbers derived for one group tend to be larger than the numbers derived for another similar or related group? Do they tend to vary more in magnitude? Is there anything abnormal about them when compared with similar numbers derived for some base or reference group? These and many other questions may need to be answered. Statistical methods are the techniques used in the attempt to arrive at the required answers.

Books on statistical methods are oriented toward a variety of fields such as business, economics, sociology, political science, geography, medicine, agriculture, and biology. The orientation of this book is toward the fields of psychology and education. This means primarily that most of the examples used to make the material concrete have been drawn from these two fields. Some statistical techniques are of much greater importance in some fields of application than in others, and in some instances a technique may even be unique to a given field of application. But for the most part, statistical techniques are of general applicability and the student who masters them thoroughly will be able to apply them as well in one area as in another. For example, the statistical problems involved in analyzing gains in milk production for a collection of cows fed a certain diet are, by and large, the same as the problems encountered in analyzing a collection of learning scores for a group of college students participating in a psychological experiment or a group of school children engaged in learning some school subject by a particular method of instruction.

Statistical techniques may be classified in different ways. One scheme that has proved helpful in bringing to the beginning student a general overview of the subject is the three-category classification of descriptive statistics, statistical inference, and prediction or regression. A few words should be said about the types of techniques that fall into each of these categories.

It is difficult, if not impossible, to glean pertinent facts from a large, unorganized collection of numerical data. Ways must be found to organize the data, to make summary statements about the general (average) level of magnitude of the numbers involved, to indicate in some way the extent to which these numbers tend to be alike or different in magnitude, and to show how they are distributed in value. Techniques that help to indicate such facts as these regarding a large collection of numbers are descriptive in character and fall into the category of *descriptive statistics.*

Still another type of descriptive statistic has to do with a somewhat different kind of collection of numerical data. This collection consists of pairs of measures for each member of a group of individuals, such as heights and weights for each of a large number of ten-year-old girls. We know from casual observation that some relationship exists between height and weight scores for the same girl. We know, for example, that there is a tendency for girls who are tall to weigh more than girls who are short. But we also can call to mind such exceptions as the tall and thin girl or the short and fat one. Just how strong is this tendency toward relationship? Techniques for assessing the degree of relationship in situations such as this also fall within the category of descriptive statistics.

Many research studies are of a type known as *sampling studies*. In such studies relatively small groups of individuals selected from larger groups are observed, investigated, or treated experimentally. From the results derived from these small groups (samples), inferences are drawn about the large groups (populations). In any such study there is always the possibility that the sample of individuals used may not be truly representative of the population, since chance factors beyond the investigator's control will always determine, to some extent, which individuals constitute the sample used. Hence, any fact derived from a sample must always be considered as only an *approximation* to the corresponding "true" fact—that is, the fact that would have been obtained had the entire population been studied. Under certain conditions of sampling, statistical techniques are available that enable investigators to determine what to expect in the way of error in the inferences about population facts that they make from examining corresponding sample facts. Such techniques represent a very important aspect of statistical methodology and belong to the category of *statistical inference*.

Finally, suppose that for a large group of individuals we know something about the relationship between a variable Y and some other variable X. For example, Y might represent some measure of a person's success as a college student and the other variable, X, some measure of success as a high school student or some measure of general intelligence or scholastic aptitude. Now suppose that we are confronted with some new individuals for whom only the X measure is currently available and that we are required to make for them some estimate or prediction of Y—in this instance, of success as a college student. This prediction problem consists in using our measure for X, together with our knowledge based on previous experience with the relationship between X and Y, to make the best possible estimate of how these new individuals will perform in terms of Y. The statistical methods designed to cope with this problem fall into the category known as *prediction* or *regression*.

Elementary techniques representative of each of these three categories are presented in this text.

1.2 The Major Aspects of Instruction in Statistics

Entirely apart from the major purposes of statistics as categorized in the preceding section, there are three aspects of statistics that have been variously stressed in introductory books on the subject. One of these has to do with the mathematical theory underlying the techniques. A second has to do with the computational procedures involved in the application of the techniques. And a third has to do with the selection of techniques most appropriate for a given purpose and set of data, and with the interpretation of the results.

The foundation of statistical methods is mathematics. The mathematical theory of statistics has, in fact, achieved recognition as an area of specialization in the general field of higher mathematics. No longer is it possible to qualify as a statistics expert and be relatively ignorant of mathematics. It does remain possible, however, to acquire some very useful information regarding the application and interpretations of certain important statistical techniques without studying their mathematical bases. In this book the mathematical bases requiring a background of more than a year or two of senior high school mathematics have been omitted in an effort to make the text understandable and the techniques available even to students having quite meager mathematical training. It is not to be inferred, however, that the treatment is wholly nonmathematical. The foundation of statistics is mathematics, and to divest a presentation of all mathematical aspects would amount to shortchanging students. Such a presentation would leave them ignorant of much of the logic underlying the techniques they are seeking to master, and would render them incapable of critical interpretation. It would also handicap them in any attempt they might make to pursue the study of statistics beyond a most elementary beginning and would leave them quite incapable of consulting many valuable statistical references. This book, therefore, does not avoid all that is mathematical (indeed the student will be expected to think mathematically), but it does require by way of background *only* that degree of mathematical sophistication which it is reasonable to expect of even the most meagerly equipped college student.[1]

The second aspect, that having to do with computational procedures, is also given rather cursory treatment in this volume. A great variety of such procedures have been developed, including many that involve the use of special equipment ranging from pocket electronic calculators to large high-speed computers. These procedures are so varied and often so complex that early consideration of them would only confuse beginning students and interfere with attainment of a real understanding of the principles underlying the techniques. In this book only the most essential, straightforward, and readily understandable computational procedures are considered. The descriptions of these procedures, moreover, are given not so much for the purpose of developing com-

---

[1] The equivalent of at least one year of senior high school mathematics plus a reasonable maturity in arithmetic.

putational skill and facility as for the purpose of contributing toward a fuller understanding of the techniques themselves.

The emphasis in this book, then, is on the third aspect—on developing a knowledge of the appropriate technique to select for a given purpose and a given set of data, and on the critical interpretation of results. For each of the techniques considered, major emphasis will be placed upon such questions as:

> What, within the limits of the mathematical background assumed, are the most significant mathematical properties and characteristics of the technique? What assumptions are involved in applying it?
>
> What specific uses may be made of it? In what types of situations is its application valid?
>
> What are its major advantages and limitations in comparison with other techniques intended for roughly the same purposes?
>
> How may the results of its application be interpreted? How must this interpretation be qualified in the light of considerations that may be unique to the particular application?
>
> What common misinterpretations are to be avoided? What common fallacies in statistical thinking are related to the use of this technique?

In short, this book has to do with the interpretation of statistical techniques. The mathematical theory of statistics and the mechanics of computation are minimized as much as is consistent with this major purpose. There are a number of reasons for this distribution of emphasis. One is that, in general, students in a first course in statistics are not likely to be engaged in any significant amount of research. Nevertheless, while they may not be immediate users of statistical techniques, they are almost certain to be consumers of the uses made by others. Certainly, if students are to attain any real insight into the problems of their fields, if they are to inform and keep themselves informed about the current research investigations and experiments, they must be prepared to read the periodical literature with understanding. If only as preparation for such reading, training in statistics is an essential part of every student's equipment. Without such training much of what students will need to read professionally would be rendered unintelligible by the frequent recurrence of such statistical terms as *variance, standard deviation, standard error, critical region, level of significance, confidence interval, errors of the first and second kind, correlation coefficient, regression coefficient, statistical significance,* etc. To read such material with comprehension, students need have no special skill in computational procedures, but they must be prepared to evaluate critically the uses that others have made of statistical techniques, and must be able to check other workers' conclusions against their own interpretations of the results reported. For the few occasions in which students at this level may need to apply statistical techniques themselves, either the limited computational procedures described in this volume will suffice or directions for the preferred procedures can readily be found in references and handbooks. The student who has achieved an understanding of the essential nature of a technique will have no difficulty in following such directions in these sources. As students progress to a point where they may become engaged in more extensive research of their own, they will in any event find it necessary to proceed to advanced courses in statistics in which the more economical computational procedures involved in large-scale research may be considered at greater length.

1.3   The Nature of This Book and the Accompanying Study Manual

This is a long book, yet it treats only the elementary statistical techniques. Many statistics books that are no greater in length have a much wider topical coverage. Such books are usually intended to serve in a dual capacity as both teaching instruments and general reference books. Because of practical limitations of space, authors of such books frequently find that in order to achieve the topical coverage demanded by a general reference work, they must give many of the topics rather cursory treatment. This book makes no pretense of serving the general reference function. It was written solely as an instructional tool. It is long mainly because it attempts to provide a genuinely complete and detailed presentation of such elementary statistical techniques and concepts as might be regarded appropriate for an introductory course. In deference to the presumed lack of mathematical background of many potential users, the accounts of the techniques and concepts are presented largely in words rather than symbols, a practice that makes for a still longer book. It is believed, however, that the student who will patiently study the sometimes rather lengthy presentations will find this form of treatment a genuine aid toward a mastery of the topics involved.

Furthermore, this book is only one part of what is intended to be a two-way approach to learning statistics. Accompanying the book is a study manual containing problems and questions designed to assist students to rediscover for themselves many of the significant properties, aspects, and underlying assumptions of the concepts and techniques presented in the text. These problems and questions are organized by chapters, and within chapters, in such a way as to follow much the same sequence of presentation as the text itself. They suggest a large number and variety of concrete situations, illustrating the uses and limitations of each technique. Also, they draw attention to how the basic assumptions underlying the derivation of the techniques affect the interpretation of results. By developing these illustrations and by formulating and stating in their own words the generalizations they support, students will in a sense develop a second text of their own writing that will contain many of the important principles and concepts of the original book. It is strongly recommended that the student do the appropriate exercises in the study manual after finishing each section of the text. Properly used, then, the study manual will provide a second presentation of at least some of the major concepts of the book and will greatly enhance the student's learning.

A special effort has been made in both book and manual to develop in the student a critical attitude toward the use of statistical techniques. Special stress has been placed on the limitations of each technique, on the frequent and unavoidable failure of many practical situations to satisfy all the basic assumptions or requirements of each technique, on the manner in which conclusions must be qualified because of such failures, and on prevalent misconceptions and fallacies in statistical reasoning. In a misguided effort to simplify statistics, many of these necessary qualifications have often been ignored in instruction, and students have been provided with a number of rule-of-thumb procedures and stereotyped interpretations. However, because of the numerous exceptions to such procedures and such interpretations, this type of presentation leads to more difficulties in the long run than it helps to avoid. Statistical techniques are an aid to, not a substitute for, common sense. Each technique is designed for a certain purpose and for use under certain conditions only. When these conditions are not satisfied, the application of the technique may and often does lead to conclusions that are obviously contradictory to common sense. It is because of such abuses of statistical techniques that people have developed a distrust of statistics and statisticians. In using these instructional materials, then, students should strive consciously to develop in themselves a highly critical attitude toward statistics and to be constantly vigilant against the tendency to overgeneralize or to depend unduly on stereotyped interpretations.

1.4   Studying Statistics

Many students may be inexperienced in reading material of the type represented by certain sections of this book. Statistics has to do with the analysis of numerical data. Obviously, then, the ideas, concepts, and techniques involved will be quantitative in nature. Since the most efficient method of presenting or dealing with quantitative concepts is through the use of symbols, the exposition will become at times rather heavily symbolic. Relatively few of the students using this book will be experienced in reading materials that deal primarily with quantitative concepts, and fewer still will be practiced in reading material that involves much use of symbolic expression.

Perhaps the thing that most discourages the unpracticed reader of materials of this type is the failure to achieve full comprehension on a first or even a second reading. Many students are accustomed to covering reading assignments with a single reading carried on at a rate of 30 to 40 or more pages an hour. To encounter reading material that requires painstaking study—that indeed may require several readings— is for them a new experience. Unaware that such material often does not come easily even to the most practiced reader, they conclude that the material is beyond their reach and give up their attempt to learn before they are actually well started. They capitulate not because they are unwilling to make the attempt but rather because they fail to realize what the attempt involves.

Possibly the best advice that can be offered to the beginning student of statistics is to slow down. Approach the subject knowing that mastery is not likely to be achieved as the result of a single reading. In studying this book, it is not a bad idea to have a pencil and scratch paper at hand. One of the best ways to check one's understanding of a concept is to verify the results of the illustrative examples. Furthermore, because of the enormous amount of condensation achieved by the use of mathematical symbols, it is always possible, in reading a given formula or symbolic expression, to overlook some crucial notation. Writing the formula down on paper is a good way to fix each element in mind. From time to time students may find it helpful to outline the steps in their own reasoning about a concept or to sketch a diagram or figure as an aid to their own thinking. They may also find it helpful to develop their own glossary of statistical terminology and to write their own summaries of the ideas studied. Such note-taking procedures can prove to be a highly efficient form of "rereading."

In the same way, use of the study manual should be most helpful. The questions and problems in the manual follow the same sectional organization as the text itself. They are designed to lead students to discover for themselves, independently of the text, at least some of the most important ideas presented in the text. At the same time, the exercises allow students to check their mastery of the exposition in the text. It will sometimes happen that students will feel they have fully understood a given section of the text when actually their understanding is incomplete or even erroneous. The study manual provides an important means of checking how adequately and how accurately the underlying concepts have been grasped.

These brief remarks may sound discouraging to beginning students.

However, they are intended not as a threat but as a promise—a promise that if beginning students will approach the unfamiliar with patience, realizing that others like them have faced the same problems and solved them, they will eventually master the field of statistics. They may in time forget the details of a given formula or computational routine, but this should not discourage them; careful statisticians do not trust their memories in such matters. The important point is that once students have achieved an understanding of the general purpose and underlying assumptions of the statistical techniques presented in this book, formulas and computational routines will all fit into a logical whole. Statistics will then become for them not a mysterious jumble of symbols and numbers cluttering up the pages of learned articles and books but rather an instrument for organizing and deepening their perception of the infinitely various collections of enumerated data with which they will continue to be confronted throughout their personal and professional lives.

2

Some Remarks about the Nature of Behavioral Science Data

2.1   Introduction: Variables and Their Measurement

On any given school day, in any given school, questions similar to the following are frequently voiced:

1 "Is Johnny working up to his potential?"
2 "Is Mary alienated from her classmates?"
3 "Is Mike ready to begin the first-level reading series?"
4 "Do the teachers in this building like the new scheduling system?"
5 "Do our students need to spend more time on spelling?"

To answer these questions, information must be gathered that describes John's potential, Mary's alienation, Mike's readiness for reading, teachers' attitudes toward the new scheduling system, and students' achievements in spelling.

In addition to these specific types of questions, the behavioral scientist is also concerned with a multitude of more general questions in a variety of areas. Typical are such questions as:

1 How do children learn?
2 How are the mores of American middle-class society changing?
3 What factors are crucial in determining how voters will vote at a coming election?
4 What personality factors are associated with various abnormalities?

To answer such questions as these, behavioral scientists must use a tremendous variety of information.

What is the nature of the data behavioral scientists use in seeking answers to these and other questions? What are the major problems these researchers face when they attempt to measure characteristics such as "potential," "alienation," "readiness," and "personality"? The primary purpose of this chapter is to examine briefly some of the characteristics of the data the behavioral scientist must collect and analyze. In this section we define variables and the measurement of variables. The next three sections discuss some of the problems related to the measurement of variables and some of the ramifications of these problems for the interpretation of data.

Before we formally define a variable, consider some specific examples of the types of data that behavioral scientists might gather. Listed below are 11 different "types."

1 Annual salaries of 100 teachers in a given school system
2 Numbers of words spelled correctly by 25 third-grade pupils on a weekly spelling test
3 Scores on an introversion-extroversion scale of a personality inventory for a group of 60 mental patients
4 Numbers of books in the libraries of a selected sample of elementary schools in the state of New York
5 Scores for 20 students (ages 11–13) on an instrument that measures "alienation from school"
6 Average lengths of sentences used by third-, fourth-, and fifth-grade pupils in writing a creative paper
7 Times required by 30 fifth-grade students to solve a particular anagram problem
8 Scores for 75 kindergarten students on an instrument that measures "reading readiness"
9 Attitudes of the members of the professional staff of Jefferson High School toward flexible modular scheduling
10 Employment classifications of professional personnel of Jefferson High School
11 Marital status of each of 100 secretaries

Although these examples represent markedly different types of data, implicit in each of them are two factors: (1) the identification of a characteristic or attribute of an individual or object, and (2) the assigning of a "value" or "score" indicative of the presence or amount of this attribute in each individual or object. Formally, characteristics or attributes of persons or objects that can assume different values (scores) for different persons or objects are called *variables.* The process of assigning such values or scores is called *measurement.* Table 2.1 indicates the variable of interest and possible hypothetical "values" or *scores* for each of two individuals or objects as obtained from an

Table 2.1   Variables and Values

Variable of Interest	Two Possible Assigned Values
1 Annual salaries of teachers	$10,000, $10,050
2 Spelling achievement	10 questions correct, 8 questions correct
3 Introversion-extroversion	50 statements checked, 52 statements checked
4 Number of books in a library	1,400 books, 1,010 books
5 Alienation from school	45 statements checked, 49 statements checked
6 Average sentence length	7.2 words, 8.3 words
7 Anagram solution time	20 seconds, 25 seconds
8 Reading readiness	21 questions correct, 32 questions correct
9 Attitude toward flexible modular scheduling	Favorable, unfavorable
10 Employment classification	Classroom teacher, principal
11 Marital status	Unmarried, married

application of the measurement process in the case of each of the 11 examples given above.[1]

Many behavioral scientists would use the word *measurement* to refer only to the assignment of numerical values for continuous attributes.[2] We agree with this position. However, for pedagogical convenience we have chosen a broader and less technical definition.

The measurement process, the process of assigning values for a variable to each member of a group, is often a very complicated procedure. In the next section we differentiate between the two major classes of variables—those whose measurement yields a meaningful ordering of members of a group and those whose measurement does not. In Section 2.3 we pursue the measurement of ordered variables in more detail.

2.2   Unordered and Ordered Variables

Data are often collected for the purpose of classifying people or objects according to membership in some category. For example, consider an

[1] The word *value* (score) is used very loosely in this section and does not necessarily imply numerical value. See, for example, variables 9, 10, and 11 in Table 2.1. Hereafter, we will not use quotation marks as reminders of this usage but will simply leave it as understood.

[2] Continuous attributes can potentially assume any value on an unbroken numerical scale. This notion will be discussed in greater detail in Section 2.4.

investigation into the attitude of school personnel toward a recently instituted flexible modular scheduling system. Such an investigation might involve contrasting the views of men and women classroom teachers. Hence, data regarding sex as well as data pertaining to attitude must be collected.

Variables such as sex are known as *unordered variables*.[3] The reason for the label should be clear. In terms of this variable, there is no underlying dimension on which people can be ordered from high to low or most to least. Measurement of such variables does not yield a meaningful ordering of persons or objects. Another example of an unordered variable is marital status (see, for example, item 11 in Table 2.1). In this instance the possible values (names) are unmarried, married, divorced, or widowed. Again there is no way to order people in terms of the variable in question. In essence, unordered variables provide merely classification-type data.

It is true that numerical values of a sort are sometimes arbitrarily assigned to unordered variables for the purpose of facilitating data analysis. This is particularly true if the data are to be analyzed by computer. Thus, in the case of the marital status variable, the four categories might be coded as follows:

$$1 = \text{unmarried}$$
$$2 = \text{married}$$
$$3 = \text{divorced}$$
$$4 = \text{widowed}$$

These numbers serve merely as identification codes that may be punched in computer cards so that responses to other questions or items may be collated with marital status.

Ordered variables, as the name implies, are variables that yield a dimensional ordering of individuals or objects. For example, it seems logical to think that teachers' attitudes toward flexible modular scheduling will not only differ but also vary in degree. Some teachers will have favorable attitudes of varying intensity, others unfavorable attitudes; still others may be more or less neutral. Thus, it is possible to consider an ordering of teachers along the dimension of attitudes from favorable to unfavorable. Or consider the number of books in a school library. Some school libraries contain more books than others, so schools can be ordered on this variable. Similarly, for the variable "anagram solution time," it is again reasonable to conceptualize pupils as being ordered (ranked) from fast to slow. Examples 1, 2, 3, 5, 6, and 8 in Table 2.1 represent other possible ordered variables.

Thus far in our discussion of ordered variables, no mention has been made of the problem of the measurement of such variables. It is clear

---

[3] Other labels for variables of this type are *categorical* and *nominal*.

that in some of the examples cited the measurement process is very simple. The measurement of the variable "number of books in a library" merely requires a counting of books. The measurement of variables 1, 6, and 7 in Table 2.1 is also straightforward. However, the development of appropriate procedures for the measurement of such variables as attitude toward flexible modular scheduling, alienation from school, or reading readiness involves complex technical problems. A comprehensive treatment of such measurement procedures is beyond the scope of this book. In the next section, however, we do mention some of these problems, briefly, for the sake of alerting students to a matter of critical importance in research, particularly in research in the behavioral sciences.

2.3   The Measurement of Ordered Variables: Some Considerations

The basic purpose of measurement is to differentiate among individuals or objects with regard to the amount of some variable. To accomplish this differentiation, a set of rules for assigning values indicative of such amounts must be developed. Some such sets of rules are easily derived and understood. Rules for the measurement of such variables as height, weight, time, and income, for example, are widely known and understood. Varying units of measurement may be used, but the procedures are well defined regardless of the units chosen. The behavioral scientist, by contrast, is frequently called upon to work with variables for which the rules for assigning values are not easily defined. How, for example, are such variables as introversion, alienation from school, reading readiness, or attitude toward flexible modular scheduling to be measured? A possible procedure involves two steps: (1) the development of a *conceptual definition* of the variable, and (2) the development of an *operational definition* of the variable that, it is hoped, bears a close, if not a one-to-one, relationship to the conceptual definition. Conceptual definitions are usually relatively abstract, whereas operational definitions are more concrete and usually embody a specification of the operations (rules) involved in the measurement of the variable. Perhaps an example will make these ideas more meaningful.

Consider the variable "alienation from school." Conceptually this might be defined as "the tendency to exhibit negative feelings toward the school."[4] Operationally, alienation might be measured by giving a list of, say, 100 statements about school to each pupil. For example, one such statement might read, "School is a good place to make new

---

[4] This, of course, is not the only possible conceptual definition.

friends." Each pupil would be directed to indicate agreement or disagreement with this statement. An indication of disagreement would be counted as a negative response. The total number of negative responses to the 100 statements would then be the value (score) assigned to each pupil for the variable "alienation from school." Clearly this measurement procedure will lead to differentiation among pupils—one may give 30 negative responses, another 20, and so on. Thus, the basic purpose of the measurement has been accomplished. However, there remains the question, "How useful are the values thus obtained?" Students familiar with the terminology of educational and psychological measurement will recognize that this question relates to the *reliability* and *validity* of the values. Two questions that might be raised are:

1 If a second set of 100 different but similar statements had been used would the pupils have been ordered in a similar way?
2 Is the ordering of pupils by this technique the same as an ordering based on a different operational definition of alienation?

Using a different operational definition, for example, we might simply ask the teacher to rank the pupils according to the degree of alienation they exhibit in their behavior and then assign each pupil a value corresponding to his or her rank. Would the results of these two procedures for ordering pupils from high to low alienation agree?

As stated previously, an adequate treatment of this and other similar questions pertaining to the development of procedures for measuring variables, and to the reliability and validity of the values they provide, is beyond the domain of this book.[5] In this book we deal only with techniques for analyzing numerical data, that is, for analyzing the scores or values obtained from an application of a measurement process. Nonetheless, it is important for the student to be hypersensitive to the fact that unless the values we analyze are meaningful, no analysis we can make, however erudite, can be of any value. This point cannot be overemphasized. The widespread availability of computers makes extremely complicated statistical analyses easy to effect. But even the most sophisticated analysis cannot make "good" data out of "bad." A statement frequently made in the computer field is applicable: "Garbage in; garbage out." Unless the measuring process provides good data, any analysis of the numbers is fruitless.

Throughout this book it is assumed that the data we are analyzing were produced by application of reliable and valid measurement procedures. However, the student should never lose sight of the basic

---

[5] The student is encouraged to read Chapter 6 of *Measurement and Evaluation in Psychology and Education* (3d ed.) by R. L. Thorndike and E. Hagen (Wiley, New York, 1969) for a more detailed discussion of reliability and validity.

fact that the reliable and valid measurement of the variables in question represents the first and perhaps the most critical step in any investigation.

2.4   Discrete and Continuous Data

In the previous section we examined briefly the measurement of ordered variables. In this section we examine two types of data that arise from making such measurements.

Continuous data arise from the measurement of continuous attributes or variables. An attribute, or trait, or characteristic, or variable is said to be *continuous* if it is possible for the *true* amount of it possessed by an individual or object to correspond to any conceivable point or value within at least a portion of an unbroken scale. Any trait in which individuals may conceivably differ by infinitesimal amounts is thus a continuous trait. Weights or heights of children, for example, may correspond to any conceivable value within a portion of an uninterrupted scale, and hence are examples of continuous variables or attributes. Intelligence, school achievement, arithmetic ability, spelling ability, personal adjustment, attitude toward flexible modular scheduling, strength, temperature, blood pressure, and alienation from school are further examples of continuous variables.

Discrete data, on the other hand, are characterized by gaps in the scale—gaps for which no real values may ever be found. Thus, though we hear such statements as "the average family has 2.7 children," we know that in reality children come only in discrete quantities. Discrete data are usually expressed in whole numbers (integers) and ordinarily represent counts of indivisible entities. Sizes of families, school enrollments, numbers of books in various libraries, and census enumerations are examples of discrete data.

The determining factor in distinguishing between continuous and discrete data is the continuity of the attribute or trait involved and *not* the continuity of the measurements reported. *Taken as a measurement of spelling achievement*, the numbers of words correctly spelled by a group of third-grade students are regarded as continuous data even though they represent counts of indivisible entities, because the trait involved is a matter of gradual continuing growth and development and the true spelling ability of an individual may be regarded as falling at any point along an unbroken scale. Since two individuals may differ with respect to a continuous attribute by an infinitesimal amount, and since it is humanly impossible to detect such differences, it follows that all measurements of continuous attributes must necessarily be approximate. It is for this reason that the measurements themselves do not provide a basis for distinguishing between discrete and continuous data.

No matter how precisely we measure, our inability to distinguish between points on the scale that are separated by infinitesimal amounts implies the inevitable existence of unassignable gaps between the very closest measurements we are able to take.

In a more concrete manner, we can say that if the variable being measured is discrete, then any two individuals (or objects) with the same measurement are absolutely identical (with respect to this variable). Thus, if the Stony Brook Elementary School library has 620 books and the Roosevelt Elementary School library has 620 books, these two schools are absolutely identical with respect to the *number* of books in their libraries. (Of course, the quality of books could differ.) On the other hand, if the measurements are continuous, two individuals assigned the same value may not be absolutely identical in terms of the variable being measured. For example, if Bill and John both receive a weight score of 125 pounds, it does not necessarily follow that their weights are precisely equal.

Ordinarily, measurements of continuous variables are reported to the nearest value of some convenient unit. Weights, for example, are usually read to the nearest pound, or ounce, or gram, or centigram, depending on the degree of precision required. Thus, when a person weighs herself and finds that the pointer on the scale is closer to 126 than to 125, she reads her weight as 126. When a person gives his weight as 181 pounds, we interpret this to mean that his real weight is nearer 181 than 180 or 182 pounds—that it is actually somewhere between 180.5 and 181.5. Similarly, heights are measured to the nearest inch, or sometimes to the nearest half or quarter of an inch, and performance in the hundred-yard dash is timed to the nearest tenth of a second. These values in terms of which measurements are read or reported are known as *units of measurement*.

Occasionally measurements of continuous variables are reported to the *last* instead of the nearest value of the unit involved. In the collecting of chronological age data, for example, it is the usual practice to express an individual's age in terms of the number of years on his last birthday. Thus, the actual age of a boy whose reported age is 13 years may be anywhere from 13 up to, but not including, 14 years, i.e., from 13 to 13.99 years. Similarly, "five years of teaching experience" could, as such data are often recorded, correspond to an actual period of experience anywhere from 5 to 5.99 years in length.

Actually, insofar as data analysis is concerned, the distinction between discrete and continuous data is not critical. The differentiation is made here more for the sake of an in-depth understanding of the nature of data than for any practical considerations. In fact, in this text, aside from some brief remarks in Chapters 3, 4, 9, 10, and 15, no distinction will be made in the statistical treatment of continuous and discrete data.

2.5   Summary Statement

The behavioral scientist must deal with a large assortment of variables. For some of these variables—people's heights, for example—the measurement procedure is well defined. For others, however, the particular measurement procedure adopted by one person may not be accepted by others. Would our paper and pencil procedure for measuring alienation from school meet with general acceptance?

The values obtained from the measurement of certain types of variables merely classify objects or persons into categories. Religious preference is such a variable. For other variables, such as number of teachers in selected school districts, the measurement procedure yields values that enable the persons or objects to be ordered. The measurement of these ordered variables yields two different types of data: continuous, and discrete. Although differences between continuous and discrete data are of some importance in a technical treatment of statistical methods, these differences are not of great concern in this book.

The most important concept in this chapter is that good measurements are essential to any data analysis procedure. Even the most sophisticated statistical analysis cannot overcome deficiencies in the quality of the measurements involved. Hence, one of the first steps in any investigation should be the development of appropriate measuring procedures. Similarly, in any critical analysis of a research study one of the first considerations is the appropriateness of the measuring procedures. Often it is not easy to evaluate the quality of the measures used in an investigation. Nor is it easy to describe the methods and procedures commonly used for assessing the validity and reliability of the data employed in a given research study. In this chapter we have introduced the concepts of reliability and validity only at the most superficial level. Our objective was not so much to make the student knowledgeable about these measurement issues as to simply make the student aware of the crucial role that measurement plays in statistical data analyses.

Such measurement issues are of utmost importance, but they are not the subject of this book and hence, will not be considered in any detail in the chapters that follow. Throughout the remaining chapters we assume that "good" measurements have been obtained. Our concern will be restricted to the appropriate statistical analysis of these good data.

3
The Frequency Distribution

3.1 Introduction

The graphical representation of numerical data is a device commonly employed by the mass media. Newspapers, weekly news magazines, and television news programs frequently use graphs to present a wide variety of types of data. The major purpose of such graphs is to present a visual summary of a collection of numbers—numbers that may pertain to commodity prices, to the time to relief produced by various analgesics, to fluctuations in the stock market, to the production of steel, to college enrollment trends, to college cost trends, and so on, and so on. Just as different readers may form different interpretations of textual material, different viewers may draw different conclusions from the visual impressions that graphical materials portray. Later in this chapter we will discuss some of the tricks that have been used to "lead" the viewer to a particular conclusion.

Only a few of the many available types of graphs are necessary for developing the statistical concepts treated in this book. We will discuss these in this and in the following chapter. First, however, it will be useful to discuss procedures for organizing a collection of numbers (data) in such a way as to facilitate interpretation. The next two sections of this chapter thus treat problems that pertain to the construction and interpretation of the so-called frequency distribution table. The remaining sections treat the construction of selected types of graphs as well as the use of such graphs in analyzing selected problems.

3.2   Rationale for and Construction of Frequency Distributions

The first step in any analysis of a set of data is to examine it in detail. Some data are easy to arrange or organize in such a way as to greatly facilitate examination. Consider, for example, a set of data obtained from a group of 100 parents who indicated their opinion regarding the influence that participation in athletics has on the moral character of children by checking one of the following:

Athletics has
_____   a strong positive influence on moral character.
_____   a slight positive influence on moral character.
_____   no influence on moral character.
_____   a slight negative influence on moral character.
_____   a strong negative influence on moral character.

One way to organize these data to facilitate their examination consists simply of indicating the number of parents checking each category. Table 3.1 shows one possible set of results. With the data so organized, it is easy to make descriptive statements about this group of parents. One such statement might be: 65 out of the 100 parents responding (or 65 percent) viewed participation in athletics as having a positive influence on the moral character of children.

The data in this example were relatively easy to organize in a fashion that shows at a glance how parents as a group feel about the effect of athletic participation on moral character. However, often in the behavioral sciences the data of interest are more difficult to organize. As an example, consider the scores of 100 high school pupils' reactions to the 200 items of an instrument designed to measure "alienation from school." (A possible form such an instrument might take was described in Chapter 2.) These scores are shown in Table 3.2.

The possible scores on this instrument range from 0 to 200. As the data are given in Table 3.2, generalizations about the scores actually

Table 3.1   Responses of 100 Parents to Statement Regarding Influence of Athletics on Moral Character

Response	Frequency of Response
Strong positive influence	30
Slight positive influence	35
No influence	20
Slight negative influence	10
Strong negative influence	5

Table 3.2   Scores of 100 High School Pupils on the
Alienation from School Instrument

132	126	87	94	97	191	174	105	133	139
171	93	112	123	106	85	105	80	93	63
138	179	95	137	88	112	170	87	154	120
56	82	131	126	141	89	92	109	138	121
164	156	121	89	146	146	163	131	75	115
137	146	56	94	102	90	71	110	134	150
159	92	65	79	126	153	112	159	132	65
139	120	147	68	102	101	96	148	108	152
153	138	93	128	92	98	108	112	67	68
145	86	112	83	103	76	157	96	134	96

obtained are difficult to make. For example, questions such as the following are difficult to answer

1 What is the most frequently occurring score?
2 How widely are the scores spread out along the possible score scale?
3 Is there anything unusual about the pattern of the score distribution?
4 What is the "middle" score?
5 Where do most of the scores tend to concentrate?

However, it would be relatively easy to organize these data into a distribution similar to that of Table 3.1 by listing the possible scores from the highest actual score to the lowest and then indicating the frequency of each. Table 3.3 shows such a distribution. In this table X is used to represent a score value and f the frequency with which it occurs. It is immediately evident that this arrangement of the data facilitates interpretation. The most frequently occurring score (112) is easily determined, as are the segments of the scale in which the scores tend to be most heavily concentrated. The total number of scores may be quickly checked simply by adding the numbers in the frequency column, and the number of scores between any given values can likewise be readily obtained by simple addition. But most important is the fact that this form of table shows clearly how the scores are *distributed* along the score scale. This last advantage would be more evident were the table not so bulky and were the scores arranged in a single vertical column (which is the usual practice) instead of six separate columns as the limitations of space here necessitated.

The bulkiness of Table 3.3 is a serious disadvantage, particularly when the data are to be presented as part of a research report. With the scores distributed over so wide a range, considerable space is needed to list all possible values. The presentation is strung out and certain

Table 3.3 Frequency Distribution of the Alienation Scores of Table 3.2

X	f	X	f	X	f	X	f	X	f	X	f
191	1	168		145	1	122		99		76	1
190		167		144		121	2	98	1	75	1
189		166		143		120	2	97	1	74	
188		165		142		119		96	3	73	
187		164	1	141	1	118		95	1	72	
186		163	1	140		117		94	2	71	1
185		162		139	2	116		93	3	70	
184		161		138	3	115	1	92	3	69	
183		160		137	2	114		91		68	2
182		159	2	136		113		90	1	67	1
181		158		135		112	5	89	2	66	
180		157	1	134	2	111		88	1	65	2
179	1	156	1	133	1	110	1	87	2	64	
178		155		132	2	109	1	86	1	63	1
177		154	1	131	2	108	2	85	1	62	
176		153	2	130		107		84		61	
175		152	1	129		106	1	83	1	60	
174	1	151		128	1	105	2	82	1	59	
173		150	1	127		104		81		58	
172		149		126	3	103	1	80	1	57	
171	1	148	1	125		102	2	79	1	56	2
170	1	147	1	124		101	1	78			
169		146	3	123	1	100		77			

meaningful characteristics of the collection of scores still remain rather difficult to grasp. This fact suggests that the interpretation would be further facilitated if we were to condense Table 3.3 by indicating the number of scores falling within equal *intervals* along the score scale instead of indicating the number of times each integral value occurs. This has been done for four different interval sizes in Table 3.4. For each distribution in this table the frequency value indicates the total number of scores contained in the corresponding interval. In this table intervals of size 5, 10, 20, and 50 have been used. Other interval sizes could, of course, have been employed. The degree of compactness of a table of this kind depends on the size of interval used.

Table 3.4 differs in one fundamental respect from Table 3.3. In Table 3.3 the exact value of *each* score is indicated. In Table 3.4 we lose in varying degrees the identity of the original scores. For example, we may read in Distribution B of Table 3.4 that there are 15 scores in the interval 90–99, but we have no way of telling from this table how these 15 scores are distributed within the interval. We are, therefore, unable to determine from this distribution the exact frequency of occurrence of any single score value. However, we can now more conveniently derive

Table 3.4   Frequency Distributions of the Alienation Scores of Table 3.2 (Intervals of Five, Ten, Twenty, and Fifty Units)

A. Intervals of 5 Units		B. Intervals of 10 Units	
X	f	X	f
190–194	1	190–199	1
185–189	0	180–189	0
180–184	0	170–179	4
175–179	1	160–169	2
170–174	3	150–159	9
165–169	0	140–149	7
160–164	2	130–139	14
155–159	4	120–129	9
150–154	5	110–119	7
145–149	6	100–109	10
140–144	1	90–99	15
135–139	7	80–89	10
130–134	7	70–79	4
125–129	4	60–69	6
120–124	5	50–59	2
115–119	1	**C. Intervals of 20 Units**	
110–114	6		
105–109	6	X	f
100–104	4	180–199	1
95–99	6	160–179	6
90–94	9	140–159	16
85–89	7	120–139	23
80–84	3	100–119	17
75–79	3	80–99	25
70–74	1	60–79	10
65–69	5	40–59	2
60–64	1	**D. Intervals of 50 Units**	
55–59	2		
		X	f
		150–199	16
		100–149	47
		50–99	37

in a general way an adequate idea of how the scores are distributed over the entire range. We may note, for example, a tendency for the scores to cluster or to be most heavily concentrated in two rather widely separated intervals, namely, 90–99 and 130–139. Moreover, the scores show a tendency to diminish in frequency to a minimum, or low point, at the interval midway between these two, while below and above, the frequencies taper off gradually to values of 2 and 1 for the extreme intervals. This picture of the scores as a group is more readily discernible from Distribution B of Table 3.4 than from Distribution A, where the number of intervals is considerably greater and the intervals themselves are narrower. The picture is also clearer in Distribution B than in Distribution D, where most of the scores fall in a single 50-unit interval and the bimodal character of the distribution of scores (that is, the fact that the scores are concentrated in two separated intervals) is obscured. In general, the coarser the interval, the greater the loss of identity of individual scores.

The size of the interval to be used is a matter of arbitrary choice, dependent on the nature of the data and the uses to which the table is to be put or the kinds of interpretations one desires to draw from it. If high precision in description is desired, if fluctuations in frequency over small parts of the range are to be studied, and if the number of scores tabulated is large enough to permit such detailed study, then the interval used should be as small as 3 or 5; even a 1-unit interval may be justified, as in Table 3.3. If, on the other hand, only a very rough picture of the distribution of scores is needed, an interval as broad as 20, or even 50 (see Distributions C and D of Table 3.4), may prove quite satisfactory. Of course, if the number of possible distinct score values is small (see, for example, Table 3.1), questions of grouping are not relevant. In such instances the frequency at each score value can easily be shown.

The purpose of the preceding discussion has been to point out briefly and simply some of the major purposes, advantages, and limitations of a technique for presenting a mass of numerical data that is known as the *frequency distribution*. A frequency distribution may be defined as *a technique for presenting a collection of classified objects in such a way as to show the number in each class.* The word *class* as used in this definition corresponds to the word *interval* (or score value) as used in the foregoing discussion; the word *object* corresponds to the word *score*. To *classify* an object is to identify the class to which it belongs. The words *object* and *class* are somewhat more general in that they extend the scheme to application with unordered data (see Table 3.5) and to ordered data without numerical values (see Tables 3.1 and 3.6). The name *frequency distribution* is clearly appropriate since the scheme

Table 3.5   Frequency Distribution of Marital Status for a Group of 70 Teachers

Marital Status	f
Married	43
Single	18
Divorced	4
Widowed	5
TOTAL	70

Table 3.6 Frequency Distribution of Ratings of
Management by 100 Employees

Rating	f
Superior	12
Excellent	22
Very good	21
Fair	21
Satisfactory	14
Barely satisfactory	7
Unsatisfactory	3
TOTAL	100

shows the *frequency* with which the objects are *distributed* among the
various classes.

It is clear that a frequency distribution consists of two basic elements:
(1) the description, identification, or definition of the classes, and (2)
the frequency counts associated with each class. Given the definitions
of the classes, it is usually nothing more than a matter of clerical labor
to classify and count the scores or objects to determine the *f*-values.
The task of defining the classes, however, is another matter. It should
be clear from the foregoing discussion that no general rule concerning
the sizes of the intervals or classes can be appropriate for all purposes
or for all types of data. It is here, then, that judgment enters, and, as
with most situations calling for sound judgment, it is here that difficulty
begins. It is impossible to anticipate all the purposes for which frequency distributions might possibly be employed as well as all conceivable types of data that might be involved. The ability to arrive at sound
judgments can come only with training and experience, and neither of
these alone can take the place of constant alertness for the unusual. In
Section 3.6 we shall consider the detailed questions that arise in the
construction of frequency distributions intended for certain specific
uses or involving certain specific types of data.

3.3   Continuous Data: Effect on Class Limits

The distinction between continuous and discrete variables was discussed
in some detail in Section 2.4. The primary purpose of this section is to
indicate the minor modifications in the interpretation of frequency
distributions that follow as the result of this distinction.

Consider a frequency distribution of weights to the nearest pound.
An interval identified by the integral limits 160 and 164 must be considered as *really* extending from 159.5 to 164.5 pounds. The value 160

represents any real, or true, or actual weight from 159.5 to 160.5 pounds and 164 any real weight from 163.5 to 164.5. Hence, whenever measurements are taken to the *nearest* value of the unit involved, the *real limits* of a class or interval in a frequency distribution should be considered as extending one-half of a unit on either side of the *integral limits.* The so-called integral limits are actually not limits at all, but only the highest and lowest unit points *within* the interval. In fact, the measurements may be reported in such a way that these integral limits are not even expressed as integers or whole numbers. Suppose, for example, that measurements of length are taken to the nearest one-fourth of an inch and that an interval or class in a frequency distribution is identified as extending from $59\frac{1}{4}$ to $60\frac{3}{4}$ inches. These values are, of course, integral limits. The real limits, which extend one-half of a unit (i.e., one-half of one-fourth) on either side of these values, are $59\frac{1}{8}$ and $60\frac{7}{8}$ inches, respectively.[1]

If measurements of continuous variables are reported to the last unit (see Section 2.4) instead of the nearest unit, then a slightly different specification of the real limits is necessary. For example, consider the questionnaire item: "How many years of teaching experience do you have? (Answer in terms of years completed.)" The response "16" could represent an actual period of experience anywhere from 16 to 16.99 years in length. For such measures the integral measure is considered as the lower real limit of the unit interval.

The real limits of an interval or class in a grouped frequency distribution involving such data would have to be considered as extending from the lowest unit point in the interval up to, *but not including*, the lowest point in the next higher interval. Thus, the real limits of the interval 16–17 would in this case be 16 and 17.99. Clearly, how an interval in a grouped frequency distribution should be interpreted depends on how the data were collected or the measurements were made.

We have noted previously that when we present a collection of measures in a grouped frequency distribution, we sacrifice information regarding their individual values. On the other hand, the grouping of data is sometimes necessary. When data are so organized it is often desirable to be able to offer some indication of the values of the scores in an interval. Perhaps the simplest and most common practice is that of using the interval midpoint as a token value for—or an *index* of—the values of the scores classified in that interval. This practice has led to the use of the term *index value* to mean interval midpoint. The

---

[1] Of course, the integral limits always represent a whole or integral number of whatever unit may be involved. Thus, in the foregoing example the integral limits are 237 and 243 quarter-inches, while the real limits are 236.5 and 243.5 quarter-inches.

midpoint, or index value, of any interval is always the point midway between the real limits, regardless of the manner in which the measurements have been taken. In the case of measurement to the nearest unit, the midpoint of the interval 16–17 would be halfway between 15.5 and 17.5, at 16.5. On the other hand, if the measurements had been recorded as of the last unit, the midpoint of this interval would be halfway between 16 and 17.99, at 17.

It would appear, because of the discontinuous character of discrete data, that the preceding suggestions for determining real limits and midpoints may not be applied when the data are discrete. Some writers, in fact, have given special consideration to the construction and interpretation of frequency distributions of discrete data, and have described modified procedures for their treatment. These modifications, however, are rarely, if ever, of any great practical consequence. In this book, therefore, no distinction will be made in the statistical treatment of continuous and discrete data, with reference to the frequency distribution.

3.4 Graphical Representation of Frequency Distributions: Histograms and Frequency Polygons

This section describes two of the schemes most commonly used for presenting pictorially, or graphically, the same information about the distribution of scores that we have until this point been presenting in tabular form.

The first of these schemes is the *histogram*.[2] In this scheme the scale of values of a variable is marked off along a horizontal line. Rectangles are then constructed above the intervals or classes. The height of each rectangle is equal to the frequency of scores in the interval or class.[3] This type of representation is illustrated in Figure 3.1. The histogram in Figure 3.1 is based on the frequency distribution shown in Table 3.4B.

The vertical and horizontal scales of the figure are known as the *axes*. In Figure 3.1 the scale along the vertical axis is that along which the frequencies of the individual intervals or classes are represented. It is referred to as the *frequency scale*. The horizontal scale is likewise divided into a number of equal units, each of which corresponds to a unit of whatever scale has been employed to measure the attribute

---

[2] You may have previously encountered this type of graph under the label *bar graph* in your high school mathematics courses.

[3] For most of the data that you will meet, the height of the rectangle can be made equal to the frequency. However, as we will illustrate in exercise 3.6.16 of the study manual, there are exceptions to this rule.

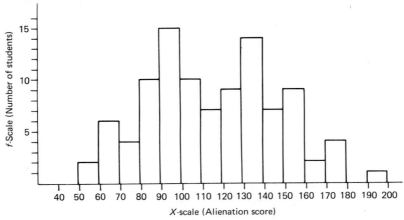

Figure 3.1   Histogram of Distribution B in Table 3.4

involved—in this case, alienation from school. This scale is referred to as the attribute scale, or *score scale*.

The manner in which a histogram representing a distribution involving equal intervals is constructed is too obvious to warrant detailed explanation. The *f*-scale is marked off to provide for the largest class frequency in the distribution. Unlike the *X*-scale, *this scale should always begin with zero*, for to start this scale with a value greater than zero would not only cut off a part of the picture but also make it impossible to compare the magnitudes of the frequencies in the different intervals by noting approximately how many times higher (or longer) one rectangle is than another. (More will be said about this point in Section 3.8.) Although it is common practice to mark off the *X*-scale in such a way as to allow an extra empty interval or two at each end of the distribution, there is no need to extend this scale to zero. To do so would often result in the presentation of a long portion of the scale where no measures or scores fall. It should be noted that the use of squared (graph) paper will usually make it easier to mark off these scales and draw the rectangles.

The second type of graphical representation is the *frequency polygon*. The frequency polygon in Figure 3.2 is based on the same distribution as the histogram of Figure 3.1.

The frequency polygon may be considered as having been derived from the histogram: if straight lines were drawn joining the midpoints of the tops of adjacent rectangles in Figure 3.1, these lines would form the polygon of Figure 3.2. The polygon may, of course, be constructed without reference to the histogram. A dot is made directly above the midpoint of each interval at a height equal to the frequency of the

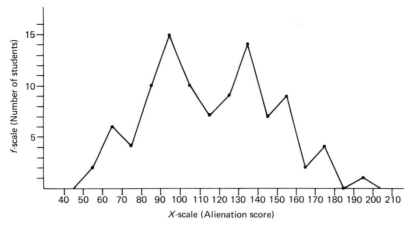

Figure 3.2 Frequency polygon of Distribution B in Table 3.4

interval. When successive dots are joined with straight lines, the polygon is formed. The figure is closed when the X-scale is extended to include the empty intervals at each extreme of the distribution. The dot for these two intervals goes at zero height above their midpoints, to correspond to their zero frequency values.

3.5 Using Histograms and Frequency Polygons to Identify Common Forms of Score Distributions

Histograms and polygons are usually constructed for the simple purpose of displaying in the most readily interpretable manner an overall picture of the way the scores are distributed along the score scale. They reveal, at a glance, what we shall refer to as the *form* of the distribution. There are a variety of ways or forms in which scores or measures may be distributed along a scale.

Figure 3.3 shows eight different histograms. While each pictures a purely hypothetical data set, the fact remains that each is representative of a type of data set that may be encountered in the real world. To reduce the possible skepticism with which this assertion may be greeted, examples of the types of measures that could give rise to these distributions are given in Table 3.7.

Later discussion will be greatly facilitated if some of the more common types of distributions can be identified by name. First, it should

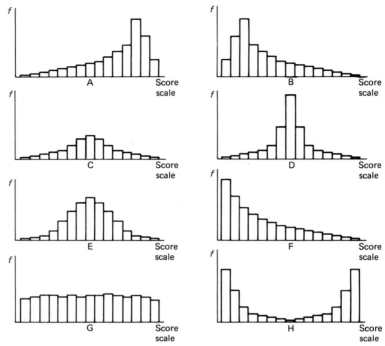

Figure 3.3   Histograms showing various forms of frequency distributions

be noted that distributions may be classified as either symmetrical or skewed. A distribution is _symmetrical_ if the polygon or histogram representing it can be folded along a vertical line so that the two halves of the figure coincide. Histograms C, D, E, and H of Figure 3.3 are illustrations of symmetrical distributions. If relatively minor fluctuations are disregarded, Distribution G may also be classified as symmetrical.

If the measures are not symmetrically distributed—that is, if they tend to be thinly strung out at one end of the score scale and piled up at the other—the distribution is said to be _skewed_. Distributions A, B, and F of Figure 3.3 are examples of skewed distributions. Two types of skewness are possible. If the scores are thinly strung out toward the right or upper end of the score scale and piled up at the lower end, the distribution is said to be skewed to the right or _positively skewed_. When the situation is reversed, the distribution is skewed to the left or _negatively skewed_. Distributions B and F of Figure 3.3 are positively skewed, and Distribution A is negatively skewed. Note that the direction or type of skewness is determined by the side on which the

Table 3.7   Measures That Would Give Rise to the Types of Histograms Shown in Figure 3.3

Histogram	Description of Distributions
A	A distribution of scores on an "easy" arithmetic test
B	A distribution of scores on a "hard" arithmetic test
C, D, or E	A distribution of scores on an arithmetic test of "medium" difficulty
F	The distribution of family incomes in a particular city
G	A distribution of monthly incidence of infant mortality in a large modern hospital
H	A distribution of ages at time of death of pedestrians killed by automobiles

scores are stretched out rather than by the side on which they are concentrated.

When the scores of a distribution are clearly more heavily concentrated in one interval than in any other, the distribution is said to be *unimodal*. In Figure 3.3, Distributions A, B, C, D, E, and F are all unimodal: A, B, and F are unimodal and skewed, while C, D, and E are unimodal and symmetrical. Note that all unimodal and symmetrical distributions are not identical. Histograms C, D, and E in Figure 3.3 are unimodal and symmetrical but exhibit various degrees of *flatness* or *peakedness*.

When the scores are concentrated at one or the other extreme end of the distribution, as in F of Figure 3.3, the distribution is said to be *J-shaped*. Histogram F illustrates a positively skewed J-shaped distribution. J-shaped distributions may be either positively or negatively skewed.

A frequency distribution is said to be *rectangular* to the degree that all its class frequencies tend to have the same value. Histogram G of Figure 3.3 is an example of a distribution approaching rectangularity.

Distributions in which the scores are heavily concentrated in two distinct parts of the scale, or in two separated intervals, are said to be *bimodal*. Histogram H of Figure 3.3 is an example of a type of bimodal symmetrical distribution often referred to as a *U-shaped* distribution. Distributions characterized by more than two pronounced concentrations of scores are said to be *multimodal*. Distributions may be bimodal or multimodal even though the concentrations are not equal. Figure 3.4 is an illustration of a bimodal distribution in which the concentration is greater at one part of the scale than at the other. Such a distribution might be obtained if a mathematical ability test were given to all education majors taking an introductory statistics course.

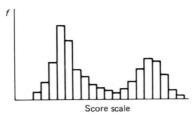

Figure 3.4   Histogram of bimodal frequency distribution

3.6   Some Considerations Related to Class Size

As stated at the end of Section 3.2, providing general rules for determining the number and size of the classes to be used in a frequency
distribution is not practical. One generality does apply: that if the
number of distinct score values is small, unit intervals (or, in the case of
unordered data, each response category) should be used and questions
pertaining to grouping do not arise. But for the most part the discussion
in this section must be based not on general rules about class size but
on considerations to be applied in particular cases.

Before the widespread availability of computing equipment, one of
the major purposes for which frequency distributions were developed
was the facilitation of certain statistical calculations. When large
amounts of data were to be used in making various computations, the
data were organized into grouped frequency distributions and the midpoint of each interval was used to represent the scores in that interval.
We have previously commented (in Section 3.2) on the loss of information regarding the nature of the score distribution when such a
procedure is used. Likewise, statistical computations based on a
grouped frequency distribution involve a certain amount of inaccuracy
(grouping error).

While the magnitude of such error can be kept reasonably low,
actually such errors need not be tolerated at all, given the computing
equipment currently available. Hence, in this book the problems of
grouping error associated with the computation of statistical indexes
from grouped data are not treated. Instead, we shall concentrate on
problems that may be involved when the purpose of grouping the data
is primarily that of presenting information about the form of the score
distribution. (It should be noted that the above comments do *not* apply
when unit intervals are used. In this circumstance no inaccuracies and
no loss of information are involved. This issue will be discussed further
in Section 5.5.)

Let us consider for now the use of frequency distributions in two
specific situations: first, the situation in which the data are markedly
skewed, and second, the situation in which observed frequency dis-

tributions are to serve as a basis for making generalizations about the form of some parent distribution. In both situations the focus will be on the definition of the classes (or intervals).

Occasionally it is necessary to set up a frequency distribution of data involving extreme skewness. Consider, for example, a collection of measures of income for a particular group of 1,000 individuals for which the following facts hold:

Largest income is	$99,950
Smallest income is	0
50% of incomes are below	1,250
90% of incomes are below	3,000

Here half of the cases are concentrated between $0 and $1,250; 40 percent fall between $1,250 and $3,000; and the remaining 10 percent are spread out between $3,000 and $99,950. If a frequency distribution involving these data is to provide any distinction at all among the lower half of the incomes, a rather fine interval—say, $200, or perhaps $250—is needed. But if intervals of this size are used throughout, the distribution will contain from 400 to 500 classes, an absurdly large number. On the other hand, if some practicable number of equalized classes is used, say 20, the bottom class will include all individuals having incomes below $5,000. This means that more than 90 percent of the individuals will be lumped into a single class. It is clear, therefore, that the only way to make distinctions among the incomes of individuals in the lower income group without at the same time using an absurd number of intervals is to permit the size of the interval to vary. Just how this should be done depends on the nature of the data and the degree of distinction to be achieved at various parts of the scale. Fine intervals are needed along those portions of the scale where the scores are most heavily concentrated and the most precise distinction is required. As the density of the scores decreases, fine distinctions become less important and the classes may be made increasingly larger. One way in which this might be done for the particular collection of data cited above is shown in Table 3.8. The right-hand column of Table 3.8 is not ordinarily presented as part of a frequency distribution and has been included only to show quickly and clearly how the classes have been varied in size. This table involves 19 classes, with relatively narrow intervals being used over that portion of the income scale where the frequencies are greatest. It thus presents fairly detailed information regarding the distribution of income among these 1,000 individuals.[4]

---

[4] If a histogram or a frequency polygon is to be constructed for the frequency distribution of Table 3.8, certain problems must be resolved. Exercise 3.6.16 in the study manual explains how these problems can be handled.

Table 3.8 Frequency Distribution 1,000 Individual Incomes

Annual Income	f	Class Size
50,000–99,999	1	50,000
25,000–49,999	2	25,000
20,000–24,999	2	5,000
15,000–19,999	4	5,000
10,000–14,999	5	5,000
7,000– 9,999	6	3,000
5,000– 6,999	8	2,000
4,000– 4,999	14	1,000
3,500– 3,999	17	1,000
3,000– 3,499	41	500
2,500– 2,999	85	500
2,000– 2,499	116	500
1,500– 1,999	124	500
1,250– 1,499	75	250
1,000– 1,249	78	250
750– 999	99	250
500– 749	104	250
250– 499	107	250
0– 249	112	250
	1,000	

Next, we consider the use of observed frequency distributions in making generalizations about the form or shape of a parent distribution. In statistics, *generalization* usually refers to the act of drawing inferences about some parent collection of data from a limited collection, or *sample*, presumably representative of the parent collection. Most research studies in psychology and education as well as in other fields involve generalizations of this type. That is, measurements or observations are made of a sample of individuals or objects in order that generalizations may be established about the larger collection, or *population*, that the sample is supposed to represent. Because the individuals or objects constituting a population differ from one another, and because chance or uncontrolled influences always play some part in determining which of these differing individuals are to be represented in the sample obtained, the characteristics of the sample are almost certain to differ to some extent from those of the population itself. Consideration of the kinds of differences, or sampling errors, that may reasonably be expected in specific situations makes up a major portion of later chapters in this book. At this point we are concerned only with a very crude technique that, if used with caution, may serve to minimize a certain type of discrepancy between sample and population.

Suppose that we are interested in the manner in which a large collection of scores (i.e., a population of scores) is distributed along the scale involved. Also suppose that for some reason it is highly impractical—if not impossible—for us to study all of the scores in the entire population. For example, assume we wish to study the variable "alienation from school" for students in a particular high school. Assume further that it is impossible to have every student take the alienation instrument, but that it is possible to obtain alienation scores from a sample of 100 students from the school. Any conclusions we may reach, then, can be the result of studying only a sample of 100 scores, and we must be alert to the possibility that what is true of this sample may not be true of the population about which we wish to make a general statement. The particular characteristic in which we are interested here is the form of the population distribution. We shall assume that we are interested in the form of the distribution only in a very general way. We wish to know simply whether the distribution is unimodal and symmetrical, or positively skewed, or negatively skewed, or bimodal, or rectangular, or whatever.

Now when a relatively few scores are classified into a large number of possible classes, general tendencies are much less likely to be discernible than when these scores are grouped into a small number of possible classes. Suppose, for example, that we regard the scores reported in Table 3.2 as our sample from a large population of such scores (i.e., all the students in the particular high school). When the number of possible classes is as great as in the distribution of Table 3.3, or for that matter Table 3.4A, it is almost impossible to discern, even with 100 scores, general population characteristics of the type with which we are here concerned. On the other hand, when the number of classes is greatly reduced, as in Distribution C of Table 3.4, we clearly gain the impression of a possible bimodal population distribution. To illustrate further how changing the class size affects the appearance of a distribution, histograms of Distributions A and C in Table 3.4 are shown in Figures 3.5 and 3.6.

Beware of making the intervals so coarse as to obscure some important population characteristic. Distribution D of Table 3.4 involves only three classes, and here the bimodal feature of the data has been completely obscured. This can be seen in Figure 3.7, which presents the histogram of this frequency distribution.

It is impossible to suggest a general rule for the optimum number of classes to be employed when the resulting distribution is to be used as a basis for making inferences about the general form of a population or parent distribution. When the number of scores in the sample is necessarily small, it is essential that the intervals be coarse and few in number, say five to ten. On the other hand, if the number of scores in the sample is large, a somewhat greater number of classes may be employed.

It is important to note that the greater the number of objects in the

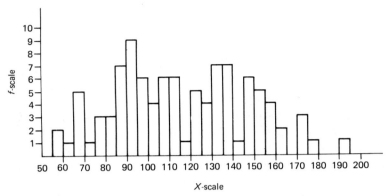

Figure 3.5   Histogram of Distribution A of Table 3.4

sample, the less likely are serious discrepancies between the sample and the population. The best insurance against attributing to the population some purely chance characteristic of the particular sample is the use of a large sample. It is only when circumstances preclude the use of large samples that one should resort to the use of a sample frequency distribution involving coarse intervals to obtain a clue to the general form of the population distribution.

These comments concerning generalizations about the shape of the parent population have been related to the selection of the "proper" interval size. In the discussion that follows, we introduce a technique that is intended to identify the shape of the parent distribution more accurately, given a specified number of intervals.

When the data involved in a sample frequency distribution are

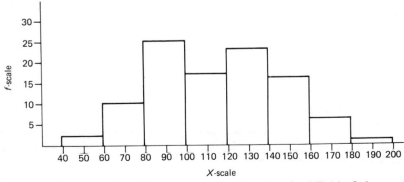

Figure 3.6   Histogram of Distribution C of Table 3.4

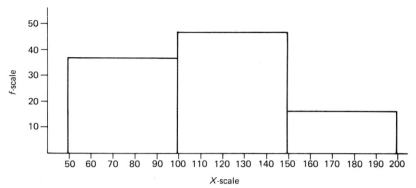

Figure 3.7 Histogram of Distribution D of Table 3.4

measurements of a continuous attribute, and when the population from which they come is extremely large and composed of individuals representing all shades of variation in the amount of the attribute being measured, then it is logical to assume that many of the irregularities of the sample are actually sampling errors or chance irregularities not truly characteristic of the entire population. This follows from the notion that if "true"—or at least extremely accurate—measurements of the attribute involved could be obtained for all members of the population, the polygon of the resulting frequency distribution would approach a smooth curve. In order to obtain a more highly generalized picture, therefore, the practice of "smoothing" the sample figure is sometimes followed. One simple means of accomplishing this smoothing consists of drawing freehand a smooth curved line that comes as close as possible to passing through all of the points used in plotting the polygon. Such a generalized curve is presented in Figure 3.8 for the frequency distribution of Table 3.4B. For purposes of comparison, the straight-line polygon has been superimposed on the generalized curve in Figure 3.8.

It should be clearly understood that such smoothing is proper only when the group of individuals involved is not being studied for its own sake but rather is being considered as a sample that presumably is representative of some larger group or population. The purpose of smoothing is to remove from the polygon for the sample any irregularities that are not characteristic of the distribution for the entire population. The principal danger in this smoothing procedure is that it sometimes removes irregularities that are not accidental but are real and perhaps significant characteristics of the distribution for the whole population. There is, of course, no way of telling by inspection whether or not a given irregularity is accidental.

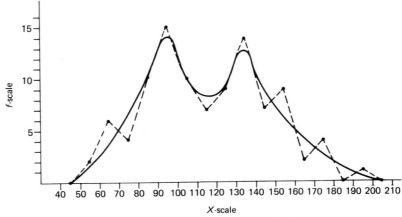

Figure 3.8 Generalized frequency distribution of alienation scores of 100 students

There are other and more objective ways of smoothing figures than the freehand method just described. For the simple purpose of describing the form of the population distribution they are not sufficiently better than the freehand method to warrant consideration here. As we have said before, the only highly dependable way to eliminate accidental irregularities is to collect data from larger numbers of cases—that is, to plot the results for larger samples. If certain irregularities disappear as the size of the sample is increased, we may be quite certain that they were accidental; if they persist, we have increasing assurance that they are truly characteristic of the population distribution.

It is also important to note in this connection that the polygon provides a more realistic picture of population distributions, even without smoothing, than does the histogram. The latter, with its flat-topped rectangles, implies an even distribution of the frequencies within a class, with an abrupt change occurring at the class boundary point. The former, with its sloping lines, implies a gradual change in the magnitudes of the frequencies—which is indeed characteristic of the type of populations we have been considering.

In summary, the foregoing discussion dealing with the selection of suitable classes for frequency distributions should be sufficient to establish the previous contention that no general rule concerning the sizes of the intervals or classes can possibly be appropriate for all purposes or types of data. The two situations treated varied both in the purposes for which the distributions were prepared and in the types of data involved. These particular situations represent only two of a great number of possible situations. They should suffice, nonetheless, to show how necessary it is to consider *the specific purpose or purposes for which a frequency distribution is to be used*, as well as the type of data involved. These examples should also show the importance of being constantly on the alert for any deviation from the ordinary. They should serve as adequate warning against the two major causes of statistical errors: carelessness, and the blanket application of rule-of-thumb procedures without regard for the peculiarities of the situation involved.

3.7   Using Graphs to Compare Frequency Distributions

Up to this point, we have considered the use of frequency distributions for describing a single set of data. However, it is probably true that the most useful outcomes of statistical analyses are those involving comparisons among various sets of data. The primary purpose of this section is to discuss and illustrate the use of graphs in making comparisons between two sets of data. The two sets of data can be from two different groups or from the same group. Interest might center on a comparison of the distribution of reading comprehension scores for boys with that for girls. On the other hand, it may be desirable to compare distributions of scores on the "alienation from school" instrument obtained for the same group of boys but at different times (e.g., ninth grade and twelfth grade). The examples that follow illustrate both situations.

Before we look at actual comparisons, it will be useful to consider what sorts of information such comparisons might yield. Basically, there are three general characteristics of distributions that lend themselves to comparison. The first has to do with shape or form: are both distributions similar in shape? (For example, are both symmetrical, or are both positively skewed?) The second has to do with the extent to which the scores constituting the distributions vary: are the scores of one distribution more variable in magnitude than those of the other? Finally, there is the matter of the overall location of the two distributions: considered more or less as a whole, does one distribution seem to be located up or down the score scale in relation to the other? Later we shall study more precise methods of making the latter two types of comparisons. For now, however, we shall be satisfied with relatively crude procedures.

Figure 3.9 shows the frequency polygons picturing the distributions of two sets of "cheating" scores for a single group of 106 sixth-grade students.[5] Although the actual experimental situation was rather

[5] Although the data in Figure 3.9 are fictitious, the idea for this example is based on: A. A. Nelsen, R. E. Grinder, and M. L. Mutterer, "Sources of Variance in Behavioral Measures of Honesty in Temptation Situations: Methodological Analyses," *Developmental Psychology*, 1, No. 3 (1969), 265–279.

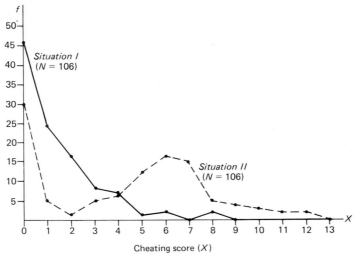

Figure 3.9   Frequency polygons representing two distributions of "cheating scores" obtained under different conditions for a group of 106 sixth-grade students

complicated, it will be adequate for our purposes to note that the experiment was designed to ascertain whether the extent of cheating was related to the type of "temptation situation" in which the students were placed.

The graphs shown in Figure 3.9 seem to warrant the following conclusions about the three characteristics in which we are interested:

> *Form:* Distribution II is bimodal and skewed to the right. Distribution I is unimodal and markedly skewed right.
> *Variability:* The scores for Distribution II range from 0 to 12. For Distribution I, the range is 0 to 8. Furthermore, most of the scores for Distribution I are either 0, 1, 2, 3, or 4.
> *Location:* Distribution II has a much larger number of students with high scores than does Distribution I.

It is possible to suggest a wide variety of situations in which comparisons between two distributions lead to useful insights. However, unless the two distributions are based on the same group of individuals (as was the case in the cheating example), it would be highly unlikely that each distribution would involve exactly the same number of people. If the groups do not differ markedly in size, comparisons between frequency distributions can still be made. But if the score distributions are based on substantially different numbers of individuals, it is necessary to compare relative frequency distributions instead. A *relative frequency distribution* gives the proportions rather than counts of individuals falling into each class.

Table 3.9 gives both the frequency counts and the relative frequencies for sets of scores made on a map reading test by the third-grade pupils of two elementary schools. The number of third-grade pupils in School B is twice that of School A. The column labeled *rf* gives the proportions of scores (relative frequencies) for each class. Thus, for School A the relative frequency (or proportion) of scores in the interval 45–47 is .15 (15/100). A polygon, too, may be used to picture relative frequencies as well as frequency counts. Figure 3.10 shows the relative frequency polygons for the two distributions of Table 3.9. Notice that the vertical scale is now labeled *rf* and not *f*. The score scale, however, remains the same. The midpoints of the intervals have been used as the score values associated with each relative frequency.[6]

The major types of comparisons to be made using relative frequency distributions are the same as for frequency distributions, namely:

1 Form: How do the distributions compare in form?
2 Variability: How do the distributions compare in the extent to which they are spread along the score scale?
3 Location: Is there a tendency for one distribution to be shifted as a whole up or down the score scale from the other?

[*Note:* It would be instructive to graph the frequency distributions (*f*-values) given in Table 3.9. It would be apparent from these graphs why relative frequency distributions are necessary when sample sizes differ.]

Before we conclude this section a few final comments are necessary. First, notice that all the graphs presented in this section were polygons. The student should consider why polygons are better suited than histograms to the kinds of comparisons we have been illustrating. (See study manual exercise 3.4.10.) Second, there is nothing that prohibits the use of more than two polygons in making such comparisons. For example, it might be desired to compare reading score distributions for a reading test given to three consecutive school grade groups. The amount of overlap usually found in such distributions is almost astonishing. Finally, when the polygons involved are based on small numbers of individuals such comparisons as we have been discussing must be made with extreme caution.

[6] It is good practice to include the sample size for each distribution as has been done in Figure 3.10. The basic reason for this is that when small samples are plotted, minor fluctuations in frequency counts are transformed into seemingly large relative frequency differences.

Table 3.9 Frequency Distributions for Two Schools on a Map Reading Test

School A			School B		
X	f	rf	X	f	rf
66–68	0	.00	66–68	0	.00
63–65	1	.01	63–65	0	.00
60–62	1	.01	60–62	0	.00
57–59	3	.03	57–59	4	.02
54–56	5	.05	54–56	12	.06
51–53	7	.07	51–53	14	.07
48–50	10	.10	48–50	18	.09
45–47	15	.15	45–47	26	.13
42–44	8	.08	42–44	24	.12
39–41	5	.05	39–41	26	.13
36–38	6	.06	36–38	20	.10
33–35	13	.13	33–35	14	.07
30–32	9	.09	30–32	12	.06
27–29	6	.06	27–29	14	.07
24–26	4	.04	24–26	10	.05
21–23	4	.04	21–23	6	.03
18–20	2	.02	18–20	0	.00
15–17	1	.01	15–17	0	.00
	$N = 100$			$N = 200$	

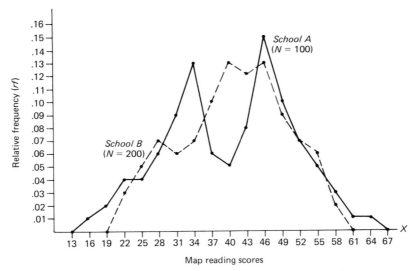

Figure 3.10   Relative frequency distributions of map reading scores for two elementary schools (third grades)

3.8 Misleading Visual Impressions

The use of graphical procedures to present data is very widespread. Hence, it is important to be aware of procedures that can be used to create misleading visual impressions. In this section we consider two such procedures.

Recall that one suggested use of frequency distributions had to do with studying score variability. If a graphical procedure is used to present the data, the choice of the physical distance representing score and frequency (or relative frequency) units is completely under the arbitrary control of the investigator. These units can be purposefully manipulated to create misleading impressions of the data. For example, Figure 3.11 shows the histogram for the data of Table 3.9 for School B. Figure 3.12 shows a second histogram for the *same data*. However, in Figure 3.12, a smaller physical distance (relative to Figure 3.11) has been used to represent a unit on the *rf*-scale and at the same time a larger physical distance has been used to represent a score scale unit. In Figure 3.11 the distribution of scores appears relatively homogeneous. Precisely the same distribution of scores appears in Figure 3.12 to be highly heterogeneous. The apparent degree of variability among the scores of a distribution is subject to pictorial manipulation. Of course, if the purpose of presenting the graphs is to facilitate comparisons among two or more distributions, there is little reason for concern since all the distributions would be plotted with reference to the same axes.

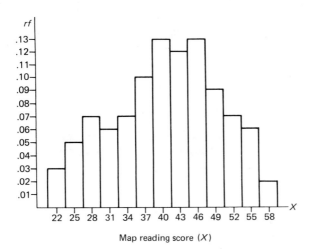

Map reading score (X)

Figure 3.11 Histogram of the relative frequency distribution of School B in Table 3.9 (with large-unit-distance on rf-scale and small-unit-distance on X-scale)

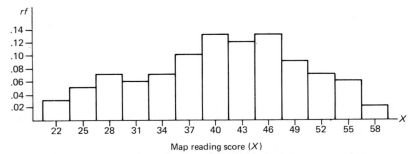

Figure 3.12 Histogram of the relative frequency distribution of School B in Table 3.9 (with small-unit-distance on rf-scale and large-unit-distance on X-scale)

In Section 3.4, it was noted that the frequency (or relative frequency) scale must have a zero point if comparisons to be made between f- or rf-values are to be based on the heights of the rectangles of a histogram. To illustrate this point consider the frequency distribution given in Table 3.10.

Figure 3.13 illustrates the misleading visual effect made when the f-scale does not start at zero. For example, from Table 3.10 we know that the number of people who indicated "disagree" was twice the number of people who indicated "strongly disagree." However, in Figure 3.13, the rectangle for the "disagree" rating is approximately four times (instead of two times) as high as the "strongly disagree" rectangle. The appropriate histogram for the data of Table 3.10 is also shown in Figure 3.13. When the missing part of the frequency scale is added, the rectangles of the histogram now indicate the proper frequency relationships.

Table 3.10 Frequency Distribution of Ratings of Agreement or Disagreement with a Bill before the State Legislature

Rating	f
Strongly agree	20
Agree	37
No opinion	13
Disagree	20
Strongly disagree	10
TOTAL	$N = 100$

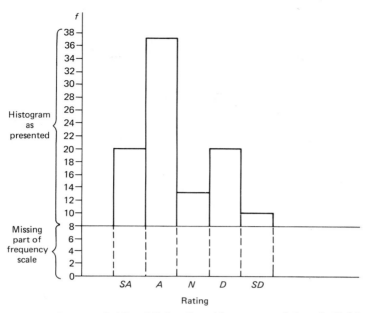

Figure 3.13   Misleading histogram of data in Table 3.10

3.9   Summary Statement

In this chapter we have described the construction of frequency distributions, relative frequency distributions, histograms, frequency polygons, and relative frequency polygons. In general, the processes involved are straightforward. Some problems may arise, however, when the number of variable score points is very large. In such situations, the appropriate size of the score interval called for may be difficult to determine. In this chapter, we explained that determination of the appropriate interval size depends on the nature of the data and the uses to be made of the data.

There are two major uses for frequency distributions and relative frequency distributions. First, since frequency distributions show at a glance how scores are distributed along the score scale, such distributions make it possible to describe certain general characteristics of the scores in some detail. For example, the highest and lowest score values can be easily noted; the score values that tend to mass or cluster are easily identified; the shape (form) of the distribution is easily ascertained.

The second major use of frequency distributions (and relative frequency distributions) is in comparing distributions of the scores on some variable obtained from two or more groups. When making such comparisons, the most common questions that arise are:

1 How do the distributions compare in shape?
2 How do the distributions compare in variability?
3 Are the distributions centered at approximately the same location on the score scale?

In this chapter we were content to answer these questions by simply setting up the frequency or relative frequency distributions for the different groups, graphing them, and then visually comparing the several graphs. As will be seen later, other more sophisticated techniques for making such comparisons are available. Some of these are treated in some detail in the following chapters.

4
Percentile Ranks and Percentiles

4.1   Introduction

In Chapter 3 we discussed frequency distributions. Most of that discussion dealt with ordered variables for which the measurement procedure provided numerical values (such ordered variables are often called *scaled* variables). However, examples of frequency distributions for unordered data (see Table 3.5) and for ordered variables that had not been scaled (had not been assigned numerical values—see Table 3.6) were also given. In this chapter, the discussion is restricted to scaled, continuous variables. The extension of the concepts presented here to other types of data is developed through study manual exercises.

Frequency distributions indicate in a general way how the scores are distributed along the score scale. However, given a frequency distribution, it is also possible to answer questions about specific score values. Consider, for example, the questions raised in the following three situations.

> *Situation 1:* The head of the English Department of a large university decides to admit freshman students to the honors program in English if their scores on the English entrance examination are sufficiently high. As a definition of "sufficiently high," she decides to use as a cutoff point the test score value that was surpassed by only 10 percent of last year's freshman students. Given the frequency distribution of test scores for last year's freshmen, how can the desired cutoff point be determined?
>
> *Situation 2:* Parents attending parent-teacher conferences fre-

quently ask how the performance of their child in various school subjects compares with that of other children in the city or state or nation. The fourth-grade students at Lincoln School recently took part in a city-wide testing program. Included in this program was a reading comprehension test. Mary Smith is in fourth grade and her parents are scheduled for a conference. The teacher wishes not only to provide Mary's parents with her reading test score but also to be able to show them how this score compares with the scores of other fourth-grade students in the city. The teacher decides that one way to make this comparison would be to estimate the percentage of fourth-grade students in the city whose test scores were poorer (or better) than Mary's score. Given the distribution of test scores for the entire city, how can the desired percentage be determined?

Situation 3: Ms. Jones teaches third grade in Longfellow School. Mr. Smith teaches third grade in Hoover School. At a recent city-wide teachers meeting they were discussing the ability of their respective classes. Since both schools had recently administered a scholastic aptitude test, the two teachers decided that a reasonable comparison between classes could be made if they each identified the score on this test above and below which 50 percent of their students scored (i.e., the middle score value). How can these score values be found?

The questions posed in these three situations are not difficult to answer. All that is needed in each case is the appropriate frequency distribution. If for example, in Situation 1, we had the frequency distribution of scores made by last year's freshman class on the English entrance examination, we would merely need to find the score value below which approximately 90 percent of last year's freshmen scored. In the previous chapter we did not focus on specific techniques for answering such questions as these. In this chapter, such techniques become the primary topic of discussion. We will show, for example: (1) how to estimate the "middle" score (Situation 3), (2) how to give relative (normative) meaning to each score by estimating the percentage of scores that are smaller (Situation 2), and (3) how to estimate the scale value that is exceeded by 10 percent of scores (Situation 1). We will also show how to estimate the two scores that are the boundary points of the middle 50 percent of the scores.

The particular technique that we have chosen is graphical. But before investigating it, we must define some terms and resolve a troublesome difficulty that arises when the scores involved are measurements of a continuous attribute.

4.2 Percentile Ranks and Percentiles: Definitions

Percentile ranks A _percentile rank_ may be formally defined as follows.[1]

> **DN 4.1** The percentile rank (PR) of a given point on a score scale is the percentage of measures in the whole distribution that are below this given point.

For example, if a particular fourth-grade pupil makes a score of 52 on a reading comprehension test and if this score has a percentile rank of 65, then we know that this pupil's score was better (in the sense of being higher or larger) than the scores of 65 percent of the pupils taking this test. "Raw" scores (usually the number right) on most educational and psychological tests have little, if any, absolute significance—they do not mean very much when considered alone.[2] Thus, we did not learn much when we read that the fourth-grade student scored 52 on the reading test. But as the above example shows, PR's can be useful aids to the interpretation of a raw score value. Such interpretations are often referred to as _norm-referenced_ interpretations, since the meaning of the PR is derived by reference to some norm group.

Given the above definition of a PR, it is not difficult to see how the PR's for particular raw score values can be found. Assume it is desired to determine the PR of a score of 33 on a particular test. Assume further that of the 50 people who took the test 40 make scores below 33. Then, according to the above definition the PR of 33 is (40/50) × 100, or 80.[3] This illustrates a perfectly legitimate method of obtaining PR's. The meaning of the PR is unambiguous: 80 percent of the scores involved are below 33. However, this is not the only method that can be justified. Another, which takes into account the characteristics of continuous-type variables, can also be justified, and it is this second technique that we will use.

Assuming, as we previously have, that a raw test score represents a measurement taken to the nearest unit, it follows that the location of a given individual's score corresponds to some scale point in the interval extending from one-half of a score unit below to one-half of a score unit above the obtained raw score. The exact location of the scale point within these limits is, of course, unknown. Suppose now that we again

---

[1] Throughout this text we will use the letters _DN_ as an abbreviation for _definition_.

[2] There are tests that yield meaningful raw scores. For example, consider a test of the 100 single-digit multiplication facts. A raw score on this test indicates the percentage of single-digit multiplication facts a pupil knows.

[3] Multiplication by 100 merely changes the proportion to a percent value.

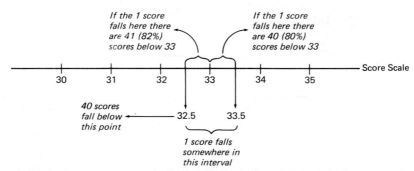

Figure 4.1   Estimating the percent of scores below a score value

wish to determine the *PR* of 33 knowing that, of the 50 scores involved, 40 are below 33 and 1 is equal to 33. The exact location of the scale point representing a test performance of 33 is known only to be somewhere in the interval from 32.5 to 33.5. If it falls in the lower half of this interval (i.e., between 32.5 and 33), the percentile rank of the score point 33 is 82 (41 expressed as a percentage of 50). On the other hand, if it falls in the upper half of this interval (i.e., between 33 and 33.5), the percentile rank of the score point 33 is 80 (40 expressed as a percentage of 50). Since its actual location is unknown and just as likely to be in one half of the interval 32.5–33.5 as in the other, a reasonable compromise is to choose a value midway between these two extreme possibilities (80 and 82) as our estimate of the percentile rank of 33. That is, we would report 81 as the percentile rank of a score of 33. The situation is diagrammed in Figure 4.1.

In the example we have just gone through, the *PR* of 81 represented an arbitrary compromise arrived at by treating the individual's score of 33 as though it were somehow evenly split between the two halves of the interval 32.5–33.5. This arbitrary compromise or convention may also be extended to apply in situations involving the determination of the percentile rank of a score point when more than one raw score corresponds to the score point. Suppose that in the foregoing example, three of the individuals, instead of one, had made raw scores of 33. Applying the convention in this situation amounts to treating these three scores as though they were evenly spaced throughout the interval 32.5–33.5. This means that one-half of these three scores, or 1.5 scores, are regarded as falling in the lower half of this score interval (i.e., between 32.5 and 33). Hence, a total of 41.5 (40 + 1.5) scores are regarded as falling below the score point 33, and the percentile rank of this point in this situation is taken to be 83 (41.5 expressed as a percentage of 50). It should be noted that percentile ranks of score points determined in accordance with the above convention are necessarily only *estimates* of the "true" percentile ranks of these points for the given group of individuals, since the true amount of the continuous attribute possessed by any individual can never be precisely assessed.

Students are sometimes disturbed by the fact that fractional parts of a number of scores (e.g., 1.5) can be used in the computation of *PR*'s. It must be remembered, however, that at best we can only *estimate* the percentage of scores below a score point. The use of fractional parts of a number of scores is simply an arbitrary aspect of the arithmetic procedure for arriving at the estimates.

Percentiles A *percentile* is the inverse of a percentile rank. Whereas the percentile rank of a particular score point is the percentage of scores falling below this point in the ordered series of scores, the value of this *point itself* is the percentile corresponding to this percentile rank. Thus, the 90th percentile is the point on the score scale below which 90 percent of the scores fall. The percentile rank of this point is 90, but the particular value of this point itself is the 90th percentile.

> **DN 4.2** The xth percentile (P_x) of a given score distribution is the point on the score scale below which x percent of the scores fall.

It is important to distinguish carefully between the terms *percentile* and *percentile rank*. The *percentile rank* of a given score point is the number representing the *percentage* of scores in the total group lying below the given score point, while the *percentile* is the *score point* below which a given percentage of the scores lie. The 28th percentile in a certain distribution of weights might, for example, be 112 pounds, but the percentile rank of an individual of this weight—that is, of the score point 112—in this distribution is 28.

Procedures for estimating percentiles are discussed in Section 4.4. At this time, it is necessary only to note that the same convention that is used in estimating percentile ranks (that scores are treated as though they are evenly spaced throughout a given interval) is also used in estimating percentiles.

4.3   Notation and Special Percentiles Defined

Percentile rank is commonly represented by "%-ile rank," "%-ile rk," or "*PR*." In this book the notation *PR* will be employed. The xth percentile may be written "xth %-ile" or "P_x." The uppercase *P* with a numerical subscript indicating the particular percentage involved will be used in this book. Thus, P_{90} indicates the score value of the 90th percentile.

Certain percentile points are of sufficient special importance to warrant being designated by special names and symbols. The nine percentile points that divide the distribution into ten equal sets of scores are known as *deciles*. The decile point below which 10 percent of the scores fall (i.e., the tenth percentile, P_{10}) is known as the *first decile* and is designated by the symbol D_1. The decile point below which 20 percent of the scores fall (P_{20}) is known as the *second decile* and is designated by the symbol D_2. And so on.

The three percentile points that divide the distribution into four equal sets of scores are known as *quartiles*. The quartile point below which 25 percent of the scores fall (i.e., P_{25}) is known as the *first* or *lower quartile* and is designated by the symbol Q_1. The quartile point below which 50 percent of the scores fall (i.e., P_{50}) is known as the *second* or *middle quartile* and is designated Q_2. The quartile point below which 75 percent of the scores fall (i.e., P_{75}) is known as the *third* or *upper quartile* and is designated Q_3.

The percentile point that divides the distribution into two equal sets of scores, that is, the point below and above which 50 percent of the scores lie, is known as the *median*. It is variously represented by the symbols *Mdn*, *Me*, *Mn*, and *Md*. In this book the first of these (*Mdn*) will be employed. The median is the equivalent of both the fifth decile (D_5) and the second quartile (Q_2).

These special percentiles are summarized in Table 4.1.

In our definition of P_x in the preceding section, no restrictions were placed on the value of x except that it lie between the limits of 0 and 100. Thus, if $x = 7$, P_x (i.e., P_7) represents the score point below which

Table 4.1   Special Percentile Points

Name	Symbol	Percentile
First decile	D_1	P_{10}
Second decile	D_2	P_{20}
Third decile	D_3	P_{30}
Fourth decile	D_4	P_{40}
Fifth decile	$D_5 = Q_2 = Mdn$	P_{50}
Sixth decile	D_6	P_{60}
Seventh decile	D_7	P_{70}
Eighth decile	D_8	P_{80}
Ninth decile	D_9	P_{90}
First (or lower) quartile	Q_1	P_{25}
Second (or middle) quartile	$Q_2 = D_5 = Mdn$	P_{50}
Third (or upper) quartile	Q_3	P_{75}
Median	$Mdn = D_5 = Q_2$	P_{50}

7 percent of the scores in the distribution lie. If $x = 14.73$, P_x (i.e., $P_{14.73}$) represents the score point below which 14.73 percent of the scores lie. Usually, however, we are interested only in those values of P_x where x is some integer from 1 to 99. Just as the 9 points that divide a distribution into 10 equal sets of scores are called deciles, the 99 points that divide a distribution into 100 equal sets of scores are referred to as *centiles*. The point below which 1 percent of the scores in the distribution lie is called the *first centile* and is designated by the symbol C_1; the point below which 2 percent of the scores lie is called the *second centile* and is designated by C_2; and so on. Obviously, C_1 is the equivalent of P_1, C_2 of P_2, etc. Centiles, then, are those special P_x points for which x takes the values of the integers 1, 2, 3, ..., 99.

It is important to note that special percentiles (deciles, quartiles, medians, centiles), like all percentiles, are points on the score scale and not intervals along this scale. Occasionally one hears an individual referred to as being "in" the first or lower quartile of a particular group on some test when actually it is intended to indicate that he is in (or among) the lowest one-fourth of this group. Again, strictly speaking, the lower quartile is a point on, and not an interval along, the score scale.[4]

4.4 A Graphical Technique for Estimating Percentile Ranks and Percentiles

In this section we will define a cumulative frequency distribution and a relative cumulative frequency distribution and consider a scheme for representing such distributions graphically. We will show also how a graph of a relative cumulative frequency distribution may be used to estimate percentiles and percentile ranks.

Table 4.2A shows a frequency distribution of the 100 alienation scores given in Section 3.2 (see Table 3.4B). Table 4.2B gives the same frequency distribution but also includes an additional column: the *cf* or "cumulative frequency" column. The *cumulative frequency* of a given interval is the frequency of this interval plus the total of the frequencies of all intervals below it. Thus, the *cf*-value of any interval indicates the number of scores in the distribution that fall below the upper real limit of that interval. For example, in Table 4.2B, where 84 is shown as the *cf* of the interval 139.5–149.5, 84 scores are below 149.5.

The cumulative frequency distribution is not the distribution of interest for estimating percentile ranks and percentiles. However, its

---

[4] This language nicety, like many others, is succumbing to common usage, and there is little point in being critical of the use of "quartile" to refer to the "lowest one-fourth" provided the meaning is contextually clear.

Table 4.2   Frequency, Cumulative Frequency, and Relative Cumulative Frequency Distributions of 100 Alienation Scores

A. Frequency Distribution			B. Cumulative Frequency Distribution		
X	f		X	f	cf
189.5–199.5	1		189.5–199.5	1	100
179.5–189.5	0		179.5–189.5	0	99
169.5–179.5	4		169.5–179.5	4	99
159.5–169.5	2		159.5–169.5	2	95
149.5–159.5	9		149.5–159.5	9	93
139.5–149.5	7		139.5–149.5	7	84
129.5–139.5	14		129.5–139.5	14	77
119.5–129.5	9		119.5–129.5	9	63
109.5–119.5	7		109.5–119.5	7	54
99.5–109.5	10		99.5–109.5	10	47
89.5– 99.5	15		89.5– 99.5	15	37
79.5– 89.5	10		79.5– 89.5	10	22
69.5– 79.5	4		69.5– 79.5	4	12
59.5– 69.5	6		59.5– 69.5	6	8
49.5– 59.5	2		49.5– 59.5	2	2

C. Relative Cumulative Frequency Distribution

X	f	cf	rcf	rcf (%)
189.5–199.5	1	100	1.00	100
179.5–189.5	0	99	.99	99
169.5–179.5	4	99	.99	99
159.5–169.5	2	95	.95	95
149.5–159.5	9	93	.93	93
139.5–149.5	7	84	.84	84
129.5–139.5	14	77	.77	77
119.5–129.5	9	63	.63	63
109.5–119.5	7	54	.54	54
99.5–109.5	10	47	.47	47
89.5– 99.5	15	37	.37	37
79.5– 89.5	10	22	.22	22
69.5– 79.5	4	12	.12	12
59.5– 69.5	6	8	.08	8
49.5– 59.5	2	2	.02	2

determination is a necessary intermediate step. It is the *relative* cumulative frequency distribution that we actually use to estimate PR's and P_x's. Table 4.2C gives the same distribution as Table 4.2B. However, an additional column (rcf) has been added [for the moment, ignore the "$rcf(\%)$" column]. The relative cumulative frequencies are merely the cumulative frequencies expressed as proportions of the total number of scores. Thus, for Table 4.2C we see that .84 (84/100) of the scores are below 149.5.

Figure 4.2 shows the graph of the relative cumulative frequency

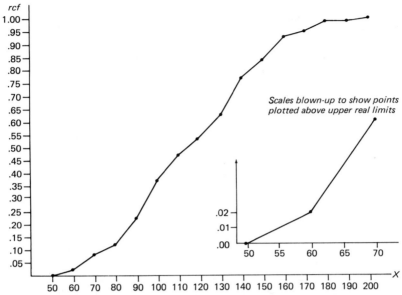

Figure 4.2   Relative cumulative frequency graph of data
in Table 4.2C

distribution of Table 4.2C. There is no need to go into detail about the
construction of this graph, since Figure 4.2 by itself should adequately
illustrate the technique. However, it is important to note that the *rcf*-
values are plotted above the upper real limits, rather than above the
midpoints, of the corresponding intervals. Relative cumulative frequency graphs as illustrated by Figure 4.2 are often referred to as
ogives, and we will use this label throughout this book.

How can the ogive be used to estimate *PR*'s and P_x's? Recall that
PR's and P_x's were defined in terms of percentages rather than proportions. Hence, to estimate *PR*'s and P_x's using graphical procedures,
the vertical axis of Figure 4.2 should be scaled in terms of percents
instead of proportions. This change is easily accomplished by multiplying each *rcf*-value by 100. We will label these new values *rcf*(%).
The last column of Table 4.2C gives these values, and Figure 4.3 shows
the corresponding ogive.

We can now use Figure 4.3 to illustrate graphical estimation of *PR*'s
and P_x's. First, consider the *PR* problem. Given some score point, say
110, we seek an estimate of the percentage of scores falling below it.
To arrive at a good estimate, first locate the point on the ogive directly
above the score point 110 (see line *A* in Figure 4.3). Then locate the
point on the *rcf*(%)-scale that corresponds to this point on the ogive
(see line *B* in Figure 4.3). The value of this point on the *rcf*(%)-scale is

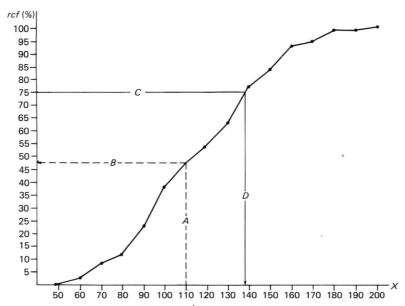

Figure 4.3 Relative cumulative frequency (%) graph of data in Table 4.2C

47. This value is the estimated percentile rank of 110. The *PR* of any other score point can be similarly estimated.

Next, consider the graphical estimation of a selected percentile. Assume it is desired to estimate the 75th percentile (P_{75}) of the distribution shown in Table 4.2C (i.e., the score value below which 75 percent of the scores of this distribution fall). We can again use the ogive of Figure 4.3. First locate the point on the ogive opposite the point 75 on the *rcf*(%)-scale (see line *C* in Figure 4.3). Then locate the point on the score scale that lies directly below this point on the ogive (see line *D* in Figure 4.3). The value of this point on the score scale is 138. This value is the estimated value of the 75th percentile of this distribution. Any other percentile can be similarly estimated.

An ogive constructed with care and with a sufficiently readable scale may be used to estimate percentile ranks and percentiles that are as accurate as can ordinarily be justified—percentile ranks accurate to the nearest whole percent and percentiles to the nearest tenth of a score unit.

Before we examine possible uses of percentiles and percentile ranks, a few remarks related to the estimation procedure developed in this section are necessary. First, it is possible to estimate *PR*'s and P_x's without using the graphical procedure presented above. Instead an interpolative procedure could be applied to the frequency table involved.[5] If the ogive is constructed with sufficient care the graphical and interpolative procedures will agree very closely. Furthermore, unless an investigator wanted to estimate only one or two values (either PR's or P_x's), the time required for the two procedures would not differ greatly. In fact, if many such values are desired, as is apt to be the case, graphical procedures are more efficient. (In Chapter 6 we will present the interpolative procedure for estimating just the median of a distribution.)

A second point to be noted is that if PR's and P_x's are estimated for the same raw data but from ogives based on markedly different interval sizes, the estimates may differ. (Study manual exercise 4.4.7 illustrates this fact.) This, of course, is simply a further instance of the loss of information that occurs when raw data are grouped (see Section 3.2).

Finally, although it is not immediately obvious, the graphical procedure employs the assumption of scores evenly distributed within an interval that was discussed in Section 4.2. Thus, for the 129.5–139.5 interval in Table 4.2C, which contains 14 scores, our estimation procedure assumes that 7 of these scores are evenly spaced below 134.5 and 7 are evenly spaced above 134.5.

4.5   Population Percentile Ranks and Percentiles

In Section 3.6 we gave some consideration to the problem of making an inference about the form of a population distribution from an inspection of the frequency distribution of a sample of scores taken from that population. In this section we shall consider a crude but nevertheless useful technique for estimating percentile ranks and percentiles of a population distribution from the distribution of scores for a sample.

It was observed in Section 3.6 that when the data involved are measurements of a continuous attribute, and when the population itself is extremely large and composed of individuals representing all shades of variations in the amount of the attribute they possess, then the population polygon approaches a smooth curve. If this is the case, it follows that the population ogive would also approach a smooth curve. Hence, just as it is possible to obtain a more highly generalized picture of the population distribution by smoothing the sample polygon, so is it possible to obtain a more highly generalized picture of the relative cumulative frequency distribution of the population by smoothing the sample ogive. As was suggested in the case of the polygon, one simple way to smooth a curve is literally to draw freehand a smooth curved

---

[5] Such a procedure was actually used on p. 50 for a very simple problem. A very thorough discussion of this procedure is given in the first edition of this book (pp. 72–79).

Table 4.3 Distribution and Percentile Ranks of Scores on Vocabulary Test for 2,000 Iowa Eleventh-Grade Pupils

X	f	cf	rcf (%)	PR (Unsmoothed)	PR (Smoothed)
29	12	2,000	100.0	100	100
28	33	1,988	99.4	99	99
27	4	1,955	97.8	98	98
26	31	1,951	97.6	97	97
25	7	1,920	96.0	96	96
24	55	1,913	95.7	94	94
23	87	1,858	92.9	91	92
22	30	1,771	88.6	88	89
21	59	1,741	87.1	86	85
20	150	1,682	84.1	80	81
19	51	1,532	76.6	75	76
18	130	1,481	74.1	71	70
17	129	1,351	67.6	64	64
16	180	1,222	61.1	57	57
15	138	1,042	52.1	49	49
14	210	904	45.2	40	40
13	155	694	34.7	31	32
12	35	539	27.0	26	25
11	103	504	25.2	23	20
10	125	401	20.1	17	15
9	90	276	13.8	12	10
8	90	186	9.3	7	7
7	10	96	4.8	5	5
6	30	86	4.3	4	4
5	4	56	2.8	3	3
4	28	52	2.6	2	2
3	9	24	1.2	1	1
2	15	15	0.8	0	0
	2,000				

line that comes as close as is reasonably possible to passing through all of the points used in plotting the sample ogive.

Consider, as an illustrative application, the problem of establishing percentile norms for test performance. *Norms* are intended to describe the performance of a specified group or population of individuals on a particular test. They are quantitative statements descriptive of a population frequency distribution of test scores. There are many ways in which these quantitative statements can be expressed. Percentiles and percentile ranks for such a population distribution of test scores are known as *percentile norms*. Such norms make possible the interpretation or evaluation of the single score made by a given individual member of the population in relation to, or in comparison with, the scores made by the other members of the population.

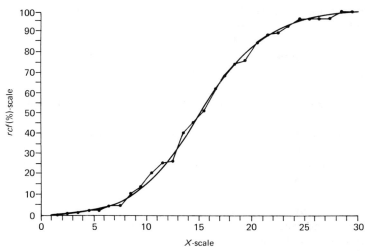

Figure 4.4 Smoothed and unsmoothed ogives based on the relative cumulative frequencies of a sample of vocabulary-test scores made by 2,000 Iowa eleventh-grade pupils

Percentile norms are population values. Since it is ordinarily impossible to administer a test to all members of a population, the percentile norms reported for a test can usually be nothing more than estimates based on a distribution of scores obtained for a sample of individuals presumed to be representative of the particular population in question. Because the individuals constituting a population differ, and because chance, or uncontrolled, influences always play some part in determining which of these differing individuals are included in the sample, it follows that the sample distribution may be expected to differ to some extent from the population distribution. If this is the case, the sample cumulative frequency distribution from which the estimates of the percentile norms are derived will also differ to some extent from the population cumulative frequency distribution. As has been suggested, one possible means of minimizing such differences consists of smoothing the sample ogive. The estimated percentile norms may be read from this smoothed ogive.

As an example, suppose it is required to estimate percentile norms for Iowa eleventh-grade pupils on a given vocabulary test. Suppose that 2,000 pupils enrolled in the eleventh grade in Iowa high schools were selected to represent this population. The frequency distribution of the scores of these 2,000 pupils on the given test is shown in Table 4.3.

Table 4.3 also gives the *PR*'s estimated from both the smoothed and unsmoothed ogives for the distribution, given in Figure 4.4. The two sets of values are not markedly different. However, the values from the smoothed ogive are probably somewhat superior as estimates of the corresponding population values, since the smoothing has probably eliminated chance irregularities.

4.6   Distances between Special Percentile Points

We have indicated previously that PR's can be used to aid in the interpretation of a given score value. Likewise, percentile points can provide useful information about the way the scores are distributed along the score scale. In this section, we provide the necessary background for using percentiles to describe the extent to which the scores of a given distribution vary in magnitude; the actual treatment of this application of percentiles is deferred to to the next section.

Figure 4.5 shows the smoothed polygon[6] of an idealized population of reading comprehension scores for a large group of sixth-grade

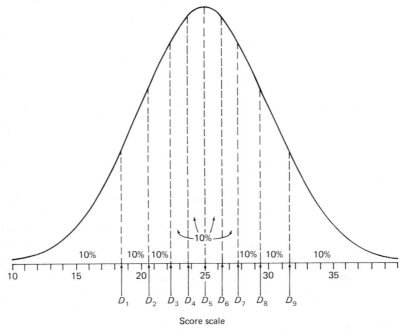

Score scale

Figure 4.5   Smoothed polygon of idealized population (unimodal symmetrical) of measures of reading comprehension showing locations of nine decile points

[6] A rationale for smoothing polygons was given in Section 3.6.

Table 4.4 Decile Points and Interdecile Distances
(Unimodal and Symmetrical Distribution)

Decile	Point	Distance between Points
D_9	31.5	
		2.2
D_8	29.3	
		1.6
D_7	27.7	
		1.4
D_6	26.3	
		1.3
D_5	25.0	
		1.3
D_4	23.7	
		1.4
D_3	22.3	
		1.6
D_2	20.7	
		2.2
D_1	18.5	

students. The distribution is unimodal and symmetrical. The nine decile points have been marked on the score scale. Inspection of this figure shows clearly that the distances between these decile points on the score scale are not equal. The actual distances between decile points are reported in Table 4.4.

Recall that the deciles are the nine points on the score scale that divide the distribution into ten equal-sized subgroups. It follows that *the distances between deciles will be largest at those portions of the scale where the frequencies are smallest, and smallest at those portions of the scale where frequencies are largest.* This principle is also applicable to quartile and centile points.

As an additional illustration of this principle, assume that the distribution of reading measures is not unimodal and symmetric, but rather unimodal and positively skewed (i.e., the test was relatively difficult for this population). Figure 4.6 pictures an idealized version of such a population distribution, and Table 4.5 provides the decile points and interdecile distances for this skewed distribution.

As a final example, assume the population distribution of reading scores to be bimodal and symmetric. Figure 4.7 pictures such a distribution, and Table 4.6 gives the decile points and interdecile distances.

Consideration of the above principle should serve to dispel any misconception that the average of, say, D_5 and D_9 is D_7. The average of D_5 and D_9 will be D_7 only if the interdecile distances are equal (equal interdecile distances imply a rectangular score distribution). In the case of Figure 4.6, for example, inspection shows D_7 to be much

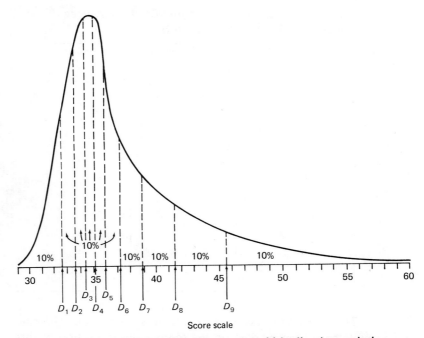

Figure 4.6   Smoothed polygon of idealized population (positively skewed) of measures of reading comprehension showing locations of nine decile points

Table 4.5   Decile Points and Interdecile Distances (Skewed Distribution)

Decile	Point	Distance between Points
D_9	45.6	
		4.2
D_8	41.4	
		2.5
D_7	38.9	
		1.7
D_6	37.2	
		1.2
D_5	36.0	
		0.9
D_4	35.1	
		0.7
D_3	34.4	
		0.8
D_2	33.6	
		1.0
D_1	32.6	

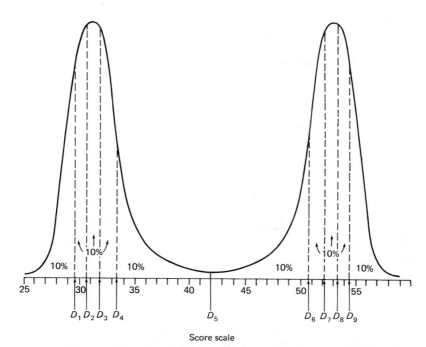

Score scale

Figure 4.7   Smoothed polygon of idealized population
(Bimodal) of measures of reading comprehension showing
locations of nine decile points

Table 4.6   Decile Points and Interdecile Distances
(Bimodal Distribution)

Decile	Point	Distance between Points
D_9	54.4	
		1.1
D_8	53.3	
		1.2
D_7	52.1	
		1.4
D_6	50.7	
		8.7
D_5	42.0	
		8.7
D_4	33.3	
		1.4
D_3	31.9	
		1.2
D_2	30.7	
		1.1
D_1	29.6	

nearer D_5 than D_9. Actually, the point midway between D_5 and D_9 is 40.8 ($\frac{1}{2}$[36.0 + 45.6] = 40.8), and 40.8 lies well *above* D_7 (D_7 = 38.9). Or in the case of Figure 4.7, D_7 is much nearer D_9 than D_5. In this situation the point midway between D_5 and D_9 is 48.2, which lies well *below* D_7 (D_7 = 52.1).

Thus, deciles, or for that matter quartiles or centiles, cannot be regarded as units in the usual sense. The actual score distances between them fluctuate, so that it cannot be said, for example, that an individual at D_9 is as much above an individual at D_8 as an individual at D_6 is above an individual at D_5. Similarly, it cannot be said that the score of an individual at D_4 is twice that of an individual at D_2. Actually D_4 may be only a few score points above D_2. In Figure 4.5, for example, D_4 is 23.7 and D_2 is 20.7.

We have seen that distances between special percentile points vary inversely with the magnitude of the frequencies at that portion of the score scale. This fact makes it possible to gain some notion of the general form of a distribution from a table of distances between special percentile points. Consideration of the interdecile distances shown in Tables 4.4 and 4.5 without reference to Figures 4.5 and 4.6 shows that the distributions involved must both be unimodal with frequencies decreasing on both sides of the modal frequencies, because the interdecile distances are smallest along one portion of the scale and become increasingly larger on both sides of this modal portion of the scale. Moreover, the interdecile distances of Table 4.4 imply that the distribution involved is symmetrical, inasmuch as these distances are themselves symmetrical—that is, the increases in one direction from the modal portion of the scale match those in the opposite direction. In the case of Table 4.5, on the other hand, the interdecile distances imply a distribution skewed to the right, for not only is the modal portion of the scale not centrally located, but the interdecile distances above this portion of the scale increase by far greater amounts than do those below it. Similar consideration of Table 4.6, without reference to Figure 4.7, suggests a symmetrical bimodal distribution.

Inferences regarding the symmetry and skewness of a frequency distribution may be drawn from a consideration of the quartile points, too, but it is not possible to determine from the quartiles whether the distribution is unimodal, bimodal, or multimodal. In all symmetrical distributions the distance between Q_2 and Q_1 is the same as that between Q_3 and Q_2, whereas in skewed distributions these distances differ. The distance between Q_3 and Q_2 will be the greater of the two in the case of positively skewed distributions, while that between Q_1 and Q_2 will be greater in negatively skewed distributions. Moreover, the more extreme the skewness of a distribution, the greater the difference between these two distances. Hence, quartile points may be used to indicate both the type and degree of the skewness of a distribution.

4.7 Distances between Special Percentile Points as an Indication of Variation Among Measures

We have previously called attention to the problem of comparing distributions of measures of some attribute for two or more groups of individuals for the purpose of determining in which group the measures are the more variable in magnitude (see Section 3.7). Later we shall devote an entire chapter to further consideration of this problem. It is appropriate at this point, however, to call attention to the fact that the principle developed in the preceding section suggests one possible means of indicating the degree to which the scores in a collection tend to vary in magnitude. Since distances between special percentile points are large in those portions of the scale where frequencies are small, and small in those portions of the scale where frequencies are large, it follows that if the distance between, say, Q_3 and Q_1 is greater in one distribution than in another, then the relative frequencies over this part of the scale must be smaller in the former distribution than in the latter. If this is the case, the scores in the distribution in which the distance between Q_3 and Q_1 is greater must vary more in magnitude. Hence, comparisons for two or more distributions of the distances between a selected pair of percentile points such as Q_3 and Q_1 provide an indication of the relative variability among the scores constituting these distributions. Other pairs of percentile points—for example, D_9 and D_1—may be used instead of Q_3 and Q_1. It is important to note that if the distances between pairs of special percentile points are to be thus compared for the purpose of determining the relative variability of two distributions, then the measures that constitute both distributions must be in terms of the same score scale.

By way of example, consider the smoothed relative frequency distributions of two idealized populations shown in Figure 4.8. Distribution A is the smoothed distribution of scores on a verbal ability test for a population of students in School District A. Distribution B is the smoothed distribution of the scores on the same test for a population of students in School District B. The scores for Population A are quite homogeneous, that is, they are concentrated over a relatively narrow segment of the score scale. The scores for Population B, by contrast, are quite heterogeneous; they are scattered over a much wider segment of the score scale. Inspection of Figure 4.8 shows clearly that the distance from Q_3 to Q_1 (or from D_9 to D_1) is much greater in the case of the heterogeneous distribution, B, than in the case of the more homogeneous distribution, A. In fact, the distance from Q_3 to Q_1 in Distribution B is 7.2 as compared with 2.8 in Distribution A (see Table 4.7). If D_9 and D_1 are used, the distances are 13.4 for B as compared with 5.6 for A (see Table 4.7).

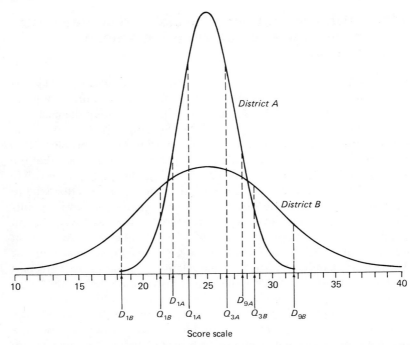

Figure 4.8   Smoothed relative frequency polygons (curves) of two idealized population distributions (A & B) of measures of verbal ability

The distance between Q_3 and Q_1 is sometimes used as a basis for describing the spread of scores for a given distribution. It is also used, as we have just illustrated, as a basis for comparing the variability of scores on some measure for two different distributions. This distance is known as the *interquartile range*. Its use will be pursued in a little more detail in Chapter 7.

Table 4.7   Special Percentile Points in Distributions of Populations A and B of Figure 4.8

Point	Population A	Distance between Points	Population B	Distance between Points
D_9	27.8		31.7	
		5.6		13.4
D_1	22.2		18.3	
Q_3	26.4		28.6	
		2.8		7.2
Q_1	23.6		21.4	

4.8   Summary Statement

In Section 4.6 we discussed the use of the distances between selected percentile points as a method of ascertaining the shape or form of a given distribution (at least in a crude manner). It follows that it is possible to compare the shapes of two distributions by comparing selected interpercentile distances determined for each distribution.

In Section 4.7 we explained how the distances between special percentile points could provide an indication of the variation among the scores. Again, it is possible to compare the variability of two distributions by comparing the distances between these special percentile points as determined for each distribution.

Finally, we noted in Section 4.3 that P_{50} is the score point that divides any distribution into two equal groups. Thus, if one distribution has a P_{50} of 100 and a second distribution a P_{50} of 150, it should be clear that the second distribution is located higher up the score scale than the first.

In summary, then, it is possible through the use of selected percentile points to compare distributions on the three characteristics we previously observed to be of frequent interest (see Section 3.7). Specifically, percentiles enable us to compare distributions in terms of shape, variability, and location. The study manual exercises for this section call upon you to make such comparisons using the percentiles for various distributions.

5

Symbolic Representation of Data

5.1   Introduction

The symbolic notation of statistics makes it possible to state and discuss statistical ideas more precisely and far more concisely than is ordinarily possible with common words. Mastering this notation and the rules governing its application may be time-consuming, but it is the price that must be paid for this superior mode of communication.

Since mathematics provides the foundation for statistics, it is to be expected that many of the symbols and rules will be those of mathematics. Others are used, however, that are unique to statistics. This chapter is primarily concerned with statistical symbols and rules that are particularly useful to the beginning statistics student. Symbols are defined, and the rules governing their application are explained. No knowledge of mathematics beyond a beginning high school course is presumed.

5.2   The Representation of Any Collection of Measures or Scores

We shall consider first a notational scheme that will serve to represent any collection of measures or scores. Since such a generalized scheme must be capable of representing collections containing varying numbers of scores, we shall use the symbol N (n is also sometimes used in this sense) to represent the number of scores involved. Since N represents counts of the number of scores, it is restricted to representing any positive integer.

The individuals or objects measured will each be assigned an identifying number. The assignment will be in a purely arbitrary order, with one individual being assigned the identifying number 1, a second individual the number 2, a third the number 3, and so on. The last individual will be assigned the number N, that is to say, the number represented by N. As a sort of general designation or identification, we shall use the letter i. This letter, then, represents any integer from 1 through N.

The score value for a given individual will be represented by an X to which that individual's identification number is affixed as a subscript. Thus, X_1 represents the score of Individual 1, X_2 the score of Individual 2, and so on. The score of the last individual is represented by X_N, and the score of *any* individual by X_i.

There are two ways in which the collection of scores may now be represented. We may write

$$X_1, X_2, X_3, \ldots, X_N \tag{5.1}$$

The dots in this statement should be read "and so on to." An alternative representation is

$$X_i \qquad (i = 1, 2, \ldots, N) \tag{5.2}$$

It should be noted that the choice of symbols used in this scheme is purely arbitrary. Letters other than N, i, and X would serve equally well and are, in fact, often used.

5.3   Expressing Computational Results in Terms of the Notational Scheme of Section 5.2

It is now possible, within the framework of the symbolic scheme of the preceding section, to represent the application of certain computational operations to the scores of *any* collection. Thus, the sum of the N scores may be represented by

$$X_1 + X_2 + X_3 + \cdots + X_N \tag{5.3}$$

To abbreviate this result further, statisticians use the upper-case Greek letter *sigma* ($\sum$) to indicate summation. Thus, the above sum may be expressed

$$\sum X_i \qquad (i = 1, 2, \ldots, N) \tag{5.4}$$

or

$$\sum_{i=1}^{N} X_i \tag{5.5}$$

The symbol $\sum$ is a sign of operation in the same sense that $+$, $-$, $\times$, and $\div$ are signs of operation. It is called a *summation operator* or *summation sign*. Expression (5.5) indicates the terms included in the sum by the $i = 1$ and the N that appear below and above the summation operator. These terms are sometimes called the *limits* of the summation, and they indicate that the X-values subscripted $1, 2, \ldots, N$ are included in the sum. The expressions (5.4) and (5.5) are alternative methods of indicating the fact that all N scores are involved in this sum. Similarly, the sum of the squares of any collection of scores may be represented by

$$X_1^2 + X_2^2 + \cdots + X_N^2 \tag{5.6}$$

or by

$$\sum X_i^2 \quad (i = 1, 2, \ldots, N) \tag{5.7}$$

or by

$$\sum_{i=1}^{N} X_i^2 \tag{5.8}$$

To illustrate this scheme, let us regard it as applying specifically to the collection of scores given in Table 3.2. In this case $N = 100$ and

$$X_i \, (i = 1, 2, \ldots, 100) = 132, 171, \ldots, 96$$

The sum of the 100 scores in this particular collection is

$$\sum_{i=1}^{100} X_i = 132 + 171 + \cdots + 96 = 11{,}538$$

The sum of the squares of these scores is

$$\sum_{i=1}^{100} X_i^2 = 132^2 + 171^2 + \cdots + 96^2$$
$$= 17{,}424 + 29{,}241 + \cdots + 9{,}216 = 1{,}427{,}186$$

Or, if we are concerned with the subsum or subtotal of only the second ten scores in this particular collection, we could write

$$\sum_{i=11}^{20} X_i = 126 + 93 + \cdots + 86 = 1{,}218$$

This last example illustrates the need for indicating the particular score values to be included in a desired sum. The identification is accomplished by indicating the first and last values involved—here

X_{11} and X_{20}. These are designated by the $i = 11$ placed below and the 20 placed above the operator as limits. It is a common practice not to designate the limits when *all* N values in a given collection are involved in a sum—that is, simply to write

$$\sum X_i \qquad (5.9)$$

to represent the sum of all the values in a given collection. In this book we shall generally follow the practice of omitting the limits of summation. The occasional exceptions to this policy occur in situations in which some ambiguity might otherwise exist, or in which there appears to be something to be gained by directing the student's attention to the precise terms involved in a given sum.

5.4 A Scheme for Representing Any Frequency Distribution

Next we shall consider a scheme for representing any frequency distribution. Such a generalized scheme must be capable of representing a frequency distribution with any number of classes and involving any number of scores. We shall represent the number of classes by the symbol c and, as before, the number of scores by the symbol N. The symbol c, like N, can represent only a positive integer. Each class will be assigned an identifying number. Again the assignment is arbitrary, but it is usually convenient to assign the number 1 to the lowest class, the number 2 to the next lowest, and so on. The last class, in this case the highest, will then be represented by c. We shall use the letter j to represent the identification number of any class. Thus, j represents any integer from 1 to c, inclusive.

The score value corresponding to the midpoint of a given class will be represented by an X to which the identification number for that class is affixed as a subscript. The frequency for that class will be represented by an f with the class identification number affixed as a subscript. The sum of the class frequencies is equal to the number of scores in the entire collection. The complete scheme for representing any frequency distribution is presented in Table 5.1.

An alternative and highly abridged presentation is

$$\left. \begin{array}{l} X_j, f_j \\[2mm] \sum f_j = N \quad (j = 1, 2, \ldots, c) \end{array} \right\} \qquad (5.10)$$

where

It should again be observed that the choice of symbols used is arbitrary and that others would serve equally well.

Table 5.1   Symbolic Representation of Any Frequency Distribution

Class Midpoint	Frequency
X_c	f_c
X_{c-1}	f_{c-1}
X_{c-2}	f_{c-2}
$\vdots$	$\vdots$
X_2	f_2
X_1	f_1
	$N = \sum\limits_{j=1}^{c} f_j$

5.5   Computation in Terms of the Notational Scheme for Frequency Distributions

As was explained at the beginning of Section 3.6, the use of grouped frequency distributions to compute statistical indexes that are a function of each score value introduces unnecessary error when the interval size is greater than the unit of measure employed. Hence, unless computing machinery is not available, or unless only grouped data are available, it is best to compute such indexes from the raw data. However, if the data are grouped by unit intervals, no computational error is introduced. Therefore, in this section we present the application of certain computational operations to a collection of scores organized into a frequency distribution but under the restriction that unit intervals are used.

In terms of the scheme under discussion, the sum of the f_1 scores in Class 1 is $f_1 X_1$, the sum of the f_2 scores in Class 2 is $f_2 X_2$, and so on. Thus, the sum of the N scores involved in any frequency distribution may be represented by

$$f_1 X_1 + f_2 X_2 + \cdots + f_c X_c \tag{5.11}$$

or

$$\sum f_j X_j \quad (j = 1, 2, \ldots, c) \tag{5.12}$$

or, if it is understood that all c products are involved, simply by

$$\sum f_j X_j \tag{5.13}$$

Similarly, the sum of the squares of the N scores of any frequency distribution may be represented by

$$f_1 X_1{}^2 + f_2 X_2{}^2 + \cdots + f_c X_c{}^2 \tag{5.14}$$

Table 5.2 Distributions of Arithmetic Quiz Scores for 50 Students

A. Frequency Distribution		B. Relative Frequency Distribution		
X	f	X	f	rf
10	2	10	2	.04
9	5	9	5	.10
8	4	8	4	.08
7	6	7	6	.12
6	9	6	9	.18
5	8	5	8	.16
4	5	4	5	.10
3	4	3	4	.08
2	2	2	2	.04
1	3	1	3	.06
0	2	0	2	.04
	$N = 50$			1.00

or

$$\sum f_j X_j^2 \qquad (j = 1, 2, \ldots, c) \tag{5.15}$$

or, simply by

$$\sum f_j X_j^2 \tag{5.16}$$

To illustrate these operations, consider the data in Table 5.2A. In this instance $c = 11$ and $N = 50$. Also, $X_1 = 0$, $X_2 = 1$, and so on, while $f_1 = 2, f_2 = 3$, and so on. Hence,

$$\sum f_j X_j = (2)(0) + (3)(1) + \cdots + (2)(10) = 272$$
$$\sum f_j X_j^2 = (2)(0)^2 + (3)(1)^2 + \cdots + (2)(10)^2 = 1,806$$

(*Note:* The student should verify these results.)

5.6 Representation of a Relative Frequency Distribution

In Section 3.7 it was observed that frequencies are sometimes reported as fractions of the total number of scores involved. To represent any such relative frequency distribution, we shall employ the same scheme as was used with an ordinary frequency distribution, except that we

Table 5.3 Symbolic Representation of Any Relative Frequency Distribution

Class Midpoint	Relative Frequency
X_c	p_c
X_{c-1}	p_{c-1}
X_{c-2}	p_{c-2}
$\vdots$	$\vdots$
X_2	p_2
X_1	p_1

shall represent the relative frequencies by $p_1, p_2, \ldots, p_c$. That is, if j represents any class identification number,

$$p_j = \frac{f_j}{N} \tag{5.17}$$

The complete scheme is shown in Table 5.3. Or if we use the form of (5.10) we have

$$X_j, p_j \quad (j = 1, 2, \ldots, c) \tag{5.18}$$

In any relative frequency distribution the sum of the c relative frequencies is 1. This may be demonstrated as follows:

$$\sum p_j = \sum \frac{f_j}{N} = \sum \frac{1}{N} f_j = \frac{1}{N} f_1 + \frac{1}{N} f_2 + \cdots + \frac{1}{N} f_c$$

$$= \frac{1}{N} (f_1 + f_2 + \cdots + f_c)$$

$$= \frac{1}{N} (N) \quad [\text{see } (5.10)]$$

$$= 1$$

5.7 Computation in Terms of the Notational Scheme for Relative Frequency Distributions

In this section we give expressions for the sum and sum of squares of the original scores in terms of the notational scheme for relative frequency distributions that we have just set forth. These expressions are equivalent to those of (5.13) and (5.16).

$$\sum f_j X_j = N \sum p_j X_j \qquad (5.19)$$

$$\sum f_j X_j{}^2 = N \sum p_j X_j{}^2 \qquad (5.20)$$

As an illustration of these rules consider Table 5.2B. In this instance, $c = 11$ and $N = 50$. Also, $X_1 = 0$, $X_2 = 1$, and so on, while $p_1 = .04$, $p_2 = .06$, and so on. Hence,

$$\sum f_j X_j = N \sum p_j X_j = 50[(.04)(0) + (.06)(1) + \cdots$$
$$+ (.04)(10)]$$
$$= 50(5.44) = 272$$

$$\sum f_j X_j{}^2 = N \sum p_j X_j{}^2 = 50[(.04)(0)^2 + (.06)(1)^2 + \cdots$$
$$+ (.04)(10)^2]$$
$$= 50(36.12) = 1,806$$

(*Note:* The student should verify these results.)

5.8 Some Simple Rules Regarding the Summation Operator*

In this section we shall consider some simple rules regarding the summation operator. These rules will prove extremely useful to students interested in following some of the derivations presented in later chapters of this book and in understanding any general reading they may do on the subject of statistics. The rules are stated in terms of the symbolic scheme for representing *any* collection of scores (see Section 5.2).

> **RULE 5.1** The value obtained from applying the summation operator, $\sum$, to the products that result from multiplying the scores of any collection by a constant multiplier is the same as the value obtained from multiplying this constant times the value that results from applying $\sum$ to the scores.

Symbolically,

$$\sum C X_i = C \sum X_i \qquad (5.21)$$

That C represents a constant is indicated by the fact that no subscript is affixed to it.

---

* Optional section. The content of this section, while most useful, is not absolutely essential to a general understanding of the topics treated in this book.

Example It will prove helpful to the student to verify this rule in the case of a specific example. Consider the following collection of six scores (here $N = 6$):

$$X_1 = 3 \qquad X_3 = 7 \qquad X_5 = 3$$
$$X_2 = 1 \qquad X_4 = 10 \qquad X_6 = 6$$

Now let $C = 2$. Then, substituting these specific values into the left-hand side of (5.21), we have

$$\sum 2X_i = (2)(3) + (2)(1) + (2)(7) + (2)(10) + (2)(3) + (2)(6)$$
$$= 60$$

and, substituting into the right-hand side,

$$2 \sum X_i = 2(3 + 1 + 7 + 10 + 3 + 6) = (2)(30) = 60$$

Proof According to the definition of the summation operator, the left-hand member of (5.21) may be written

$$\sum CX_i = CX_1 + CX_2 + \cdots + CX_N$$

Now by the distributive axiom of ordinary algebra,

$$CX_1 + CX_2 + \cdots + CX_N = C(X_1 + X_2 + \cdots + X_N)$$

And using the operator $\sum$ to express the quantity in the parentheses, we have

$$\sum CX_i = C \sum X_i$$

which is, of course, the equality we wished to establish.

> **RULE 5.2** Given two or more scores for each member of a group of N individuals. The value obtained from applying the summation operator, $\sum$, to the algebraic sums of each individual's two or more scores is the same as the algebraic sum of the results of applying $\sum$ to the separate collections of scores.

Symbolically,

$$\sum (X_i + Y_i - Z_i) = \sum X_i + \sum Y_i - \sum Z_i \qquad (5.22)$$

Example To verify this rule in the case of a specific example, consider the following three collections of scores, each of which involves the same group of four individuals:

$$X_1 = 2 \quad Y_1 = 1 \quad Z_1 = 3$$
$$X_2 = 7 \quad Y_2 = 4 \quad Z_2 = 5$$
$$X_3 = 3 \quad Y_3 = 2 \quad Z_3 = 2$$
$$X_4 = 3 \quad Y_4 = 3 \quad Z_4 = 5$$

Then

$$\sum (X_i + Y_i - Z_i) = (2 + 1 - 3) + (7 + 4 - 5)$$
$$+ (3 + 2 - 2) + (3 + 3 - 5)$$
$$= 0 + 6 + 3 + 1$$
$$= 10$$

And

$$\sum X_i + \sum Y_i - \sum Z_i = (2 + 7 + 3 + 3) + (1 + 4 + 2 + 3)$$
$$- (3 + 5 + 2 + 5)$$
$$= 15 + 10 - 15$$
$$= 10$$

Proof According to the definition of the summation operator, the left-hand member of (5.22) may be written

$$\sum (X_i + Y_i - Z_i) = (X_1 + Y_1 - Z_1)$$
$$+ (X_2 + Y_2 - Z_2) + \cdots + (X_N + Y_N - Z_N)$$

Now, simply rearranging and grouping terms (i.e., by applying the commutative and associative axioms of ordinary algebra), we have

$$\sum (X_i + Y_i - Z_i)$$
$$= X_1 + X_2 + \cdots + X_N + Y_1 + Y_2 + \cdots$$
$$+ Y_N - Z_1 - Z_2 - \cdots - Z_N$$
$$= (X_1 + X_2 + \cdots + X_N) + (Y_1 + Y_2 + \cdots + Y_N)$$
$$- (Z_1 + Z_2 + \cdots + Z_N)$$

And using the operator $\sum$ to express the three quantities in the parentheses, we obtain

$$\sum (X_i + Y_i - Z_i) = \sum X_i + \sum Y_i - \sum Z_i$$

which is the equality we wished to establish.

Remark: This rule is analogous to the distributive axiom used in proving Rule 5.1. Verbally this axiom states that the operation multiplication is distributive over addition. Note that Rule 5.2 indicates that the operation summation ($\sum$) is distributive over addition.

RULE 5.3   The application of the summation operator, $\sum$, to N values of some constant is the same as the product of N times this constant.

Symbolically,

$$\sum C = NC \tag{5.23}$$

Proof Note that

$$\sum C = C + C + \cdots + C \quad \text{(for } N \text{ terms)}$$

But the sum of NC's is the same as N times C. Hence,

$$\sum C = NC$$

In statistical work the application of these rules often occurs in combination. Hence we shall conclude this section with several examples illustrating their joint application.

Example 1 For a collection of N values of X show that

$$\sum (X_i - C) = \sum X_i - NC$$

Solution

$$\sum (X_i - C) = \sum X_i - \sum C \qquad \text{[by Rule (5.2)]}$$

$$= \sum X_i - NC \qquad \text{[by Rule (5.3)]}$$

Example 2 For a collection of N pairs of values of X and Y show that

$$\sum X_i(Y_i + a) = \sum X_i Y_i + a \sum X_i$$

Solution

$$\sum X_i(Y_i + a) = \sum (X_i Y_i + aX_i) \qquad \text{(multiplying)}$$

$$= \sum X_i Y_i + \sum aX_i \qquad \text{[by Rule (5.2)]}$$

$$= \sum X_i Y_i + a \sum X_i \qquad \text{[by Rule (5.1)]}$$

Example 3 For a collection of k values of W show that

$$\sum (aW_i - b)^2 = a^2 \sum W_i^2 - 2ab \sum W_i + kb^2$$

Solution

$\sum (aW_i - b)^2$

$$= \sum (a^2 W_i^2 - 2abW_i + b^2) \qquad \text{(squaring)}$$

$$= \sum a^2 W_i^2 - \sum 2abW_i + \sum b^2 \qquad \text{[by Rule (5.2)]}$$

$$= a^2 \sum W_i^2 - 2ab \sum W_i + \sum b^2 \qquad \text{[by Rule (5.1)]}$$

$$= a^2 \sum W_i^2 - 2ab \sum W_i + kb^2 \qquad \text{[by Rule (5.3)]}$$

5.9 Summary Statement

In this chapter we have considered notational schemes for representing any collection of scores, any frequency distribution, and any relative frequency distribution. For each of these schemes we have shown how the sum and the sum of the squares of the scores involved may be represented. We have also presented and illustrated three properties or rules applying to the summation operator, $\sum$. Students will find that mastery of this material will facilitate their reading of the remaining chapters of this text.

It is important that the student appreciate the fact that the particular choice of symbols (letters) used in these schemes is purely arbitrary. Any other selection would serve equally well. There is no well-established standard practice followed by all writers in these respects. It is regarded as sufficient for an author to define a notational scheme and then to follow it consistently. Thus, in each instance, it becomes the responsibility of readers (students) to acquaint themselves with and to continually keep in mind the notational scheme adopted by the particular author of the material they are studying at the time.

6

Indexes of Location or Central Tendency

6.1 Introduction: The Concept of an Average Related to Indexes of Location or Central Tendency

The familiar term *average* is one for which the popular meanings are extremely loose and ambiguous. Popularly we use this same term indiscriminately in speaking, for example, of the "average American," the "average personality," the "average yield of corn per acre," the "average household," the "average high school," the "average of a distribution of test scores," the "average length of life." Synonyms for the term in its popular usages are such expressions as "typical," "usual," "representative," "normal," and "expected." If asked to define the term more accurately, the "average man" might respond that it is the single measure, or individual, or object, or characteristic that best represents a group of such measures, or individuals, or objects, or characteristics. However, if he is then asked to *select* this most representative object or measure from the group, he is likely to become less specific. He may say that in order to find the average of a group of measures you simply "add them all up and divide by the number of them." But such a concept becomes meaningless when applied to characteristics that cannot be numerically represented, as in the case of the "average American" or the "average personality." As we shall subsequently show, even if the characteristic involved may be measured or numerically represented, this process of dividing the sum by the number does not in all cases yield the most "typical" or "representative" result.

Whatever may be the specific meanings of the word *average*, it is clear from the popular meaning of the term that the use of an average adds greatly to the convenience with which we can reason about groups or make comparisons between groups. No person can bear in mind simultaneously the individual characteristics of all the objects constituting a large collection or group, but we have little difficulty in handling such groups in our thinking when we can let a single quantitative index represent the whole—that is, when we can use an "average" as a concise and simple picture of the large group from which it is derived.

Suppose, for example, that we are faced with the problem of comparing two large collections of numerical data. We could, of course, organize the two sets of data into relative frequency distributions and superimpose the two corresponding polygons on the same axes. Consideration of the resulting figure would reveal whether the scores of one of the collections tended on the whole to be larger—that is, to be placed or located higher on the score scale—than the scores of the other; or whether the scores in one collection were more variable than the scores in the other; or whether there were any notable differences in the form of the two score distributions (see Section 3.7). But even though general comparisons of these types may be made, the fact remains that it would be convenient and useful to have some single quantitative index of the location of a collection of scores considered as a whole, or of the degree to which the scores in such a collection differ in magnitude. Indexes of the latter type, that is, indexes of variability or dispersion, will be treated in the following chapter. In this chapter we shall be concerned with indexes of the former type. In the past a variety of such indexes have been labeled "averages." However, as will become clear, it is more descriptive to label these indexes as *indexes of location* or *indexes of central tendency*.

There are at least five indexes of location in common use—the *mode*, the *median*, the *arithmetic mean*, the *geometric mean*, and the *harmonic mean*.[1] Of these, only the first three are considered in this text. While these various indexes are all points on the score scale indicative of the placement (or location) of the collection of scores as a whole, they possess different individual properties or characteristics. Under one set of circumstances one index may be preferable to the others; under another set of circumstances some other one of the indexes may be preferable. In the sections of this chapter that follow, we shall define the first three of the indexes cited, investigate their properties, and consider the circumstances under which they should be employed.

---

[1] In recent years several additional indexes have been suggested. Two of these are described in footnote 13 on p. 101.

6.2   Median: Definition and Computation

The median is a special percentile point and has been defined in Section 4.3. We shall state a slightly modified definition of the median here.

> **DN 6.1**   The median (*Mdn*) of a distribution is a point on the score scale such that the number of scores below it is the same as the number above it.

This definition should make it quite clear that the median is a location index. The point on the score scale that splits the distribution into equal parts is certainly indicative of the placement of the distribution on the score scale.

In Section 4.4, we presented a graphical technique for estimating any percentile point. This procedure could, of course, be used to estimate the *Median*. However, it is also possible to estimate the median (or, for that matter, any percentile) without drawing an ogive.

Consider the following collection of six scores, arranged in order of ascending magnitude: 5, 7, 9, 12, 14, 15. What is the median of this collection? What point on the scale of values has the same number of scores below it as above it? Is 10 the median? Is 11? Both of these score points have three scores below them and three above. In fact, any point between the two middle scores 9 and 12 satisfies DN 6.1. Thus, there is no unique value for the median. This state of indeterminacy is resolved by the purely arbitrary convention that specifies the median as the point midway between the two middle scores.[2] Application of the convention to the six scores above fixes the median at 10.5.[3] (*Note:* this convention was also discussed in study manual exercise 4.4.9.)

In the preceding example, the number of scores (N) was even. What is the median of a set of scores when N is odd? Consider the following seven scores: 5, 7, 9, 12, 14, 15, 19. The number of scores below 12 is the same as the number above it so that by definition 12 is the median.

In both of the above examples no two subjects had the same score. This is, of course, an unusual circumstance. Frequently we find several subjects having the same score value. Consider, for example, the data in Table 6.1, which gives the scores made in a 25-word anticipation test by 50 subjects participating in a psychological experiment on

---

[2] The student may wonder how the median would be found if the frequency of some of the scores were greater than one. For example, what is the median of the collection 5, 7, 7, 9, 9, 9, 12, 12? We will provide a solution to this question later in this section.

[3] Note that the median of this collection is a function of the two "middle scores" only. If, in fact, the highest score had been 25 instead of 15, the median is still 10.5.

Table 6.1   Scores of 50 Subjects on a 25-Word Anticipation Test

18	15	10	12	9	13	11	17	8	9
10	7	15	5	16	8	12	10	12	10
9	14	21	11	9	18	4	15	11	13
8	13	6	10	11	8	12	7	14	10
11	10	9	11	10	8	10	9	9	16

serial learning.[4] The first two columns of Table 6.2 give the unit-interval frequency distribution of the scores of Table 6.1. Obviously, with such data, it usually will be impossible to identify a given obtained score value as the middle score. In Table 6.2, for example, 17 persons had scores below the value of 10, 24 persons had scores above this value, and 9 persons had scores of 10. None of the scores obtained can be identified as the middle score value in such situations. If the data are continuous, however, we can use the convention we employed in Section 4.2 in estimating percentiles and percentile ranks for *estimating* the median, too. You may recall that this convention stipulates that with continuous data it is reasonable to assume that the scores in a given interval are spread evenly throughout the interval. (See pp. 49–51 for more details on this convention.) Thus, for the data in Table 6.2 (assuming that the data are continuous), the 9 scores with a value of 10 can be thought of as being spaced evenly throughout the interval 9.5–10.5.

Now, how does using this convention help us identify the median point for the data of Table 6.2? The median is that score value which has the same number of scores above it as below it; and the distribution in Table 6.2 is based on 50 scores. Thus, in this instance, the median is the score point that has 25 scores below it and 25 scores above it. We see from Table 6.2 that 17 scores are below 9.5 and 9 scores are between 9.5 and 10.5. These 17 plus 9 scores total 26, so we now know that the estimated score value that has 25 scores below it is in the interval 9.5–10.5. Where in the interval? Since there are 17 scores below 9.5, we need to locate the point in the interval 9.5–10.5 that has 8 (8 = 25 − 17) of the 9 scores below it. Since we are assuming that the scores

----

[4] The anticipation method is frequently used in psychological research on serial learning. While many variations are possible, the method consists essentially in presenting one at a time and always in the same fixed order a series of words, or syllables, or numbers, to be learned. After a period of learning the subjects are tested by being asked to state, or "anticipate," the next item in the series while viewing or hearing its immediate predecessor. The number of items correctly anticipated becomes the subject's score, which is taken to be indicative of learning success or of retention, depending upon the time lapse between the end of the learning period and the administration of the test.

Table 6.2   Unit-Interval Frequency Distribution of 50 Scores Given in Table 6.1

X (Score)	f	cf	fX
21	1	50	21
20	0	49	0
19	0	49	0
18	2	49	36
17	1	47	17
16	2	46	32
15	3	44	45
14	2	41	28
13	3	39	39
12	4	36	48
11	6	32	66
10	9	26	90
9	7	17	63
8	5	10	40
7	2	5	14
6	1	3	6
5	1	2	5
4	1	1	4
	50		554

are evenly spread throughout the interval, it seems legitimate to estimate that this point is eight-ninths of the way up the interval from 9.5. Since the interval size is 1 unit, eight-ninths of the interval is $(8/9)(1 \text{ unit}) \approx .9$ units. Therefore, the median is estimated as 10.4 $(10.4 = 9.5 + .9)$. This situation is diagrammed in Figure 6.1.

The above procedure for estimating the median can be restated as a formula. Our example illustrates that only a small amount of information about a frequency distribution is essential to the determination of its median. Actually only four pieces of information are required. These may be presented in a variety of ways, but in the final analysis they may be reduced to the following

1 N, the total number of scores in the collection
2 f_{50}, the frequency of the interval containing the median
3 U_{50} and L_{50}, the upper and lower real limits of the interval containing the median
4 $cf_{L_{50}}$, the cumulative frequency up to but not including the interval containing the median

Then,

$$Mdn = L_{50} + \frac{.5N - cf_{L_{50}}}{f_{50}} (U_{50} - L_{50}) \tag{6.1}$$

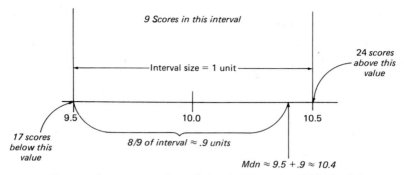

Figure 6.1   A portion of the score scale of Table 6.2

The use of this formula requires first the identification of the interval containing the median. As noted above, for the data in Table 6.2, this interval is 9.5–10.5. The formula calls for the following information:

$$N = 50 \qquad f_{50} = 9 \qquad cf_{L_{50}} = 17 \qquad L_{50}, U_{50} = 9.5, 10.5$$

Hence, for this distribution

$$Mdn = 9.5 + \frac{(.5)(50) - 17}{9}(10.5 - 9.5)$$

$$= 9.5 + \frac{25 - 17}{9}(1)$$

$$= 9.5 + \frac{8}{9} = 9.5 + .89$$

$$= 10.39$$

$$\approx 10.4$$

Although this example involved a unit-interval distribution, formula (6.1) can also be applied to any grouped frequency distribution. As a general rule, however, it is best to compute the median using only unit-interval frequency distributions. This follows from our earlier concern with the error that is introduced into the calculated values of indexes for data grouped into classes or intervals that span more than one unit. Because of "grouping error," a median value calculated from data so grouped is almost certain to differ from a median calculated for the same data organized into a unit-interval distribution.

6.3   Mode Defined

In many large collections of numerical data there is a clear-cut tendency for a certain score value to occur with greater frequency than
any other. If such a collection is organized into a *unit-interval* frequency
distribution the value of this score is readily determined, since it is
simply the score corresponding to the largest frequency value. Often
such scores are more or less centrally located with reference to the other
score values, which tend to occur with decreasing frequency in either
direction from this most frequently occurring value. Such a most
frequently occurring score clearly provides an indication of the placement along the score scale of the distribution as a whole and, hence,
may be used as an index of location. This index, which in effect
indicates the location along the score scale of a pile-up of score values,
is called a *mode*.

Consider the distribution of reading scores shown in Figure 6.2. In
this distribution 25 is the modal value. Many people studying statistics
for the first time seem determined to regard the value of the largest
frequency itself as the value of the mode. In Figure 6.2, 12 is the
frequency count of scores at the modal value of 25. *Modal values are
score values!*

Occasionally the scores constituting a collection will tend to pile up
at two distinctly separate places on the score scale. In such situations
the distribution is regarded as having two modes, that is, as being
bimodal, even though the concentration at one place may be considerably greater than that at the other. Some distributions may even
involve more than two distinctly separate concentrations of scores.
Such distributions, of course, have more than two modes. In general,

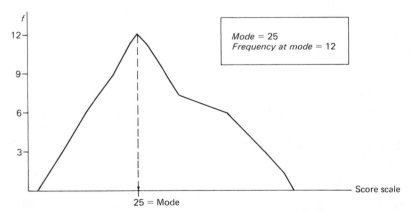

Figure 6.2   Frequency polygon for a set of reading
comprehension scores

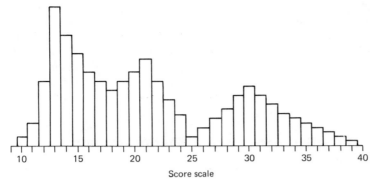

Figure 6.3   Histogram of a frequency distribution of scores on a statistics test

distributions having more than one mode are referred to as *multimodal* distributions. Figure 6.3 shows the histogram of a distribution of scores on a statistics exam. This distribution has modes at 13, 21, and 30, because each of these score values is the most frequently occurring score in a distinctly separate concentration of score values.[5]

A formal summary of the foregoing concepts is contained in the following definition.

> **DN 6.2**   A mode (*Mo*) of a frequency distribution is a point on the score scale corresponding to a frequency that is large in relation to other frequency values in its neighborhood.

Most of the population distributions of interest to the psychologist or educator are unimodal. Of course, because of chance sampling fluctuations, the score distributions of samples taken from these populations often appear multimodal. A number of frequencies in the sample distributions will be larger than adjoining or neighboring frequencies simply owing to accidental sampling fluctuations. Such chance large frequencies should, of course, *not* be regarded as determining the modes of such distributions. Only those large frequencies that are clearly the peaks of major concentrations of scores should be considered as establishing modal points.

It is clear, then, that the determination of the mode or modes of a distribution often involves a *judgment* as to which large frequencies should be ignored. In doubtful situations it is best to increase the size of the sample for the purpose of noting whether or not the questionable

---

[5] The modal values in a multimodal distribution are often divided into two categories. The *absolute mode* is the score value with the largest frequency (in Figure 6.3 this would be 13). The other modal values are labeled *relative* modes (21 and 30 are relative modes for the distribution of Figure 6.3).

concentrations of scores persist. When this cannot be done it is perhaps best to follow an earlier suggestion (see Section 3.6) and either set up a grouped frequency distribution with relatively coarse intervals or resort to freehand smoothing. *When a grouped frequency distribution with coarse intervals is used as a basis for fixing a mode, the value of this mode is taken to be the midpoint of the interval whose frequency is large in relation to the frequencies of neighboring intervals.*

6.4   The Arithmetic Mean: Definition and Computation

The arithmetic mean is generally the most useful of the three means.[6] For this reason it is common practice to refer to it simply as *the* mean. It is the only mean treated in this book.

> **DN 6.3**   The mean of a distribution of scores is the point on the score scale corresponding to the sum of the scores divided by their number.

In popular usage the mean is often referred to as the "average."[7] It is variously designated by the symbols $\overline{X}$ (where the individual scores are represented by X's), $X.$, m, and M. In this book we shall usually represent the mean of a given real collection of X-scores by the symbol $\overline{X}$, or of a given real collection of Y-scores by $\overline{Y}$. Later we shall find it necessary to deal with certain theoretical or hypothetical score distributions. Such theoretical score distributions will usually apply to some population all members of which are not actually available for measurement. We shall use the Greek letter μ (mu) to represent the means of such theoretical distributions.

It is possible to state the above definition symbolically. Let any collection of N scores be represented by

$$X_1, X_2, X_3, \ldots, X_N \hspace{3cm} [\text{see } (5.1)]$$

Then the sum of these N scores may be represented by

$$\sum X_i = X_1 + X_2 + \cdots + X_N \hspace{2cm} [\text{see } (5.3), (5.5)]$$

Hence, the definition of the mean of any distribution of N scores may be written

$$\overline{X} = \frac{\sum X_i}{N} \hspace{5cm} (6.2)$$

---

[6] Arithmetic, geometric, and harmonic.

[7] Such a designation is reasonable since it is the only index (of the three considered here) that uses the mathematical process of averaging.

We will use the data given in Table 6.1 to illustrate the computation of the mean. Following the instructions of the definition of the mean, we see that it is necessary only to determine the sum of these 50 scores and to divide this sum by 50, i.e., by the number of scores. How the instructions of the symbolic statement of the definition given in (6.2) may be applied to determining the mean of the scores given in Table 6.1 is shown below.

$$\bar{X} = \frac{\sum X_i}{N} = \frac{18 + 10 + 9 + \cdots + 10 + 16}{50} = \frac{554}{50} = 11.08$$

Sometimes the analysis of the data may call for the preparation of a unit-interval frequency distribution. For example, it may be necessary to determine the percentile rank of each score point. When the situation calls for the preparation of such a frequency distribution, it is usually more convenient to defer the computation of the mean until the frequency distribution is prepared, for it is a simple matter to compute the mean of data organized in this form.

Table 6.2 shows the unit-interval frequency distribution of the collection of scores given in Table 6.1. If we represent the frequency distribution symbolically, using the notational scheme described in Section 5.4, the total of the N scores involved is as given in (5.13), i.e., $\sum f_j X_j$. Hence, if we adapt the definition of the mean to this situation we obtain the following computational formula:[8]

$$\bar{X} = \frac{\sum f_j X_j}{N} \tag{6.3}$$

The application of this formula to our example (Table 6.2) is spelled out below.

$$\bar{X} = \frac{\sum f_j X_j}{N}$$

$$= \frac{(1)(4) + (1)(5) + (1)(6) + (2)(7) + \cdots + (1)(21)}{50}$$

$$= \frac{554}{50} = 11.08$$

[8] It is also possible to use (6.3) with a grouped frequency distribution—that is, with a frequency distribution the classes of which span more than one unit—by letting X_j be the midpoint of the jth class. In this case, however, the mean resulting from the application of (6.3) will be only an approximation of the mean obtained by (6.2)—that is, of the mean of the original ungrouped scores. As has been previously indicated, there is little justification for introducing such grouping error.

Table 6.3   Relative Frequency Distribution of 50 Scores Given in Table 6.1

X (Score)	rf
21	.02
20	.00
19	.00
18	.04
17	.02
16	.04
15	.06
14	.04
13	.06
12	.08
11	.12
10	.18
9	.14
8	.10
7	.04
6	.02
5	.02
4	.02

It is also possible to compute the mean of a set of scores when the data are presented as a relative frequency distribution (see Section 5.6). If p_j represents the proportion (relative frequency) of the total N with scores X_j, then by (5.19)

$$\sum f_j X_j = N \sum p_j X_j$$

Substituting in (6.3) gives

$$\overline{X} = \frac{N \sum p_j X_j}{N} = \sum p_j X_j \tag{6.3a}$$

Table 6.3 shows the relative frequency distribution of the scores of Table 6.1. The application of (6.3a) to these data is shown below

$$\overline{X} = \sum p_j X_j = (.02)(4) + (.02)(5) + (.02)(6)$$
$$+ (.04)(7) + \cdots + (.02)(21)$$
$$= 11.08$$

6.5   Properties of the Mean

To understand the mean as an index of location or central tendency it may be helpful to observe that the mean is that score value which would be assigned each individual or object if the total for the entire collection were to be evenly distributed among all the individuals involved. It may be thought of as an amount "per individual" or "per object." Per capita figures, then, are actually means. Thus, the statement that the per capita debt of a particular state government is $1,900 simply implies that at a given time the total debt divided equally among the individuals of the state is $1,900. Since this amount corresponds to the total debt divided by the number of "debtors," it is by definition a mean.

The definition of a mean has two important implications. First, the mean is the only one of the three indexes of location considered here that is dependent upon the exact value of each and every score in the entire distribution. Any change in the value of any score in the collection will be reflected in the sum of the scores and, hence, in the mean. The median, on the other hand, will reflect a change in the value of a score only if that change results in a shift of that score past the original position of the median. When such a shift occurs, the percentage of scores below the original position of the median will no longer be 50, and consequently the median point will have to be relocated to conform to the requirement that exactly 50 percent of the scores lie below it. But if changes in the values of certain scores do not shift them from one half of the distribution to the other, the location of the median will remain unchanged, regardless of how great these changes may be.

Consider, for example, the following collection of five scores arranged in order of magnitude:

17, 21, 22, 26, 29

The median of these scores is 22. Their sum is 115 so that their mean is 23. Now suppose it is discovered that an error has been made and that the top score should have been 39 instead of 29. The median remains at 22 as before, but the mean now becomes 25, thus reflecting the upward change in the value of this single score.

Similarly, changes may occur in the values of certain scores in a distribution without affecting the mode, so that, again, of the three averages treated here, only the mean depends upon the exact value of each score in the collection.

The second implication of the definition of the mean that should be noted at this point is that it is the only one of the indexes that is a function of the total, or aggregate, of the scores constituting the collection. Since by definition the mean is the sum—i.e., the total or aggregate—of the scores in the collection divided by the number, it follows that the total or aggregate of the collection of scores is the product of their mean times their number. This relationship may be stated symbolically as follows:

$$\sum X_i = N\overline{X} \qquad (6.2a)$$

Because of these aspects of the definition of the mean, it may be said that of the three indexes considered here, only the mean is arithmetically or algebraically defined. It is largely this characteristic of the mean that gives it such a great advantage over the mode and the median in both applied and theoretical statistics.

This algebraic characteristic of the mean makes it possible to obtain the mean of a given collection of scores organized into subgroups when only the subgroup numbers and means are available. For example, assume a school superintendent wishes to use both last year's ninth-grade class and this year's ninth-grade class to compute the ninth-grade mean on a standardized test of reading. The following data are available

Last Year's Class (Subgroup 1)	This Year's Class (Subgroup 2)
$\overline{X}_1 = 20$	$\overline{X}_2 = 22$
$n_1 = 80$	$n_2 = 100$

Here, the subscripts affixed to the symbols $\overline{X}$ and n identify the particular subgroup involved. Now let M represent the mean for the combined classes. Then,

$$M = \frac{n_1\overline{X}_1 + n_2\overline{X}_2}{n_1 + n_2} = \frac{(80)(20) + (100)(22)}{80 + 100} = 21.11 \qquad (6.4)$$

It should be noted that the numerator of the above equation is nothing more than the sum of scores for people in both subgroups. That is, by (6.2a), $n_1\overline{X}_1$ is the sum of scores for Subgroup 1 and $n_2\overline{X}_2$ is the sum of scores for Subgroup 2. The denominator is the total number in both groups. It is clear that this formula may be extended to apply to any number of subgroups.

One final property of the mean will be considered at this point. Suppose that some point is selected on the scale of values of a given collection of scores. We shall call this point A. Now suppose that for each score larger than A the distance between the score value and A is determined, and that these distances are summed. Suppose further that the corresponding sum is determined for all scores smaller than A. It is a characteristic of the mean that these two sums will be equal if, and only if, the point A is located at the mean. In other words, *the mean possesses the property that the aggregate of the distances from it of the scores lying above it is the same as that of the scores lying below it.*

In statistical terminology the distance of a score from a point on the score scale is referred to as the *deviation of the score* from that point. It is customary to compute these deviations by subtracting the value of the point from that of the score. Hence, if algebraic signs are retained, the deviations of scores having values greater than that of the point are positive, whereas those of scores having values less than that of the point are negative. If the point involved is taken at the mean, the net (algebraic) sum of all the deviations will be exactly zero, for the sum of the positive deviations will be exactly canceled by the sum of the negative deviations. A formal statement of this property of the mean together with an illustrative example and a formal proof follow.

RULE 6.1 The algebraic sum of the deviations of N scores from their mean, $\overline{X}$, is zero.

Symbolically,

$$\sum (X_i - \overline{X}) = 0 \tag{6.5}$$

We shall represent the deviation of a score, say X_i, from the mean of the collection to which it belongs by the lower-case x_i. That is,

$$x_i = X_i - \overline{X} \tag{6.6}$$

Hence, (6.5) may also be written

$$\sum x_i = 0 \tag{6.7}$$

Example Consider the scores 10, 7, 12, 15, and 11, of which the mean is 11. The deviations of these scores from their mean are respectively -1, -4, $+1$, $+4$, and 0. To verify the application of (6.5) in the case of this example, we need only find the algebraic sum of these deviations. That is,

$$\sum x_i = -1 - 4 + 1 + 4 + 0 = 0$$

---

*Proof**

$$\sum x_i = \sum (X_i - \overline{X})$$

$$= \sum X_i - \sum \overline{X} \qquad \text{[by (5.22)]}$$

$$= \sum X_i - N\overline{X} \qquad \text{[by (5.23)]}$$

$$= N\overline{X} - N\overline{X} \qquad \text{[by (6.2a)]}$$

$$= 0$$

---

* Optional.

6.6 An Additional Property of the Median

In the introductory section of this chapter we stated that many individuals interpret the term *average* in the sense of "typical." It was further pointed out, however, that most such individuals, confronted with the problem of selecting a score value typical of a given collection of such values, would not possess a sufficiently precise notion of what they meant by "typical" to enable them to attack the problem systematically. That is, most such individuals would have no notion of any criteria of typicalness or representativeness that could be applied to the solution of this problem.

In the foregoing sections of this chapter we have considered three such criteria, each leading to the selection of a typical value. The first of these criteria, equal numbers of smaller and larger scores, led to the selection of a value called the median. The second, frequency of occurrence, led to the selection of a value called the mode. And the third, an equal division per item of the aggregate of the scores, led to the selection of a value called the mean. In this section we shall investigate still another criterion of typicalness, namely, the "aggregate proximity" to all the scores. In other words, *we shall select as a typical score value the score point to which all the scores are closest, or the score point from which the total distance to all the scores in the collection is least*.

Perhaps a clearer understanding of this criterion can be acquired from a consideration of the score scale shown in Figure 6.4, along which score values have been plotted. We shall arbitrarily select the value 10 on this scale and determine the aggregate of the absolute values of the deviations of the scores in the collection from this value.[9] The absolute deviations of these scores from 10 are shown in the accompanying table.[10]

Score	Absolute Deviation
A	$\|2 - 10\| = 8$
B	$\|3 - 10\| = 7$
C	$\|13 - 10\| = 3$
D	$\|17 - 10\| = 7$
E	$\|21 - 10\| = 11$
F	$\|23 - 10\| = 13$
G	$\|26 - 10\| = 16$
	$\sum \|X_i - 10\| = 65$

[9] Absolute values are values considered without regard to algebraic sign.

[10] The vertical bars enclosing the differences or deviations are used instead of parentheses by mathematicians when it is desired to designate only the absolute value of the difference.

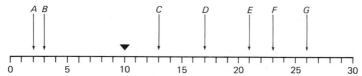

Figure 6.4 Scale showing values of a collection of seven scores

The sum of the deviations here is seen to be 65. Had we selected the value 20 instead of 10 from which to measure the deviations, $\sum |X_i - 20|$ would have been considerably smaller—55 instead of 65. Or suppose we use the mean, 15, of these seven scores as a point from which to measure the absolute deviations. Then $\sum |X_i - 15|$ would be 54. *What we seek, according to the criterion of typical under consideration, is the value that gives us the smallest figure for the aggregate of the absolute deviations.* By continuing the process used above, we could show that no value on the scale of Figure 6.4 that anyone might select would lead to a smaller aggregate than the value 17, for which the total of the absolute deviations is 52. But this value, 17, is the same value that arises from the application of the criterion of equal numbers of smaller and larger scores, i.e., the value previously defined as the median. We have arrived at the following rule.

RULE 6.2 The aggregate of the absolute values of the deviations of the scores of a given collection from a point on the score scale is least when that point is the median of the collection.

Symbolically,

$$\sum |X_i - A| \text{ is least when } A = Mdn \tag{6.8}$$

The application of the criterion of aggregate proximity, that is, the use of a score value to which all the scores in a collection are closest, as a definition of typicalness is a practice that would meet with general acceptance. Hence, when the purpose of an index of central tendency is to portray or represent the "typical" score in a collection, the median of the collection should usually be the index employed. Further justification for this recommendation is given in subsequent sections of this chapter.

Rationale*   We shall not present a rigorous proof of this rule. We shall instead attempt to present arguments that will hold for two

* Optional.

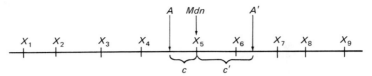

Figure 6.5   Scale showing values of a collection of nine scores

special collections of scores. It is hoped that these arguments will at least serve to make the rule plausibly acceptable.

Case I: A collection consisting of nine (an odd number) scores. Consider the score scale shown in Figure 6.5, along which nine scores have been plotted. In this collection the score represented by X_5 is the median and A is any point on the scale not the median. The distance between X_5 and A is represented by c.

Now it is clear that the aggregate of the absolute deviation of the scores X_5, X_6, X_7, X_8, and X_9 from A is $5c$ greater than that of these same scores from the median, whereas the aggregate of the absolute deviations of the scores X_1, X_2, X_3, and X_4 from A is $4c$ less than that of these latter scores from the median. Hence, the aggregate of the absolute values of the deviations of all nine scores from A is greater than that of the nine scores from the median by an amount equal to $5c - 4c$, or c. Therefore, in this situation the sum of the absolute values of the deviations of these nine scores is smaller when these deviations are measured from the median than when they are measured from A.[11]

Case II: A collection consisting of eight (an even number) scores. Consider the score scale shown in Figure 6.6, along which eight scores have been plotted. Since this collection consists of an even number of scores, the median is indeterminate in the sense that any score point between X_4 and X_5 satisfies the definition of the median. The argument that follows holds for any value between X_4 and X_5, but so that it may be stated as definitely as possible, we shall follow the convention previously suggested (see Section 6.2) and locate the median at a point midway between X_4 and X_5. As before, A is some point on this scale not a median so that A cannot be located in the interval between X_4 and X_5, all points of which are median points. The distance between A and the arbitrarily selected median point is c.

Again it is clear that the aggregate of the absolute deviations of the scores X_5, X_6, X_7, and X_8 is $4c$ greater when these deviations are measured from A than when they are measured from the median,

[11] The student may find it instructive to repeat this argument using the point A' shown in Figure 6.5.

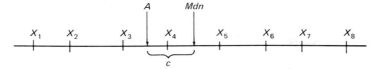

Figure 6.6   Scale showing values of a collection of eight scores

whereas the aggregate of the absolute deviations of the scores X_1, X_2, and X_3 is $3c$ less when the deviations are measured from A instead of the median. Hence, for these seven scores the aggregate of the absolute value of their deviations from A is $4c - 3c$, or c more than from the median. Now the remaining score, X_4, may be closer to A than to the median, but since it lies between A and the median, the amount by which it is closer to A must be less than c. Hence, again in this situation the sum of the absolute values of the deviations of these eight scores is smaller when the deviations are measured from the median than when they are measured from A.

6.7   Selection of a Location Index: Representing the Typical Score of a Unimodal Distribution Containing Extreme Scores

In this section, we shall first consider the effect of extreme scores on the mode, median, and mean in the case of some simple numerical examples. The extreme scores included in these illustrative collections are quite unrealistic in the sense that they differ so markedly from the other scores involved that they clearly do not appropriately belong in the same collection. This was permitted, nonetheless, in order to provide examples that would be particularly striking in demonstrating the effects under consideration. In more realistic collections these effects would not be as extreme, but they would still be of the same general character.

Figure 6.7 shows the histograms of four collections of scores. The numbers entered in the rectangles are the frequencies associated with each score value. Each collection pictured involves 20 scores, and below each histogram are the values of the three indexes for that distribution as well as the percentile rank of the mean. Distribution A is a symmetrical unimodal distribution. In such a distribution, of course, all three indexes locate the exact center of the distribution and must coincide or have the same value. Distribution B is the same as Distribution A except that one score has been changed from 85 to 145. This change would obviously have no effect on the mode; and since the score

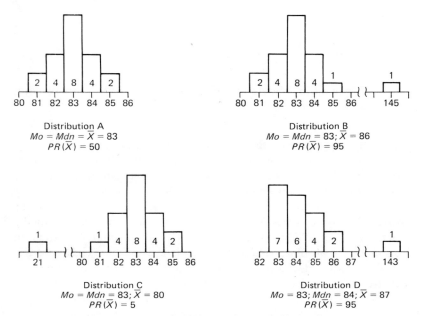

Figure 6.7 Distributions showing effect of extreme scores on indexes of location

changed was and remains above the median, the value of that index will also be unaffected. But the effect of this one extreme score on the mean is very marked—so marked, in fact, that the value of the mean is now larger than that of 95 percent of the scores in the collection, and hence can scarcely be regarded as a "typical" or "representative" value. Distribution C, which is the mirror image of Distribution B, shows that an extremely small score can pull the value of the mean downward just as markedly as an extremely large score can raise it.

Distribution D is J-shaped, one score being extremely larger than the rest. The modal value remains at 83, but since scores that in Distribution A were below the median have now been shifted above it, the median of Distribution D will necessarily be higher than that of Distribution A. The change in the median, however, is not nearly as marked as the change in the mean—a change due almost entirely to the presence in the distribution of a single extreme score.

The question naturally arises in the case of a distribution like D as to which index should be employed if the purpose is to select or provide a value *typical* of the values of the scores constituting the collection. Clearly the mean value is atypical. Some might argue that the modal, or most frequently occurring, value is more appropriate to this purpose than the median. It will be noted, however, that while the mean value is larger than 95 percent of the scores in this distribution, the modal value is smaller than 82.5 percent of the scores. Moreover, in terms of the criterion of most frequent occurrence, there is very little basis for choice between the modal value of 83 and the median value of 84. This is usually the case in most unimodal distributions, even in instances of rather marked skewness. Consequently, the most appropriate of the indexes in situations of this type is the median, which satisfies not only the criterion of equal numbers of smaller and larger values, but also the criterion of aggregate proximity (6.8). (In Distribution D the aggregate of the score distances from the mean value of 87 is 112, from the modal value of 83 is 80, and from the median value of 84 is 74.)

For an example of the relative magnitudes of the three indexes in more realistic distributions involving extreme scores, the student should refer to Table 3.8. (Additional examples of distributions of this type are given in the study manual.) For the distribution of annual incomes shown in Table 3.8, the modal value is $125,[12] the median value is $1,250, and the mean value is approximately $1,795. Here approximately 94 percent of the values in the distribution are above the modal value and approximately 65 percent are below the mean value. The aggregates of the score differences from the mode and mean are 1,669,875 and 1,282,035, respectively, while from the median this aggregate is only 1,207,875. It is again clear that the median value is most appropriate for the purpose of representing the typical individual.

6.8 Selection of an Index: Interest Centered on Total Rather than Typical

In Section 6.5 we pointed out that of the three indexes considered, only the mean depends on the value of each score. It is, of course, this property that makes the mean sensitive to extreme scores. The mode is completely unaffected by any change in a score value that does not alter the location of the major concentration of scores. The median is insensitive to any changes in score values that do not affect the equality of the proportions of scores above and below it. Hence, the median of a given collection of scores will be affected only by such changes in score values as may result in a shifting of these scores past the original value of the median. Thus, a teacher seeking to raise the median performance of a class on some test will find it profitable to concentrate her instructional efforts on individuals whose initial performance

---

[12] $125 is the midpoint of the modal class. Since the classes vary in size, it is necessary, in order to determine the portion of the scale in which the greatest concentration of values occurs, to express the class frequencies as proportions of the class size (or interval length). When this is done the class that has the greatest concentration of scores per unit of class size is this lowest class.

levels are near—especially just below—the original value of the median, for it is this group of pupils whose performances she will be most likely to succeed in raising past this original median value.

But this, of course, represents an instructional procedure of dubious value, for as a teacher she should be concerned with improving the performance levels of *all* her pupils. This example thus illustrates the inappropriate selection of an index for the true basic purpose at hand. This basic purpose is, or certainly should be, to raise the performance level of a class as a whole. Hence, if the success with which this purpose is accomplished is to be reported in the form of an index of location of the final test scores, the index that should be employed is the index that is based on the total performance level of the class as a whole. This, of course, implies the use of the mean, which is the only one of the three indexes considered here that is based on the aggregate, or total, of the score values. This index, unlike the median or mode, is sensitive to *any* change in the performance level of *any* individual pupil.

As a second example of a situation in which the total is of greater concern than the typical, consider two communities of comparable size: one, Community A, in which the ownership of real and personal property is largely concentrated in the hands of a relatively small number of individuals, and another, Community B, in which ownership is much more widely dispersed. Suppose, then, that in Community A the *median* assessed value of real and personal property owned by each individual is $250, while the corresponding value for Community B is $2,500. Suppose further, however, that in Community A there are a few extremely valuable properties so that the *mean* assessed value of property owned by each individual is $3,500, while for Community B this mean value is $3,000. Now, if the school programs in these communities are supported by a direct millage levy on the property owners, which community is in the stronger financial position? That is, in which community will a given millage levy produce the greater income? The answer is clearly that community which has the greater *total* assessed valuation, for the total tax income (assuming no tax delinquency) is simply the product of the millage levy times the total assessed valuation. Now, since the mean is the index related to total, the community that has the greater mean assessed valuation will also have the greater total assessed valuation (the two communities being of the same size). Hence, other factors (such as indebtedness) being equal, Community A is in the stronger financial position as regards the support of its school program.

In short, when the purpose to which an index is to be put has to do with the total or aggregate of the collection of scores involved, then the appropriate index to employ is the mean. It alone of the three indexes considered here is related to total.

6.9   Selection of an Index: Case of Multimodal Distributions

Suppose that we are concerned with a multimodal distribution (for example, see Figure 6.3) and that we wish to use an index for the purpose of representing the *typical* score value. If the situation further demands the use of a single-valued index, as would be the case were our purpose to compare the typical score value for this distribution with that of some other distribution for which only a single-valued average could be obtained, the appropriate choice would be the median—i.e., the comparison should be made between the medians of the two distributions.

If, on the other hand, the situation does not demand the use of a single-valued index, a more complete picture of the typical score of a multimodal distribution would be the multi-valued index consisting of all the modal values of the distribution. Our job would amount to reporting the location of each major concentration of scores. Thus, given the modal values 13, 21, and 30 (see Figure 6.3), we know that whereas the score value 13 is typical of a substantial portion of the distribution, the score value 21 is typical of another substantial portion of the distribution, and the score value 30 of still another such portion.

6.10   Selection of an Index: Summary

We have previously called attention to the necessity in statistical work of selecting procedures that are consistent with the purpose of the work and appropriate for the type of data involved. As the foregoing sections have indicated, the selection of an index of location permits no exception to this basic principle. We have not attempted in these sections to catalogue completely the various purposes to which indexes of location may be applied or the various types of data that may be involved. It is hoped, however, that the variety of purposes and situations considered is sufficient to demonstrate that there is no single index that is best for all purposes and all types of data, and thus to demonstrate, too, the necessity of constant, careful attention to purpose and to the nature of the data. The summary presented in Table 6.4 is limited to the purposes and types of data specifically treated in the three foregoing sections.[13]

---

[13] The summary, of course, is limited also to the three indexes specifically treated in this chapter. In recent years some statisticians have presented additional indexes of location. For example, Tukey (in *Exploratory Data Analysis*, Addison-Wesley Publishing Company, Reading, Mass., 1970) discusses a "trimean" as a measure of central tendency. The trimean is defined as follows:

Table 6.4 Summary of Conclusions of Sections 6.7, 6.8, and 6.9 on the Selection of an Index of Location

Purpose	Nature of Distribution	Appropriate Index
To represent typical score value	Unimodal, symmetrical	Choice immaterial since $\bar{X} = Mdn = Mo$.[a]
	Multimodal, symmetrical	Modes if multi-valued index usable, otherwise either Mdn or $\bar{X}$, since $Mdn = \bar{X}$.
	Unimodal, skewed	Mdn.
	Multimodal, skewed	Modes if multi-valued index usable, otherwise Mdn.
To support an interest in aggregate of score values	All types	Mean

[a] *Unless sampling from a population is involved. In this case, for reasons which will be developed in later chapters, it is usually best to use the mean.*

6.11 Joint Use of Indexes

As would be expected, a particular statistical analysis may be carried out with more than one purpose in view. If these purposes conflict insofar as the selection of an index of location is concerned, the only sensible way to resolve the conflict is to use the index appropriate to each purpose, that is, to use more than one index.

The joint use of indexes may have bonus advantages. For example, the mean and median considered jointly contain information regarding the asymmetry of a distribution. In Section 6.7 (see particularly Figure 6.7) we pointed out that while in symmetrical distributions the values of the mean and median are the same, in asymmetrical or skewed distributions the values of these indexes differ due to the greater sensitivity of the mean to the extreme score values present in such distributions. It was observed that in distributions skewed to the right, the value of the mean exceeds that of the median, while the reverse is true in the case of distributions skewed to the left. Because the median

$$\text{Trimean} = \frac{\frac{1}{2}(P_{25} + P_{75}) + Mdn}{2}$$

Tukey also discusses a "midmean," which is defined as follows:

$$\text{Midmean} = \frac{\text{sum of middle } 50\% \text{ of the scores}}{(50\%)(N)}$$

It is not difficult to see that each of these quantities does reflect a central tendency concept. These quantities have not been pursued in this book basically because they are not widely used in the literature of educational and psychological research at this time.

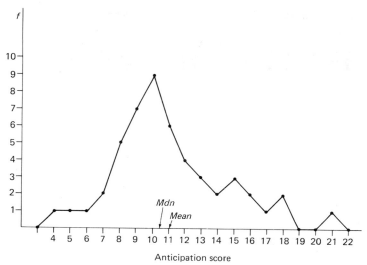

Figure 6.8   Frequency polygon for the scores given in
Table 6.1

and mean behave in this manner, a comparison of these two indexes
for any distribution provides an indication of the direction in which the
distribution is skewed.

For example, Figure 6.8 shows the frequency polygon for the 50 word
anticipation scores given in Table 6.1. This distribution is unimodal
and skewed to the right. You may recall from previous calculations in
this chapter the following facts about this distribution:

Mean = 11.08   Median = 10.4

The mean has, in essence, been "pulled" in the direction of the skew.

7

Measures of Variability

7.1   Introduction

It should be readily apparent that considered alone, a measure of
central tendency or group location can describe only one of the important characteristics of a distribution of scores. It is often equally
essential to know how *compactly* the scores are distributed about this
point of location or, conversely, how far they are scattered away from
it. Consider, for example, the two smoothed relative frequency distributions shown in Figure 7.1. Assume these are distributions of
scholastic aptitude test scores for two different schools.

It is easily seen from Figure 7.1 that the "average" aptitude scores
(mean, median, or mode) for Schools A and B are approximately the
same. However, the scores of the students of School B are much more
varied (spread out over more of the score scale) than those of students
at School A. Such differences in variation have obvious implications
for instructional practices in each school.

As a second example of the need to consider how scores are spread
along the score scale, consider the smoothed relative frequency distributions shown in Figure 7.2. These two distributions were obtained
when an "authoritarian" measure[1] was administered to a group of
college students during their freshman year and again during their
senior year. Basically, the investigator was interested in assessing the
effect of college attendance on this trait. If we consider only changes
in "average" values (seniors are more authoritarian than freshmen) we
are evaluating only one type of effect. In fact, on the basis of these
graphs, it appears that in addition to being more authoritarian, seniors
are also more alike in this respect than they were as freshmen.

[1] Authoritarian instruments presumably measure degree of dependency on
clearly delineated hierarchies of authority.

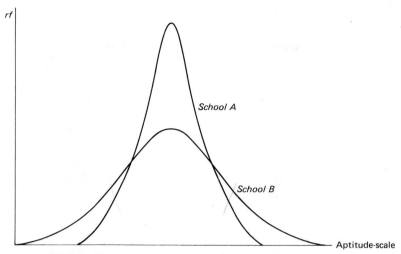

Figure 7.1   Scholastic aptitude distributions for two schools

Thus, in addition to describing distributions with respect to location, it is also important to describe how widely the scores are spread out along the same scale. This latter characteristic of a distribution is variously referred to as *dispersion*, *scatter*, *deviation*, and *variability*. In this chapter we shall define and discuss several quantitative indexes of this characteristic.

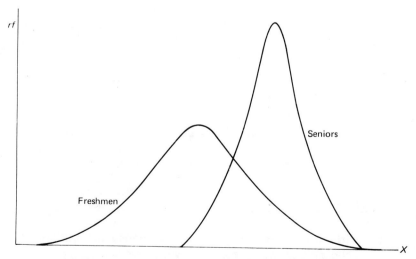

Figure 7.2   Distributions of authoritarian scores for freshmen and seniors

7.2   The Range Type of Index

While any quantitative index of location is necessarily a *point* on the score scale, any meaningful index of variability must be a *distance* along the score scale. This distance will be small or large as the variability in the score values is small or large. A distance sometimes used as an index of variability is that from the smallest to the largest score in the collection. If the scores of a collection are compactly or homogeneously distributed—if, that is, they are much alike in magnitude—then the distance from the smallest to the largest score will be much smaller than the corresponding distance for a collection of scores that differ markedly in magnitude. This distance is known as the *range*. If the lowest score of a collection is represented by L and the highest score by H, then the range, R, is defined by[2]

$$R = H - L \qquad (7.1)$$

This index has the advantage of great simplicity. But it is weak in the sense that it ignores or fails to take into account any of the distances between scores except the distance between the smallest and largest. Between these extreme scores almost anything could be true of the distribution; all the other scores may or may not be very compactly distributed. For example, consider the two smoothed distributions of scholastic aptitude scores shown in Figure 7.3. The range

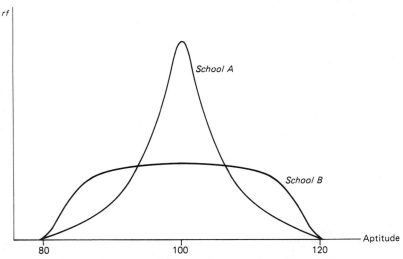

Figure 7.3   Smoothed relative frequency distributions of scholastic aptitude scores for two schools

[2] Some statistics books define the range as $R = H - L + 1$.

for both schools is 40 (120 − 80). However, the variability of the scores between 120 and 80 is markedly different for the two schools.

This weakness may be lessened to some extent by the use of the distance (i.e., range) between some pair of score values other than the highest and lowest. Two such ranges were suggested in Section 4.7. These were the distance from Q_1 (the first quartile) to Q_3 (the third quartile) and the distance from D_1 (the first decile) to D_9 (the ninth decile). Although we are less likely to be misled by these ranges than by the one defined in (7.1), the fact remains that they still fail to take into account much of the total available information regarding variability.

For a reason to be mentioned in the following section, *one-half* the range from Q_1 to Q_3 is sometimes used as an index of variability.[3] This index, known as the *semi-interquartile range* (Q), is defined by

$$Q = \frac{Q_3 - Q_1}{2} \tag{7.2}$$

[3] The only technique we have presented for estimating Q_1 and Q_3 involves the use of an ogive. If the only use for an ogive in any particular case is in connection with the determination of two percentile points such as Q_1 and Q_3 or D_1 and D_9, more efficient techniques are available. The general formula for calculating any percentile point is analogous to formula (6.1). If X represents the percentile rank of the point P_X in a collection of N scores, if f_X is the frequency of the interval containing P_X, if U_X and L_X are respectively the upper and lower real limits of this interval, and if cf_{L_X} is the cumulative frequency up to but not including this interval, then:

$$P_X \approx L_X + \frac{(X/100)(N) - cf_{L_X}}{f_X} (U_X - L_X)$$

Note that the use of this formula requires first the identification of the interval containing the point P_X. To identify this interval first find $(X/100)(N)$. Then the interval in question is the first one that has a cf-value exceeding the amount $(X/100)(N)$.

As an example, consider the data in Table 4.2 (p. 54). Assume we want to compute Q_3 (i.e., P_{75}) for these data. In this example, $X = 75$, $N = 100$, and $(X/100)(N) = 75$. Thus, the interval containing P_{75} is 130–139. Substituting in the above formula we have:

$$P_{75} \approx 129.5 + \frac{(75/100)(100) - 63}{14} (139.5 - 129.5)$$

$$\approx 129.5 + \frac{75 - 63}{14} 10$$

$$\approx 129.5 + \frac{12}{14} 10$$

$$\approx 129.5 + 8.6 \approx 138.1$$

On page 56, using the ogive of Figure 4.3, we estimated the value of P_{75} to be 138.

Insofar as use of available information on variability is concerned, Q is no better than $Q_3 - Q_1$. In the next section we shall consider a different approach to the problem of devising indexes of variability. This approach will not be as simple as the use of ranges, but it is capable of providing indexes that make more complete use of the available information on variability. Ordinarily, range indexes are useful only in situations in which a rather crude indication of variability is sufficient for the purpose of the particular analysis.

7.3   The Deviation Type of Index

Another type of distance value indicative of variability is the average of the distances of certain score values from some central point (location index). Suppose, for example, that we determine the mean of the distances of Q_1 and Q_3 from the median. These distances are respectively

$$Mdn - Q_1 \qquad \text{and} \qquad Q_3 - Mdn$$

Adding these distances and dividing by two to find their mean, we obtain

$$\frac{(Q_3 - Mdn) + (Mdn - Q_1)}{2} = \frac{Q_3 - Q_1}{2}$$

We now see that the semi-interquartile range defined in (7.2) is simply the mean of the distances of Q_3 and Q_1 from the median. (Actually any point between Q_1 and Q_3 would serve as well as the median.)

The mere change from a range to an average-distance approach in deriving Q, obviously, cannot in any way alter the usefulness or meaningfulness of Q as an index of variability. In applying the distance approach, however, there is no need to limit the number of score values involved to two, as was done in the case of Q. There is no reason, in fact, why the average distance could not be made to involve *all* the score values and thereby take into more complete account the information on variability contained in the data.

By way of providing a simple example the histograms of two hypothetical score distributions are shown in Figure 7.4. The ten scores of Distribution A are clearly more widely dispersed (more heterogeneous) than those of B. Both distributions have means of 20. We shall arbitrarily use this value as a central point from which to measure the distances of the scores. The scores of each of these distributions and the absolute distance of each score from $\overline{X} = 20$

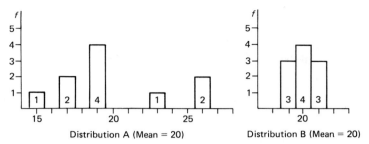

Figure 7.4   Heterogeneous (A) and homogeneous (B) hypothetical score distributions

are shown in Table 7.1.[4] For the more variable Distribution A the mean of the ten score distances is 30/10, or 3.0. For the more homogeneous Distribution B this mean is 6/10, or .6, a value one-fifth as large as that obtained for Distribution A.

In the terminology of statistics the distance of a score from a central point is called a *deviation*, and the index of variability just described is the average absolute deviation, or, more commonly, the *mean deviation*. Symbolically, the mean deviation may be defined as follows:

$$MD = \frac{\sum |x_i|}{N} \qquad (|x_i| = |X_i - \overline{X}|) \qquad (7.3)$$

where

N = the number of scores

X_i = the score value for an individual i $(i = 1, 2, \ldots, N)$

$\overline{X}$ = the mean of the collection

Comments

1. As noted previously, the vertical bars indicate that only the numerical or absolute values of such deviations are to be considered. Reference to (6.7) should reveal at once why it was necessary to ignore the sign of the deviations in defining the mean deviation: had the sign been retained, their sum, and hence their mean, would always be zero regardless of the variability of the scores involved.

2. A notational practice first introduced in Section 6.5 (see Rule 6.1) is again used in (7.3). Since this practice, which is widespread, will be used throughout this book, it is important that the student have it thoroughly in mind. The practice referred to is that of representing

---

[4] The meaning of the vertical bars that appear in Table 7.1 has been discussed in some detail on p. 94.

Table 7.1   Absolute Distances of Scores of Distributions A
and B from $\overline{X} = 20$

Distribution A		Distribution B	
Score (X)	$\lvert X - 20 \rvert$	Score (X)	$\lvert X - 20 \rvert$
15	5	19	1
17	3	19	1
17	3	19	1
19	1	20	0
19	1	20	0
19	1	20	0
19	1	20	0
23	3	21	1
26	6	21	1
26	6	21	1
$\Sigma \lvert X_i - 20 \rvert = 30$		$\Sigma \lvert X_i - 20 \rvert = 6$	

any score in a collection by an upper-case letter and its deviation from
the mean of the collection by the corresponding lower-case letter.
    3. It is perfectly reasonable to compute deviations from the
median. Thus, another index of spread is

$$\frac{\Sigma \lvert X_i - Mdn \rvert}{N}$$

This index represents the average absolute deviation from the median.

In the mean deviation we have an index of variability that clearly
takes more thoroughly into account the information on variability
contained in the data than does any range type of index. Indeed, if our
sole purpose in determining an index of variability were simply to
describe the extent to which the scores of a collection are dispersed or
scattered along the score scale, we would look no further. Unfortunately,
however, the mean deviation, due to the involvement of absolute
values, has proven to be most stubborn, if not unmanageable, in the
development of more complicated statistical theory. This is particularly
true for various aspects of inferential statistics, and also for correlation
theory. Both inferential statistics and correlation theory are needed at
a rather early stage in the study of statistics and are dealt with at some
length in subsequent chapters of this text. It is essential, therefore,
that we introduce at this point an index of variability that is free from
the involvement of absolute values and hence more tractable in the
development of statistical theory.

We have seen that the mean of the signed $X_i - \overline{X}$ deviations must
be zero for all distributions of scores (see Rule 6.1) and is consequently

useless as an index of variability. Inasmuch as the product of two negative numbers is a positive number, this difficulty can be circumvented by using as an index of variability the mean of the squares of these deviations. The squaring of each deviation is an added complication. But it is nevertheless true that such a mean-square deviation is fully as sensitive to changes in variation as the mean deviation itself. Again consider Distributions A and B of Figure 7.4. Table 7.2 shows the scores of each of these distributions together with their algebraic (signed) deviations from $\overline{X} = 20$ and the squares of these deviations. In each case the sum of the algebraic deviations is zero. However, the sum of the squares of the deviations of the ten scores of the more variable Distribution A is 128, so that the mean of the squared deviation is 12.8. For the more homogeneous Distribution B, the sum of the squared deviations is 6, and the mean of these squares is only .6, a value less than one-twentieth of that of Distribution A.

The index we have just described is known as the _variance_. A variety of symbols have been employed to represent the variance. Among the more common are V, S^2, s^2, and σ^2. We have elected to use S^2. Thus, the symbolic definition of the variance is:[5]

$$S^2 = \frac{\sum x_i^2}{N} \qquad (x_i = X_i - \overline{X}) \qquad (7.4)$$

A disadvantage of the variance in certain applications is the fact that it is not a value that is expressed in terms of the units of the original score scale. For example, if the original measures are in units of inches, then the squaring of the deviations produces a series of numbers representing _square inches_, and the variance, which is the mean of these numbers, is, therefore, also a value expressed in terms of square inches. In general, the variance is expressed in units that are the squares of the units of the scores involved. Consequently, unlike the other measures of variability considered, it cannot be interpreted as a distance along the score scale. This characteristic of the variance, however, is easily modified. To return the index to the

---

[5] Many writers of applied statistics books define the variance as follows:

$$\text{Variance} = \frac{\sum x_i^2}{N - 1}$$

That is, instead of using the mean of the squared deviations they use the sum of the squared deviations divided by one less than their number. Of course, when the sample size is large such a minor difference is of very little importance. The theoretical reason for this variation will be discussed in Chapter 11. For the moment it is necessary for the student only to be aware that some books do define the variance in a slightly different way.

Table 7.2 Squares of Algebraic Deviations of Scores of Distributions A and B from $\bar{X} = 20$

Distribution A			Distribution B		
Score (X)	$X - 20 = x$	x^2	Score (X)	$X - 20 = x$	x^2
15	−5	+25	19	−1	+1
17	−3	+ 9	19	−1	+1
17	−3	+ 9	19	−1	+1
19	−1	+ 1	20	0	0
19	−1	+ 1	20	0	0
19	−1	+ 1	20	0	0
19	−1	+ 1	20	0	0
23	+3	+ 9	21	+1	+1
26	+6	+36	21	+1	+1
26	+6	+36	21	+1	+1
Σ	0	128	Σ	0	6

original scale it is necessary only to extract its square root. The resulting index of variability, which is amenable to interpretation as a distance along the original score scale, is known as the *standard deviation*. Symbolically, its definition may be written[6]

$$S = \sqrt{\frac{\sum x_i^2}{N}} \qquad (x_i = X_i - \bar{X}) \tag{7.5}$$

Throughout this book we will use the capital S to represent the standard deviation of a distribution of scores.

The standard deviation of Distribution A of Figure 7.4 is simply the square root of its variance 12.8, or 3.58. The standard deviation of Distribution B is the square root of .6, or .77, a value between one-fourth and one-fifth as large as that of the more variable Distribution A.

The standard deviation is by far the most important and most widely used index of variability. It makes complete use of the information on variability contained in the data. Furthermore, it is quite manageable mathematically—a characteristic of great importance in the development of statistical theory. The cost of these advantages is, primarily, a slight loss in simplicity.

7.4   Computation of Variance and Standard Deviation

To illustrate the computation of the variance and standard deviation of a set of scores we shall use the 50 scores made by 50 subjects on a

---

[6] The standard deviation is always defined as the *positive* square root of S^2.

25-word anticipation test that were reported in Table 6.1 (p. 83). The mean of these 50 scores is 11.08 (see Section 6.4). To compute the variance of this set of scores we may follow directly the instructions of the symbolic statement of the definition given in (7.4). That is,

$$S^2 = \frac{\sum x_i^2}{N}$$

$$= \frac{(18 - 11.08)^2 + (10 - 11.08)^2 + \cdots + (16 - 11.08)^2}{50}$$

$$= \frac{(6.92)^2 + (-1.08)^2 + \cdots + (4.92)^2}{50}$$

$$= \frac{47.8864 + 1.1664 + \cdots + 24.2064}{50} = \frac{589.6800}{50}$$

$$= 11.7936$$

The standard deviation of this distribution is, therefore,

$$S = \sqrt{11.7936} \approx 3.43$$

It is apparent that the direct computation (computation according to the definition) of the variance is a tedious task. When the mean involves a decimal fraction, the deviations are not only awkward to obtain but also troublesome to square.[7] Fortunately it is possible to obtain the sum of the squares of the deviations of the scores from their mean without actually finding the deviations.

We shall present the rule for obtaining the needed sum of squares both verbally and symbolically. Then we shall verify it in the case of a specific example. Finally we shall provide a general proof. This rule is among the most useful of all elementary statistical rules. Although the student may wish to omit study of its proof, it is essential that all students understand the statement of this rule and master its application.

RULE 7.1 In any collection of scores, the sum of the squares of the deviations of the scores from the mean of the collection is given by the difference between the sum of the squares of the scores and the square of the sum of the scores divided by their number.

Symbolically,

$$\sum x_i^2 = \sum X_i^2 - \frac{(\sum X_i)^2}{N} \qquad (x_i = X_i - \overline{X}) \qquad (7.6)$$

---

[7] Of course, the use of a calculator or even a table of squares (see Table I, Appendix C) will greatly reduce the labor involved.

It is important to understand the difference between $\sum X_i^2$ and $(\sum X_i)^2$. The first of these expressions represents the quantity obtained when each of the N scores is *first squared* and then these squares are summed. The second represents the quantity obtained when the N scores are *first summed* and then the resulting sum is squared. The distinction between these two expressions is misunderstood by many beginning students. Careful consideration of the following example may be helpful in overcoming this difficulty.

Example Consider the following ten scores (here $N = 10$):

12, 7, 13, 13, 5, 2, 8, 5, 5, 10

For these data:

$$\sum X_i^2 = (12)^2 + (7)^2 + \cdots + (10)^2 = 774$$
$$(\sum X_i)^2 = (12 + 7 + \cdots + 10)^2 = (80)^2 = 6,400$$

Applying Rule 7.1 we have

$$\sum x_i^2 = \sum X_i^2 - \frac{(\sum X_i)^2}{N}$$

$$= 774 - \frac{6,400}{10} = 774 - 640$$

$$= 134$$

To verify this result we must first determine the mean, $\overline{X}$, of these ten scores. This mean is

$$\overline{X} = \frac{\sum X_i}{N} = \frac{80}{10} = 8$$

Next we determine the deviation from the mean (i.e., $x_i = X_i - 8$) of each score. These deviations are 4, -1, 5, 5, -3, -6, 0, -3, -3, and 2. The squares of these deviations are 16, 1, 25, 25, 9, 36, 0, 9, 9, and 4. Hence,

$$\sum x_i^2 = 16 + 1 + \cdots + 4 = 134$$

which is the quantity previously obtained by application of the rule. The foregoing calculations are displayed in full in Table 7.3.

Proof of Rule 7.1 * Given a collection of N scores, $X_1, X_2, \ldots,$ X_N. Let X_i represent the value of any score in this collection [see (5.1) or (5.2)] and let x_i represent its deviation from the mean $\overline{X}$. That is,

$$x_i = X_i - \overline{X}$$

* Optional.

Table 7.3 The Direct Calculation of $\sum x_i^2$ and Its Calculation by Rule 7.1

X	$x = X - 8$	x^2	X^2
12	$+4$	$+16$	144
7	-1	$+ 1$	49
13	$+5$	$+25$	169
13	$+5$	$+25$	169
5	-3	$+ 9$	25
2	-6	$+36$	4
8	0	0	64
5	-3	$+ 9$	25
5	-3	$+ 9$	25
10	$+2$	$+ 4$	100
$\sum X_i = 80$	$\sum x_i = 0$	$\sum x_i^2 = 134$	$\sum X^2 = 774$

By Rule 7.1: $\sum x^2 = 774 - 80^2/10 = 134$

Then

$$x_i^2 = (X_i - \overline{X})^2$$
$$= X_i^2 + \overline{X}^2 - 2\overline{X}X_i$$

Now summing all N such squares we obtain

$$\sum x_i^2 = \sum X_i^2 + N\overline{X}^2 - 2\overline{X} \sum X_i \tag{a}$$

[See (5.21), (5.22), and (5.23).] But by definition [see (6.2)],

$$\overline{X} = \frac{\sum X_i}{N} \tag{b}$$

Hence,

$$\overline{X}^2 = \frac{(\sum X_i)^2}{N^2}$$

If we multiply both members of this equality by N we obtain

$$N\overline{X}^2 = \frac{(\sum X_i)^2}{N} \tag{c}$$

Now substituting from (b) and (c) into (a) we have

$$\sum x_i^2 = \sum X_i^2 + \frac{(\sum X_i)^2}{N} - \frac{2(\sum X_i)^2}{N}$$

And upon combining terms we obtain

$$\sum x_i^2 = \sum X_i^2 - \frac{(\sum X_i)^2}{N}$$

which proves the rule.

We shall now show how this rule can be used to facilitate the computation of the variance (or standard deviation). If we substitute from (7.6) into (7.4) we have

$$S^2 = \frac{\sum x_i^2}{N} = \frac{\sum X_i^2}{N} - \left(\frac{\sum X_i}{N}\right)^2 \tag{7.7}$$

or

$$S^2 = \frac{\sum X_i^2}{N} - \overline{X}^2 \tag{7.8}$$

Thus, to obtain S^2 it is no longer necessary to carry out the tedious process of determining the square of the amount by which each score deviates from the mean. Instead we need simply (1) square each score, (2) find the mean of these squares, and (3) subtract from it the square of the mean of the scores. Applying this procedure to the data of Table 6.1 we have

$$S^2 = \frac{18^2 + 10^2 + \cdots + 16^2}{50} - 11.08^2$$

$$= \frac{6,728}{50} - 11.08^2 = 134.56 - 122.7664$$

$$= 11.7936$$

which is identical with the result obtained earlier.

If for some reason the data are to be organized into a unit-interval frequency distribution, it is usually more convenient to defer the computation of the variance until the frequency distribution is prepared. We have already considered the computation of the mean of data organized into such a frequency distribution (see Section 6.4). To illustrate the procedure as it applies to the computation of the variance, the data of Table 6.1 have been organized into a frequency distribution involving unit intervals. This distribution is shown in Table 7.4. To find the $\sum X_i^2$ called for by either (7.7) or (7.8), we first obtain the X^2 subtotal for each class just as we obtained the X subtotal for each class in computing $\overline{X}$. For example, the X^2 subtotal for the class 15 is 675 since there are three scores in this class ($f = 3$), and the sum $15^2 + 15^2 + 15^2$ is 675. It is, of course, more efficient to use multiplication instead of addition to obtain the class subtotals, that is, simply to find the product of the class frequency (f) and the square of the class value (X^2). In the case of the class 15, for example, we have 3×15^2,

Table 7.4 Unit-Interval Frequency Distribution of 50
Scores Given in Table 6.1

X (Score)	f	fX	fX²
21	1	21	441
20	0	0	0
19	0	0	0
18	2	36	648
17	1	17	289
16	2	32	512
15	3	45	675
14	2	28	392
13	3	39	507
12	4	48	576
11	6	66	726
10	9	90	900
9	7	63	567
8	5	40	320
7	2	14	98
6	1	6	36
5	1	5	25
4	1	4	16
	50	554	6,728

or $3 \times 225 = 675$. Obviously, the grand total of these subtotals for all
classes is the required $\sum X_i^2$. Table 7.4 shows these subtotals in the
column headed fX^2. The fX column of this same table gives the X
subtotal for each class, and the grand total for this column is the $\sum X_i$
required in computing the mean. Thus we have in the grand totals for
the fX and fX^2 columns of Table 7.4 all the information needed to
apply (7.7) or (7.8). For example, applying (7.7) we have

$$S^2 = \frac{6{,}728}{50} - \left(\frac{554}{50}\right)^2 = 134.56 - 122.7664 = 11.7936$$

as before.

If we use the symbolic scheme for representing a frequency distribution described in Section 5.4, the total of the N scores involved is
as given in (5.13), i.e., $\sum f_j X_j$, and the total of the squares of these N
scores is as given in (5.16), i.e., $\sum f_j X_j^2$. Adapting this notation to
formulas (7.7) and (7.8) we obtain the following computational
formulas for the variance; these formulas are directly applicable to
data organized into a frequency distribution.

$$S^2 = \frac{\sum f_j X_j^2}{N} - \left(\frac{\sum f_j X_j}{N}\right)^2 \tag{7.9}$$

$$S^2 = \frac{\sum f_j X_j^2}{N} - \bar{X}^2 \tag{7.10}$$

The application of formula (7.10) to our example is shown below:

$$S^2 = \frac{(1)(4)^2 + (1)(5)^2 + (1)(6)^2 + (2)(7)^2 + \cdots + (1)(21)^2}{50}$$
$$- 11.08^2$$

$$= \frac{6{,}728}{50} - 11.08^2 = 134.56 - 122.7664 = 11.7936$$

It is also possible to compute the variance of a set of scores when the data are presented as a relative frequency distribution (Section 5.6). If p_j represents the proportion (relative frequency) of the total N with score X_j, then by (5.19)

$$\sum f_j X_j = N \sum p_j X_j$$

Also, by (5.20),

$$\sum f_j X_j{}^2 = N \sum p_j X_j{}^2$$

Substituting these quantities into 7.9 gives

$$S^2 = \frac{N \sum p_j X_j{}^2}{N} - \left(\frac{N \sum p_j X_j}{N}\right)^2$$
$$= \sum p_j X_j{}^2 - (\sum p_j X_j)^2 \qquad (7.9a)$$

Since $\sum p_j X_j = \bar{X}$ [see equation (6.3a)], we also have

$$S^2 = \sum p_j X_j{}^2 - \bar{X}^2 \qquad (7.10a)$$

We shall illustrate the use of (7.10a) using the data in Table 6.3 (p. 90), which gives the relative frequencies for the distribution of Table 7.4.

$$S^2 = (.02)(4)^2 + (.02)(5)^2 + (.02)(6)^2 + (.04)(7)^2 + \cdots$$
$$+ (.02)(21)^2 - (11.08)^2$$
$$= 134.56 - 122.7664$$
$$= 11.7936$$

7.5   Comparison of Q and S

In the previous chapter, it was noted that the mean, median, and mode are identical if the distribution is unimodal and symmetrical. Of course, most observed distributions are not perfectly symmetrical

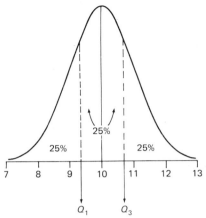

Figure 7.5 Smoothed polygon of hypothetical continuous symmetrical score distribution with $\overline{X} = 10$

and hence these quantities are usually only approximately equal. The magnitudes of Q and S, by contrast, are not usually equal. Even in unimodal symmetrical distributions like the one shown in Figure 7.5, the values of Q and S are different. The value of Q in this distribution is approximately .7; the value of S is 1.0.

When extreme scores are involved, the difference in magnitude between S and Q may become very marked, owing to the fact that S is so much more sensitive than Q to the presence of such scores. This greater sensitivity of S follows, of course, from the fact that S and Q behave in a manner comparable to the mean and median, and from the fact that the mean is much more sensitive than the median to the presence of extreme scores (see Section 6.7). The sensitivity of S to the presence of extreme scores is a characteristic that is important to keep in mind. As was true of the mean, the effect may be so marked in cases of extreme skewness as to invalidate the use of S as a descriptive index.

To illustrate the sensitivity of S to extreme scores, the values of S and Q have been obtained for each of the score distributions shown in Figure 6.7 (p. 98). These results are given in Table 7.5. The difference between the values of S and Q for the unimodal symmetrical Distribution A of Figure 6.7 is of about the same order of magnitude as was noted in the case of the continuous unimodal symmetrical distribution of Figure 7.5. Distribution B of Figure 6.7 is like A except that one of the two highest scores of the A distribution is shifted to an extreme position far up the scale (from a value of 85 to a value of 145). This change of a single score had no effect upon the value of Q_3 and hence none upon the value of Q. The value of S, however, increased

Table 7.5   Values of S and Q for the Distributions of
Figure 6.7

Distribution	S	Q
A. Unimodal, symmetrical	1.10	.75
B. One extreme score at right	13.57	.75
C. One extreme score at left	13.57	.75
D. J-shaped	12.88	.90

by more than 12 times and, except for the single extreme score, exceeds twice the range of the rest of the distribution. Distribution C is the mirror image of B, while Distribution D is a positively skewed J-shaped distribution; in both these cases, too, the value of S varies significantly from that of Q.

It must, of course, be recognized that the distributions of Figure 6.7 are extreme hypothetical examples. For a comparison of the relative magnitudes of S and Q in the case of skewed distributions that are more realistic, attention is directed to the distribution shown in Table 3.8. Table 3.8 shows the distribution of 1,000 individual incomes in dollars for a particular year. The value of S in this distribution is approximately \$3,450 as compared with \$825 for Q. If a distance equal to Q is marked off to either side of the mean of this distribution, the resulting section of the scale contains about 43 percent of the distribution. If, on the other hand, a distance equal to S is marked off to either side of the mean, the section of scale thus established encompasses over 97 percent of the scores involved.

In markedly skewed distributions, measures are quite compactly distributed over one portion of the scale (either the lower or higher portion) and widely scattered over the other portion. This fact suggests that in such distributions a single index of variability may not be as useful as several interpercentile distances. Inspection of several selected percentiles would provide much more insight into the nature of the distribution than would consideration of S or Q alone. Table 7.6 gives approximate values of selected percentiles for the distribution of Table 3.8. In this instance the fact that Q_3 and P_{95} are much farther

Table 7.6   Approximate Values of Selected Percentile
Points for Distribution of Table 3.8

PR	Percentile
95	\$3,765
75	\$2,220
50	\$1,250
25	\$575
5	\$110

above the median than Q_1 and P_5 are below it indicates a highly variable upper portion of the distribution and a highly compact lower portion. Thus we not only have information about the variability of the distribution not revealed by S or Q alone, but we also have information regarding its form (see Sections 4.6 and 4.7).

7.6 Uses of Measures of Variability: Comparing Variability

Quantitative indexes of variability may serve simply in providing a quantitative index of the degree of variation among the scores of a particular collection. They may also serve, in a very practical way, in comparing the relative degree of variability among the scores on some measure for two (or more) groups of individuals (see Section 7.1 for two examples of such comparisons).

This application is possible only if the measures are expressed in terms of the same unit for both groups. Suppose, for example, that the standard deviations of the heights of two groups of children are reported as 2 and 4. Clearly, no one would contend that the second group was twice as variable as the first if it were known that the height scores for the second group were expressed in centimeters while those for the first group were expressed in inches. It is just as unreasonable to infer that a group of children is twice as variable in ability to read as in ability to solve arithmetic problems, simply because the standard deviation of their scores on a given reading test is twice that of their scores on some arithmetic test. Such an inference ignores completely the possibility of a total lack of comparability between the two measuring scales involved.

7.7 Uses of Measures of Variability: Reliability of Measurement or Estimate

A very important application of variability arises in connection with the study of the accuracy of certain measuring or estimating procedures. Consider the problem of measuring the amount of some continuous trait possessed by some individual or object. We have explained in Section 2.4 how it is impossible to take a measurement of the *true* amount of a continuous trait that is possessed by a given object and that any such measurement is, therefore, approximate. This being the case, it is similarly impossible to study errors of measurement by comparing obtained (measured) amounts with true amounts. An analogous situation arises when it is desired to estimate some population characteristic by studying a sample taken from the population. For example, suppose it is desired to estimate the mean IQ for all children in the United States of age 3 through age 15 by obtaining as the estimate the mean of a sample of children taken from this population. Since the determination of the IQ of all the children in the population is a practical impossibility, the true or population mean can never be known, and in this situation, too, it is impossible to investigate error by comparing the obtained and true values. How then, in any situation involving the approximation of a true value that ever remains unknown, can error be investigated?

One possible method of attack consists of making a number of independent repetitions of the measuring or estimating procedure. Then, if it can be assumed that the procedure itself does not give rise to systematic error (that it is free from bias), the variation in the values thus obtained provides a basis for assessing the accuracy of the procedure. If the values arising from a number of repetitions are in close agreement, then the procedure may be regarded as an accurate one. On the other hand, if the values differ markedly there can be little confidence in its accuracy. Obviously then, some index of variability (e.g., S or Q) applied to a collection of values resulting from a number of independent repetitions of a measuring or estimating procedure provides, in turn, a quantitative index of the accuracy of the procedure. Comparison of such indexes for different measuring or estimating procedures provides a basis for evaluating their relative accuracy.

By way of illustration, let us suppose that it is desired to know in advance of an election the proportion of eligible voters in the United States who favor presidential Candidate A over Candidate B. It is, of course, a practical impossibility to question each eligible voter in advance of the election in order to determine whether or not that voter prefers A over B. Hence, the true value of the required proportion can never be predicted, and some estimate of it, based on only a small portion of the entire population of eligible voters, will necessarily have to do. Suppose that it is decided to use a sample of 1,000 eligible voters. Suppose further that some bias-free method of selecting this sample has been invented. This means that while this method of sample selection would not, if repeated, lead to the selection of precisely the same individuals, it would nevertheless produce estimates of the true proportion that would not differ from it any more in one direction than in the other. Let us suppose that by means of this selection technique 1,000 eligible voters have been identified and asked for their preference between A and B, and that, of these, 485, or 48.5 percent, favored A. This, of course, represents only an estimate of the true proportion favoring A; the actual magnitude of the error involved cannot be determined in advance of the election.

Now ordinarily, this is the only sample we would select; we would stand or fall on the accuracy of this estimate. For if we could afford to study more eligible voters, we would undoubtedly prefer to expand the size of our sample and thereby improve the accuracy of the estimate, rather than to obtain additional independent estimates of this same true proportion simply to enable us to make some statement about the degree to which our estimates vary. Just what may be done in a situation of this type to enable us to base our estimates on all individuals selected and yet obtain some indication of the degree to which several independent determinations of such estimates would vary is the subject of a later chapter. For purposes of completing our illustration of the points in question, we shall turn from the practical example of polling preference for presidential candidates to an analogous but purely hypothetical situation.

Suppose that instead of a population of eligible voters, we have a large collection of beads that are alike except for the fact that some are white and some are red. Suppose further that one wants to estimate the proportion that are red by means of a sampling procedure known to be free from bias. To provide a basis for assessing the accuracy of this procedure, we shall repeat it a number of times, thus obtaining a number of estimates of the same true value. The standard deviation of these estimates provides a quantitative estimate of the accuracy of the estimating (actually the sample-selecting) procedure. Quantitatively this index is inversely related to accuracy. That is, a large value of this standard deviation implies marked variation in estimated values and consequent inaccuracy, while a small value implies close agreement among the estimated values and a high degree of accuracy.

This experiment was actually conducted on a small scale. First, 25 samples, each containing 50 beads, were selected by a purely chance or random procedure that would be free from bias. The proportion of red beads was determined for each sample, so that 25 independent estimates of the true proportion of red beads in the "population" were available. Then 25 additional samples, each containing 100 beads, were selected by the same procedure and used to provide 25 other estimates of the actual proportion of red beads in the population. Now, obviously, samples of 100 beads should provide estimates that are more accurate than estimates based on samples of 50 beads. Consequently, we may predict that the standard deviation of the 25 estimates based on the samples of 100 beads will be smaller than the standard deviation of the 25 estimates based on the samples of 50 beads. Thus we have an illustration of the use of an index of variability both as an indicator of the accuracy of a particular estimating procedure and as a basis for comparing the accuracy of two estimating procedures.

The results of this experiment are presented in Figure 7.6. In this

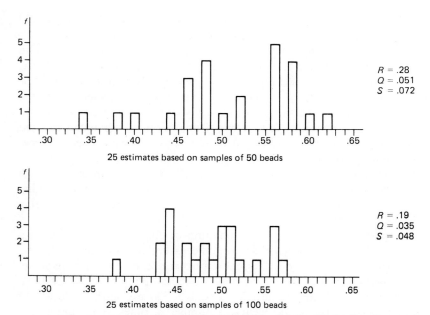

Figure 7.6 Histograms showing distribution of estimates of the true proportion of red beads in a collection of red and white beads for samples of 50 and 100 beads

figure the upper and lower histograms picture the distributions of estimates based on samples consisting of 50 and 100 beads, respectively. It is clear that the estimates based on samples of 50 beads vary more than the estimates based on samples of 100. The range (R), semi-interquartile range (Q), and standard deviation (S) for each distribution are also shown in Figure 7.6. Regardless of which of these indexes of variability is used as basis for comparison, it is clear, as was predicted, that estimates based on the larger samples are less variable and hence more accurate.

The above illustration represents a very useful application of indexes of variability. As will be seen in later chapters dealing with sampling error theory, such estimates of variability are absolutely essential in inferential statistics.

7.8   Uses of Measures of Variability: Standardized Scores

In our discussion of percentiles and percentile ranks (see Chapter 4), we attempted to give meaning to a particular score value by finding the percentage of scores below that value. This was necessary because the raw scores from most tests have little or no meaning.[8] Another method frequently used by standardized test publishers is the *standard score*. Standard scores involve the use of an index of variability as a unit in a new scale. Here we merely note this use. The next chapter treats this idea in some detail.

7.9 Summary Statement

Probably the two most important characteristics of a distribution of scores are its central tendency and its variability. In Chapter 6 we considered indexes of central tendency. In this chapter we discussed indexes of variability. The most commonly used index of variability is the standard deviation (or its square, the variance). Other relatively common indexes include the range, the semi-interquartile range, and the mean deviation.

In addition to providing an estimate of the degree of variability among the scores of a given distribution, indexes of variability can be used to compare the variabilities of different distributions. For example, such indexes can be employed to help answer the following question: Are a group of college students more alike (less variable) on a measure of authoritarianism as seniors than they were as freshmen (see Section 7.1)?

As implied above, measures of variability are useful as descriptive statistics. Such indexes are also extremely useful in inferential statistics. Section 7.7 illustrated, in some detail, how measures of variability are helpful in assessing the accuracy of a particular estimating procedure. It is this use of variability indexes that is of utmost importance in this book. A major portion of the remaining chapters is devoted to the definition and use of indexes of variability in inferential statistics.

[8] See footnote 2 in Chapter 4.

8

Linear Transformations

8.1 Introduction

At first glance, the title of this chapter may seem a little imposing. The word *transformation* tends to convey the impression that a fairly sophisticated technique is involved. We shall attempt to show, however, that this is not really the case. There are many ways in which scores can be transformed into new scores. Here, however, we shall consider only the type known as a linear transformation.

It is impossible to proceed very far in the study of statistics without some knowledge of linear transformations. The primary purpose of this chapter is to develop an understanding of such transformations. In many ways this chapter serves a purpose similar to that of Chapter 5. That is, it is a tool chapter that develops concepts necessary to the understanding of material to be presented later. However, for the sake of concreteness, we will relate the notion of a linear transformation to a practical problem that arises in educational and psychological measurement, even though this particular application is not of great importance to the specific topics treated in this book.

8.2 A Use of Linear Transformations in Educational and Psychological Measurement

We have previously noted (see Section 4.2) that in many instances the raw scores yielded by educational or psychological tests have little meaning in themselves. Even with physical measures (such as length or weight) additional information about a particular measurement is helpful. In Chapter 4, we saw that one technique for making scores more meaningful consisted of determining their *PR*'s. If it is reported that John is 60 inches tall, the meaning of this number can be enhanced by indicating that for all boys of John's chronological age his height score has a *PR* of 80. That is, John is taller than approximately 80 percent of the boys of his chronological age. The interpretation of a score, then, either requires or is enhanced by some indication of its placement or position in a reference collection.

The *PR* is only one possible technique for making a score value (measurement) more meaningful. A *PR* indicates the position of a score in a distribution by stating the percentage of scores that are lower. Another possible approach might be to indicate the position of a score by reporting its location with reference to a central point such as the mean. Suppose, for example, that the mean of a certain score distribution is 80. A score of 72 in this distribution might be reported as −8, indicating a value eight score points below the mean. Or a raw score of 86 might be reported as +6, indicating a value six score points above the mean.

Another method of imparting this information consists of adjusting the scores of a collection so as to change their mean to some standard value. Such an adjustment might consist simply of adding some constant amount to each score. Suppose, for example, that it is decided to use 100 as the standard value for the mean. If the mean of the original score values is 80, it is necessary only to add 20 to each score to form a new collection with the mean having this desired standard value.[1] Scores of 72 and 86 in the original collection assume values of 92 and 106, respectively, in the new collection. Since it is known that the mean of the new collection has the standard value 100, scores of 92 and 106 are immediately recognized as being respectively 8 points below and 6 points above the mean.

Such a scheme results in score values that embody some information not contained in the original scores, namely, information regarding location with reference to the mean of the distribution. While some gain has thus been achieved, the meaningfulness of such scores remains clouded by failure to relate them to the variability of the distribution involved. If, for example, the distribution is quite homogeneous so that most of the scores are crowded closely about the mean 100, a score of 92 may represent an extremely low value in relation to the other scores. On the other hand, if the distribution is highly variable, much of that part of it below the mean may extend far below 92, in which case a score of 92 would represent a more nearly typical score value. In short, a score of 92 in one collection having a mean of 100 could mean something very different from a score of 92 in another having a mean of 100, owing to differences in the variability of the two collections.

---

[1] A formal proof of this assertion is given later.

This inadequacy of the scheme can be overcome by altering the original score values of the distributions so as to cause them to exhibit some same standard degree of variability as well as some standard mean value. Once this is accomplished, a score of a given magnitude would have more nearly comparable meaning from one distribution to another.

Scores whose distributions have means and standard deviations of some standard value are known as standard scores. The operation by which the original or raw scores (X-values) are converted into such standard scores is known as a *linear transformation.* After presenting the formal procedures for making any linear transformation, we shall consider how original scores may be transformed into new scores having means and standard deviations that are of some standard value.

8.3   Linear Transformation: Formal Definition

It will be easier to follow the technique of linear transformation if we work with a concrete example first, and then generalize the procedure. Assume that we have a set of achievement test scores as shown in Table 8.1. Further assume that it is desired for some reason to form a new score by multiplying the original score by 2 and then adding 5 to the result. (Although we may seem, in setting up such an example, to be playing games with numbers, the previous section should provide some hint as to why this sort of thing might be done.)

If we label the original scores X and the new scores Y, then the following equation provides a symbolically stated rule for obtaining the desired Y-values:

$$Y_i = 2X_i + 5 \qquad (i = 1, 2, \ldots, 10)$$

Table 8.2 shows both the original and new scores.

The Y-scores so determined are said to be *linear* transformations of the X-scores, because if the Y-scores are plotted against the X-scores they fall on a straight line (see Figure 8.1).

To generalize the procedure, we merely need to note the two parts of the process: (1) multiplication by a fixed number, and (2) the subsequent addition of a fixed number. That is, each X-value is multiplied by a constant (in the example, by 2), and then a second constant (in the example, 5) is added to the resulting product. A general

Table 8.1   Hypothetical Set of Ten Test Scores

7	8	9	10	5
4	5	8	9	6

Table 8.2 Original and Transformed Scores for Data of
Table 8.1

Original Score (X)	New Score (Y)
7	19
8	21
9	23
10	25
5	15
4	13
5	15
8	21
9	23
6	17

formula for the linear transformation of any variable, say X, into a
new variable, say Y, is:

$$Y_i = bX_i + c \qquad\qquad (8.1)$$

where b and c represent any constants (any fixed numbers).

8.4 Means and Variances of New Distributions Formed by a Linear Transformation

A linear transformation involves multiplication by and addition of a
constant. Since linear transformations may be applied to distributions
of scores, we should examine the relationships that exist between

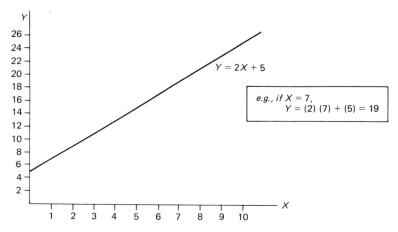

Figure 8.1 Plot of X and Y values in Table 8.2

certain statistical indexes of the original score (X) distribution and the new score (Y) distribution.

In a sense we start backwards by first considering the effect of the addition of a constant to each X-score. In this instance $b = 1$, and equation (8.1) is $Y_i = X_i + c$.

> **RULE 8.1**   Let a constant amount, c, be added to each of N X-scores. Then the mean of the new set of scores thus formed is equal to the mean of the original set plus this constant amount.

Or symbolically,

$$M_{X+c} = \bar{X} + c \qquad (8.2)$$

Example 1 Consider the five scores 16, 4, 12, 8, and 10, of which the mean is 10. (Here $N = 5$.) Now let $c = 3$. Then by (8.2) the mean of the new set of scores formed by adding 3 to each of these scores is

$$M_{X+3} = 10 + 3 = 13$$

To verify this we shall actually form the new set of scores and determine its mean by application of (6.2). The new set is 19, 7, 15, 11, and 13, for which the mean is

$$M_{X+3} = \frac{19 + 7 + 15 + 11 + 13}{5} = \frac{65}{5} = 13$$

Example 2 Let $c = -2$. Then the mean of the new set as given by (8.2) is

$$M_{X+(-2)} = 10 + (-2) = 8$$

Verifying as before, the new set is 14, 2, 10, 6, and 8, for which the mean is

$$M_{X+(-2)} = \frac{14 + 2 + 10 + 6 + 8}{5} = \frac{40}{5} = 8$$

Proof* By (6.2)

$$M_{X+c} = \frac{\sum (X_i + c)}{N}$$

* Optional.

Now applying (5.22) we have

$$M_{X+c} = \frac{\sum X_i + \sum c}{N}$$

And by (5.23)

$$M_{X+c} = \frac{\sum X_i + Nc}{N}$$

And dividing by N we obtain

$$M_{X+c} = \overline{X} + c$$

which establishes the rule.

It should be noted that c may be either a positive or a negative number (see Example 2) and hence the rule holds in the case of subtracting a constant from each score as well as in the case of adding a constant to each score.

RULE 8.2   Let a constant, c, be added to each of N scores. Then the variance of the new set of scores thus formed remains the same as the variance of the original set.

Or symbolically,

$$S^2_{X+c} = S_X{}^2 \tag{8.3}$$

RULE 8.2a   Let a constant, c, be added to each of N scores. Then the standard deviation of the new set of scores thus formed remains the same as the standard deviation of the original set.

Symbolically,

$$S_{X+c} = S_X \tag{8.4}$$

Example 1 Again consider the five scores 16, 4, 12, 8, and 10, the mean of which is 10. The deviations of these five scores from 10 are $+6$, -6, $+2$, -2, and 0, respectively. The squares of these deviations are 36, 36, 4, 4, and 0, and the mean of these squares is 16. Thus, the variance of these five scores is 16 and the standard deviation is 4. Now let $c = 3$. Then, according to (8.3) and (8.4), the variance and the standard deviation of the new set of scores formed by adding 3 to each of the given scores also have the values 16 and 4 respectively. That is,

$$S^2_{X+3} = S_X{}^2 = 16 \quad \text{and} \quad S_{X+3} = S_X = 4$$

To verify, we shall form the new set of scores and determine its variance and standard deviation by direct application of (7.4) and (7.5). The new set of scores is 19, 7, 15, 11, and 13. The mean of this new set is 13. Hence,

$$S^2_{X+3} = \frac{(19 - 13)^2 + (7 - 13)^2 + (15 - 13)^2 \\ + (11 - 13)^2 + (13 - 13)^2}{5}$$

$$= 16$$

and, of course,

$$S_{X+3} = 4$$

Example 2 Using the same five scores as in Example 1, let $c = -2$. The variance and standard deviation of the new set should remain 16 and 4. Verifying as before, the new set now becomes 14, 2, 10, 6, and 8. The mean of this new set is 8. Hence,

$$S^2_{X+(-2)} = \frac{(14 - 8)^2 + (2 - 8)^2 + (10 - 8)^2 \\ + (6 - 8)^2 + (8 - 8)^2}{5}$$

$$= 16$$

and

$$S_{X+(-2)} = 4$$

Comment: To see the plausibility of this result it is necessary only to recall that the variance (or standard deviation) is an index of the degree to which the scores in a collection differ in magnitude, and to note that such differences remain wholly unchanged when all scores in the collection are altered by adding the same amount to each.

Proof* By definition of variance [see (7.4)],

$$S^2_{X+c} = \frac{\sum (X_i + c - M_{X+c})^2}{N}$$

But by (8.2)

$$M_{X+c} = \overline{X} + c$$

* Optional

Hence,

$$S^2_{\bar{X}+c} = \frac{\sum (X_i + c - \bar{X} - c)^2}{N}$$

$$= \frac{\sum (X_i - \bar{X})^2}{N}$$

$$= S_X{}^2$$

which proves the rule.

Next, we examine the effect of multiplying each X-value by a constant. In this case $c = 0$, and (8.1) is $Y_i = bX_i$.

> **RULE 8.3**   Let each of N scores be multiplied by a constant amount b. Then the mean of the new set of scores thus formed is equal to the mean of the original set multiplied by this constant amount.

Or symbolically,

$$M_{bX} = b\bar{X} \tag{8.5}$$

Example 1   Again consider the five scores 16, 4, 12, 8, and 10, of which the mean is 10. (Here $N = 5$.) Now let $b = 2$. Then by (8.5) the mean of the new set of scores formed by multiplying each of these scores by 2 is

$$M_{2X} = (2)(10) = 20$$

To verify this result we shall form the new set of scores and determine its mean by application of (6.2). The new set is 32, 8, 24, 16, and 20, for which the mean is

$$M_{2X} = \frac{32 + 8 + 24 + 16 + 20}{5} = \frac{100}{5} = 20$$

Example 2   Let $b = 1/2$. Then the mean of the new set as given by (8.5) is

$$M_{(1/2)X} = (1/2)(10) = 5$$

Verifying as before, the new set is 8, 2, 6, 4, and 5, for which the mean is

$$M_{(1/2)X} = \frac{8 + 2 + 6 + 4 + 5}{5} = \frac{25}{5} = 5$$

Proof By (6.2)

$$M_{bX} = \frac{\sum bX_i}{N}$$

Applying (5.21) we may write

$$M_{bX} = \frac{b \sum X_i}{N} = b\bar{X}$$

which establishes the rule.

It should be noted that b may be either an integer or a fraction. Hence, by letting b be a fraction of the type $1/d$, we show that the relationship holds in the case of dividing each score by a constant as well as in the case of multiplying each score by a constant.

> **RULE 8.4**   Let each of N scores be multiplied by a constant amount b. Then the variance of the new set of scores thus formed is equal to the variance of the original set multiplied by the square of this amount.

Or symbolically,

$$S_{bX}^2 = b^2 S_X^2 \tag{8.6}$$

> **RULE 8.4a**   Let each of N scores be multiplied by a constant amount b. Then the standard deviation of the new set of scores thus formed is equal to the standard deviation of the original set multiplied by the absolute value of this amount.

Symbolically,[2]

$$S_{bX} = |b|S_X \tag{8.7}$$

Example 1 Again consider the five scores 16, 4, 12, 8, and 10, the variance of which is 16. Now let $b = 2$. Then, according to (8.6) the variance of the new set formed by multiplying each of these scores by 2 is

$$S_{2X}^2 = (2)^2(16) = 64$$

---

* Optional.

[2] You may recall that the standard deviation of a set of scores is defined as the positive square root of the variance (see p. 112). Thus, since b may be negative, it is necessary to include the absolute-value sign in this equation to ensure that S_{bX} is always positive.

and according to (8.7) the standard deviation is

$$S_{2X} = |2|(4) = 8$$

To verify this result we shall form the new set of scores and determine its variance by application of (7.4). The new set is 32, 8, 24, 16, and 20. The mean of this new set is 20 and hence

$$S_{2X}{}^2 = \frac{(32 - 20)^2 + (8 - 20)^2 + (24 - 20)^2 + (16 - 20)^2 + (20 - 20)^2}{5}$$

$$= \frac{320}{5} = 64$$

and

$$S_{2X} = 8$$

Example 2 Let $b = 1/2$. Then the variance and standard deviation of the new set as given by (8.6) and (8.7) are

$$S_{(1/2)X}^2 = (1/2)^2(16) = 4$$

and

$$S_{(1/2)X} = |1/2|(4) = 2$$

Verifying as before, the new set is 8, 2, 6, 4, and 5. The mean of this new set is 5 and hence,

$$S_{(1/2)X}^2 = \frac{(8 - 5)^2 + (2 - 5)^2 + (6 - 5)^2 + (4 - 5)^2 + (5 - 5)^2}{5}$$

$$= \frac{20}{5} = 4$$

and

$$S_{(1/2)X} = 2$$

Proof* By definition of variance [see (7.4)],

$$S_{bX}{}^2 = \frac{\Sigma (bX_i - M_{bX})^2}{N}$$

But by (8.5)

$$M_{bX} = b\overline{X}$$

* Optional.

Hence,

$$S_{bX}^{2} = \frac{\sum (bX_i - b\overline{X})^2}{N}$$

Now removing the common factor b we have

$$S_{bX}^{2} = \frac{\sum b^2(X_i - \overline{X})^2}{N}$$

$$= \frac{b^2 \sum (X_i - \overline{X})^2}{N} \qquad\qquad \text{[see (5.21)]}$$

$$= b^2 S_X^{2}$$

which proves the rule.

Of course, in the general linear transformation, defined by (8.1), each score of a set is first multiplied by a constant, say b, and then increased by a constant, say c. Thus, using the results of Rules 8.1 through 8.4 in combination we have[3]

$$M_{bX+c} = b\overline{X} + c \qquad\qquad (8.8)$$

$$S_{bX+c}^{2} = b^2 S_X^{2} \qquad\qquad (8.9)$$

$$S_{bX+c} = |b|S_X \qquad\qquad (8.10)$$

The verification of these equations in the case of a specific example is left as an exercise (see study manual exercise 8.4.3).

8.5   A Useful Linear Transformation

One of the most useful transformations in statistics is of the following form.

$$Y_i = \frac{1}{S_X}X_i + \frac{-\overline{X}}{S_X} \qquad\qquad (8.11)$$

In this example $b = 1/S_X$ and $c = -\overline{X}/S_X$. That is, each X-score is first multiplied by the reciprocal of the standard deviation and then

---

[3] For a brief explanation of why the absolute-value sign is used in expression (8.10), see footnote 2 in this chapter.

$-\overline{X}/S_X$ is added to this product. Expression (8.11) is more commonly given in another form.

$$Y_i = \frac{1}{S_X} X_i - \frac{1}{S_X} \overline{X}$$

$$= \frac{1}{S_X}(X_i - \overline{X})$$

$$Y_i = \frac{X_i - \overline{X}}{S_X} \tag{8.12}$$

In fact, this transformation is so frequently used that it has been given a special label. Instead of being given the general label Y, the scores obtained by this transformation are referred to as z-scores. That is,

$$z_i = \frac{X_i - \overline{X}}{S_X} \tag{8.13}$$

Formulas (8.8), (8.9), and (8.10) can be used to compute the mean, variance, and standard deviation of a z-score distribution. Remember $b = 1/S_X$ and $c = -\overline{X}/S_X$. By (8.8), the mean of the z-scores is

$$M_z = \frac{1}{S_X} \overline{X} + \frac{-\overline{X}}{S_X} = 0$$

By (8.9), their variance is

$$S_z^2 = \left(\frac{1}{S_X}\right)^2 S_X^2 = 1$$

And by (8.10), their standard deviation is

$$S_z = \left|\frac{1}{S_X}\right| S_X = 1$$

Thus, a distribution of z-scores has the very convenient characteristic that its mean is 0 and its standard deviation is 1.[4] Therefore, a given z-value is directly interpretable as indicative of the number of standard deviations a score is above or below the mean. It should also be noted

[4] The student may wish to verify these results with a real collection of scores. The five scores given in the previous section (16, 4, 12, 8, 10) have a mean of 10 and a standard deviation of 4 and can be used to verify that the z-scores have a mean of 0 and a standard deviation of 1.

from (8.13) that a z-score is a pure or abstract (dimensionless) number as distinguished from a concrete or denominate number (i.e., a number giving some specific dimension such as 6 inches or 114 IQ points).

Recall that at the end of Section 8.2 standard scores were defined as scores whose distributions have means and standard deviations of some standard value. Hence, z-scores are standard scores having standard values of 0 and 1 for the mean and standard deviation, respectively. A z-score of +1.0 is directly interpretable as a value that is one standard deviation above the mean of the distribution to which it belongs, since this distribution is known to have a mean of 0 and a standard deviation of 1.[5] Standard scores whose distributions have means and standard deviations other than 1 and 0 are also frequently encountered in the educational and psychological literature. For example, Wechsler Intelligence Scale for Children (WISC) scores are standard scores with a mean of 100 and a standard deviation of 15. Originally Graduate Record Examination (GRE) scores were standard scores with a mean of 500 and a standard deviation of 100.

It is easy to convert z-scores to any desired set of standard scores by using a linear transformation. Formula (8.14) can be used to make the desired transformation.

Let Z_i = desired standard score for person i.[6] Then

$$Z_i = S_Z z_i + M_Z \tag{8.14}$$

where

S_Z = desired standard deviation
M_Z = desired mean

For example, to transform z_i scores into standard scores having the standard values 500 and 100 for mean and standard deviation respectively, formula (8.14) becomes

$$Z_i = 100z_i + 500$$

An individual with a z-score of +1 has a Z-score of 600.[7]

---

[5] Since a person's z-score is interpretable only with reference to the particular distribution (or norm group) to which it belongs, such scores are sometimes called *norm-referenced* scores. (We have referred to this idea earlier in discussing percentile ranks; see p. 49.)

[6] Note that Z_i is used to represent the score for individual i in any set of standard scores. However, z_i represents the score for person i in the special set of standard scores that has mean 0 and standard deviation 1.

[7] Since z-scores are derived from raw scores (X's), it is possible to compute Z-scores directly from X's also. The formula is $Z_i = S_Z[(X_i - \bar{X})/S_X] + M_Z$.

8.6   The Form of a Distribution of Linearly Transformed Scores

In Section 8.3, we showed how a linear transformation of a set of X-scores produced a set of Y-scores (in Section 8.5, we also labeled these new scores z or Z) having some desired mean and standard deviation. In this final section of Chapter 8, we examine, through a specific example, what happens to the form of the distribution when a set of scores are subjected to a linear transformation.

Table 8.3 shows the frequency distribution of a hypothetical collection of 200 test scores. The particular distribution involved is markedly skewed to the right. Table 8.3 also shows the computation of the mean and standard deviation of this set of scores. The procedures employed involve the application of formulas (6.3) and (7.10).

Table 8.4 shows the z- and Z-values (with mean = 500 and standard deviation = 100) corresponding to each X-value of Table 8.3. The z-values corresponding to each X were obtained by first multiplying each X-value by $1/S$, that is, by .29 (see third column of Table 8.4), and then adding to each of these products the negative of $\overline{X}/S$, that is, -2.30. [See (8.11).] The Z-values were obtained from the z-values by application of (8.14). Notice that the frequencies are distributed in precisely the same pattern regardless of which scale is involved. In other words, *the form of the distribution is unaffected by the linear transformation.* Figure 8.2 shows the polygon for this frequency

Table 8.3   The Frequency Distribution of a Hypothetical Set of 200 Test Scores and the Computation of $\overline{X}$ and S

X	f	fX	fX²	
20	1	20	400	
19	1	19	361	
18	2	36	648	
17	2	34	578	$\overline{X} = \dfrac{1,572}{200} = 7.86$
16	3	48	768	
15	4	60	900	
14	5	70	980	$S^2 = \dfrac{14,694}{200} - 7.86^2$
13	6	78	1,014	$= 73.47 - 61.7796$
12	7	84	1,008	$= 11.6904$
11	8	88	968	$S = 3.42$
10	9	90	900	$1/S = .29$
9	12	108	972	$-\overline{X}/S = -2.30$
8	18	144	1,152	
7	26	182	1,274	
6	46	276	1,656	
5	35	175	875	
4	15	60	240	
	200	1,572	14,694	

Table 8.4   The z- and Z-Values Corresponding to Each X-Value of the Distribution of Table 8.3

X	f	.29X	z = .29X − 2.30	Z = 100z + 500
20	1	5.80	3.50	850
19	1	5.51	3.21	821
18	2	5.22	2.92	792
17	2	4.93	2.63	763
16	3	4.64	2.34	734
15	4	4.35	2.05	705
14	5	4.06	1.76	676
13	6	3.77	1.47	647
12	7	3.48	1.18	618
11	8	3.19	.89	589
10	9	2.90	.60	560
9	12	2.61	.31	531
8	18	2.32	.02	502
7	26	2.03	− .27	473
6	46	1.74	− .56	444
5	35	1.45	− .85	415
4	15	1.16	−1.14	386
	200			

distribution with reference to all three scales, which have been placed in juxtaposition at the base of the figure. In the figure, as in the table, it can be seen that the form of the distribution is invariant under a linear transformation.

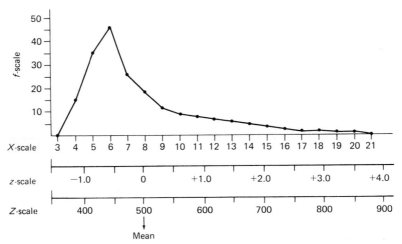

Figure 8.2   Polygon of hypothetical score distribution of Table 8.3 with reference to X-, z-, and Z-scales

8.7   Summary Statement

A linear transformation of a set of scores yields a new set of scores having a mean and a standard deviation that are functionally related to the mean and standard deviation of the original set [see (8.8) and (8.10)]. In addition, a linear transformation does not change the shape of a distribution of scores. If the original set of scores was unimodal, skewed left, the new set formed by a linear transformation will be unimodal, skewed left.

In this chapter the only illustrative application of the linear transformation technique treated the development and interpretation of standard scores for educational and psychological measuring instruments. This particular application was employed primarily because the prerequisites for understanding it are minimal. However, it happens that knowledge of this particular application will enhance an understanding of many research studies in psychology and education, since many of these studies use measuring instruments for which standard scores are reported.

In later chapters of this book, we shall be concerned with two somewhat different applications of the linear transformation concept. First, in Chapters 9 through 17, we will frequently use such transformations in inferential statistics. In this setting, for example, transformations very similar to (8.13) can be used to help test statistical hypotheses. Second, in Chapter 18, linear transformations similar to (8.1) are employed to predict scores on a particular variable (say, college grade-point average) given scores on another variable (say, high school grade-point average). It should be apparent, then, that an understanding of linear transformations will be important to an understanding of much that is to follow.

9

Introduction to Some Probability Concepts

9.1 The Need for Probability Theory in Inferential Statistics

Our previous work in this book has been limited to the description of observed data. The indexes and techniques that have been presented are useful in describing the characteristics of a particular collection of numerical data. If interest is limited to the particular group of individuals for whom measures on some variable are available, these descriptive procedures probably would be sufficient and no additional inferential techniques would be needed. However, most research studies in education and psychology, or for that matter in many other fields, are of the type known as *sampling studies*. In such studies, measurements or observations are made of a limited number, or *sample*, of individuals or objects in order that generalizations, or *inferences*, may be drawn about larger groups, or *populations*, of the individuals or objects that these samples are supposed to represent. Because the individuals or objects constituting these populations differ from one another, and because chance or uncontrolled influences always play some part in determining which of these differing individuals constitute the particular sample used, any single fact obtained from the examination of the sample is almost certain to differ by some amount from the corresponding fact for the whole population. Such "sample facts," therefore, may never be accepted as exactly descriptive of, or equivalent to, the corresponding facts for the whole population.

Consider, for example, the type of sampling study most widely known to the general public, the public opinion survey. Assume one of the public opinion polls has asked a representative sample[1] of 1,000

---

[1] A brief discussion of one possible sampling plan designed to ensure a representative sample will be presented in Chapter 11.

U.S. citizens in the 18–25 age bracket the following question: "Do you favor the passage of the Smith amendment?" Assume 51 percent of the sample answered "Yes." It should be clear that 51 percent is merely an estimate of the true percentage of the entire population of citizens 18–25 years old who favor the passage of this amendment. That is, if all citizens age 18–25 were asked this question, the percentage responding "Yes" would in all likelihood not be exactly 51 percent. Thus, when a sample from some population is used to estimate facts about the population, these sample estimates almost always contain some error, called *sampling error*. How much error? We cannot know the answer to this question unless we obtain responses from the entire population.

The dilemma is obvious. It is almost always totally impracticable to poll an entire population; and yet if we poll only a sample, there is almost certain to be some degree of error in the result.

The solution to this dilemma is not absolute. In a sampling study we will never be able to specify the exact amount of sampling error in the findings. However, if appropriate theory is available, it may be possible to make a statement about the probable magnitude of errors in our estimate. Consider a statement such as the following: "The results of this opinion poll are accurate within 2 percent." This statement is at this time somewhat difficult to interpret precisely but the idea conveyed is that the maximum amount of error is 2 percent. But this idea is not as categorical as it sounds. It is actually only *highly probable* that the maximum error is 2 percent. The determination of this value of 2 percent is made through the use of what is called *probability theory*.

This example used the public opinion poll to suggest how probability theory may be useful in analyzing the results of sampling studies. Another example, more typical of research studies in education and psychology, follows.

Each year at the beginning of the fall semester, the newspapers of many campus communities contain advertisements for speed reading courses. According to the advertisements, students completing such courses are able to read faster and comprehend more fully. One of the student personnel workers at a particular university decides to investigate some of the claims made in such an advertisement. Specifically, he wants to answer the question: "Does this speed reading course actually improve reading comprehension?" He develops a procedure that he could follow to answer this question. First, he decides, he will select (by appropriate procedures) 60 students from the freshman class. These 60 students will be asked if they will consent to take a reading comprehension test on a date approximately two weeks hence. Then 30 of the 60 students will be selected by lot and asked to take a two-week speed reading course at no cost. All 60, the worker assumes, will agree to cooperate. After the group of 30 has completed the two-week course, the reading comprehension test will be administered to all 60 students.

How can the results of the test be used to answer the personnel worker's question? He reasons as follows. If the reading course neither improves nor hurts comprehension (if the course has neither a positive nor a negative effect), then the mean score for the group that took the course ($\overline{X}_C$) should be approximately the same as the mean score for the group that did not take the course ($\overline{X}_{NC}$). If the reading course actually improves comprehension, then $\overline{X}_C$ should be greater than $\overline{X}_{NC}$. On the other hand, if the reading course should actually have a negative effect on comprehension—perhaps as a result of overemphasizing speed—$\overline{X}_C$ should be less than $\overline{X}_{NC}$.

At first thought, it might seem reasonable for the investigator simply to look at the observed means (i.e., at $\overline{X}_C$ and $\overline{X}_{NC}$) and then, if $\overline{X}_C > \overline{X}_{NC}$, conclude that the course had a positive effect; or, if $\overline{X}_C < \overline{X}_{NC}$, conclude that the course had a negative effect. In fact, if interest is restricted to this particular set of 60 students, such a procedure might be defensible. It seems obvious, however, that the investigator must really be interested in generalizing his findings beyond these 60 students. Perhaps the population of interest is the entire freshman class at this particular university, or perhaps it consists of the freshman classes at a number of similar universities, or perhaps of all college freshman regardless of type of institution.[2] If this is the case, the study is a sampling study.

What population facts are of interest to the investigator? The investigator would like to know the mean score on the comprehension test for all freshmen before they took the speed reading course and the mean score for all after taking the course. Clearly, it is not practicable to obtain these population means. Estimates of these means can, however, be found from the 30 students who took the two-week course and the 30 students who did not. However, as in the case of the opinion poll example, such estimates almost certainly contain some sampling error. Precisely how much can be determined only if all freshmen are involved in the investigation—which would be totally impracticable.

Here again, probability theory can help an investigator escape a vicious circle. Probability theory can provide an estimate of the maximum amount of sampling error the investigator can expect in this experiment if he assumes the course offers students no benefits. For example, suppose that by using appropriate probability theory it is determined that if the reading treatment has no effect, then it is "highly" probable that the observed difference between $\overline{X}_C$ and $\overline{X}_{NC}$ will be between -4 and $+4$. Now, if the observed difference,

[2] In Chapter 11, more will be said about what constitutes a population of interest.

$\overline{X}_C - \overline{X}_{NC}$, is found to be 2, there is little support for the effectiveness of the reading course. The fact that the observed means differ by two units might be easily explained as sampling error. However, if the observed difference is 6, the probability theory indicates that something most unusual has happened—so unusual, indeed, as to cast grave doubt on the assumption of no positive course effects. Such a finding, if the doubt is sufficiently great, is supportive of the competing conclusion that the course produces positive effects.

It is the purpose of this chapter to introduce a few probability concepts that are essential for understanding the inferential procedures treated in Chapters 11 through 16. No attempt is made to develop these probability concepts beyond the minimal level necessary for this understanding.

9.2 Experiment as a Technical Term in Probability and Statistics

In the college edition of Webster's *New World Dictionary*, one can find that an *experiment* in one sense is a *test*, that a *test* in one sense is a *trial*, and that a *trial* in one sense is an *experiment*. Given this set of facts about these three terms, any person who understands the meaning, in the sense necessary to these equivalences, of any one of these terms understands also the meaning in this sense of the other two. On the other hand, this set of facts is useless to the person who does not understand this sense of the meaning of any one of these terms. Definitions of words are made of simpler words, and are useful to an individual only to the degree to which he understands the simpler words of which they are made. It is inevitable as one progresses along the hierarchy of simplicity that sooner or later one must encounter instances in which word *A* is defined by word *B* and word *B* in its turn is defined by word *A*. Mathematicians evade this dilemma by the simple device of leaving either *A* or *B* undefined.[3] This is not to say that they begin from nothing, that they use as a foundation block a completely meaningless symbol or term. On the contrary they may go to some lengths to develop the sense of *A* (or *B*) by citing instances of what is *A* and what is not *A*. This is the way in which the term *experiment* will be dealt with here. No formal definition of the sense in which the term *experiment* is used in a probability or statistical context will be given, but an attempt will nonetheless be made to explain clearly the sense in which the term is so employed.

Consider a describable and repeatable act or concurrence of circumstances the result of which cannot be predicted with certainty on any

---

[3] Consider, for example, the notion of set membership as it is used in modern algebra.

Table 9.1   Examples of Repeatable Acts or Concurrences of Circumstances, the Nature of the Observations, and the Sets of All Possible Observations

Act or Concurrence of Circumstances	Nature of Observations (Outcome of Interest)	Set of All Possible Observations
1 Toss or cast of an ordinary die	Number of dots facing up	1, 2, 3, 4, 5, and 6 dots
2 Draw of a single card from an ordinary 52-card bridge deck	Color of card	Red (R) and not red ($\bar{R}$), i.e., black
3 Ten persons assembled in a room[a]	Number who are left-handed	0, 1, 2, . . . , 10 left-handed
4 An instant in time at an office phone switchboard controlling 25 phones[b]	Number of phones in use	0, 1, 2, . . . , 25 phones in use
5 N persons assembled in a room	Number who are smokers	0, 1, 2, . . . , N smokers
6 The instant at which an instructor enters a classroom	The position of the second hand (X) of the classroom clock	$0 \leq X < 60$
7 N persons assembled in a room	Mean ($\bar{X}$) of their heights in inches	$0 < \bar{X} < 120$

[a] *Repetition here involves a new assemblage of ten persons.*
[b] *Repetition here involves other instants in time.*

given occasion but the set of all possible outcomes of which can be specified in advance. For example, consider the clearly repeatable act of tossing a coin. The result—the way the coin lands—cannot be predicted with certainty on any given toss, but the set of all possible results consists simply of the elements "heads up" and "tails up."[4] Or consider the repeatable act of tossing two coins designated as 1 and 2. Again the result, how the coins land, cannot be predicted with certainty for a given toss. It is clear, however, that this result must be one of the following: both coins heads up (H_1, H_2); coin 1 heads up and coin 2 tails up (H_1, T_2); coin 1 tails up and coin 2 heads up (T_1, H_2); and both coins tails up (T_1, T_2). These examples, together with the additional ones given in Table 9.1, are representative of what we shall refer to as an experiment.

An experiment is characterized by (1) repeatability, (2) uncertainty of outcome on a given occasion, and (3) specifiability of all possible outcomes. Note that the outcomes of all the examples given in Table 9.1 are discrete except for those of examples 6 and 7. In the case of example 7, the outcome is continuous in the sense that it can be any positive

[4] Strictly speaking, "on edge" is also a member of the set. For the sake of simplicity, however, we shall not admit "on edge" as a possible outcome.

real number over some finite range. Whatever this range actually may be, it is included within the range that is specified.

9.3   Some Definitions and Basic Concepts of Probability Theory

With the background provided in the foregoing sections, it is now possible to state somewhat more formal definitions of certain of the terms and concepts that are needed in a treatment of probability. We shall illustrate most of these definitions with fairly simple experiments. In later chapters we shall discuss the concepts in more realistic settings.

DN 9.1   A set ($\mathscr{S}$) of elements such that any outcome of an experiment corresponds to exactly one element in the set is called a *sample space*.

DN 9.2   An element in a sample space is called a *sample point*.

Example 1 Consider experiment 1 in Table 9.1. As stated in the table, the outcome of interest is the number of dots facing up. Thus, the sample space $\mathscr{S}$ is $\{1, 2, 3, 4, 5, 6\}$.[5] And the six sample points are 1, 2, 3, 4, 5, and 6. However, consider a slight modification of the experiment. Assume that the outcome of interest is whether the number of dots facing up is either odd or even. Then, $\mathscr{S} = \{\text{odd, even}\}$. The two sample points are odd and even.

Example 2 Consider the second experiment in Table 9.1. As stated, the outcome of interest is the color of the card. Therefore, $\mathscr{S} = \{\text{red (R), not red } (\bar{R})\}$, and the sample points are R, $\bar{R}$. If the outcome of interest had been the value and suit of the drawn card, then the sample space of interest would be

$$\mathscr{S} = \{2, 3, 4, 5, 6, 7, 8, 9, 10, \text{J, Q, K, A of clubs,}$$
$$2, 3, 4, 5, 6, 7, 8, 9, 10, \text{J, Q, K, A of diamonds,}$$
$$2, 3, 4, 5, 6, 7, 8, 9, 10, \text{J, Q, K, A of hearts,}$$
$$2, 3, 4, 5, 6, 7, 8, 9, 10, \text{J, Q, K, A of spades}\}$$

The sample points of this sample space are the 52 elements of this set.

Example 3 Consider experiment 7 in Table 9.1. The outcome of interest is the mean height of N persons. As we noted previously, this outcome is continuous in the sense that it can be any positive number over some finite range. A sample space for this outcome is $\mathscr{S} = \{0 < \bar{X} < 120\}$. Technically, there are an infinity of elements

---

[5] We shall use braces around the elements of the sample space.

(sample points) in this sample space. Assume the outcome of interest in this experiment is merely whether the average height is greater than or equal to 69 inches or less than 69 inches. Then, $\mathscr{S} = \{\overline{X} \geq 69, \overline{X} < 69\}$, and the two sample points are $\overline{X} \geq 69$ and $\overline{X} < 69$.

> **DN 9.3** An *event* is a subset of the sample points that constitute the sample space of an experiment. It may consist of one or more of the sample points.

Example 1 Again consider experiment 1 in Table 9.1. Here, $\mathscr{S} = \{1, 2, 3, 4, 5, 6\}$. Possible events may be

$$E_1 = 1 \text{ dot} \qquad E_2 = 2 \text{ dots} \qquad E_3 = 3 \text{ dots}$$
$$E_4 = 4 \text{ dots} \qquad E_5 = 5 \text{ dots} \qquad E_6 = 6 \text{ dots}$$
$$E_7 = 2 \text{ dots or 4 dots or 6 dots (number of dots even)}$$
$$E_8 = 1 \text{ dot or 3 dots or 5 dots (number of dots odd)}$$
$$E_9 = 1 \text{ dot or 2 dots or 3 dots (number of dots 3 or less)}$$
$$E_{10} = 4 \text{ dots or 5 dots or 6 dots (number of dots more than 3)}$$

Example 2 Consider an experiment that consists of tossing two coins, say a penny (p) and a dime (d). A sample space of interest may be $\mathscr{S} = \{H_p, H_d; T_p, T_d; H_p, T_d; T_p, H_d\}$. Possible events of interest may be

$$E_1 = H_p, H_d$$
$$E_2 = T_p, T_d$$
$$E_3 = H_p, T_d$$
$$E_4 = T_p, H_d$$
$$E_5 = H_p, H_d \text{ or } T_p, T_d \text{ (both fall alike)}$$
$$E_6 = H_p, T_d \text{ or } T_p, H_d \text{ (penny and dime fall differently)}$$
$$E_7 = H_p, H_d \text{ or } H_p, T_d \text{ or } T_p, H_d \text{ (at least one head)}$$

From the above two examples, it can be seen that it is possible to distinguish between two types of events. These types are labeled as simple and compound events.

> **DN 9.4** An event that is a sample point is called an *elementary* or *simple* event. That is, sample points are simple events. A *compound* event is one that consists of more than one sample point and, hence, is itself decomposable into simple events.

Example In the first example after DN 9.3, E_1, E_2, E_3, E_4, E_5, and E_6 are simple events; E_7, E_8, E_9, and E_{10} are compound events.

Remark: It is important to note that simple and compound events are defined in terms of the sample space of an experiment. Thus, for example, in experiment 2 of Table 9.1 the sample space is $\mathscr{S} = \{R, \bar{R}\}$. The simple events of this experiment are

$$E_1 = R \quad \text{and} \quad E_2 = \bar{R}$$

There are no compound events that would be of interest for this experiment. (Why?) However, if experiment 2 is modified so that the outcome of interest is the value and suit of the drawn card, then the sample space consists of 52 sample points and a large number of compound events are possible. For example, consider the event that consists of the subset of points club A, diamond A, heart A, and spade A (i.e., any ace).

We next give a rather formal definition of a probability value. The student should be satisfied at this point to understand *what* the definition says; he should not pause in an effort to figure out *why* it is true. The "why" of this definition should become clear as the following pages are studied. Perhaps at the end of Section 9.4 the student should reconsider this definition with the question as to the "why" of it foremost in mind.

DN 9.5 Probability. Given a sample space, $\mathscr{S}$, consisting of the sample points (simple events) s_j ($j = 1, 2, \ldots, n$). Let some number designated by $P(s_j \mid \mathscr{S})$, or simply by $P(s_j)$,[6] be assigned to—i.e., paired or associated with—each sample point where

$$P(s_j) \geq 0$$

and

$$P(s_1) + P(s_2) + \cdots + P(s_n) = \sum_{j=1}^{n} P(s_j) = 1$$

Then $P(s_j)$ is said to be the probability or the probability value of the sample point s_j.

DN 9.6 The probability of a compound event E, designated $P(E \mid \mathscr{S})$ or simply $P(E)$, is the sum of the probabilities of the sample points in E.

DN 9.7 The equally likely outcomes model. Given a sample space, $\mathscr{S}$, with n sample points s_j ($j = 1, 2, \ldots, n$). Let $P(s_j) = 1/n$ for every sample point. Then the outcomes (simple events or sample points) of the experiment having this sample space are said to be equally likely.

Before stating the last two definitions of this section, it may be helpful to consider examples that illustrate the concepts and terms already defined.

---

[6] This simpler designation may be used when and only when there can be no possible misunderstanding regarding the sample space involved.

Example 1 Consider an *experiment* that consists of drawing a single card from an ordinary 52-card bridge deck. Assume the outcome of interest is the value and suit of the card. Then the *sample space* of this experiment consists of the 52 possible outcomes. More specifically it consists of

2, 3, 4, 5, 6, 7, 8, 9, 10, J, Q, K, A of clubs
2, 3, 4, 5, 6, 7, 8, 9, 10, J, Q, K, A of diamonds
2, 3, 4, 5, 6, 7, 8, 9, 10, J, Q, K, A of hearts
2, 3, 4, 5, 6, 7, 8, 9, 10, J, Q, K, A of spades

Each of these outcomes is a *sample point*. In the *equally likely outcomes model* each of these 52 sample points is assigned or associated with the number 1/52. Note that this number is nonnegative and that the sum of all 52 of these numbers is 1. Hence, these numbers are *probabilities* (see DN 9.5). Some possible instances of *compound events* include an ace (A), a club (C), and a red card (R). Note that by DN 9.6

$$P(A) = \frac{1}{52} + \frac{1}{52} + \frac{1}{52} + \frac{1}{52} = \frac{4}{52} = \frac{1}{13}$$

$$P(C) = \sum_{i=1}^{13} \frac{1}{52} = 13\left(\frac{1}{52}\right) = \frac{13}{52} = \frac{1}{4}$$

$$P(R) = \sum_{i=1}^{26} \frac{1}{52} = 26\left(\frac{1}{52}\right) = \frac{26}{52} = \frac{1}{2}$$

Example 2 Given an *experiment* that consists of drawing a single score from the collection of 100 scores shown in Table 9.2. Note that in this collection there are 5 nines. Let these nines be labeled $9_1, 9_2, 9_3, 9_4,$ and 9_5. Similarly the 10 eights may be labeled $8_1, 8_2, \ldots,$ 8_{10}, the 20 sevens $7_1, 7_2, \ldots, 7_{20},$ and so on. The outcome of interest is the particular score drawn. Thus, we have in all 100 distinguishable outcomes, each of which is a *sample point* and which together specify the *sample space*. If we now adopt the *equally likely outcomes model*, we must assign to or associate with each of the 100 sample points the number $1/100 = .01$. Then .01 is the *probability* of any sample point. Some instances of *events* include a nine (9), an odd number, $X < 6$, $5 \leq X \leq 7$, and $5 < X < 7$. By DN 9.6

$$P(9) = .01 + .01 + .01 + .01 + .01 = .05$$
$$P(\text{odd number}) = .50$$
$$P(X < 6) = .35$$
$$P(5 \leq X \leq 7) = .70$$
$$P(5 < X < 7) = .30$$

Table 9.2   Collection 100 Scores

Score (X)	f
9	5
8	10
7	20
6	30
5	20
4	10
3	5
	100

Let us verify that $P(\text{odd number}) = .50$. In the sample space the odd numbers consist of 5 nines, 20 sevens, 20 fives, and 5 threes. Hence, the subset of odd numbers contains 50 sample points each having the probability .01 and, by DN 9.6, the probability of an odd number is the sum of these fifty probability values of .01, which is .50. It is left to the student to verify the last three probability values.

The student should recognize that other models are possible within the framework of DN 9.5. For example, with each of the 5 nines, we could associate the number .2, and with all the remaining X-values the number 0. Each of the numbers so used is equal to or greater than 0 and their sum over the sample space is 1. Hence, by DN 9.5 they are *probabilities*.

We conclude this section with two additional definitions.

DN 9.8   An experiment that is repeatable under the same conditions is said to be a *random experiment*.

A coin tossing experiment by its very nature is a random experiment so long as the same coin or coins are used and so long as the same individual tosses these coins on the same surface, in the same environment, with the same technique.[7] If the particular individual uses a technique that enables him to toss the coin so that it falls heads up a substantially greater proportion of times than it falls tails up, this does *not* alter the fact that a toss constitutes a random experiment.

The type of random experiment that is of particular interest in statistics is the random sampling experiment as represented by examples 3, 5, and 7 in Table 9.1. It is much more difficult to conceive of repetition under the same conditions in such experiments. First, it is necessary to have some population of objects or individuals from which the N to be assembled are presumed to have come. These assembled objects or

---

[7] It must be assumed that the coins do not become worn in the process, for then they are no longer the *same* as the coins used in the previous runs of the experiment and, hence, repetition cannot be claimed.

individuals are called the *sample*. Second, it is necessary to devise some scheme for selecting the sample members from the population. This must be a scheme that can be repeated. It must further be a scheme with results or outcomes that *cannot* be predicted with certainty for any given repetition but that *can* be specified in advance as a totality of all possible outcomes. More will be said about this situation in a later chapter.

> **DN 9.9**   If the outcome of a random experiment can be expressed as a real number, this number is called a *random variable*.

It is clear that except for example 2 the outcomes of the experiments cited in Table 9.1 are expressed in terms of numbers. In example 2 the outcome is a color, more specifically one of two colors: red, and not red (i.e., black). It is possible, however, to express even the outcome of example 2 as a number by agreeing (quite arbitrarily, of course) to score a red as 1 and a not red as 0. If such an agreement regarding experiment 2 is reached, and if all the experiments cited in Table 9.1 are assumed to be repeatable under the same conditions, they are all instances of *random experiments* of the type that give rise to *random variables*.

9.4   Intuitive Interpretation of and Assignment of Probability Values

In the preceding section we considered a rather abstract (axiomatic) definition of a probability or of a probability value (DN 9.5). In this section we shall consider the question of what it is that these values might indicate. Unfortunately there is no unequivocal answer to this question. We first examine a relative frequency point of view.

The key to the relative frequency interpretation of probability lies in the repeatability characteristic of an experiment. What is needed is some numerical value that indicates the frequency of occurrence of a particular experimental outcome (sample point) of the experiment, given the ideal of theoretical totality of experience with that experiment. "Theoretical totality of experience" refers to the experience with the outcomes of an experiment that would accrue were the experiment somehow to be repeated indefinitely.

Clearly, a convenient and meaningful number to assign to, or associate with, a given possible experimental outcome is simply the *relative frequency* with which this outcome occurs in the universe that consists of the ideal totality of experience with this experiment. It will be observed that the restrictions placed on probability values as they were defined earlier are applicable to numbers so assigned. No relative frequency can possibly be negative (no outcome can occur fewer than zero times), and the combined relative frequencies of all possible outcomes must always be unity (see Section 5.6).

The question at once arises as to how such relative frequencies can be determined, if theoretical totality of experience implies indefinite (infinite) repetition. Two possibilities exist.

Consider first the empirical or *Monte Carlo* method. This method consists of (1) actually causing the experiment to be repeated some "large" number of times, say $\mathcal{N}$, (2) recording or tabulating the numbers of times $n_1, n_2, \ldots, n_k$ $\left(\sum_{j=1}^{k} n_j = \mathcal{N} \right)$ each of the k possible sample points (outcomes) occurs, and (3) assigning to or associating with these sample points the probability values $n_1/\mathcal{N}, n_2/\mathcal{N}, \ldots, n_k/\mathcal{N}$ that are the relative frequencies of their respective occurrences. Apart from the fact that this method may be very costly, it suffers from the weakness that the probability values it furnishes are neither unique nor representative of the totality of all possible experience. Some other experimenter running this same experiment under the same conditions and repeating it some other "large" number of times, say $\mathcal{N}'$, may observe different probability values. Experience appears to indicate, however, that if the two experimenters are indeed independently repeating the same experiment under the same conditions, the corresponding probability values they observe will tend to become more and more alike as $\mathcal{N}$ and $\mathcal{N}'$ increase. Sometimes, because of the complexity of the possible experimental outcomes, the Monte Carlo method is the only practicable one for assigning probability values. In such cases a large high-speed computer may be programmed to simulate the experiment and keep track of the results so as to make possible a large number of repetitions over a relatively short space of time.[8]

Second, consider a purely hypothetical or theoretical method. This method consists simply of assigning a probability value to each sample point on the basis of some assumed or hypothetical model. Of course, the values assigned must satisfy the conditions of DN 9.5 and DN 9.6, that is, they must be nonnegative and they must add up to 1. One such model has already been defined and illustrated, namely, the *equally likely outcomes model* (see DN 9.7 and the examples that follow it). Values assigned using such models are interpreted in precisely the same way as values derived by the more direct Monte Carlo method. That is, they are interpreted as the relative frequencies with which the various sample points and compound events would occur if the experiment were indeed to be repeated indefinitely. Of course, with this method it is not necessary to conduct even a single trial of the experiment in order to arrive at the probability values. To summarize, the

---

[8] We discuss such a simulation in Section 15.9.

hypothetical method consists simply of more or less arbitrarily assigning probability values to the sample points. These probability values are then interpreted as the relative frequencies with which these points (outcomes) would occur were the experiment involved repeated indefinitely.

To be useful in a practical sense, hypothetically assigned probability values must be at least good approximations of the probabilities that would arise from indefinite repetition of the experiment. Fortunately, when the assignments are made on the basis of a well-chosen model, experience indicates that assigned values *do* approximate "true" values; for many random experiments, the equally likely outcomes model has been found to be highly satisfactory when empirically checked by the Monte Carlo method. In fact, if the hypothetical approach as applied to a specific experiment is based on a valid model, the probability values it assigns are superior to those that would be obtained by the empirical approach, because (1) the values are unique and (2) they are *the* relative frequencies of the various possible outcomes for the ideal totality of all possible experience with this experiment. Neither of these claims can be made for empirically derived values. Of course, if the model is not true, empirically determined values are more meaningful in a practical sense.

One of the important features of the hypothetical model approach lies in the fact that the model adopted may stem from some scientific theory. That is, the model used may be one that is known to be true if the theory is true. An important application of statistical inference is in checking the truth of a probability model, and thus in turn checking the truth of the theory that gave rise to that model, by actually conducting, some "large" number of times, the experiment for which the model was built.

An entirely different approach to both the interpretation and the assignment of probability values has gained considerable attention recently. In this approach, although values are assigned to or associated with events in a manner fully consistent with DN 9.5 and DN 9.6, they are not interpreted as indicating the relative frequencies with which the events occur in the universe of outcomes established by the ideal totality of experience with a particular experiment. Instead, they are viewed as quantitative indexes of one's personal and rational degree of belief that some event will occur or has occurred, or that some assertion is true. For example, suppose that one observed a certain coin being tossed ten times and that the outcome on each toss was a head. One might then say that the probability that the coin has heads on both sides is .9 or perhaps even .99, thereby expressing a very strong belief that such is the case. In the same sense a meteorologist might aver that the probability of a storm occurring in a certain area within a certain time is .80, or a historian might assert that the probability that a particular one of the *Federalist Papers* was written by Hamilton instead of Madison is .75. It is possible for a personalist (or *Bayesian*, as advocates of this approach are sometimes called) to associate probability values with events that are obviously not repeatable. Indeed some personalists deny the notion that any situation or experiment giving rise to events of practical interest is truly repeatable.

It is the applicability of the personalistic interpretation of a probability value to the possible outcomes of a nonrepeatable concurrence of circumstances that lends it its appeal, since this interpretation is certainly consistent with the vernacular sense in which the word *probability* is used. It would appear that the personalistic approach might give rise to the frequent assignment of ill-considered if not frivolous probability values. It can be shown, however, that if probabilities are systematically and objectively revised as more information becomes available, the original values assigned, however frivolous they may be, will make very little difference in the end result. If this is indeed the case, then it would seem more appropriate to start with some judgment regarding a probability value, however subjective that judgment may be, than to behave as if one had no knowledge whatever as to the probability's magnitude. A more detailed discussion of this approach to probability will be presented in Chapter 16.

9.5   Probability Distributions for Experiments with a Finite Number of Sample Points

A *probability distribution* is simply the pairing of the elements of a sample space (i.e., the sample points) with the probability values assigned to each of them. This distribution may be represented by a graph, table, or formula.

Example 1 Consider the first experiment in Table 9.1. In this situation an ordinary die is tossed. The outcome of interest (i.e., the random variable) is the number of dots showing on the top side of the die. Here, the sample space of interest is $\mathscr{S} = \{1, 2, 3, 4, 5, 6\}$.[9] If the equally likely model is assumed, then $P(s_j) = 1/n = 1/6$ (see p. 149). In this instance the probability distribution is as shown in Table 9.3. This probability distribution could also be presented as a graph as shown in Figure 9.1.

In Figure 9.1 the *height* of the point (dot) above a particular outcome represents the probability of this particular outcome. An alternative

[9] Of course, other random variables may be of interest. For example, we may be concerned only in noting if the number of dots is even (assign a value of 1) or odd (assign a value of 0). In this instance, $\mathscr{S} = \{1, 0\}$.

Table 9.3   Probability Distribution for Experiment 1 in Table 9.1

Sample Point (s_j)	$P(s_j)$
1	1/6
2	1/6
3	1/6
4	1/6
5	1/6
6	1/6

method of representing such a probability value graphically consists of erecting on a set of axes a rectangle whose base, measuring one unit, is centered above the particular outcome value and whose height corresponds to the probability value. Then either the height *or the area* (since the base is unity) of the rectangle represents the probability value graphically. We will see later (Section 9.10) that there is some advantage in certain situations in using areas rather than heights to represent probability values. Figure 9.2 shows a graphical presentation of the probability distribution of Table 9.3 that involves this use of rectangles to represent the probability values.

Finally, this probability distribution can be presented as a formula:

$$P(s_j) = \tfrac{1}{6} \qquad (s_j = 1, 2, 3, 4, 5, 6)$$

Example 2 Consider the experiment that consists of drawing a score from the collection of 100 scores shown in Table 9.2 (see p. 151). Assume that the random variable of interest is the score value. Thus,

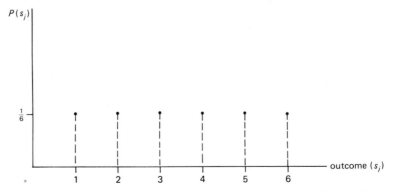

Figure 9.1   Probability distribution for experiment 1 in Table 9.1

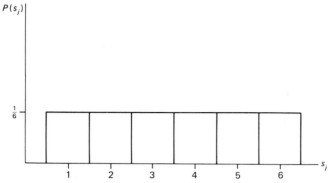

Figure 9.2   Probability distribution for experiment 1
in Table 9.1

the sample space of interest is $\mathscr{S} = \{3, 4, 5, 6, 7, 8, 9\}$. What probability values are associated with each s_j? One set that meets the requirements of DN 9.5 and DN 9.6 is shown in Table 9.4.[10] Or graphically, we have either Figure 9.3 or 9.4.

We end this section with a more formal definition of a probability distribution.

DN 9.10   Let the set of sample points in the sample space of an experiment be s_j $(j = 1, 2, \ldots, n)$ and let the respective probability values assigned to these events be represented by $P(s_j)$. Then the set of pairs $\{[s_j, P(s_j)]; j = 1, 2, \ldots, n\}$ is the probability distribution (PD) of the experiment.

Remark: The word *distribution* is clearly appropriate because this pairing reveals the manner in which the aggregate of the probability values (i.e., unity) is apportioned among the possible sample points of an experiment.

Table 9.4   Probability Distribution for experiment of
Example 2

s_j	3	4	5	6	7	8	9
$P(s_j)$	.05	.10	.20	.30	.20	.10	.05

[10] It may be noted that these probability values are equal to the relative frequency of a given score in the total collection of 100 scores.

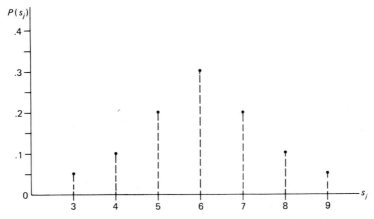

Figure 9.3 Graphical representation of probability distribution given in Table 9.4

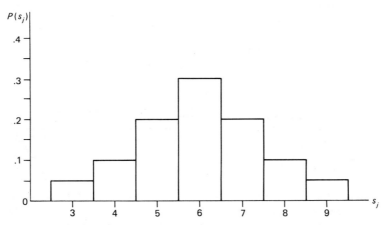

Figure 9.4 Graphical representation of probability distribution given in Table 9.4

9.6   The Concept of Expected Value

In Section 9.4, we noted that it is possible to interpret a probability value assigned to a given outcome of an experiment as the relative frequency of that outcome in repeated runs of the experiment. Consistent with this interpretation is the conceptualization of a probability distribution as the relative frequency distribution of the random variable of interest. Thus, for example, in Example 2 of Section 9.5, the random variable of interest is the score value drawn from a collection of 100 scores. The probability distribution presented in Table 9.4 can be conceptualized as the relative frequency distribution of the random variable for an infinity of runs of the experiment.

Since probability distributions can be thought of as relative frequency distributions, it seems reasonable to describe such distributions in terms of selected summary indexes of central tendency and variability. Two of the most commonly used indexes are the mean and variance (or standard deviation) of the probability distribution.

A special name is often given the mean of a probability distribution of a random variable, say X. The mean of the probability distribution of X is frequently referred to as the *expected value of X* and is symbolically represented by $E(X)$. Keep in mind that a probability distribution describes the theoretical totality of experience regarding outcomes under indefinite repetition of a random experiment. That is, the probability distribution is construed as the *universe* or population of values of some random variable generated by repeating an experiment indefinitely. Consequently, we may think of $E(X)$ as the mean of the universe of X-values (outcomes of the experiment) arising from indefinitely repeating a random experiment. This notion is formalized in the following definition.

DN 9.11 Given a random variable X capable of taking on the specific numerical values X_j ($j = 1, 2, \ldots, n$) with corresponding probability values $P(X_j)$. Then the expected value of X, designated $E(X)$, is defined by $E(X) = \sum_{j=1}^{n} X_j P(X_j)$.

Example Consider the probability distribution displayed in Table 9.4 (p. 157). For this distribution

$$
\begin{aligned}
E(X) = \sum_{j=1}^{n} X_j P(X_j) &= (3)(.05) + (4)(.10) + (5)(.20) \\
&\quad + (6)(.30) + (7)(.20) + (8)(.10) \\
&\quad + (9)(.05) \\
&= 6
\end{aligned}
$$

That is, the mean of the probability distribution of Table 9.4 is 6.

Remarks: 1. Note that the formula defining $E(X)$ and the relative frequency formula for $\bar{X}$ (6.3a) are highly similar. (*Note:* $\bar{X} = \sum p_j X_j$.) There is, however, an important distinction. A p_j-value in (6.3a) is the relative frequency of occurrence of the X_j-value in a specific collection (sample) of such values. The $P(X_j)$-values in the formula defining $E(X)$ are, on the other hand, the probability values associated with the specific outcomes X_j ($j = 1, 2, \ldots, n$) of a random experiment.

2. The term *expected value* (also called "mathematical expectation") probably originated in connection with games of chance. Consider a game (random experiment) that consists of drawing a single card from a well-mixed deck of 20 cards marked with dollar payoff values as follows:

$ Payoff	$0	$1	$5	$100
Frequency in deck	10	7	2	1

If we apply the equally likely model to each card and then apply DN 9.6, we obtain the following probability distribution for this experiment (game):

$ Payoff (X_j)	$0	$1	$5	$100
$P(X_j)$	.50	.35	.10	.05

These $P(X_j)$-values may be interpreted as the relative frequencies of occurrence of the X_j-values if the game were played indefinitely. By definition

$$E(X) = (0)(.5) + (1)(.35) + (5)(.10) + (100)(.05) = \$5.85$$

This $5.85 is not the most probable outcome (the most probable outcome is zero dollars). Indeed $5.85 is not even a possible outcome. It is simply the mean payoff value of the cards the player would draw were he to play the game indefinitely. A player charged a $5.85 fee for each play of the game would, therefore, expect to break even in the long run.

3. $E(X)$ is sometimes represented by the Greek letter μ (mu), which corresponds to the English *m*, the initial letter of the word *mean*.

4. The definition as stated holds only for discrete random variables. The notion of a continuous random variable is discussed at an intuitive level in Section 9.10.

Next we ask, "What is the expected value of the square of the deviation of a random variable from its expected (mean) value?" For example, using the probability distribution of Table 9.4, which we have seen to have the expected value 6, we apply DN 9.11 to the new random variable

$$Y = [X - E(X)]^2 = (X - \mu)^2$$

Thus, we calculate

$$E(Y) = E[(X - \mu)^2] = \sum_{j=1}^{7} (X_j - 6)^2 P(X_j)$$
$$= (3 - 6)^2(.05) + (4 - 6)^2(.10) + (5 - 6)^2(.20)$$
$$+ (6 - 6)^2(.30) + (7 - 6)^2(.20) + (8 - 6)^2(.10)$$
$$+ (9 - 6)^2(.05)$$
$$= 2.10$$

This result is the expected or mean value of $Y = (X - \mu)^2$ for the probability distribution of Table 9.4. This particular expected value is known as the *variance of a probability distribution* and is commonly designated by σ^2. The positive square root of this variance, σ, is its standard deviation. This Greek letter sigma corresponds to the English letter s, which is the initial letter of the word *standard* in "standard deviation." In this example

$$\sigma = \sqrt{2.10} \approx 1.4491$$

We now formalize this notion by stating two definitions.

DN 9.12 Given a random variable X that is capable of taking the specific values X_j ($j = 1, 2, \ldots, n$), which have the corresponding probability values $P(X_j)$. Then the variance of the probability distribution of X is

$$\sigma^2 = E[(X - \mu)^2] = \sum_{j=1}^{n} (X_j - \mu)^2 P(X_j)$$

DN 9.13 The standard deviation, σ, of the probability distribution of a random variable X is the positive square root of σ^2.

Remarks: 1. As an exercise, show for the probability distribution of the "draw-a-card" game described in remark 2 following DN 9.11 that $\sigma^2 = E[(X - \mu)^2] = 468.6275$ and that $\sigma \approx \$21.6478$.

2. The definition of σ^2 as stated in DN 9.12 holds only for discrete random variables.

9.7 Another Experiment with a Finite Number of Sample Points: The Binomial Experiment

Consider the following modification of experiment 2 in Table 9.1. Instead of drawing one card only, assume the experiment consists of drawing three cards in the following manner:

1 Shuffle the deck
2 Draw a card. Note its color (R or R̄)
3 Replace the card

4 Reshuffle the deck

5 Draw a card. Note its color (R or $\bar{R}$)

6 Repeat the above process to draw a third card

Assume the outcome of interest consists of the sequence in which the R and $\bar{R}$ cards are drawn. For example, one outcome is the sequence (R, $\bar{R}$, R). We ask, "What is the probability of obtaining this sequence?" In this specific example it is not difficult to answer this question, since we can use the equally likely model. Note, first, that the following set of eight outcomes consists of all possible outcomes and, hence, is the sample space of the experiment.

(R, R, R)	(R, $\bar{R}$, $\bar{R}$)
(R, R, $\bar{R}$)	($\bar{R}$, R, $\bar{R}$)
(R, $\bar{R}$, R)	($\bar{R}$, $\bar{R}$, R)
($\bar{R}$, R, R)	($\bar{R}$, $\bar{R}$, $\bar{R}$)

If each of these outcomes is taken to be equally likely, the probability of each is 1/8.[11]

Now assume that instead of the sequence in which the R and $\bar{R}$ cards are drawn, the outcome of interest is merely the number of red cards. Then, $\mathscr{S} = \{0, 1, 2, 3\}$, since in the three draws we can have either 0 reds, 1 red, 2 reds, or 3 reds. Now we can ask, "What is the probability of drawing 1 red card out of three draws?" Or, more generally, "What is the probability distribution (PD) for the sample space (i.e., $\{0, 1, 2, 3\}$) of this experiment?"

In the previously considered sample space of eight outcomes, one outcome had 3 red cards, three had 2 red cards, three had 1 red card, and one had 0 red cards. Thus, in this instance, applying DN 9.6 to the equally likely outcomes model of the first experiment gives us the following PD:

Sample Point (s_j)	$P(s_j)$
0	1/8 ·
1	3/8 ·
2	3/8 ·
3	1/8 ·
	$\sum P(s_j) = 1$

If the experiment had consisted of drawing four instead of three cards in this manner, the sample space for the sequence in which R and $\bar{R}$

---

[11] The application of the equally likely model is appropriate in this instance because $P(R) = P(\bar{R})$ at each draw. Consider, for example, a deck of 52 cards where 50 of the cards are red and only 2 are black. In this instance, it should be obvious that $P(R, R, R) \neq P(\bar{R}, \bar{R}, \bar{R})$, and that the equally likely model would not be appropriate.

cards are drawn would have been

4 Red	3 Red	2 Red	1 Red	0 Red
(R, R, R, R)	(R,R, R, $\bar{R}$)	(R, R, $\bar{R}$, $\bar{R}$)	(R, $\bar{R}$, $\bar{R}$, $\bar{R}$)	($\bar{R}$, $\bar{R}$, $\bar{R}$, $\bar{R}$)
	(R,R, $\bar{R}$, R)	(R, $\bar{R}$, R, $\bar{R}$)	($\bar{R}$, R, $\bar{R}$, $\bar{R}$)	
	(R, $\bar{R}$, R, R)	($\bar{R}$, R, R, $\bar{R}$)	($\bar{R}$, $\bar{R}$, R, $\bar{R}$)	
	($\bar{R}$,R, R, R)	($\bar{R}$, R, $\bar{R}$, R)	($\bar{R}$, $\bar{R}$, $\bar{R}$, R)	
		($\bar{R}$, $\bar{R}$, R, R)		
		(R, $\bar{R}$, $\bar{R}$, R)		

If each of these outcomes is equally likely, the probability of each is 1/16.

Now redefine the outcome to be the number of R cards drawn. Then the new $\mathscr{S}$ is {0, 1, 2, 3, 4}, and applying DN 9.6 gives the *PD* of this $\mathscr{S}$ as

s_j	$P(s_j)$
0	1/16
1	4/16
2	6/16
3	4/16
4	1/16
	$\sum P(s_j) = 1$

Note that in either of these examples the outcome could have been expressed as the proportion of R cards drawn instead of the number. If this is done, the sample space for the first example becomes {0, 1/3, 2/3, 1}, and for the second example $\mathscr{S} = \{0, 1/4, 2/4, 3/4, 1\}$. The *PD*'s for these sample spaces are clearly the same as those previously given—for example 1:

s_j	$P(s_j)$
0	1/8
1/3	3/8
2/3	3/8
1	1/8
	1

and for example 2.

s_j	$P(s_j)$
0	1/16
1/4	4/16
2/4	6/16
3/4	4/16
1	1/16
	1

It should be clear that this procedure will become increasingly tedious as the number of cards drawn increases. Moreover, the procedure is not directly applicable if the probability of each sequence is not the same, as would be the case if the numbers of R and $\bar{R}$ cards in the deck were not the same. Mathematical statisticians have developed a rule for obtaining probability values for outcomes of experiments similar to the above that is applicable regardless of the number of cards drawn even when $P(R)$ on a single draw differs from $P(\bar{R})$.

᛫ Before presenting this rule, we shall review the general characteristics of this experiment. An experiment described by these characteristics is known as a *binomial experiment*.

1 Given a universe of N objects of two types or kinds, A and $\bar{A}$ (not A). (In our example above, $N = 52$, A = red, and $\bar{A}$ = not red.)

   Remark: The following are examples of universes of this type that might occur in practical work:
   a All elementary school children in a certain school system who have had (A-type) and who have not had ($\bar{A}$-type) red measles
   b Voters in a certain community who are for (A-type) and who are against ($\bar{A}$-type) a bond issue
   c All high school pupils in a certain district who do (A-type) and who do not ($\bar{A}$-type) smoke
   d All cars of a certain make, model, and year that have (A-type) and do not have ($\bar{A}$-type) a specific mechanical defect
   e All fourth-grade children in a certain school system who can (A-type) and who cannot ($\bar{A}$-type) spell a given word (or solve a given arithmetic problem, or perform some given task)

2 By some chance (random[12]) procedure select an object from this universe and note its type. Replace this object in the universe and by the procedure used before select a second object and note its type. Continue this process until the desired number (n) of objects have been drawn and classified according to type.

   Remarks: (i) If N (the number of objects in the universe) is large in relation to n (the number of objects selected), replacement of the objects drawn becomes unnecessary.[13] (ii) In the

---

[12] This concept is developed in Chapter 11.

[13] If n is less than 10 percent of N (i.e., $n < 0.1N$), then replacement of the objects is not a critical requirement. See O. A. Liberman and D. B. Owen, *Tables of the Hypergeometric Probability Distribution*, Stanford University Press, Stanford, 1961, p. 17.

card examples above the values of n were 3 and 4, respectively.
3 The probability of an A-type object (i.e., the proportion of A's) in the universe is ϕ. That is, $P(A) = \phi$ and $P(\bar{A}) = 1 - \phi$.

Remark: In the card examples $P(R) = \phi = 26/52 = .5$ and $P(\bar{R}) = 1 - \phi = 1 - .5 = .5$. Here, $P(R) = P(\bar{R})$. This was an essential condition of our solutions to these examples. However, it is not a condition necessary to the applicability of the rule we are about to state.
4 $P(A)$ must remain constant over the n repetitions of the selection process.

Remark: This is the reason that replacement is required when N is not large in relation to n. For example, if on the first draw in our card example an R were obtained and not replaced, then on the second draw $P(R) = 25/51 \approx .49$ rather than the required $26/52 = .5$.
5 The random variable (outcome of interest) can be expressed as either the number or the proportion of A-type objects selected. If the former, the sample space of the experiment is

$$\mathscr{S} = \{0, 1, 2, \ldots, n - 2, n - 1, n\}$$

If the latter, the sample space is

$$\mathscr{S} = \left\{0, \frac{1}{n}, \frac{2}{n}, \ldots, \frac{n-2}{n}, \frac{n-1}{n}, 1\right\}$$

Remark: For the two card examples given above, the sample spaces expressed as counts of the number of red cards drawn are $\mathscr{S} = \{0, 1, 2, 3\}$ and $\mathscr{S} = \{0, 1, 2, 3, 4\}$. Expressed as proportions of cards drawn that are red, they are $\mathscr{S} = \{0, 1/3, 2/3, 1\}$ and $\mathscr{S} = \{0, 1/4, 2/4, 3/4, 1\}$.

We are now ready to state the mathematical rule that can be used to calculate the probability value associated with any specific outcome from a binomial experiment.

RULE 9.1 Given a binomial experiment involving the selection of n objects from a universe in which the proportion of A-type objects is ϕ. If r is some specific number of A-type objects selected, then the probability of r given some specific value of ϕ, designated $P(r \mid n, \phi)$, is

$$P(r \mid n, \phi) = \binom{n}{r}\phi^r(1 - \phi)^{n-r} \tag{9.1}$$

To use (9.1) there are certain mathematical facts that must be known. These are:

1 The factor $\binom{n}{r}$ is defined as follows:

$$\binom{n}{r} = \frac{n!}{r!\,(n-r)!}$$

where the symbol !, read *factorial*, is defined for any positive integer $n > 1$ by $n! = (n)(n-1)(n-2)\cdots(2)(1)$. For example,

$$3! = (3)(2)(1) = 6$$
$$4! = (4)(3)(2)(1) = 24$$
$$\binom{5}{2} = \frac{5!}{2!\,(5-2)!} = \frac{(5)(4)(3)(2)(1)}{(2)(1)(3)(2)(1)} = 10$$

2 The quantities 1! and 0! are, by definition, both equal to unity (i.e., to 1). Thus,

$$\binom{5}{0} = \frac{5!}{0!\,(5-0)!} = \frac{(5)(4)(3)(2)(1)}{(1)(5)(4)(3)(2)(1)} = 1$$
$$\binom{5}{1} = \frac{5!}{1!\,(5-1)!} = \frac{(5)(4)(3)(2)(1)}{(1)(4)(3)(2)(1)} = 5$$

3 Any number, say X, raised to the zero power is, by definition, unity (i.e., $X^0 = 1$).

Of course, in algebra these definitions have a logical basis. Here, however, we shall be content with simply using them to apply Rule 9.1. To illustrate, we shall show how Rule 9.1 could be applied to give the probability distributions of the two card examples given above.

Example 1 Here $n = 3$ and $\phi = 26/52 = 1/2$. The sample space is $\{0, 1, 2, 3\}$.

$$\text{For } r = 0, \quad P(0 \mid 3, 1/2) = \frac{3!}{0!\,(3-0)!}\left(\frac{1}{2}\right)^0\left(1 - \frac{1}{2}\right)^{3-0}$$
$$= \frac{(3)(2)(1)}{(1)(3)(2)(1)}(1)\left(\frac{1}{2}\right)^3 = \frac{1}{8}$$
$$\text{For } r = 1, \quad P(1 \mid 3, 1/2) = \frac{3!}{1!\,(3-1)!}\left(\frac{1}{2}\right)^1\left(1 - \frac{1}{2}\right)^{3-1}$$
$$= \frac{(3)(2)(1)}{(1)(2)(1)}\left(\frac{1}{2}\right)^1\left(\frac{1}{2}\right)^2 = \frac{3}{8}$$

For $r = 2$, $P(2 \mid 3, 1/2) = \dfrac{3!}{2!\,(3-2)!} \left(\dfrac{1}{2}\right)^2 \left(1-\dfrac{1}{2}\right)^{3-2}$

$$= \dfrac{(3)(2)(1)}{(2)(1)(1)} \left(\dfrac{1}{2}\right)^2 \left(\dfrac{1}{2}\right)^1 = \dfrac{3}{8}$$

For $r = 3$, $P(3 \mid 3, 1/2) = \dfrac{3!}{3!\,(3-3)!} \left(\dfrac{1}{2}\right)^3 \left(1-\dfrac{1}{2}\right)^{3-3}$

$$= \dfrac{(3)(2)(1)}{(3)(2)(1)(1)} \left(\dfrac{1}{2}\right)^3 (1) = \dfrac{1}{8}$$

The *PD* for the sample space is seen to be precisely the same as previously obtained.

Example 2 Here $n = 4$, $\phi = 1/2$, and $\mathscr{S} = \{0, 1, 2, 3, 4\}$. In this example, we display the substitutions into (9.1) but we leave as an exercise the task of verifying the probability values shown.

For $r = 0$, $P(0 \mid 4, 1/2) = \dfrac{4!}{0!\,(4-0)!} \left(\dfrac{1}{2}\right)^0 \left(1-\dfrac{1}{2}\right)^{4-0} = \dfrac{1}{16}$

For $r = 1$, $P(1 \mid 4, 1/2) = \dfrac{4!}{1!\,(4-1)!} \left(\dfrac{1}{2}\right)^1 \left(1-\dfrac{1}{2}\right)^{4-1} = \dfrac{4}{16}$

For $r = 2$, $P(2 \mid 4, 1/2) = \dfrac{4!}{2!\,(4-2)!} \left(\dfrac{1}{2}\right)^2 \left(1-\dfrac{1}{2}\right)^{4-2} = \dfrac{6}{16}$

For $r = 3$, $P(3 \mid 4, 1/2) = \dfrac{4!}{3!\,(4-3)!} \left(\dfrac{1}{2}\right)^3 \left(1-\dfrac{1}{2}\right)^{4-3} = \dfrac{4}{16}$

For $r = 4$, $P(4 \mid 4, 1/2) = \dfrac{4!}{4!\,(4-4)!} \left(\dfrac{1}{2}\right)^4 \left(1-\dfrac{1}{2}\right)^{4-4} = \dfrac{1}{16}$

Note that if the outcomes constituting the sample space of this example had been expressed as proportions, then $\mathscr{S}$ would be $\{0/4, 1/4, 2/4, 3/4, 4/4\}$. If p represents a sample point of this $\mathscr{S}$, then $p = r/4$ and $r = 4p$. Hence, given $\mathscr{S}$ in this latter form, Rule 9.1 can still be used to obtain the probability values associated with the sample points: simply use the relationship $r = 4p$ to convert the p-value to the corresponding r-value called for by the rule. For example, to find $P(p = 3/4 \mid 4, 1/2)$ we see that $r = np = 4 \times 3/4 = 3$. Now using Rule 9.1 with $n = 4$, $r = 3$, and $\phi = 1/2$, we find $P(3/4 \mid 4, 1/2) = 4/16$.

In general, Rule 9.1 may be used to find $P(p \mid n, \phi)$ (the probability value associated with the outcome of a binomial experiment expressed as the proportion of A-type objects selected) by simply entering (9.1) with $r = np$.

We shall present one further example. Given a binomial experiment with $n = 8$ and $\phi = 1/4 = .25$, we ask, "What is the probability that exactly three of the objects selected are of the A type?" The answer is

$$P(3 \mid 8, 1/4) = \binom{8}{3}\left(\frac{1}{4}\right)^3\left(\frac{3}{4}\right)^{8-3} = \frac{8!}{3!\,(8-3)!}\left(\frac{1}{4}\right)^3\left(\frac{3}{4}\right)^5$$

$$= \frac{(8)(7)(6)(5!)}{(3)(2)(1)(5!)}\left(\frac{1}{64}\right)\left(\frac{243}{1,024}\right) = (56)\left(\frac{1}{64}\right)\left(\frac{243}{1,024}\right)$$

$$= \frac{13,608}{65,536} \approx .2076$$

It is clear that as n increases, even the use of Rule 9.1 becomes tedious. Fortunately, most large computer facilities have "canned" programs for computing binomial probabilities. Furthermore, values of $P(r \mid n, \phi)$ have been rather extensively tabulated.[14] We have chosen not to include such a table in the appendix of tables of this book. However, some indication of the form such a table may take may be obtained by examining Table 9.5. The value of $P(3 \mid 8, 1/4)$ that we just obtained by using (9.1) can be read directly from this table. As a second example we ask, "What is the value of $P(.4 \mid 10, .2)$?" Entering Table 9.5 with $n = 10$, $\phi = .2$, and $p = .4$ (or $r = 4$) we see that the required value correct to four places is .0881.

We conclude this section with an example of the usefulness of the binomial probability distribution using a situation taken from the field of educational and psychological measurement. (The study manual exercises provide additional examples.) Suppose we have given a ten-item multiple choice test and that each item has five responses, one of which is correct. We are interested in making some probability statements about the performance on this test of individuals who know absolutely nothing about the concepts tested and who, therefore, make a purely haphazard response to each item. If an individual applies this chance response procedure to a given item a "large" number of times, it is reasonable to assume that he will succeed (answer the item correctly), and hence be an A-type, 20 percent or one-fifth of the time, and that he will fail, and hence be an $\bar{A}$ type, 80 percent or four-fifths of the time.[15] This follows from the fact that there are five

---

[14] *Tables of the Binomial Probability Distribution*, National Bureau of Standards, U.S. Government Printing Office, Washington, D.C., is the most extensive of such tabulations. Less extensive tables are more common and appear in a variety of sources.

[15] The designation of a success of an A type and a failure as an $\bar{A}$ type is purely arbitrary.

Table 9.5 Probability Values for Selected Binomial Distributions

			Probabilities (Four Places) for ϕ of:						
n	r	p	.1	.2	.25	.30	$.33\frac{1}{3}$	.40	.50
5	0	.0	.5905	.3277	.2373	.1681	.1317	.0778	.0312
	1	.2	.3280	.4096	.3955	.3602	.3292	.2592	.1562
	2	.4	.0729	.2048	.2637	.3087	.3292	.3456	.3125
	3	.6	.0081	.0512	.0879	.1323	.1646	.2304	.3125
	4	.8	.0004	.0064	.0146	.0284	.0412	.0768	.1562
	5	1.0	.0000	.0003	.0010	.0024	.0041	.0102	.0312
8	0	.0	.4305	.1678	.1001	.0576	.0390	.0168	.0039
	1	.125	.3826	.3355	.2670	.1977	.1561	.0896	.0312
	2	.25	.1488	.2936	.3115	.2965	.2731	.2090	.1094
	3	.375	.0331	.1468	.2076	.2541	.2731	.2787	.2188
	4	.50	.0046	.0459	.0865	.1361	.1707	.2322	.2734
	5	.625	.0004	.0092	.0231	.0467	.0683	.1239	.2188
	6	.750	.0000	.0011	.0038	.0100	.0171	.0413	.1094
	7	.875	.0000	.0001	.0004	.0012	.0024	.0079	.0312
	8	1.00	.0000	.0000	.0000	.0001	.0002	.0007	.0039
10	0	.0	.3487	.1074	.0563	.0282	.0173	.0060	.0010
	1	.1	.3874	.2684	.1877	.1211	.0867	.0403	.0098
	2	.2	.1937	.3020	.2816	.2335	.1951	.1209	.0439
	3	.3	.0574	.2013	.2503	.2668	.2601	.2150	.1172
	4	.4	.0112	.0881	.1460	.2001	.2276	.2508	.2051
	5	.5	.0015	.0264	.0584	.1029	.1366	.2007	.2461
	6	.6	.0001	.0055	.0162	.0368	.0569	.1115	.2051
	7	.7	.0000	.0008	.0031	.0090	.0163	.0425	.1172
	8	.8	.0000	.0001	.0004	.0014	.0030	.0106	.0439
	9	.9	.0000	.0000	.0000	.0001	.0003	.0016	.0098
	10	1.0	.0000	.0000	.0000	.0000	.0000	.0001	.0010

possible ways to answer the item, one of which is correct and four of which are wrong. Thus, we have $\phi = P(A) = 1/5$ and $1 - \phi = P(\bar{A}) = 4/5$.[16] Now, since the individual concerned is one who knows nothing about any of the ten items, it is immaterial whether he answers the same item ten times, independently applying the same chance response procedure each time, or whether he so answers the ten different items. In either case, his ten attempts may be thought of as selecting ten objects from a universe of objects, .2 of which are A-type and .8 of which are $\bar{A}$-type. Thus, the n of this experiment is 10.

---

[16] Consider the item sample space as consisting of five sample points corresponding to the five possible responses, one of which is right (A) and four of which are wrong ($\bar{A}$). Since a purely chance procedure is followed, it is reasonable to use the equally likely model in assigning probability values to the five points. Now consider the space of interest to be simply $\mathscr{S} = \{A, \bar{A}\}$. Application of DN 9.6. gives $P(A) = 1/5$ and $P(\bar{A}) = 4/5$.

Suppose we want to know the probability value associated with the outcome that consists of exactly two correct answers. From Table 9.5 we read that $P(2 \mid 10, .2) = .3020$. Or suppose we ask for the probability of the event (subspace) that consists of two or fewer correct answers. By DN 9.6 we know that

$$P(r \leq 2 \mid 10, .2) = P(2 \mid 10, .2) + P(1 \mid 10, .2) + P(0 \mid 10, .2)$$

Now using Table 9.5 we find

$$P(r \leq 2 \mid 10, .2) = .3020 + .2684 + .1074 = .6778$$

Such probability values for performance outcomes of "know-nothing" chance responders can be compared with actual performances to help in determining whether or not a particular individual does indeed possess some real knowledge of the material covered by the test. Ways of making such determinations are described in later chapters.

9.8   A Derivation of Rule 9.1*

It should be clear from the examples given at the outset of the previous section that our problem is basically a counting problem. Two counting rules will be needed to solve it. We shall state these rules without proof. The first might more properly be called a principle than a rule, but we shall use the latter designation.

> **COUNTING RULE 1**   If one thing can be done n_1 ways, a second thing n_2 ways, and so on with a kth thing capable of being done n_k ways, then the total number of ways in which these things can be done together is simply the product $n_1 \times n_2 \times \cdots \times n_k$.

For example, a penny can be tossed two ways (heads up; tails up) and a die can be cast six ways (one dot up, two dots up, ..., six dots up). Hence, by the above rule the number of ways in which a penny and a die can be tossed together is 2×6, or 12. These are displayed in the accompanying table.

		Die					
		1 dot	2 dots	3 dots	4 dots	5 dots	6 dots
Coin	Head	H, 1	H, 2	H, 3	H, 4	H, 5	H, 6
	Tail	T, 1	T, 2	T, 3	T, 4	T, 5	T, 6

* Optional section.

COUNTING RULE 2 Given a collection of n objects of two kinds, namely A's and $\bar{A}$'s. Assume r are A's so that $n - r$ are $\bar{A}$'s. Then the total number of sequences in which r A's and $(n - r)$ $\bar{A}$'s can be selected is

$$\binom{n}{r} = \frac{n!}{r!(n - r)!}$$

This will be recognized as a factor of (9.1). We now apply these two rules to obtaining (9.1). Since we have a universe of N objects from which we use a chance procedure to select n with replacement, it follows that there are N ways in which the first object can be selected, N ways in which the second can be selected, and so on to N ways in which the nth can be selected. Hence, by the first counting rule there are $N \times N \times \cdots \times N$ (for n factors), or N^n, ways in which n objects can be selected from N with replacement. Now applying the equally likely model we assign to each of these ways the same probability value $1/N^n$.

Next, suppose that m of the N objects in the universe are of the A type and that we select r of them. By the same reasoning as just used, the number of ways in which this can be done is

$$m^r \tag{a}$$

Now, since we are selecting n objects in all, and since r are of the A type, it follows that $n - r$ must be of the $\bar{A}$ type. Also, since m of the N objects in the universe are of the A type, it follows that $N - m$ are of the $\bar{A}$ type. Again, by the same reasoning as used before, we know that the number of ways in which $(n - r)$ $\bar{A}$-type objects can be selected from $N - m$ is

$$(N - m)^{n-r} \tag{b}$$

The counts (a) and (b) apply to any given sequence of r A's and $(n - r)$ $\bar{A}$'s. But according to counting rule 2 the number of possible sequences in which r A's and $(n - r)$ $\bar{A}$'s can be selected is

$$\binom{n}{r} \tag{c}$$

Now by counting rule 1 the total number of ways in which r A's and $(n - r)$ $\bar{A}$'s can be selected is the product of the number of ways in which r A's can be selected from m [see (a)] times the number of ways in which $(n - r)$ $\bar{A}$'s can be selected from $N - m$ [see (b)] times the number of sequences in which r A's and $(n - r)$ $\bar{A}$'s can be selected [see (c)], i.e.,

$$\binom{n}{r} m^r (N - m)^{n-r} \tag{d}$$

With each of these ways we have associated the same probability value $1/N^n$. Hence, by DN 9.6, the probability of selecting exactly r A's and $(n - r)$ $\bar{A}$'s from a universe of m A's and $(N - m)$ $\bar{A}$'s is the sum of as many $1/N^n$ values as is indicated by (d).

This sum is simply the product of (d) times $1/N^n$, or

$$\frac{\binom{n}{r} m^r (N - m)^{n-r}}{N^n} = \frac{\binom{n}{r} m^r (N - m)^{n-r}}{(N^r)(N^{n-r})}$$

$$= \binom{n}{r} \left(\frac{m}{N}\right)^r \left(\frac{N - m}{N}\right)^{n-r}$$

But $m/N = \phi = $ the proportion of A's in the universe, and $(N - m)/N = 1 - m/N = 1 - \phi$. Hence, we have

$$\binom{n}{r} \phi^r (1 - \phi)^{n-r}$$

which is the value of $P(r \mid n, \phi)$ as given by (9.1).

9.9 The Mean and Variance of the Binomial Probability Distribution

In this section we state, without proof, formulas for determining the expected or mean value—$E(r)$ or μ—and variance—σ^2—of a binomial probability distribution (BPD).

$$E(r) = \mu = n\phi \tag{9.2}$$

$$\sigma^2 = n\phi(1 - \phi) \tag{9.3}$$

For example, for the BPD for which $n = 5$ and $\phi = .5$,

$$E(r) = (5)(.5) = 2.5$$

and

$$\sigma^2 = (5)(.5)(1 - .5) = 1.25$$

We shall verify the results by applying DN 9.11 and DN 9.12, which apply to any probability distribution. From Table 9.5 we see that the BPD for $n = 5$ and $\phi = .5$ is

r	$P(r \mid 5, .5)$
0	.0312
1	.1562
2	.3125
3	.3125
4	.1562
5	.0312
	$.9998 \approx 1$

Now applying DN 9.11 we have

$$
\begin{aligned}
E(r) = \mu &= \sum r_j P(r_j \mid 5, .5) \\
&= (0)(.0312) + (1)(.1562) + (2)(.3125) + (3)(.3125) \\
&\quad + (4)(.1562) + (5)(.0312) \\
&= 2.4995 \approx 2.5
\end{aligned}
$$

And applying DN 9.12 we have

$$
\begin{aligned}
\sigma^2 = E[(r - \mu)^2] &= \sum (r_j - \mu)^2 P(r_j \mid 5, .5) \\
&= (0 - 2.5)^2(.0312) + (1 - 2.5)^2(.1562) \\
&\quad + (2 - 2.5)^2(.3125) + (3 - 2.5)^2(.3125) \\
&\quad + (4 - 2.5)^2(.1562) + (5 - 2.5^2)(.0312) \\
&= 1.249150 \approx 1.25
\end{aligned}
$$

9.10   Probability Distributions for Experiments with Continuous Random Variables

To this point the sample spaces considered have been composed of some finite number of sample points. Often in practical work the random variable (outcome) is based on or is a function of measurements of some continuous attribute. Whenever this is the case, the random variable is also continuous and the sample space may consist of an infinity of points (see experiment 6 of Table 9.1). While a rigorous extension of probability concepts to this situation involves certain technical problems, it is not difficult to so extend these concepts at an intuitive level.

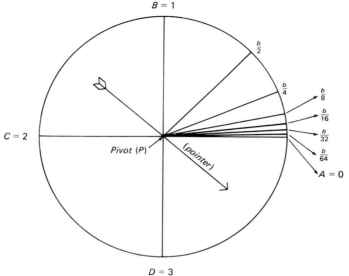

Figure 9.5 Diagram of the device for the experiment described in Section 9.10

Consider an experiment that consists of spinning a pointer mounted on a pivot located at the center of a circle that is divided into some number of sectors (pie slices) of equal area (such a gadget is sometimes substituted for dice in games based on the principle of Parcheesi). An idealized diagram of such a device is shown in Figure 9.5. In this figure the only *complete set* of such equal sectors that is pictured consists of the four sectors APB, BPC, CPD, and DPA. However, single members of such sets of sectors having successively smaller areas are also shown in the figure. Thus the sector $AP(b/2)$ is a member of a set of 8 sectors of equal area, $AP(b/4)$ is a member of a set of 16 sectors of equal area, ..., $AP(b/64)$ is a member of a set of 256 sectors of equal area. Theoretically, we could continue indefinitely the formation of new sets of successively smaller-sized sectors by simply cutting in half the sectors of the preceding set. As a limit, the area of these sectors would approach zero. That is, if this method of cutting sectors were continued indefinitely, the pictured member of the set of sectors would approach APA, which is nothing more than the radius of the circle to point A.

Suppose 0, 1, 2, and 3 are assigned as numerical values corresponding to the points A, B, C, and D, respectively. Then if the pointer is set at A and turned through one full rotation in a counterclockwise direction, it will point in succession toward each of the infinity of points on the circle. These points in turn may be thought of as bearing a one-to-one relationship with the members of the set of real numbers $\{X\}$, where

$(0 \leq X < 4)$.[17] Thus, it is possible to conceive of the outcome of the experiment (spinning the pointer) as a random variable (say, X) with possible values $0 \leq X < 4$. In this instance the sample is composed of an infinity of sample points, the real numbers from 0 up to but not including 4. The problem with which we are here basically concerned consists of assigning probability values to the various outcomes (possible values of the random variable) of an experiment of this type.

To help us solve this problem we will begin with a redefinition of the experiment in order to make the sample space of interest finite and then repeatedly redefine the sample space to contain a larger and larger number of sample points.

First, consider the following modification. Proceeding in a counter-clockwise direction from A, let each member of a set of equal-sized sections be assigned a number equal to the numerical value corresponding to the terminal point on the circle of that radius of the sector that is closest to A. Thus in the set of four sectors each member of which is pictured in Figure 9.5, sector APB is assigned the value 0, sector BPC the value 1, sector CPD the value 2, and sector DPA the value 3. Now let the experiment consist of spinning the pointer, and let the random variable (the outcome expressed as a numerical value) be the number assigned to that member of the four sectors APB, BPC, CPD, and DPA in which the pointer comes to rest. For example, the pointer as shown in Figure 9.5 has come to rest in sector DPA. The numerical value of the outcome (random variable) of this particular run of the experiment is 3.

In this experiment the sample space of interest is $\mathscr{S} = \{0, 1, 2, 3\}$. If the set of sectors chosen consists of just these four, we want to know what the probability is that the random variable, say X, is equal to 0, 1, 2, or 3. Since these four sectors are all of the same area it would seem intuitively reasonable that assigning 1/4 as the probability value of each of these outcomes would be reasonable. In other words, the equally likely model applies. Thus, for this sample space the probability distribution is as follows:

Outcome s_j	$P(s_j)$
0	1/4
1	1/4
2	1/4
3	1/4

Consider a slightly different sample space. Assign the value 0 to the sector $AP(b/2)$, which is a member of a set of eight equal-sized sectors.

[17] Note that 0 and 3.999 as well as any number between 3.999 and 4 are members of this set but 4 is not.

Proceeding in a counterclockwise direction the remaining seven members of this set of sectors would be assigned in succession the values 1/2, 2/2 or 1, 3/2, 4/2 or 2, 5/2, 6/2 or 3, and 7/2. The sample space is now $\mathscr{S} = \{0, \frac{1}{2}, 1, 1\frac{1}{2}, 2, 2\frac{1}{2}, 3, 3\frac{1}{2}\}$. Here it seems reasonable to assign 1/8 as the probability value corresponding to each of these sample points (value of the random variable), since the eight sectors are of equal area. The only member of this set pictured in Figure 9.5 is $AP(b/2)$.

The above procedure could, in fact, be extended indefinitely. We could define a sample space consisting of the set of 16 sectors of equal area [the only member of this set pictured is $AP(b/4)$]; or a space consisting of the set of 256 sectors of equal area; and so on. The probability values assigned to the sample points of these sample spaces would be 1/16 and 1/256, respectively.

The ultimate conclusion of this procedure would be to define the sample space as $\mathscr{S} = \{X; 0 \le X < 4\}$—that is, the set of "sectors" that consists of the infinity of points on the circle. Now we ask, "What is the probability that the needle comes to rest *precisely at the point* $A = 0$?" The "sector" APA has an area of zero and is actually not a sector at all but a radius. If we follow the practice of assigning probability values that are proportional to areas, then we must write $P(X = 0) = 0$. Similarly, the probability is also zero that the needle comes to rest at precisely any specific one of the infinity of possible points on the circle indicating some specific member s_j of the sample space $\mathscr{S} = \{X; 0 \le X < 4\}$.

The difficulties are obvious. In the first place, there is no question that the needle comes to rest at some specific point on the circle. In other words, an event to which we have assigned a probability of zero actually occurs. Second, since zero is the probability associated with each point in this sample space, the sum of the probability values is itself zero and not unity as DN 9.5 requires.

Now although these difficulties can be overcome in a rigorous way only with special mathematical tools, they do not present particularly serious problems in the realm of the "real world" when considered intuitively. First of all, while a person may conceive of adjacent points on a continuum, he cannot "see" them or visually differentiate them. That is, he cannot determine precisely *the* point at which the needle comes to rest. He can only indicate an interval (in our example, an arc) of some "length" within which the needle stops. It is true that he may succeed in making this interval quite small (say with the help of a microscope), but the fact remains that in any "real world" situation he can at best do no more than specify some interval called the "unit of measurement." Then, by the rules of geometry, he can associate an area with an interval on the scale of values of the random variable. This permits him to exploit the possibility that we have already

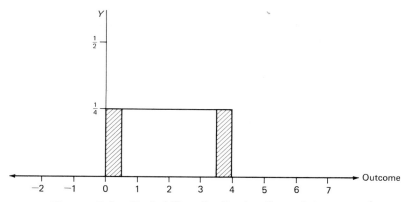

Figure 9.6   Probability distribution for pointer example

illustrated of assigning probability values to intervals that are proportional to areas.

In view of these considerations, we shall adopt the strategy of conceiving of the probability distribution of continuous random variables as represented by a continuous figure (graph)[18] located in a positive direction from (i.e., above) the scale of all possible values of the random variable and of such size that the total area between this figure and this scale is unity. Moreover, we shall regard that proportion of this total area which is directly over some specified interval on the scale as the probability value associated with the subset of outcomes constituting this interval. In this way we achieve probability values that are consistent with the probabilities developed in our study of sample spaces involving some finite number of sample points (i.e., nonnegative values that total unity—see DN 9.5 and also DN 9.6). This achievement obtains no matter how small the interval so long as it does not vanish into a point.

To illustrate we shall display the graph of the probability distribution for the pointer example using the analogue of the equally likely outcomes model. Here the range of the random variable is four units, since the sample space is $\{0 \leq X < 4\}$. Hence, the figure representing the probability values consists of a rectangle extending from $X = 0$ up to but not including $X = 4$ and having a height of $1/4$. For all intervals not in this range the probability values are zero. Figure 9.6 is a graphical display of the probability distribution of the pointer experiment.[19]

---

[18] Continuous only in the sense that there is a one-to-one correspondence between the points of the figure and the continuum of the random variable.

[19] In Figure 9.6, the vertical axis is labeled Y. We have previously labeled this axis $P(s_j)$. Why $P(s_j)$ is not used for this graph is discussed later.

With this graph, we can now answer such questions as: "What is the probability that $0 \leq X < 1$?" This subset of outcomes corresponds to the pointer's coming to rest anywhere in the sector APB and gives rise to $X = 0$ when the circle is divided into just four sectors of equal area, that is, when the interval or "unit of measurement" is one quarter of the circumference of the circle. Since the area under that portion of the graph above this interval is $1/4$, the answer to the question is $1/4$. Moreover, we can answer such questions for any specific interval— including intervals of a type quite different from any that we have specifically illustrated or referred to up until now. For example, consider the question: "What is the probability that the needle comes to rest within an interval extending .5 to either side of the point on the circle designated A or 0?" This event is equivalent to a value of X, where $0 \leq X < .5$ or $3.5 < X < 4$ (see shaded portions of Figure 9.6). The area over each of these intervals is $1/8$, so that the required probability value is $1/8 + 1/8$, or $1/4$.

Remarks:

1. The vertical axis in Figure 9.6 does *not* represent probability values. In our previous graphs where the number of sample points was finite we used a histogram approach for graphically representing probability distributions. In these instances, the vertical axis was used to represent probability values. In experiments for which the sample space consists of an infinity of sample points (i.e., the random variable is continuous), the probability distribution will be represented by a continuous graph with the total area between the graph and the outcome scale equal to unity.[20] (Figure 9.6 is one type of continuous graph. Any smoothed relative frequency polygon is also a continuous graph of this type.) The vertical axis of such a continuous graph cannot be considered a probability value. Rather, as indicated previously, the probability values are obtained by finding the areas above certain segments of the score scale.

What, then, do the values on the vertical axis used in the graphical representation of a probability distribution for a continuous random variable represent? In mathematical terms, the Y-values are simply the values of the mathematical function used to plot the continuous graph. A particular Y-value is the height (called the *ordinate*) of the graph at a particular value of the random variable X. In our example:

For $0 \leq X < 4$, $Y = 1/4$
Elsewhere, $Y = 0$

---

[20] That is, this total area is equal to the area of a square with sides of unit length, or one square unit.

The vertical axis, then, is simply a scale of the heights of the graph of the probability distribution corresponding to the various possible values of the random variable.

2. Since the probability value associated with any point of the continuum is zero, it follows that

$$P(3.5 < X < 4) = P(3.5 \leq X < 4)$$

Therefore, in dealing with probability values associated with an interval a–b of the scale of values of a continuous random variable, it is immaterial whether the interval be designated

$$a < X < b \qquad \text{or} \qquad a \leq X \leq b$$

Most writers of mathematical treatments of probability employ the first of these designations.

3. $P(X = a) = 0$; i.e., the probability that a continuous X takes precisely the value of the point a is zero. In a "real world" sense, such a point outcome is indeed impossible in that there is no way in which observed values of a continuous variable can be determined with point precision.

4. Again, the idea of most importance in this discussion is the use of the area to represent the probability of a given subset (interval) of outcomes.

5. The concepts of expected value and variance apply to probability distributions of continuous random variables. If X is a continuous random variable, then $E(X)$ (or μ) is the mean and σ^2 is the variance of the probability distribution of X. The actual computation of these values requires the use of calculus and is beyond the scope of this book.

9.11   Summary Statement

In this chapter we have presented the probability concepts necessary for understanding the inferential procedures discussed in the next few chapters. Most of these inferential procedures involve continuous random variables. Thus, the ideas of Section 9.10 are especially important. In addition, our discussion of these inferential processes will depend heavily on the concept of an experiment, particularly the repeatability characteristic, and the interpretation of probability values as relative frequencies.

10

The Normal Probability Distribution

10.1 Introduction

In Section 9.10, we discussed a specific probability distribution of the continuous type called the *uniform probability distribution*. Although this particular probability distribution was useful for illustrating the concepts underlying continuous probability distributions, we will have little use for it in this book. For the purposes of this book a much more useful probability distribution of the continuous type is the so-called *normal probability distribution* (*NPD*). Before we discuss this particular probability distribution, it will be beneficial to describe an experiment whose outcomes can be seen intuitively to follow a particular type of relative frequency distribution. Then, the formal presentation of the *NPD* can be made using this experimental situation as a concrete example.

Consider an experiment designed to estimate the mean IQ of all children of ages 3 through 15 in a particular state. The experiment consists of selecting a sample of 200 children from this population and then obtaining their IQs. The method of selection must be one that establishes the experiment as a random one. The outcome or random variable of this experiment is the mean IQ for the sample obtained. The number of different possible outcomes is for all practical purposes infinite. Is it possible to use some theoretical model to assign probability values to possible outcomes?

Before answering this question, consider intuitively what the form of the probability distribution of outcomes will be like. Recall that this distribution is the relative frequency distribution of the outcomes of a large number of repetitions of the experiment. Now, suppose that the method of sampling is such that the selection of a particular child as a member of the sample is purely a matter of chance. Then it would

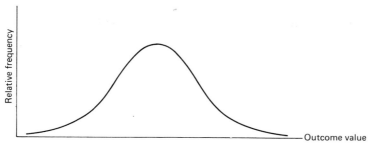

Figure 10.1   Idealized smoothed relative frequency
polygon for the IQ experiment described in Section 10.1

seem intuitively plausible that the outcomes arising from repetition of
the experiment would tend to cluster about the unknown true value of
the population mean. In other words, many of the outcomes would
fall relatively close to the true value. Occasionally, however, the
vagaries of chance may make some outcomes more deviant; and on
relatively rare occasions, even large variations may occur. It is plausible
that deviations of a given magnitude would occur about as frequently
in one direction as in the other. A probability distribution of the
outcomes of this experiment would, therefore, be unimodal and
symmetrical, that is, bell-shaped (see Histograms C, D, and E of
Figure 3.3, p. 30). The idealized smoothed relative frequency polygon
of such a distribution of outcomes could look like the curve shown in
Figure 10.1.

In the remaining sections of this chapter, we shall discuss the
properties of a mathematical function the graph of which has the
properties just described. We shall also show how this mathematical
model can be used to make probability statements about various
possible outcomes of an experiment. In a later chapter we shall pursue
the use of this model as an aid in the process of statistical inference.

10.2   The Normal Probability Distribution Function Defined

The normal probability distribution function (NPD) is

$$Y = \frac{1}{\sigma\sqrt{2\pi}}\, e^{-(X-\mu)^2/2\sigma^2} \qquad (-\infty < X < \infty\,; \sigma^2 > 0) \quad (10.1)$$

where

$X =$ the magnitude of an outcome (or estimate) arising from a run of some experiment

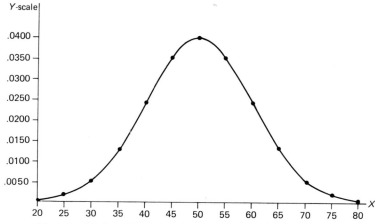

Figure 10.2   Plot of function of (10.1) when $\mu = 50$ and $\sigma = 10$ for selected values of X

$Y =$ the value of the function at X

$\mu =$ the mean of the X's (or the expected value of X)[1]

$\sigma =$ the standard deviation of the X's[1]

$\pi \approx 3.1416$, i.e., the ratio of the circumference of a circle to its diameter

$e \approx 2.7183$, an important mathematical constant used as the base of the system of natural logarithms

Remark: The nonmathematician may find (10.1) difficult to evaluate. As will be shown, this need not be a cause for anxiety, since tables have been developed that make a direct evaluation of (10.1) unnecessary.

Once μ and σ are specified, a particular normal distribution is completely determined. For example, Figure 10.2 shows a graph of (10.1) for $\mu = 50$ and $\sigma = 10$. The function has been evaluated only for selected values of X at intervals of 5 on the X-scale. These values are presented in Table 10.1 and are represented in the figure by large dots. The complete curve has been sketched in with these dots as guides. It is not important that the student be able to verify the Y-values given in Table 10.1. They were determined with the help of tables giving the value of e^{-t} for various values of t. Later, we shall introduce tables that will make direct evaluation of (10.1) unnecessary; the student need

---

[1] We have noted previously (see Section 9.6) that the mean and standard deviation are meaningful concepts to apply to probability distributions. Remember, we have chosen to represent these hypothetical values using Greek letters and to reserve the use of the Latin letters such as $\overline{X}$ and S to describe observed sets of data.

Table 10.1 Values of Function of (10.1) when $\mu = 50$
and $\sigma = 10$ for Selected Values of X as Plotted in Figure 10.2

X	Y
20	.0004
25	.0018
30	.0054
35	.0130
40	.0242
45	.0352
50	.0399
55	.0352
60	.0242
65	.0130
70	.0054
75	.0018
80	.0004

feel no compulsion to master the mathematics needed for such evaluation.

Remarks:

1. Not obvious from formula (10.1) is the fact that the total area under the graphic plot of (10.1)—that is, the area between the curve and the X-axis—is unity. Thus, (10.1) is a model of the relative frequency distribution of outcomes. Hence, as with the continuous probability distribution in Section 9.10, it is possible to assign probability values to intervals by finding the area under the curve between the endpoints of the intervals. (We will pursue this idea in a later section.)

2. The domain of this function is $-\infty < X < \infty$. Technically, random variables that conform to this model must be capable of assuming all values on a continuous scale from positive to negative infinity. We have previously noted that no one can distinguish adjacent points on a continuous scale. Thus, no real collection of real outcomes can be truly normally distributed, that is, truly represented by the model of (10.1). However, our primary interest in (10.1) will be as a model for assigning probability values to possible outcomes of particular types of experiments. Thus, (10.1) serves the same purpose as the equally likely model or the uniform probability model. That is, the outcomes of repeated runs of certain types of experiments (see Section 10.1 for one example) can be thought of as following the probability model represented by (10.1), so that (10.1) can be used as a theoretical model for making probability statements about the outcomes of such experiments.

3. We will frequently refer to the graph of the normal probability distribution function as simply the *normal curve* or the *normal distribution*.

10.3   Another Form of the Normal Probability Distribution Model

We have previously noted that a linear transformation of the scores of a given distribution does not alter the shape of the distribution (see Section 8.6). Also, we have seen that the transformation of X-scores to z-scores results in a distribution having a mean of zero and a standard deviation of one unit.

In the last section we noted that μ and σ are the mean and standard deviation of a hypothetical set of outcomes (i.e., the mean and standard deviation of the X-values). Thus, in this situation the X-values can be transformed into z-values by the formula $z = (X - \mu)/\sigma.^2$

The *NPD* in terms of z-scores is given by

$$y = \frac{1}{\sqrt{2\pi}} e^{-z^2/2} \tag{10.2}$$

The function (10.2) is obtained from (10.1) by letting $z = (X - \mu)/\sigma$ and remembering that, for any collection of z-scores, $\mu = 0$ and $\sigma = 1$. The value of the mathematical function has been represented by the lower-case y to call attention to the fact that y is expressed in terms of a

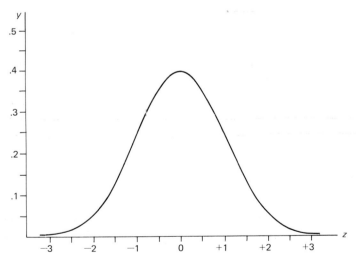

Figure 10.3   Values of *y* for given values of *z*

---

[2] Recall (see Section 8.5) that for a given collection of scores X having mean $\bar{X}$ and standard deviation S, $z = (X - \bar{X})/S$. This same transformation can be applied to the hypothetical normally distributed set of X-values having mean μ and standard deviation σ.

Table 10.2 Values of y for Selected Values of z as Plotted in Figure 10.3

z	y
-3.0	.004
-2.5	.018
-2.0	.054
-1.5	.130
-1.0	.242
$-\ .5$	.352
$.0$	.399
$+\ .5$	.352
$+1.0$	.242
$+1.5$	.130
$+2.0$	.054
$+2.5$	.018
$+3.0$	.004

unit different from that of Y. This follows simply from the fact that z is expressed in terms of a unit different from that of X. The function (10.2), which is known as the *standard normal distribution*, is pictured in Figure 10.3. The y-values plotted as guide points are shown in Table 10.2. The change in the z- and y-scales is of such character as to maintain a single unit of area under the curve. Hence, like (10.1) the function (10.2) may be used as a model for assigning probability values to sets of outcomes expressed in z-units. It is important to recall from Chapter 8 that z-scale values may be interpreted as indicating distances from the mean in units of standard deviation.

10.4   Some Properties of the Normal Probability Distribution

It is clear from Figure 10.2 that the maximum value of the *NPD* function occurs when $X = \mu$ (when the random variable equals the population mean) and that the graph is symmetrical and unimodal. Furthermore, we have already noted that the *NPD* is a continuous function and that the area between its graph and the X-axis is unity. Also, we have indicated that the domain of the function is $-\infty < X < \infty$. In addition, an inspection of Figure 10.2 will show that the area under the two parts of the curve that are more than three σ's away from μ is very small. In fact, the probability that outcomes (X's) will deviate by more than three σ's from μ is approximately .0026. Since this is a negligible probability, it is common practice to regard the range of possible outcomes as six σ's (i.e., as extending from three σ's

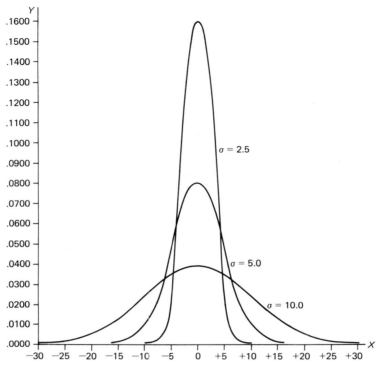

Figure 10.4   Three normal curves with $\mu = 0$ and unit area but with varying values of σ

below μ to three σ's above μ). Three additional characteristics of the *NPD* are discussed below.

First, it should be noted that formula (10.1) represents many different distributions, each of which can be labeled a normal curve. There is no such thing as *the* normal curve; rather, there is a family or class of curves each of which is a normal curve. The members of the family differ with respect to μ and σ. Variation in μ does not affect the appearance of the curve but simply determines its central location on the scale. Variation in σ, however, has considerable effect on the appearance of the curve, making it broad (spread out) or narrow (compact). This characteristic of the function is essential if the function is to be useful as a model of distributions of outcomes. Clearly, depending on the accuracy of the estimating procedure, the outcomes will or will not differ markedly. By varying the size of σ, we can make our model represent the product of either accurate or inaccurate estimating procedures. Figure 10.4 shows three normal curves with the same mean ($\mu = 0$) but with different σ-values superimposed on the same axes. All these curves are centered on zero and are of unit area. What

Table 10.3   Value of Y Expressed as a Percentage of Center Height, for Selected σ-Distances above μ

σ-Distance above μ	Percentage
.0	100.0
.5	88.3
1.0	60.7
1.5	32.5
2.0	13.5
2.5	4.4
3.0	1.1

makes them look different is that their standard deviations are different: 2.5, 5, and 10. Considering the marked variation in the appearance of these three normal curves, it should be obvious that it is extremely difficult to tell by visual inspection alone whether a given unimodal symmetrical curve satisfies the conditions of (10.1) or (10.2), that is, is a normal curve. This difficulty is aggravated by the fact that the appearance of any curve may be manipulated to a degree by the choice of the physical distances representing units along the X- and Y-scales (see Section 3.8; note particularly Figures 3.11 and 3.12). It is not surprising then, to learn that certain real collections of measures that are more or less bell-shaped have been mistakenly described as normally distributed when in actuality they are not.

A second important characteristic of the *NPD* is that, for any normal curve, the value of Y at a point deviating from μ by some specified σ-distance is always the same percentage of the height of the curve at μ (the center height).[3] The values of these percentages for a few selected σ-distances from the center are given in Table 10.3.[4] These percentages make it relatively simple to sketch a curve that will satisfy the specifications of a normal curve. It is necessary only to select some center height and then, at the various σ-distances from center, locate guide points that are the stated percentage of this center height above the X-axis. The curve may then be drawn through these guide points. An illustrative sketch is shown in Figure 10.5. It should be obvious that, by varying the physical distances representing the center height and one standard deviation, it is possible to make curves ranging from very

[3] The student with some training in mathematics will recognize that this must be so from an inspection of (10.1). The nonmathematical student need feel responsible only for understanding the point being made and should simply assume its mathematical accuracy.

[4] Since the curve is symmetrical, the percentages need be given only for distances above μ.

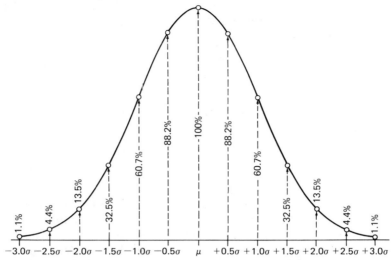

Figure 10.5   Sketch of normal curve using a center height of $2\frac{1}{2}$ inches and representing one σ by using $\frac{5}{8}$ of an inch

flat and broad to very peaked and narrow. Yet, so long as the specifications of Table 10.3 are followed, the resulting curves will be normal. One other point should be noted with regard to normal curves thus constructed. Regardless of the physical distance selected to represent the center height, unless that center height is considered as having the value $1/\sigma\sqrt{2\pi}$ (i.e., $.3989/\sigma$), the area under the curve will not be unity.

The final characteristic to be considered in this section is definitely the most important of all. Without any attempt to provide a mathematical basis, we refer to the fact that in any normal curve, the probability of obtaining a value of X between μ and a point deviating from μ by some specified σ-distance is always the same. The values of these probabilities for a few selected σ-distances are shown in Table 10.4.[5] Figure 10.6 shows the probability (represented by the area)[6] between the center (0) of a standard normal distribution (10.2) and $z = 1$, that is, a point 1σ above center. This probability is .3413 (see Table 10.4), and this fact is true of any normal curve regardless of the values of μ and σ. Thus, for any normal curve $P(\mu \leq X \leq \mu + 1\sigma) = .3413$. For example, if the outcome of an experiment (say X) follows a *NPD* with $\mu = 50$ and $\sigma = 10$, then $P(50 \leq X \leq 60) = .3413$.

---

[5] Since the curve is symmetrical, the probabilities need be given only for distances above μ.

[6] If you don't remember why these probability values can be represented by areas, review Section 9.10. See also Remark 1 in Section 10.2.

Table 10.4   Probability That X Is Between μ and Points That Are Selected σ-Distances above μ

σ-Distance above μ	Probability (or Area)
.0	.0000
.5	.1915
1.0	.3413
1.5	.4332
2.0	.4772
2.5	.4938
3.0	.4987

10.5   Tables for the Normal Distribution Defined by (10.2)

We have seen that for *any* normal distribution there exists a set relationship between the Y at a specified σ-distance from μ and the height at μ. We have also seen that for *any* normal distribution the probability of obtaining an outcome between μ and a point at a specified σ-distance from μ is always the same. Thus, if we know these height relationships and probability values for one normal distribution, we know them for all normal distributions. We shall present these facts for the normal distribution in standard-score form, that is, for the function (10.2). As we shall subsequently illustrate, it is a simple matter to apply these facts to any normal curve by transforming from one scale (z) to another (X). These facts together with other information regarding (10.2) are presented for selected z-values in Table 10.5.

Column 1 gives selected z-values from the upper half of the curve (10.2).

Column 2 gives the probability of obtaining a value between 0 and z_1 (i.e., a particular value of z).

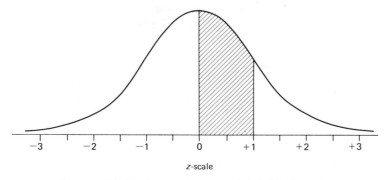

z-scale

Figure 10.6   Normal curve of (10.2) showing area between 0 and 1

Table 10.5   Normal Distribution Probabilities and Ordinates

Col. 1	Col.2	Col. 3	Col. 4	Col. 5	Col. 6	Col. 7	Col. 8
$+z_1$	$P(0 \leq z \leq z_1)$	$P(\lvert z \rvert \geq z_1)$	y	y as a % of y at μ	$P(z \leq +z_1)$	$P(z \leq -z_1)$	$-z_1$
0.0	.0000	1.0000	.3989	100.00	.5000	.5000	0.0
+0.5	.1915	.6170	.3521	88.25	.6915	.3085	−0.5
+1.0	.3413	.3174	.2420	60.65	.8413	.1587	−1.0
+1.5	.4332	.1336	.1295	32.47	.9332	.0668	−1.5
+2.0	.4772	.0456	.0540	13.53	.9772	.0228	−2.0
+2.5	.4938	.0124	.0175	4.39	.9938	.0062	−2.5
+3.0	.4987	.0026	.0044	1.11	.9987	.0013	−3.0

Column 3 gives the probability of an outcome in either of the two extremes (ends or tails) of the distribution.[7]

Column 4 gives the y-value for the curve (10.2) corresponding to the given z_1.[8]

Column 5 expresses the height of the curve (y) at z_1 as a percentage of the center height.

Column 6 gives the probability of a z smaller than a specified positive value ($+z_1$).

Column 7 gives the probability of a z smaller than a specified negative value ($-z_1$).

Column 8 gives selected negative z-values.

The points below should be made here.

1 The z-values may be interpreted as σ-distances.
2 The z-value corresponding to any X may be found by

$$z = \frac{X - \mu}{\sigma} \tag{10.3}$$

3 The X-value corresponding to any z may be found by

$$X = \sigma z + \mu \tag{10.4}$$

---

[7] The vertical bars designate that the absolute value of z is to be considered.

[8] In algebra these values are called *ordinates*.

4 When z-values are interpreted as σ-distances as given by (10.3), columns 2, 3, 5, 6, and 7 apply to any normal distribution function.

5 The y-values given in column 4 apply only to the standard normal curve (10.2). To obtain the ordinate (height) values (Y's) for any normal curve, it is necessary only to divide the y values by σ.[9] That is,

$$Y = \frac{y}{\sigma} \qquad (10.5)$$

6 Columns 2, 4, and 5 apply for plus or minus z-values, that is, for z-values either above or below μ.

7 Column 6 applies only to positive z-values.

8 Column 7 applies only to negative z-values.

Remarks:

1. Table 10.5 is part of a more comprehensive table given in Appendix C and labeled Table II.

2. It should be noted that the values in columns 3, 6, and 7 can be found from those in column 2. For example, given a z-score of $+1$, the probability of a smaller z (column 6) can be found by adding .5000 to the value in column 2. (Study manual exercises are based on this fact.) The values in column 5 can be obtained from the values in column 4 by expressing each column-4 value as a percentage of .3989 (that is, as a percentage of the value of y at $z_1 = 0$). Hence, all necessary information is contained in columns 2 and 4. The information in the other columns has been included only for convenience.

3. We have previously noted the relationship between probability values and area. Thus, it is perfectly reasonable to view the values in column 2 of Table 5 as representing the proportion of the area of the curve between 0 and z_1. (See graph at top of column 2.) Likewise, the values in column 3 can be viewed as representing the proportion of the area of the curve beyond a specified positive and negative z-value. (See graph at top of column 3.)

10.6 Using Tables to Obtain Various Facts about Normal Probability Distributions

In this section, we shall illustrate the use of Table II of Appendix C by presenting the solutions to selected types of problems. In each of

[9] Compare (10.1) and (10.2). Note that the formulas for these curves differ only by the factor $1/\sigma$.

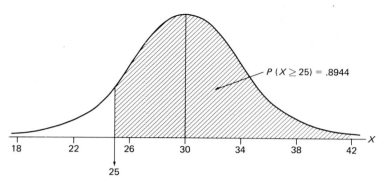

$P(X \geq 25) = .8944$

Figure 10.7   Normal distribution with $\mu = 30$, $\sigma = 4$

these examples, X represents the outcome of a random experiment. We assume that X follows a normal probability distribution model. That is, if the experiment were repeated indefinitely, a particular normal curve could be used to represent the relative frequency distribution of outcomes. (Section 10.1 described one such experiment.) Also, each of these problems is accompanied by a diagrammatic representation of the problem, showing how the area under the portion of the curve above a particular segment of the score scale represents the probability of an outcome in that segment of the scale.

Type 1: Probability that X is greater than some specified value

Example 1 If $\mu = 30$ and $\sigma = 4$, what is $P(X \geq 25)$?

Solution As the diagram labeled Figure 10.7 shows, we need simply to determine the fraction of the area of the appropriate *ND* over that portion of the X-scale which exceeds 25. Since $z = (25 - 30)/4 = -1.25$, the fraction required is the same as that of the area of the standard *ND* (i.e., *ND*: $\mu = 0$, $\sigma = 1$) that exceeds -1.25. Column 2 of Table II shows that $P(-1.25 \leq z \leq 0)$ is .3944. To this must be added the .5000 that represents the probability of an outcome greater than $\mu = 0$. Hence, we have $P(X \geq 25 \mid ND: \mu = 30, \sigma = 4) = .8944.$[10]

Comment: It should be observed that the information necessary to the solution of this type of problem may be read from Table II in a variety of ways. For example, column 7 shows that the probability of

---

[10] This notation should be read as follows: "The probability that X is greater than or equal to 25 given that X is normally distributed with $\mu = 30$ and $\sigma = 4$ is .8944."

$z \leq -1.25$ is .1056. Hence, the required probability is given by $1.0000 - .1056 = .8944$. Or, since the curve is symmetrical, the probability of a score larger than any negative z is the same as the probability of a score smaller than the corresponding positive z, so that the required probability may be read directly from column 6. In the following examples only one method of solution will be indicated. Students should, however, consider various alternative ways in which Table II provides a given item of information about a normal distribution. In this way they not only will fully familiarize themselves with the character of the information contained in Table II but also can learn the most efficient ways in which to use it.

Type 2: Probability that X is between two specified values

Example 2 If $\mu = 40$ and $\sigma = 6$, what is $P(36 \leq X \leq 48)$?

Solution In Figure 10.8, the shaded area represents the desired probability. Since the z-value corresponding to 36 is $(36 - 40)/6 = -.67$ and the z-value corresponding to 48 is $(48 - 40)/6 = +1.33$, the required probability value is the same as $P(-.67 \leq z \leq +1.33)$. We see from column 2 of Table II that the $P(-.67 \leq z \leq 0) = .2486$ and that the $P(0 \leq z \leq +1.33) = .4082$. Hence,

$$P(-.67 \leq z \leq +1.33) = P(36 \leq X \leq 48 \mid ND: \mu = 40, \sigma = 6)$$
$$= .2486 + .4082 = .6568$$

Example 3 In the distribution of the foregoing example, what is $P(27 \leq X \leq 35)$?

Solution The area of the curve representing this probability is the shaded area in Figure 10.9. First note that the z-value corre-

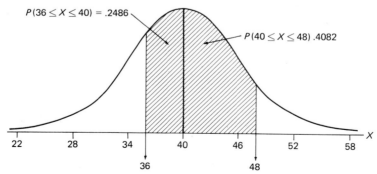

$P(36 \leq X \leq 40) = .2486$

$P(40 \leq X \leq 48) .4082$

Figure 10.8 Normal distribution with $\mu = 40$, $\sigma = 6$

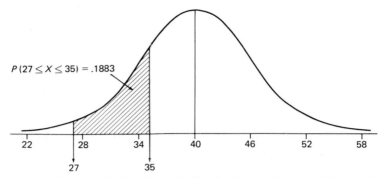

$P(27 \le X \le 35) = .1883$

22   28   34   40   46   52   58

27   35

Figure 10.9   Normal distribution with $\mu = 40$, $\sigma = 6$

sponding to 27 is $(27 - 40)/6 = -2.17$, and that the z-value corresponding to 35 is $(35 - 40)/6 = -0.83$. Hence, the required probability is the same as $P(-2.17 \le z \le -0.83)$. Now from column 2 of Table II we see the $P(-2.17 \le z \le 0) = .4850$ and the $P(-0.83 \le z \le 0) = .2967$. Hence,

$$P(-2.17 \le z \le -0.83) = .4850 - .2967 = .1883$$

Therefore,

$$P(27 \le X \le 35 \mid ND: \mu = 40, \sigma = 6) = .1883$$

Example 4 If $\mu = 50$ and $\sigma = 10$, what is $P(X = 34)$?

Solution Whenever we use the normal curve as a model of a probability distribution, the probabilities are represented by areas. But, the score point having no width, there can be no segment of area above a score point. However, in reporting measurements of continuous attributes we usually report to the nearest unit point. Thus a score of 34 reported for a particular object implies that we have determined the "true" amount of this attribute as possessed by this object to be somewhere between 33.5 and 34.5. That is to say, in terms of this X-scale any object measured as possessing between 33.5 and 34.5 units of the trait in question is reported as possessing 34 units. Hence, the probability of 34 is represented in the normal curve model by the proportion of the area between 33.5 and 34.5 (see Figure 10.10). The solution of this example now follows precisely that sketched for the foregoing example. First note that since $X = 33.5$ corresponds to $z = (33.5 - 50)/10 = -1.65$, and $X = 34.5$ corresponds to $z = (34.5 - 50)/10 = -1.55$, it follows that the required probability is the same as $P(-1.65 \le z \le -1.55)$. Now from Table II, column 2, we

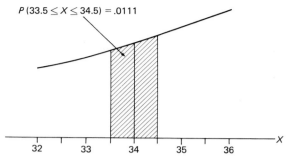

$P(33.5 \leq X \leq 34.5) = .0111$

Figure 10.10 Section of X-scale for the normal distribution with $\mu = 50$, $\sigma = 10$

read that $P(-1.65 \leq z \leq 0)$ is .4505 and that $P(-1.55 \leq z \leq 0)$ is .4394. Hence,

$$P(-1.65 \leq z \leq -1.55) = .4505 - .4394 = .0111$$

Therefore,

$$P(33.5 \leq X \leq 34.5 \mid ND: \mu = 50, \sigma = 10) = .0111$$

Type 3: Probability that X is beyond (either above or below) two values

Example 5 If $\mu = 60$ and $\sigma = 8$, what is the probability that X differs from the mean (60) by 10 or more points?

Solution We seek the proportion of the area of a ND that is below 50 and above 70 (see Figure 10.11). Here 10 score points correspond to a σ- or z-distance of $10/8 = 1.25$. From column 3 of Table II we read directly that the $P(z \geq 1.25) + P(z \leq -1.25) = P(|z| \geq 1.25)$ is .2113. Hence, $P(X \leq 50 \text{ or } X \geq 70 \mid ND: \mu = 60, \sigma = 8) = .2113$.

Type 4: Given the probability that X is smaller (or larger) than some X-value, find this X-value

Example 6 If X is ND with $\mu = 25$ and $\sigma = 5$, find an X-value, say X_1, such that $P(X \leq X_1) = .20$.

Solution Here we seek a value on the X-scale such that .20 of the area of the given ND lies below it (see Figure 10.12). Since this X_1 will necessarily fall in the lower half of this ND, the value of the

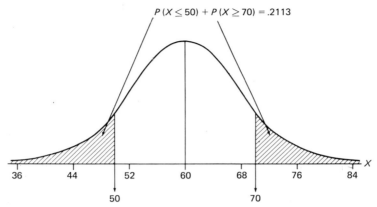

$$P(X \le 50) + P(X \ge 70) = .2113$$

Figure 10.11   Normal distribution with $\mu = 60$, $\sigma = 8$

corresponding z will be negative. We therefore look into column 7 of Table II for .20. The exact value .20 is not to be found, but we shall be satisfied to use the nearest value, namely, .2005. This value corresponds to $z = -.84$. Now applying formula (10.4) we have $X_1 = (5)(-.84) + 25 = 20.8$. Hence, in this ND, $X_1 = 20.8$. That is, $P(X \le 20.8 \mid ND: \mu = 25, \sigma = 5) \approx .20$.

   Comment: In this and all remaining examples we are using Table II in reverse. In all previous examples we entered Table II with a z-value and read out a probability value. Now we are entering Table II with a probability value and reading out a z-value.

   Example 7 In the ND of the foregoing example, what is the value of X_1 such that $P(X \ge X_1) = .1$?

   Solution Here the z-value corresponding to the required X_1 lies in the upper half of the ND and hence is positive. The z-value

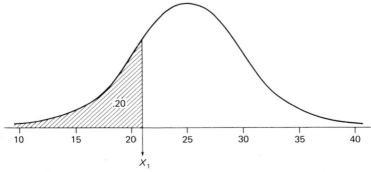

Figure 10.12   Normal distribution with $\mu = 25$, $\sigma = 5$

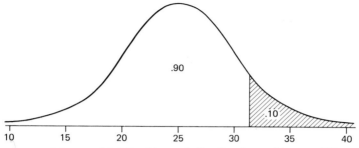

Figure 10.13 Normal distribution with $\mu = 25$, σ

required is the same as that for which $P(z \leq z_1) = .90$ (see Figure 10.13). The value closest to .90 in column 6 of Table II is .8997, which corresponds to $z = +1.28$. Hence, application of (10.4) gives $X_1 = (5)(+1.28) + 25 = 31.4$, and in this ND, $P(X \geq 31.4) \approx 0.1$.

Type 5: Score distance to either side of μ corresponding to a given central probability value

Example 8 Given a ND universe with $\mu = 50$ and $\sigma = 10$, what is the value of X_1 such that in this universe $P(|x| \leq x_1) = .95$, where $x = X - \mu$?

Solution Here, we seek a score distance[11] x_1 which, if measured in both a positive and a negative direction from 50, will encompass .95 of the area under the curve (see Figure 10.14). One way to obtain this information from Table II would be simply to

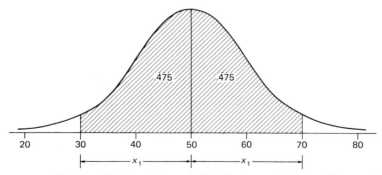

Figure 10.14 Normal distribution with $\mu = 50$, $\sigma = 10$

[11] Remember, lower-case letters represent deviations from the mean (see Rule 6.1, p. 93).

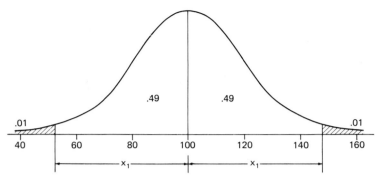

Figure 10.15   Normal distribution with $\mu = 100$, $\sigma = 20$

locate the value nearest to .4750 in column 2. This value happens to appear exactly in column 2; it corresponds to a z- or σ-distance of 1.96. Since $\sigma = 10$, it follows that $x_1 = 19.6$. That is, in this *NPD*, $P(|x| \leq 19.6) = .95$.

Type 6: Score distance to either side of μ corresponding to a given extreme area probability value

Example 9 Given a *ND* universe with $\mu = 100$ and $\sigma = 20$, what is the value of x_1 such that in this universe $P(|x| \geq x_1) = .02$?

Solution Here we seek a score distance x_1 which, measured in either a positive or a negative direction from 100, will be exceeded by .02 of the score distances from 100 (see Figure 10.15). One way to obtain this information from Table II is to locate the value nearest to .02 in column 3. This value is .0198 and corresponds to a z-value or σ-distance of 2.33. Hence, $x_1 = (20)(2.33) = 46.6$ so that in this *NPD* the $P(|x| \geq 46.6) = .02$.

10.7 The Normal Probability Distribution as an Approximation of the Binomial Probability Distribution

The normal probability distribution is the third fundamental probability model that we have presented. The other two, the equally likely model and the binomial model, were discussed in some detail in Chapter 9. There we noted that when the number of trials (n) of a binomial experiment is large, the solution of the binomial equation (9.1) (see p. 165) becomes very tedious. Tables of binomial probabilities are not commonly available for $n > 50$. The widespread availability of computer programs for calculating binomial probability values has alleviated this problem somewhat. However, when such computing equipment is not readily accessible, an alternative solution may be possible. This alternative procedure involves the use of the normal probability distribution to obtain probability values that closely approximate the actual probability values given by the binomial rule.

Consider a large population consisting of two types of voters: those who favor the passage of a particular bond issue (A-type), and those who oppose the passage of this bond issue ($\overline{A}$-type). Assume a binomial experiment is conducted with n, the number of draws (i.e., people selected), equal to 10. (See pp. 164 and 165 for the criteria of a binomial experiment.) We now ask: "If ϕ (the proportion of A types in the population) equals .50, what is the probability distribution for the random variable r (i.e., the number of A types in the sample) when $n = 10$?" Table 9.5 provides these probability values, and a graphical representation of them is shown in Figure 10.16 (see just the histogram in Figure 10.16). Next, we ask: "What normal distribution provides the best approximation of the binomial probability values?" It seems reasonable that we should use a normal distribution with the same mean and standard deviation as this binomial distri-

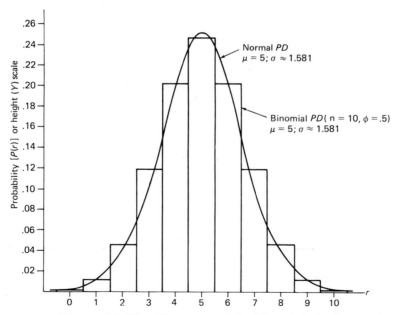

Figure 10.16 Histogram of the binomial distribution for $n = 10$ and $\phi = .5$ and a plot of the normal distribution with $\mu = n\phi = 5$ and $\sigma = \sqrt{n(\phi)(1 - \phi)} \approx 1.581$

bution. By (9.2) (p. 172) we know that the mean for the binomial probability distribution of r is

$$E(r) = \mu = n\phi$$

Likewise, by (9.3),

$$\sigma^2 = n\phi(1 - \phi)$$

Hence, for the example under consideration,

$$\mu = (10)(.5) = 5 \quad \text{and} \quad \sigma^2 = (10)(.5)(.5) = 2.5$$

In Figure 10.16, the plot of a normal curve with $\mu = 5$ and $\sigma = \sqrt{2.5} \approx 1.581$ is superimposed on the histogram representing the binomial probability distribution for $n = 10$ and $\phi = .5$.[12] The "fit" of the normal curve looks good. A closer examination of the fit of the NPD to the BPD can be obtained by comparing some actual probability statements derived from each model.

For example, find $P(r \geq 8)$. Using the BPD (see Table 9.5),

$$P(r \geq 8 \mid BD : n = 10, \phi = .5) = .0439 + .0098 + .0010 \approx .0538$$

Using the NPD,

$$P(r \geq 8 \mid ND: \mu = 5, \sigma = 1.58)$$
$$= P\left(z \geq \frac{8 - 5}{1.58} \approx 1.90 \mid ND: \mu = 0, \sigma = 1\right) \approx .0287$$

In this instance, the true probability value obtained from the BPD is about twice as great as the approximate value obtained from the NPD. Most researchers would not be satisfied with such a degree of inaccuracy. It appears that in this specific situation the normal curve cannot be used to estimate binomial probabilities. However, the degree of inaccuracy can be markedly reduced if one simple modification is made in the procedure.

Whereas the normal PD is a model for random variables of a continuous nature, the binomial PD serves as model for a discrete random variable. If, as in the above example, we are interested in the probability $P(r \geq 8)$ and if r is a discrete random variable, then we are interested in the probability that $r = 8$, 9, or 10. This probability

---

[12] The procedure for superimposing the NPD on the binomial distribution is not discussed in this text. Nor is it essential to an understanding of the concept being developed. The student interested in this procedure is referred to the first edition of this text (pp. 208–212).

is represented in Figure 10.16 by the sum of the areas of the rectangles above 8, 9, and 10. This is the sum of the areas of the rectangles having the unit bases 7.5–8.5, 8.5–9.5, and 9.5–10.5. However, if we treat r as a continuous random variable and assume that specific values of r are measured to the nearest unit, then instead of asking "What is $P(r \geq 8)$?", we should ask "What is $P(r \geq 7.5)$?" Therefore, we should use the area above the interval 7.5–∞ in the NPD with $\mu = 5$ and $\sigma = 1.58$ as an approximation of the total area of the three rectangles cited. More formally, we write

$$P(r \geq 7.5 \mid ND: \mu = 5, \sigma = 1.58)$$
$$= P\left(z \geq \frac{7.5 - 5}{1.58} \,\middle|\, ND: \mu = 0, \sigma = 1\right)$$
$$\approx P(z \geq 1.58 \mid ND: \mu = 0, \sigma = 1)$$
$$\approx .0571$$

This value compares very favorably with the actual binomial probability of .0538.

Mathematical statisticians have shown that if this modification is used and if ϕ does not differ markedly from .5, the normal PD provides very accurate approximations to binomial PD's even when n is relatively small. However, when ϕ differs markedly from .5 (say, $\phi \leq .1$ or $\phi \geq .9$), much larger sample sizes are needed.[13]

Remark: The above discussion does not outline a general procedure for approximating binomial probability values using the appropriate normal curve. Such a general procedure is as follows. If r_1 is a particular outcome of the binomial experiment and if we are interested in the probability of outcomes greater than r_1, then $P(r \geq r_1 \mid BD: n, \phi)$ is approximated by

$$P\left(z \geq \frac{(r_1 - .5) - n\phi}{\sqrt{n\phi(1 - \phi)}} \,\middle|\, ND: \mu = 0, \sigma = 1\right)$$

Likewise, if r_1 is the outcome and if we are interested in the probability of outcomes less than r_1, then $P(r \leq r_1 \mid BD: n, \phi)$ is approximated by

$$P\left(z \leq \frac{(r_1 + .5) - n\phi}{\sqrt{n\phi(1 - \phi)}} \,\middle|\, ND: \mu = 0, \sigma = 1\right)$$

[13] Novick and Jackson (*Statistical Methods for Educational and Psychological Research*, McGraw-Hill, New York, 1973, p. 106) state that for many purposes the normal approximation is adequate even with an n as small as 10, if ϕ is close to .5. If ϕ is close to .1 or .9, then much larger sample sizes (in the thousands) are needed. A conservative rule of thumb would be to require $n \geq 100$ when ϕ differs from .5 so long as this difference is not too marked, say no more than .3.

Finally, if it is of interest to compute the probability that the outcome is between two specific values, say r_1 and r_2 (where $r_1 < r_2$), then $P(r_1 \leq r \leq r_2 \mid BD: n, \phi)$ is approximated by

$$P\left(\frac{(r_1 - .5) - n\phi}{\sqrt{n\phi(1 - \phi)}} \leq z \leq \frac{(r_2 + .5) - n\phi}{\sqrt{n\phi(1 - \phi)}} \;\middle|\; ND: \mu = 0, \sigma = 1\right)$$

Example 1 $P(r \geq 6 \mid BD: n = 10, \phi = .5) = .3770$ (see Table 9.5). The normal curve approximation is

$$P\left(z \geq \frac{(6 - .5) - 5}{1.58} \;\middle|\; ND: \mu = 0, \sigma = 1\right)$$
$$= P\left(z \geq \frac{.5}{1.58} \;\middle|\; ND: \mu = 0, \sigma = 1\right)$$
$$= P(z \geq .316 \approx .32 \mid ND: \mu = 0, \sigma = 1) \approx .3745$$

(See Table II, Appendix C.)[14]

Example 2 $P(r \leq 3 \mid n = 10, \phi = .5) = .1719$ (see Table 9.5). The normal curve approximation is

$$P\left(z \leq \frac{(3 + .5) - 5}{1.58} \;\middle|\; ND: \mu = 0, \sigma = 1\right)$$
$$= P(z \leq -.95 \mid ND: \mu = 0, \sigma = 1) \approx .1711$$

(See Table II, Appendix C.)

Example 3 $P(3 \leq r \leq 6 \mid n = 10, \sigma = .5) = .7735$ (see Table 9.5). The normal curve approximation is

$$P\left(\frac{(3 - .5) - 5}{1.58} \leq z \leq \frac{(6 + .5) - 5}{1.58} \;\middle|\; ND: \mu = 0, \sigma = 1\right)$$
$$= P(-1.58 \leq z \leq .95 \mid ND: \mu = 0, \sigma = 1) \approx .7718$$

Remarks:
1. The adjustment of the obtained r-values by adding or subtracting .5 is frequently referred to as Yate's correction.

---

[14] Accuracy may be further improved by using a linear interpolation. Note from Table II that $P(z \geq .32) = .3745$. Also, $P(z \geq .31) = .3783$. Therefore, $P(z \geq .316)$ is approximately $.3783 - (.6)(.3783 - .3745) \approx .3783 - .23 \approx .3760$. It is not essential that the student master this procedure, since for most practical purposes a z-value to the nearest hundredth provides sufficiently accurate probability values. However, a detailed discussion of this process is presented in the first edition of this text (pp. 205–208).

2. Obviously, the normal approximation should not be used when the exact binomial probabilities can be calculated easily.

3. When n is large (say $n > 500$) and ϕ is between .1 and .9, it is not necessary to use Yate's correction.

10.8   The Lack of Generality of the Normal Curve as a Distribution Model

We have presented the normal curve as providing a suitable model of the probability distributions of the outcomes of certain types of experiments (see, for example, Section 10.1). As such a model the normal curve has proved to be highly satisfactory. (In subsequent chapters we will pursue this in some detail.) Unfortunately, however, certain early statisticians formed the view that this curve could be used to describe almost any mass collection of data. Adolphe Quetelet (1796–1874), for example, believed that data from anthropometry, economics, criminology, the physical sciences, botany, and zoology were all fundamentally "normal" in form of distribution.[15] He was further convinced that the same was true of mental and moral traits and that verification of this point of view waited only the development of suitable measuring techniques. The identity of the individual who first applied the adjective "normal" to the particular curve we are considering is not definitely known, but the choice undoubtedly stemmed from a point of view like that of Quetelet. Both this adjective and this point of view have tended to persist.

Actually, if we were to make a broad and representative collection of frequency distributions of real data found in the research literature of education, psychology, sociology, anthropometry, and other related fields, and if we were to construct a histogram or even a smoothed polygon for each, we would find that our collection contained a wide variety of forms of distributions. Some curves would be skewed positively, others negatively; some would be bimodal, some U-shaped, some J-shaped, and some almost rectangular. It is true that many could be roughly described as bell-shaped, but among these would be some too peaked and others too flat-topped to be represented by the normal curve model. The great variation in forms of distributions, even of a single trait, is strikingly illustrated by the age distributions presented in Figure 10.17. Because of this extreme variation in form, we would find it impossible to phrase a *single* generalized description that would apply accurately to more than a small portion of the distributions we had collected. There is, then, no universal "law" of any kind, not to mention

[15] Helen M. Walker, "Bicentenary of the Normal Curve," *Journal of the American Statistical Association*, 29 (March 1934).

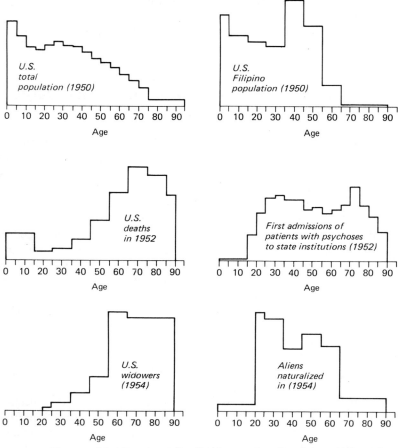

Figure 10.17   Age distributions of various populations in the United States based on data reported in Statistical Abstract of the United States, 1955

an underlying "law of normality," concerning the form of frequency distributions in general.

Two fundamental facts explain why there can be no *single* universally applicable frequency distribution model—at least not for distributions of measures of any human trait. In the first place, it is clear that the measures of a given trait may be distributed in different ways (forms) for different populations. This is illustrated by the age distributions pictured in Figure 10.17. Second, not only do distributions of a given trait differ for different populations, but they differ according to the particular scale employed in the measurement of the trait. Since the choice of scale is arbitrary, distributions of different sets of measurements of the same trait for the same group of individuals may be made to differ in form in almost any way by simply varying the measuring scale employed.

We have seen, for example, that distributions of incomes in dollars may be markedly skewed positively (see Table 3.8). And yet economists have found that if they measure incomes in terms of the logarithms of dollars, they obtain distributions that quite closely approximate the normal curve model.

One of the most striking instances of the deliberate construction of scales so as to produce normally distributed scores is to be found in educational and psychological measurement. A distribution can be made to fit the "normal" model either by an adjustment of the difficulty of the items that will make the distribution of raw scores normal, or by some transformation of the raw scores that will tend to yield scores that are normally distributed.[16] If the test author so desired, sets of items that would yield distributions skewed positively or negatively could be easily prepared. Choosing items that tend to be too difficult would yield a positively skewed distribution of scores. Likewise, selecting very easy items would yield a negatively skewed distribution.

In most educational and psychological test scales, the amount of the trait involved that corresponds to a scale unit varies in an unknown way from one part of the scale to another. Consequently, it is impossible to use distributions of scores along such scales as a basis for inferring the character of the distribution of the "true" amounts of the trait possessed by the members of a given group—assuming that somehow measurements of these "true" amounts could be determined. In seeking to construct scales that produce normally distributed scores, educators and psychologists are implicitly assuming the "true" amounts to be normally distributed for the groups involved; they make their scales bear out this assumption. They are somewhat abetted in this as a result of the fact that the scores yielded by their tests usually involve rather large chance-error components, which tend to be normally distributed. The random addition of normally distributed components to any set of nonnormally distributed scores can result only in a set of scores that is more nearly normally distributed than before. Thus, the very inaccuracy of the scores yielded by educational and psychological tests contributes to the tendency of such scores to be normally distributed.

The foregoing remarks do not constitute a blanket criticism of the practice of deliberately constructing educational and psychological

---

[16] In Chapter 8 we introduced the concept of a linear transformation of raw scores. As was noted in Section 8.6, such a transformation does *not* change the shape of the frequency distribution. Thus, a transformation of raw scores which yields scores that are normally distributed will not, in general, be a linear transformation.

scales so as to yield normal score distributions. If there is some logical basis for the *a priori* assumption that "true" amounts of some trait are normally distributed for a given population, then it would not appear unreasonable that a measuring scale yield a distribution of scores that conforms to this hypothesis.

10.9   Summary Statement

The normal probability distribution is one of the most important probability models in inferential statistics. In this chapter, we discussed the characteristics of normal curves, presented methods for using normal curves to make probability statements, and indicated how normal curves can be used to approximate binomial probability distributions. Although we attempted to show (in Section 10.1) why such a distribution may be needed as a model of the distribution of the outcomes of some experiments, our presentation focused more on the mechanics of how to use a normal curve to make probability statements than on the practical applications of the normal curve model in inferential statistics. These practical inferential applications of this distribution will be examined in detail in subsequent chapters (particularly Chapters 11 through 14). In these chapters the normal curve will serve as a model of the distribution of outcomes from repeated runs of certain random experiments. This is the situation for which the formula of the curve was originally developed. Its importance as a model in such situations cannot be overemphasized.

11
Introduction to Sampling Theory

11.1 Introduction

As we stated in Section 9.1, a large majority of the research studies in education and psychology are of the type known as sampling studies. In such studies, the usual procedure is as follows. A sample of individuals is selected from some population and data relevant to the question being studied are gathered. These sample data are then used to make generalizations or inferences about the population from which the sample was selected. (At this time, we urge the rereading of Section 9.1, which gives concrete examples of the types of inferences with which we will be concerned.)

Most sampling studies can be viewed as experiments. That is, the three characteristics of an experiment—repeatability, uncertainty of an outcome on any one run, and specifiability of all possible outcomes (see Section 9.2)—are all also characteristic of such studies. Hence, the outcome of a sampling study can be viewed as an outcome (random variable) of an experiment. In sampling studies, repetition of the experiment implies the selection of a new sample from which a new set of data is gathered. Since it is assumed (more will be said about this assumption in the subsequent sections of the chapter) that only chance factors determine the identity of the specific units selected for the sample, the outcomes of each repetition are likely to differ from the true value because of these chance factors. The difference between a given outcome (estimate) and the true value is called *sampling error*. As was explained in Section 9.1, this problem of sampling error in the outcome of a given experiment provided the basic motivation for developing the probability concepts presented in the preceding two chapters.

In this chapter, we extend our discussion of sampling error and the entire sampling process. First, we present a brief discussion to clarify the concept of a population. Then, we define the basic concepts of sampling-error theory. Third, we present the necessary theory for solving certain inferential problems when the outcome (random variable) of the sampling experiment is either a mean, a median, or a proportion. This theory will involve the normal curve probability model.

11.2   The Concept of a Population

We begin this section with a definition and then discuss a few important factors that will help clarify the definition.

Population

DN 11.1   By population we mean the aggregate or totality of objects or individuals regarding which inferences are to be made through a sampling study.

One of the important steps in the design of a sampling study is the specification of the population to be studied. It may be that this can be easily accomplished, as in the case of a population of H78 × 15 radial tires produced by a certain manufacturer where it is desired to estimate the mean mileage for the population; or in the case of a population of fourth-grade pupils enrolled in the Catholic parochial schools of a certain state where it is desired to estimate the mean performance for the population on a certain test of ability to spell. Quite often, however, the specification of the population presents difficulties. Consider, for example, a population of farms, where it is desired to estimate the mean annual income for the population. The difficulty, of course, has to do with the definition of a farm. Questionable cases will arise, and the investigator will be in doubt about whether or not a particular object belongs to the population—that is, is a "farm." It is essential that the population be specified to a point that eliminates such doubt. The investigator is responsible for the development of a set of rules that clearly determine whether or not a given object belongs to the population under investigation. These rules, then, prescribe this population.

In recent years, a very useful distinction between two types of populations has been made. This distinction is extremely helpful in understanding the validity of the generalizations that can be made in a research study. Bracht and Glass[1] have presented an excellent discussion

[1] G. H. Bracht and G. V. Glass, "The External Validity of Experiments," *American Educational Research Journal*, 5 (1968), 437–473. Reprinted by permission of the American Educational Research Association.

of these two types of populations, and a small segment of their paper (which is based on the ideas of Kempthorne)[2] is quoted below.

> Kempthorne (1961) has distinguished between the *experimentally accessible population and the target population*. The former is the population of subjects that is available to the experimenter for his study. The target population is defined as the total group of subjects about whom the experimenter is empirically attempting to learn something. It is the group that he wishes to understand a little better and to whom he wants to apply the conclusions drawn from his findings. For example, an educator has discovered a new approach to teaching fractions to fourth graders. Probably he would like to conclude that his method is better for all fourth-grade students in the United States—the target population. However, he randomly selects his sample from all fourth graders in the local school district—the experimentally accessible population.
>
> The experimenter must make two "jumps" in his generalizations: (1) from the sample to the experimentally accessible population, and (2) from the accessible population to the target population. The first jump, a matter of inferential statistics, usually presents no problem if the experimenter has selected his sample randomly from the accessible population.
>
> In the previous example, the experimenter may have chosen all fourth-grade students in the state as his experimentally accessible population and randomly selected a sample of fourth-grade classrooms. Then the accessible population would probably be more like the target population and inference could be made to the target population with more confidence than in the first example. (However, the experimenter now has a problem in managing the research procedures and maintaining precise control over the treatment because the experiment is being conducted throughout the state.) . . .
>
> The second jump, from the experimentally accessible population to the target population, can be made with relatively less confidence and rigor than the first jump. The only basis for this inference is a thorough knowledge of the characteristics of both populations and how these characteristics interact with the experimental treatment. If the mean IQ of fourth graders in the accessible population is 115, can the experimenter generalize to a target population in which the mean

---

[2] O. Kempthorne, "The Design and Analysis of Experiments with Some Reference to Educational Research," in *Research Design and Analysis: Second Annual Phi Delta Kappa Symposium on Educational Research*, ed. R. O. Collier, Jr., and S. M. Elam, Phi Delta Kappa, Bloomington, Ind., 1961, pp. 97–126.

IQ is 100? The answer depends, of course, on what findings one wishes to generalize and the relationship between the treatment variable and the characteristics of the target population.

The degree of confidence with which an experimenter can generalize to the target population is never known because the experimenter is never able to sample randomly from the true target population. Kempthorne (1961) pointed out that, even if we could draw a random sample from the target population, by the time the results were analyzed the target population would not be that which had been sampled. "Just how different it will be is a matter of inference about the processes which lead to the target populations. Such an inference is in my opinion impossible to validate in any strict sense." (p. 101).

As an illustration of the possible effects of generalizing to a target population from an inappropriate experimentally accessible population, consider the results of a public opinion survey taken in 1948. In that year, the American Institute of Public Opinion, popularly known as the Gallup Poll, reported in the press its prediction of the outcome of the presidential election of that year. This prediction was based on a sample presumed to represent the population of individuals who would cast their ballots for president on November 2, 1948. The individuals constituting this sample were asked, in advance of November 2, who they would vote for if the election were assumed to be in progress, that is, to be taking place on the day the question was asked. The percentages of individuals in the sample indicating they would vote for Dewey, Truman, Thurmond, Wallace, or some other candidate were reported as predictive of the election outcome.

Table 11.1 shows the sample percentages as they were published by the American Institute of Public Opinion and corresponding population percentages as reported in *Statistics of the Presidential and Congressional Election of November 2, 1948* (Government Printing Office, 1949). It will be observed that the discrepancies between the sample and population percentages are sufficiently great to invalidate the election forecasts based on these sample percentages.

In this example, it is clear that the experimentally accessible population was not representative of the target population. In this instance, the target population consisted of individuals who voted in the presidential election of November 2, 1948. At the time Dr. Gallup's organization selected the sample, this population did not yet exist. The sample was taken from an experimentally accessible population and interpreted as representing the target population. This was, in this case, done deliberately and with the hope that the two populations would be sufficiently alike that generalizations extended to the pop-

Table 11.1   Sample and Population Percentages of Votes
for 1948 Presidential Candidates

Candidate	Sample Percentage (Gallup Poll)	Population Percentage (National Vote)
Dewey	49.5	45.1
Truman	44.5	49.5
Thurmond	2.0	2.4
Wallace	4.0	2.4
Other	—	0.6
	100.0	100.0

ulation actually sampled could also be extended to the then-nonexistent population of actual voters. The erroneous forecast given by the poll on this particular occasion was probably due to differences between these two populations. On another occasion the populations may be sufficiently alike to permit a generalization of this type to be accurate.

Another more extreme example of the use of a sample taken from an experimentally accessible population as a basis for drawing inferences about a different target population is to be found in medical experimentation conducted with animals. A sample of rats or guinea pigs provides a basis for generalizations regarding, say, the effect of some new drug on the development of cancer in a population of such rats or pigs. Populations of other animals—even human beings—may then be regarded as sufficiently like this population of rats insofar as the effect of the particular drug is concerned to permit the second generalization to take place. Often—at least at certain stages of theory development—this represents the only practicable means of experimentally checking theory. When this is the case, it ultimately becomes essential for the investigator to collect comparative information about the two populations for the purpose of determining whether generalizations may reasonably be extended from one to the other.

A similar situation is often encountered in educational experimentation, particularly in experimentation having to do with evaluating the relative effectiveness of two ways of doing something—such as teaching and developing a particular skill in arithmetic at the fourth-grade level. The two methods may be tried out on samples of fourth-grade children, and one of them may prove better than the other insofar as the experimentally accessible population of children involved is concerned. To then recommend this method in preference to the other implies a generalization of sample fact to a target population of children who will be attending similar fourth grades in the future—a population that is, of course, nonexistent at the time of experimentation. The success of such a generalization depends on the degree to which the experiences and abilities of the members of this future population conform and continue to conform to the experiences and abilities of the members of the population studied.

Conceivably, there are times when the experimentally accessible population is identical to the target population. Consider, for example, an experiment conducted for the specific purpose of ascertaining how undergraduates currently enrolled in a particular university feel about a proposed bill before the state legislature. In this instance, the target population (undergraduates now) and the experimentally accessible population (undergraduates now) are the same. This assumes, of course, that all undergraduates are accessible as potential participants in the experiment. But this is a most atypical example. No matter how carefully the investigator may restrict the stated generalizations, the implication almost always remains that they are somehow applicable to other groups of undergraduates.

Throughout the remaining sections of this book, we shall limit our attention to the problem of generalizing to the experimentally accessible population. After all, such generalizations are a *sine qua non* to target population generalizations. We shall simply assume that the experimentally accessible population is representative of some meaningful target population. This is not a "cop-out" in a book of this character, but it would be a cop-out on the part of a researcher who completely ignored the issue.

11.3   Definitions and Basic Concepts of Sampling-Error Theory

Sample

DN 11.2 By *sample* we mean a collection consisting of a part or a subset of the objects or individuals of a population which is selected for the express purpose of representing the population, that is, as a basis for making inferences about or estimates of certain population characteristics.

The statement that a sample ought to be selected from the population it is intended to represent may seem a truism. The fact is, however, that selecting a sample from the population involved may be impossible. As our examples in the previous section showed, the experimentally accessible population is not always representative of the target population. However, our work in this book assumes that an appropriate sample (as defined above) can be obtained.

Sampling unit We have indicated that the populations we seek to study consist of a number of individuals or objects. Each individual or object is a *population unit*. For the purpose of selecting a sample, the population is divided into a number of parts called *sampling units*. Sampling units usually contain one or more population units; no population unit may belong to more than one sampling unit. The aggregate of sampling units is the whole population.

In the simplest situation, the population unit *is* the sampling unit. For example, in the illustration of the population of tires previously suggested, the sampling unit could be a single tire. On the other hand, in the population of fourth-grade pupils enrolled in the Catholic parochial schools of a certain state, the sampling unit might be a classroom, or perhaps a school building, or even the children residing in some governmental subdivision such as a township. It is clear that if the township were used as the sampling unit, any such given unit could contain none, one, or more than one population units (children).

Score To begin with, we are, of course, interested in determining some population characteristic. Our interest may be no more clearly defined than a generally expressed desire to determine the life of a certain type of tire produced by a certain company. What do we mean by the life of a tire? Do we have in mind miles of wear before it becomes useless beyond repair? If so, what kind of wear, on what kinds of roads, at what kinds of speeds, and bearing what kinds of loads? What does the phrase "useless beyond repair" mean? By what criteria may one judge this state in a tire? These are only indicative of the many questions that must be answered if our general purpose is to be satisfied.

Somehow, for each sampling unit in our sample, we must accurately count or measure the characteristic or trait in which we are fundamentally interested. We shall call the counts or measurements we obtain *scores*. These scores constitute the basic data from which our generalizations will stem.

How such measurements should be taken and how valid and reliable they should be are topics that were treated very briefly in Chapter 2. It seems important to repeat, however, that the most erudite statistical analysis can only help to *interpret* the information contained in the scores. *It can never add information.* If the scores are inappropriately or inaccurately determined, the study is doomed to failure and the money, time, and energy expended will have been wasted.

Parameter

DN 11.3   Parameter is the name given to the population characteristic we seek to estimate.

A parameter is not the estimate we may obtain but the population characteristic itself. The parameter can be obtained only by determining the scores for all of the units that constitute the population.

In our illustration regarding the life of a certain brand of automobile tire, the pertinent population parameter might be taken as the mean number of miles of service the tires give before wearing out. Let us assume, for the sake of economy as well as of achieving uniformity of condition, that the tires are tested on a machine designed to simulate actual highway use, and that the machine is calibrated to indicate for each tire tested the number of miles it is used. Let us further assume that a tire is defined, for the purpose of this investigation, to be worn out when it first blows out. Then the score for a given unit (tire) is obtained by placing the unit on the machine, setting the indicator dial at zero, letting the machine run until the tire blows out, and reading from the indicator dial the number of miles elapsed.

Now to obtain the population parameter in which we are interested—that is, the mean number of miles of service—we must obtain such a score for every unit in the entire population. The value of the parameter, then, is the mean of these scores. This implies exposing to machine wear until blown out each and every tire of the specified size produced by the particular manufacturer involved. But then there would be no tires to sell. Obviously the value of the parameter in this situation can never be determined practically. We are forced to be content with an estimate based on a sample of units taken from the population.

In other situations reasons dictating the use of a sample estimate may include (a) the fact that the population is so large that obtaining a score for all the population units is physically and/or economically impracticable, and (b) the fact that the target population units may be nonexistent at the time of the investigation (recall the experiment designed to evaluate the relative effectiveness of two methods of teaching a particular arithmetic skill).

Statistic

DN 11.4   A statistic is a sample fact that depends on the scores of the particular sampling units constituting a sample.

Just as *parameter* is the name given to a population fact, so is *statistic* the name given to a sample fact.

In our illustration regarding the wearing qualities of tires, a value of the statistic corresponding to the parameter described could be determined by selecting a number of tires as a sample, obtaining the scores for the tires chosen, and then finding the mean of these scores. As we noted in Section 11.1, the outcome of a sampling study can be viewed as a particular value of the random variable of an experiment. Thus a statistic, too, can be viewed as a particular value of the random variable of an experiment. The mean number of miles for our sample of tires is, then, both a statistic and a random variable of this experiment.

Now if there is one thing about which we may be certain, it is that the units that make up our population vary in durability. No matter how the manufacturer may have striven for uniformity of quality, the fact remains that some of the tires will wear better than others. It is clear that the value of the statistic in this example will depend on the quality of the sample units chosen. If these units are on the whole more durable than usual, their mean (the statistic) will be large in relation to the population mean. If they are less durable, it will be small. Moreover, if a second sample of units were to be selected from this same population (i.e., if the experiment were repeated) and the scores of these units were determined, it is extremely *unlikely* that the distribution of the values of these new scores would be identical to the score distribution of the first sample. Hence the statistic based on the second sample would almost certainly differ from the previous statistic. Thus, while a particular parameter can have one and only one value, the corresponding statistic may assume many different values. For any given population, then, the value of a parameter is a *constant* while that of the corresponding statistic *varies* for different samples selected from this population.

Sampling error

DN 11.5   Sampling error is simply the difference between the value of a population parameter and that of the corresponding statistic.

So that the direction of the error may be taken into account, this difference should always be determined in the same way. The, conventional procedure consists of subtracting the value of the parameter (θ) from that of the statistic (T). That is, if E represents sampling error,

$$E = T - \theta \tag{11.1}$$

This convention identifies sampling errors associated with underestimates of the parameter as negative errors and those associated with overestimates as positive errors.

Sampling distribution   We have noted that the value of a statistic may be expected to vary from one sample to another even if the samples are selected by the same procedure from the same population. Let us suppose that by means of some prescribed procedure we select a sample of 100 units from some population. Then we obtain a score for each unit selected and compute for this sample the value of a statistic, such as the mean of the 100 scores. Now suppose we repeat this process 1,000 times. Each time we select (by the same procedure) a new sample of 100 units from this same population,[3] and each time determine the mean of the 100 scores obtained for the selected set of sample units. The 1,000 means thus obtained will, of course, vary somewhat from sample to sample. Now let us organize these 1,000 means into a relative frequency distribution. We have in this distribution a start toward the empirical derivation of a particular *sampling distribution*—the sampling distribution of the means of 100 scores obtained for samples of 100 units selected according to the same prescribed procedure from the same population. We can claim only to have made a start toward the empirical derivation of this particular sampling distribution because the notion of a sampling distribution incorporates the relative frequency distribution of the infinity of statistics that would arise from an infinity of repetitions of a particular sampling routine. In our case, the true sampling distribution would represent the totality of all possible experience with variation in the values of the means that arise from the repeated application of the particular sampling experiment to the particular population. A sampling distribution is, then, a theoretical construct. We may be able to set up a model of one, but we could never empirically derive one because no experiment can be repeated to infinity.[4]

A sampling distribution may be based on any experimentally obtained statistic. Thus, if the medians, rather than the means, of each sample of 100 scores had been obtained in our experiment, we could have made a similar start toward the empirical derivation of a sampling distribution of medians. In the same way it is possible to base sampling distributions on semi-interquartile ranges, or on standard deviations, or on percentages, as on percentages of individuals in the samples who indicate their intention to vote for a particular candidate for public office.

We are now ready to state a somewhat more formal definition of a sampling distribution.

> **DN 11.6** The sampling distribution of a statistic (random variable) is the relative frequency distribution of an infinity of determinations of the value of this statistic, each determination being based on a separate sample of the same size and selected independently but by the same prescribed procedure from the same population.

[3] If the population is "very large" (i.e., infinite), the removal of sample units will not affect its character. It can be assumed, therefore, that each new sample is selected from the same population as its predecessor, even if the units previously selected are not returned to the population. If the population is not large, the experimenter must, of course, return to it the units selected for any given sample before selecting the succeeding sample, in order to satisfy the condition that each sample be selected from the same population.

[4] It is, of course, possible to make useful approximations of sampling distributions empirically.

For a fairly concrete illustration of the above concepts, the student is urged to reread Section 10.1. Figure 10.1 can be viewed as a picture of the sampling distribution of means for the experiment described in Section 10.1.

From DN 11.6 it should be clear that a sampling distribution is a probability distribution. A sampling distribution indicates the probability (relative frequency) of all the possible different outcomes (values of the statistic) of a random experiment. We shall use the terms "sampling distribution" and "probability distribution" synonymously in this book.

Bias A sampling distribution is a probability distribution. As discussed in Section 9.6, a particular probability distribution may be described (1) in terms of its placement along the scale of possible values of the statistic (i.e., in terms of its mean or expected value); (2) in terms of the extent to which the values are spread along the scale (i.e., in terms of its variability); and (3) in terms of its symmetry, or skewness, or peakedness, or flatness (i.e., in terms of its form). If the expected value (mean) of the sampling distribution of a statistic coincides with or equals the corresponding population parameter, the statistic is said to be *unbiased*. If, on the other hand, the expected value of the sampling distribution of that statistic does not coincide with the parameter, the statistic is said to be *biased*.

It is important not to confuse bias and sampling error. Sampling errors are the chance differences between the values of some sample statistic and the corresponding population parameter. Bias refers to a single difference, namely, the difference between the expected value of the statistic (i.e., the mean of its sampling distribution) and the true value of the corresponding parameter. In other words, bias refers to the overall or long-run tendency of the sample results to differ from the parameter in a particular way. Obviously, the presence of bias in a sampling investigation is a thing either to be avoided or to be fully taken into account.

Bias may arise in two ways. The most troublesome way is as a result of the method of sample selection. Suppose, for example, that the procedure used in selecting the sample for our automobile tire illustration somehow consistently gives us tires that tend to be more durable than usual: suppose that all tires selected are inspected for durability and that only those passing this preliminary screening are retained for use in the sample. Then the mean of the sampling distribution of the statistic[5] will be larger than the parameter. The bias here

[5] The statistic in this example is itself a mean, the mean of the numbers of miles of use the tires in a sample will give before blowout occurs. The mean of the sampling distribution, on the other hand, is the mean or expected value of an infinite collection of such sample means.

is due to the sampling procedure. To say that the procedure *tends* to produce samples of tires that are more durable than usual is not to say that every sample contains only extra-durable tires. Some samples produced by the procedure may involve tires whose average durability is the same as that of the population. The sampling error in the case of such samples is, of course, zero. Occasionally the procedure may even select tires having an average durability lower than that of the population. The sampling error in the case of such samples is in an opposite direction from the bias. This illustrates why the term *bias* is not applicable to the result of a single sample. *Bias refers, instead, to long-run tendency as reflected by the expected value of the outcomes of an infinity of samples.*

Bias due to the method of selecting samples from the experimentally accessible population is troublesome because there is no way to assess its magnitude and consequently there can be no way to make due allowance for it or to take it into account in interpreting the sample results. Craftsmanly and honest designers of sampling procedures take every precaution to avoid bias. But bias resulting from the sampling procedure can be extremely subtle. It may escape the notice of the sampler until—too late, really—some inconsistency in results begins to suggest that it is there. To design sampling routines that are free of bias is not always an easy undertaking. Some attention is given this problem in the following section.

The second source of bias is a less troublesome one. It has to do with the character of the statistic itself. Certain statistics are of such a nature that the expected values of their sampling distributions will differ from the corresponding population parameter even if the sampling procedures involved are unbiased. The sample range, for example, could never exceed the population range; it could at most equal it, and then only if both the smallest and largest population scores happened to be included in the particular sample. Hence, the mean of a sampling distribution of ranges is bound to be smaller than the population range. The sample range illustrates an inherently biased statistic.

Bias inherent in a statistic is not a troublesome problem, because its direction and magnitude can be deduced mathematically. When the direction and magnitude of a bias are known, it is a simple matter to make allowance for it in interpreting results.

Standard error We have already discussed briefly the use of measures of variability as indexes of the reliability of a measuring or sample estimating procedure (see Section 7.7). In so doing we pointed out that neither errors of measurement nor sampling errors could ever be determined quantitatively because their determination would require knowledge of the true value (parameter) being measured or estimated. We suggested that a study of the consistency of the results arising from repetition of a given measuring or sampling procedure would provide a useful basis for evaluating the reliability or accuracy of that procedure. In keeping with this approach we shall use as a quantitative index of the accuracy (actually, the inaccuracy) of a sampling procedure the standard deviation of the sampling distribution of the statistic (T) involved. Since this standard deviation is used as an index of the degree of precision or degree of error with which a parameter may be estimated by a statistic, it is called a *standard error*.

DN 11.7 The standard error of any statistic is the standard deviation of its sampling distribution.

Since the sampling distribution of a statistic is a theoretical construct, the standard error of a statistic must also be a theoretical construct. We can, however, estimate its value for any statistic derived from a specified sampling procedure by actually carrying out this procedure a number of times. Here we are in effect regarding the sampling distribution as a hypothetical population of values from which we select a sample by repeating a specified sampling routine and determining the value of the statistic for each repetition. The values of the statistic that constitute this sample may then be used to estimate a particular parameter—the standard deviation—of this hypothetical population (the sampling distribution). As we shall later learn, it is possible in the case of certain statistics based on samples selected in a certain way to obtain useful estimates of their standard errors from the information contained in a single sample, thus saving oneself the time and costs of repeating a sampling routine.

11.4 Selecting the Sample

There are many ways in which a sample may be selected. In the example about the automobile tires, for instance, we might simply go to the company stockpile and take from it the needed number of most conveniently accessible tires. Or we might go to the end of the plant production line and take the needed number of tires in succession as they come off the line. The usefulness of these or any other procedures depends on the effectiveness with which the resulting samples represent the population involved. Both procedures cited, for example, ignore tires that may have been in retailers' stockrooms for an appreciable period of time. In other words, tires thus chosen represent only the more recently manufactured portion of the population. If the wearing qualities of a tire are in any way a function of recency of manufacture, then samples chosen according to the above procedures will be biased in the direction of the qualities that are characteristic of only the more recently manufactured tires.

The task of devising selection procedures that will result in samples from the experimentally accessible population that are free from bias is, as we have already pointed out, extremely difficult and subject to subtly concealed sources of error. There is no substitute for a soundly conceived plan. Not even the use of an extremely large sample can be counted on to mitigate the bias arising from an invalid sampling scheme. In 1936, the editors of a weekly news periodical known as the *Literary Digest* undertook to forecast the outcome of the presidential election of that year. They put their faith in sample size, believing, it would seem, that if a sample were simply made big enough the manner of its selection would be immaterial. They obtained straw ballots from some ten million people using telephone directories as the primary source of names. This procedure not only ignored people who had no telephone but also resulted in the inclusion in the sample of disproportionate numbers in the older age groups. Since the issues of the 1936 campaign were drawn largely along economic lines, it is not surprising that the forecast based on this sample was a victory for the Republican candidate, Landon. Roosevelt's subsequent sweep of all states save Maine and Vermont and the *Literary Digest's* subsequent failure are a matter of record.

But procedural errors in selecting samples are not always so obvious. Even the foregoing example has been oversimplified and incompletely reported. It is, perhaps, unfair to imply that the conductors of the *Literary Digest* poll of 1936 were blind to the possibility that their technique of sample selection would result in the inclusion of a disproportionate number of individuals favoring the economic philosophy of the Republican party. Besides their faith in the extreme size and the widespread distribution of their sample (names were selected from every phone book in the United States), they could point with pardonable pride to the past success of their technique. In 1932, for example, another election year in which economic issues were paramount, the same sampling technique produced a phenomenally accurate forecast of the outcome of the presidential election. How is it possible that a scheme that proved so satisfactory in forecasting one election failed so miserably in another? Post-mortem analysis provided an answer. Unlike modern polls that make use of interviewers, the *Literary Digest* poll was conducted through the mails. This procedure, of course, leaves the return of the ballot to the whim of the recipient. It was soon discovered that, perhaps as a form of voicing protest, members of the party out of power are far more likely to return such ballots than members of the "ins."[6] In 1932, a far greater proportion of the then-out-of-power Democrats receiving *Literary Digest* ballots

---

[6] J. D. Cahalan, *Literary Digest Presidential Poll*, unpublished Master's thesis, State University of Iowa, 1936.

returned them than did the Republicans receiving these ballots. Thus the bias resulting from the use of the phone directory as a primary source of sampling units was canceled by the opposite bias resulting from the use of the mails in collecting the straw ballots. In 1936, on the other hand, the then-out-of-power Republicans returned the ballots in greater proportion. The two sources of bias, instead of canceling each other out, became additive. The bias due to allowing people to decide for themselves whether or not to be included in the sample is one that most present-day designers of sampling studies seek to avoid. It is not uncommon, however, particularly in the case of questionnaire studies, to find this method of sampling extant today, which explains in part the skepticism with which the results of such studies are generally regarded. To the operators of the *Literary Digest* poll this particular source of bias was apparently unknown. While obvious enough once pointed out, it illustrates the subtlety of sources of bias against which the sampler must be continually on guard.

In general, sampling schemes may be classified according to two types: (1) those in which sample elements are automatically selected by some scheme under which a particular sample of a given size from a specified population has some known probability of being selected; and (2) those in which the sample elements are arbitrarily selected by the sampler because in his judgment the elements thus chosen will most effectively represent the population. Samples of the first type are known as *probability* samples; those of the second type are referred to as *judgment* samples.[7] Of these two general types of sampling procedure, only the first is amenable to the development of any theory regarding the magnitudes of the sampling errors that may be expected in a given situation.

In this book we shall confine our attention to a special case of probability sampling known as *simple random sampling.* Simple random sampling refers to a method of selecting a sample of a given size from a given population in such a way that all possible samples of this size that could be formed from this population have an equal probability of being selected. Suppose a population consists of only five elements named *a, b, c, d,* and *e.* It is possible to form ten different samples of two elements each from this population, so the probability of any sample in this universe of samples is .1. The ten possible samples are

ab	*ad*	*bc*	*be*	*ce*
ac	*ae*	*bd*	*cd*	*de*

Next we must prescribe some procedure (experiment) for selecting one of these samples such that if the procedure is repeated an infinity of times, each of the possible samples will occur with the same relative

---

[7] L. Kish, *Survey Sampling,* John Wiley & Sons, New York, 1965.

frequency in the new hypothetical universe thus generated—a new universe representing the totality of all possible experience with this sampling procedure in this situation. In other words, we are positing an experiment that consists of drawing one of the ten possible samples that can be listed. The outcome of one run of the experiment is the particular sample drawn. The probability value associated with each of the ten possible outcomes under indefinite repetition of the experiment is to be the same (.1). That is, the equally likely outcomes model is to apply. Under these conditions, any sample drawn is said to be a simple random sample.

To select our random samples, we might assign each of the ten possible samples a number from 1 to 10, write each sample identification number on one of ten identical cards, place these cards in a container, mix them thoroughly, and then, blindfolded, draw one of them from the container. Since, with repetition of this procedure we would expect each sample to be drawn one-tenth of the time in the long run (i.e., in the infinity of repetitions), the resulting sample would be, by definition, a simple random sample.

Actually, to draw a simple random sample, it is not necessary to identify all possible samples as in the above example. It is sufficient to identify the elements in the population and then, as a first step, to draw a single element by a procedure of the character just suggested. The single element thus chosen is, by definition, a simple random sample of one object taken from the given population. The element thus chosen is set aside as the first member of the sample to be drawn. The process is then repeated with what is left of the population. From this new population, which differs from the original only in that it lacks the element just drawn, a second element is chosen by this same procedure. This element is also set aside as a member of the sample desired. This process is repeated until a sample of the desired size is attained. While we shall not attempt here to detail the argument involved, it can be shown that this procedure fully complies with the definition of simple random sample previously stated and that the probability associated with a sample selected from a given population by this latter procedure has the same numerical value as that of a sample selected by the procedure that requires the identification of all possible samples.

To apply the procedure just suggested we must not only assign some identifying number to each population element but we must also prepare for each element a corresponding card bearing this number. Except for this number, these cards must be made as nearly identical as possible in order to avoid any effect that physical differences in the cards might have on the long-run frequency with which some would be selected. Obviously the task of preparing such cards can become a tedious one. The practical difficulties associated with it mount as the population becomes large.

To circumvent this task, tables of random digits have been developed to take the place of cards or slips of paper. A *random digit* is the outcome of an experiment that consists of selecting a simple random sample of one case (one digit) from the universe of the ten digits 0, 1, 2, . . . , 9. A table of random digits records the outcomes in order of occurrence of some large but finite number of independent repetitions of this experiment. A very large table of random digits may itself be thought of as a universe in which the ten digits occur with nearly equal frequency in a random order. This implies that if N digits are read successively either by rows or by columns or in any other systematic way, and from any arbitrarily selected starting point in the table, the N digits thus read would constitute a simple random sample from this universe.

Computers may be programmed to generate tables of random digits. Perhaps the largest such table is one prepared by the Rand Corporation.[8] A small table of random digits is given in Table III of Appendix C.

To use a table of random digits to select a simple random sample of, say, 25 objects from a universe of, say, 1,000 objects, it is first necessary to identify all objects in the universe by assigning each a successive number beginning at 000, 001, 002, . . . , up to 999.[9] Then choosing any three columns (or rows) of the table—it is usually most convenient to use successive columns—and arbitrarily selecting any row of these columns as a starting point, record the first 25 successive rows of three digits appearing in these columns. Now take as the sample from the universe the 25 objects whose identification numbers correspond to the 25 numbers thus recorded. It may be necessary to record more than 25 numbers if it develops that some of the numbers recorded are the same.

While this technique saves the preparation of cards and the invention of some scheme for mixing and drawing them, it does not eliminate the task of numerically identifying each element of the experimentally accessible population. Also, it must be remembered that the selection of a random sample from the experimentally accessible population does not guarantee that a random sample from the target population has been obtained. The validity of any generalizations to the target population must be defended by the investigator.

[8] Rand Corporation, *A Million Random Digits with 100,000 Normal Deviates*, Free Press, Glencoe, Ill., 1955.

[9] All the identifying numbers must involve the same number of digits—in this example, three digits.

11.5   Sampling Theory as It Applies to the Means of Random Samples

The basic purpose of this section and the two sections that follow is to describe the sampling distributions of three statistics: the mean, the proportion, and the median. These distributions will then aid us in making inferences about population parameters.

We use the notion of sampling theory *as it applies to some statistic* to refer to the nature and characteristics of the theoretical sampling distribution (probability distribution) of this statistic. In other words, we use this notion to refer to a description of the theoretical totality of experience with the values of this statistic that arise when a given sampling experiment is repeatedly applied to a given population. The development of such theory is the work of the mathematical statistician, who is often forced to employ advanced mathematical procedures to accomplish this purpose. Throughout this text we shall limit our treatment of sampling-error theories as they apply to selected statistics to a description of the mathematician's findings without any attempt at presenting the mathematical bases. We shall, moreover, confine our attention to the theory as it has been developed for infinitely large populations.

This is not as restricting as might be presumed. In the first place, unless the target population is quite small and the sample so large as to take in a substantial portion of the population, there is very little practical difference in the theory for finite and infinite populations. In the second place, such errors as will occur in estimating the reliability of a sampling routine applied to a finite population will tend to be on the conservative side. That is, estimates of standard error based on the theory developed for infinite populations will tend to be too large when this theory is applied to finite populations. Finally, most of the target populations of concern to psychologists and educators are either quite large or entirely hypothetical. It is usually logically defensible to view a hypothetical population as very large if not infinite.

In this section we shall be specifically concerned with the sampling theory that has been developed for the mean of a simple random sample. Some concrete illustrations are cited, but consideration of the practical applications of this theory is deferred to Chapters 12 through 15.

We shall consider first the case in which the population of scores (X's) involved is normally distributed.[10] We shall represent the mean

---

[10] As we have indicated previously (see Section 10.2), no real collection of real outcomes can be truly normally distributed. However, distributions of certain scores are for all practical purposes normally distributed. For example, the heights in inches of all nine-year-old Canadian boys (see Figure 11.1), or the intelligence scores in mental age units of all ten-year-old girls in the state of New York, can be considered normally distributed.

and variance of this population of scores by μ and σ^2, respectively. Now let a simple random sample of N scores be selected from this population, and let the mean of these N scores be represented by $\overline{X}$. Mathematical statisticians have rigorously demonstrated that were this sampling procedure to be repeated indefinitely, the resulting infinite collection of $\overline{X}$-values would also be normally distributed with mean $\mu_{\overline{X}} = \mu$.[11] Since the population and this theoretical collection are both normally distributed, the *NPD* will serve as a model of what is called the "sampling distribution of means."

Intuitively it would seem that the variability of this theoretical collection of $\overline{X}$-values should depend on (1) the variability of the scores that make up the population, and (2) the size of the sample, N. The greater the variation among the population scores, the more variation we would expect to observe among the $\overline{X}$-values. And since a large sample provides a more precise estimate of μ than a small one, it would also be true that the larger the value of N, the less variation we would expect to observe among the $\overline{X}$-values. In other words, we would expect the degree of variation among the $\overline{X}$-values to be *directly* proportional to the degree of variation among the population scores and *inversely* proportional to the size of the sample. Mathematical statisticians have shown that the *variance* of the sampling distribution of $\overline{X}$'s ($\sigma_{\overline{X}}^2$) is directly proportional to the variance of the population (σ^2) and inversely proportional to the size of the sample (N).

By way of summary we shall express the foregoing theory in the form of a rule.

> **RULE 11.1** The sampling distribution of means ($\overline{X}$) of simple random samples of N cases each taken from a normally distributed population of scores (X-values) with mean μ and variance σ^2 is a normal distribution with mean $\mu_{\overline{X}} = \mu$ and variance

$$\sigma_{\overline{X}}^2 = \frac{\sigma^2}{N} \tag{11.2}$$

> **RULE 11.1a** The standard error of the sampling distribution of Rule 11.1 is

$$\sigma_{\overline{X}} = \frac{\sigma}{\sqrt{N}} \tag{11.3}$$

By way of concrete illustration consider the theoretical population of height scores of nine-year-old Canadian boys, which is pictured in Figure 11.1.[12] For random samples of 16 height scores selected from

---

[11] The subscript identifies the statistic of interest.

[12] Based on data from *A Height and Weight Survey of Toronto Elementary School Children, 1939*, Department of Trade and Commerce, Dominion Bureau of Statistics, Social Analysis Branch, Ottawa, Canada, 1942. The normal curve was derived from the measurement of 4,451 boys.

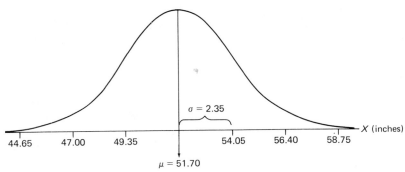

Figure 11.1   Normal curve of heights in inches of
Canadian boys age 9. $\mu = 51.7$, $\sigma = 2.35$

this population, the sampling distribution of the statistic $\overline{X}$ should be
a normal distribution with mean at 51.7 and a variance of $2.35^2/16 \approx$
.3452, or a standard error of $2.35/\sqrt{16} \approx .59$ (see Figure 11.2). From
this distribution we may note, for example, that in the long run .6826
(or 68.26 percent) of the means of random samples of 16 cases selected
from this population will involve sampling errors of less than .59
inches; or that the probability of a sample mean being in error by .59 or
more is .3174.

If Figure 11.2 is compared to Figure 11.1, the two distributions look
identical. The similarity in shape is due to an adjustment of the score
scale. The physical distance that represented one σ-distance (2.35 score
units) in Figure 11.1 was also used to represent one $\sigma_{\overline{X}}$ distance
(.59 score units) in Figure 11.2. In fact, if the two curves were plotted
on a comparable scale, the distribution of $\overline{X}$ would be much narrower
than the distribution of X. Figure 11.3 illustrates the differences between
these two distributions.

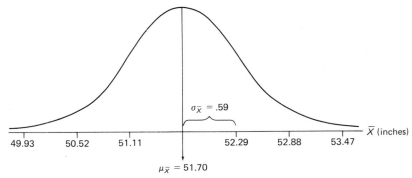

Figure 11.2   Sampling distribution of means of samples
of 16 cases selected at random from a normally distributed
population having $\mu = 51.7$ and $\sigma = 2.35$

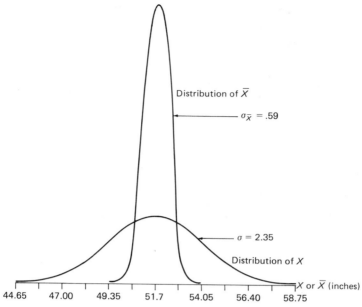

Distribution of $\overline{X}$

$\sigma_{\overline{X}} = .59$

$\sigma = 2.35$

Distribution of X

X or $\overline{X}$ (inches)

| 44.65 | 47.00 | 49.35 | 51.7 | 54.05 | 56.40 | 58.75 |

Figure 11.3 A comparison of the distribution of X and the distribution of $\overline{X}$ when $N = 16$

Rule 11.1 specifies the mean, the standard error (or standard deviation), and the shape (normal) of the sampling distribution of means when random samples are selected from a normally distributed population of scores. The question naturally arises: "What are the characteristics of the sampling distribution of $\overline{X}$ if samples are selected from populations of scores that are *not* normally distributed?" In fact, the mean of the sampling distribution of X remains equal to the mean of the population of scores. Also, $\sigma_{\overline{X}}$ remains equal to $\sigma/\sqrt{N}$. However, the shape of the sampling distribution of X is not necessarily normal when the population distribution of scores is not normal. Since we may expect to find relatively few of the "real world" populations in which we are interested to be normally distributed, the applicability of the theory specified by Rule 11.1 is quite limited. Fortunately, however, there exists a useful theory that has a much more extensive range of applicability. This theory is the subject of Rule 11.2.[13]

[13] This important result follows from a theorem known to statisticians as the central-limit theorem. Technically, the central-limit theorem states that the random variable z [where $z = (\overline{X} - \mu)/(\sigma/\sqrt{N})$] approaches a normal distribution with mean $= 0$ and variance $= 1$ as N increases. However, in this introductory course we shall consider the random variable $\overline{X}$ as approaching a normal distribution with mean μ and variance σ^2/N as N increases. While the transformation of $\overline{X}$ to z is technically essential to the central-limit theorem, it is of virtually no practical consequence insofar as the applicability of Rules 11.2 and 11.2a is concerned.

RULE 11.2   The sampling distribution of means ($\overline{X}$) of simple random samples of N cases taken from any infinite population having mean μ and finite variance σ^2 approaches a normal distribution with mean $\mu_{\overline{x}} = \mu$ and variance σ^2/N as N increases.

RULE 11.2a   The standard error of the sampling distribution of Rule 11.2 is

$$\sigma_{\overline{x}} = \frac{\sigma}{\sqrt{N}} \tag{11.4}$$

This theory, which belongs to the class of theories labeled "large-sample theory," differs from the theory of Rule 11.1 in that it is applicable to any infinite population whatever, regardless of the form of the score distribution, so long as the variance of this population is finite. Since almost any population in which we are likely to have a practical interest will have a finite variance, the theory becomes almost completely general in its applicability. Nevertheless, this theory leaves something to be desired. Its shortcoming lies in the fact that it is extremely difficult to say just how large N must be in order for the normal distribution to provide a sufficiently accurate model. If the population distribution is roughly normal, the theory is sufficiently accurate even when N is quite small. If, on the other hand, the population distribution is far from normal—say, J-shaped—a much larger N is necessary to justify the application of the normal approximation. Empirical investigations have shown that, for most of the populations encountered, $N \geq 50$ is sufficient to warrant the use of this theory.

11.6   Sampling Theory as It Applies to a Proportion: A Special Application of the Theory of Rules 11.2 and 11.2a

Consider a population consisting of only two types of objects, say A's and not A's. The population may consist of just two types of fourth-grade pupils—those who can spell a given word (A's) and those who cannot (not A's), or those who correctly answer a particular test question (A's) and those who do not (not A's), or those who have had mumps (A's) and those who have not (not A's). Or the population may consist of voters who vote for Candidate A and those who do not, or of United States citizens who are church members and those who are not, or of teen-agers who are delinquent (a definition of delinquency is, of course, necessary) and whose who are not. Populations of this type, that is, populations whose units may be classified into one or the other of two mutually exclusive classes, are known as *dichotomous populations*.

Suppose that for some dichotomous population we wish to determine the proportion of units belonging to one of the two classes, but that it is impractical for us to examine all of the units in the population. We can obtain an approximation of the value of the desired proportion by selecting a sample from the population, counting the sample units belonging to the class in which we are interested, and expressing this count as a proportion of the number of units in the sample. It should be recognized, of course, that this sample proportion may involve a sampling error and that a repetition of the sampling procedure would almost certainly yield a proportion different from that of the first sample. In fact, all the sampling-error concepts that we have thus far developed may be applied to the sample proportion considered as a statistic (random variable).

The sampling theory for a proportion is a special case of the sampling theory for a mean (Rules 11.2 and 11.2a). This follows from the fact that the population proportion of A's can be viewed as the mean of a set of scores taking on only one or the other of two values, 0 or 1. If we assign the score of unity (one) to population units classified as A's and the score of zero to units that are not A's, then the proportion of A's is the mean of this set of zeros and ones.[14] We shall use the symbol ϕ to represent the proportion of A's in the population. That is, ϕ is the mean of a population of scores that are either 0 or 1. The proportion of A's (or 1's) in the sample will be represented by the symbol p. Hence, p is a sample mean.

Furthermore, the variance of the population distribution of zeros and ones is $\phi(1 - \phi)$. Likewise, the variance of a set or sample of observed scores consisting of only zeros and ones is $p(1 - p)$.[15]

We can now state the sampling theory as it applies to a proportion (mean) calculated for large samples as a special case of Rule 11.2.

---

[14] If this result is not clear, consider a population consisting of 1,000 students, some of whom can spell a given word and some of whom cannot. Assume 600 of the 1,000 students can spell the word (they are classified as A's). Then, the proportion of A's is .60. Likewise, if a score of unity is assigned to these 600 students and a score of zero is assigned to the remaining 400, then the mean $\sum X/N$ is 600/1,000 = .60.

[15] For any relative frequency distribution the variance is $\sum_{j=1}^{c} (rf)_j X_j^2 - \bar{X}^2$ [see (7.10a)]. Now consider the dichotomous (i.e., $c = 2$) relative frequency distribution shown in the accompanying table. Since the mean of this distribution is ϕ, it follows that the variance σ^2 is equal to $\phi - \phi^2 = \phi(1 - \phi)$.

Type of Object	Score (X)	rf	$(rf)X^2$
A	1	ϕ	ϕ
Not A	0	$1 - \phi$	0
		1	ϕ

RULE 11.3   Given an infinite dichotomous population, the units of which are assigned a score of one if they belong to Class A[16] and a score of zero if they do not belong to Class A. The sampling distribution of the proportion (p) of A-type units in random samples of N units taken from this population approaches a normal distribution with mean ϕ and variance

$$\sigma_{p2} = \frac{\phi(1 - \phi)}{N} \tag{11.5}$$

as N increases.

RULE 11.3a   The standard error of the sampling distribution of Rule 11.3 is

$$\sigma_p = \sqrt{\frac{\phi(1 - \phi)}{N}} \tag{11.6}$$

As an example of this theory, consider a population of school pupils 40 percent of whom can solve a given test exercise correctly. Here the pupils who are able to solve the exercise correctly are the A's and $\phi = .4$. For random samples of 600 pupils taken from this population, the sampling distribution of p, the proportion of A's in a sample, is a normal distribution (approximately) with mean at .4 and standard error of .02 (i.e., $\sigma_p = \sqrt{(.4)(.6)/600} = .02$). This theoretical sampling distribution is pictured in Figure 11.4. From this distribution we may

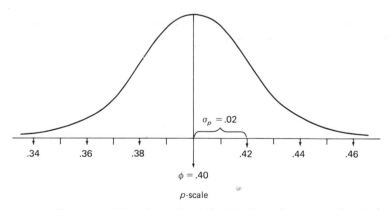

$\sigma_p = .02$

.34   .36   .38   .42   .44   .46

$\phi = .40$

p-scale

Figure 11.4   Sampling distribution of a proportion (p) for random samples of 600 units selected from a dichotomous population containing .4 A's

---

[16] Belonging to Class A means having the characteristic under study (e.g., being above 100 on a test; voting "yes" for increased Social Security benefits, passing the life-saving test).

note, for example, that the probability of a sample p-value being in error (i.e., differing from ϕ) by .02 or more is approximately .3174.

Remarks:

1. In Section 9.7 we discussed the binomial experiment. The characteristics of a binomial experiment were listed on pages 164 to 165. You may already have recognized that these characteristics hold true for the sampling experiments described in this section. In these examples, the sample size, N, represents the number of trials (previously designated by n); and ϕ, the proportion of A types in the populations, represents the probability of an A type on each trial.[17] Thus, on the basis of the material presented in Section 9.7, it would have been possible to show that the sampling distribution of p, the sample proportion, is, in fact, a binomial distribution with mean = ϕ and variance = $\phi(1 - \phi)/N$.[18]

2. It is known (see Section 10.7) that the normal probability distribution provides a good approximation of the binomial distribution when N is large. Here, we have chosen to use the normal probability distribution as the approximate sampling distribution of p rather than its true binomial sampling distribution. There were three basic reasons for this decision.

First, as noted earlier, the proportion of A types can be viewed as the mean of a set of scores consisting of only two values, 0 and 1. Hence, a sampling theory for p is easily derived from the sampling theory for $\overline{X}$. Second, using the normal probability distribution as the approximate sampling distribution of p enables us to use just one probability model (the normal curve) for the inferential procedures we develop in the remaining part of this chapter and also in Chapters 12, 13, and 14. Finally, all the inferential procedures we consider in the next several chapters are based on the condition that "large" samples are involved. In such situations, if the outcome of the experiment is p (the proportion of A types), the calculation of exact binomial probabilities by (9.1) becomes impractical. Instead, the normal curve, which provides good approximations to binomial probabilities, may

---

[17] Note that if the population is large relative to N, ϕ remains essentially constant from trial to trial.

[18] In Section 9.9, it was stated that the mean of the binomial distribution for the number of A types was $N\phi$ (see equation 9.2) and that the variance of the number of A types was $N\phi(1 - \phi)$ (see equation 9.3). However, in this section we are concerned with the distribution of p, the proportion of A types. Note that $p = (\text{No. of } A \text{ types})/N$. Thus, p is a linear transformation of the number of successes (with $b = 1/N$ and $c = 0$; see Chapter 8). Therefore, by Rule 8.3 (p. 133), the mean of the sampling distribution of p is $(1/N)(N\phi) = \phi$ and the variance is (by Rule 8.4) $(1/N)^2[N\phi(1 - \phi)] = \phi(1 - \phi)/N$.

be used.[19] In Chapter 15, a chapter specifically treating sampling-error theory for "small" samples, we will illustrate the use of the exact binomial probability distribution as the sampling distribution of p (see Section 15.11).

11.7 Sampling Theory as It Applies to the Median of Random Samples

RULE 11.4 The sampling distribution of medians (*Mdns*) of simple random samples of N cases taken from any continuous infinite population having median ξ approaches a normal distribution with mean ξ as N increases.

RULE 11.4a If y_ξ is the ordinate (height) of the population probability distribution curve at the median ξ, the variance of the sampling distribution of Rule 11.4 is

$$\sigma^2_{Mdn} = \frac{1}{4y_\xi^2 N} \tag{11.7}$$

RULE 11.4b The standard error of the median is

$$\sigma_{Mdn} = \frac{1}{2y_\xi \sqrt{N}} \tag{11.8}$$

RULE 11.4c If the population is normally distributed with standard deviation σ, the standard error of the median is

$$\sigma_{Mdn} = \frac{\sqrt{\pi}}{\sqrt{2}} \frac{\sigma}{\sqrt{N}} = \sqrt{\frac{\pi}{2}} \sigma_{\bar{x}} \approx 1.25 \sigma_{\bar{x}} \tag{11.9}$$

Proof * If the population distribution is as specified by (10.1), then, since $\xi = \mu$,

$$y_\xi = \frac{1}{\sigma\sqrt{2\pi}}$$

and direct substitution into (11.8) gives (11.9).

This theory is very similar to the theory for the mean, given as Rule 11.2. The remarks made at the close of Section 11.5 with regard

[19] Footnote 13 in Chapter 10 discusses how large the sample size must be in order to justify the use of the normal approximation.

* Optional.

to sample size apply here as well. It will be observed that the theory does not require that the population variance be finite as does the theory of Rule 11.2. On the other hand, Rule 11.4 is limited to use with scores representing measures of continuous attributes, whereas the theory pertaining to the mean is applicable to both discrete and continuous data. It is also important to note that *when the population involved is normally distributed*, the sample mean is a more reliable estimate of μ than is the sample median, the standard error of the median being approximately one and one-fourth times larger than that of the mean (11.9). This is why the mean is usually preferred over the median as the statistic in sampling studies having to do with the characteristic of central tendency.

To illustrate the theory of Rule 11.4, we shall again make use of the theoretical population of height scores of nine-year-old Canadian boys shown in Figure 11.1. In Section 11.5 we saw that the sampling distribution of $\overline{X}$ for random samples of 16 taken from this population was normal with mean at 51.7 and a standard error of .59. Since the median of this population of height scores is also 51.7, it follows from Rule 11.4 that the sampling distribution of the median for random samples of 16 taken from this population is also a normal distribution with a mean (or median) of 51.7. Moreover, since the population from which the samples are taken is itself normally distributed, it further follows, from Rule 11.4c, that the standard error of this sampling distribution is approximately $1.25 \times .59 = .74$. This theoretical sampling distribution is pictured in Figure 11.5. From this distribution we may note, for example, that the probability of a sample median being in error by .74 or more is .3174.

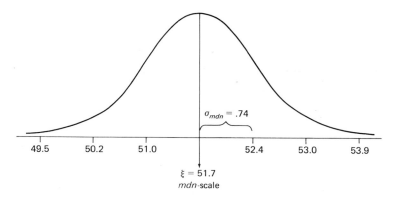

Figure 11.5 Sampling distribution of medians of samples of 16 cases selected at random from a normally distributed population having $\mu = 51.7$ and $\sigma = 2.35$

11.8   Approximating Descriptions of Sampling Distributions

Except for the limited case of the sampling distribution of the mean for random samples from a normally distributed population (Rule 11.1), all the theoretical sampling distributions presented in the foregoing sections are approximate. All the sampling distributions, except this one, only *tend toward* or *approach* the normal distribution model as the sample size increases. In each case, however, suggestions were made regarding the minimum sample size necessary to make the use of the theoretical model sufficiently accurate for practical purposes.

There remains another aspect of all the sampling distributions as they have thus far been described (including those of Rule 11.1) that restricts their practical usefulness. This is the fact that the specification of any of these distributions in a particular case requires knowledge of certain population facts (parameters). For example, specification of the distributions involving means of random samples implies knowledge of the means and the variances of the populations involved; and specification of sampling distributions involving the proportions of A's in random samples from a dichotomous population of A's and not A's implies knowledge of these very proportions. Obviously, knowledge of this type is not generally available. If it were, sample estimates would not be needed and sampling theory would not be of interest to the practical researcher.

And yet it *is* possible to make useful applications of these models, if the researcher is willing to accept further approximations—namely, such approximations of the needed population parameters as can be derived from the information contained in the sample at hand.

An indication of the value of a population mean, median, or proportion is readily obtainable from the sample. For example, we note from either Rule 11.1 or 11.2 that the mean of the sampling distribution of means of random samples is the same as the mean of the population from which the samples come. Hence, the expected value (Section 9.6) of the mean of a random sample $[E(\overline{X})]$ is the population mean. Thus, the mean of a random sample provides an unbiased estimate of the population mean. Similar conclusions apply in the case of medians and proportions.

By way of summary we have the following rule.

> **RULE 11.5**   The following statistics derived from random samples selected from a given population provide unbiased estimates of the corresponding population parameters: $\overline{X}$, *Mdn*, and p.

In addition to these estimates of location or central tendency, the specification of the approximate sampling distributions under consideration also implies the availability of an estimate of the variance or standard deviation of the populations involved. The expected value (mean) of the sampling distribution of the variances of random samples is *not* equal to the population variance. In other words, the sample variance—unlike the sample mean, median, and proportion—does not provide an unbiased estimate of the population variance. Consideration of the sampling distribution of variances of random samples is beyond the scope of this test, but the solid curve in Figure 11.6 shows what such a distribution would look like for S^2-values based on random samples of five scores ($N = 5$) drawn from a normally distributed population having $\sigma^2 = 4$. One fact about the sampling distribution of S^2 is of great importance: its expected value is given by

$$E(S^2) = \frac{N-1}{N}\sigma^2$$
(11.10)

where

$E(S^2)$ = the expected value (mean) of the sampling distribution of S^2

σ^2 = the variance of the population from which the samples come

N = the sample size

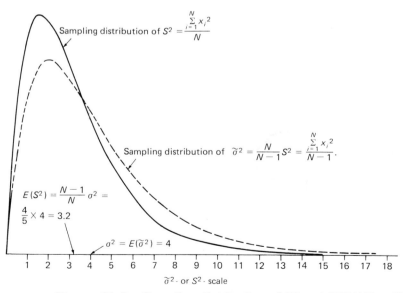

Figure 11.6 Sampling distribution of S^2 and $NS^2/(N-1)$ for random samples of size 5 selected from a normal distribution with $\sigma^2 = 4$

Formula (11.10) shows that the expected value of the sampling distribution of random sample variances is somewhat smaller than the population variance, since the factor $(N - 1)/N$ must always be less than unity. For example, if N is 5, the expected value of the distribution of sample variances is 80 percent of the population variance [in the sampling distribution of S^2 in Figure 11.6, $E(S^2) = .8\sigma^2 = 3.2$]; and if N is 100, the mean of the sample variances is 99 percent of the population variance. It is also clear that as N increases, the magnitude of this bias decreases. We have previously learned (see Rule 8.3) that if each score in a collection is multiplied by some constant, the mean of the new collection thus formed is equal to the mean of the original scores multiplied by this constant. Suppose now that instead of considering a distribution of S^2-values, we consider a distribution of values consisting of the product of each S^2 times the constant $N/(N - 1)$. Then the expected value (mean) of this new distribution is equal to the mean of the S^2-distribution multiplied by this same constant. That is,

$$E\left(\frac{N}{N-1}S^2\right) = \frac{N}{N-1}E(S^2) = \frac{N}{N-1}\cdot\frac{N-1}{N}\sigma^2 = \sigma^2$$

It follows that the population variance is the mean (expected value) of the sampling distribution of the statistic $NS^2/(N - 1)$. That is, $NS^2/(N - 1)$ is an unbiased estimate of the population variance σ^2. The dotted curve in Figure 11.6 pictures the sampling distribution of $NS^2/(N - 1)$ for random samples of five scores ($N = 5$) drawn from a normally distributed population having $\sigma^2 = 4$. We will represent this new statistic by the symbol $\tilde{\sigma}^2$. In this example $E(\tilde{\sigma}^2) = \sigma^2 = 4$. We shall again summarize in the form of a rule.

> **RULE 11.6** Let S^2 represent the variance of a random sample of size N from a population having variance σ^2, and let $\tilde{\sigma}^2$ represent an unbiased estimate of σ^2. Then
>
> $$\tilde{\sigma}^2 = \frac{N}{N-1}S^2 \qquad\qquad (11.11)$$

Three distinct types of quantitative facts enter into this rule: (1) the population fact or parameter, σ^2, (2) the sample fact or statistic, S^2, and (3) an unbiased estimate of the population fact based on information contained in the sample, $\tilde{\sigma}^2$. To represent these facts we have, in keeping with common practice, generally employed a Greek letter to represent the parameter and an English letter (where possible, the corresponding one) to represent the statistic. Where the estimate differs from the sample fact (the statistic), a third symbol is needed. To represent an estimate of a population parameter in such cases, we shall use its Greek representational character superposed by a tilde ($\sim$).

We shall continue to employ this notational scheme throughout the remainder of this book.

RULE 11.6a

$$\tilde{\sigma}^2 = \frac{\sum\limits_{i=1}^{N} x_i^2}{N-1} \qquad (x_i = X_i - \bar{X}) \qquad\qquad (11.12)$$

This result follows directly from substituting into (11.11) the equivalent of S^2 as stated in (7.4).

Many writers follow the practice of defining the variance of any collection of scores by (11.12), that is, as involving division by $N - 1$ rather than by N. This practice has the advantage of simplifying some of the formulas that arise in sampling theory. For reasons stated in the preface to the first edition, we have elected not to follow this practice. In keeping with the above remarks on notation, the writers who do follow this practice have generally used the lower-case English s^2 to represent the sample variance and σ^2 to represent the population variance. They have no need for the third symbol ($\tilde{\sigma}^2$) to represent the estimate of the population variance since the sample variance, as they define it, *is* this estimate. We have used the upper-case English S^2 to represent the sample variance as a reminder that the definition we are using differs from that which is usually represented by the lower-case s^2.

> **RULE 11.6b** If p represents the proportion of A's in a random sample from a dichotomous population of A's (ones) and not A's (zeros), then the estimated variance of the population is
>
> $$\tilde{\sigma}^2 = \frac{Np(1-p)}{N-1} \qquad\qquad (11.13)$$

This result follows from the fact that the sample $S^2 = p(1 - p)$. (See footnote 15 on p. 229 and substitute S^2 for σ^2 and p for ϕ.)

We are now in a position to write formulas providing unbiased estimates of the variances of the sampling distributions thus far considered. For the sampling distributions of Rules 11.1 and 11.2 we have, on substituting (11.11),

$$\tilde{\sigma}_{\bar{X}}^2 = \frac{\tilde{\sigma}^2}{N} = \frac{S^2}{N-1} \qquad\qquad (11.14)$$

For the sampling distribution of the median where the population is normally distributed, we have (see Rule 11.4c)

$$\tilde{\sigma}_{Mdn}^2 = \frac{\pi}{2}\tilde{\sigma}_{\bar{X}}^2 = \frac{\pi}{2}\frac{S^2}{N-1} \approx \frac{1.57S^2}{N-1} \qquad\qquad (11.15)$$

For the sampling distribution of Rule 11.3 we have, on substituting the estimate of $\phi(1 - \phi)$ as given in (11.13) into (11.5),

$$\tilde{\sigma}_p{}^2 = \frac{1}{N} \frac{Np(1 - p)}{N - 1} = \frac{p(1 - p)}{N - 1} \tag{11.16}$$

It should not be inferred from (11.11) and (11.13) that the square roots of these unbiased variance estimates are also unbiased estimates of the population standard deviations. That is,

$$E\left(S\sqrt{\frac{N - 1}{N}}\right) \neq \sigma$$

in spite of the fact that

$$E\left(\frac{N - 1}{N} S^2\right) = \sigma^2$$

This follows from the fact that the mean of the square roots of a collection of values is not *in general* equal to the square root of their mean. For example, consider the scores 4, 25, and 121. Here $\bar{X} = 50$ and $\sqrt{\bar{X}} = 7.071$. But the square roots of these scores are 2, 5, and 11, and the mean of these square roots is 6.

In spite of the fact that the square roots of (11.11) and (11.13) do not provide unbiased estimates of the population standard deviation, they have been shown to provide estimates of great theoretical and practical usefulness. Consequently we shall use as an estimate of a population standard deviation the square root of the unbiased estimate of the population variance. For sake of completeness, we list below the formulas for estimating population standard deviations and also for estimating standard errors of sampling distributions. In each case these are simply the square root of the corresponding variance estimate.

$$\tilde{\sigma} = S\sqrt{\frac{N}{N - 1}} \tag{11.17}$$

Or, for dichotomous populations,

$$\tilde{\sigma} = \sqrt{\frac{Np(1 - p)}{N - 1}} \tag{11.18}$$

The estimated standard errors are:

$$\tilde{\sigma}_{\bar{X}} = \frac{S}{\sqrt{N-1}} \qquad (11.19)$$

$$\tilde{\sigma}_{\bar{X}} = \frac{\tilde{\sigma}}{\sqrt{N}} \qquad (11.19a)$$

$$\tilde{\sigma}_{Mdn} = \sqrt{\frac{\pi}{2}} \cdot \frac{S}{\sqrt{N-1}} = \frac{1.25S}{\sqrt{N-1}} \qquad (11.20)$$

$$\tilde{\sigma}_{Mdn} = 1.25\tilde{\sigma}_{\bar{X}} \qquad (11.20a)$$

$$\tilde{\sigma}_p = \sqrt{\frac{p(1-p)}{N-1}} \qquad (11.21)$$

By employing these estimates of population parameters together with those of Rule 11.5, it is possible to describe approximately in a particular case the nature of the sampling distribution of a mean, median, or proportion.

All the necessary information can be gleaned from a single run of the sampling experiment. As previously indicated, the accuracy of such descriptions depends on the size of the sample. Our previous remarks regarding minimum values for N were made in anticipation of the use of these estimated parametric values and hence are still applicable. We shall conclude this section with one example.

Example Consider a population of voters, a certain proportion of whom favor a particular candidate for a political office. Suppose that in a random sample of 530 individuals selected from this population, 244 identified themselves as being in favor of this candidate. On the basis of this information, describe the approximate character of the sampling distribution of the proportion of individuals favoring this candidate.

Solution Here $p = 244/530 = .46+$ and hence $\phi \approx .46$ (see Rule 11.5). Applying (11.21),

$$\tilde{\sigma}_p = \sqrt{\frac{(.46)(.54)}{530-1}} \approx .02+$$

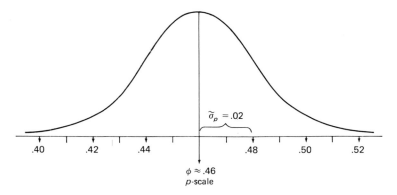

$\tilde{\sigma}_p = .02$

.40   .42   .44   .48   .50   .52

$\phi \approx .46$
p-scale

Figure 11.7 Approximate sampling distribution of proportions of voters favoring a particular candidate in random samples of 530 cases

Finally we know from Rule 11.3 that this sampling distribution is approximately normal in form. This approximate distribution is pictured in Figure 11.7.

    Comment: The distribution in Figure 11.7 is approximate in three respects: (1) the actual sampling distribution is only approximately normal in form; (2) the placement of the actual sampling distribution along the scale (i.e., its mean) may differ somewhat from that of the pictured distribution; and (3) the standard error of the actual sampling distribution may also differ from that shown.

11.9   Summary Statement

This chapter consisted of two major parts: (1) definitions of the basic concepts of inferential statistics (population, parameter, statistic, random sampling, etc.); and (2) sampling theory for means, medians, and proportions. The importance of these basic concepts for using and interpreting inferential statistical procedures should be apparent. However, the rather abstract presentation of the sampling-theory material may have left the reader wondering how such theory can be applied to practical problems. The next chapter illustrates the usefulness of this theory for a widely used inferential technique, namely, hypothesis testing.

12
Testing Statistical Hypotheses: The Classical Hypothesis Testing Procedure

12.1 The Problem of the Principal and the Superintendent

One day the principal of an elementary school in a city school system approached the superintendent, contending that the population of children that fed into his building were, on the whole, subnormal in intelligence and, as a consequence, almost impossible to bring up to the educational level of pupils of other elementary schools in the city. He directed attention to the fact that this population lived, for the most part, in a slum environment that (he contended) gave children no incentive for achieving educational success and offered them no opportunity for enriching extra-school experience. As further evidence in support of his contentions, he pointed to the low standing of his school as measured by city-wide testing programs, to the disproportionate number of pupils from his school who failed in junior high school, and to the high incidence of delinquency among these pupils. He vigorously rejected as a possible alternative explanation any lack of efficiency on the part of his staff or in the operation of his school's program. As a solution to the problem, he urged that special funds be appropriated to enable him to construct special rooms, to engage special teachers in addition to his regular staff, and to purchase special equipment, aids, and materials adapted to the needs of slow learners. He argued that only through such measures could his school hope to raise its pupils to the educational level achieved by the pupils of other elementary schools in the system.

The superintendent gave sympathetic audience but reserved personal doubt regarding the principal's notions of the character of the school's population. She asked the principal for time to consider and decided to undertake a statistical investigation of the intelligence characteristics of this population. This implied selecting a sample from the population, measuring the intelligence of its units (children), and inferring from the results whether or not the principal's characterization of the population was accurate. She decided that she would use the IQ score yielded by the Wechsler Intelligence Scale for Children (WISC) as a measure of intelligence. The WISC is a generally accepted measure of intellectual ability that must be administered individually to each child by a specially trained expert. The superintendent estimated that it would be impossible to administer this test to more than four pupils per school day. At this rate it would require the full time of one school psychologist for 16 school days (more than three work-weeks) to obtain IQs for 64 children. She felt hard pressed to justify this great an investment of time on the part of the school psychologist. She decided, nevertheless, to ask the psychologist to obtain WISC IQs for a random sample of 65 children selected from among those currently enrolled in the school in question. She felt that it was reasonable to assume that the children currently enrolled (the experimentally accessible population) constituted a random sample from the hypothetical population of children who would attend the school during the expected life of the special facilities recommended by the principal (the target population), and that, by extension, a random subset of the pupils currently enrolled could reasonably be regarded as a random sample from the target population.

In due time the 65 IQ scores arrived on her desk. The uses she made of them in attempting to arrive at a decision about the principal's recommendation are described in following sections. Before investigating them, we need some basic tools. These are developed in the next two sections. Then in Section 12.4 we return to a consideration of the problem of the principal and the superintendent.

12.2   The Notion of Indirect Proof

The student may recall from studying plane geometry in high school a method of proof known as indirect proof or *reductio ad absurdum*. This method of proof consists simply of listing *all* possibilities and showing that all, save one, lead to an absurdity. The steps in the procedure are as follows:

1 List all possibilities.
2 Hypothesize one of these possibilities to be true.
3 Seek to determine whether this hypothesis leads to a contradiction to known fact.
4 If such a contradiction is discovered, reject the hypothesis as false.

5 Repeat steps 2, 3, and 4 with other possibilities until only one possibility remains in the list. This one remaining possibility must then be true.

The success of this method of proof depends on (1) a *complete* listing of all possibilities and (2) successful discovery of a contradiction. Failure to discover a contradiction to a hypothesized possibility does not in any sense constitute proof that this possibility is true. Other possibilities may be equally tenable in the sense that they, too, do not appear to lead to contradiction. Besides, failure to discover a contradiction does not necessarily mean that one does not exist. The most that can be said for an uncontradicted possibility is that it remains a *tenable* possibility since it cannot be eliminated from the list. Proof of its truth occurs only when it remains as the only uncontradicted possibility among a complete listing of all possibilities.

Let us first consider a nonmathematical application of this form of proof. Defendant C is charged with the commission of a certain crime, and his trial by jury is in progress. The attorney for his defense states that two, and only two, possibilities exist: either C is guilty of the crime, or C is not guilty. The attorney opens the defense by hypothesizing the first, that C is guilty. Then C must have been present at the scene of the crime at the time of its occurrence. After establishing the scene and time of the crime, the attorney proceeds, through reliable witnesses, to show that at this particular time C was elsewhere and thus establishes a contradiction to the hypothesized possibility. The only other possibility—C's innocence—is proved.

As a second example (drawn from plane geometry) suppose we wish to prove that in a triangle having two sides of unequal length, the angle opposite the longer of these two sides is larger than the angle opposite the shorter. In terms of Figure 12.1, suppose that it is a known fact that *BC* is longer than *AB*. Our problem, then, is to prove that Angle *A* (which is opposite side *BC*) is larger than Angle *C* (which is opposite side *AB*). Or stated symbolically, we wish to prove that $A > C$.

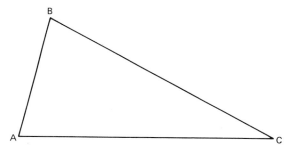

Figure 12.1   Triangle with side *BC* longer than side *AB*

Let us assume that the following facts are known or have been previously proved and are, therefore, at our disposal: (1) if two angles of a triangle are equal, the sides opposite them are equal; and (2) if two angles of a triangle are unequal, the sides opposite them are unequal, the longer being that which lies opposite the larger angle.

We begin by a complete listing of possibilities.

> *Possibility 1: $A = C$*
> *Possibility 2: $A < C$*
> *Possibility 3: $A > C$*

Next we hypothesize Possibility 1 to be true. If this possibility is true, then, from fact 1 above, it follows that side AB equals side BC. But this is contradictory to the known fact that side BC is longer than side AB, and hence Possibility 1 is eliminated from the list. We continue by hypothesizing Possibility 2 to be true. But if this possibility is true, it follows from fact 2 that side AB must be longer than side BC, which again contradicts the known fact that BC is longer than AB. Thus Possibility 2 is eliminated. Possibility 3, the only remaining possibility, is *proved* true.

12.3   Testing Statistical Hypotheses: Introductory Remarks

The testing of a statistical hypothesis is a process for drawing some inference about the value of a population parameter from the information contained in a sample selected from the population.

The logic involved is in many respects similar to that of indirect proof. In one major aspect, however, it differs markedly. In indirect proof, a hypothesis is rejected only when it is found to lead to a definite contradiction of known fact. In statistical hypothesis testing, the hypothesis is rejected if a specific occurrence of an event can be shown to be highly unlikely if the hypothesis is assumed true. In other words, if this event is inconsistent with the hypothesis because the probability of its occurring is low when the hypothesis is assumed true, then the hypothesis is rejected as a possibility. The "event" referred to is always the value obtained for some statistic for a particular sample; the "hypothesis" is a particular value of some parameter selected from among all possible values. The value of the obtained statistic is referred to the sampling distribution that would apply if the hypothesis were true. If this value is found to be an unusual or improbable one, its occurrence is regarded as sufficiently inconsistent with the hypothesis to justify rejection of the hypothesis as a possible value of the parameter. This technique does not afford rigorous and incontrovertible proof in the sense of indirect proof, since possibilities are eliminated because of the occurrence of events that are only *unlikely* rather than *impossible* under the conditions hypothesized.

Difficult as they may be to appreciate when presented void of illustration, we shall next outline the steps involved in testing statistical hypotheses. Illustrative examples, definitions of certain terminology, and further discussions of the logical aspects of the process will be presented in subsequent sections.

Step 1. State the statistical hypothesis to be assumed true and list the alternative possibilities.

Comment: This is a combination of steps 1 and 2 of the method of indirect proof. It calls for selecting a value from among all the values a population parameter could take, and assuming this value to be the true one. It also calls for specifying possible alternative hypotheses. We shall follow the convention of labeling the statistical hypothesis to be tested as H_0. Possible alternative hypotheses will be labeled H_1, H_2, and so on.

DN 12.1 The hypothesis to be tested (H_0) is commonly called the *null hypothesis*.

This is a natural choice of terminology, since the objective of the process is to nullify (eliminate, contradict) this hypothesis.

Step 2. Specify the level of significance to be used.

DN 12.2 In general terms, *level of significance* is some arbitrarily selected, small probability value that defines the degree of improbability deemed necessary to cast sufficient doubt on the possible truth of the null hypothesis to warrant its rejection.

Comment: The level of significance is stated in terms of some small probability value such as .10 (one in ten), or .05 (one in twenty), or .01 (one in a hundred), or even .001 (one in a thousand). The choice of a particular probability value is a purely arbitrary one. Considerations influencing the choice will be treated in a later section. It is customary to represent this probability value by the Greek letter *alpha* (α). There is no corresponding step in the process of indirect proof for the obvious reason that absolute contradiction rather than improbability is the criterion for rejection. It should be appreciated that in selecting a level of significance we are simply indicating what we mean by the phrase "sufficiently improbable" when we state that, under the terms of the hypothesis being considered, the observed value of the statistic is "sufficiently improbable" of occurrence to discredit this hypothesis. A more precise definition of the level of significance will be presented in Section 12.11.

Step 3. Specify the critical region to be used.

DN 12.3 A *critical region* is a portion of the scale of possible values of the statistic, so chosen that if the particular obtained value of the statistic falls within it, rejection of the null hypothesis is indicated.

Comment: There are two criteria for choosing the critical region. First, it must be made consistent with the level of significance adopted. This implies that it must be so located that *if the null hypothesis is true*, the probability that the statistic will fall within it equals (or at least does not exceed) this level of significance. Second, it should be so located that *if the null hypothesis is not true*, the probability that the statistic will fall within it is a maximum. The ideal critical region is such that if the null hypothesis is false, the chances of rejecting this false hypothesis become as large as possible within the limits of the framework of the particular investigation. The task of locating critical regions so as best to comply with these criteria will be discussed later.

Step 4. Carry out the sampling study as planned and compute the particular value of the test statistic for the data gathered.

Comment: The term "test statistic" here refers to the statistic employed in effecting the test of the null hypothesis. The sampling study may be viewed as constituting one run of a random experiment, the random variable of which is the test statistic.

Decisions regarding the three preceding steps can—in fact, should—be made before the sample is selected and data are gathered.

Step 5. Refer the particular value of the test statistic as obtained in Step 4 to the critical region adopted. If the value falls in this region, reject the hypothesis. Otherwise, retain the hypothesis as a tenable (not disproved) possibility.

12.4   The Problem of the Principal and the Superintendent: Solution I

In Section 12.1 we described a situation that we called "the problem of the principal and the superintendent." In Sections 12.4 through 12.10 we use this situation to illustrate the application of the basic concepts of hypothesis testing outlined in the preceding section.

Step 1. The statement of the null hypothesis.

The superintendent recognizes that "on the whole" the population of children concerned can be below normal in intelligence, normal in intelligence, or above normal in intelligence. She reasons that for the problem at hand, there is no difference between the latter two possibilities; certainly she would not wish to approve the principal's recommendation if either of these were true. Hence, she decides to reduce the problem to the consideration of just two possibilities: (1) that the population of children is, "on the whole," normal in intelligence, and (2) that the population of children is, "on the whole," below normal in intelligence.

She next considers the question of the meaning of the phrase "on the whole." She quickly discards, as invalid for the purpose of this problem, the notion that "on the whole" means *all* or even a large majority of the children constituting the population. After some consideration she decides, quite arbitrarily, to define "on the whole" to apply to the mean IQ for the population. Since an IQ of 100 implies normal intellectual ability, the two possibilities can now be translated into the statements: (1) the mean IQ score for the population is 100, and (2) the mean IQ score for the population is less than 100. Stated symbolically, these possibilities are

$$\mu = 100 \quad \text{and} \quad \mu < 100$$

The superintendent chooses to test statistically the first possibility. That is, she hypothesizes that $\mu = 100$. The alternative is that $\mu < 100$. Symbolically,

$$H_0 : \mu = 100 \quad \text{and} \quad H_1 : \mu < 100$$

Step 2. The selection of the level of significance.

The considerations entering into the choice of a level of significance can best be presented later. At this point we shall simply state that the superintendent is concerned lest she approve the principal's proposal only to discover later that the population is *not* below normal in intelligence. In other words, she is afraid that she may err by rejecting a true hypothesis. As a reasonable safeguard against this possibility, she decides to choose a rather small probability value as a definition of the degree of improbability sufficient to discredit the hypothesis. The value she selects is .01 (one in a hundred). That is, she lets $\alpha = .01$.

Step 3. The specification of the critical region.

To specify a critical region, it is first necessary to at least approximate the sampling distribution that the test statistic would follow if the hypothesis under test were actually true. Because the test statistic involved is the mean of a "large" random sample, Rule 11.2 applies. That is, the sampling distribution is approximately normal in form with a mean of 100 (the hypothesized value of the mean IQ of the population from which the sample is presumed to have been randomly

$\sqrt{N}$

selected) and a standard error of $\sigma/\sqrt{65}$, where σ is the standard deviation of the population of IQ scores (see Rule 11.2a). The superintendent does not know the value of σ, nor is she interested in its value except for the purpose of determining the standard error ($\sigma_{\bar{x}}$) of the sampling distribution. Consequently, she is compelled to use an estimate of σ based on the sample. Formula (11.17) indicates an appropriate estimate that could be divided by $\sqrt{65}$ to provide the required estimated value of the standard error. But since the only use the superintendent has for an estimate of σ is to obtain an estimate of the required standard error, she can take advantage of the computational short cut provided by formula (11.19). This requires that she first determine the sample standard deviation, S. Working with the 65 IQ scores and applying formula (7.5), she finds the value of S to be 20. Then by (11.19)

$$\tilde{\sigma}_{\bar{x}} = \frac{S}{\sqrt{N-1}} = \frac{20}{\sqrt{65-1}} = 2.5$$

She then sketches the approximate sampling distribution shown in Figure 12.2. Now since the only admissible possibilities about the value of μ are that either $\mu = 100$ or $\mu < 100$, the only explanation for an obtained value of $\bar{X} > 100$ is the operation of chance in determining the composition of the sample. On the other hand, two possible explanations exist for any obtained value of $\bar{X} < 100$, namely, (1) the operation of chance and (2) the possibility that μ is less than instead of equal to 100. The smaller the obtained value of $\bar{X}$, the more plausible the second of these two explanations becomes. Hence, in this situation the logical location for a critical region is somewhere down the $\bar{X}$-scale from the 100 point. Just how far down the upper limit of the region

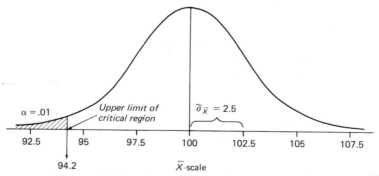

Figure 12.2 Approximate sampling distribution of $\bar{X}$ for random samples of 65 cases selected from a population having $\mu = 100$

should be located is governed by the level of significance. Here the superintendent has adopted an α of .01. In the standard normal distribution (10.2), 1 percent of the area lies below a point 2.33 standard deviations below the mean—i.e., below $z = -2.33$ (see Table II, Appendix C). To translate this z-value into terms of the $\overline{X}$-scale, the superintendent applies formula (10.4) as follows:[1]

$$\overline{X}_R = (2.5)(-2.33) + 100$$
$$= -5.83 + 100$$
$$= 94.17 \approx 94.2$$

The critical region (R) is: $R: \overline{X} \leq 94.2$. The portion of the sampling distribution over the critical region thus established is the blackened portion of Figure 12.2.

Step 4. The determination of the particular value of the test statistic for the data gathered.

In this first solution, the test statistic is the mean of the 65 IQ scores of the sample at hand. Assume the superintendent finds this value of $\overline{X}$ to be 94.

Step 5. The decision.

The superintendent now refers the obtained value of $\overline{X} = 94$ to the critical regions she has established and notes that it falls in this region. Hence, she rejects the hypothesis that $\mu = 100$. This decision implies that $\mu < 100$, since this is the only other remaining possibility. The action implied by the outcome of this particular solution to the problem is the approval of the funds requested by the principal.

12.5 The Problem of the Principal and the Superintendent: A Modification of Solution I

We shall consider here a slight modification in the mechanics of the solution just described. The solution as we shall modify it is the equivalent of that employed by the superintendent. However, the modified solution will have the advantage of being somewhat more like other tests of statistical hypotheses that the student may later encounter in this or more advanced books on statistics. For this reason, this modified approach will be followed in most of the examples of testing statistical hypotheses that follow.

---

[1] To represent the boundary point of a critical region we shall use the symbol representing the statistic involved with R written as a subscript.

The first procedural change occurs in Step 3, in which the critical region is established. Since the normal distribution provides an approximate model of the sampling distribution of the test statistic involved ($\overline{X}$), and since any normally distributed variable can be transformed into a standard normal distribution (10.2), we shall simply establish the critical region in terms of the z-scale instead of the $\overline{X}$-scale. In terms of the z-scale, the critical region chosen by the superintendent extends downward from -2.33. This may be expressed symbolically as $R: z \leq -2.33$.[2]

The second procedural change occurs in Step 4, in which the value of the test statistic for the sample at hand is determined. Since R is now in terms of the z-scale rather than the $\overline{X}$-scale, we must use the sample data to determine the particular z-value for the sample. This is done by application of formula (10.3). In the superintendent's problem, the particular value of z (the test statistic) is obtained as follows:

$$z = \frac{\overline{X} - \mu}{\hat{\sigma}_{\overline{X}}} = \frac{94 - 100}{2.5} = \frac{-6}{2.5} = -2.4$$

Now to reach a decision (Step 5), we refer this value of z to the critical region R. Since -2.4 is less than -2.33,[3] the obtained value of z falls in R—an outcome that dictates rejection of the hypothesis, as before.

12.6 The Problem of the Principal and the Superintendent: Solution II

Let us suppose that in Step 1 the superintendent had chosen to define "on the whole" as the median (ξ) IQ for the population. Stated symbolically the two possibilities now become

$$\xi = 100 \quad \text{and} \quad \xi < 100$$

The solution to the problem with "on the whole" thus defined is outlined below.

Step 1. $H_0: \xi = 100$; $H_1: \xi < 100$

Step 2. $\alpha = .01$, as before.

Step 3. $R: z \leq -2.33$

---

[2] Read "critical region (R) is z equal to or less than -2.33."

[3] The larger the absolute value of a negative number, the smaller its algebraic value.

Comment: Here we find the superintendent using the modification suggested in Section 12.5. She is justified in using the normally distributed z as a test statistic since the test statistic involved—the sample median (*Mdn*)—is known to be approximately normally distributed (see Rule 11.4), with mean ξ (i.e., with a mean equal to the median of the population sampled).

Step 4. The test statistic, z, for the sample at hand is given by

$$z = \frac{Mdn - \xi}{\tilde{\sigma}_{Mdn}}$$

Before we can apply this formula it is necessary to obtain an estimate of the standard error of the sampling distribution of medians $(\tilde{\sigma}_{Mdn})$. For this purpose the superintendent elects to use formula (11.20a) as follows:

$$\tilde{\sigma}_{Mdn} = 1.25\tilde{\sigma}_{\bar{X}} \approx (1.25)(2.5) \approx 3.13$$

This formula is appropriate only if the population of IQ scores sampled is normally distributed. This assumption is not unreasonable in this situation, since for standard populations of children, IQ scores are known to be approximately normally distributed.

In addition to $\tilde{\sigma}_{Mdn}$ the superintendent also needs to determine the value of the median (*Mdn*) for the sample at hand. Let us suppose that this median has the value 93, a value slightly smaller than that of the sample mean, which was 94. Then, the value of the test statistic, z, is:

$$z = \frac{93 - 100}{3.13} = -2.24$$

Step 5. Decision: Retain the hypothesis as a tenable possibility.

Since -2.24 is larger than -2.33, the obtained value of z does not fall in the R as specified. This outcome dictates retention of the hypothesis that $\xi = 100$ in the list of possible values of ξ. *This outcome does not constitute proof that $\xi = 100$. It means only that the evidence is not sufficiently inconsistent with the possibility that $\xi = 100$ to warrant eliminating this possibility from the list.* In fact, no value belonging to the family of values lumped into the other possibility (the possibility that $\xi < 100$) could be eliminated on the basis of the evidence at hand. Both possibilities remain in the list.[4]

---

[4] For any hypothesized value of $\xi < 100$, the value of z for the sample at hand would be greater than the value -2.24 obtained for the hypothesis $\xi = 100$. Since any $z > -2.33$ indicates retention, no hypothetical value of $\xi < 100$ could be rejected.

It is important to note that the decision dictated by this second solution to the problem differs from that dictated by the first solution in spite of the fact that the sample median (93) differed from the hypothesized value of the population median (100) by a greater amount than the sample mean (94) differed from the hypothesized value of the population mean (100). It is clear, then, that the outcome of a test of a statistical hypothesis may vary with certain arbitrary decisions made in the course of setting up the test. These arbitrary decisions almost always represent subjective judgments on the part of the person conducting the test. The considerations basic to such judgments will be treated in later sections.

12.7   The Problem of the Principal and the Superintendent: Solution III

In this solution, we shall assume that all of the judgmental decisions made by the superintendent are the same as in Solution I except for the sample size employed. We shall here suppose that in an effort to be as economical as possible of the school psychologist's time, the superintendent elects to base her decision on a sample of 50 instead of 65. Suppose that for this sample of 50, the mean and standard deviation turn out to have the same values as before, namely, 94 and 20 respectively.[5]

Step 1. $H_0: \mu = 100; \quad H_1: \mu < 100$

Step 2. $\alpha = .01$

Step 3. $R: z \leq -2.33$

Step 4. $\tilde{\sigma}_{\bar{X}} = \dfrac{S}{\sqrt{N-1}} = \dfrac{20}{\sqrt{50-1}} = 2.86 \qquad$ [see (11.19)]

$$z = \frac{\bar{X} - \mu}{\tilde{\sigma}_{\bar{X}}} = \frac{94 - 100}{2.86} = -2.10 \qquad \text{[see (10.3)]}$$

Step 5. Decision: Retain hypothesis. (Why?)

Once again the course of action dictated differs from that of Solution I—in spite of the fact that the sample mean and standard deviation have the same values as before. The difference in outcome arises from the fact that the smaller the sample is, the larger we would expect the

[5] Ordinarily one would expect some sample-to-sample variation to occur in these values. We have elected to assume the same values in order to simplify comparisons that we wish to make later.

chance sample-to-sample variations in the values of the sample means to become. It follows that *a discrepancy between statistic and hypothesized value of parameter that satisfies the definition of "sufficiently improbable to discredit the hypothesis" in the case of a large sample may not satisfy this definition in the case of a smaller sample.*

12.8   The Problem of the Principal and the Superintendent: Solution IV

Step 1. The statement of the statistical hypothesis.

In this solution we shall have the superintendent adopt quite a different line of attack. We shall have her reason that children with an IQ of 90 or above should experience no particular difficulty in keeping reasonably well apace with the normal program of their school grade, while pupils with IQ scores below this level—at least those five or more points below—may indeed experience considerable difficulty in maintaining normal progress. In keeping with this line of reasoning, we shall have the superintendent approach the problem by inquiring into the proportion of children in the population having IQs below 90. A larger-than-normal proportion will constitute evidence in support of the principal's contention; an equal or smaller proportion will imply refutation.

The superintendent is aware that in the normative population, WISC IQ scores are approximately normally distributed with mean 100 and standard deviation 15. Hence, in the usual population an IQ score of 90 corresponds to a normally distributed z of $-.67$. From Table II, Appendix C, $P(z \leq -.67) = .2514$. Therefore, viewing the population as a dichotomous population of ones (A type) and zeros ($\bar{A}$ type), with children having IQ < 90 being designated as ones and children having IQ ≥ 90 being designated as zeros, the superintendent decides that she will approve the principal's recommendation only if the population proportion of children with IQ scores below 90 is greater than one-fourth (.25). This amounts to considering only the following possible values of the population proportion (ϕ) of children with IQ scores below 90:[6]

$$\phi = .25 \quad \text{and} \quad \phi > .25$$

---

[6] It is possible, of course, that $\phi < .25$. However, the superintendent would be even less justified in approving the principal's recommendation in this event than she would if $\phi = .25$. Hence, for the purpose of making the decision called for by the problem at hand, the possibility that $\phi < .25$ is the same as the possibility that $\phi = .25$.

The superintendent elects to test as a statistical hypothesis the possibility that $\phi = .25$. The alternative is that $\phi > .25$. Then

$$H_0: \phi = .25 \qquad \text{and} \qquad H_1: \phi > .25$$

Step 2. Selection of the level of significance.

Here we shall simply have the superintendent make the same choice as in the previous solutions: $\alpha = .01$.

Step 3. The specification of the critical region.

The superintendent knows that as the sample size becomes large, the sampling distribution of a proportion (p) tends toward a normal distribution with mean ϕ (see Rule 11.3) and standard error

$$\sigma_p = \sqrt{\frac{\phi(1 - \phi)}{N}} \qquad\qquad [\text{see (11.6)}]$$

She instructs the school psychologist to obtain IQ scores for 100 randomly selected pupils.[7] Then, if the hypothesis is true, that is, if $\phi = .25$, it follows that

$$\sigma_p = \sqrt{\frac{(.25)(.75)}{100}} = \sqrt{.001875} = .0433$$

Comment: Students frequently fall into the error of using the obtained (sample) value of p in computing this standard error rather than the hypothesized value of ϕ. Recall that the sampling distribution used in locating the critical region must be the distribution that would arise were the hypothesis under test actually true. Since the standard error of a proportion is a function of the population proportion (ϕ), the specification of the sampling distribution of p that would arise were the hypothesis true requires the use of the hypothesized value of ϕ in determining its standard error. The standard error thus determined (note that the symbol σ_p and not $\bar{\sigma}_p$ was used) is not an estimate but is rather the exact value that would apply if the hypothesis were true. It is true that the sample standard deviation (S) was used in estimating

---

[7] In Section 15.11, we will show that when the principal and superintendent problem is investigated using the procedures outlined at the beginning of this section, the problem can be classified as a binomial experiment. Then, if H_0 is true, the true sampling distribution of p is a binomial distribution with $N = 100$ and $\phi = .25$. However, we have previously noted (see Section 10.7, particularly footnote 13 on p. 201, and Section 11.6, particularly Remark 2 on p. 231) that if N is as large as 100 and if ϕ is not too far from .5 (say more than .3), then the normal distribution defined by Rule 11.3 provides an adequate model for the sampling distribution of p.

the standard error of the sampling distributions involved in the preceding solutions of this problem. In none of these solutions, however, were the standard errors functions of the parameter in question (i.e., of μ or ξ). Nor was the value of the population standard deviation, which is necessary to the determination of the standard errors of the sampling distributions, specified by any of the hypotheses tested. Therefore, the use of the sample S in estimating the standard error was not inconsistent with, nor did it in any way violate, these hypotheses.

The sampling distribution of p is, therefore, approximately as shown in Figure 12.3. Now since the only admissible possibilities with respect to the value of ϕ are $\phi = .25$ and $\phi > .25$, the only explanation for an obtained value of $p < .25$ is the operation of chance in determining the composition of the sample. On the other hand, an obtained value of $p > .25$ may be due either to the operation of chance or to the fact that ϕ is actually greater than .25. The larger the value obtained for p, the more plausible the latter of these explanations becomes. Hence, the logical location for the critical region is somewhere up the p-scale from the .25 point. Since the level of significance is to be .01, the lower bound of the critical region must correspond to the point $z = +2.33$ in the standard normal distribution. In terms of the p-scale, this point is

$$p_R = (.0433)(+2.33) + .25 = .3509 \qquad [\text{see } (10.4)]$$

and, hence,

$$R: p \geq .3509$$

The portion of the sampling distribution over this critical region is the blackened portion of Figure 12.3.

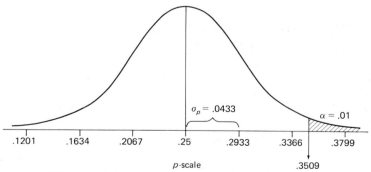

Figure 12.3 Approximate model of the sampling distribution of a proportion (p) when $\phi = .25$ and $N = 100$

Or, if we have the superintendent follow the modified procedure described in Section 12.5 and express R in terms of the z-scale, the region may simply be specified as follows:

$$R: z \geq +2.33$$

Step 4. The determination of the value of the test statistic.

If p is the test statistic, the superintendent has only to count the number of IQ scores in the sample that are below 90 and to express this number as a proportion of the total number of cases in the sample (i.e., 100). Suppose that 36 such scores are found. Then $p = 36/100 = .36$.

Or, if we have the superintendent use the modified procedure, the test statistic is the z-value for the sample. This is computed by formula (10.3) as follows:

$$z = \frac{p - \phi}{\sigma_p} = \frac{.36 - .25}{.0433} = +2.54$$

Step 5. The decision.

The superintendent now refers the obtained value $p = .36$ to the critical region ($R: p \geq .3509$). Noting that this value falls in R, she rejects the hypothesis that $\phi = .25$. This decision implies that $\phi > .25$, since this is the only other possibility. The action dictated by this outcome is approval of the principal's recommendation.

Or, if the modified procedure is followed, the sample value of the statistic $z = +2.54$ is referred to the critical region, $R: z \geq +2.33$, and the same decision is again reached.

12.9 The Problem of the Principal and the Superintendent: Solution V

In this solution we shall again have the superintendent view the population as a dichotomous one consisting of children who are below and not below normal in intelligence, with those below normal again being designated as ones (A type) and those not below normal being designated as zeros ($\bar{A}$ type). However, we shall here have her define "below normal intelligence" as IQ < 100. If the population concerned is like the usual one, the proportion of its members having IQ scores below 100 is one-half. With this definition of below normal, the superintendent's interest is in the possibilities $\phi = .5$ and $\phi > .5$. The solution to the problem now proceeds as follows.

Step 1. $H_0: \phi = .5$; $H_1: \phi > .5$

Step 2. $\alpha = .01$, as before.

Step 3. $R: z \geq +2.33$

Step 4. Determine the value of the test statistic.

The z for the sample at hand is again given by

$$z = \frac{p - \phi}{\sigma_p}$$

If we assume that a sample of 100 is again used, the value of σ_p for $\phi = .5$ is

$$\sigma_p = \sqrt{\frac{(.5)(.5)}{100}} = .05 \qquad\qquad [\text{see (11.6)}]$$

Now suppose that 61 of the 100 IQ scores constituting the sample are below 100. Then the sample value of p is .61 and

$$z = \frac{.61 - .5}{.05} = +2.20$$

Step 5. Decision: Retain the hypothesis. (Why?)

Note that the decision dictated by this solution is the opposite of that dictated by Solution IV in spite of the fact that in each case the difference between the obtained value of the statistic (p) and the hypothesized value of the parameter (ϕ) is the same. (In Solution IV, $p - \phi = .36 - .25 = .11$; and in Solution V, $p - \phi = .61 - .50 = .11$). This is due to the fact that sample-to-sample chance variation in the value of p becomes greater as the value of ϕ approaches .5—see formula (11.6). On the other hand, it should be observed that the normal distribution provides a more accurate model of the sampling distribution of p for samples as small as 100 when $\phi = .5$ than when $\phi = .25$ (see Section 11.6).

12.10 The Problem of the Principal and the Superintendent: Solution VI

In this, the last solution to this problem that we will consider, we shall have the superintendent follow the line of the preceding solution, with one exception. We shall here have her take the position that although the principal's contention may be true, the very opposite of his contention may also be true: it may be that the population of children involved is actually *above* normal in intelligence, and that the true explanation of the school's low standing as measured by city-wide testing programs and the disproportionate number of junior high school failures lies in the direction of inefficiency and maladministration. We shall have the superintendent wonder if it may not be that the high incidence of delinquency among the pupils involved is symptomatic of failure to challenge them up to the true level of their abilities, of failure to keep them properly motivated and occupied, and of failure to maintain adequate discipline. We shall have her reason that if these things are true, then the principal and perhaps at least certain members of his staff should be subject to dismissal for incompetent performance of their duties.

The effect of such an attitude on the part of the superintendent is to introduce, along with a third possibility, a third course of action. The three possibilities and their attendant courses of action may be summarized as follows:

> *Possibility 1:* The population is of normal intelligence.
> *Action 1:* Deny the principal's request. Undertake to help him trouble-shoot along other lines.
> *Possibility 2:* The population is below normal in intelligence.
> *Action 2:* Grant the principal's request.
> *Possibility 3:* The population is above normal in intelligence.
> *Action 3:* Dismiss the principal and certain members of his staff.

We shall now have the superintendent translate these possibilities into terms amenable to statistical test. She lets ϕ represent the proportion of children in the population whose IQ scores are below 100. Then the three possibilities stated as hypotheses become, respectively,

$$H_0: \phi = .5 \qquad H_1: \phi > .5 \qquad H_2: \phi < .5$$

Now the only change the superintendent need make in the preceding solution is in the specification of the critical region (Step 3). As before, two possible explanations exist for an observed value of $p > .5$, namely, (1) the operation of chance in determining the composition of the sample at hand, and (2) the possibility that $\phi > .5$. Now, however, there are also two possible explanations for an observed value of $p < .5$, namely, (1) the operation of chance as before, and (2) the possibility that $\phi < .5$. In this situation, therefore, the greater the amount by which p exceeds .5, the more plausible becomes the possibility that $\phi > .5$; and the greater the amount by which p falls below

.5, the more plausible becomes the possibility that $\phi < .5$. If the critical region is to function with respect to both possibilities, part of it must be located toward the upper end of the p-scale and part toward the lower end. We shall have the superintendent split the region equally between the two ends. She places the lower bound of the upper part of the region at $z = +2.58$, since in the standard normal distribution the probability of $z \geq +2.58$ is .005. Similarly, she places the upper bound of the lower part of the region at $z = -2.58$. Now, if the null hypothesis (H_0) is true, the probability that p will fall in either part of the region is $.005 + .005 = .01$, which is the selected value of α. Symbolically this critical region may be written as follows:

$$R: z \leq -2.58 \quad \text{and} \quad z \geq +2.58; \quad \text{or } |z| \geq 2.58$$

Now, using the same data as in the preceding solution (i.e., using $p = .61$), we obtain for the value of the test statistic $z = +2.20$ as before. Since this z does not fall in either part of the critical region, the null hypothesis ($\phi = .5$) must be retained as a tenable possibility.

To round out the discussion, let us suppose that instead of 61 there are 65 IQ scores in the sample that are below 100. Now the sample value of the test statistic, z, becomes

$$z = \frac{.65 - .50}{.05} = +3.00$$

This value of z falls in the upper part of R, dictating rejection of the null hypothesis $\phi = .5$. This leaves two possibilities in the list, namely, $H_1: \phi > .5$ and $H_2: \phi < .5$. However, for any hypothesized value of $\phi < .5$, the value of the test statistic z would only be still greater than $+3.00$.[8] Therefore, rejection of $H_0: \phi = .5$ when p falls into the upper part of R also automatically implies rejection of $H_2: \phi < .5$, leaving $H_1: \phi > .5$ as the only remaining possibility. If our superintendent is willing to reject $H_0: \phi = .5$ because of the inconsistency between it and the observed value of p (.65), her behavior would be capriciously inconsistent indeed were she to take the position that this same evidence was not sufficiently inconsistent with $H_2: \phi < .5$ to justify its rejection also.

Similarly, rejection of the hypothesis $H_0: \phi = .5$ as a result of a value of p falling into the lower part of R would also automatically imply rejection of $H_1: \phi > .5$, leaving $H_2: \phi < .5$ as the only remaining possibility.

[8] For example, if $\phi = .49$, $z = (.65 - .49)/.04999 = +3.20$.

12.11 Choosing the Level of Significance: The Two Types of Error

The choice of a level of significance (α)—that is, the selection of some small probability value as the definition of what is meant by "sufficiently improbable of occurrence to discredit the hypothesis"—is a non-statistical problem in the sense that it calls for a purely arbitrary subjective judgment. The levels most commonly judged suitable are .01 and .05. Occasionally .001, .02, .10, and even .20 are selected. The types of considerations that enter into the formulation of this judgment can best be appreciated in the perspective of an analysis of the kinds of errors that may arise in connection with tests of statistical hypotheses.

One of two possibilities applies to any statistical hypothesis H_0: either it is true, or it is false. If it is true, there are still two courses of action to which our test may lead: either we retain this true H_0—the desired correct action; or we reject it—the undesired erroneous action. Similarly, if H_0 is false, there are also two courses of action to which our test may lead: either we reject this false H_0—the desired correct action; or we retain it—the undesired erroneous action. The situation is displayed diagrammatically in Table 12.1. The two undesired erroneous actions here are clearly different. Since one can occur only if the H_0 under test is false, and the other only if it is true, they are mutually exclusive in any given situation; both cannot occur at the same time. These two kinds of errors are known as errors of the first and second kind (or type).

DN 12.4 A Type I error, or an error of the first kind, consists in rejecting H_0 when it is actually true.

DN 12.5 A Type II error, or an error of the second kind, consists in retaining H_0 when it is actually false.

Table 12.1 A Diagrammatic Display of the Two Types of Error That May Occur in Statistical Hypothesis Testing

		Outcome	
		Retain H_0	Reject H_0
Actual state of nature	H_0 true	A correct decision	An erroneous decision; a Type I error
	H_0 false	An erroneous decision; a Type II error	A correct decision

If the H_0 under test is in fact true, the probability of the value of the test statistic (T)[9] falling in the critical region (R) is equal to α, that is, to the level of significance chosen (e.g., see Figures 12.2 and 12.3). If T falls in R, rejection of this true H_0 is indicated. That is, H_0 being true, the occurrence of a T in R implies the occurrence of a Type I error, and, hence, α represents the relative frequency with which Type I errors would occur with long-run repetition of the particular statistical test. We are now in a position to present a more precise definition of level of significance.

> ⌐DN 12.6   In situations in which Type I errors are possible, the level of significance (α) is the probability of such an error.

In considering this definition the student should recognize that a Type I error can occur only if H_0 is true; and that if H_0 is true, T will fall in R approximately 100α percent of the time for many independent repetitions of this particular statistical test. Thus, through the selection of α, we have at our disposal a means of controlling the likelihood of a Type I error.

At this point the student may wonder why an α as large as .05 is common, or why an α of .10 or .20 would ever be used, when choosing smaller probability values for α would markedly reduce the likelihood of occurrence of a Type I error. It is, in fact, possible to eliminate the occurrence of Type I errors entirely. To accomplish this, all we have to do is to let $\alpha = 0$. This, of course, implies that no critical region exists. It amounts to deciding, regardless of the strength of the evidence to the contrary, always to retain any H_0 tested. Under such a rule of operation, no one would ever bother to analyze, or, for that matter, even to collect any data. All that would be necessary would be to state H_0 and then retain it. Obviously, while such a procedure would completely eliminate the possibility of making a Type I error, it does not provide a guarantee against error, for every time that the H_0 stated was false, a Type II error would necessarily occur. Similarly, by letting $\alpha = 1$ it would be possible to eliminate entirely the occurrence of Type II errors at the cost of committing a Type I error for every true H_0 tested.

It is clear that the choice of a level of significance must represent a compromise aimed at controlling both of the two types of error. Just what compromise is most appropriate in a given situation depends on an evaluation of the seriousness of the consequences of these two types of error in that situation.

For the purposes of illustration, consider again the problem of the principal and the superintendent. If we suppose that the implementation of the principal's recommendations would involve a very considerable

---

[9] Here, the symbol T is used to represent any test statistic (e.g., z, $\bar{X}$, p, Mdn).

outlay of cash from funds for which many important competing demands exist, we might list, at least partially, the consequences of the two types of error somewhat as follows.

Consequences of a Type I Error (Consequences of approving the principal's recommendations when the appropriate action is disapproval):
Purposeless expenditure of a large sum of tax money when other important needs for this money exist and, when the error becomes known, the attendant:

1 public criticism
2 loss of school board members' confidence
3 loss of staff members' confidence
4 possible creation of staff dissension resulting from singling out one building for special aid
5 general overall damage to professional reputation
6 possible loss of superintendency

Consequences of a Type II Error (Consequences of disapproving the principal's recommendations when the appropriate action is approval):
Failure to provide needed special facilities that may, in the end, by reducing the incidence of delinquency and by offering the children involved a better start on the road toward good citizenship, represent an actual saving to the taxpayers; and, when the error becomes known, the attendant:

1 public criticism
2 loss of school board members' confidence
3 loss of staff members' confidence
4 loss of principal—and perhaps some of his teachers—owing to their unwillingness to continue in an intolerable situation that could have been remedied
5 general overall damage to professional reputation
6 possible loss of superintendency

Although the two lists of attendant consequences appear almost identical, they stem from differing basic causes and hence may differ markedly in degree. For example, if, as we have assumed, the cash outlay is great and other important needs for the money exist, the superintendent may regard the public criticism attendant on a Type I error as much more serious than the criticism that would follow a Type II error. Under such circumstances, a Type II error might be excused as representing a not-too-unreasonable degree of conservatism in the management of tax monies, while a Type I error would appear to be almost inexcusable. Similarly, all other consequences of making a Type I error become more serious than their Type II error counterparts. The superintendent would, therefore, feel a very strong need for preventing a Type I error. In this situation, she would choose a small α. While we have had her use $\alpha = .01$, it might well be that in the situation we have just described $\alpha = .001$ would be even more defensible.

On the other hand, suppose that the principal's recommendations are relatively inexpensive to implement and that money represents no particular problem. Now the various consequences of a Type II error may become the more serious, since failure to provide needed facilities may now be attributed to lack of insight, to lack of wisdom, or even to neglect, rather than to justifiable conservatism in the management of tax funds. Thus, a Type I error may become a matter of much less concern, justifying an α of .10 or even .20.

Though exceptional situations may arise, it is usually true that the consequences associated with Type I errors are the more serious. Retention of H_0, unless necessarily accompanied by some critical action, is an inconclusive sort of result. The H_0, while retained, is not proved, a fact that may serve to invite further research with perhaps improved methods. On the other hand, rejection of H_0 represents a somewhat more conclusive type of action that may have a greater tendency to lead to general acceptance of the finding and the discouragement of further research on the problem. Thus, most investigators prefer to be cautious rather than precipitous about rejecting a hypothesis.

There exists an even more important reason for exercising caution with respect to Type I errors. It may be possible, in certain instances at least, to exercise some degree of control over a Type II error quite independent of that exercised over a Type I error. That is, for a given choice of α, we may be in a position to manipulate the probability (β) of a Type II error. In situations in which a Type II error might become a matter of real concern, we may be able to choose a fairly small α and at the same time maintain a small β—i.e., a small likelihood of a Type II error.

It is for these reasons that α-values in excess of .05 are rarely used. As will be explained in the next section, it is actually only the Type I error over which we can exercise a complete arbitrary control. While there are ways in which we may, for a given α, reduce the likelihood of a Type II error, we can never be certain of the exact degree of control we are exercising over this type of error.

12.12 Controlling Type II Errors

The probability, β, of a Type II error depends on four factors: (1) the value of α selected, i.e., the degree of protection against a Type I error,

(2) the location of the critical region, R, (3) the variability of the sampling distribution of the test statistic, T, and (4) the amount by which the actual value, θ, of the parameter differs from the value, θ_0, hypothesized for it. Because in any real situation θ is unknown, the last of these four factors can never be known. It is for this reason that the degree of control exercised by a given statistical test over a Type II error can never be determined. We can only indicate, in the case of a particular statistical test, what this degree of control would be for an assumed discrepancy between θ and θ_0.

To illustrate, we shall determine the value of β in Solution I of the problem of the principal and the superintendent in the special case in which the actual mean for the population involved is assumed to be 90 IQ points. In Solution I, R, in terms of the $\overline{X}$-scale, extended downward from 94.17. If, as we have assumed, $\mu = 90$, the approximate sampling distribution of $\overline{X}$ will be a normal distribution with mean at 90 instead of 100 and an estimated standard error of 2.5, as before. This distribution is pictured in Figure 12.4a. In this situation a Type II error will occur when $\overline{X} > 94.17$, since values greater than 94.17 lead to retention of H_0. The proportion of the area of the sampling distribution above 94.17 (see shaded portion of Figure 12.4a) is approximately .0475.[10] Hence, the approximate probability, β, of a Type II error is .0475. If in this situation our particular statistical test were to be repeated indefinitely, 4.75 percent of the decisions it would direct us to make would be errors of the second kind.[11]

To illustrate how the choice of α affects the value of β we shall suppose that in Solution I the superintendent had selected an α of .001. In this case R would have extended downward from approximately 92.28 [since by (10.4), $\overline{X}_R = (2.5)(-3.09) + 100 = 92.28$]. In the distribution of Figure 12.4a, an $\overline{X}$-value of 92.28 corresponds to a z-value of $+0.91$. The approximate value of β now becomes .1814. Had the superintendent elected to use $\alpha = .05$, the approximate value of β would be only .0091.[12] In short, the use of a smaller α (.001) increases the probability of a Type II error, whereas the use of a larger α (.05) decreases it.

To illustrate the effect of the location of R on the value of β, let us suppose that in Solution I the superintendent's approach to the problem was similar to that described in Solution VI, in that she wished to consider not only the alternative possibility that $\mu < 100$ but also the alternative possibility that $\mu > 100$. In this case she would, of course, locate R so that part of it would lie at each end of the hypothesized

---

[10] $\overline{X} = 94.17$ corresponds to $z = +1.67$. The area above $z = +1.67$ may be obtained from Table II, Appendix C.

[11] If $\mu = 90$ and the θ_0-value is taken to be 100, errors of the first kind are impossible. Why?

[12] The student should verify this result.

sampling distribution. The lower part would extend downward from $\overline{X} = 93.55$ [since $\overline{X}_R = (2.5)(-2.58) + 100 = 93.55$], and the upper part would extend upward from $\overline{X} = 106.45$ [since $\overline{X}_R = (2.5)(+2.58) + 100 = 106.45$]. If, as before, we assume the actual value of μ to be 90, then the value of β is the probability of $\overline{X}$ in that part of the scale between 93.55 and 106.45. This is the same as the probability of z between $+1.42$ and $+6.58$, which, for all practical purposes, is simply the probability of $z > +1.42$. Hence, in this situation, the approximate value of β is .0778, and we see that the price for guarding against the additional alternative that $\mu > 100$ is an increase in β from .0475 to .0778. (See Figure 12.4b.)

As an illustration of the effect of the variability of the sampling distribution on the value of β, consider Solution II to the problem of the principal and the superintendent. In this solution, which was based on the median rather than the mean, the approximate standard error of the sampling distribution was 3.13 as compared with 2.5 in Solution I. In terms of the scale of values of the median, R extends downward from 92.71 [since $Mdn_R = (3.13)(-2.33) + 100 = 92.71$]. If the population median, ξ, is 90, the approximate sampling distribution of the median is a normal distribution with mean at 90 and an estimated standard error of 3.13. In this situation β is the probability of a median value greater than 92.71, or the probability of a z-value greater than $+0.87$. Hence, $\beta = .1922$. We see that we pay for using this less stable statistic (Mdn) by an increase in β from .0475 to .1922. (See Figure 12.4c.)

Finally, we shall illustrate the effect on β of the amount by which the actual value of the parameter differs from the value hypothesized for it. Assume the actual value of the population mean to be 95 instead of 90, which is only 5 points, rather than 10, below the hypothesized value. Then, of course, the sampling distribution of $\overline{X}$ will be centered on 95 and the upper limit of R (i.e., 94.17—see Solution I) will be in the lower half of this distribution. In this situation β is the probability of a $\overline{X}$-value greater than 94.17 or of a z-value greater than $-0.33+$. Hence, β is approximately .6293. (See Figure 12.4d.) On the other hand, if the actual value of the population mean is assumed to be 85, that is, a distance of 15 IQ points below the hypothesized value, then the probability of a $\overline{X}$-value greater than 94.17 corresponds to the probability of a z-value greater than $+3.67$. Here $\beta = .0001$. We see that the closer μ is to the hypothesized value (μ_0), the more likely we are to commit a Type II error; and the farther μ is from μ_0, the less likely we are to commit such an error. This is clearly a desirable feature of the test procedure.

The variations in the value of β associated with the situations we have presented are summarized in Table 12.2 on p. 267.

It should now be clear that Type II errors cannot be controlled in the same arbitrary manner as Type I errors can be. In fact, the probability of a Type II error in a given situation can only be estimated for

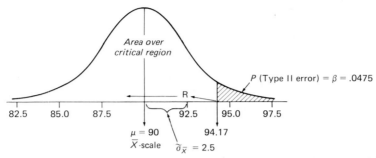

Figure 12.4a   Approximate sampling distribution of $\overline{X}$ for random samples of 65 cases from a population having $\mu = 90$

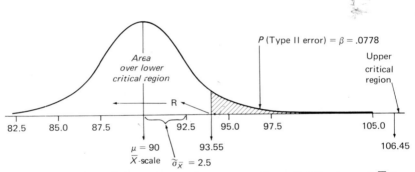

Figure 12.4b   Approximate sampling distribution of $\overline{X}$ for random samples of 65 cases selected from a population having $\mu = 90$

particular assumed values of the population parameter. It may occur to the student, therefore, that our discussion of this problem is more theoretical than practical. Although this may be true to some extent, there is, nevertheless, much that an analysis of the expected frequency of Type II errors for various possible alternative values of the parameter can contribute to the planning of an experiment. How such analyses can be accomplished with tests of the type we have been illustrating will be shown in the following section.

12.13 The Power of a Statistical Test

Suppose that the actual value of a population parameter, θ, differs by some particular amount from the value, θ_0, hypothesized for it. This fact, of course, is not known to the statisticians testing H_0, and they select a level of significance (α) that will afford them the degree of protection against a Type I error that they deem appropriate. We have

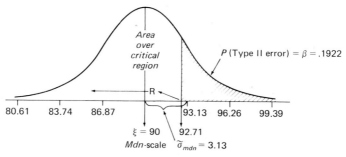

Figure 12.4c Approximate sampling distribution of *Mdn* for random samples of 65 cases selected from a population having $\xi = 90$

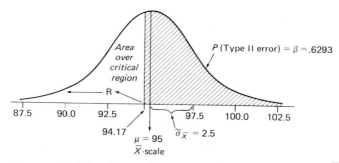

Figure 12.4d Approximate sampling distribution of $\overline{X}$ for random samples of 65 cases selected from a population having $\mu = 95$

illustrated how, in such a situation, the probability (β) of occurrence of a Type II error may still vary according to the critical region (R) chosen and the variability of the sampling distribution of the test statistic (T) employed. In this situation, rejection of H_0 is the desired correct outcome. The probability that this outcome will be reached is

Table 12.2 Summary of Variations in β in Seven Selected Illustrative Situations

μ	α	R	T	$\tilde{\sigma}_T$	β
90	.01	Lower end	$\overline{X}$	2.5	.0475
90	.001	Lower end	$\overline{X}$	2.5	.1814
90	.05	Lower end	$\overline{X}$	2.5	.0091
90	.01	Both ends	$\overline{X}$	2.5	.0778
90	.01	Lower end	*Mdn*	3.13	.1922
95	.01	Lower end	$\overline{X}$	2.5	.6293
85	.01	Lower end	$\overline{X}$	2.5	.0001

the probability that T falls in R. We shall refer to this probability as the *power (P)* of the test.[13] Since β represents the probability that T does not fall in R, and since T either does or does not fall in R, it follows that $P = 1 - \beta.$

> **DN 12.7** The *power* of a test of a statistical hypothesis, H_0, is the probability, P, that it will lead to rejection of H_0 when the true value of the parameter is θ_1 rather than θ_0, the hypothesized value. Or, the power of a statistical test is the probability that the statistic, T, will fall in the critical region, R, when θ is equal to θ_1 rather than θ_0.

In other words, the power of a test is the probability that it will detect a specified degree of falsity in the hypothesis. Now since $P = 1 - \beta$, and since β can be evaluated only for assumed alternative values of θ, it follows that P, also, can be evaluated only for such assumed alternative values of θ. This does not in any way prevent the concept of the power of a statistical test from being a useful criterion for the evaluation of such tests. One way, in fact, to compare statistical tests is simply to determine their respective powers for all values of θ that are possible alternatives to θ_0. Such determinations are usually presented graphically in the form of *power curves*.

> **DN 12.8** The *power curve* of a test of a statistical hypothesis, H_0, is the plot of the *P*-values that correspond to all θ-values that are possible alternatives to θ_0.

Let us construct the power curve for the statistical test employed in Solution I of the problem of the principal and the superintendent. In this solution there exists an infinite collection of μ-values ($\mu < 100$) that are possible alternative values to the hypothesized value of 100 (here $\mu_0 = 100$). Obviously, in this situation we cannot determine the *P*-values associated with all possible alternative μ-values. We shall content ourselves, therefore, with determining the *P*-values that correspond to selected possible alternative μ-values. After plotting these *P*-values we shall use them as guide points to sketch the smooth continuous curve which is the locus of all such *P*-values.

We shall begin by determining the *P*-value corresponding to $\mu = 98$.

> 1 *Determination of P for* $\mu = 98$. R in Solution I is $\overline{X} \leq 94.17$, and if $\mu = 98$, then the actual $\overline{X}$-distribution is as pictured in Figure 12.5. Here $P = P(\overline{X} \leq 94.17 \mid ND: \mu = 98, \hat{\sigma}_{\overline{X}} = 2.5)$[14]—see the shaded area in Figure 12.5. But 94.17 cor-

[13] In previous sections of this text, P was used to indicate a probability value. However, this symbol never appeared alone. It was always used in conjunction with a statement giving the referent for the probability value: $P(3 \text{ red cards}) = .20$, $P(\overline{X} \geq 101) = .50$, and so on. Therefore, the use of P by itself to indicate the power of a statistical procedure should not lead to confusion.

[14] Read "power equals the probability of an $\overline{X}$-value of 94.17 or less, given a normally distributed universe having a mean of 98 and an estimated standard deviation of 2.5."

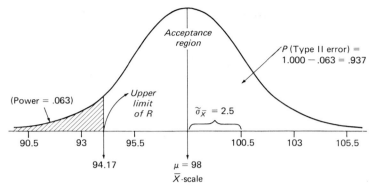

Figure 12.5 Approximate sampling distribution of $\bar{X}$ for random sample of 65 cases from a population having $\mu = 98$

responds to $z = (94.17 - 98)/2.5 = -1.53$. Therefore,

$$P = P(z \leq -1.53 \mid ND: \mu = 0, \sigma = 1) = .063$$

2 *Determination of P for* $\mu = 96$. Here $P = P(\bar{X} \leq 94.17 \mid ND: \mu = 96, \tilde{\sigma}_{\bar{X}} = 2.5)$. Since in this situation the sampling distribution is centered on 96, it follows that 94.17 corresponds to $z = (94.17 - 96)/2.5 = -0.73$. Therefore,

$$P = P(z \leq -0.73 \mid ND: \mu = 0, \sigma = 1) = .233$$

3 *Other values of P determined similarly are*[15]

For $\mu = 94$, $P = .527$
For $\mu = 92$, $P = .808$
For $\mu = 90$, $P = .953$
For $\mu = 88$, $P = .993$

The *P*-values corresponding to these selected μ-values have been plotted in Figure 12.6. The smooth curve sketched through these *P*-values is the power curve of the particular statistical test used in Solution I of the problem of the principal and the superintendent. The *D*-scale placed below the μ-scale simply indicates the discrepancies between the possible alternative μ-values and $\mu_0 = 100$. The order of subtraction used was $D = \mu - \mu_0$, so that negative *D*-values indicate μ-values of less than μ_0. This power curve may be used to read the probability of rejecting H_0 for any given possible alternative value of μ. It will be observed that the power of the test increases as the discrepancy (*D*) between μ and μ_0 increases in absolute value. Thus, for a *D* of -5, the

[15] The student ought to verify these values.

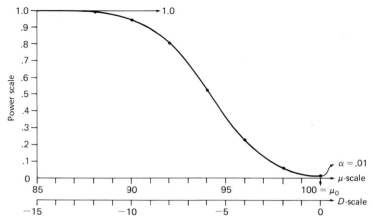

Figure 12.6   Power curve of statistical test of Solution I of
the problem of the principal and the superintendent

chances that the test will detect the falsity of $\mu_0 = 100$ are only about
four out of ten (actually 371 in a thousand), whereas for a D of -10,
the chances become better than nine out of ten (actually 953 in a
thousand).

To illustrate how power curves may be used to assess the relative
effectiveness of various statistical tests, we have superimposed the
curves for the first three solutions to the problem of the principal and
the superintendent on the same axes (see Figure 12.7). For each of these
tests the *P*-values corresponding to selected alternative values of the
parameter are given in Table 12.3. These are the values that were plotted

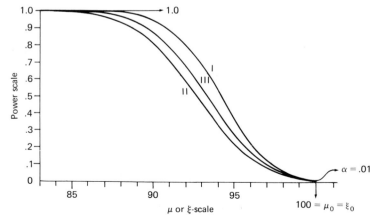

Figure 12.7   Power curves of Solutions, I, II, and III
of the problem of the principal and the superintendent

Table 12.3 Values of P Corresponding to Selected Values of μ or ξ for Solutions I, II, and III of the Problem of the Principal and the Superintendent

μ or ξ	P_I	P_{II}	P_{III}
$100 = \mu_0 = \xi_0$	.01	.01	.01
98	.063	.046	.052
96	.233	.147	.176
94	.527	.341	.409
92	.808	.591	.681
90	.953	.808	.879
88	.993	.933	.969
86		.984	.995
84		.997	

as guide points in sketching the curves. We have already shown how the P-values were computed for Solution I. We will show how the values for P_{II} and P_{III} were determined for ξ or $\mu = 98$.

To determine P_{II} for $\xi = 98$ we will first express R in terms of the scale of values of the statistic used (Mdn).[16] The upper limit of R in terms of the Mdn scale is given by:

$$Mdn_R = (3.13)(-2.33) + 100 = 92.71$$

Therefore,

$$R: Mdn \leq 92.71$$

Then

$$P_{II} = P(Mdn \leq 92.71 \mid ND: \mu = \xi = 98, \tilde{\sigma}_{Mdn} = 3.13)$$

But in this ND, 92.71 corresponds to $z = (92.71 - 98)/3.13 = -1.69$. Therefore,

$$P_{II} = P(z \leq -1.69 \mid ND: \mu = 0; \sigma = 1) = .046$$

Similarly, to determine P_{III} for $\mu = 98$ we first determine R in terms of the $\overline{X}$-scale. Here we have

$$\overline{X}_R = (2.86)(-2.33) + 100 = 93.34$$

---

[16] In Solution II the modified solution described in Section 12.5 was used: R was expressed in terms of z-units rather than in terms of IQ units. While it is possible also to express alternatives to H_0 in z-scale units, their interpretation is more straightforward when they are expressed in terms of IQ units. Hence, we have chosen here to express R in terms of the IQ scale.

Or

$$R: \overline{X} \leq 93.34$$

Then

$$P_{III} = P(\overline{X} \leq 93.34 \mid ND: \mu = 98, \tilde{\sigma}_{\overline{x}} = 2.86)$$

But in this ND, 93.34 corresponds to $z = (93.34 - 98)/2.86 = -1.63$. Therefore,

$$P_{III} = P(z \leq -1.63 \mid ND: \mu = 0, \sigma = 1) = .052$$

Inspection of the power curves in Figure 12.7 shows the statistical test of Solution I to be the most powerful of the three for any value of the parameter alternative to $\mu_0 = 100$, and the test of Solution II to be the least powerful for any alternative value of the parameter. It should also be observed that if μ or ξ equals the hypothesized value of 100, then for all three tests the probability of the test statistic falling to R is equal to the selected level of significance ($\alpha = .01$). That is, *the tests are all equally effective at an arbitrarily predetermined level insofar as control over Type I error is concerned*—which, of course, is the only type of error possible when μ or ξ equals μ_0 or ξ_0.

The test of Solution I is the most powerful because the standard error of the statistic employed is the smallest. For a given N, the standard error of the median (which was the test statistic used in Solution II) is about 1.25 times larger than that of the mean—see (11.9). The mean was again used as the test statistic in Solution III but this time with a smaller sample so that a sampling distribution more variable than that of Solution I resulted.

Figure 12.8 shows graphically how the variability of the sampling distribution affects the power of statistical tests. The curve on the right in the upper part of the figure represents the hypothesized sampling distribution of $\overline{X}$ for the statistical test of Solution I of the problem of the principal and the superintendent. The other upper curve represents the actual sampling distribution of $\overline{X}$ as it would appear if the population value of μ were 95. The shaded portion of this latter curve represents the probability of $\overline{X}$ in R—that is, the power of the test when $\mu = 95$. When $\mu = 95$ this test has only about four chances out of ten (actually $P = .371$) of detecting the falsity of $\mu_0 = 100$.

Suppose the investigation had been conducted in such a way as to reduce the standard error of the sampling distribution from 2.5 to 1.[17] The right-hand curve in the lower part of Figure 12.8 represents the hypothesized sampling distribution of $\overline{X}$ as it would now appear.

---

[17] This could be done by increasing the sample to about 400 cases. For, assuming S to remain fairly stable (in Solution I we assumed S to be 20), we have by (11.19) $\sigma_{\overline{x}} \approx 20/\sqrt{401 - 1} = 1$.

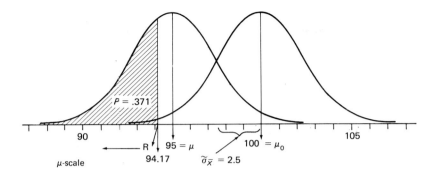

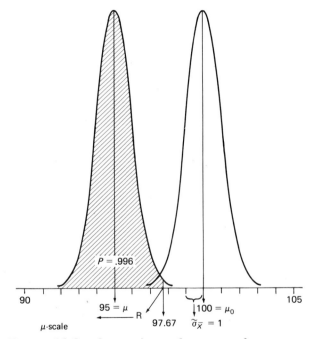

Figure 12.8   Comparison of powers of two tests of $H_0 = 100$ if $\mu = 95$ and where standard error of one test is 2.5 times that of the other

Note that R in this situation has the upper limit 97.67, since

$$(1)(-2.33) + 100 = 97.67$$

The other lower curve represents the actual sampling distribution of $\overline{X}$ as it would appear if $\mu = 95$. It is clear that the effect of thus reducing the standard error is to provide a test that is almost certain ($P = .996$) to detect the falsity of $\mu_0 = 100$ when actually $\mu = 95$.

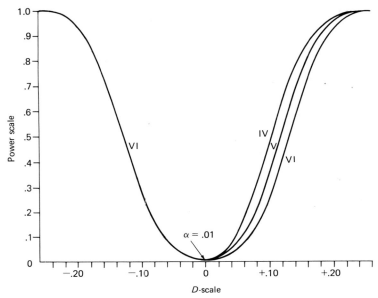

Figure 12.9   Power curves for Solutions IV, V, and VI
of the problem of the principal and the superintendent

We shall conclude this section with a comparison of the powers of
the statistical tests used in Solutions IV, V, and VI of the problem of
the principal and the superintendent. The powers corresponding to
selected differences between ϕ_0 and possible alternative values of the
population parameter are given in Table 12.4. These P-values are
plotted and the power curves shown in Figure 12.9. We shall present
the computation of P_{IV}, P_V, and P_{VI} for $D = .12$. The student should
at least spot-check some of the other P-values.

1 P_{IV} *for* $D = \phi - \phi_0 = .37 - .25 = .12$. Here, $R: p \geq .3509$
(see p. 255). Now, if $\phi = .37$, the actual sampling distribution
of p is approximately a normal distribution with $\mu_p = .37$ and

$$\sigma_p = \sqrt{\frac{(.37)(.63)}{100}} = .0483$$

Therefore, $P_{IV} = P(p \geq .3509 \mid ND: \mu_p = .37, \sigma_p = .0483)$.
But in this ND, $p = .3509$ corresponds to $z = (.3509 - .37)/.0483 = -.40$. Therefore,

$$P_{IV} = P(z \geq -.40 \mid ND: \mu = 0, \sigma = 1) = .655$$

Table 12.4 Values of P Corresponding to Differences (D) between ϕ_0 and Selected Possible Alternative Values of ϕ for Solutions IV, V, and VI of the Problem of the Principal and the Superintendent

$D = \phi - \phi_0$	P_{IV}	P_V	$D = \phi - \phi_0$	P_{VI}
.0	.01	.01	.0	.01
+.02	.034	.027	±.02	.016
+.04	.090	.062	±.04	.037
+.06	.189	.127	±.06	.082
+.08	.330	.230	±.08	.161
+.10	.492	.367	+.10	.278
+.12	.655	.528	±.12	.425
+.14	.788	.688	±.14	.591
+.16	.885	.821	±.16	.742
+.18	.945	.913	±.18	.862
+.20	.977	.966	±.20	.939
+.22	.992	.990	±.22	.979
+.24	.997	.998	±.24	.994

2 P_V for $D = \phi - \phi_0 = .62 - .50 = .12$. Here, $R: z \geq 2.33$ or $p \geq (.05)(2.33) + .5 = .6165$. Now, if $\phi = .62$, p is approximately normally distributed with $\mu_p = .62$ and

$$\sigma_p = \sqrt{\frac{(.62)(.38)}{100}} = .0485$$

Therefore, $P_V = P(p \geq .6165 \mid ND: \mu_p = .62, \sigma_p = .0485)$. But in this ND, $p = .6165$ corresponds to $z = (.6165 - .62)/.0485 = -.07$. Therefore,

$$P_V = P(z \geq -.07 \mid ND: \mu = 0, \sigma = 1) = .528$$

3 P_{VI} for $D = \phi - \phi_0 = .62 - .50 = .12$. Here, $R: z \leq -2.58$ and $z \geq +2.58$, or $p \leq (.05)(-2.58) + .50 = .371$ and $p \geq (.05)(+2.58) + .50 = .629$. Now, if $\phi = .62$, p is approximately normally distributed with $\mu = .62$ and

$$\sigma_p = \sqrt{\frac{(.62)(.38)}{100}} = .0485$$

Therefore,

$$P_{VI} = P(p \leq .371 \mid ND: \mu = .62, \sigma_p = .0485) \\ + P(p \geq .629 \mid ND: \mu_p = .62, \sigma_p = .0485)$$

But in this ND, $p = .371$ corresponds to $z = (.371 - .62)/.0485 = -5.13$ and $p = .629$ corresponds to $z = (.629 - .62)/.0485 = +.19$. Therefore,

$$\begin{aligned} P_{VI} = {} & P(z \leq -5.13 \mid ND\colon \mu = 0,\ \sigma = 1) \\ & + P(z \geq +.19 \mid ND\colon \mu = 0,\ \sigma = 1) \\ = {} & .000 + .425 = .425 \end{aligned}$$

We see from an inspection of Figure 12.9 that of these three last solutions to the problem of the principal and the superintendent, IV is the most powerful for alternative values of ϕ greater than the values hypothesized. Solution IV is more powerful than Solution V for such alternative values, owing to the fact that the standard error of the sampling distribution of p decreases as the value of the parameter ϕ differs more and more from .5 [see (11.6)]; recall that both ϕ_0 and the possible alternative values differed more from .5 in Solution IV than in Solution V.[18] This advantage of Solution IV over V may, however, be more apparent than real. It is real only if we can regard the difference between, say, .25 and .27 as representing a difference of the same order of magnitude as that between .50 and .52. Furthermore, the normal distribution is a less accurate model of the sampling distribution of p in Solution IV than in Solution V (see Section 10.7).

Solution V is more powerful than Solution VI for possible alternative values of ϕ greater than ϕ_0. This is because Solution VI provides protection against a Type II error not only for possible alternative values of ϕ greater than ϕ_0, but also for possible alternative values of ϕ less than ϕ_0. Solution V, like IV, provides no protection at all against the possibility of alternative values of ϕ less than ϕ_0. The choice between Solutions V and VI, therefore, clearly depends on whether the conditions of the problem demand a statistical test that will be sensitive to possible alternative values of the parameter on both sides of ϕ_0.

12.14 The Arbitrary Aspects of Statistical Tests: A Summary

In this section we shall attempt to pull together ideas developed in the foregoing sections by directing attention to the arbitrary decisions that enter into tests of statistical hypotheses.

Arbitrary decision 1: choice of statistic In presenting the various possible solutions to the problem of the principal and the

---

[18] In Solution IV, $\phi_0 = .25$ and the possible alternative values were $\phi > .25$. In Solution V, $\phi_0 = .50$ and the possible alternative values were $\phi > .50$.

superintendent, we have attempted to illustrate how different statistics may be applied to the solution of the same general problem. Two considerations are of major importance. First, it is essential that the statistic chosen be *valid* as an index of the general or research hypothesis, as distinguished from the statistical hypothesis, involved. In the problem of the principal and the superintendent, for example, we might express the *research hypothesis* by saying that the population that will attend a particular elementary school during some limited period in the future (a period determined by the expected useful life of certain physical facilities and equipment) is made up predominantly of children who are sufficiently retarded mentally to require special handling by a specially trained staff using special facilities and materials costing approximately X dollars. The *statistical hypotheses, on the other hand, are negations of research hypotheses, so that rejection of a statistical hypothesis implies acceptance of the research hypothesis*. The statistical hypotheses that we have tested in the different solutions represented a variety of attempts to express the negation of this research hypothesis in valid quantitative terms amenable to test. Some of our attempts are perhaps more valid in this sense than others. For example, in Solution IV, the superintendent defined "below normal" as $IQ < 90$, whereas in Solution V "below normal" was defined as $IQ < 100$. In view of the general nature of the research problem, the definition used in Solution IV appears to be more valid than that used in Solution V. It may be that there exist approaches not chosen by us that are more valid still. In any case, the practical usefulness of the statistical test depends on the degree to which it provides a valid attack on the general problem.

The second consideration in the selection of a statistic has to do with its *efficiency*, in the sense of its having a small standard error. The reason for this requirement was developed in the preceding section in the discussion accompanying Figure 12.8.

Arbitrary decision 2: choice of level of significance (α) The possibilities in choosing a level of significance are unlimited, since any conceivable probability value between zero and one may be adopted. The consideration determining the choice is the relative seriousness of the consequences of Type I and Type II errors. When Type I errors appear to be the more serious, small values (.001, .01, or .02) are used. When Type II errors appear to be the more serious, larger values (.10 or .20) are used. A commonly employed compromise value is .05.

The choice of a level of significance determines the degree of control over a Type I error, which is the only type of error over which it is possible to exercise complete arbitrary control. As we explained in the concluding paragraphs of Section 12.11, the consequences of a Type I error are ordinarily more serious than those of a Type II error. It is unusual, therefore, to find the larger values (.10 or .20) employed. Their selection should always be accompanied by special justification.

Arbitrary decision 3: choice of critical region (R) For a given level of significance (α), the possibilities for choosing a critical region are unlimited. Any R, however chosen, will be as good as any other R for controlling a Type I error if the same α applies, since for all such R's the probability of the statistic falling in the region is α *if the hypothesis is true*. However, we have shown in the foregoing sections that all such R's are not equally effective with respect to controlling Type II errors. Hence, the consideration governing the choice of R is the effectiveness of the control it provides over Type II errors. The most effective R's from this standpoint are located at the extremes of the sampling distribution of the test statistic. Whether R should be located entirely at one end of the sampling distribution or whether it should be divided into two portions, one at each end, depends on whether the general conditions of the problem are such that the value of the parameter could differ from the value hypothesized for it in only one or in both directions.

A word of caution is in order at this point. The examples with which we have introduced tests of statistical hypotheses may suggest that one-ended R's are commonly employed. Actually, in most research situations that involve tests of statistical hypotheses (at least in psychology and education), the possible alternative values of the parameter lie to either side of the value hypothesized. In such situations, of course, a two-ended R is mandatory.

12.15 Estimating Sample Size*

In this section we shall present the steps involved in estimating the size of sample necessary to bring the power of a statistical test up to some desired level for a given discrepancy (D) between the value of the parameter and the value hypothesized for it. The solution to this problem requires that we first decide

1 the value of α
2 the location of R—whether R is to be located entirely at one end or divided between both ends of the sampling distribution
3 the value of the critical discrepancy, D—an amount such that if the actual value of the parameter differs from the value hypothesized for it by this amount, the probability of rejecting the hypothesis is P
4 the value of P, or $\beta = 1 - P$.

* Optional section.

In addition it is necessary for us to obtain—either through previous research or by means of a small preliminary sample—such information about the population as may be necessary to an approximation of the standard error of the sampling distribution of the test statistic involved.

We shall first illustrate the procedure using the situation of Solution I of the problem of the principal and the superintendent. Again we shall let $\alpha = .01$ and locate R entirely at the lower end of the sampling distribution of the statistic, $\overline{X}$. In addition we shall let $D = -10$ and $\beta = .05$. That is, if the actual mean IQ for the population is 10 points below the hypothesized value of $\mu_0 = 100$, we wish the probability of a Type II error to be .05. In terms of power this corresponds to $P = .95$ when $\mu = 90$. Suppose further that for a small preliminary sample of 10 cases the superintendent obtains $S = 19.1$. Then a rough approximation of the population standard deviation is

$$\tilde{\sigma} = 19.1 \sqrt{\frac{10}{9}} = 20.1 \qquad\qquad [\text{see } (11.17)]$$

Now consider Figure 12.10. The normal curve on the right provides an approximate model of the sampling distribution of the statistic, $\overline{X}$, as it would appear if the hypothesis, $\mu = 100$, were true. The model is approximate, both because $\tilde{\sigma} = 20.1$ is not reliably determined when based on a small preliminary sample, and because the population of IQs sampled may not be normally distributed. In this figure R_U is the upper limit of the critical region R. Note that if H_0 is true, the probability of $\overline{X}$ falling in R is $\alpha = .01$; i.e., the probability of a Type I error

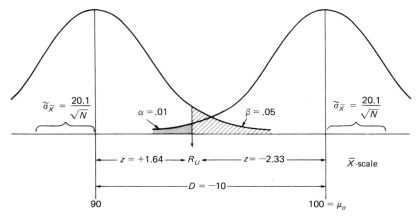

Figure 12.10 Diagram of situation involved in estimating N for Solution I of the problem of the principal and the superintendent

is .01. It is clear that for the curve on the right in Figure 12.10

$$R_U = \tilde{\sigma}_X z + \mu_0 = \frac{20.1}{\sqrt{N}}(-2.33) + 100 = \frac{-46.8}{\sqrt{N}} + 100$$

If, however, there is a discrepancy of $D = -10$ between the actual value of the parameter and μ_0, then the normal curve at the left in Figure 12.10 is the approximate model of the sampling distribution. Note that in this situation the probability of $\bar{X}$ not falling in R is $\beta = .05$; i.e., the probability of a Type II error is .05. Or the probability of $\bar{X}$ falling in R, i.e., the probability of correctly rejecting H_0, is $P = .95$. In this alternative distribution

$$R_U = \tilde{\sigma}_X z + (\mu_0 + D)$$
$$= \frac{20.1}{\sqrt{N}}(+1.64) + (100 - 10) = \frac{33.0}{\sqrt{N}} + 90$$

Now to estimate (roughly) the size sample necessary to provide the specified control over a Type I error, as well as the specified control over a Type II error in the case of the given critical discrepancy, it is necessary only to equate these two expressions for R_U and to solve for N as follows:

$$\frac{33.0}{\sqrt{N}} + 90 = \frac{-46.8}{\sqrt{N}} + 100$$
$$\frac{79.8}{\sqrt{N}} = 10$$
$$10\sqrt{N} = 79.8$$
$$\sqrt{N} = 7.98$$
$$N \approx 64$$

Thus, we see that the sample size actually used by the superintendent ($N = 65$) was about right for the specifications selected in the above example.

As a second example, involving a different statistic and a two-ended R, we shall estimate for the case of Solution VI to the problem of the principal and the superintendent the sample size necessary for an α of .01, a β of .05, and a D of .1 in either direction.

Figure 12.11 represents the situation for a D-value of $+.1$. It is immaterial whether we work with a positive or negative D-value of .1 since either leads to the same estimate of N. We begin by writing two expressions for R_U, the beginning of the upper portion of R.[19] In the

---

[19] When $D = +.1$ the lower portion of R may be ignored since the probability of the statistic (p) falling in it when $\phi = .6$ is negligible.

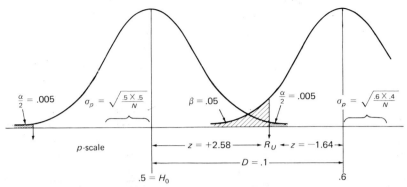

Figure 12.11 Diagram of situation involved in estimating *N* for Solution VI to the problem of the principal and the superintendent

hypothesized distribution

$$R_U = \sigma_p z + \phi_0 = \sqrt{\frac{(.5)(.5)}{N}}\,(+2.58) + .5$$

In the alternative distribution

$$R_U = \sigma_p z + (\phi_0 + D) = \sqrt{\frac{(.6)(.4)}{N}}\,(-1.64) + (.5 + .1)$$

Equating these two expressions and solving for *N*, we have:

$$\sqrt{\frac{(.5)(.5)}{N}}\,(2.58) + .5 = \sqrt{\frac{(.6)(.4)}{N}}\,(-1.64) + (.5 + .1)$$

$$\frac{2.58\sqrt{.25}}{\sqrt{N}} + \frac{1.64\sqrt{.24}}{\sqrt{N}} = .1$$

$$\frac{1.29}{\sqrt{N}} + \frac{.80}{\sqrt{N}} = .1$$

$$\frac{1.29 + .80}{\sqrt{N}} = .1$$

$$\frac{2.09}{\sqrt{N}} = .1$$

$$\frac{4.37}{N} = .01$$

$$.01N = 4.37$$

$$N = 437$$

Thus we see that to meet this selected set of specifications the superintendent would have needed a sample of approximately 437. In Solution VI we had her using only 100 cases. Our previous investigation of this solution showed its power for $D = \pm.1$ to be only .278 (see Table 12.4). In other words, if $D = \pm.1$, the probability of a Type II error when $N = 100$ is .722. Actually, sample size is not as important to the control of Type I errors as it is to the control of Type II errors. For proper control of Type I errors it is necessary only that the sample be large enough to justify the use of the normal curve as a model of the sampling distribution. On the other hand, as this example shows, sample size is extremely critical as a factor controlling Type II errors. This follows as a result of the effect of sample size on the standard error (see discussion relating to Figure 12.8).

One other comment is pertinent. The usefulness of this procedure in much psychological and educational research work is somewhat lessened by the difficulties encountered in determining an appropriate value for the critical difference (D) in terms of the type of scale units commonly involved. Whenever possible, however, it is advisable to attempt to establish some reasonably suitable value for D and to use the routine described to obtain at least a rough notion of the sample size necessary to the desired degrees of control over the two types of error.

12.16 Summary Statement

The major purpose of the preceding sections was to introduce classical hypothesis testing procedures and some related concepts. We followed the commonsense pedagogical principle of beginning with the simplest possible situation, namely, the situation involving the selection of a single random sample from a single well-defined experimentally accessible population. (This situation is often referred to as the *one-sample case*.) To give our examples an aura of practicality we chose a situation that involved a criterion measure (IQ) for which normative data are available. That is, our examples were reasonable because information external to the experiment was available. But consider a case in which external information is not available. What if our problem involved formulating a plausible hypothesis about the population mean in the case of the problem of the principal and superintendent where the measurements involved were obtained by using an instrument developed by the principal for assessing the level of "defeatist attitude"? Assuming no previous widespread experience with this instrument, what is a reasonable hypothesis? Is $\mu_0 = 100$ reasonable? Of course, we cannot know. In such a situation, the hypothesis testing procedure is obviously not appropriate.

What type of inferential procedure is appropriate in situations in which reasonable hypotheses do not exist? One such procedure is presented in Chapter 14. It focuses on the problem of obtaining an estimate of the parameter of interest rather than on testing a hypothesis about it.

Actually, situations analogous to the problem of the principal and superintendent as described in this chapter are not common in practical work. You may recall, however, that in preceding chapters of this book we have emphasized the practical importance of developing procedures for comparing groups. The technique of statistical hypothesis testing plays an important role in such comparisons. Consider an experiment designed to assess the effect of a speed reading course on reading comprehension. In Section 9.1 one experimental procedure that could be used to check on the effectiveness of such a course was described. Basically, the experiment consisted of having two randomly selected groups take part in the experiment. One group was given the speed reading course; the other was not. After the one group had completed the course, a reading comprehension test was given to both groups. Is there a reasonable hypothesis that can be tested in this situation? One such hypothesis might be that the mean of the comprehension test scores of the population of students represented by the sample group that took the course is the same as the corresponding mean of the population of students represented by the sample group that did not take the course. Symbolically, this hypothesis can be stated as follows:

$$\mu_C = \mu_{NC}$$

where μ_C = the mean of the comprehension test scores of a population of students who have taken the speed reading course, and μ_{NC} = the corresponding parameter for a population of students who have not taken this course. Another way of symbolically stating this hypothesis is:

$$\mu_C - \mu_{NC} = 0$$

The important point is that in experimental situations such as this, it is not essential that we hypothesize specific values for μ_C and μ_{NC}. Instead, the hypothesis of interest pertains to the difference, or rather the lack of difference, between the population means, regardless of what the magnitude of these means may be. Situations analogous to this are widespread in psychological and educational research. Experiments designed to investigate such situations are often referred to as *two-sample cases* of hypothesis testing. In the next chapter of this text, hypothesis testing procedures for the two-sample case will be presented.

A final comment is important. In Section 12.13 the notion of the power of a statistical test was discussed in some detail. In Section 12.15 (an optional section) the determination of sample size was treated. These are considerations of great practical importance to researchers whose investigations involve hypothesis testing. Unfortunately, procedures for determining power and sample size are quite complicated in all but the simplest situations, and consequently any extensive consideration of them is beyond the scope of an elementary book.[20]

[20] These topics are treated extensively in Jacob Cohen's *Statistical Power Analysis for the Behavioral Sciences* (Academic Press, New York, 1969).

13

Sampling Theory as It Applies to Differences between Means and Proportions: Large Samples

13.1   Introduction

In the last three sections of Chapter 11, we presented a sampling-error theory for p, $\overline{X}$, and Mdn. This theory enabled us to describe the sampling distributions of these statistics. In Chapter 12 we examined one practical application of this sampling theory: hypothesis testing. In this chapter we present some sampling-error theory as it applies to differences between two normally distributed random variables and show how this theory can also be used to test selected hypotheses.

13.2   Sampling Theory for $\overline{X}_1 - \overline{X}_2$ and $p_1 - p_2$

Suppose we have two normally distributed populations of scores (X's) designated Population 1 and Population 2. Let the means and variances of these two populations be represented by μ_1 and $\sigma_1{}^2$, and μ_2 and $\sigma_2{}^2$. Now consider an experiment that consists of selecting a single score at random from each of these populations. Let the difference $X_1 - X_2$ between these two scores, designated D, be the random variable (outcome) of this experiment. Repetition of this experiment would result in the generation of a collection of D-values; and an infinity of such repetitions would lead to a sampling distribution of D's. Mathematicians have demonstrated the following facts regarding this sampling distribution.

1 It is a normal distribution.
2 It has a mean equal to the difference between the means of the two populations. That is, it has the mean

$$\mu_D = \mu_1 - \mu_2$$

3 It would have a variance equal to the sum of the two population variances. That is,

$$\sigma_D^2 = \sigma_1^2 + \sigma_2^2$$

We shall summarize this theory as a rule.

> **RULE 13.1**   Given two normally distributed independent[1] random variables X_1 and X_2 having respective means μ_1 and μ_2 and variances σ_1^2 and σ_2^2. Then the sampling distribution of the random variable $D = X_1 - X_2$ is a normal distribution with mean $\mu_1 - \mu_2$ and variance $\sigma_1^2 + \sigma_2^2$.

The importance of this theory is that it in turn provides us with a very important sampling theory regarding the difference between the means of two random samples selected independently from two populations. Let us approach this latter theory in terms of a more concrete situation.

Suppose that we are interested in investigating the difference in mean reading comprehension, as measured by the score on some reading test, of a population of college freshmen who take a speed reading course and a population of similar freshmen who do not take the speed reading course. (This situation was described in considerable detail to show the need for probability concepts in inferential statistics; see Section 9.1.) To be consistent with the notation above, we shall designate these populations as Populations 1 and 2, respectively. Since the means of these populations are unknown to us, we shall simply represent them by μ_1 and μ_2. The difference we wish to investigate is the difference $\mu_1 - \mu_2$.

Now suppose we select from Population 1 a random sample of 50 freshmen for whom the mean score on the reading comprehension test $(\overline{X}_1)$ is 72. Also suppose that for a random sample of 60 freshmen taken independently from Population 2, the corresponding mean score $(\overline{X}_2)$ is 65. The difference $\overline{X}_1 - \overline{X}_2 = 72 - 65 = 7$ gives us some indication of the difference $\mu_1 - \mu_2$, but we recognize that it may involve a certain amount of sampling error. We know that were we to repeat the procedure, taking a new pair of independent random samples of 50 and 60 cases from the two populations, the new value of $\overline{X}_1 - \overline{X}_2$ would almost certainly not be 7, owing to chance variation in the composition of the two sets of samples.

---

[1] We cannot at this point define precisely the word *independent* in terms that would be meaningful to the student. Perhaps the word *unrelated* could serve as a substitute, for now. Relationship would occur if the selection of a large X_1 tended to be accompanied by the selection of a large X_2, or the selection of a small X_1 tended to be accompanied by the selection of a small X_2. At this point it is sufficient to understand that if both values are selected at random from their respective distributions, the condition of independence necessary for the rule will be satisfied.

Now by Rule 11.2 (p. 228) we know that $\overline{X}_1$ and $\overline{X}_2$ are both approximately normally distributed with respective means μ_1 and μ_2. We also know that the variance of $\overline{X}_1$ ($\sigma_{\overline{X}_1}^2$) is $\sigma_1^2/N_1 = \sigma^2/50$ and that the variance of $\overline{X}_2$ ($\sigma_{\overline{X}_2}^2$) is $\sigma_2^2/N_2 = \sigma_2^2/60$.

Note that Rule 13.1 applies to any two normally distributed independent random variables. Since $\overline{X}_1$ and $\overline{X}_2$ are normally distributed independent random variables, Rule 13.1 applies to $\overline{X}_1$ and $\overline{X}_2$. Therefore, by substituting $\overline{X}_1$ for X_1, $\overline{X}_2$ for X_2, $\sigma_{\overline{X}_1}^2$ for σ_1^2, and $\sigma_{\overline{X}_2}^2$ for σ_2^2 in Rule 13.1, we arrive at the following characteristics of the sampling distribution of $\overline{X}_1 - \overline{X}_2$:

1 This distribution is approximately normal.
2 The mean is $\mu_1 - \mu_2$.
3 The variance is $\sigma_{\overline{X}_1}^2 + \sigma_{\overline{X}_2}^2 = \sigma_1^2/N_1 + \sigma_2^2/N_2$.

For our speed reading example, the difference $\overline{X}_1 - \overline{X}_2$ has an approximately normal sampling distribution with mean $\mu_1 - \mu_2$ and variance $\sigma_1^2/50 + \sigma_2^2/60$. If we now knew the values of the variances of these populations (the values of σ_1^2 and σ_2^2), we could describe quite precisely the sampling distribution for the infinity of the $\overline{X}_1 - \overline{X}_2$ differences that would be generated by repeating this experiment indefinitely.

For the sake of concreteness, assume that we somehow know the variances to be 250 and 240, respectively. Then by Rule 11.2, $\overline{X}_1$ is a normally distributed variable with mean μ_1 and variance 5 (since $250/50 = 5$). Also by this same rule, $\overline{X}_2$ is a normally distributed variable with mean μ_2 and variance 4 (since $240/60 = 4$). Hence, by Rule 13.1, $\overline{X}_1 - \overline{X}_2$ has a normal sampling distribution with mean $\mu_1 - \mu_2$ and a variance of 9 (since $5 + 4 = 9$) or a standard error of 3 (since $\sqrt{9} = 3$). The sampling distribution of $\overline{X}_1 - \overline{X}_2$ is pictured in Figure 13.1. The positive and negative values shown along the scale represent distances above and below the "true" difference $\mu_1 - \mu_2$. That is, the point $+3$ represents a point three units above $\mu_1 - \mu_2$ on the $\overline{X}_1 - \overline{X}_2$ scale. Similarly, the point -6 corresponds to the value six units below $\mu_1 - \mu_2$ on this scale. In this situation we may note, for example, that the probability of a given $\overline{X}_1 - \overline{X}_2$ difference being in error by 5.9 (since $1.96 \times 3 = 5.88)^2$ or more is approximately .05.

The sampling theory that we have just illustrated can be summarized as in the rule that follows.[3]

---

[2] In the standard normal distribution $P(|z| \geq 1.96) = .05$.

[3] To this point we have usually used an upper-case N to represent the number of scores in a collection or the number of cases in a sample. However, when the total collection of scores may be viewed as consisting of subsets of scores, we shall use a lower-case n to represent the number of scores in a subset. This leaves us free to use N to represent the total number of scores in all subsets. In the present situation we may regard the total collection of data at hand as consisting of two subsets—namely, the two samples.

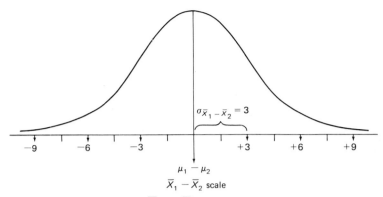

$$\mu_1 - \mu_2$$

$$\bar{X}_1 - \bar{X}_2 \text{ scale}$$

Figure 13.1 $\bar{X}_1 - \bar{X}_2$ sampling distribution

RULE 13.2   Let $\bar{X}_1$ represent the mean of a random sample of n_1 cases taken from any infinite population having mean μ_1 and finite variance $\sigma_1{}^2$, and let $\bar{X}_2$ represent the mean of an independently selected random sample of n_2 cases from any other infinite population having mean μ_2 and finite variance $\sigma_2{}^2$. Then, as n_1 and n_2 increase, the sampling distribution of $\bar{X}_1 - \bar{X}_2$ approaches a normal distribution with mean $\mu_1 - \mu_2$ and variance given by

$$\sigma^2_{\bar{X}_1 - \bar{X}_2} = \sigma_{\bar{X}_1}{}^2 + \sigma_{\bar{X}_2}{}^2 = \frac{\sigma_1{}^2}{n_1} + \frac{\sigma_2{}^2}{n_2} \tag{13.1}$$

RULE 13.2a   The standard error of the sampling distribution of Rule 13.2 is[4]

$$\sigma_{\bar{X}_1 - \bar{X}_2} = \sqrt{\sigma_{\bar{X}_1}{}^2 + \sigma_{\bar{X}_2}{}^2} = \sqrt{\frac{\sigma_1{}^2}{n_1} + \frac{\sigma_2{}^2}{n_2}} \tag{13.2}$$

In a similar fashion, through the application of Rules 13.1 and 11.3 it is possible to derive a sampling theory for the difference between sample proportions. We shall simply state this theory in the form of a rule without illustrative elaboration.

RULE 13.3   Given dichotomous Populations 1 and 2, each consisting of A's (ones) and not A's (zeros). Let ϕ_1 and ϕ_2 represent the respective proportions of A's in these populations. Also let p_1 and p_2 represent the proportions of A's in independent random samples of n_1 and n_2 cases taken from Populations 1 and 2, respectively. Then as n_1 and n_2 increase,

---

[4] If the population distributions are roughly normal, the theory of Rule 13.2 is sufficiently accurate even when n_1 and n_2 are quite small. If, however, the population distributions are far from normal—say, J-shaped—much larger sample sizes are required in order to justify the normal approximations. Empirical investigations have shown that for most of the populations encountered, if n_1 and n_2 are ≥ 50, this theory can be used without fear of gross inaccuracies in the results.

the sampling distribution of $p_1 - p_2$ approaches a normal distribution with mean $\phi_1 - \phi_2$ and variance given by

$$\sigma^2_{p_1 - p_2} = \frac{\phi_1(1 - \phi_1)}{n_1} + \frac{\phi_2(1 - \phi_2)}{n_2} \tag{13.3}$$

RULE 13.3a The standard error of the sampling distribution of Rule 13.3 is

$$\sigma_{p_1 - p_2} = \sqrt{\frac{\phi_1(1 - \phi_1)}{n_1} + \frac{\phi_2(1 - \phi_2)}{n_2}} \tag{13.4}$$

13.3 Approximating the Sampling Distributions of $\overline{X}_1 - \overline{X}_2$ and $p_1 - p_2$

Rules 13.2, 13.2a, 13.3, and 13.3a are not very useful as they are stated. To use these rules, we would need to know the means and variances of the two populations of X-values or the proportion of A's in each of the dichotomous populations. The situation is the same as that described in Section 11.8 with respect to the sampling distributions of $\overline{X}$, Mdn, and p. At that point we indicated that it was possible to use certain estimates of the parameters in order to describe the sampling distributions at least approximately. The same holds in the present case. Here, it is possible to obtain useful approximations of the sampling distributions of $\overline{X}_1 - \overline{X}_2$ and $p_1 - p_2$ by using sample data. The needed estimates are given below.

RULE 13.4 The following differences derived from independent random samples selected from Populations 1 and 2 provide unbiased estimates of the differences between the corresponding parameters:

$$\overline{X}_1 - \overline{X}_2 \qquad \text{and} \qquad p_1 - p_2$$

Also, by applying (11.14) we have an approximation of the variance of the sampling distribution of Rule 13.2:

$$\tilde{\sigma}^2_{\overline{X}_1 - \overline{X}_2} = \tilde{\sigma}_{\overline{X}_1}{}^2 + \tilde{\sigma}_{\overline{X}_2}{}^2 = \frac{S_1{}^2}{n_1 - 1} + \frac{S_2{}^2}{n_2 - 1} \tag{13.5}$$

Or, taking the positive square root of (13.5), we have the estimated standard error of $\overline{X}_1 - \overline{X}_2$:

$$\tilde{\sigma}_{\overline{X}_1 - \overline{X}_2} = \sqrt{\frac{S_1{}^2}{n_1 - 1} + \frac{S_2{}^2}{n_2 - 1}} \tag{13.6}$$

And applying (11.16) we have an approximation of the variance of the sampling distribution of Rule 13.3:

$$\tilde{\sigma}^2_{p_1 - p_2} = \frac{P_1(1 - P_1)}{n_1 - 1} + \frac{P_2(1 - P_2)}{n_2 - 1} \tag{13.7}$$

The estimated standard error of $p_1 - p_2$ is

$$\tilde{\sigma}_{p_1 - p_2} = \sqrt{\frac{p_1(1 - p_1)}{n_1 - 1} + \frac{p_2(1 - p_2)}{n_2 - 1}} \qquad (13.8)$$

Example Consider two hypothetical populations of fourth-grade school pupils. Suppose that the pupils constituting one of these populations have been taught a particular skill in arithmetic by Method 1 while those belonging to the other population were taught this same skill by Method 2, and that the pupils of both populations have been given the same criterion test to determine the extent to which this skill has been mastered. Assume that random samples of 50 and 65 cases, respectively, are drawn from the populations taught by Method 1 and by Method 2, that the means of the criterion scores for these samples are 100 and 80, and that the standard deviations are 28 and 24. On the basis of this information, describe the approximate sampling distribution of the difference between means.

Solution What we want to describe is the approximate sampling distribution of the statistic $\overline{X}_1 - \overline{X}_2$. Here $\overline{X}_1 - \overline{X}_2 = 100 - 80 = 20$, and hence (see Rule 13.4) $\mu_1 - \mu_2 \approx 20$. Also, applying formula 13.6, we obtain

$$\tilde{\sigma}_{\overline{X}_1 - \overline{X}_2} = \sqrt{\frac{28^2}{50 - 1} + \frac{24^2}{65 - 1}} = 5$$

Finally we know from Rule 13.2 that the sampling distribution involved is approximately normal in form. This approximate distribution is pictured in Figure 13.2.

Comments: First, it should be noted that the sampling distribution of Figure 13.2 is approximate in three respects: (1) the actual sampling distribution is only approximately normal in form; (2) the placement of the actual distribution along the scale (i.e., its mean) may differ somewhat from that of the pictured distribution; and (3) the standard error of the actual distribution may also differ from that shown. Second, it should be observed that in a practical situation in which the purpose is to evaluate experimentally the relative effectiveness of the two methods of instruction, there would exist only a single hypothetical population consisting not only of pupils now attending fourth grade (the experimentally accessible population), but also of such pupils as may attend similar fourth-grade classes in the future (the target population). Two groups of pupils selected from the currently enrolled group of fourth-grade pupils (these would usually have to consist of

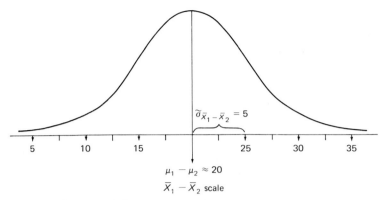

Figure 13.2   Approximate sampling distribution of difference between means of two random samples

intact classes) would then be *assumed* to be random samples from this hypothetical target population. The methods of instruction would be assigned to these groups by some random procedure, and the criterion scores for these groups of pupils would provide the information necessary for specifying the approximate sampling distribution. Thus, there always exists the additional danger in an experimental design of the type described in the example that the groups cannot, as we assumed, be reasonably regarded as random samples from two hypothetical populations of fourth-grade pupils—populations that differ only in that the pupils constituting them have been taught a particular arithmetic skill by different methods. If the assumption of randomness cannot be reasonably defended, the sampling theory that we have described is not applicable.

13.4   Testing Hypotheses about μ_1 and μ_2: An Example

In this section we show how the sampling theory developed in the previous two sections can be used to test hypotheses about $\mu_1 - \mu_2$. Consider the following problem.[5]

[5] Although the situation described in this example is imaginary and the data later presented are fictitious, it is based on experimental work conducted by Cecil M. Freeburne and J. E. Taylor ["Discrimination Learning with Shock for Right and Wrong Responses in the Same Subjects," *Journal of Comparative and Physiological Psychology*, 45 (June 1952), 264–268]; and by C. M. Freeburne and Marvin Schneider ["Shock for Right and Wrong Responses During Learning and Extinction in Human Subjects," *Journal of Experimental Psychology*, 49 (March 1955), 181–186]. It is hoped that violences done to psychological learning theory will be overlooked in the interest of developing a pedagogical example.

A psychologist reviewing reports of experimentation on the effect of punishment on learning speed was impressed by the fact that in designing their experiments the researchers endeavored to associate the punishments with failures and even with successes, but never with both failures and successes at the same time. The experimental evidence appeared to be clear that punishment following either failure or success increased the speed of learning over that occurring when no punishment was involved. What was very probably happening, the psychologist reasoned, was that the punishment itself was becoming a response cue. The increase in speed of learning, then, might be explained either in terms of differential secondary reinforcement or in terms of drive heightened by anxiety induced by punishment. At least it appeared to him that these factors had been thoroughly confounded in the experiments thus far conducted.

It occurred to him that if both successes and failures were punished, the possibility of differential secondary reinforcement would be removed. Any differences in speed of learning as compared with a no-punishment situation would be due to some motivational component such as anxiety induced by the punishment. The psychologist reasoned that the anxiety thus induced might operate in either of two ways: (1) it might heighten the drive to learn as quickly as possible, or (2) it might so frustrate the subject that speed of learning would be impeded. If the effect of punishing both successes and failures could be shown experimentally to increase speed of learning, it might be inferred that the first of these ways dominates. If the effect of such punishment could be shown to impede learning, it might be inferred that the second of these ways dominates. Finally, if such punishment had no effect, it might be inferred that these ways either tend to cancel each other out or are inoperative. In thus reviewing the situation, the psychologist also reasoned that severity of punishment would operate as a variable to influence the balance between these ways.

The psychologist decided to attack the problem experimentally with two groups of human subjects: a no-punishment group (NP), and a punishment group (P). As a learning task he decided to use a series of 20 successive right-left choices between two punch keys. He arbitrarily selected the following series, in which the total number of right (R) and left (L) were the same: R L R R L L R L L R L R L L R R L R R L.

To indicate to the subject whether or not a given choice was correct, he decided to rig his apparatus so that a buzzer tone would accompany each correct choice. Thus, the task involved trial-and-error learning of the correct sequence. As a form of punishment he decided upon an electric shock, to be applied immediately following each choice regardless of whether it was correct or incorrect. He decided a preliminary trial would enable him to determine the maximum shock each subject could stand without displaying evidence of severe discomfort. The punishment used with a given subject at the start of the experiment was this maximum shock as specifically determined for that subject. The experimenter further decided that during the course of the learning activity he would gradually increase the shock to compensate for the subject's adaptation to it. In this way he hoped to induce and maintain a maximum anxiety without at the same time causing the complete disintegration of the learning situation. As a criterion measure of learning speed he decided to use the number of trials required for two successive series of 20 correct choices. One experiment (Experiment I) designed to investigate this problem is described below.

A psychological problem: Experiment I   From a large class of college sophomores enrolled in an introductory psychology course, the psychologist selected two groups of 50 and 65 at random, and assigned them respectively to the punishment (P) and no-punishment (NP) conditions. The criterion scores he obtained are shown in Table 13.1.

Before we have the psychologist apply the technique of testing statistical hypotheses to these data, we should consider the character

Table 13.1   Criterion Scores for Two Experimental Groups in Experiment I on the Effect of Punishment on Speed of Learning

	P Group				NP Group			
28	21	23	22	40	22	16	75	11
19	18	17	18	63	34	16	40	7
9	21	16	24	8	51	33	27	58
23	14	7	15	21	23	15	45	9
14	28	17	25	27	40	76	46	34
24	19	13		88	63	16	100	
24	10	27		57	63	39	75	
21	20	19		9	45	21	75	
34	13	17		22	27	7	17	
28	16	16		16	94	28	21	
18	27	19		34	33	70	21	
30	21	6		15	8	39	69	
15	28	27		8	40	16	70	
14	15	10		22	39	10	28	
20	24	28		40	64	75	22	

P Group	NP Group
$\Sigma X = 982$	$\Sigma X = 2{,}443$
$\overline{X} = 19.64$	$\overline{X} = 37.58$
$\Sigma X^2 = 21{,}216$	$\Sigma X^2 = 129{,}685$
$(\Sigma X)^2/n = 19{,}286.48$	$(\Sigma X)^2/n = 91{,}819.22$
$\Sigma x^2 = 1{,}929.52$	$\Sigma x^2 = 37{,}865.78$
$S^2 = 38.5904$	$S^2 = 582.5505$
$S = 6.21$	$S = 24.14$

of the possible target populations. Because the problem lies in the field of human learning, the psychologist will naturally wish to be able to generalize his findings as widely as possible—perhaps to the entire population of all human beings capable of mastering the particular task. The situation might be expressed as follows.

Suppose that all human beings capable of learning the task could somehow be required to do so under the no-punishment condition. Next suppose this learning, together with any experiences accruing from it that might affect future learning, is somehow completely extinguished from all these people. Then suppose the task is relearned by all these people under the punishment condition. We thus conceptualize two hypothetical sets of learning scores. Although only one human population is involved, it will be convenient for us to think of the two sets of performance scores—one representing the totality of experience with human performance on a learning task under one condition, and the other representing this totality of experience under another condition—as *two populations* of scores to which sample findings might be generalized. These two populations of scores will be alike only if the effects of the conditions are the same.

Now it is clear that if the psychologist wishes to generalize his sample findings to two such hypothetical populations of scores, he is in the position of wishing to generalize findings based on samples taken from one pair of populations (experimentally accessible populations) to a different pair of populations (target populations). His samples must be regarded as having been taken from two hypothetical populations of scores such as might be generated from all sophomores enrolled in an introductory course in psychology in a particular college at a particular time. Therefore, before he can generalize to the target populations of scores representing all human beings, he must assume that these populations are respectively like those from which he may be presumed to have selected his samples. Clearly, if such an assumption is to be made, some justification is mandatory.

One important consideration may be of help here. People differ greatly in ability to learn. Some subjects are able to master a given learning task more quickly than others, regardless of differences in conditions. The issue at stake is not how Subject A, learning under one condition, compares with Subject B, learning under another, but rather how the overall performance of the Condition 1 population compares with that of the Condition 2 population. The concern, moreover, and this is the helpful thing, is simply a matter of *relative* comparison. Our psychologist has no special interest in the precise magnitude of the differences between whatever indexes of overall performance may be used. This magnitude, after all, is unique to the particular task. What actually matters is the answer to the question "Which, if either, of the two overall indexes is the larger?" While it may be inconceivable that either of the hypothetical populations of scores generated from the particular group of college sophomores is like its counterpart generated from all human beings, it may not be at all inconceivable that the difference between the overall indexes is in the same direction for both pairs of populations.

If this should still appear to the psychologist too strong an assumption, his only recourse is to limit his generalization. He might redefine the target populations of scores as being generated from all human adults living in the United States, or as being generated from all human adults living in the United States who are from 20 to 22 years of age, or as being generated from all college sophomores in the United States, or as being generated from all college sophomores enrolled in colleges of the same type as that which provided the subjects actually used, or as being generated from all such college sophomores enrolled in introductory psychology courses, or from the college sophomores actually studied plus all who will enroll in introductory psychology at the particular college involved during the next four or five years. Each successive suggested source is more restrictive. It is also more like the experimentally accessible population actually studied and hence involves a more easily acceptable assumption.

It is, of course, up to the psychologist to decide how far he wishes to generalize his findings. Whatever he decides, it is essential that he describe the population actually sampled so that other potential users of his findings will be in a position to make their own generalizations if his do not satisfy them. For purposes of this example we shall have him define his populations as if generated from all college sophomores enrolled in introductory psychology courses in colleges of the type that provided the subjects used. It is necessary in this case to assume that subjects taken at random from among such students in one particular college are in effect a random sample from among such students in all such colleges. This assumption is not unreasonable in view of the particular learning task under investigation. (The psychologist is well aware, however, that for many learning tasks the populations and also the overall performances would differ markedly from college to college. When this is the case, the generalizations must be limited to such students as have attended or will attend this one particular college at a time not too far removed from the year of the experiment.)

We shall now show how the psychologist applied the technique of testing statistical hypotheses.

Step 1. Statement of hypothesis.

The psychologist wished to compare the general level of two hypothetical populations of learning scores. As an index of general level, he arbitrarily selected the mean. Two means may be compared in different ways. One mean may be said to be a certain number of times smaller than the other (ratio method). Or the difference between the two means may be observed (difference method). Since the psychologist was familiar with sampling-error theory as it applies to the difference between sample means (see Rule 13.2), he decided on the latter method. Three possibilities existed: (1) that the conditions are on the average equally effective in increasing learning speed; (2) that the no-punishment condition (NP) is on the average the more effective; and (3) that the punishment condition (P) is on the average the more effective. If $\mu_P - \mu_{NP}$ represents the difference between the means of the hypothetical populations of P and NP scores, these three possibilities may be stated symbolically in terms of this difference as follows:[6]

1 $\mu_P - \mu_{NP} = 0$
2 $\mu_P - \mu_{NP} > 0$
3 $\mu_P - \mu_{NP} < 0$

The psychologist elected to test statistically the first of these possibilities. Thus, the null hypothesis is $H_0: \mu_P - \mu_{NP} = 0$. The alternatives are $H_1: \mu_P - \mu_{NP} > 0$, and $H_2: \mu_P - \mu_{NP} < 0$.

   Step 2. Selection of α.

We shall assume this experiment to be the first of its kind. We shall further assume that at the time it was conducted the thought of punishing both successes and failures would have been viewed by most authorities as an extremely radical departure from sound practice. Consequently, the psychologist would have been very greatly concerned about rejecting H_0 (the possibility that P and NP are equally effective), especially in favor of the possibility that P is more effective, if H_0 were actually true. Being extremely anxious to avoid a Type I error, he elected to let $\alpha = .001$.

   Step 3. Specification of R.

The situation as we have described it clearly calls for a two-ended R. The simplest way to specify R is in terms of the z-scale. However, to help the student see clearly the application of the sampling-error theory involved, we shall first have the psychologist specify it in terms of the scale of values of the statistic $\overline{X}_P - \overline{X}_{NP}$. According to Rule 13.2, the sampling distribution of $\overline{X}_P - \overline{X}_{NP}$ tends toward a normal distribution as the sample sizes increase (the psychologist's samples of 50 and 65 are adequate for this theory). The rule further states that this distribution has a mean equal to the difference between the means of the

---

[6] Note in the second and third possibilities that the fewer the number of trials required to learn, the faster the learning. Hence, a positive $\mu_P - \mu_{NP}$ difference indicates superiority for the NP condition, while a negative $\mu_P - \mu_{NP}$ difference indicates superiority for the P condition.

two populations involved. This implies that *if H_0 is true*, this distribution has a mean of zero. Finally, an estimate of its standard error may be made by means of formula (13.6). The computation of the values needed for (13.6) is outlined in Table 13.1. The $\sum x^2$-values were obtained by application of (7.6), and the S^2-values by application of (7.4). Substituting in (13.6) we have

$$\tilde{\sigma}_{\bar{X}_P - \bar{X}_{NP}} = \sqrt{\frac{38.5904}{50 - 1} + \frac{582.5505}{65 - 1}}$$
$$= \sqrt{.7876 + 9.1024}$$
$$= \sqrt{9.8900}$$
$$= 3.14$$

With this information the psychologist was able to graph the sampling distribution approximately as it would appear, *assuming H_0 to be true*. The sketch is shown in Figure 13.3. An obtained $\bar{X}_P - \bar{X}_{NP}$ difference greater than zero may be due either to (1) the chance composition of the particular samples drawn, or to (2) the fact that $\mu_P - \mu_{NP} > 0$, in which case H_0 is false. This latter possibility, which indicates superiority for the NP condition, will be adopted should the obtained $\bar{X}_P - \bar{X}_{NP}$ difference fall into the upper portion of R. Similarly, an obtained $\bar{X}_P - \bar{X}_{NP}$ difference less than zero may be due either to (1) chance, as before, or to (2) the fact that $\mu_P - \mu_{NP} < 0$, in which case H_0 is false. The latter possibility, which indicates superiority for the P condition, will be adopted if the $\bar{X}_P - \bar{X}_{NP}$ difference falls into the lower portion of R.

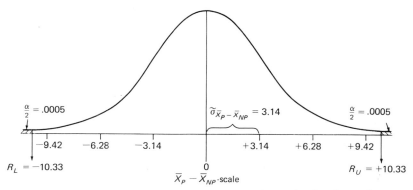

Figure 13.3 Approximate sampling distribution of $\bar{X}_P - \bar{X}_{NP}$ for $H_0 = 0$ showing starting point of upper position (R_U) and starting point of lower position (R_L) of R

Using a table of areas (probabilities) for a normal distribution (such as Table II, Appendix C), the psychologist found that .0005 (i.e., $\alpha/2$) of the area extends upward from $z = +3.29$ and that a like fraction extends downward from $z = -3.29$. He converted these two values into terms of the $\overline{X}_P - \overline{X}_{NP}$ scale by means of formula (10.4), thus for R_U, the starting point of the upper portion of R,

$$R_U = (3.14)(+3.29) + 0 = +10.33$$

For R_L, the starting point for the lower portion of R,

$$R_L = (3.14)(-3.29) + 0 = -10.33$$

Hence, R is

$$\overline{X}_P - \overline{X}_{NP} \geq +10.33 \qquad \text{and} \qquad \overline{X}_P - \overline{X}_{NP} \leq -10.33$$

To specify R in terms of the z-scale, we have only to write

$$z \geq +3.29 \qquad \text{and} \qquad z \leq -3.29$$

Step 4. Determination of the value of the test statistic.

To determine the value of the test statistic when R is specified in terms of the $\overline{X}_P - \overline{X}_{NP}$ scale, the psychologist had only to compute $\overline{X}_P$, $\overline{X}_{NP}$, and $\overline{X}_P - \overline{X}_{NP}$. He found $\overline{X}_P$ to be 19.64 and $\overline{X}_{NP}$ to be 37.58. Hence, $\overline{X}_P - \overline{X}_{NP}$ was -17.94.

Had R been expressed in terms of the z-scale the value of the test statistic z would have been obtained by application of (10.3) as follows:

$$z = \frac{(\overline{X}_P - \overline{X}_{NP}) - (\mu_P - \mu_{NP})}{\tilde{\sigma}_{\overline{X}_P - \overline{X}_{NP}}} = \frac{(19.64 - 37.58) - 0}{3.14}$$

$$= \frac{-17.94}{3.14} = -5.71$$

Step 5. Decision.

The psychologist now referred the value of the statistic (-17.94) to R and found it to lie in R. Hence, he rejected the hypothesis that $\mu_P - \mu_{NP} = 0$. The fact that the value of the statistic fell into the lower portion of R indicates further that the possibility $\mu_P - \mu_{NP} > 0$ may also be rejected, for the only acceptable explanations for a $\overline{X}_P - \overline{X}_{NP}$ difference of less than zero are chance or the fact that $\mu_P - \mu_{NP} < 0$. Chance is eliminated as an acceptable explanation when $\overline{X}_P - \overline{X}_{NP}$ falls in R. In other words, if the obtained $\overline{X}_P - \overline{X}_{NP}$ is so far below zero as to warrant rejection of zero, its value also warrants rejection of any hypothetical difference greater than zero, for it would be still further removed from any such hypothetical difference. Thus the only remaining possibility is that $\mu_P - \mu_{NP} < 0$. This, of course, means that learning occurred more rapidly—fewer trials were required—under the punishment condition than under the no-punishment condition.

Had the psychologist used z as the test statistic, he would have referred the obtained value of z (-5.71) to R expressed in terms of z. In all respects the outcome is the same.

13.5   Some Possible Explanations of the Result $\overline{X}_P - \overline{X}_{NP} < 0$

In this section we shall consider some of the possible reasons for the occurrence of an obtained value of $\overline{X}_P - \overline{X}_{NP}$ of less than zero, that is, an obtained difference in favor of the punishment (P) condition.[7]

1 The particular set of individuals in the P sample may have been more intelligent, and hence more rapid learners, than those in the NP sample.

2 The particular set of individuals in the P sample may have had more previous experience with a learning task of the type involved than those in the NP sample.

3 The particular set of individuals in the P sample may have been in better physical condition at the time of the experiment than those in the NP sample.

4 The experimenter may have unwittingly given the instructions to the subjects in such a way as to favor the P condition.

5 In scheduling the subjects the experimenter may have allotted more favorable times to the members of the P sample. (For example, the P subjects may all have been scheduled for about 9 A.M.—a time of day when all were mentally fresh and alert. The members of the NP sample, on the other hand, may all have been scheduled for about 1:00 P.M.—a time of day when all were somewhat logy following noon lunch.)

6 The room in which the P condition was carried out may have been more conducive to learning (e.g., it may have been more quiet) than that used for the NP condition.

7 The P condition may have been more favorable to rapid learning than the NP condition.

Now, of these possible reasons, only items 1, 2, and 3 may be eliminated as a result of the outcome of the statistical test, that is, as a

---

[7] It must be kept in mind that the criterion measure is such that small values indicate fast learning and large values slow learning.

result of the obtained difference falling in R. These three items give reasons why individuals differ in their ability to learn a given task at a given time. Whether one or the other of the experimental groups has an advantage as a result of any reason such as these depends entirely on the operation of chance in the selection of the particular individuals who constitute the particular samples studied. It is only reasons of this type that we eliminate when we reject statistical hypotheses.

On rejecting H_0 as a result of $\overline{X}_P - \overline{X}_{NP}$ falling in the lower portion of R, the psychologist would, of course, like to be able to point to item 7 as the explanation. Before he can validly do this, he must be in a position to show that he has conducted his experiment in such a way as to have avoided such possible competing explanations as items 4, 5, and 6. For example, he must be able to state that the same set of instructions was used with both experimental groups, that the time schedule was equally favorable to both, and that the same room was used by both. This, of course, requires careful planning. Any factor that might operate to give one group an overall advantage over the other must be either eliminated or allowed to affect both groups equally. Failure to anticipate and take into account such factors has voided much costly experimental work.

In concluding this section, we shall present a term that, up to this point, we have not employed. We refer to the term *significant*, or preferably *statistically significant*, as it is commonly applied to an observed difference. When a statistical test leads to rejection of a hypothesis of no difference between corresponding parameters of two populations, the observed difference is said to be *significant*. When such a hypothesis cannot be thus rejected, the observed difference is said to be *nonsignificant*. The term *significant* thus used simply implies that the observed difference differs from zero by an amount greater than can reasonably be explained in terms of random sampling fluctuation— that is, by an amount greater than can reasonably be explained by causes of the type represented by items 1, 2, and 3 of the above list.

Thus used, *significant* is a technical term, the meaning of which is not to be confused with that of the word *significant* as it is employed in common usage. In interpreting findings regarding significant differences, the student should be extremely careful not to infer that all such differences are necessarily of practical importance or consequence. Clearly, statistical significance is a *necessary condition* to the practical importance of any observed difference; a difference that is not large enough to warrant the elimination of chance sampling fluctuations as a possible explanatory cause can hardly be of practical importance. On the other hand, statistical significance can in no sense be regarded as a *sufficient condition* of the practical importance of an observed difference. A difference between the values of corresponding parameters of two populations may exist and, if investigated by a sufficiently powerful statistical test, may give rise to a statistically significant observed difference. Yet this real difference may not be sufficiently large to be of any practical importance in the real world.

For example, a sufficiently powerful statistical test might conceivably enable us to demonstrate that an observed difference in the mean heights of samples of United States and Canadian adult males was statistically significant. Yet the real difference in the mean heights of the two populations involved would almost certainly be so small as to be of no practical importance whatever to, say, clothing manufacturers, who in spite of the statistically significant difference can use the same distributions of clothes sizes for the two populations. On the other hand, an observed significant difference between the mean height of a sample of adult United States males and that of a sample of adult Japanese males would almost certainly relate to a real difference of some practical consequence to clothing manufacturers seeking to supply both markets. It should also be obvious in this connection that a much less powerful test would be sufficient to demonstrate significance in the case of the latter comparison than in the case of the former.[8]

13.6   A Modification of Experiment I: Experiment II

In view of the outcome of Experiment I, the psychologist wondered whether the punishment of both successes and failures was any more effective in increasing the speed of learning than punishment of failures alone. He decided to conduct a second experiment (Experiment II), similar to the first except that the experimental conditions would now involve punishment of *both* successes and failures (PB) and punishment of failures only (PF). From among students who had not participated in the first experiment he selected two groups of 50 at random and assigned them to the PB and PF conditions. The criterion scores he obtained are shown in Table 13.2.

Since, save for the change in experimental conditions, the circumstances are the same as those of Experiment I, we shall simply outline the test of the null hypothesis involved without further comment.

Step 1. $H_0: \mu_{PB} - \mu_{PF} = 0;$ $H_1: \mu_{PB} - \mu_{PF} > 0;$
$H_2: \mu_{PB} - \mu_{PF} < 0$

---

[8] Actually, when sample sizes become extremely large (say, 500) there is probably little need for testing hypotheses. Any observed difference that is of practical importance will in all likelihood be statistically significant. (Of course, performing the statistical test does no harm.) However, one of the most difficult questions to answer in educational and psychological research is: "How big a difference is important?" Unless the measuring instruments have been extensively studied, this question may be impossible to answer.

Table 13.2   Criterion Scores for Two Experimental Groups in Experiment II on the Effect of Punishment on Speed of Learning

PB Condition					PF Condition				
25	19	20	16	23	24	31	24	23	15
21	27	25	19	20	37	22	21	23	16
15	12	25	18	13	24	26	11	29	10
21	10	17	21	22	27	21	26	21	26
27	26	24	15	17	17	24	23	14	20
25	20	20	24	23	23	18	25	31	21
17	16	24	12	12	27	12	19	22	29
28	28	19	23	22	18	22	23	25	27
12	15	6	19	16	14	14	18	25	11
22	21	16	22	12	22	26	25	20	35

$$\begin{aligned}
\Sigma X &= 972 \\
\overline{X} &= 19.44 \\
\Sigma X^2 &= 20,176 \\
(\Sigma X)^2/N &= 18,895.68 \\
\Sigma x^2 &= 1,280.32 \\
S^2 &= 25.6064 \\
S &= 5.06
\end{aligned}$$

$$\begin{aligned}
\Sigma X &= 1,107 \\
\overline{X} &= 22.14 \\
\Sigma X^2 &= 26,215 \\
(\Sigma X)^2/N &= 24,508.98 \\
\Sigma x^2 &= 1,706.02 \\
S^2 &= 34.1204 \\
S &= 5.84
\end{aligned}$$

Step 2. $\alpha = .001$, as before.

Step 3. The critical region (in terms of z) is $R: z \geq +3.29$ and $z \leq -3.29$.

Step 4. Computation of test statistic, z, for the sample at hand.

$$z = \frac{(\overline{X}_{PB} - \overline{X}_{PF}) - (\mu_{PB} - \mu_{PF})}{\tilde{\sigma}_{\overline{X}_{PB} - \overline{X}_{PF}}}$$

Applying (13.6) we obtain:

$$\tilde{\sigma}_{\overline{X}_{PB} - \overline{X}_{PF}} = \sqrt{\frac{25.6064}{50 - 1} + \frac{34.1204}{50 - 1}} = 1.10$$

Therefore, if H_0 is true:

$$z = \frac{(19.44 - 22.14) - 0}{1.10} = \frac{-2.70}{1.10} = -2.45$$

Step 5. Retain hypothesis. (Why?)

13.7   Reporting the Extreme Area

The outcome of Experiment II was inconclusive. The evidence did not justify the rejection of the hypothesis at the selected level of significance, so the psychologist must retain the possibility $\mu_{PB} - \mu_{PF} = 0$ in the list of possibilities. Yet the fact remains that in the particular samples studied the PB condition was superior.[9] In fact, assuming the hypothesis to be true, the probability of a value for $\overline{X}_{PB} - \overline{X}_{PF}$ as large as the one obtained is rather small. This probability is represented by the area at the extremes of the normal distribution, that is, by the combined segments of area below and above $z = -2.45$ and $z = +2.45$. Using Table II, Appendix C, we may find this extreme area (EA) as follows:

$$
\begin{aligned}
EA &= P(z \leq -2.45 \mid ND: \mu = 0, \sigma = 1) \\
&\quad + P(z \geq +2.45 \mid ND: \mu = 0, \sigma = 1) \\
&= .0071 + .0071 \\
&= .0142
\end{aligned}
$$

This EA corresponds to the smallest value of α that could have been chosen and yet lead to a decision to reject H_0, given the particular collection of data at hand. This probability value is often included as part of the published findings of research investigations. The practice of reporting this value serves as a convenience for those readers who may disagree with the researchers' arbitrary choice of a level of significance (α), and who consequently wish to know what the outcome of the test would be had some other value of α been selected. Thus, a reader who feels that an α of .05 would have been appropriate in this experiment would in his own mind arrive at a decision to reject the hypothesis—a decision different from that made by the experimenter. The decision rule stated with reference to any arbitrarily selected α and its relation to EA is simply:

Reject if $EA \leq \alpha$; retain if $EA > \alpha$

It is important that the student realize that under no circumstances can a researcher properly delay the choice of α until the EA has been determined. The degree of control to be exercised over a Type I error, while a matter of subjective judgment, ought always to be established with complete independence of the outcome of the statistical test; the outcome of the test should in no way influence the selection of α. In the theory of testing statistical hypotheses, the level of significance, α, is an arbitrarily selected constant and not a variable. It should never

[9] Keep in mind that the fewer the trials necessary to reach the learning criterion, the faster the learning.

be confused with the EA-value, which is a random variable whose value varies from sample to sample; and this EA-value, in turn, should never be referred to as a level of significance. No information is ever gained as a result of conducting an experiment that provides an additional basis for the selection of an α-value, because all information bearing on this selection is available prior to the actual analysis of the data. It is for this reason that the selection of α has been established as a second step in the procedure. With the selection of α thus ordered, prior to the collection and analysis of the data, the temptation to manipulate α to fit the findings is removed.

Small EA-values should be interpreted with caution. A small EA is, of course, associated with a large $|z|$. While such a z implies a small likelihood of a Type I error in rejecting $H_0: \theta = \theta_0$, it does *not* *necessarily* also imply that the discrepancy between the hypothesized value (θ_0) and the observed value of the corresponding statistic (T) is of any practical importance in the real world. A large absolute value of z may result from a small difference between T and θ_0, provided σ_T is very small, that is, provided the test is very powerful. It is indeed tempting to interpret large values of absolute z or small values of EA as implying a difference of great practical importance between T and θ_0. But such an interpretation may be quite invalid.[10]

13.8   A Modification of Experiment II Using Related Samples: Experiment III

In considering the outcome of Experiment II (a difference of 2.7 in favor of the mean of the PB condition, with which an EA of .0142 was associated), the psychologist wondered if perhaps the PB condition was actually more effective in increasing the speed of learning than the PF condition. Had the statistical test resulted in a Type II error? He realized that such an error might have occurred as a sampling accident. Such an accident would result if, in spite of overall superiority of the PB condition for the population, the particular PB sample just happened to contain an unusual number of individuals who under any condition were inferior as learners to those in the particular PF sample. The psychologist knew that the probability of such a chance occurrence could be reduced by increasing the power of the statistical test. He decided, therefore, to run Experiment II a second time but to employ, this time, a variation in the experimental design that would reduce the

---

[10] In this connection the student is advised to reread the concluding remarks of Section 13.5.

standard error and thus increase the power of the test.[11] He called this modified test Experiment III.

The variation the psychologist decided to use involved attempting to control one of the possible causes of difference between the two sets of individuals who would constitute the samples to be studied. The particular cause he elected to control was the subjects' intelligence. (In Experiments I and II, this had been a random factor; see item 1, Section 13.5.) In theory, controlling for intelligence would have to be accomplished by some process such as the following.

1 Select an individual at random from the population and obtain for that individual a measure of the amount of the control variable (intelligence) he or she possesses.

2 From among the subset of individuals in the population who possess this same measured amount of the control variable, select one at random and pair him or her with the individual selected in step 1.

3 Repeat steps 1 and 2 until the desired number of pairs of individuals is obtained.

4 By a random process (e.g., the toss of a coin) assign the members of the pairs to one or the other of the two experimental groups.

The student will at once recognize the practical impossibility of carrying out this process in a real situation. In the first place, in a real situation the total pool of individuals available for experimental purposes (e.g., college sophomores enrolled in an introductory psychology course) is not usually the population to which it is desired to generalize, but is rather by assumption a random sample from this population. Thus, in step 1, the individual is selected at random from a sample rather than from the population. If this sample is, as assumed, a random sample from the population, we may assume practical compliance with step 1. The principal difficulty arises in step 2. The population subset referred to in this step is, of course, not available. The experimenter may be able to identify a sample subset from which a matching subject may be randomly selected. But what if there is no individual in the sample pool who has the same measured amount of the control variable as the individual selected in step 1? This is particularly likely to occur when the available sample pool is not very large. When this situation arises there is no way to carry out step 2. The experimenter can, of course, either discard the subject initially selected

---

[11] It should be noted that he could have accomplished this within the framework of the design previously used by simply increasing the numbers of cases in the samples.

and start over or select some subject who matches the initial subject approximately. The discard method would be the better one here. If he proceeds according to this method, he is in effect selecting matching pairs at random from the matching pairs in the sample pool. Only if the matching pairs in the sample pool may reasonably be assumed to be a random sample of such pairs as they exist in the population can the conditions necessary to the use of a control variable be regarded as having been satisfied.

Although we shall proceed with our example assuming the conditions necessary for the analysis to be satisfied, it is important for the student to recognize that this is not likely to be the case in many real situations. The method of analyzing the data that we shall present is, nevertheless, a most important one, for it is the appropriate procedure to follow in situations in which the two experimental treatments may both be applied to the same individual[12] or in which before- and after-treatment scores are to be compared for a given sample of individuals. In such situations each subject is, of course, paired or matched with himself, and the problems associated with obtaining a random set of accurately matched pairs do not exist.

In our illustrative example, let us say that the psychologist decided to delay running the experiment until the fall semester of the following year so that an entirely new class of students in introductory psychology would be available from which he could select his sample of matched pairs. Shortly after the opening of this term, he administered an intelligence test to all these students. He then selected at random a single student from among them. Next, he selected at random a single student from among the subgroup of students whose scores on this test were the same as that of the first student selected. These two students, matched in intelligence as measured by their performance on the test, became the first pair of subjects selected. The psychologist repeated this procedure until he had in all selected 50 pairs of subjects matched on the basis of their intelligence-test scores. He then randomly assigned one member of each pair to the PB condition and the other to the PF condition.

The criterion scores for each pair of subjects on the same learning task as was used in the preceding experiment, together with the differences ($D = X_{PB} - X_{PF}$) between these scores for each pair, are shown in Table 13.3. It is clear that had the psychologist picked both members of each pair purely at random without equating them, the expected variability of the D-values would be greater than that shown in the table. This follows from the fact that the matching process used

---

[12] This, of course, implies that the administration of either one of the experimental treatments to a subject has no effect on the outcome of the administration of the other.

Table 13.3   Criterion Scores and Differences between Them for Two Matched Groups in Experiment III on the Effect of Punishment on Speed of Learning

PB	PF	D	PB	PF	D	PB	PF	D
23	26	−3	21	24	−3	18	20	−2
18	16	+2	10	24	−14	24	22	+2
27	21	+6	25	25	0	23	24	−1
30	25	+5	24	24	0	21	21	0
15	17	−2	12	20	−8	22	22	0
16	14	+2	31	25	+6	23	26	−3
21	31	−10	20	24	−4	15	22	−7
24	25	−1	18	14	+4	20	28	−8
19	24	−5	24	21	+3	22	13	+9
22	26	−4	11	20	−9	24	32	−8
20	15	+5	25	31	−6	$\Sigma(-D) =$		−185
20	28	−8	25	27	−2	$\Sigma(+D) =$		+57
12	19	−7	8	25	−17	$\Sigma D =$		−128
16	20	−4	19	15	+4	$\bar{D} =$		−2.56
30	24	+6	17	24	−7	$\Sigma D^2 =$		1,796
13	21	−8	27	30	−3	$(\Sigma D)^2/N =$		327.68
23	23	0	16	23	−7	$\Sigma d^2 =$		1,468.32
20	23	−3	25	24	+1	$S_D{}^2 =$		29.3664
16	23	−7	15	21	−6	$S_D =$		5.42
17	25	−8	27	25	+2			

by the psychologist had eliminated one of the factors causing variation in D-values derived from purely random pairs. Consequently, the standard error of the sampling distribution of the means of the samples of D-values shown in the table must be smaller than that of the means of the samples of D-values derived from purely random pairs. Hence, *a test of the hypothesis that the mean of a population of D-values is zero is more powerful when the D-values are derived from equated pairs than when they are derived from random pairs.*

The extent to which an increase in power may be achieved by equating depends on the extent to which the equating factor contributes to variation in the performances of individual subjects on the experimental task. If this factor has little to do with individual variation in performance on this task, the effect of equating on the variability of D-values will be slight. That is, there will be little difference between the variability of D-values derived from equated pairs and that of D-values derived from purely random pairs. On the other hand, if the equating factor is one of the major factors contributing to individual differences in performance on the experimental task, the variability of D-values derived from equated pairs will be considerably smaller than that of D-values derived from purely random pairs. It is important, therefore, if an increase in power is to be achieved, that the factor with reference to which the members of the pairs are equated be one that makes an appreciable contribution to individual differences in performance on the experimental task. Unless this is the case there is little to be gained through application of this equating procedure.

Understanding of the experimental design under consideration requires further that the student appreciate the fact that the mean of a population of D-values is the same as the difference between the means of the two populations of X-values that form the pairs of scores. Symbolically stated in terms of our example,

$$\mu_D = \mu_{PB} - \mu_{PF}$$

where $D = X_{PB} - X_{PF}$.[13] Hence, whether we test a hypothesis about $\mu_{PB} - \mu_{PF}$ as we did in Experiment II, or about μ_D as we now propose to do, we are actually testing a hypothesis about the same value. In other words, testing the hypothesis that $\mu_D = 0$ is the equivalent of testing the hypothesis that $\mu_{PB} - \mu_{PF} = 0$.

We shall now present, step by step, the procedure followed by the psychologist in testing this hypothesis using the data of Experiment III (see Table 13.3).

Step 1. $H_0: \mu_D = 0$; $H_1: \mu_D > 0$; $H_2: \mu_D < 0$

Step 2. $\alpha = .001$, as before.

Step 3. The critical region (in terms of z) is $R: z \geq +3.29$ and $z \leq -3.29$.

Step 4. Computation of test statistic, z, for the sample of D-values at hand.

$$z = \frac{\bar{D} - \mu_D}{\tilde{\sigma}_{\bar{D}}}$$

Applying (11.19) we obtain

$$\tilde{\sigma}_{\bar{D}} = \frac{S_D}{\sqrt{N-1}} = \frac{5.42}{\sqrt{50-1}} = .774$$

---

[13] Given scores on two dimensions, X_1 and X_2, for each of N individuals ($i = 1, 2, \ldots, N$). Then for any individual, say individual i, $D_i = X_{1i} - X_{2i}$. Therefore,

$$\sum_{i=1}^{N} D_i = \sum_{i=1}^{N} (X_{1i} - X_{2i}) \qquad \text{(adding equals to equals)}$$

$$\sum_{i=1}^{N} D_i = \sum_{i=1}^{N} X_{1i} - \sum_{i=1}^{N} X_{2i} \qquad \text{(see Rule 5.2)}$$

$$\bar{D} = \bar{X}_1 - \bar{X}_2 \qquad \text{(dividing by } N)$$

(*Note:* N here is the number of D-values, i.e., the number of pairs.) Therefore,

$$z = \frac{-2.56}{.774} = -3.31$$

Step 5. Reject the hypothesis. (Why?)

Since the z-value obtained falls in the lower portion of R, the rejection of $\mu_D = 0$ implies also rejection of any μ_D-value greater than zero. Hence, the only remaining possibility is that $\mu_D < 0$, and the psychologist is able to report the finding that the PB condition is more effective in increasing the speed of learning the experimental task than the PF condition.

We thus have an example showing how the power of a statistical test may be improved without increasing sample size by means of an experimental design involving equated groups. The designs of Experiments II and III are equally effective insofar as control over a Type I error is concerned, but Experiment III is superior in the degree of control exercised over a Type II error. The power curves for these two tests are shown in Figure 13.4. The P-values plotted are given in Table 13.4.[14] It may be seen from Figure 13.4 that for $P = .95$ (i.e., for

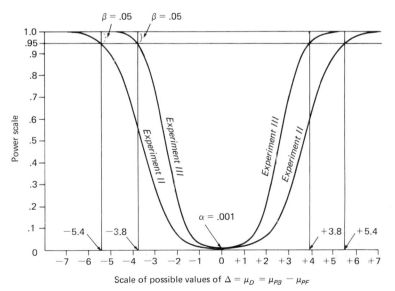

Figure 13.4 Power curves of tests used in psychological experiments II and III

---

[14] It is suggested that the student verify some of these values.

Table 13.4   Values of P Corresponding to Differences (Δ) between H_0 and Selected Possible Alternative Values of $\mu_D = \mu_{PB} - \mu_{PF}$ for Psychological Experiments II and III

$\Delta = \mu_D - \mu_{D_0}$ $= \mu_D - 0$	P_{II} $R: \overline{D} \geq +3.62$ $\overline{D} \leq -3.62$	P_{III} $R: \overline{D} \geq +2.55$ $\overline{D} \leq -2.55$
.0	.001	.001
± .5	.002	.004
± 1.0	.009	.023
± 1.5	.027	.087
± 2.0	.071	.239
± 2.5	.154	.476
± 3.0	.288	.719
± 3.5	.456	.891
± 4.0	.637	.969
± 4.5	.788	.994
± 5.0	.894	.999
± 5.5	.956	
± 6.0	.984	
± 6.5	.996	
± 7.0	.999	

β = probability of a Type II error = .05) the discrepancy between the hypothesized value of μ_D (zero) and the actual value of μ_D would have to be 5.42 trials in the case of Experiment II as compared with only 3.82 trials in the case of Experiment III.

13.9   A Problem Involving the Comparison of Two Proportions

An investigator was interested in comparing the educational achievement of present-day high school students with that of the high school students of 20 to 25 years ago.[15] He located certain achievement tests that had been used in certain high schools 20 to 25 years ago and for which results were still available. He repeated these tests with students currently enrolled in these same schools.

One of the tests thus repeated was a proofreading test of English correctness originally given in 1931. One of the sentences in the test copy read: "In my own case my greatest triumph has been the study of the old ways of working mettle."

The investigator discovered that in a random sample of 1,000 students taking this test in 1931, .36 had detected and properly corrected

[15] Joseph R. Sligo, *Comparison of Achievement in Selected High School Subjects in 1934 and 1954*, unpublished doctoral dissertation, State University of Iowa, 1955.

the spelling error involved. He further found that in a random sample of 500 students taking this same test in 1954, .54 detected and properly corrected this particular error. He wished to determine whether the difference in these two proportions was larger than could reasonably be attributed to random sampling fluctuation. To accomplish this he tested the statistical hypothesis that the proportions for the two populations represented were the same. The procedure he used and the results he obtained were as follows.

Step 1.[16] $H_0: \phi_{31} - \phi_{54} = 0; \quad H_1: \phi_{31} - \phi_{54} > 0;$
$H_2: \phi_{31} - \phi_{54} < 0$

Step 2. $\alpha = .01$

In justifying this choice the investigator wrote: "It was felt that the mistake of retaining an hypothesis of no difference between then and now populations when such a difference actually exists would be of less serious consequence than the converse error of rejecting such an hypothesis when it was actually true. Hence, to guard against the type of error felt to be the more serious, a .01 value was chosen as the critical level of significance."

Step 3. $R: z \leq -2.58$ and $z \geq +2.58$

Step 4. Computation of the test statistic, z.

Here

$$z = \frac{(p_{31} - p_{54}) - (\phi_{31} - \phi_{54})}{\tilde{\sigma}_{p_{31}-p_{54}}}$$

The standard error of the difference between two proportions may be estimated by means of (13.8). In this particular situation, however, *the two population proportions involved are hypothesized to be equal.* Hence, if the data are to be analyzed in a manner consistent with the hypothesis, the same value should be used for both p_1 and p_2 in formula (13.8).

The value to be so used should be the best possible estimate of the proportion hypothesized to be common to both populations that can be derived from the data at hand. This estimate is simply the proportion for both samples considered as one. Since p_{31} and p_{54} are means (see Section 11.6), the simplest way to obtain p for both samples combined is to apply (6.4). As it applies to the problem at hand, (6.4) may be written:

$$p = \frac{n_{31}p_{31} + n_{54}p_{54}}{n_{31} + n_{54}}$$

[16] The subscripts 31 and 54 identify the 1931 and 1954 groups.

Table 13.5 Summary of Classical Hypothesis Testing
Procedures—Large Samples

Hypothesis of Interest[a]	Test Statistic	Shape of Sampling Distribution
$H_0: \mu = \mu_0$	$\bar{X}$	$\sim ND$[b]
$H_0: \mu_1 - \mu_2 = 0$	$\bar{X}_1 - \bar{X}_2$	$\sim ND$
$H_0: \mu_D = 0$	$\bar{D}$	$\sim ND$
$H_0: \xi = \xi_0$	Mdn	$\sim ND$
$H_0: \phi = \phi_0$	p	$\sim ND$
$H_0: \phi_1 - \phi_2 = 0$	$p_1 - p_2$	$\sim ND$

[a] μ_0 = a specific value hypothesized for μ; ξ_0 = a specific value hypothesized for ξ; ϕ_0 = a specific value hypothesized for ϕ.
[b] Read "approximate normal distribution."
[c] In the equation for $\tilde{\sigma}_{p_1 - p_2}$, $p = (n_1 p_1 + n_2 p_2)/(n_1 + n_2)$.

Or

$$p = \frac{(1000)(.36) + (500)(.54)}{1000 + 500} = .42$$

Now application of (13.8) gives

$$\tilde{\sigma}_{p_{31} - p_{54}} = \sqrt{\frac{.42(1 - .42)}{1000 - 1} + \frac{.42(1 - .42)}{500 - 1}}$$
$$= \sqrt{.0002438 + .0004882}$$
$$= \sqrt{.0007320}$$
$$= .027$$

Therefore, if H_0 is assumed to be true

$$z = \frac{(.36 - .54) - 0}{.027} = -6.67$$

Step 5. Reject hypothesis. (Why?)

In this situation rejection of $\phi_{31} - \phi_{54} = 0$ also implies rejection of the alternative possibility that $\phi_{31} - \phi_{54} > 0$. (Why?) Hence, the

Table 13.5   (continued)

Mean of Sampling Distribution, if H_0 Is True	Standard Error[c]	Test Statistic in Terms of z
μ_0	$\tilde{\sigma}_{\bar{X}} = \dfrac{S}{\sqrt{N-1}}$	$z = \dfrac{\bar{X} - \mu_0}{\tilde{\sigma}_{\bar{X}}}$
0	$\tilde{\sigma}_{\bar{X}_1 - \bar{X}_2} = \sqrt{\dfrac{S_1{}^2}{n_1 - 1} + \dfrac{S_2{}^2}{n_2 - 1}}$	$z = \dfrac{(\bar{X}_1 - \bar{X}_2) - 0}{\tilde{\sigma}_{\bar{X}_1 - \bar{X}_2}}$
0	$\tilde{\sigma}_{\bar{D}} = \dfrac{S_D}{\sqrt{N-1}}$	$z = \dfrac{\bar{D} - 0}{\tilde{\sigma}_{\bar{D}}}$
ξ_0	$\tilde{\sigma}_{Mdn} = 1.25 \tilde{\sigma}_{\bar{X}}$	$z = \dfrac{Mdn - \xi_0}{\tilde{\sigma}_{Mdn}}$
ϕ_0	$\tilde{\sigma}_p = \sqrt{\dfrac{\phi(1 - \phi)}{N}}$	$z = \dfrac{p - \phi_0}{\sigma_p}$
0	$\tilde{\sigma}_{p_1 - p_2} = \sqrt{\dfrac{p(1-p)}{n_1 - 1} + \dfrac{p(1-p)}{n_2 - 1}}$	$z = \dfrac{(p_1 - p_2) - 0}{\tilde{\sigma}_{p_1 - p_2}}$

investigator concluded that $\phi_{31} - \phi_{54} < 0$, that is, that the proportion of success on this particular test item was greater in the 1954 population than in the 1931 population.

13.10 Some Remarks on the Truth of the Null Hypothesis

In recent years there has been some debate in the psychological and educational literature regarding the usefulness of the classical hypothesis testing procedure.[17] One of the most frequently voiced criticisms of the procedure is that the null hypothesis is never exactly true and, therefore, there is no need to test it. For example, in the experiment described in Section 13.4, it is certainly not likely that the mean of the population of scores under the P condition (μ_P) and the mean of the

[17] See, for example, D. Bakan, "The Test of Significance in Psychological Research," *Psychological Bulletin*, 66 (1966), 423–437; W. Wilson, H. Miller, and J. Lower, "Much Ado about the Null Hypothesis," *Psychological Bulletin*, 67 (1967), 188–196; and W. Coats, "A Case against the Normal Use of Inferential Models in Educational Research," *Educational Researcher*, 21 (1970), 6–7. Some critical responses to Coats' paper are given in the October 1970 issue of *Educational Researcher*.

population of scores under the NP condition (μ_{NP}) could be absolutely identical (i.e., $\mu_{NP} - \mu_P = 0$ precisely). In other words, it is highly unlikely that any two "treatments" could produce precisely identical results; some difference, however small, probably exists. Therefore, given sufficiently accurate measuring instruments and sufficiently large samples, such differences ultimately could be identified.

However, when an experimenter tests $H_0: \mu_1 - \mu_2 = 0$, he is really not interested in the integrity of this hypothesis at all. Rather, he is looking for evidence of its falsity. Kennedy (1970) put it this way:

> In the performance of a test on a hypothesis, the researcher desires to obtain evidence pertaining to the credibility of his alternative (or research) hypothesis. Unfortunately, the modes of logic available to precise minds at this point in history rarely permit a direct test of the research (alternative) hypothesis so as to result in a conclusion approaching proof. However, if the hypothesis of interest is structured so as to constitute the logical alternative of the null, and if the null is subjected to direct test resulting in rejection, then the credibility of the alternative hypothesis is indirectly enhanced. In short, the null hypothesis is nothing more than a "straw man" created for the purpose of being rejected so that chance artifacts may be ruled out as a determinant of the effect.[18]

13.11 Summary Statement

In this chapter we have presented some sampling-distribution theory for the difference between two normally distributed random variables. We illustrated the application of this theory to testing hypotheses about the difference between the means of two populations and also about the difference between the proportions of A-type objects in two dichotomous populations. These are instances of so-called two-sample problems as distinguished from the one-sample problems treated in Chapter 12. Table 13.5 summarizes the hypothesis testing procedures treated in both Chapters 12 and 13.

---

[18] J. Kennedy, "A Significant Difference Can Still Be Significant," *Educational Researcher*, 21 (1970), 7–9. Reprinted by permission of the American Educational Research Association.

14
Interval Estimation

14.1 Introduction

In the two preceding chapters we considered the problem of tests appropriate for determining whether certain logical *a priori* values, called hypotheses, were tenable as values of certain population parameters. The whole procedure was based on the premise that such logical *a priori* values did exist. Occasions arise in which information about the magnitude of a population parameter is of great interest and yet no logical *a priori* notion regarding its possible value exists. In such situations there can be no hypotheses to test. The problem becomes simply one of making the most informative statement possible about the magnitude of the parameter by studying a sample.

Consider the following situations.

1 A senator wants to estimate the percentage of voters in her state who favor giving foreign aid to a particular country.
2 The student personnel director at a large university wants to estimate the "average" score for the student population on each of several instruments that measure attitude toward certain aspects of the college environment (e.g., social aspects, academic aspects).
3 The State Department of Public Safety desires to estimate the percentage of fatal accidents caused by drunken driving.
4 A state vocational rehabilitation agency wishes to estimate the percentage of all clients served over the past five years who are currently "gainfully" employed.

5 An insurance firm desires to estimate the "average" yearly dental costs for families with two or more children.

In each of the above examples it should be obvious that there is no logical hypothesis to test about the specific value of a population parameter. These examples are representative of a group of problems that are problems of statistical estimation.

Situations in which there are no logical hypotheses to test are not the only situations in which statistical estimation may play an important role. In fact, they may not even be the most important. Consider the situation in which a hypothesis ($H_0 : \theta = \theta_0$) regarding a parameter (θ) of some population has been tested and rejected. Let us suppose that the value of the statistic (T) was considerably greater than θ_0 so that rejection implies elimination of the possibilities $H_0 : \theta = \theta_0$ and $H_1 : \theta < \theta_0$. This leaves us with the knowledge that $\theta > \theta_0$, provided, of course, that a Type I error has not been made. But the simple fact that θ is greater than some value θ_0 may not tell us what we need to know about θ. In fact, it may represent only a crude preliminary first stage in the development of some theory. As this development progresses toward refinement, the critical issue may well be not that $\theta > \theta_0$, but rather precisely *how much* greater. A natural second stage in our investigation consists of making the best possible estimate of the magnitude of θ from the information contained in a sample.

Consider again, for example, the problem of the principal and the superintendent as analyzed in Section 12.4. Here the outcome of the hypothesis test as reported by the superintendent to the board of education was reject $H_0 : \mu = 100$ and accept $H_1 : \mu < 100$. But suppose the president of the board says, "So the results of your investigation show that the children passing through this school are on the average subnormal in ability to learn. So far so good. *But* before I can intelligently vote on your recommendation I need to know just how far below normal this average is." Immediately the superintendent is confronted with a problem in estimation. Or consider the psychological experiment dealing with learning under a punishment condition (P) and a no-punishment condition (NP) that was described in Section 13.4. In this instance the experimenter rejected $H_0 : \mu_P - \mu_{NP} = 0$ and $H_1 : \mu_P - \mu_{NP} > 0$, and accepted $H_2 : \mu_P - \mu_{NP} < 0$. A natural extension of this experiment of possible great importance to motivation theory would be the provision of an estimate of the true value of $\mu_P - \mu_{NP}$ using the sample data.

In this chapter we shall be concerned with the problem of making such estimates. Although a comprehensive attack on this problem is beyond the scope of this book, the student should not minimize its great importance. In fact, the more refined the theories with which the student seeks to deal, the more important the issues involved in statistical estimation become.

14.2   Two Approaches to Estimation

There are two approaches to the problem of estimating the magnitude of some population parameter, θ, from the information contained in a sample: the *point* or single-valued approach, and the *interval* or range-of-values approach. The first approach yields a single value that, according to some criterion or criteria, is the "best" estimate that can be made from the information contained in the sample. Since the selection of a criterion—that is, of a definition of "best"—is arbitrary, and since a number of possibilities exist, there are a variety of ways in which point or single-valued estimates of θ may be obtained from a sample. Some of these ways lead to the use of T, the sample fact (statistic) corresponding to θ; others do not. Some indicate the use of T in the case of some parameters but not in the case of others. The theory of point estimation is extensive and is, to a large degree, based on fairly advanced mathematical concepts. Treatment of this theory is, therefore, beyond the scope of this book. In situations in which we may find it necessary to employ point estimates, we shall be content simply to accept and apply the theorists' findings. This we have already done—for example, in estimating the standard errors of the various sampling distributions we have used in testing statistical hypotheses. Rules 11.5 and 13.4 and formulas (11.11) through (11.21) all provide point estimates of certain population parameters.

The second approach involves the determination of an interval, or range of values, within which the "true" or population value is presumed to fall. Such intervals may be prescribed simply in terms of their lower and upper limits. Thus we might present the values 90 and 95 as the limits of an interval presumed to contain the value of the mean, μ, of some population. (Or the values 60 percent and 70 percent as the limits of an interval presumed to contain the true percentage of clients served by a state vocational rehabilitation agency over the past five years who are currently "gainfully" employed.) In presenting such limits, we are in effect saying that, according to the information contained in a particular sample, μ is probably some value in the interval 90 to 95.

This approach has the advantage not only of implying the fact that estimation is involved, but also, through the width of the interval, of providing some indication of the accuracy of the estimation. For example, to present the interval 85–100 as an estimate of μ suggests a less accurate estimate than would be provided by the interval 90–95. Interval estimates are at a disadvantage—in fact, cannot be used—when the estimate is required for use in subsequent calculation. An estimate of the population standard deviation is needed in order to estimate the standard error of the mean, which in turn is used in estimating the value of the statistic z that is referred to a critical region R in testing a hypothesis about the mean of some population; and the theory of testing statistical hypotheses required that all of these estimates ($\tilde{\sigma}$, $\tilde{\sigma}_{\overline{X}}$, and z) be single-valued, *not* interval. However, in all situations in which single-valued estimates are not required, interval estimates are to be preferred. In this chapter we shall consider only the technique of interval estimation.

14.3   Introduction to the Concept of a Confidence Interval

Let θ represent the value (unknown to us) of a population parameter we wish to estimate (e.g., μ, μ_D, or ϕ). That is, we wish to determine from the information contained in a sample an estimate of θ. We shall use the interval approach. This implies that we must determine lower and upper limits on the value of θ in such a way that we can be "reasonably confident" that θ lies between them. Before we can do this, we should indicate more precisely what is meant by "reasonably confident."

It would be a simple matter to specify the limits of an interval that would be *absolutely certain* to contain θ. All we would need to do is write $-\infty$ and $+\infty$ for the lower and upper limits, respectively. Of course, such an interval would be of no use whatever as an estimate. It would be like a description of the location of New York City as "somewhere in the universe." Such statements may obviously be made without collecting any information at all. We have available for use the information contained in our sample, and we would certainly be willing to sacrifice some degree of certainty to secure an estimate that would be of some practical value. Such sacrifice of some degree of certainty should always be accommpanied by a fairly precise indication either of the extent of the sacrifice or of the degree of certainty that remains after the sacrifice has been made; it is usually customary to specify the degree of certainty remaining. In the discussion that follows, the term *confidence* will be used in lieu of the phrase "degree of certainty."

In deriving an interval estimate of θ from a given random sample, we are dealing with an event of uncertain outcome in the sense that the particular interval obtained either does or does not include the value θ. If the sampling and estimating procedures were to be repeated a second time, the sample scores and consequently the interval limits would almost certainly differ to some extent from those previously obtained, owing to the operation of chance; and again the interval either would or would not contain θ. If, through repetition of the sampling and estimating procedures, a "large" number of intervals were obtained, a certain proportion of them would contain θ and a certain proportion would not. As a quantitative index of our confidence that an interval contains θ, we shall use the relative frequency (probability) with which intervals containing θ occur in the theoretical universe of such intervals that would arise from an infinity of repetitions of the sampling and estimating procedures.

Suppose that in such a universe of intervals, .95 contained θ. We shall refer to any particular one of these intervals as a 95 percent confidence interval. This does not mean that the probability that this particular interval contains θ is .95. Either this particular interval contains θ or it does not. However, we do know that for the infinite universe of intervals derived by repeated application of the same procedure as led to the particular interval at hand, the probability of intervals containing θ is .95. In other words, our procedures are of such a nature as to yield intervals .95 of which contain θ, and the particular interval at hand is a member of this universe. Indeed it may be viewed as having been randomly selected from this universe. It is important to recognize that *the value .95 may be interpreted as a probability only with reference to the theoretical universe of all such intervals.*

In a practical sense, then, our problem is one of prescribing a procedure for deriving interval limits from the information contained in a random sample—a sampling and estimating procedure which, if repeated indefinitely, would lead to a universe of intervals, some arbitrarily selected proportion of which would contain the value of the parameter (θ) being estimated. It is common practice to use either .95 or .99 as the arbitrarily selected proportion, though other values may be selected.

Before presenting the procedures for computing confidence intervals, we will use the problem of the principal and the superintendent (see Section 12.1) to illustrate the concept of a confidence interval in a relatively concrete manner. Assume that the superintendent asked the school psychologist to estimate the value of μ (the population mean IQ score) for the students who are or will be attending the principal's school. Assume further that the psychologist decided to select 65 students at random from the current student body and to administer the WISC to each child. After obtaining the IQ scores for the 65 children, the psychologist (using appropriate procedures) used the results to compute a 95 percent confidence interval for μ. Assume this is the interval 90.3–98.6. What meaning can be attached to this interval? First, we might ask, "Is μ between 90.3 and 98.6?" The answer should be apparent: we don't know, since the value of μ is unknown. What do we know? We know that if the sampling experiment were to be repeated a very large number of times, and if an appropriate estimating procedure has been used, then 95 percent of the intervals computed would contain the true value of μ. Knowing this, we can label the one interval we have computed (90.3–98.6) a 95 percent confidence interval.

The psychologist could have selected a degree of confidence other than 95 percent. A 50 percent confidence interval, for example, could have been chosen. In this instance, only 50 percent of the intervals in the universe of intervals would contain μ.

So that our discussion may be presented in general terms, we shall let the Greek letter γ (gamma) represent the arbitrarily selected proportion of intervals that would contain a particular parameter θ. While γ may be interpreted as a probability value only with reference to a universe of intervals, its magnitude certainly suggests the confidence we feel that a particular interval contains θ. If, for each interval in the universe, we were to make the statement "this interval contains θ," we would be correct 100γ percent of the time. Clearly, the more frequently our statements are correct, the more *confident* we feel about them. It is for this reason that such interval estimates are referred to as *100γ percent confidence intervals*, and that the value γ is referred to as a *confidence coefficient*.

We have already pointed out how absolute certainty ($\gamma = 1$) leads to a trivial interval estimate extending from negative to positive infinity. It should be fairly obvious that the larger the value of γ, the wider the resulting intervals will be. On the other hand, the use of a small value of γ, while resulting in narrower intervals, indicates that we lack confidence that any given interval contains θ, since we know that only a small proportion (γ) of the intervals in the universe of such intervals actually contain θ. The selection of γ, then, represents an arbitrary compromise between the degree to which we wish to be confident that the interval contains θ and the degree to which we wish to pin down our estimate of θ to a narrow range of possible values. While we naturally wish to pin down our estimate as much as possible, there is no point in doing so at the sacrifice of at least a reasonable degree of confidence that the resulting interval contains θ. As we have previously indicated, γ is usually taken to be either .95 or .99. Occasional use has also been made of the value of .90 and even of the value .50, but as a general rule the selection of any values less than .90 ought to be accompanied by special justification. As one might intuitively expect, it is always possible to improve estimates by increasing the size of the sample. If interval estimates for γ-values of .99 or .95 are too wide to suit our purpose, we should seek to narrow them by collecting more information rather than by further reducing the value of γ.

14.4   Definition of a 100γ Percent Confidence Interval

In this section we consider the general definition of a confidence interval. In the remaining sections of this chapter, we will apply this definition to obtain 100γ percent confidence intervals for specific parameters.

If we are given a random sample from some population, suppose we let

θ = the value of the population parameter to be estimated
$\underline{\theta}_1$ = the lower limit of a 100γ percent confidence interval
$\bar{\theta}_1$ = the upper limit of a 100γ percent confidence interval
T = the statistic corresponding to θ[1]
T_1 = the particular value of T for the given sample

Now suppose that the sampling distribution of T is as shown in Figure 14.1. Then $\underline{\theta}_1$ and $\bar{\theta}_1$, which prescribe a 100γ percent confidence interval for the given sample, may be defined as follows:

$$\underline{\theta}_1 = T_1 - d \quad \text{and} \tag{14.1a}$$

$$\bar{\theta}_1 = T_1 + c \tag{14.1b}$$

where d and c are distances as defined by Figure 14.1; i.e., d and c are distances such that the probability of T in the range extending from a point that is a distance c below θ (point C) to a point that is a distance d above θ (point D) is γ.

Figure 14.1 shows that, in the universe of such intervals, 100γ percent of them contain θ. This follows from two facts: (1) that for every sample yielding a T-value in the range bounded by C and D, the interval as defined by (14.1) will contain θ, while for every sample yielding a T-value not in this range the interval as defined will not contain θ (see Figure 14.1), and (2) that the probability of samples that yield a T-value in the range bounded by C and D is γ.

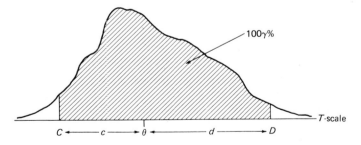

Figure 14.1 Sampling distribution of a statistic, T, corresponding to a parameter, θ

---

[1] Actually, T should be some "best" point estimate of θ. While some such point estimates are not the sample counterparts of the parameter involved, no such situations are treated in this text.

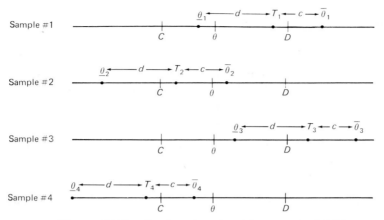

Figure 14.2 Scales showing placement of 100γ percent confidence intervals for different obtained values of T

The particular interval bounded by $\underline{\theta}_1$ and $\bar{\theta}_1$ is a 100γ percent confidence interval, since in the universe of all such intervals 100γ percent of them contain θ.

Figure 14.2 is intended to help the student grasp fact 1 above. This figure shows how the placement of a 100γ percent confidence interval varies in the case of four imaginary samples yielding for T the values represented by T_1, T_2, T_3, and T_4. The four scales shown are like the scale of Figure 14.1. The values T_1 and T_2 both fall in the range bounded by C and D, and the $\underline{\theta}$–$\bar{\theta}$ intervals are seen to contain θ. The values T_3 and T_4 fall outside of this range, and consequently the $\underline{\theta}$–$\bar{\theta}$ intervals do not contain θ. If γ were set equal to 90, then 90 percent of an infinitely large number of such intervals would contain θ within their limits.

It is important to note that (14.1) does not define a unique range from C to D for the given value of γ, because it is possible to select different sets of c- and d-distances each of which establishes a range of values (C to D) on the T-scale such that the probability of T in this range is γ. The c- and d-distances shown in Figure 14.1 could, for example, be varied by making an increase in the length of c and a compensating decrease in the length of d. The best selection of the c- and d-distances for a given value of γ is that which results in the shortest distance from C to D. In some situations this criterion may prove difficult to apply. However, if the distribution of the statistic (T) is symmetrical, the best selection consists simply in making c and d equal. This, of course, amounts to determining c and d in such a way as to make the proportion of the distribution below C equal to that above D. In fact, the practice of making the proportions of the distribution below C and above D equal is, because of its convenience, very commonly used in the case of asymmetric distributions, too—despite the fact that this may not result in the best values for c and d in the sense that the intervals are not of minimum width. The situations considered in this text are limited to situations in which the sampling distributions are symmetrical. Consequently, the values we shall obtain for c and d by making the proportions below C and above D equal are best values.

The use of (14.1) to determine $\underline{\theta}$ and $\bar{\theta}$ obviously requires that we be able to determine c and d. This implies that we must know the form of the sampling distribution. It also implies that the distances c and d must be independent not only of θ but also of any other parameters that may control the form of the sampling distribution. When c and d are functions of θ or other parameters, either a different technique must be employed or we must be content with a procedure that leads to intervals that are only approximately 100γ percent confidence intervals—that is, to a universe of intervals in which the proportion containing θ is only approximately γ. We shall use (14.1) even when c and d are functions of θ or other parameters. When the samples are large, such application of (14.1) is quite satisfactory for practical purposes—at least when applied to the problems of estimation treated in this text. In the sections that follow, we will show how values of c and d may be determined to provide approximately 100γ percent confidence intervals for a population mean (μ), a population median (ξ), a population proportion (ϕ), and the difference between two population means ($\Delta = \mu_1 - \mu_2$).

14.5 The 100γ Percent Confidence Interval for a Population Mean

Suppose we are given a large random sample of N cases from some "large" population having a finite variance. Then suppose we let

μ = the population mean
$\underline{\mu}_1$ = the lower limit of a 100γ percent confidence interval
$\bar{\mu}_1$ = the upper limit of a 100γ percent confidence interval
$\overline{X}$ = the mean of any such sample
$\overline{X}_1$ = the mean of the particular sample at hand
$\sigma_{\overline{X}}$ = the standard error of the $\overline{X}$ sampling distribution

Then by Rule 11.2 we know the sampling distribution of $\overline{X}$ to be approximately a normal distribution. This approximate sampling distribution is pictured in Figure 14.3.

Two facts are apparent in this situation. First, since the distribution is symmetrical, the distances c and d should be made equal. Second, these distances are determined entirely by the choice of γ and by the magnitude of $\sigma_{\overline{X}}$ and, hence, are independent of μ. To determine c

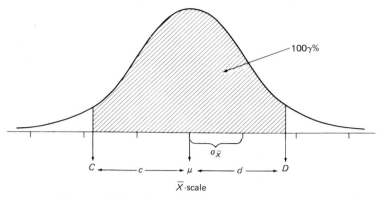

Figure 14.3 Location of C and D in the case of the approximate sampling distribution of $\overline{X}$ for large random samples

(or d) we need only (1) refer to Table II, Appendix C, to obtain the value of z such that the probability of a z in the range bounded by C and μ is $\gamma/2$, and (2) transform this z-value into units of the $\overline{X}$-scale by finding the product of this z-value and $\sigma_{\overline{X}}$. If we let $z_{\gamma/2}$ represent this z-value, we may write the following formulas for the limits of a 100γ percent confidence interval for the sample at hand.

$$\mu_1 = \overline{X}_1 - \sigma_{\overline{X}} z_{\gamma/2} \qquad \text{and} \qquad (14.2a)$$

$$\bar{\mu}_1 = \overline{X}_1 + \sigma_{\overline{X}} z_{\gamma/2} \qquad (14.2b)$$

Before we can use (14.2) to determine $\bar{\mu}_1$ and μ_1 we need to know the value of $\sigma_{\overline{X}}$. If the sample is large, we can obtain a satisfactory approximation by using (11.19) to obtain an estimate of $\sigma_{\overline{X}}$ based on the sample. This results in the following formulas.

$$\mu_1 = \overline{X}_1 - \tilde{\sigma}_{\overline{X}} z_{\gamma/2} = \overline{X}_1 - \frac{S}{\sqrt{N-1}} z_{\gamma/2} \qquad (14.3a)$$

$$\bar{\mu}_1 = \overline{X}_1 + \tilde{\sigma}_{\overline{X}} z_{\gamma/2} = \overline{X}_1 + \frac{S}{\sqrt{N-1}} z_{\gamma/2} \qquad (14.3b)$$

The values of μ_1 and $\bar{\mu}_1$ as prescribed by (14.3) are the limits of a confidence interval for which the confidence coefficient is only *approximately* γ. The approximate character of this interval is due (1) to the fact that the sampling distribution of $\overline{X}$ only tends toward a normal distribution as N becomes large, and (2) to the use of an estimate for the value of $\sigma_{\bar{x}}$. For remarks on the size sample necessary to justify the use of (14.3) the student is referred to the concluding paragraph of Section 11.5. Illustrations of the application of (14.3) follow.

Example 1 Using the data of Solution I of the problem of the principal and the superintendent, determine the 99 percent confidence interval for the mean IQ of the population of school children involved. (See Sections 12.1 and 12.4.)

Solution Here $N = 65$, $\bar{X}_1 = 94$, and $S = 20$. Also from column 2 of Table II, Appendix C, we see that $z_{.495} = 2.58$. Hence, application of (14.3) gives:

$$\mu_1 = 94 - \frac{20}{\sqrt{65 - 1}} \, 2.58 = 94 - 6.45 = 87.55$$

$$\bar{\mu}_1 = 94 + \frac{20}{\sqrt{65 - 1}} \, 2.58 = 94 + 6.45 = 100.45$$

Thus, the 99 percent confidence interval extends from 87.55 through 100.45.

Remarks:
1. As previously explained, μ either is or is not between 87.55 and 100.45. If μ is between these particular values, the only correct probability statement we can make is the trivial one

$$P(87.55 \leq \mu \leq 100.45) = 1$$

If μ is not between these particular values, the only correct probability statement we can make is the trivial one

$$P(87.55 \leq \mu \leq 100.45) = 0$$

Given the relative frequency notion of probability that we have adopted, there is no way in which the statement

$$P(87.55 \leq \mu \leq 100.45) = .99$$

can be construed as correct. Since we do not know the actual value of μ, we do not know which of the two potentially correct trivial probability statements holds. What do we know? Simply that if the sampling experiment were repeated indefinitely, and if on each repetition a pair of μ- and $\bar{\mu}$-values were obtained, then of this "large" universe of pairs 99 percent would contain μ. Table 14.1 gives intervals resulting from

Table 14.1   99 Percent Confidence Intervals for Ten Runs of the Experiment Described in Example 1

Run	$\bar{X}$	S	99% Confidence Interval
1	94	20	87.55–100.45
2	95	19	88.87–101.13
3	97	18	91.20–102.80
4	98	20	91.55–104.45
5	94	18	88.20– 99.80
6	101	17	95.52–106.48
7	99	17	93.52–104.48
8	97	21	90.23–103.77
9	100	22	92.91–107.09
10	96	19	89.87–102.13

ten imaginary repetitions of this experiment. For each repetition the interval obtained either contains or does not contain μ. We do not know μ, and hence we do not know what proportion of these ten intervals contain μ. Any particular one of the intervals (e.g., 87.55–100.45) may be viewed as having been randomly selected from the "large" universe of intervals. The larger the confidence coefficient (in this case .99), the more confident we feel that the particular interval at hand is one that contains μ. Hence the name confidence interval or, more fully, 99 percent confidence interval.

2. We shall write a specific confidence interval in symbolic form as follows:

$$C(87.55 \leq \mu \leq 100.45) = 99\%$$

This statement contains two signals reminding the reader that it is not a probability statement. First, the parenthetic expression indicating that μ is some value between 87.55 and 100.45 inclusive is preceded by the letter C (for confidence) rather than by the letter P, which is traditionally used to indicate probability. Second, the confidence coefficient γ has been multiplied by 100 to convert it to a percent, because probability values are expressed as either common or decimal fractions rather than as percentages.

3. How is it possible that Solution I, with $\alpha = .01$, led to the decision to reject the hypothesis that $\mu = 100$ while the value 100 falls in the 99 percent confidence interval just obtained? Recall that in this solution the superintendent elected, for the purpose of the decision required of her, to ignore the possibility that $\mu > 100$. Hence, the level of significance she adopted ($\alpha = .01$) actually corresponds to the use of $\gamma/2 = .49$, that is, to a γ-value of .98. As an exercise the student may wish to obtain the 98 percent confidence interval for μ using the

data of the above example. If this is done it will be found that the resulting interval does not contain the rejected hypothetical value of 100.

As was explained in the foregoing section, the 99 percent confidence interval, which we have just established by making c equal to d, is only one of an unlimited number of 99 percent confidence intervals that could be established for the particular collection of data at hand. It is possible to establish 100γ percent confidence intervals using unequal c and d or even to establish 100γ percent confidence intervals that are open at one end. For example, we might let $d = \infty$ and c be a distance such that the probability of $\bar{X}$ between μ and C is $\gamma - .50$. Then in our example,

$$c = \tilde{\sigma}_{\bar{X}} z_{.49} = \frac{20}{\sqrt{65 - 1}} \, 2.33 = 5.83$$

Now applying (14.3) we have

$$\mu_1 = \bar{X}_1 - d = 94 - \infty = -\infty$$

and

$$\bar{\mu}_1 = \bar{X}_1 + c = 94 + 5.83 = 99.83$$

Hence, $C(-\infty < \mu \leq 99.83) = 99\%$, or more simply $C(\mu \leq 99.83) = 99\%$.

This amounts to estimating the value of μ as being something less than 99.83. While this interval has the same confidence coefficient ($\gamma = .99$) as the interval previously determined, it provides a less precise estimate of μ because of its greater width resulting from the fact that its lower end is left open. By allowing c and d to differ, we could obtain different intervals all having γ confidence coefficients. As we have previously indicated, the best confidence interval for a given value of γ is in general the narrowest one, though occasional situations may arise in which only an upper (or lower) limit is needed. When the sampling distribution is symmetrical, the narrowest 100γ percent confidence interval is the one for which $c = d$.

Example 2 Using the data of Solution III of the problem of the principal and the superintendent, determine the 95 percent confidence interval for the mean IQ of the population of school children involved. (See Section 12.7.)

Solution Here $N = 50$, $\bar{X}_1 = 94$, and $S = 20$. Also from column 2 of Table II, Appendix C, we see that $z_{.475} = 1.96$. Hence, application of (14.3) gives:

$$\bar{\mu}_1 = 94 - \frac{20}{\sqrt{50-1}} \, 1.96 = 94 - 5.6 = 88.4$$

$$\bar{\mu}_1 = 94 + \frac{20}{\sqrt{50-1}} \, 1.96 = 94 + 5.6 = 99.6$$

That is, $C(88.4 \le \mu \le 99.6) = 95\%$.

14.6   The 100γ Percent Confidence Interval for the Median of a Normally Distributed Population

By rule (11.4) we know that the sampling distribution of the median tends to be approximately a normal distribution when N becomes large. Moreover, by Rule (11.4c) we know that the standard error of this sampling distribution (σ_{Mdn}) is given by $1.25\sigma_{\bar{x}}$ if the population is normal. Hence, given a large ($N > 50$) random sample, the reasoning of the foregoing section may be applied to the problem of approximating a 100γ percent confidence interval for the median (ξ) of a normally distributed population. The formulas for the lower ($\underline{\xi}_1$) and upper ($\bar{\xi}_1$) limits are as follows:

$$\underline{\xi}_1 = Mdn_1 - \frac{1.25S}{\sqrt{N-1}} \, z_{\gamma/2} \tag{14.4a}$$

$$\bar{\xi}_1 = Mdn_1 + \frac{1.25S}{\sqrt{N-1}} \, z_{\gamma/2} \tag{14.4b}$$

where Mdn_1 is the median of the particular sample at hand.

Example Using the data of Solution II of the problem of the principal and the superintendent, determine the 99 percent confidence interval for the median IQ of school children involved. (See Section 12.6.[2])

Solution

$$\underline{\xi}_1 = 93 - \frac{(1.25)(20)}{\sqrt{65-1}} \, 2.58 = 93 - 8.06 = 84.94$$

$$\bar{\xi}_1 = 93 + \frac{(1.25)(20)}{\sqrt{65-1}} \, 2.58 = 93 + 8.06 = 101.06$$

$$C(84.94 \le \xi \le 101.06) = 99\%$$

[2] In this solution $Mdn_1 = 93$, $S = 20$, and $N = 65$.

Comment: Notice that the width of this interval is 16.12, as compared with a width of 12.90 for the 99 percent confidence interval of μ obtained in Example 1 of the preceding section, in spite of the fact that N and S are the same in both instances. This is, of course, due to the fact that in this situation the median varies more from sample to sample than the mean ($\sigma_{Mdn} \approx 1.25\sigma_{\bar{x}}$) and hence cannot be as accurately estimated from a sample of a given size.

14.7 The 100γ Percent Confidence Interval for a Population Proportion

Suppose we are given an infinite dichotomous population, the units of which either do or do not belong to Class A. Then by Rule 11.3 we know that as N becomes large,[3] the sampling distribution of the sample proportion, p, of A-type units tends toward a normal distribution. The standard error of this distribution is given by

$$\sigma_p = \sqrt{\frac{\phi(1 - \phi)}{N}} \qquad \text{[see (11.6)]}$$

where ϕ is the proportion of A-type units in the population. If we apply the reasoning of Section 14.5 to the problem of approximating a 100γ percent confidence interval for the population proportion (ϕ), the formulas for the lower (ϕ_1) and upper ($\bar{\phi}_1$) limits are as follows:

$$\phi_1 = p_1 - \sigma_p z_{\gamma/2} \qquad \text{and} \qquad (14.5a)$$

$$\bar{\phi}_1 = p_1 + \sigma_p z_{\gamma/2} \qquad (14.5b)$$

where p_1 is the proportion of A-type units in the particular sample at hand.

It is obvious that these formulas cannot be applied, since the magnitude of σ_p is itself based on ϕ, the very value we seek to estimate. In other words, we are here confronted with a situation in which our method of determining confidence intervals fails, owing to the fact that the magnitudes of the c- and d-distances depend on the magnitude of the parameter we wish to estimate. However, if N is large, it can be shown that the use of

$$\tilde{\sigma}_p = \sqrt{\frac{p_1(1 - p_1)}{N - 1}} \qquad (14.6)$$

[3] For remarks regarding the size of sample necessary to the practical application of this theory, see Section 11.6.

in place of σ_p in (14.5) leads to values of $\underline{\phi}_1$ and $\bar{\phi}_1$ that, for all practical purposes, serve quite adequately as approximations of the limits of the 100γ percent confidence interval.[4] Hence, if the availability of large random samples is presumed, formulas (14.5) may be revised as follows:

$$\underline{\phi}_1 = p_1 - \tilde{\sigma}_p z_{\gamma/2} \qquad \text{and} \tag{14.7a}$$

$$\bar{\phi}_1 = p_1 + \tilde{\sigma}_p z_{\gamma/2} \tag{14.7b}$$

where $\tilde{\sigma}_p$ is as given by (14.6).

Example 1 Using the data of Solution IV of the problem of the principal and the superintendent (see Section 12.8), determine the 99 percent confidence interval for the population proportion of school children having IQ scores below 90.

Solution Here $N = 100$ and $p_1 = .36$. Hence, application of (14.7) gives:

$$\underline{\phi}_1 = .36 - \sqrt{\frac{.36(1 - .36)}{100 - 1}}\, 2.58 = .36 - .124 = .236$$

$$\bar{\phi}_1 = .36 + \sqrt{\frac{.36(1 - .36)}{100 - 1}}\, 2.58 = .36 + .124 = .484$$

$$C(.236 \le \phi \le .484) = 99\%$$

Example 2 Using the data of Solution V of the problem of the principal and the superintendent (see Section 12.9), determine the 95 percent confidence interval for the population of school children having IQ scores below 100.

Solution Here $N = 100$ and $p_1 = .61$. Hence, applying (14.7) we obtain:

$$\underline{\phi}_1 = .61 - \sqrt{\frac{.61(1 - .61)}{100 - 1}}\, 1.96 = .61 - .096 = .514$$

$$\bar{\phi}_1 = .61 + \sqrt{\frac{.61(1 - .61)}{100 - 1}}\, 1.96 = .61 + .096 = .706$$

$$C(.514 \le \phi \le .706) = 95\%$$

[4] Application of a different and more general technique for establishing 100γ percent confidence intervals, a technique beyond the scope of this text, leads to the following formula for $\underline{\phi}_1$ and $\bar{\phi}_1$.

$$\frac{2Np_1 + z_{\gamma/2}^2 \mp z_{\gamma/2}\sqrt{4Np_1 + z_{\gamma/2}^2 - 4Np_1^2}}{2(N + z_{\gamma/2}^2)}$$

14.8 The 100γ Percent Confidence Interval for the Difference between the Means of Two Populations

Given a random sample of n_1 cases from a population having mean μ_1 and an independent random sample of n_2 cases from a second population having mean μ_2, let $\bar{X}_1$ and $\bar{X}_2$ be the respective means of these samples. Then by Rule 13.2 we know that as n_1 and n_2 become large, the sampling distribution of the difference $\bar{X}_1 - \bar{X}_2$ tends toward a normal distribution having a mean of $\Delta = \mu_1 - \mu_2$, and a standard error of $\sqrt{\sigma_{\bar{X}_1}^2 + \sigma_{\bar{X}_2}^2}$ [see (13.2)]. Hence, given large independent random samples from each of two populations, it is possible to apply the reasoning of Section 14.5 to the problem of approximating the 100γ percent confidence interval for the difference between the two population means. If we let $\underline{\Delta}_1$ and $\bar{\Delta}_1$ represent respectively the lower and upper limits of this interval estimate and $(\bar{X}_1 - \bar{X}_2)_1$ represent the difference for the particular set of samples at hand, and if we use formula (13.6) to estimate the standard error of the $\bar{X}_1 - \bar{X}_2$ sampling distribution, we have the following formulas for the approximate 100γ percent confidence interval of the $\mu_1 - \mu_2$ difference:

$$\underline{\Delta}_1 = (\bar{X}_1 - \bar{X}_2)_1 - z_{\gamma/2} \sqrt{\frac{S_1^2}{n_1 - 1} + \frac{S_2^2}{n_2 - 1}} \qquad (14.8a)$$

$$\bar{\Delta}_1 = (\bar{X}_1 - \bar{X}_2)_1 + z_{\gamma/2} \sqrt{\frac{S_1^2}{n_1 - 1} + \frac{S_2^2}{n_2 - 1}} \qquad (14.8b)$$

Example 1 Using the data of the psychological problem Experiment I (see Table 13.1), obtain the 99 percent confidence interval for the difference between the means of the hypothetical punishment (P) and no-punishment (NP) populations.

Solution Here $n_P = 50$, $n_{NP} = 65$, $(\bar{X}_P - \bar{X}_{NP})_1 = 19.64 - 37.58 = -17.94$, $S_P^2 = 38.5904$, and $S_{NP}^2 = 582.5505$. Hence, applying (14.8) we obtain:

$$\underline{\Delta}_1 = -17.94 - 2.58 \sqrt{\frac{38.5904}{50 - 1} + \frac{582.5505}{65 - 1}}$$

$$= -17.94 - 8.11 = -26.05$$

$$\bar{\Delta}_1 = -17.94 + 2.58 \sqrt{\frac{38.5904}{50 - 1} + \frac{582.5505}{65 - 1}}$$

$$= -17.94 + 8.11 = -9.83$$

$$C(-26.05 \leq \Delta \leq -9.83) = 99\%$$

Comment: The minus signs simply indicate the direction of the difference. In this example they imply that the mean of the punishment population is the smaller. Since the criterion scores consisted of the number of trials required for learning, it follows that the negative limits indicate more rapid learning on the average for the punishment population.

Example 2 Using the data of the psychological problem Experiment II (see Table 13.2), obtain the 95 percent confidence interval for the difference between the means of the hypothetical punishment-of-both[5] (PB) and punishment-of-failures-only (PF) populations.

Solution Here $n_{PB} = n_{PF} = 50$, $(\bar{X}_{PB} - \bar{X}_{PF})_1 = 19.44 - 22.14 = -2.70$, $S_{PB}{}^2 = 25.6064$, and $S_{PF}{}^2 = 34.1204$. Hence, applying (14.8) we obtain:

$$\underline{\Delta}_1 = -2.70 - 1.96 \sqrt{\frac{25.6064}{50 - 1} + \frac{34.1204}{50 - 1}}$$

$$= -2.70 - 2.16 = -4.86$$

$$\bar{\Delta}_1 = -2.70 + 1.96 \sqrt{\frac{25.6064}{50 - 1} + \frac{34.1204}{50 - 1}}$$

$$= -2.70 + 2.16 = -.54$$

$$C(-4.86 \leq \Delta \leq -.54) = 95\%$$

Example 3 Using the data of the psychological problem Experiment III (see Table 13.3), obtain the 95 percent confidence interval for the mean (μ_D) of the hypothetical population of D-scores ($D = X_{PB} - X_{PF}$) for matched pairs of subjects representing the hypothetical punishment-of-both (PB) and punishment-of-failures-only (PF) populations.

Solution Here we are actually dealing with a single sample of D-scores so that (14.3) applies. Since $N = 50$, $\bar{D}_1 = -2.56$, and $S_D = 5.42$, the application of (14.3) gives:

$$\mu_{D_1} = -2.56 - \frac{5.42}{\sqrt{50 - 1}} 1.96 = -2.56 - 1.52 = -4.08$$

$$\bar{\mu}_{D_1} = -2.56 + \frac{5.42}{\sqrt{50 - 1}} 1.96 = -2.56 + 1.52 = -1.04$$

$$C(-4.08 \leq \mu_D \leq -1.04) = 95\%$$

---

[5] That is, both successes and failures.

Comment: The limits obtained here actually provide an estimate of the same parametric difference that was estimated in Example 2 above. However, the width of the interval is only 3.04, as compared with 4.32 in the case of Example 2. The increase in precision that is indicated by the greater narrowness of the interval of Example 3 may be attributed to the use of a design that has the effect of reducing the standard error of the sampling distribution through the equating of one of the factors (intelligence) that in Experiment II contributed to random variation. Just as reduction in the magnitude of a standard error improves the power of a test of a statistical hypothesis, so also does such a reduction increase the precision of an interval estimate.

14.9   Summary Statement

This chapter was primarily concerned with the definition and interpretation of confidence intervals. Specific procedures for establishing confidence intervals for μ, $\mu_1 - \mu_2$, μ_D, ξ, and ϕ were presented. These procedures are straightforward. Once the appropriate formula is identified, it is necessary only to "plug-in" the appropriate values for the data at hand and perform the arithmetic computations prescribed by this formula.

The correct interpretation of a confidence interval is a more difficult feature of the concept than its calculation. We have repeatedly emphasized that for any given confidence interval the parameter being estimated is either in the interval or not in the interval. For example, if a particular 90 percent confidence interval for μ is $C(25 \leq \mu \leq 35)$, then either μ is between 25 and 35 or it is not. The 90 percent indicates only that if the experiment were repeated a "large" number of times and for each repetition a 90 percent confidence interval for μ were calculated, then 90 percent of the universe of intervals thus formed would contain μ. Since 90 percent of all possible intervals would contain μ, 90 percent represents the degree of confidence we feel that a specific interval actually contains the μ-value of interest.

15

Some Small-Sample
Theory and Its Application

15.1　Introduction

In the chapters on testing statistical hypotheses and on interval estimation, repeated references were made to the approximate character of the techniques presented. Consider the test of a statistical hypothesis about the mean of *any* population.[1] As one test statistic we used

$$z = \frac{\overline{X} - \mu_0}{\tilde{\sigma}_{\overline{X}}}$$

Assuming the hypothesis to be true (i.e. assuming $\mu = \mu_0$), we interpreted this z as a normally distributed random variable with mean zero and variance one. Actually, this interpretation is only approximately correct. In order for it to be exactly correct, $\overline{X}$ would have to be normally distributed and its standard error ($\sigma_{\overline{X}}$) would have to be known. Thus our interpretation is approximate on two counts. First, unless the population sampled is normal, the sampling distribution of $\overline{X}$ only *tends* toward a normal distribution as N becomes large (see Rule 11.2); and second, an estimate is used in place of the true value of the standard error of this $\overline{X}$ sampling distribution.

Now there is nothing wrong with using approximations, so long as they are sufficiently accurate to meet the practical demands of the situation. This is true of our interpretation of the above z so long as the samples used are fairly large, say at least 50. If, however, circumstances preclude securing large samples, our interpretation may become too inaccurate to be of practical use. In such situations, we need a new theory that will provide a test statistic that can be more accurately interpreted regardless of the sample size.

In testing statistical hypotheses we establish a critical region in

---

[1] The population must be large and have a finite variance (see Rule 11.2).

terms of the scale of values of the test statistic, such that, if the hypothesis under test is true, the probability of a value of the test statistic in this region would correspond to some arbitrarily selected probability value (α) called the level of significance. This probability value represents the degree of control exercised over a Type I error. Thus if, as in Solution III (Section 12.7) of the problem of the principal and the superintendent, we let $\alpha = .01$ and establish the critical region (R) as that portion of the z-scale extending downward from -2.33, and if the hypothesis (H_0) under test is true, then we could expect to obtain values of z in R one one-hundredth of the time in a large number of repetitions of the test. That is, we would reject this true H_0 1 percent of the time in the long run. Now, if the test statistic is only approximately normally distributed with mean zero and variance one, then it follows that our control over a Type I error is only *approximately* α. In short, our only approximate knowledge of the sampling behavior of the test statistic means that we are able to exercise only approximate control over Type I errors. If the actual control corresponds closely to the selected value of α, the test is appropriate in spite of its approximate character. On the other hand, if the actual probability of the test statistic falling in R differs markedly from this value of α, the test is inappropriate. For example, if with a small sample the actual probability of a z below -2.33 is, say, ten instead of one per hundred, then the use of z as a test statistic would be clearly inappropriate, for instead of the desired degree of control of .01 over the relative frequency of occurrence of a Type I error, the actual long-run relative frequency of such errors would be .10.

> **DN 15.1**   Statistical hypothesis tests based on test statistics for which the sampling distributions are exactly known if the hypothesis is true are called *exact tests*.

With exact tests we are in a position to determine exactly the probability of the test statistic (T) falling in some specified critical region (R) if the hypothesis (H_0) is true. That is to say, we are able to control exactly the probability of a Type I error for a given R. This, in turn, implies that whenever the exact sampling distribution involved is continuous, we can establish an R for any selected level of significance and know that the probability of T in this R is exactly α if H_0 is true.[2]

---

[2] Some very useful statistics—the sample proportion, for one—have exact probability (sampling) distributions that are discrete. In situations involving these statistics, the critical region consists of a set of discrete points rather than a portion of a continuous scale, and it may not be possible to establish an R for any value of α such that the probability of T in R is exactly α if H_0 is true. Nevertheless, the use of the exact sampling distribution in such situations does make it possible to determine exactly the probability of T in any R if H_0 is true, so that while we may not have complete freedom in the choice of α, at least we can determine the exact probability of a Type I error for a given R. An exact sampling distribution that is discrete is discussed in Section 15.11.

15.2   A New Interpretation of an Old Test Statistic

Consider again the test of a statistical hypothesis about a population mean. We pointed out in the foregoing section that our interpretation of the test statistic $z = (\overline{X} - \mu_0)/\hat{\sigma}_{\overline{X}}$ was approximate for two reasons. First, the sampling distribution of $\overline{X}$ only tends toward a normal distribution as N becomes large; and second, an estimated rather than true value of the standard error is employed. Now, if the populations with which we deal *are normally distributed*, the first of these reasons for the approximate character of our interpretation of z is eliminated. This follows from the fact that means of random samples taken from normally distributed populations are also normally distributed regardless of sample size (see Rule 11.1). Hence, if we are willing to restrict ourselves to dealing with normally distributed populations, we can in a sense cut our problem in half. We need be concerned only with the effect on our interpretation of z of using an estimated rather than a true value of the standard error of the mean.

Limiting ourselves, then, to dealing with normally distributed populations, the problem becomes one of describing how an infinity of values of the test statistic

$$\frac{\overline{X} - \mu_0}{\hat{\sigma}_{\overline{X}}} = \frac{\overline{X} - \mu_0}{S/\sqrt{N - 1}} = \frac{\overline{X} - \mu_0}{S}\sqrt{N - 1}$$

would be distributed if it is assumed that the hypothesis is true. Of course, when N is large, this test statistic may be approximately interpreted as a z, i.e., as having an approximately normal sampling distribution with mean zero and variance one. But the smaller the value of N, the less valid this approximate interpretation becomes. This suggests that different interpretations may be needed for different size samples.

It is customary to designate this "new" test statistic by the letter t in order to distinguish between it, as we shall come to interpret it for small samples, and z. Assuming the population to be normally distributed and the hypothesis to be true, mathematical statisticians have determined the exact manner in which t is distributed for samples of any given size.[3] This means that it is possible to establish a critical region (R) in terms of the t-scale in such a way that if the hypothesis is true, the probability of a t in R is exactly α. Hence, through the use of t as

---

[3] The original derivation of this distribution is due to an eminent British statistician, William Sealy Gosset, who, because of a ruling of his employers (Guinness Brewery, Dublin) regarding publication of research findings, wrote under the pseudonym of "Student." As a result, the sampling distribution of t has come to be known as "Student's distribution."

a test statistic, we have a test of a hypothesis about the mean of a normally distributed population which provides for exact control over the expected or long-run frequency of a Type I error.

Instead of describing at this point the distribution of this particular t, we shall turn our attention to a somewhat more general treatment of this test statistic.

15.3   The *t*-Statistic and Its Sampling Distribution

Let T represent any normally distributed statistic and let μ_T represent the mean of its distribution. Also let $\tilde{\sigma}_T$ represent a *particular* estimate of the standard error of this statistic. We shall not attempt here a general statement of the particular type of estimate of standard error required by this theory. Instead we shall present for each application of this theory a specific formula for the estimate ($\tilde{\sigma}_T$) involved. It is sufficient for our purpose that the student simply recognize that not all conceivable estimates of the standard error of T are appropriate to the theory.

Mathematicians have shown that the sampling distributions of the statistic

$$t = \frac{T - \mu_T}{\tilde{\sigma}_T} \tag{15.1}$$

is exactly described by the mathematical curve

$$y = \frac{C}{[1 + (t^2/df)]^{(df+1)/2}} \tag{15.2}$$

where df is a function of sample size and C is a rather complicated constant the value of which depends on that of df.[4] Table 15.1 shows the values of y corresponding to selected values of t for df-values of 3, 15, 29, and infinity. Plots of these curves except for $df = 29$ are shown in Figure 15.1. For the purpose to which we will put this theory it is not necessary that students be able to verify the values given in Table 15.1. It is sufficient that they acquire a general knowledge of the

---

[4] This value is as follows.

$$C = \frac{[(df - 1)/2]!}{\sqrt{\pi df}[(df - 2)/2]!}$$

The df-value is discussed in Section 15.4. Note here that df is to be interpreted as a single symbol and not as the product of d times f.

Table 15.1   Ordinates of t-Curve for Selected Values of t and df

t	$df = 3$	$df = 15$	$df = 29$	$df = \infty$
.0	.368	.392	.396	.399
± .5	.313	.344	.348	.352
±1.0	.207	.234	.238	.242
±1.5	.120	.128	.129	.130
±2.0	.068	.059	.058	.054
±2.5	.039	.024	.021	.018
±3.0	.023	.009	.007	.004
±3.5	.014	.003	.002	.001
±4.0	.009	.001	.001	.000

characteristics of sampling distributions modeled by (15.2). The more important of these characteristics are as follows.

1 *As the value of df approaches infinity, the t-curve approaches the normal curve for which $\mu = 0$ and $\sigma = 1$.* In other words, as df becomes large, t-values may be interpreted as z-values.[5] That the approach is quite rapid is obvious from a comparison of the curves for $df = 15$ and for $df = \infty$ as shown in Figure 15.1, and also from a comparison of the y-values given in Table 15.1 for the curves for which $df = 29$ and $df = \infty$.

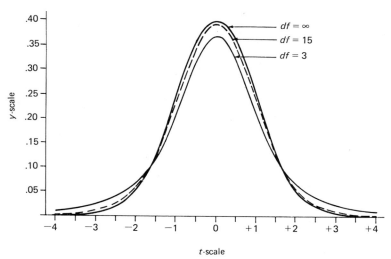

Figure 15.1   The t-curves for the df-values of 3, 15, and ∞

[5] Compare the ordinates corresponding to the t-values for $df = 29$ and for $df = \infty$ in Table 15.1 with the ordinates (the y-values) corresponding to the same z-values in Table II, Appendix C.

2 *The t-curve is symmetrical and bell-shaped with center at $t = 0$. It varies in form with the value of df.* When *df* is small, the proportion of the area of the *t*-curve beyond extreme *t*-values is much greater than that of the normal curve beyond corresponding *z*-values. For example, in the normal curve, .023 of the area lies above $z = +2$, but in the *t*-curve for $df = 3$, .070 of the area lies above $t = +2$. There are, then, many different *t*-curves represented by (15.2)—one for each value of *df*.

3 *For t-values arising from the repetition of a particular sampling experiment, there is a particular t-curve that provides an exact model of the sampling distribution of the statistic t for that experiment.* The problem, of course, is to select from among all *t*-curves the particular one that is appropriate as a model in the given situation. This is done through use of the *df*-value. Section 15.4 treats the role of the *df*-value in this sampling theory.

4 *The area under any t-curve is unity.* This must be true of any curve that serves as a model of a sampling distribution, since such distributions are by definition relative frequency distributions (or probability distributions). Since the area of the portion of the curve above a designated segment of the *t*-scale is interpreted in the model as representing the frequency of *t*-values in this segment of the scale, and since the total area under the curve is unity, it follows that the area above such a segment represents the relative frequency or probability of *t*-values occurring in this segment of the scale (see Section 9.10).

15.4   Degrees of Freedom

Thus far we have simply referred to the *df* of (15.2) as representing some value that affects the form of the *t*-curve. The letters *df* are the initials of the key words in the phrase *degrees of freedom*. The concept of degrees of freedom as it applies to a statistic is fundamentally mathematical and is difficult to explain intuitively. We shall, therefore, not attempt a rational development of this concept. Instead we shall be content to state that *the number of degrees of freedom of a statistic is always some function of the number of observations from which the statistic is computed*, a function that enters into the mathematical formula for the sampling distribution of the statistic in such a way as to influence the form of this distribution. Thus a particular statistic may not have a single sampling distribution but rather a *family* of distributions, each member of which is the appropriate distribution for a given value of this function, that is, for a given number of degrees of freedom.

The number of degrees of freedom of a statistic is used in statistical work simply to identify the particular mathematical curve that serves as an appropriate model for the sampling distribution of the given statistic. If the *df*-value for a particular *t*-statistic were 3, the *t*-curve for which $df = 3$ (see Figure 15.1) would be used as the model of the sampling distribution of this statistic. If the *df*-value for a particular *t* were 15, the *t*-curve for which $df = 15$ would be used. A rule for determining the number of degrees of freedom of a statistic follows.

RULE 15.1   The number of degrees of freedom of a given statistic (T) is equal to the number of observations involved minus the number of necessary auxiliary values used in the computation of T. These auxiliary values are themselves derived from the observations.

Consider as an example the estimated standard error of the sampling distribution of $\overline{X}$ as given by

$$\tilde{\sigma}_{\overline{X}} = \frac{S}{\sqrt{N-1}} = \frac{1}{\sqrt{N-1}} \sqrt{\frac{\sum (X_i - \overline{X})^2}{N}}$$

This statistic ($\tilde{\sigma}_{\overline{X}}$) is based on N scores or observations. To compute $\tilde{\sigma}_{\overline{X}}$ it is first necessary to compute S. But in order to compute S, *one* auxiliary value is necessary. This is the value of the point from which the deviation of each observation is measured in computing S. We use as the value of this point the mean of the observations ($\overline{X}$). Hence, the number of degrees of freedom of the statistic $\tilde{\sigma}_{\overline{X}}$ is simply *one less than the number of observations*, i.e., $N - 1$.

The beginning student of statistics may expect to experience some difficulty in applying this rule. Hence, we shall follow the practice of providing a formula for *df* that is specific to each application of *t* as a test statistic that we present in this text.

In concluding this section we shall state a rule for selecting that member of the *t*-curve family of (15.2) that is appropriate as a model for the sampling distribution of *t* as defined by (15.1) in a particular sampling situation.

RULE 15.2   The *t*-curve that is appropriate as a model of the sampling distribution of *t* in a given sampling experiment is that *t*-curve for which the value of *df* is the same as that of $\tilde{\sigma}_T$.

15.5   Tables of Areas for *t*-Curves

As we have indicated, we shall use *t*-curves as models of sampling distributions of the *t*-statistic. In using *t* as a statistic to test statistical hypotheses, we shall need to designate portions of the *t*-scale as critical regions. This implies that we must have information regarding the

Table 15.2   Probability Points of t-Curves

$P^a = .25$	.20	.10	.05	.025	.01	.005	.001	.0005
df $2P^b = .50$	.40	.20	.10	.05	.02	.01	.002	.001
3 .77	.98	1.64	2.35	3.18	4.54	5.84	10.21	12.92
15 .69	.87	1.34	1.75	2.13	2.60	2.95	3.73	4.07
29 .68	.85	1.31	1.70	2.04	2.46	2.76	3.40	3.66
∞ .67	.84	1.28	1.64	1.96	2.33	2.58	3.09	3.29

[a] *One-ended probability values.*
[b] *Two-ended probability values.*

areas of the portions of the various t-curves lying above designated segments of the t-scale, for otherwise we have no basis for establishing critical regions corresponding to our selected levels of significance.

It would, of course, be possible to develop for each t-curve a table of areas similar to that given for the normal curve in Table II, Appendix C. This would imply a voluminous collection of at least 30 such tables (perhaps after $df = 30$ the t-curve would be enough like the normal curve to justify the use of z as an approximate test statistic). However, we usually select our levels of significance from among the values .001, .01, .02 or .025, .05, .10, and .20, and our critical regions are simply located at one, or the other, or both ends of the t-scale. Hence, the only information we really need about t-curve areas is that which would enable us to establish critical regions for these selected levels of significance. We can organize all the area information we need for at least 30 t-curves into a one-page table. Table 15.2 shows how such a table may be organized. A complete table is given as Table IV, Appendix C.

In Table 15.2 (and in Table IV, Appendix C), the df-values by means of which we select the appropriate curve are given in the left-hand column. Thus each row of this table applies to a different t-curve. There are two headings for each of the other columns of this table. Those labeled P are one-ended probability values; those labeled $2P$ are two-ended probability values. The df and P (or $2P$) values are values with which the table is entered. The value read out is the particular value of t, say t_1, such that $P(t \geq t_1 \mid df) = P$ when the table is entered with P. When the table is entered with $2P$ the value read out is the value t_1 such that $P(|t| \geq t_1 \mid df) = 2P$. The table is designed to give the point on the appropriate t-scale at which the critical region (R) of a hypothesis test would start. If the R is to be located entirely at the upper end, the table is entered with $P = \alpha$ and the t_1-value read out is the starting point of the R that extends upward from that point. Since the t-curve is symmetrical about zero, the negative of t_1 is the starting point when R is located entirely at the lower end of the distribution; in this case the region extends downward from $-t_1$. For two-ended R's the table is entered with $2P = \alpha$. The positive value of the t_1 read out is the starting point of the upper portion of the R, and the negative value of this t_1 is the starting point of the lower portion.

Example 1 If df is 3 and the level of significance (α) is .05, establish a critical region (R) that is located entirely at the upper end of the t-scale.

Answer $R: t \geq +2.35$.

Example 2 If $df = 3$ and $\alpha = .05$, establish an R that is located in its entirety at the lower end of the t-scale.

Answer $R: t \leq -2.35$.

Example 3 If $df = 3$ and $\alpha = .05$, establish a two-ended R with area of $\alpha/2$ at each end.

Answer $R: t \leq -3.18$ and $t \geq +3.18$.

Comment: This R could also be designated $|t| \geq 3.18$. Here the vertical bars indicate that the absolute value (i.e., the value without regard to sign) of t must equal or exceed 3.18.

15.6   The Use of *t* as a Test Statistic to Test a Hypothesis about the Mean of a Normally Distributed Population

If we restrict ourselves to dealing with normally distributed populations, the sampling distribution of $\overline{X}$ for random samples of size N will be normally distributed with mean corresponding to the population mean μ (see Rule 11.1). Hence, $\overline{X}$ and μ comply with the requirements established for T and μ_T in Section 15.3. Moreover, it is shown in mathematical statistics that $\tilde{\sigma}_{\overline{X}} = S/\sqrt{N-1}$ is an estimate of the standard error of $\overline{X}$ that satisfies the conditions imposed on the $\tilde{\sigma}_T$ of (15.1). Also, as we have already shown in Section 15.4, the number of degrees of freedom associated with $\tilde{\sigma}_{\overline{X}}$ is $N - 1$. Hence, substituting respectively $\overline{X}$, μ, and $S/\sqrt{N-1}$ for T, μ_T, and $\tilde{\sigma}_T$ in (15.1), we obtain

$$t(df = N - 1) = \frac{\overline{X} - \mu}{\tilde{\sigma}_{\overline{X}}} = \frac{\overline{X} - \mu}{S/\sqrt{N-1}}$$

$$= \frac{\overline{X} - \mu}{S}\sqrt{N-1} \qquad (15.3)$$

To use this t as a test statistic to test a hypothesis about the mean of a normally distributed population, we substitute for μ in (15.3) the value hypothesized for it. If this hypothesis is true, the long-run probability of a t in the critical region will correspond exactly to the selected level of significance. If this hypothesis is false, the probability of a t in the critical region will be somewhat greater, depending, of course, on the magnitude of the error in the hypothesized value.

Example Consider once again the problem of the principal and the superintendent. Suppose that the superintendent follows the approach previously described as Solution I, except that instead of instructing the school psychologist to obtain WISC IQ scores for a random sample of 65 children, she instructs her to obtain such scores for a random sample of only 5 children. Assume the scores reported by the psychologist are 59, 65, 107, 89, and 80. The superintendent's application of t as a test statistic to the solution of her problem is outlined below.

Step 1. $H_0: \mu = 100;\quad H_1: \mu > 100$

Step 2. $\alpha = .01$ (as in Solution I).

Step 3. $R: t \leq -3.75$

(*Note: df* $= N - 1 = 5 - 1 = 4$. The R for $df = 4$ and $\alpha = .01$ is given in Table IV, Appendix C.)

Step 4. Calculation of the test statistic, t, for the sample at hand.

$$\sum X = 59 + 65 + 107 + 89 + 80 = 400$$
$$\overline{X} = 80 \quad \text{and} \quad (\sum X)^2/N = 32,000$$
$$\sum X^2 = 3,481 + 4,225 + 11,449 + 7,921 + 6,400 = 33,476$$
$$\sum x^2 = 33,476 - 32,000 = 1,476 \qquad [\text{see } (7.6)]$$
$$S^2 = 1,476/5 = 295.2$$

and

$$S = 17.18 \qquad\qquad [\text{see } (7.4) \text{ and } (7.5)]$$

Therefore,

$$\tilde{\sigma}_{\overline{X}} = \frac{17.18}{\sqrt{5-1}} = \frac{17.18}{2} = 8.59$$

and

$$t = \frac{80 - 100}{8.59} = \frac{-20}{8.59} = -2.33 \qquad [\text{see } (15.3)]$$

Step 5. Decision. Retain the hypothesis. (Why?)

It will be instructive to indicate R in terms of the scale of possible values for $\overline{X}$. From (15.3), we have

$$\overline{X} = \left(\frac{S}{\sqrt{N-1}}\right) t + \mu_0 \qquad (df = N - 1) \qquad (15.4)$$

Substituting in (15.4), we obtain

$$\overline{X} = \frac{17.18(-3.75)}{\sqrt{5-1}} + 100 = -32.21 + 100 = 67.79$$

Hence, in terms of the $\overline{X}$-scale the critical region is

$$R: \overline{X} \leq 67.79 \approx 67.8$$

In Solution I, with a sample of 65 children, the critical region was found to be

$$R: \overline{X} \leq 94.2$$

That is, in Solution I ($N = 65$), a sample mean of 94.2 or less constitutes sufficient evidence to discredit the hypothesis that $\mu = 100$, whereas when N is as small as 5 (as in the present example), a sample mean of 67.8 or less is necessary to discredit this same hypothesis. This suggests that our small-sample test is not very powerful: unless the difference between the parameter and the value hypothesized for it is very great, our small-sample test is not likely to detect it. The use of small samples is likely to lead to frequent commission of Type II errors (retention of false hypotheses).

Figure 15.2 provides a more definite indication of what may be expected in the way of power from a small-sample test of a hypothesis about a population mean. The figure shows the power curves for the statistical test used in Solution I of the problem of the principal and the superintendent and for the small-sample statistical test as applied above to the solution of this same problem. The power curve labeled $N = 65$ is the same curve as is pictured in Figure 12.6, the appearance of greater steepness being due entirely to the choice of scale unit. The curve labeled $N = 5$ is the power curve for a t-test based on samples of five cases applied to the same problem. The technique of constructing this latter curve is beyond the scope of this text. Its interpretation, however, follows precisely along the same lines as that of the other power curves we have studied. From Figure 15.2 we may note that:

1 Both tests are equally effective with respect to control over a Type I error. This, of course, follows from the fact that a .01

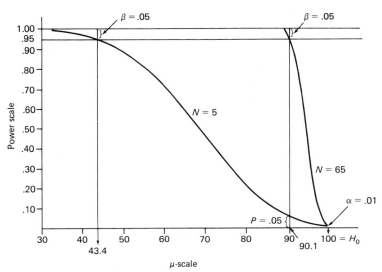

Figure 15.2 Power curves for statistical tests regarding a population mean

level of significance was used in both instances. The figure shows that when $\mu = 100$ (the value hypothesized) the probability of wrongly rejecting the hypothesis (i.e., of making a Type I error) is .01.

2 The probability ($\beta = 1 - P$) of a Type II error in the case of the test of Solution I ($N = 65$) is .05 when $\mu = 90.1$. That is, when μ differs from the value hypothesized for it by 9.9, the probability of wrongly retaining the false hypothesis that $\mu = 100$ is .05 when $N = 65$.

3 When μ differs from the value hypothesized by 9.9, the probability of a Type II error in the case of the t-test is between .95 and .96.

4 In order for the probability of a Type II error in the case of the t-test to be as small as .05, the actual value of μ must be 43.4; it must differ from the value hypothesized by 56.6 IQ points.

It is obvious from the foregoing that the use of small samples results in an extremely severe loss in terms of the power of the test to detect falsity in the hypothesis. Clearly, *small samples should be employed only when circumstances preclude the selection and use of large samples.*

It is also very important to keep in mind the fact that the foregoing small-sample theory is valid only for normally distributed populations. Strictly speaking, if it is not reasonable to assume that the population involved is normally distributed, the use of t as a test statistic is inappropriate. We shall have more to say about this later.

15.7   The Use of t as a Test Statistic to Test the Hypothesis of No Difference between the Means of Two Normally Distributed Populations

In this section we are concerned with the application of small-sample t-test theory to the problem of testing the hypothesis that the means of two populations are equal. As in the case of the application of this theory to the testing of hypotheses about the magnitude of a population mean, we must restrict our area of operation to populations that are normally distributed. We shall consider this problem in two cases.

Case I: Independent random samples from equally variable populations In this first case it is assumed that we have selected our samples independently and at random from two populations that are equally variable, i.e., have equal variances. The requirement that the populations have equal variances can only impose a further limitation on the general applicability of our test. The test now is completely appropriate only in situations in which the two populations involved are both equally variable and normally distributed.[6]

Let the populations be designated as 1 and 2. We shall use these numbers as subscripts in identifying various population or sample characteristics. For example, we shall use μ_1 and μ_2 to represent respectively the means of Populations 1 and 2. Similarly, $\overline{X}_1$ and $\overline{X}_2$ will be used to represent means of independent random samples selected respectively from Populations 1 and 2. Now if the populations are normally distributed it follows from Rule 11.1 that the sampling distribution of both $\overline{X}_1$ and $\overline{X}_2$ are also normally distributed regardless of sample sizes. It further follows from Rule 13.1 that the sampling distribution of $\overline{X}_1 - \overline{X}_2$ is normally distributed with mean equal to $\mu_1 - \mu_2 = \Delta$. Therefore, $\overline{X}_1 - \overline{X}_2$ and Δ satisfy the requirements imposed on the T and μ_T of (15.1). Hence, to apply (15.1) to this situation it remains for us only to discover the particular estimate of the standard error $(\tilde{\sigma}_{\overline{X}_1 - \overline{X}_2})$ of the sampling distribution of $\overline{X}_1 - \overline{X}_2$ that meets the requirements of the t-theory and then to establish its degrees of freedom.

It is in connection with the problem of obtaining $\tilde{\sigma}_{\overline{X}_1 - \overline{X}_2}$ that mathematical statisticians found it necessary to impose the restriction

---

[6] We shall have more to say about the importance of these assumptions in Section 15.9.

that the populations be equally variable. If the populations are equally variable, that is, if $\sigma_1{}^2 = \sigma_2{}^2 = \sigma^2$, the best estimate that we can obtain for this common variance (σ^2) is one based on a pooling of the information contained in both samples. The mathematical statisticians have shown that an unbiased estimate of this common variance results from a sort of weighted averaging of the sample variances. If we let the variances of the samples from Populations 1 and 2 be represented by $S_1{}^2$ and $S_2{}^2$, and if we let n_1 and n_2 represent the sizes of the respective samples, then an unbiased estimate of the common population variance is given by

$$\tilde{\sigma}^2 = \frac{n_1 S_1{}^2 + n_2 S_2{}^2}{n_1 + n_2 - 2} \tag{15.5}$$

The mathematical statisticians have further shown that if this $\tilde{\sigma}^2$ is used in place of both $\sigma_1{}^2$ and $\sigma_2{}^2$ in (13.2), i.e., if we write

$$\tilde{\sigma}_{\overline{X}_1 - \overline{X}_2} = \sqrt{\frac{\tilde{\sigma}^2}{n_1} + \frac{\tilde{\sigma}^2}{n_2}} = \sqrt{\tilde{\sigma}^2 \left(\frac{1}{n_1} + \frac{1}{n_2}\right)} \tag{15.6}$$

we have an estimate of the standard error of the sampling distribution of $\overline{X}_1 - \overline{X}_2$ that satisfies the requirements imposed on the $\tilde{\sigma}_T$ of (15.1). This estimate is based on the n_1 observations that enter into the determination of $S_1{}^2$ plus the n_2 observations that enter into the determination of $S_2{}^2$, or a total of $n_1 + n_2$ observations. Two auxiliary values based on the observations are necessary for determining $S_1{}^2$ and $S_2{}^2$, namely, $\overline{X}_1$ in the case of $S_1{}^2$ and $\overline{X}_2$ in the case of $S_2{}^2$. Hence, the number of degrees of freedom of the statistic $\tilde{\sigma}_{\overline{X}_1 - \overline{X}_2}$, as indicated by the rule given in Section 15.4, is $n_1 + n_2 - 2$. We may now apply (15.1) to the problem at hand as follows.

$$t(df = n_1 + n_2 - 2) = \frac{(\overline{X}_1 - \overline{X}_2) - (\mu_1 - \mu_2)}{\tilde{\sigma}_{\overline{X}_1 - \overline{X}_2}}$$

$$= \frac{(\overline{X}_1 - \overline{X}_2) - (\mu_1 - \mu_2)}{\sqrt{\tilde{\sigma}^2 \left(\dfrac{1}{n_1} + \dfrac{1}{n_2}\right)}}$$

$$= \frac{(\overline{X}_1 - \overline{X}_2) - (\mu_1 - \mu_2)}{\sqrt{\dfrac{n_1 S_1{}^2 + n_2 S_2{}^2}{n_1 + n_2 - 2} \left(\dfrac{1}{n_1} + \dfrac{1}{n_2}\right)}} \tag{15.7}$$

This t may be used as a test statistic to test any hypothesis about $\Delta = \mu_1 - \mu_2$. If we are concerned specifically with the hypothesis that

$\mu_1 - \mu_2 = 0$, we may write (15.7) as follows:

$$t(df = n_1 + n_2 - 2) = \frac{\overline{X}_1 - \overline{X}_2}{\sqrt{\dfrac{n_1 S_1{}^2 + n_2 S_2{}^2}{n_1 + n_2 - 2}\left(\dfrac{1}{n_1} + \dfrac{1}{n_2}\right)}} \qquad (15.8)$$

Example Consider the psychological problem described in Sections 13.4 and following. We cannot validly apply the above t-test theory to the situation of Experiment I, since the data appear to indicate that the hypothetical punishment (P) and no-punishment (NP) populations are different in variability (see Table 13.1).[7] This difficulty does not, however, appear to exist in the case of Experiment II (see Table 13.2). As an illustration of an application of (15.8) we shall, therefore, consider a rerun of Experiment II involving respective samples of seven and five cases from the hypothetical punish-both[8] (PB) and punish-failures-only (PF) populations. Assume the criterion scores for the two samples to be as follows:

PB *sample:* 20, 17, 10, 25, 24, 22, 15
PF *sample:* 26, 31, 23, 35, 20

Step 1. $H_0: \Delta = \mu_{PB} - \mu_{PF} = 0$

Alternative hypotheses are $H_1: \Delta > 0$ and $H_2: \Delta < 0$.

Step 2. $\alpha = .01$

We previously used .001 as the level of significance. In this example, however, we shall use the somewhat less stringent value of .01.

Step 3. $R: t \leq -3.17$ and $t \geq +3.17$

(*Note:* $df = n_{PB} + n_{PF} - 2 = 7 + 5 - 2 = 10$. The R for $df = 10$ and $\alpha = .01$ is given in Table IV, Appendix C.)

Step 4. Calculation of the test statistic, t, for data at hand.

For PB Sample	For PF Sample
$\Sigma X = 133$	$\Sigma X = 135$
$\overline{X} = 19$	$\overline{X} = 27$
$\Sigma X^2 = 2,699$	$\Sigma X^2 = 3,791$
$(\Sigma X)^2/n = 2,527$	$(\Sigma X)^2/n = 3,645$
$\Sigma x^2 = 172$	$\Sigma x^2 = 146$
$S^2 = 24.5714$	$S^2 = 29.2$

[7] We have not studied a test of $H_0: \sigma_1{}^2 = \sigma_2{}^2$ but it can be seen from Table 13.1 that the observed variance for the NP group is approximately 15 times greater than that for the P group.

[8] Both successes and failures.

Hence,

$$t = \frac{19 - 27}{\sqrt{\dfrac{(7)(24.5714) + (5)(29.2)}{7 + 5 - 2}\left(\dfrac{1}{7} + \dfrac{1}{5}\right)}} \qquad [\text{see } (15.8)]$$

$$= \frac{-8}{3.30} = -2.42$$

Step 5. Decision. Retain the hypothesis. (Why?)

Comment: We shall not at this point consider in detail the power of this test. It is sufficient to note that in spite of a difference of 8 between the sample means as compared with a difference of 2.7 for the data of the original experiment, and in spite of the use of $\alpha = .01$ instead of .001, the value of t still falls well within the region of acceptance. It is clear that *sample differences must indeed be large before our small-sample test indicates a statistically significant difference.*

Case II: Randomly selected matched pairs The situation here is precisely as described under Experiment III regarding the psychological problem (see Section 13.8). We obtain a sample of matched pairs by some process such as the following.

1 Select an object at random from the population and measure it with respect to some control variable thought to contribute to individual differences in the criterion variable being studied.
2 From among all objects in the population that possess this same measured amount of this control variable, select one at random and pair it with the object selected in step 1.
3 Repeat steps 1 and 2 until the desired number of matched pairs is obtained.
4 By a random process, assign the members of the pairs to the two experimental groups.

In this design we deal directly with pairs rather than individual objects. The score for a pair is taken to be the difference (D) between the criterion score (X_1) for the member of the pair assigned to Group 1 and the criterion score (X_2) for the member of the pair assigned to Group 2. Thus, if there are N pairs, we have a random sample of N D-scores from a hypothetical population of D-scores such as might be generated by a long-run continuation of this selection procedure. As was explained in Experiment III, a test of the hypothesis that the mean of such a population of D-scores (μ_D) is zero is equivalent to a test of the hypothesis of no difference between the means of the two hypothetical populations represented in each of the pairs.

Now if the two hypothetical populations of X-scores are normally distributed with respect to the criterion measure, we know from **Rule 13.1** that the population of D's is normally distributed with $\mu_D = \mu_1 - \mu_2$. This is true regardless of sample size and regardless of whether the original populations are equally variable. Hence, our problem becomes simply one of testing a hypothesis about the magnitude of the mean of a single, normally distributed population of D-values. The solution involves a straightforward application of the theory and techniques of the preceding section (15.6). We shall, nevertheless, rewrite (15.3) in terms of the following notation.

Let

N = number of D-values (pairs) in the sample
$\bar{D}$ = the mean of the sample of D-values
S_D = the standard deviation of the sample of D-values
μ_D = the mean of the population of D-values

Then (15.3) becomes

$$t(df = N - 1) = \frac{\bar{D} - \mu_D}{\tilde{\sigma}_{\bar{D}}} = \frac{\bar{D} - \mu_D}{S_D/\sqrt{N - 1}}$$

$$= \frac{\bar{D} - \mu_D}{S_D}\sqrt{N - 1} \tag{15.9}$$

This t may be used to test any hypothesis about $\mu_D = \mu_1 - \mu_2$. If we are concerned specifically with the hypothesis that $\mu_D = \mu_1 - \mu_2 = 0$, we may write (15.9) as follows:

$$t(df = N - 1) = \frac{\bar{D}\sqrt{N - 1}}{S_D} \tag{15.10}$$

Example Consider a rerun of the psychological problem of Experiment III involving eleven randomly selected pairs, one member of which is assigned to the punish-both (PB) condition and the other member of which is assigned to the punish-failures-only (PF) condition. Assume the data to be as shown in Table 15.3. The solution is as follows.

Step 1. $H_0: \mu_D = 0;$ $H_1: \mu_D > 0;$ $H_2: \mu_D < 0$

Step 2. $\alpha = .01$

An α of .001 was used in Experiment III. Here, as in the preceding example, we have used .01.

Step 3. $R: t \leq -3.17$ and $t \geq +3.17$

Table 15.3   Criterion Scores and Differences between
Them for 11 Matched Pairs in Experiment III on the Effect
of Punishment on Speed of Learning

Pair	PB	PF	D		
1	24	37	− 13		
2	29	35	− 6	$\Sigma D = -75$	
3	19	16	+ 3	$\bar{D} = -6.82$	
4	14	26	− 12		
5	30	23	+ 7	$\Sigma D^2 = 1,005$	
6	19	27	− 8	$(\Sigma D)^2/N = 511.3636$	
7	19	30	− 11	$\Sigma d^2 = 493.6364$	
8	20	20	0	$S_D{}^2 = 44.8760$	
9	16	28	− 12	$S_D = 6.70$	
10	11	24	− 13		
11	11	21	− 10		

(*Note:* $df = N - 1 = 11 - 1 = 10$. The R for $df = 10$ and $\alpha = .01$
is given in Table IV, Appendix C.)

Step 4. Calculation of the test statistic, t, for data at hand.

Using (15.10) we obtain

$$t = \frac{-6.82}{6.70} \sqrt{11 - 1} = -3.22$$

Step 5. Decision. Reject H_0. (Why?)

This decision also implies rejection of the alternative $\mu_D > 0$. (Why?)
Hence, the only remaining possibility is $\mu_D < 0$, indicating that the
PB condition is more effective in reducing the number of trials required
for learning than the PF condition.

In this example we clearly have a more powerful test than in the
preceding example. The test here "saw" or "interpreted" a $\bar{D}$-value
of -6.82 as sufficiently different from zero (the value hypothesized) to
warrant rejection of zero as a possible value of μ_D, whereas the test of
the preceding example did not interpret a value for $\bar{X}_1 - \bar{X}_2$ of -8 as
sufficiently different from zero to warrant such a rejection. As was
explained in the discussion relating to Experiment III (Section 13.8),
this increase in power is due to the decrease in $\tilde{\sigma}_{\bar{D}}$ that results from
controlling one of the factors (in our example, the factor of intelligence)
contributing to individual differences in learning scores. It should be
noted, however, that in order to keep the number of degrees of freedom
the same in both examples it was necessary to employ more subjects
in the latter example (11 pairs implies 22 subjects) than in the former
(12 subjects). Had the same number of subjects (12) been used in both

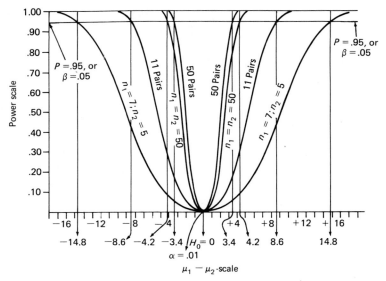

Figure 15.3 Power curves for two *t*-tests and two large-sample tests of the hypothesis of no difference between means of two populations

examples, the latter would have involved only six pairs of subjects and consequently only five degrees of freedom. Unless the control variable is extremely effective in reducing the standard error, this loss in degrees of freedom may result in a loss in power that would negate any gain in power resulting from the equating procedure.

To provide a comparison of the powers of these two *t*-tests and their large-sample counterparts, the four power curves are shown in Figure 15.3. So that the comparisons would be on the same basis throughout, a .01 level of significance was adopted for the large-sample as well as for the small-sample tests. Also, it was assumed that both populations had the common variance 25. Finally, it was assumed in the case of tests based on matched pairs that the effect of the factor controlled was such as to make a 20 percent reduction in the standard error of the $\bar{D}$-sampling distribution. It follows that the large-sample power curves differ somewhat from those shown in Figure 13.4.

From the power curves shown in Figure 15.3, it is again clearly evident that the small-sample tests do not offer much protection against Type II errors unless the true value of $\mu_1 - \mu_2$ differs markedly from the hypothesized value of zero. For the *t*-test based on independent random samples of 7 and 5 cases, $\mu_1 - \mu_2$ must differ from zero by 14.8 in order for the probability of a Type II error (β) to be reduced to .05. The corresponding amount in the large-sample test based on independent random samples of 50 is only 4.2. When matched samples are used, $\mu_1 - \mu_2$ must differ from zero by 8.6 in order to reduce β to .05 in the case of a t-test based on 11 pairs; the corresponding amount in the case of a large-sample test based on 50 pairs is 3.4.

The power superiority of the matched-sample t-test over the t-test involving independent random samples is here due primarily to the fact that more subjects were studied. The power curve for a matched-sample t-test involving 12 subjects (6 pairs) is not shown in Figure 15.3, for the reason that it is so nearly the same as that for the t-test based on independent random samples of 7 and 5 cases that the two curves could not have been distinguished in a graph drawn to this scale. This implies that *for samples of the size involved, a 20 percent reduction in standard error is fully offset by the reduction in degrees of freedom from* 10 ($n_1 + n_2 - 2 = 10$) *to* 5 ($N - 1 = 6 - 1 = 5$). That is to say, in problems involving samples of this order of size, the matching design would not result in increased power unless it also resulted in a reduction in the size of the standard error of considerably more than 20 percent.

In concluding this section, it is important to recall remarks made in Section 13.8 to the effect that the sampling routine necessary to make this matching design valid in a real-world situation is difficult to achieve, and that by far the most common application of (15.9) is consequently to be found either in situations in which the two experimental conditions may both be applied to the same individual, or in situations in which the concern is with the same individual before and after the administration of some treatment or experimental condition. In such situations the scores in a pair are both derived from the same individual, and (15.9) is appropriate as a test statistic for testing hypotheses about the mean of a population of differences between such pairs of scores (see study manual exercise 15.7.17).

15.8 A Comparison of Large-Sample Theory and Small-Sample Theory

In this section we compare the large-sample theory treated in Chapters 11, 12, and 13 with the small-sample theory described above. The presentation is divided into two sections. The first deals with hypotheses about μ or μ_D. The second discusses hypotheses related to $\mu_1 - \mu_2$.

Hypotheses about μ or μ_D   When the hypothesis under test has to do with the value of the mean of a population either of X-scores or of D-values for matched pairs, the large-sample test statistic z is computed by precisely the same formula as the small-sample test statistic t. In other words, for a given set of data, the observed values of z and t will be identical. For a true hypothesis, the large-sample z-value is interpreted as a random variable that is normally distributed with a mean of zero and a variance of one. Even if the population from which the sample is drawn is itself normally distributed, this interpretation is approximate, owing to the use of an estimate of the standard error of the sampling distribution of $\overline{X}$ or $\overline{D}$ in the computation of z. The t-statistic, by contrast, is interpreted as a random variable distributed like the member of the family of t-curves for which the df-value is the same as that of $\tilde{\sigma}_{\overline{X}}$ or $\tilde{\sigma}_{\overline{D}}$. The theory takes into account the use of the estimates $\tilde{\sigma}_{\overline{X}}$ and $\tilde{\sigma}_{\overline{D}}$ in the computation of t, and the interpretation is exact.

Suppose now that the population from which the sample is drawn is not normally distributed. Then a second source of inexactness enters into the interpretation of z, because of the fact that the $\overline{X}$ (or $\overline{D}$) sampling distribution only tends toward or approaches a normal distribution as N increases. Under this circumstance, the interpretation of t also becomes inexact for precisely the same reason. Even so, *the interpretation of t for a sample of a given size is less inexact than that of z for a sample of this size, since the interpretation of z is approximate on two counts, while that of t is approximate on only one.* As sample size increases, the approximate character of the interpretation of t that is due to the nonnormality of the population becomes less and less a matter for concern. In fact, when N becomes quite large, say 50 or more, the interpretation of z—an interpretation that is approximate both because of the nonnormality of the population and because of the use of an estimated standard error—becomes sufficiently accurate to provide a practicable test of hypotheses about means. This, of course, is the large-sample theory treated in Chapters 11, 12, and 13. This large-sample theory is actually a special case of the t-theory, the normally distributed z being that member of the family of t-curves for which $df = \infty$. The approach of the form of the t-distribution to that of the z-distribution is quite rapid, so that even for df-values as small as 30 the z-distribution provides a useful approximation of the t-distribution unless a high degree of accuracy is required. Thus we see that large-sample theory as applied to tests of hypotheses about the value of a population mean actually amounts to the use of the normal-distribution approximation of any t-distribution for which $df > 30$.[9]

Hypotheses about $\mu_1 - \mu_2$ When the hypothesis involved has to do with the difference between the means of two populations and the test is based on the use of independent random samples, the situation is altered somewhat. This is because different estimates of the standard error of the $\overline{X}_1 - \overline{X}_2$ sampling distribution are in general

[9] We have recommended against $N < 50$. See Section 11.5.

used in computing t and z.[10] However, in the case in which n_1 and n_2 are equal, the two estimates of standard error are the same,[11] so in this situation the remarks of the preceding discussion still apply. In general, the t-curve model is exact only if the two populations involved are (1) normally distributed and (2) equally variable. The normal curve model would be exact only if (1) the populations were normally distributed and (2) their variances were known. Since in practical work the population variances are not known, the normal curve model is in general approximate because of the use of an estimated standard error. If the populations are not normally distributed, both curves provide only approximate models, the normal curve model now becoming approximate on two counts. If the populations are not equally variable, the t-curve model also becomes approximate on two counts.

The situations discussed in the foregoing paragraphs are summarized in Table 15.4.

15.9   Effects of the Violation of the Normality and Equality of Variance Conditions for the Exactness of the t-Test for H_0: $\mu_1 = \mu_2$

When samples are large, the probability values provided by the normal curve model are sufficiently accurate for practical purposes. But samples, of course, are not always conveniently large. Statisticians have given much attention to the accuracy of probability statements made on the basis of the t-curve when samples are small and the assumption

[10] Compare formulas (13.6) and (15.6).

[11] Remember that for large samples [formula (13.6)],

$$\tilde{\sigma}_{\bar{x}_1 - \bar{x}_2} = \sqrt{\frac{S_1{}^2}{n_1 - 1} + \frac{S_2{}^2}{n_2 - 1}}$$

If $n_1 = n_2 = n$, this becomes

$$\sqrt{\frac{S_1{}^2 + S_2{}^2}{n - 1}}$$

Likewise, for small samples [formula (15.6)],

$$\tilde{\sigma}_{\bar{x}_1 - \bar{x}_2} = \sqrt{\frac{n_1 S_1{}^2 + n_2 S_2{}^2}{n_1 + n_2 - 2} \left(\frac{1}{n_1} + \frac{1}{n_2} \right)}$$

If $n_1 = n_2 = n$, this becomes

$$\sqrt{\frac{n(S_1{}^2 + S_2{}^2)}{2(n - 1)} \left(\frac{2}{n} \right)} = \sqrt{\frac{S_1{}^2 + S_2{}^2}{n - 1}}$$

Table 15.4   Summary Comparison of t and Normal Curves
with Regard to Characteristic of Exactness

Hypothesis about:	Conditions	t-Curve Model	z-Curve (Normal) Model
μ	Population normally distributed	Exact	Approximate because of: 1 Use of $\tilde{\sigma}_{\bar{x}}$
	Population nonnormal	Approximate because of: 1 Nonnormality of population	Approximate because of: 1 Use of $\tilde{\sigma}_{\bar{x}}$ 2 Nonnormality of population
$\mu_1 - \mu_2$	Populations normally distributed and equally variable	Exact	Approximate because of: 1 Use of $\tilde{\sigma}_{\bar{x}_1 - \bar{x}_2}$
	Populations nonnormal but equally variable	Approximate because of: 1 Nonnormality of populations	Approximate because of: 1 Use of $\tilde{\sigma}_{\bar{x}_1 - \bar{x}_2}$ 2 Nonnormality of populations
	Populations normally distributed but not equally variable	Approximate because of: 1 Inequality of population variances	Approximate because of: 1 Use of $\tilde{\sigma}_{\bar{x}_1 - \bar{x}_2}$
	Populations nonnormal and not equally variable	Approximate because of: 1 Nonnormality of populations 2 Inequality of population variances	Approximate because of: 1 Use of $\tilde{\sigma}_{\bar{x}_1 - \bar{x}_2}$ 2 Nonnormality of populations

of normality or equal variability has been violated. One very useful procedure for studying the effects of these violations is to perform a simulation or Monte Carlo study. You may recall that we discussed the use of Monte Carlo procedures for assigning probability values in Section 9.4. The Monte Carlo method consists of actually causing the experiment to be repeated a very "large" number of times, say $\mathcal{N}$, and recording the number of times each of the possible sample points occurs (n_j). Then, the probability of a particular sample point is merely the relative frequency of that sample point (i.e., $n_j/\mathcal{N}$). As you might suspect, Monte Carlo studies require the use of electronic computers to be economically feasible.

To illustrate the use of Monte Carlo procedures for the purpose noted above, assume an investigator wishes to study the effect of the

violation of the equal variability assumption on the accuracy of the
t-statistic for testing $H_0: \mu_1 - \mu_2 = 0$.

It is not a difficult task to store in the computer two artificial populations of scores with specified shapes, means, and variances. Assume
the investigator stores the following two populations in the computer:

Population 1	Population 2
(Normal = Shape)	(Normal = Shape)
$\mu_1 = 20$	$\mu_2 = 20$
$\sigma_1{}^2 = 4$	$\sigma_2{}^2 = 1$

Notice that the two populations differ only in variability. The investigator now performs the following steps.

1 Select, at random, a sample of size 8 from Population 1.
2 Compute $\overline{X}_1$ and $S_1{}^2$.
3 Select, at random, a sample of size 16 from Population 2.
4 Compute $\overline{X}_2$ and $S_2{}^2$.
5 Compute t using (15.8).
6 Repeat steps 1 through 5 10,000 times.
7 Form the relative frequency distribution of the 10,000
  outcomes.
8 Compare the rf distribution of the 10,000 outcomes with the
  theoretical model that is known to be true if all conditions
  were satisfied.

Table 15.5 shows one possible set of results for a Monte Carlo study
following these eight steps.

It is easily seen from Table 15.5 that the Monte Carlo experiment
produced more outcomes in the tail regions and fewer outcomes in the
middle range than predicted by the theoretical model. What are the
implications of this for the researcher using t-distribution theory?
Consider a researcher who plans to use the t-statistic to test H_0:
$\mu_1 = \mu_2$. If $n_1 = 8$ and $n_2 = 16$, then the appropriate t-curve is one
with 22 df. Assume that $\alpha = .05$ and that the critical region is two-
ended. In this instance, the critical region is $t \geq 2.07$ and $t \leq -2.07$.
If the normality and equal variability conditions hold, we know that
$P(t \geq 2.07) + P(t \leq -2.07) = .05$. However, what if these conditions are not met? In our example, the normality conditions were
met, but the variance of one population was four times greater than the
variance of the other. Under these conditions, what is $P(t \geq 2.07) +
P(t \leq -2.07)$? The results in Table 15.5 indicate that this probability
is very close to .11. Thus, instead of P(Type I error) $= .05$, this probability for the populations described above is probably closer to .11.
Obviously, such a difference between the selected α-value and the

Table 15.5   Results of a Monte Carlo Study of the Violation of the Equal Variance Assumption

Outcome	Theoretical Relative Frequency[a] [Equation (15.2): $df = 22$]	Empirical Relative Frequency[b] (from Monte Carlo Experiment)
$t < -3.79$	.0005	.0031
$-3.79 < t < -3.50$	.0005	.0021
$-3.50 < t < -2.82$	.0040	.0144
$-2.82 < t < -2.51$	.0050	.0121
$-2.51 < t < -2.07$	.0150	.0246
$-2.07 < t < -1.72$	.0250	.0358
$-1.72 < t < -1.32$	.0500	.0572
$-1.32 < t < -.86$	.1000	.0965
$-.86 < t < -.53$	.1000	.0872
$-.53 < t < -.26$	.1000	.0851
$-.26 < t < .0$	.1000	.0809
$.0 < t < .26$	.1000	.0840
$.26 < t < .53$	.1000	.0822
$.53 < t < .86$	.1000	.0874
$.86 < t < 1.32$	.1000	.0964
$1.32 < t < 1.72$	.0500	.0584
$1.72 < t < 2.07$	.0250	.0360
$2.07 < t < 2.51$	.0150	.0269
$2.51 < t < 2.82$	.0050	.0118
$2.82 < t < 3.50$	.0040	.0127
$3.50 < t < 3.79$	.0005	.0022
$3.79 < t$	.0005	.0030

[a] *The values in this column were taken from G. Isaacs, D. Christ, M. Novick, and P. Jackson,* Tables for Bayesian Statisticians. *Iowa Testing Programs, Iowa City, Iowa, 1974.*

[b] *The values in this column were adapted from J. Bradley,* Studies in Research Methodology: VI. The Central Limit Effect for a Variety of Populations and the Robustness of z, t, and F. Behavioral Sciences Laboratory, Air Force Systems Command, Wright-Patterson Air Force Base, Ohio, 1964.

"true" α-value cannot be tolerated and alternative procedures must be found. In this instance, the t-test was not what might be called robust. "A 'robust' statistical test preserves the validity of the probability statements applied to it even though the assumptions upon which it is based are violated."[12] It seems obvious from Table 15.5 that the probability statements for various outcomes made on the basis of the t-model differ fairly markedly (particularly in the tail regions) from the Monte Carlo results.

Statisticians have studied the robustness of the t-test fairly extensively. On the basis of theoretical considerations and a large number of Monte Carlo studies such as the one described above, the following

[12] G. Glass, P. Peckham, and J. Sanders, "Consequences of Failure to Meet Assumptions Underlying the Analysis of Variance and Co-variance," *Review of Educational Research*, 42 (1972), 284.

conclusions seem justified for testing $H_0: \mu_1 = \mu_2$ by using the t-statistic of (15.8).

1 If $n_1 > 25$ and $n_2 > 25$, always use the large-sample theory presented in Chapter 13 for testing $H_0: \mu_1 = \mu_2$. The probability statements made on the basis of normal curve theory are accurate enough.

2 If $n_1 < 25$ and $n_2 < 25$, but $n_1 = n_2$, the use of the t-theory discussed in this chapter will be accurate enough for most purposes even if the populations are not normal and the variances do differ somewhat.[13]

3 If $n_1 < 25$ and $n_2 < 25$ and if $n_1 \neq n_2$, and if the conditions of normality and variability seem likely to be violated, other available test techniques that are not subject to these restrictions should be used.[14]

4 The t-test is far more vulnerable to the effects of non-normality—especially skewness—when one-ended critical regions are used than when two-ended regions are used. If a one-ended region is required, t-tests should be used with small samples only in situations in which it is reasonable to assume that the population distribution is at least symmetrical in form.

It should be clear that t-test theory (for $H_0: \mu_1 = \mu_2$) in the case of small samples is somewhat restricted in the generality of its applicability, and the investigator who uses small samples must face the fact that an analysis based on this theory is appropriate only when the conditions under which it is exact are satisfied at least to the extent indicated above.

But the most costly aspect of the use of small samples, even in situations in which the conditions necessary to making t-test theory exact are satisfied, lies in their extreme lack of power as compared with large samples. While the appropriate application of t-test theory to small samples does provide for exact control over a Type I error, it cannot be expected, on the basis of the limited information inherently contained in such samples, to detect consistently a discrepancy between the parameter and the value hypothesized for it unless that discrepancy is very large. Of course, if Type II errors are of concern only when the difference between parameter and hypothesis becomes very great, then the use of small samples may prove practicable. In general, however,

---

[13] It is difficult to be more precise than this at this time.

[14] Discussion of these techniques is beyond the scope of this text. For a discussion of one of these techniques, see B. J. Winer, *Statistical Principles in Experimental Design*, 2d ed., McGraw-Hill, New York, 1971, pp. 41–44.

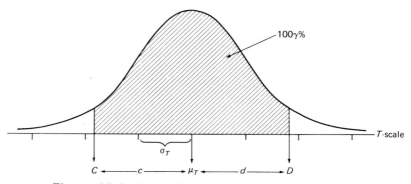

Figure 15.4   Sampling distribution of T

the use of a small sample is justifiable only in situations in which circumstances preclude the use of a large sample.

15.10 Interval Estimation Based on the t-Statistic

Let T be a normally distributed statistic with mean μ_T and standard error σ_T and let it be required to establish the limits $\underline{\mu}_T$ and $\bar{\mu}_T$ of the 100γ percent confidence interval for μ_T (see Figure 15.4). In this situation

$$z_{\gamma/2} = \frac{\mu_T - C}{\sigma_T} = \frac{D - \mu_T}{\sigma_T} = \frac{c}{\sigma_T} = \frac{d}{\sigma_T}$$

Hence, $c = d = z_{\gamma/2}\sigma_T$, and applying (14.1) we obtain

$$\underline{\mu}_{T_1} = T_1 - z_{\gamma/2}\sigma_T \quad \text{and} \quad \bar{\mu}_{T_1} = T_1 + z_{\gamma/2}\sigma_T \qquad \text{(a)}$$

where T_1 is the particular value of T that arises in the case of a particular sample.

Now suppose that σ_T is not known but that an estimate of it, $\tilde{\sigma}_T$, is obtainable from the information contained in the particular sample at hand. If we use this estimate in place of σ_T in (a) we have

$$\underline{\mu}_{T_1} = T_1 - z_{\gamma/2}\tilde{\sigma}_T \quad \text{and} \quad \bar{\mu}_{T_1} = T_1 + z_{\gamma/2}\tilde{\sigma}_T \qquad \text{(b)}$$

We can no longer claim, of course, that the $\underline{\mu}_{T_1}$- and $\bar{\mu}_{T_1}$-values given in (b) are the limits of a 100γ percent confidence interval. Such a claim is precluded by our use of an estimate of σ_T. If, as we have previously explained (see Section 14.5), the sample is sufficiently large to provide a reliable estimate of σ_T, then the application of (b) leads to limits for which the actual confidence coefficient is sufficiently close to γ to satisfy the demands of most practical situations. If, on the other hand, the sample is small and the estimate of σ_T unreliable, the application of (b) leads to limits for which the actual confidence coefficient differs considerably in value from that selected for γ. Therefore, in situations involving small samples, it becomes necessary to alter the procedure.

An appropriate alteration is easily accomplished if the estimate of σ_T is one appropriate to t-distribution theory. If $\tilde{\sigma}_T$ is appropriate to t-distribution theory, then (15.1) applies, and we may write

$$t_{\gamma/2} = \frac{\mu_T - C}{\tilde{\sigma}_T} = \frac{D - \mu_T}{\tilde{\sigma}_T} \qquad \text{(for } df \text{ equal to that of } \tilde{\sigma}_T)$$

Therefore,

$$\mu_T - C = D - \mu_T = t_{\gamma/2}\tilde{\sigma}_T$$

or

$$c = d = t_{\gamma/2}\tilde{\sigma}_T$$

Application of (14.1) gives

$$\mu_{T_1} = T_1 - t_{\gamma/2}\tilde{\sigma}_T \qquad \qquad \text{(15.11a)}$$
$$\bar{\mu}_{T_1} = T_1 + t_{\gamma/2}\tilde{\sigma}_T \qquad \qquad \text{(15.11b)}$$

where df for t is that of $\tilde{\sigma}_T$. If the statistic involved is normally distributed, intervals established by (15.11) have a confidence coefficient exactly equal to γ since the use of t takes into full account the use of an appropriate sample estimate of σ_T.

We shall now use (15.11) to write formulas for the limits of the 100γ percent confidence interval for the mean of a normally distributed population. Here, of course, the statistic represented by T_1 is the mean, $\bar{X}_1$, of the sample at hand, and $\tilde{\sigma}_T$ is $\tilde{\sigma}_{\bar{x}}$ as given by (11.19). Hence,

$$\mu_1 = \bar{X}_1 - t_{\gamma/2}\frac{S}{\sqrt{N-1}} \qquad \qquad \text{(15.12a)}$$

$$\bar{\mu}_1 = \bar{X}_1 + t_{\gamma/2}\frac{S}{\sqrt{N-1}} \qquad \qquad \text{(15.12b)}$$

where $df = N - 1$.

Example Using the data of the example of Section 15.6, establish the 99 percent confidence interval for the mean of the population involved. Here $N = 5$ so that $df = 4$; also $t_{\gamma/2} = t_{.495}$. In the t-table given in Appendix C, $P = .500 - \gamma/2$. Referring to this table for $df = 4$ and $P = .500 - .495 = .005$, we find $t = 4.60$. Since for the given data $\overline{X}_1 = 80$ and $S = 17.18$, the application of (15.12) gives

$$\mu_1 = 80 - (4.60) \frac{17.18}{\sqrt{5-1}} = 80 - 39.51 = 40.49$$

$$\bar{\mu}_1 = 80 + (4.60) \frac{17.18}{\sqrt{5-1}} = 80 + 39.51 = 119.51$$

Therefore,

$$C(40.49 \le \mu \le 119.51) = 99\%$$

Comment: It will be observed that the length of this interval is 79.02 IQ units as compared with 12.9 IQ units in the case of the corresponding large-sample estimate (see Example 1, Section 14.5). Again we have rather striking evidence of the lack of precision of small-sample results as compared with the precision yielded by more informative large samples. In the case of small samples, the procedure just illustrated is appropriate only with reference to normally distributed populations.

We shall next write formulas for the limits of the 100γ percent confidence interval for the difference between the means of two normally distributed and equally variable populations. Here the T_1 of (15.11) is the obtained value of $\overline{X}_1 - \overline{X}_2$, and $\tilde{\sigma}_{\overline{X}_1 - \overline{X}_2}$ is given by (15.6). Hence,

$$\underline{\Delta}_1 = (\overline{X}_1 - \overline{X}_2)_1 - t_{\gamma/2} \sqrt{\frac{n_1 S_1{}^2 + n_2 S_2{}^2}{n_1 + n_2 - 2} \left(\frac{1}{n_1} + \frac{1}{n_2} \right)}$$

$$(15.13\text{a})$$

$$\overline{\Delta}_1 = (\overline{X}_1 - \overline{X}_2)_1 + t_{\gamma/2} \sqrt{\frac{n_1 S_1{}^2 + n_2 S_2{}^2}{n_1 + n_2 - 2} \left(\frac{1}{n_1} + \frac{1}{n_2} \right)}$$

$$(15.13\text{b})$$

where $df = n_1 + n_2 - 2$.

Example Using the data of the example under Case I in Section 15.7, obtain the limits of the 99 percent confidence interval for the difference between the means of the populations involved. Here $n_{PB} = 7$ and $n_{PF} = 5$ so that $df = 7 + 5 - 2 = 10$. Also, $t_{\gamma/2} = t_{.495}$. Referring to the t-table for $df = 10$ and for $P = .500 - .495 = .005$, we find $t = 3.17$. Since for the given data $\overline{X}_{PB} - \overline{X}_{PF} = 19 - 27 =$

-8, and $S_{PB}{}^2$ and $S_{PF}{}^2$ are respectively 24.5714 and 29.2, the application of (15.13) gives

$$\underline{\Delta}_1 = -8 - (3.17) \sqrt{\frac{(7)(24.5714) + (5)(29.2)}{7 + 5 - 2} \left(\frac{1}{7} + \frac{1}{5}\right)}$$

$$= -8 - (3.17)(3.30)$$
$$= -8 - 10.46 = -18.46$$
$$\bar{\Delta}_1 = -8 + 10.46 = +2.46$$

Therefore,

$$C(-18.46 \le \Delta \le +2.46) = 99\%$$

Comment: Note that these limits are opposite in sign. The negative sign associated with the lower limit indicates a difference in favor of the PB condition, while the positive sign of the upper limit indicates a difference favoring the PF condition.[15] The fact that these limits lie on opposite sides of zero is consistent with our previous finding (Section 15.7) that the zero hypothesis could not be rejected. The applicability of the procedure just illustrated is limited not only to normally distributed populations but also to equally variable populations.

Finally we shall consider the problem of determining the limits of the 100γ percent confidence interval for the mean of a normally distributed population of differences resulting from forming a random sample of matched pairs. Actually, of course, (15.12) applies. Nevertheless, we shall write the formulas in terms of the notation previously developed for this situation.

$$\mu_{D_1} = \bar{D}_1 - t_{\gamma/2} \frac{S_D}{\sqrt{N-1}} \tag{15.14a}$$

$$\bar{\mu}_{D_1} = \bar{D}_1 + t_{\gamma/2} \frac{S_D}{\sqrt{N-1}} \tag{15.14b}$$

for $df = N - 1$, where N = number of pairs.

Example Using the data of the example under Case II in Section 15.7, obtain the limits of the 95 percent confidence interval for the mean of the population of differences involved.

Here, $N = 11$ so that $df = 10$. Also $t_{\gamma/2} = t_{.475}$. Referring to the t-table for $df = 10$ and for $P = .500 - .475 = .025$, we find $t = 2.23$.

---

[15] Recall that in the psychological experiment here involved, the smaller criterion scores indicated superior performance—i.e., more rapid learning.

Since for the given data $\bar{D}_1 = -6.82$ and $S_D = 6.70$, the application of (15.14) gives

$$\mu_{D_1} = -6.82 - (2.23)\frac{6.70}{\sqrt{11-1}}$$

$$= -6.82 - 4.73$$

$$= -11.55$$

$$\bar{\mu}_{D_1} = -6.82 + 4.73$$

$$= -2.09$$

Therefore,

$$C(-11.55 \leq \mu_D \leq -2.09) = 95\%$$

15.11 Testing Hypotheses about ϕ Using the Binomial Probability Distribution

The previous sections of this chapter were concerned either with testing hypotheses about, or with establishing confidence intervals for, μ, μ_D, and $\mu_1 - \mu_2$ when small samples were used. In this section, we examine procedures for testing hypotheses about ϕ when samples are small. In Sections 12.8, 12.9, and 12.10 we tested hypotheses about ϕ using the normal probability distribution. We have noted previously (see Sections 10.7 and 11.6) that the normal probability model provides an adequate approximate description of the sampling distribution of p when the sample size is large,[16] so that this model can be used to approximate the binomial probability distribution when large samples are involved. However, when the sample size is not large, the normal approximation is not adequate. Therefore, in situations involving small samples, the binomial probability distribution itself must be used. We shall demonstrate with two examples.

Example 1 Consider the speed reading example described in Section 9.1. The basic question in this example had to do with the effectiveness of a particular speed reading course for freshman students. Assume the following procedure is used to evaluate effectiveness.

1 From the freshman class of 8,000 students select two students by some random procedure.

2 For this pair of students, toss a coin to decide which member of the pair will take the speed reading course.

[16] For a discussion of what is "large" and "small" see footnote 13 on page 201.

3 Repeat steps 1 and 2 until 10 students have been assigned to the speed reading course.

4 After the course is completed, give the reading comprehension test to all 20 students.

5 Count the number of times that the reading comprehension score for the member of the pair who took the course was greater than the score for the member of the pair who did not take the course.

We will first consider whether or not this particular experiment is a binomial experiment (Section 9.7). First, note that the universe can be conceptualized as consisting of 4,000 pairs of students. Each pair of students may be thought of as participating in the experiment. Even though only 10 pairs actually take part in the experiment, we are interested in what would happen if all 4,000 pairs constituting the universe had participated.

Now assume that the pairs constituting the universe are of two kinds, namely, Type A if the difference for the test score of the member of the pair who took the reading course minus that for the member who did not is positive $(+)$, and Type $\bar{A}$ if this difference is negative $(-)$.[17] Thus we have the first characteristic of a binomial experiment (see p. 164).

The second characteristic of a binomial experiment requires that an object be selected from the universe by some random procedure and that, after its type (A or $\bar{A}$) is determined, it be returned to the universe. In this example, although an object (pair) is selected by a chance procedure and its type (A or $\bar{A}$) ultimately noted, it cannot be returned to the universe before a second selection is made. It was observed previously (see p. 164) that if N (4,000 in this example) is large relative to n (10 in this example), replacement of the objects is unnecessary. Since 4,000 is certainly large relative to 10, it seems reasonable to assume that the second characteristic is also satisfied.

The third characteristic of a binomial experiment requires that the proportion of A's (i.e., ϕ) in the universe be known. The only possible way we could determine this population value would be to have all 4,000 pairs participate in the experiment. This would be totally impracticable. However, since we are performing the experiment for the purpose of evaluating the effectiveness of the speed reading course, it may be possible to arrive at a value of ϕ that would be true under certain conditions. For example, we may start with the hypothesis that the speed reading course neither improves nor impairs com-

----

[17] What about tie scores (zero differences)? In theory, if the trait in question (reading comprehension) is continuous, the probability of such differences is zero. In practice, because of the approximate character of the test scores, ties may occur. Later we suggest one way of dealing with tie scores.

prehension (i.e., that the course has neither a positive nor a negative effect). If this is true, the proportion of A's ($+$ differences) and the proportion of $\bar{A}$'s ($-$ differences) in the population should be equal, because the selection of the pairs and the assignment to the reading course were strictly on a random basis. In such a situation, ϕ would equal .50.

The fourth characteristic of a binomial experiment requires that the ϕ-value remain constant over the n repetitions of the selection process. If we assume that the course is neither effective nor harmful (the hypothesis we are going to test), the proportion of A's ($+$ differences) in the universe of 4,000 pairs is .50. For the selection of the first pair, $P(A) = .50 = 2,000/4,000$. However, for the selection of the second pair, $P(A)$ is equal to either $1,999/3,999$ or $2,000/3,999$, depending on whether an A- or $\bar{A}$-type pair was selected on the first trial.

But even if A-type pairs were selected on the first nine draws, the $P(A)$ on the tenth draw is still very close to .50 ($1,991/3,991 \approx .499$). Likewise, if $\bar{A}$-type pairs were selected on the first nine draws, the $P(A)$ on the tenth draw remains approximately .50 ($2,000/3,991 \approx .501$). Considering this range of possible $P(A)$-values, it seems reasonable to conclude that this characteristic of a binomial experiment is satisfied.

The fifth and final characteristic of a binomial experiment requires that the outcome (statistic) of interest be expressed as either the number or the proportion of A types selected. In this experiment we will obtain the proportion of A types.

Given these conditions, it follows that the experiment described is a binomial experiment. Hence, the binomial rule (9.1) can be used to assign probability values to the possible outcomes of the experiment.

Testing the hypothesis of this experiment

Step 1. The statement of the statistical hypothesis.

In discussing the third characteristic of this binomial experiment, we noted that the hypothesis $\phi = .50$ implies that the speed reading course neither improves nor impairs comprehension. Therefore, we test

$$H_0: \phi = .50$$

against the alternatives

$$H_1: \phi > .50 \quad \text{and} \quad H_2: \phi < .50$$

Comment: It is assumed that the actual universe value of ϕ may be either greater or less than .50 (i.e., the course may have either a positive or a negative effect).

Step 2. Selection of α-level

Let us select $\alpha = .10$. This simply represents an arbitrary selection for purposes of illustration.

Step 3. Location of the critical region.

To specify the critical region it is necessary to specify the sampling distribution of the test statistic given that the hypothesis is true. The test statistic in this experiment is p, the proportion of A-types (+ differences) in the sample. Since this is a binomial experiment, it is known (see Sections 9.7 and 11.6) that p has a binomial probability distribution. To identify the particular appropriate binomial distribution we must know ϕ and n (the number of trials or the sample size). In this experiment, $n = 10$ and $\phi = .50$ (if H_0 is true). Thus, if H_0 is true, the sampling distribution of p in this experiment is a binomial distribution with $\phi = .50$ and $n = 10$. This distribution is shown in

Statistic (p)	Probability
.00	.0010
.10	.0098
.20	.0439
.30	.1172
.40	.2051
.50	.2461
.60	.2051
.70	.1172
.80	.0439
.90	.0098
1.00	.0010

the accompanying table. Given this sampling distribution, the critical region (R) is located in such a way that (1) if the hypothesis is true, the probability of the test statistic falling in it equals the level of significance, and (2) if the hypothesis is not true, the probability of the test statistic falling in it is a maximum. This second criterion leads to the placement of the R in the tails of the sampling distribution. (For a review of these points, see pp. 246 and 278).

In all our previous work, it was easy to meet the first criterion since all the test statistics considered were random variables of the continuous type. Hence, all the sampling distributions used to establish critical regions were continuous. However, the binomial probability distribution is not a continuous distribution. Hence, it will not always be possible to establish a critical region in such a way that the probability of the test statistic falling in it is exactly equal to α.

To illustrate this point, consider the example at hand. In this example

$\alpha = .10$ and a two-tailed test is to be used. Referring to the lower part of the distribution, note the following facts:

$$P(p = .00) = .0010$$
$$P(p = .00 \text{ or } .10) = .0010 + .0098 = .0108$$
$$P(p = .00 \text{ or } .10 \text{ or } .20) = .0010 + .0098 + .0439 = .0547$$

Thus, it is impossible to identify a region in this tail such that the probability that the test statistic (p) will fall in this region is exactly .05 (i.e., $\alpha/2$).

There are two possible solutions to this problem. First, we could identify that region (in the tail) with probability closest to $\alpha/2$ (or α, in the case of a one-tailed test). If this procedure is followed in the above example, the R for the lower tail would be $p \le .20$. (In this instance the actual tail probability is .0547.) The second possible procedure would be to identify that region (in the tail) with probability closest to $\alpha/2$ (or α, in the case of a one-tailed test) with the added restriction that this probability cannot be greater than $\alpha/2$ (or α). If this second procedure is followed in the example above, the R for the lower tail would be $p \le .10$. (In this instance the actual tail probability is only .0108.)

In this book, we shall follow the first procedure. Hence, the R for the speed reading example is $R: p \ge .80$ and $p \le .20$.

Step 4. Determination of the test statistic for the data.

Assume that eight A types ($+$ differences) were found (i.e., for eight of the ten pairs of students participating in the experiment, the student taking the speed reading course had the higher comprehension score). Hence, p (the test statistic) $= 8/10 = .80$.

Step 5. The decision.

Since $p = .8$ falls in the R, the hypothesis $H_0: \phi = .50$ and the alternative $H_2: \phi < .50$ are rejected, and the alternative $H_1: \phi > .50$ is accepted as the only remaining possibility.

Remarks:

1. Note that in hypothesis testing procedures using discrete random variables such as p as the test statistic, the actual α-level may not be equal to the selected or nominal α-level even when all assumptions and conditions for the procedure are met. In the above example, the nominal α-level was .10; however, the actual α-level is .1094 (.0547 + .0547).

2. In applying this procedure, an investigator may find that both members of a pair have the same score on the criterion task. If such ties occur, one thing that can be done is simply to drop those pairs from the analysis. For example, assume that for one of the ten pairs

selected, both members had the same score on the reading comprehension test. Then, this pair is dropped from the sample and the binomial distribution for $n = 9$ and $\phi = .50$ is used to test H_0. (See study manual exercise 15.11.28.)

3. The procedure presented above is often referred to as the "sign test," since it is based only on the signs of the differences between the pairs of test scores.

4. It would have been possible to use the actual scores on the reading comprehension test for the 20 students to test $H_0: \mu_C - \mu_{NC} = 0$ using the t-statistic (15.9). In fact, this latter procedure is probably to be preferred, since it will in general be more powerful than the procedure using only the sign of the differences. However, this t-test is exact only if the population of pair differences sampled is normal, whereas the sign test is exact regardless of the form of this distribution. Both procedures deal with the same basic research question: Is the course effective?

5. It is possible to use the above procedure when the members of each pair have actually been matched on some variable (in our example the matching was random). In the speed reading experiment, for example, we could match people on college entrance examination scores and then randomly assign one member of each matched pair to the experimental group (see study manual exercise 15.11.27). Likewise, this procedure can be used in situations in which the concern is with the same individual before and after the administration of some treatment or experimental condition (see study manual exercise 15.11.30).

Example 2 Consider Solution IV of the problem of the principal and the superintendent (see Section 12.8). In this solution the population was viewed as dichotomous, with A-type students being those having WISC IQ scores < 90 and $\bar{A}$-type students those having WISC IQ scores ≥ 90. In Section 12.8, the psychologist was instructed to randomly select 100 students. Here we shall reduce this number to 20. The procedure may be outlined as follows.

1 By some random procedure select a student from the experimentally accessible population.
2 Give the WISC test to this student.
3 Repeat the above two steps until 20 students have been selected.
4 Count the number of IQ scores below 90 and express this number as a proportion.

Now under the hypothesis that the population of students in this school is really not different (with respect to IQ scores) from the normative population, the superintendent decides to hypothesize that

Table 15.6   Binomial Distribution for $n = 20$ and $\phi = .25$

Test Statistic (p)	Probability	Test Statistic (p)	Probability
.00	.0032	.55	.0030
.05	.0211	.60	.0008
.10	.0669	.65	.0002
.15	.1339	.70	.0000
.20	.1897	.75	.0000
.25	.2023	.80	.0000
.30	.1686	.85	.0000
.35	.1124	.90	.0000
.40	.0609	.95	.0000
.45	.0271	1.00	.0000
.50	.0099		

$\phi = .25$ (see Section 12.8 for the derivation of this proportion). Thus, if H_0 is true, the above experiment can be viewed as a binomial experiment with $\phi = .25$ and $n = 20$. Therefore, the binomial rule (9.1) can be used to obtain the probability values for all possible outcomes of this experiment.[18] The resulting binomial distribution ($\phi = .25$ and $n = 20$) is shown in Table 15.6.

Testing the hypothesis

Step 1. The statement of the statistical hypothesis: H_0: $\phi = .25$; H_1: $\phi > .25$.

Comments:

1. In the original discussion of this experiment (Section 12.8) it was noted that if the population of this school was "normal" with respect to IQ scores, then .25 of the population would have IQ scores less than 90 (i.e., be A type).

2. See footnote 6 on p. 253 for a discussion of why only one alternate hypothesis is admitted.

Step 2. Selection of α-level: $\alpha = .05$.

Comment: This is an arbitrary selection made for sake of illustration.

Step 3. Location of critical region.

The sampling distribution for the experimental outcome (random variable), p, is shown in Table 15.6. The R is to be located in the upper

---

[18] *Note*: The target population is very large. Therefore, the binomial probability model can be used even though each student tested was not returned to the population before the next student was drawn.

tail of this distribution. Since p is a discrete random variable, it may not be possible to find an upper-tail region of this sampling distribution the total probability of which is exactly equal to .05. Note that $P(p \geq .40) = .0609 + \cdots + .0000 = .1019$. Also, $P(p \geq .45) = .0271 + \cdots + .0000 = .041$. If we follow the procedure of identifying the R as that portion of the outcome space for which the total probability is closest to α, the R is $p \geq .45$.

Step 4. Determination of the test statistic.

Assume that 10 of the 20 students selected had IQs less than 90. Then the value of the test statistic, p, is .50.

Step 5. The decision.

The observed value of p (.50) is in the R. Therefore, H_0 is rejected and H_1 is accepted as the only other possibility.

15.12 Summary Statement

The first seven sections of this chapter introduced a new statistic, t, and showed how it could be used to make exact tests of hypotheses about the means of a normally distributed population and about the difference between the means of two normally distributed and equally variable populations, given small samples. The point was made that these applications of t using small samples from nonnormal populations, although approximate, were usually to be preferred over the use of z. These ideas are summarized in Section 15.8—see particularly Table 15.4.

The remaining sections dealt with (1) the use of t in making confidence interval estimates of μ, μ_D, and $\Delta = \mu_1 - \mu_2$, and (2) the use of the binomial probability distribution in making exact tests of hypotheses about the proportion of A-type objects in dichotomous populations of A's and not-A's given small samples.

It is worth mentioning that in the last example given on the use of the binomial distribution (Example 2, Section 15.11) the situation developed is not one that occurs frequently in practical work. Basically, this situation represents a one-sample problem, and in most situations of this type interest would center on estimating a parameter rather than on testing a hypothesis about it. (See Section 12.16.) Thus, while this second situation does provide an additional illustration of the use of the binomial probability distribution in testing statistical hypotheses, this was not the major motivation for using this particular example. Rather, we have chosen to use this second example because it will serve as a basis for a comparison of a new approach to statistical inference, to be presented in the next chapter. The major study manual example illustrative of this new approach, called Bayesian inference, will again be the problem of the principal and the superintendent.

16

Introduction to Bayesian Inference

16.1   Introduction

In Chapter 9 of this book, the basic ideas of probability theory were introduced, first for events and later for random variables. From this base a theory and method of statistical inference were developed in Chapters 11 through 15. This theory and method derive largely from the work of Jerzy Neyman and Egon S. Pearson, and their approach is generally referred to as the Neyman-Pearson approach. The working methods of this approach to statistics are point estimates, interval estimates, and tests of point hypothesis. The Neyman-Pearson procedures presented in these chapters are those most frequently used by statisticians and by educational researchers, psychologists, and other behavioral scientists engaged in quantitative research. These methods have a proven record of accomplishment over an extended period of time and in a wide range of applications. Yet statistics has always been a developing and dynamic discipline in which methods other than those adopted by a majority have found acceptance and profitable use. The authors of this book (Blommers and Forsyth) and the author of this chapter (Novick) feel that students of educational statistics should be introduced to other data analysis procedures.

Many approaches to statistics have, of course, been proposed, and for each major approach there are numerous variants. This fact should not alarm or disturb students, nor should it in any way bring into question the importance and relevance of statistical methodology. In every important field of scientific activity there can be found distinct

The author is grateful to Paul Blommers and Robert Forsyth for their suggestions in the preparation of this chapter.

schools of thought with substantial controversy between them. Those with interests in the particular areas will know of the disagreement between the formalists and the intuitionists in mathematics, the monetary policy and the fiscal policy advocates in economics, and the stimulus-response and cognitive theorists in the psychological study of learning. Even in medicine we find much controversy. Internists are more inclined to treat our ills with drugs, and surgeons are more inclined to adopt methods within their specialty. Those who have need of counsel from the fields of mathematics, economics, psychology, medicine—or statistics—are well advised to shop well, even if in many instances equally beneficial advice may come from consultants having very different theoretical orientations.

By providing our readers with a broader perspective in this chapter, we believe we can accomplish two things. First, we can introduce readers to a large body of additional statistical methods that they may find useful on occasion or encounter in their reading. Although we treat in detail only a single application of one method here, we provide sources that make similar techniques available for other applications. Second, an understanding of alternative approaches will help students appreciate the limitations of the methods presented in earlier chapters. As a result of this, we believe that we shall be helping users of this book to attain a more mature understanding of the value and limitation of all statistical methods.

16.2   The Fisherian Alternative to Neyman-Pearson Statistics

It is generally acknowledged that the foremost contributor to statistical theory and method was Sir Ronald Fisher. His texts *Statistical Methods for Research Workers* (14th ed., Oliver and Boyd, Edinburgh, 1970) and *The Design of Experiments* (8th ed., Hafner, New York, 1960) have had enormous influence on successive generations of statisticians and can be read today with as much profit as in the years in which they were originally published. Yet Fisher would, and did, object to most of the logical structure of the Neyman-Pearson theory. To Fisher, a statistical test was a very different sort of thing, with a very different meaning, from what it was (and is) to Neyman and Pearson. To assure readers that this 50-year-old controversy remains unresolved, we need only note that a very well-attended symposium on the meaning of the "significance test" was held at the August 1975 meetings of the American Statistical Association.

We shall now, at some risk, attempt to describe the differences in these two points of view. The risk arises because even within the Fisher and Neyman-Pearson camps there are minor variations in points of view and emphasis, so that it is likely that others may have stated the two positions differently. The Fisherian position in particular has had varying interpretation.

In Neyman-Pearson theory, a statistician performs his job by making statements as the result of a statistical analysis. The statements of primary interest result from the computations involved in testing hypotheses and computing confidence intervals. The following are typical statements.

1 Assuming that we are dealing with normally distributed observations with an unknown mean and unknown variance, we reject the null hypothesis that the unknown mean is some constant (e.g., $\mu = 100$) with a specific probability (α) of a Type I error. (See Chapter 15.)

2 Assuming as above but with a different population and sample, we assert that the interval 95–105 is a 100γ percent confidence interval for the unknown mean (μ). By this we mean that if many such intervals were determined by repeating the experiment, approximately 100γ percent of them will contain μ. (See Chapter 14.)

In a professional lifetime a statistician will make many such assertions. Let us suppose, for simplicity, that a particular statistician always presets the same α-level for his statements. Values of .10, .05, .01, or .001 are common, depending on the nature of the field of application. Then the Neyman-Pearson theory correctly tells us that in the long run the proportion of incorrect statements that the statistician will make will be at most α.

The ultimate theoretical formulation of the Neyman-Pearson theory can be found in Abraham Wald's approach to statistical decision theory,[1] which not only incorporates the ideas of error probabilities, but also makes it possible to take into account the relative losses associated with Type I and Type II errors.

The Fisherian approach, which antedates the Neyman-Pearson approach by some years, is less formal and hence less mechanistic. Our understanding of the Fisherian approach is that it is concerned primarily with the concepts of error and evidence. A scientist wishes to draw inferences from data, but he knows that sample estimates may contain sampling errors. He does not want to believe that an observed difference between sample means indicates any true difference, unless he can reasonably be sure that it has not arisen as a result of sampling error. The question, then, is whether the observed difference present in the sample data is large relative to the sampling error. This is determined

[1] Abraham Wald, *Statistical Decision Functions*, John Wiley and Sons, New York, 1950.

using the same arithmetic and the same statistics as in the Neyman-Pearson theory. Only the interpretation and emphasis are different. In Fisherian statistics we do not so seriously entertain the possibility that the null hypothesis is true. It is, after all, only a straw man, put up with the intention of forcing us to get enough data to knock it down before any serious inferences are drawn from the data. (See Section 13.10.)

Some further concrete differences in the implications of the two theories may be usefully noted. In a strict Neyman-Pearson approach, the α-level must be set before the experiment is conducted, and if precise control of the β-error given a specified alternative to H_0 is desired, the precise sample size is determined by the choice of α and β. In this approach it is illegitimate to continue accumulating data until the null hypothesis is rejected, unless one adopts the special and relatively complicated methods of sequential analysis developed by Wald.[2]

In the Fisherian approach, data provide evidence and we should continue to gather evidence until either the issue is settled or we cannot afford further observation. Again this is what is done in practical work in the behavioral sciences, though practitioners, fearing the reproach of some statisticians, will not feel inclined to mention prominently that sample sizes were not irrevocably set before the experiment began.

In Fisherian statistics it is common to draw a sample, test a null hypothesis, and report the probability of the observed discrepancy given that H_0 is true. This probability indicates the smallest value that could be used for α for which the data are sufficient to reject the null hypothesis. [This smallest value of α was called the *extreme area (EA)* in Section 13.7.] Levels of α are not necessarily set before the experiment is conducted. In the example in Section 15.7 (Case I), the data would be judged significant at a level of about .04; there might not have been any *a priori* setting of $\alpha = .01$. The rejection of the null hypothesis at the .04 level is some evidence of a nonzero difference. If the extreme area had been .01 the evidence would have been deemed stronger.

In Fisherian statistics, the confidence interval has an added valid interpretation not available in the Neyman-Pearson approach. To understand this we must begin with some remarks about the Fisherian test of significance. To Fisher the logic of the significance test was that of the disjunction. If we obtain a large "t" statistic under the null hypothesis, one of two things has happened: (1) the null hypothesis is true but we have gotten a very unusual sample, or (2) the null hypothesis is false. The conclusion that the null hypothesis is false is based on the assumption that we have *not* gotten an unusual sample, and so we proceed in the belief that we have enough evidence to

---

[2] Abraham Wald, *Sequential Analysis*, John Wiley and Sons, New York, 1947.

conclude reasonably that the null hypothesis is untrue. This in itself, of course, does not tell us much, since no particular point value has much credibility. If we are comparing two teaching methods, we really do not believe, even tentatively, that they are absolutely equally effective. We expect that there will be some difference. The important question is: How much difference is there? The Neyman-Pearson confidence interval and the Fisherian confidence interval both attempt to answer that question, but the permissible verbal statements differ.

We have previously given the permissible Neyman-Pearson statement: "A 100γ percent confidence interval is a random interval that covers the true parameter value with probability at least γ." Notice that the subject of this statement is not the parameter; the subject is the random interval. Most of us would prefer to use statistics to make meaningful statements about parameters, not about random intervals. The former are of interest, the latter are not. For example, in the problem of the principal and the superintendent (see Section 12.1), rather than say that a 95 percent confidence interval for ϕ (i.e., the population proportion of children with IQ scores below 100) is the interval .514–.706 (see Example 2 in Section 14.7), it would seem more reasonable to be able to say that the probability that ϕ is between .514 and .706 is .95. The second statement concerns the parameter ϕ; the first statement concerns a set of random intervals.

In Fisherian statistics, the $100\gamma\% = 100(1 - \alpha)\%$ confidence interval is the set of parameter points that would not be rejected by a two-sided α-level test of significance. The confidence interval procedure in Fisherian statistics divides the parameter space into two sets of points, those that are tenable given the data, and those that are not. In the confidence interval for ϕ given in the preceding paragraph, $C(.514 \leq \phi \leq .706) = 95\%$. In Fisherian statistics, this can be interpreted as follows. Consider the H_0 that ϕ is equal to some constant. If any value of ϕ from .514 to .706 is used as the constant, then the H_0 will be retained as a possibility. Use of any other value of ϕ as the constant would lead to the rejection of the hypothesis at an α-level of .05 (i.e., $1 - \gamma$).[3]

This interpretation, we feel, is clear and useful, though later we shall show that even more useful statements are possible using other methods. These other methods will permit us to make direct probability statements about the parameter of interest. The weakness of the classical confidence interval is that it does not give us any indication of which

[3] Of course, these probability statements are only approximate since the normal curve is being used to estimate exact binomial probabilities. Also presumed is the use of the formulas given in footnote 4 on page 330. These formulas take into account the fact that the σ_p is a function of ϕ.

subsets of the set of tenable parameter points (in our example, the possible ϕ-values from .514 to .706) are more likely to be near the true value. Methods discussed in the next sections make this distinction possible.

We hope that this brief discussion will have helped to provide a perspective regarding two methods, the Fisher and the Neyman-Pearson, that together have come to be known as "classical" statistical methods. Most statistical practitioners draw heavily on a mixture of such methods, giving interpretations to statements that may (or may not) be valid from either or both points of view. One invalid interpretation frequently occurs after the hypothesis $\mu_1 = \mu_2$ has been tested and rejected. Following such a result the declaration is frequently made that a "significant difference" between the means has been found. Generally such a statement is nonsense, because an α-level "test of significance" in itself tells us nothing about the magnitude or importance (that is, the practical significance) of the true difference. (The issue of practical versus statistical significance was discussed in some detail in Section 13.5. See also study manual exercises 13.5.17–13.5.19.) A valid statement in the Fisherian sense is that the *sample difference* is sufficiently large, relative to probable sampling error, to provide reasonable assurance that there is some degree of difference between the population values.

An advantage of the approach we shall next describe is that the significance of a difference depends on an appropriate judgment of importance and *not* on a measure of the amount of evidence gathered to reject, or on the probability of incorrect rejection of a hypothesis that nobody ever believed. Furthermore, in this approach, the investigator must declare what true difference constitutes for him a significant (important) difference. Others are free to disagree with this judgment.

16.3 Bayesian Statistics—An Alternative to Neyman-Pearson / Fisherian Methods

The major problem with both Neyman-Pearson and Fisherian classical statistics is that neither system makes it possible to construct direct probability statements about the parameter of interest. Using classical statistics, we can talk about the probability of a random interval covering the mean, but we cannot talk about the probability of the mean being within a specified interval. This seems very peculiar indeed. We are not to be permitted to make statements about those things that are the subject of our investigation. This is an unsatisfactory state of affairs. What we want is a system that permits us to say: "The probability that the unknown proportion is greater than ϕ_1 and less than

ϕ_2 is $1 - \alpha$." But to make probability statements about ϕ, we must have a probability distribution for ϕ. In Bayesian statistics such a distribution is possible and meaningful and indeed is the central objective of a statistical investigation.

A second problem with the classical procedures is that they provide no mechanism for incorporating into the statistical process any prior information we may have about the parameter. But is it reasonable to evaluate evidence from an experiment while ignoring other available information extraneous to the particular experiment? Upon reflection, this does not seem reasonable. Consider a six-sided die used in Las Vegas. Suppose we roll it ten times and observe the following numbers of occurrences of the faces bearing one through six dots each: 2, 1, 1, 0, 3, 3. Would we be likely to conclude from this that the probability of these six faces was even approximately 2/10, 1/10, 1/10, 0/10, 3/10, 3/10? This does not seem reasonable. We know that the House does not need to use crooked dice to win and that manufacturing techniques can be very precise. And so uniform probabilities of 1/6, 1/6, 1/6, 1/6, 1/6, 1/6 seem much more reasonable, even given the data. No evidence, in short, can be evaluated in a vacuum. We cannot generally pretend, as classical statistics insists we must, that we had no information before beginning an experiment. In the problem of the principal and superintendent (Section 12.1), for example, it seems unreasonable to believe that the superintendent has no information already at hand concerning the ability level of students under study. However, since any background information we may have is apt to be limited, we must also demand that our system of statistical inference insure that experimental data can, in the long run, overrule our background information. We shall see that this is precisely what happens in Bayesian statistics.

In summary, we require an inferential procedure that provides experimenters with

    1 The capability of making probability statements about parameters

    2 A mechanism for combining prior information with new information to enable them to make new probability statements about parameters

Schematically, we require a system having the paradigm

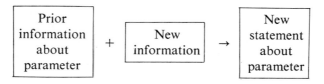

Neither of the two capabilities mentioned above is part of the classical procedures.

16.4 Personal Probabilities and Propensities

Suppose you have before you two solid objects. The first (I) is an ordinary die manufactured to Las Vegas standards with the standard inscriptions on the six faces. The second (II) is similar to a die, but the six faces are not at right angles and they have different areas. Also this figure seems to have been made by joining six irregularly shaped solids composed of substances of different weight per unit mass.

In the case of Solid I, you might anticipate that in a very large number of tosses of the solid, each of the sides, conveniently inscribed with 1, 2, 3, 4, 5, and 6 dots, will appear about one-sixth of the time. Thus, if you were to bet on the occurrence of the event "side 1 up" you would want betting odds of 5 to 1; in fact, you would want such odds for any of the six sides. Betting odds are ratios that relate the dollars you expect to receive if you win to the dollars you are willing to pay if you lose. They are related to probabilities in the following way. If the probability of an event A is $P(A)$, then the odds you should receive for betting on A are determined from the quantities $1 - P(A)$ and $P(A)$. For example, if you bet on a 1 occurring when Solid I is tossed, you would expect odds of $(1 - 1/6)$ to $1/6$, or $5/6$ to $1/6$, or 5 to 1. That is, you would demand five dollars if a 1 occurs and would be willing to pay one dollar if a 1 does not occur. On the other hand, if you were betting that a 2, 3, 4, 5, or 6 will occur (i.e., betting against a 1) your odds would be $(1 - 5/6)$ to $5/6$, or 1 to 5. That is, you would expect to receive only one dollar if a 1 did not occur and pay five dollars if a 1 did occur. In the first example you are receiving odds, and in the second example you are giving odds.

The reason that you are willing to accept the bets described above is that you believe as a result of an inspection of the die, and possibly because of some assurances as to the circumstances of manufacture, that the long-run relative frequency of occurrence of the six faces will be 1/6 for each face, and thus that in the long run such bets will leave you even. Of course, if someone offered better odds you would certainly accept them.

In the case of a toss of Solid II, you have a more difficult problem. You cannot act as if you knew the long-run relative frequencies for each of the six sides, and thus you would not so quickly name the odds at which you might consider a gamble to be reasonable. Nevertheless, if forced to do so you might assign six nonnegative (probably positive) numbers whose sum was one and use these to determine your betting behavior. Let us suppose that those numbers are .04, .10, .12, .18, .24, and .32, corresponding respectively to faces 1 through 6 of the solid. Then you would require odds of about 2.13 to 1 if you were to bet on face 6 against faces 1 through 5.[4] If you were to bet on faces 1 to 4 against faces 5 or 6 you would want odds of about 1.27 to 1.[5]

The student will no doubt wonder how the numbers .04, .10, .12, .18, .24, and .32 were obtained. The following game might help you begin to understand how this could have been done. Suppose I say to you that we shall have one toss of Solid II and that a bet will be made in the following way. You will decide what the appropriate odds are for a "6" against a "1, 2, 3, 4, or 5," and then I shall decide, considering the odds you have specified, which of the two possibilities "6" or "1, 2, 3, 4, or 5" I wish to choose. In this situation it seems clear that you will want to think very carefully about the odds you identify with face 6. If the odds are too high you are going to be unhappy if I bet on 1, 2, 3, 4, or 5, and if they are too low you will be unhappy if I bet on 6. Thus, in trying to determine a numerical value for each of the six numbers to be associated with each of the six faces, you will consider carefully the possible implications of these numbers with respect to gambles. It is this careful consideration in terms of possible gambles that provides the disciplined inquiry through which the six numbers are obtained.

After an extremely long string of observations of rolls of Solid II, you would have available a set of long-run relative frequencies of occurrence of the six faces. These numbers might be .06, .12, .14, .16, .22, and .30. If this string of observations was sufficiently long, you would disregard any inferences you might have drawn from the size, shape, and feel of the faces and rely solely on these long-run relative frequencies to govern your betting behavior. You would offer and accept bets using the same kinds of calculations as were illustrated above. You would expect to receive odds of about 2.33 to 1 (.70 to .30) to bet on face 6 and odds of 1.08 to 1 (.52 to .48) to bet on faces 1, 2, 3, or 4.

But what if you have only a limited number of observations? Perhaps in ten throws of Solid II you observe the following numbers of occurrences of each of the faces: 0, 1, 0, 2, 4, 3. Converting these to observed relative frequencies you have .00, .10, .00, .20, .40, .30.

[4] In this instance, you are betting on face 6, and $P(\text{face } 6) = .32$. Therefore, the odds you should receive for betting on face 6 are $[1 - P(\text{face } 6)]$ to $P(\text{face } 6)$. Thus, the odds are $(1 - .32)$ to .32, or .68 to .32, which is the same as 2.13 to 1.

[5] In this example, you are betting on faces 1, 2, 3, or 4, and $P(\text{face } 1, \text{face } 2, \text{face } 3, \text{or face } 4) = .04 + .10 + .12 + .18 = .44$. Therefore, the odds you should receive are $(1 - .44)$ to .44, which is .56 to .44 or 1.27 to 1.

Would you use these frequencies alone to guide your betting behavior? Probably not. Nor would you be likely to want to ignore the data and rely solely on your original judgments. Somehow you would like to be able to combine your original judgments with the observations to arrive at new numbers to be used as a guide for your betting behavior.

It will now be useful to introduce a distinction between two concepts that in their behavior satisfy the same system of rules or axioms. This will then make it possible to introduce a system in which judgments based on nonexperimental data can be coherently combined with observational data to provide a framework for inference and behavior. With respect to Solid I you assumed that you knew (to a sufficiently good approximation) the relative frequency with which each face would appear in a very, very long sequence of throws. This number, known to you approximately for a precisely and fairly constructed solid, is a piece of information that may be known by everyone observing the solid. In fact, it is a physical property of the solid and of the process of throwing it. Solid II also has such numbers associated with each of its faces, but you cannot make good guesses about their value just by examining the solid. These numbers exist and in principle are determinable to any required degree of accuracy through experimentation, but they are unknown to you.

We now depart from conventional terminology and refer to these physical characteristics (the long-run relative frequencies) of the faces of a solid within the framework of the experiment of rolling the solid as the *propensities* of these faces. We say that the propensity of face 6 for Solid I is 1/6 and the propensity of face 6 for Solid II is .30.[6] We next note that each of the two sets of propensities satisfies the probability rules given in Chapter 9. The propensity of face 1 or 2 for Solid I is 1/3 (1/6 + 1/6) and for Solid II .18. Also, each of the propensities is a number between zero and one, and the sum of the propensities for each die is one. We can also see that these propensities conform to the addition law of probability theory and in fact are formally probabilities in the sense that this word was used in Section 9.3. We emphasize that the propensities for the faces of Solid I can be taken as known (approximately) on examination of the solid and its source, whereas those for solid II cannot, except perhaps by some extremely clever physicist-geometrician.

In addition to propensities you have some other numbers. For both Solid I and Solid II, you have the numbers you would use to guide your betting behavior. For Solid I these numbers are the same as the propensities for each of the six faces. For Solid II, for which the propensities initially are unknown, these numbers could not be deter-

---

[6] The .30 is taken from the set of long-term relative frequencies for Solid II given previously, namely, .06, .12, .14, .16, .22, and .30.

mined except through a judgmental process similar to that described above. However, given these numbers, you would use them in combination, with respect to compound events, in precisely the same way as was done with probabilities in Chapter 9 and with propensities in the preceding paragraphs. As indicated above, with initial quantities of .24 and .32 for faces 5 and 6 of Solid II, you would want odds of about 2.13 to 1 to bet on face 6, and odds of 1.27 to 1 to bet on faces 1, 2, 3, or 4.[7]

Thus we have two kinds of quantities satisfying the same axioms. We referred to the first as *propensities* and we shall refer to the second as *personal probabilities*, or, for brevity, simply as probabilities. It must be stressed that propensities and probabilities are very different concepts. Propensities are physical properties of the object and the experiment. Probabilities are judgmental values supplied by a person (you) that describe his or her (your) betting behavior for uncertain events. If propensities are known to you, they will determine your probabilities. If they are unknown, you must find some way of quantifying your beliefs about them and of combining these beliefs with new data to provide revised judgments.[8]

16.5   Conditional Probabilities

We next need to reconsider the statement of the axioms of probability in light of the discussion in the previous section. Immediately we recognize that the probability value you work with depends on the information available to you. If we denote all available background information by the symbol H, then we write the probability of an event E given the background information H as

$$P(E \mid H)$$

The vertical line | means "given," and we read this expression as "the probability of E given H." Most textbooks will refer to this as a *conditional* probability, i.e., the probability of E, conditional on being given the background information H. But in our theory all probabilities depend on available information, and hence all probabilities are conditional probabilities obeying the usual axioms of probability theory.

---

[7] See footnotes 4 and 5 for the derivation of these odds.

[8] The distinction between probability and propensity has been refined by D. V. Lindley and M. R. Novick, in *Conditional Probabilities in Exchangeable Subpopulations*, unpublished manuscript, 1976.

As a review, let us restate these axioms in our new notation. Let A be an event and H the background information. Then the following axioms apply.

1 The probability of any event is not less than zero nor more than one: $0 \leq P(A \mid H) \leq 1$.

2 If A is an event that includes all possible outcomes of an experiment, it is called the *universal event*, U; and for any background information H,

$$P(U \mid H) = 1$$

3 Suppose that A and B are *independent events* given H. By this we mean that, given H, our probability for A is not affected by our knowing whether or not B has occurred. Then the probability that both A and B will occur given H is the product of the probabilities that A will occur given H, and that B will occur given H. We write this as

$$P(A \text{ and } B \mid H) = P(A \mid H) \cdot P(B \mid H)$$

This is called the *multiplication law for independent events*. As an example, consider two tosses of a fair die. The probability of a 6 on toss one and of a 6 on toss two are each individually $1/6$ and these probabilities are unaffected by previous (or subsequent) tosses. Thus the probability of getting a 6 on throw one *and* a 6 on throw two is $1/6 \cdot 1/6 = 1/36$. There is nothing new in this statement of the multiplication law except our present interpretation that it applies both to propensities and to *probabilities*.

4 If the occurrence of either A or B logically precludes the occurrence of the other, these are called *exclusive events*. For any background information H, and for exclusive events A and B,

$$P(A \text{ or } B \mid H) = P(A \mid H) + P(B \mid H)$$

That is, the probabilities for exclusive events are additive. We read this symbolic statement as "the probability that A or B will occur given H is the sum of the probabilities of A given H and B given H." More generally if E_1, E_2, and so on, are such that the occurrence of any one of these events precludes the possibility of the occurrence of any other, then these events are said to be mutually exclusive and

$$P(E_1 \text{ or } E_2 \text{ or } \ldots) = P(E_1) + P(E_2) + \cdots$$

This is called the *addition law for mutually exclusive events*. Consider the example of a fair die and suppose the events $E_1, E_2, \ldots, E_6$ correspond to the appearance of $1, 2, \ldots, 6$, respectively. The probability for each of these events is $1/6$ and we write

$$P(E_1) = P(E_2) = \cdots = P(E_6) = \frac{1}{6}$$

We have suppressed the notation "given H" but understand that even if unstated this condition H is always present. In this case, the background information is the set of six known propensities inferred from the shape and history of the die. The universal event is

$$E_1 \text{ or } E_2 \text{ or } E_3 \text{ or } E_4 \text{ or } E_5 \text{ or } E_6$$

and using axiom 4 we have

$$P(U) = P(E_1) + P(E_2) + \cdots + P(E_6)$$
$$= \frac{1}{6} + \frac{1}{6} + \cdots + \frac{1}{6} = 1$$

Suppose A is the event "E_1 or E_2" and B is the event "E_1 or E_2 or E_3 or E_4," and suppose you are told that B has occurred. What would you then say is the probability that A has occurred? Presumably you would argue that if B has occurred, then, on the information given, the four remaining events must still be equally probable. Hence each must have probability $1/4$, since their probabilities must add to 1. Then using axiom 4 with the new probabilities, we find that the probability of A is equal to $1/4 + 1/4$, or $1/2$.

To provide a way of writing this, we again adopt the notation for conditional probability and write

$$P(A \mid B)$$

which is read "probability of A given B" or "probability that A will occur (or has occurred) given that B will occur (or has occurred)." Then we have

$$P(A \mid B) = P(E_1 \text{ or } E_2 \mid B)$$
$$= P(E_1 \mid B) + P(E_2 \mid B)$$
$$= \frac{1}{4} + \frac{1}{4} = \frac{1}{2}$$

where the individual conditional probabilities were obtained by the argument given above.

Motivated by this simple example, and perhaps only after seeing that this computation makes sense generally, we are led to introduce a definition.

DN 16.1 The conditional probability of A given B, written $P(A \mid B)$, is defined by

$$P(A \mid B) = \frac{P(A \text{ and } B)}{P(B)} \tag{16.1}$$

where $P(A \text{ and } B)$ is the probability that both A and B occur and it is assumed that $P(B) > 0$.

In general $P(A \mid B)$ will not equal $P(A)$. But suppose A and B are independent. Then $P(A \text{ and } B) = P(A) \cdot P(B)$, and (16.1) yields

$$P(A \mid B) = \frac{P(A) \cdot P(B)}{P(B)} = P(A)$$

which indeed gives an intuitive meaning to the idea of the independence of events A and B.

Now consider again the previous example.

$$P(B) = P(E_1 \text{ or } E_2 \text{ or } E_3 \text{ or } E_4)$$
$$= \frac{1}{6} + \frac{1}{6} + \frac{1}{6} + \frac{1}{6} = \frac{2}{3}$$
$$P(A \text{ and } B) = P([E_1 \text{ or } E_2] \text{ and } [E_1 \text{ or } E_2 \text{ or } E_3 \text{ or } E_4])$$
$$= P(E_1 \text{ or } E_2) = \frac{1}{6} + \frac{1}{6} = \frac{1}{3}$$

Thus

$$P(A \mid B) = \frac{1/3}{2/3} = \frac{1}{2}$$

as previously determined by direct argument.

Statistical inference in the Bayesian system will involve the computation of conditional probabilities. We shall begin with certain conditional probabilities based on background information. These are usually called *prior probabilities*. Then we shall combine these probabilities with data obtained from an experiment and determine new probabilities, usually called *posterior probabilities*. These new probabilities are also conditional probabilities. They are conditional both on the background information *and* on data from the experiment. The words *prior* and *posterior* are just convenient adjectives to indicate whether the probability statements are being made before (prior to) or after (posterior to) the particular experiment. Schematically we again have

| Prior probability | + | New data | → | Posterior probability |

To begin to see just how we can combine prior probabilities with new data to arrive at posterior probabilities, we now introduce a fundamental law of probability theory.

16.6   Bayes' Theorem for Events

Suppose A is an event of interest and $P(A)$ is your probability for A. Then suppose an event B occurs that you believe bears some relationship to A and thus can be expected to affect your probability for A. What we need is a formal mechanism for computing the conditional probability that A will occur given that B occurs. In some situations, the computation can be made as illustrated in the previous section. In more complicated situations, direct calculation is less easy and a general formula will be helpful. Suppose that, using (16.1), we write

$$P(A \mid B) \cdot P(B) = P(A \text{ and } B) \tag{16.2}$$

But then we can surely also write

$$P(B \mid A) \cdot P(A) = P(A \text{ and } B) \tag{16.3}$$

since this is only a relabeling of events. Then equating the left-hand sides of these two equations and dividing both sides by $P(B)$, which we assume to be greater than zero, we have

$$P(A \mid B) = \frac{P(B \mid A) \cdot P(A)}{P(B)} \tag{16.4}$$

Consider an example. We know that in a certain town .4 of the people support a program of sex education in the schools and .6 oppose it. Among the supporters of the sex education program, .7 favor a proposed bond issue, and among those opposed to the program, only .2 support the bond issue. These are propensities that, being somehow known to you and me, determine your probabilities and mine. At a cocktail party you meet a person, and after some conversation you learn that she supports the bond issue. What is your probability that she also supports sex education? Let A be the event that she supports sex education in the schools and B be the event that she supports the bond issue. Then we can use (16.4) to make the necessary computation.

Before receiving the information B, we would already have

$$P(A) = .4$$

Next we know that among those supporting sex education (event A), .7 support the bond issue (event B). Thus we write

$$P(B \mid A) = .7$$

Finally we need to compute $P(B)$, the probability that the person supports the bond issue. This requires some care. We begin by noting that the event B can be broken down into two exclusive events, namely, "B and A" and "B and $\bar{A}$," where $\bar{A}$ is read as "not A" and means that A has not occurred. The first is the event that the person supports both the bond issue and sex education, and the second is the event that the person supports the bond issue but not sex education. These events are exclusive and together they make up the event B. Thus using the addition law we can write

$$P(B) = P(B \text{ and } A) + P(B \text{ and } \bar{A})$$

Next we use equation (16.3) and write this as

$$P(B) = P(B \mid A)P(A) + P(B \mid \bar{A})P(\bar{A})$$

where $P(\bar{A}) = 1 - P(A)$. Since each of these probabilities is known, we can compute $P(B)$. We have $P(A) = .4$, $P(\bar{A}) = 1 - .4 = .6$, $P(B \mid A) = .7$, and $P(B \mid \bar{A}) = .2$. Thus we can compute

$$P(B) = (.7)(.4) + (.2)(.6)$$
$$= .28 + .12 = .40$$

Finally we compute

$$P(A \mid B) = \frac{(.7)(.4)}{.4} = .7$$

Thus the additional information that the guest favors the bond issue raises your probability that she favors sex education from .4 to .7. Note that the incorporation of the information B involves the use of the probability of $B \mid A$.

It may be useful to emphasize again the difference between a probability statement and a propensity statement. The propensity statement is a statement concerning a property of an entity—for example, the long-run relative frequency of heads for tosses of a coin. The probability statement is the statement about your judgment relative to that entity, in this case the particular coin in question, and this statement does not necessarily have any long-run relative frequency interpretation. In the example just given, $P(A \mid B) = .7$ is at the same time *both* a propensity (that is, a long-run relative frequency) *and* your probability, because this propensity is known to you.

The form in which equation (16.4) is usually given incorporates the computations needed to compute $P(B)$ in very general situations. If A_1, A_2, A_3, and so on are such that precisely one of them must occur, they are mutually exclusive and exhaustive. In the previous example we had $A_1 = A$ and $A_2 = \bar{A}$. Then the event B is the same as the event "B and A_1" or "B and A_2" or "B and A_3" and so on. Then we can write

$$
\begin{aligned}
P(B) &= P(B \text{ and } A_1) + P(B \text{ and } A_2) + \cdots \\
&= P(B \mid A_1)P(A_1) + P(B \mid A_2)P(A_2) + \cdots \\
&= \sum P(B \mid A_i)P(A_i)
\end{aligned}
$$

Substituting this in equation (16.4) we have

$$
P(A_1 \mid B) = \frac{P(B \mid A_1)P(A_1)}{P(B)} = \frac{P(B \mid A_1)P(A_1)}{\sum P(B \mid A_i)P(A_i)} \tag{16.5}
$$

with similar statements for $P(A_2 \mid B)$ and so on. Equation (16.5) is the standard statement of *Bayes' theorem for events*. This formula is a generalization of formula (16.4). In (16.4) we considered only the two possibilities A and $\bar{A}$. In (16.5) we consider the possibilities A_1, A_2, ... [Study manual exercise 16.6.12 illustrates the applications of (16.5).]

Thus we have seen that Bayes' theorem provides a mechanism for combining prior beliefs $P(A)$ with new information, the observation B, to arrive at posterior beliefs $P(A \mid B)$. In the example of this section, we wanted to make a probability statement about whether or not a particular person supported a sex education program. Since it was known that .4 of the people favored this sex education program, your prior probability that this particular person supported the program was .4 [i.e., $P(A_1) = .4$]. The additional information in the example was that this particular person supported the bond issue. Given this new information, the application of Bayes' theorem indicated that your posterior probability (i.e., your probability after receiving this new information) that this particular person supported the sex education program was .7. Schematically, we have:

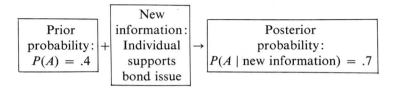

This schematic diagram represents the essential core of Bayesian statistics.

16.7   Bayes' Theorem for Continuous Random Variables: Introduction

The preceding section developed Bayes' theorem for events. To use this theorem we needed the specific probability values for particular events. Then these values were used in equation (16.5) to find the posterior probability of the event of interest.

This application of Bayes' theorem was useful as an introduction to the basic process of Bayesian inference, which involves combining prior information and observational information to yield a posterior set of beliefs. However, frequently in a Bayesian inference procedure we are interested in more than the occurrence of a single event. What interests us is the development of a probability distribution for a parameter. In Bayesian statistics parameters are considered as continuous random variables. This implies that we must be concerned with making probability statements about a very large (infinite) number of events—one for each possible value of the parameter. When we are concerned with this type of problem, certain modifications must be made in equation (16.5). In this section we present a situation that will serve as the illustrative example for this new application of Bayes' theorem. The actual implementation of Bayes' theorem for continuous random variables will be illustrated in a later section.

Consider the following situation. A school system has implemented an individualized math program in the elementary school. The program consists of a series of instructional units that each pupil must learn. A simplified view of this teaching and learning process recognizes the following three components:

  1 A pretest over a given unit of instruction to decide if the instruction is needed

2 A period of instruction, given if needed

3 A posttest to decide if the unit objectives have been achieved

Our primary concern will be with the last of these steps. We will want to use the results from the posttest to decide whether or not a particular student has "mastered" the objectives of the unit. We shall call this posttest a mastery test and assume, for simplicity, that it contains n items, all of equal difficulty. We shall use the symbol ϕ to denote the unknown propensity of a correct response on an item for the particular student. If this propensity were known, it would be our probability that the student would answer *any* particular item correctly, because all items are judged equally difficult.

This unknown propensity (ϕ) for a student to answer items correctly may also be thought of as an ability or achievement parameter, and any decision we might make about a student with regard to advancing her or him to the next unit or providing remedial work on the present unit would depend on our beliefs about the true value of this ability parameter. Now because each student's ability is unknown, the best we can hope to do is to make some probabilistic statement about it. For example, if we decide that students will not be labeled "masters" unless $\phi \geq .80$, we might want to indicate the probability that a student's ability (ϕ) is greater than .80.[9]

How can these probabilistic statements be made? What we need is a probabilistic representation of our beliefs about the student's ability parameter. Then, if we have a large enough probability that this ability parameter is above a certain point (the mastery criterion; say, $\phi = .80$), we will label the student a master. How can we arrive at this representation of our beliefs about the ability parameter? We have the student's responses to the mastery test. Also, we may have prior information about this student. For example, the teacher may have worked with the student during the unit of instruction and passed her judgment about the student's performance on to us. What we need is a way to quantify our prior beliefs and then incorporate the information obtained from the mastery test to arrive at our posterior beliefs about the student's ability parameter. While Bayes' theorem provides us with a mechanism for incorporating new information into our prior beliefs, it does not help us characterize our prior beliefs. In the next several sections, we examine procedures for representing prior beliefs and then use the mastery testing situation to illustrate the application of Bayes' theorem to random variables.

---

[9] The difficult problem of defining the specific value of ϕ that will be used to decide whether or not a student can be labeled "master" will not be discussed in this chapter.

16.8   The Beta Distribution

As noted in the preceding section, in a Bayesian analysis we must find a way to quantify our beliefs about the parameter of interest. Specifically, we need a probability distribution that is indicative of our beliefs about a particular parameter. In general, we would need a family of probability distributions that could be used to represent a variety of possible different beliefs about the parameter. For example, in the mastery testing situation discussed in Section 16.7, the parameter of interest is ϕ, where ϕ is some value between .0 and 1.0. In this instance, we must find a way to quantify our beliefs about ϕ, whatever they may be.

In previous chapters of this book we have examined three families of probability distributions: normal, t, and binomial. It seems reasonable to consider whether any of these families would be flexible enough to represent a variety of beliefs about ϕ. One minor reason why the normal distribution and the t-distribution families might not be ideal is that all members of these families are symmetrical distributions. Thus, it would be impossible to represent certain types of asymmetrical "beliefs" with these curves. For example, in the mastery testing situation we might feel that ϕ is most likely to be around .75, moderately likely to be around .95, and most unlikely to be around .55. However, the symmetry of these distributions is not a major reason for rejecting these families as prior distributions; indeed, the normal and t-distributions do serve as prior distributions for other problems. The true reason for not using these distributions will emerge later.

What about the binomial family of probability distributions? Remember that the binomial probability distribution serves as a model for discrete random variables (e.g., number of successes in n trials). As was noted at the beginning of Section 16.7, the parameter of interest in a Bayesian analysis is treated as a continuous random variable. In the mastery testing problem, for example, ϕ is considered a continuous random variable. Thus, the binomial probability distributions are not satisfactory models for our prior beliefs about ϕ.

It seems, then, that we need a new family of distributions to represent our beliefs about ϕ. What family? Consider the distributions shown in Figure 16.1. For the moment ignore the a- and b-values on the left and upper margins. Assume that the horizontal axis of each curve represents possible ϕ-values from .0 to 1.0. Note, first, the variety of curves in Figure 16.1. Even a casual look suggests that a wide variety of beliefs should be at least approximately describable by distributions selected from this family. Recall that the area under the curve between any two values gives the probability that the random variable is between these two values. For these curves, the random variable is the parameter ϕ

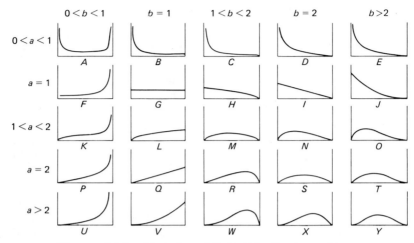

Figure 16.1   Varieties of Beta Distributions. (From
*Statistical Methods for Educational and Psychological
Research* by Novick, M. R. and Jackson, P. H. Copyright
1974, McGraw-Hill. Used by permission of McGraw-Hill
Book Company)

and the area between two ϕ-values, say ϕ_1 and ϕ_2, gives the probability
that ϕ is between ϕ_1 and ϕ_2. For example, if $\phi_1 = .1$ and $\phi_2 = .2$,
then from Figure 16.1 it can be seen that Distributions U and V assign
very little probability to this interval and Distributions D and E
assign very high probability.

The curves shown in Figure 16.1 are from a family of distributions
called *beta distributions*. As the figure suggests, a wide range of beliefs
can be characterized by a beta distribution. What we need to do, then,
is choose a beta distribution that gives probabilities we would find
reasonable in making bets about the value of the parameter ϕ. However,
before we can begin to select a reasonable beta distribution we must
be able to describe these distributions.

In Section 10.2 we defined the normal probability distribution
function as

$$Y = \frac{1}{\sigma\sqrt{2\pi}} e^{-(X-\mu)^2/2\sigma^2} \qquad \text{[see (10.1)]}$$

And, in Section 15.3 we defined the t probability distribution function as

$$y = \frac{C}{[1 + (t^2/df)]^{(df+1)/2}} \qquad \text{[see (15.2)]}$$

Table 16.1   Characteristics of the Beta Distribution: Measures of Central Tendency and Variability

---

If ϕ has the distribution $\beta(a, b)$, then

1 The expected value of ϕ = the mean = $\dfrac{a}{a + b}$

2 The mode = $\dfrac{a - 1}{a + b - 2}$, provided a and b are both greater than 1

3 The median $\approx \dfrac{2}{3}\left(\dfrac{a}{a + b}\right) + \dfrac{1}{3}\left(\dfrac{a - 1}{a + b - 2}\right)$, provided a and b are both greater than 4

4 The variance = $\dfrac{ab}{(a + b)^2(a + b + 1)}$

5 The standard deviation = $\sqrt{\dfrac{ab}{(a + b)^2(a + b + 1)}}$

Sample Calculation Suppose our prior beliefs about ϕ can be represented by $\beta(21, 6)$. The characteristics of this distribution are

1 The mean = $\dfrac{21}{21 + 6} = .778$

2 Mode = $\dfrac{21 - 1}{21 + 6 - 2} = .80$

3 Median $\approx \dfrac{2}{3}\left(\dfrac{21}{21 + 6}\right) + \dfrac{1}{3}\left(\dfrac{21 - 1}{21 + 6 - 2}\right) \approx .785$

4 Variance = $\dfrac{(21)(6)}{(21 + 6)^2(21 + 6 + 1)} \approx .0062$

5 Standard deviation = $\sqrt{.0013} \approx .079$

---

where C was some constant. For each of these functions, the value of the function (Y or y) could be thought of as representing the height of the probability distribution at values of X or t, respectively. These functions were used to obtain the probabilities that the random variables X or t lie between any two specified values.

You may recall that it was not necessary to work with either of the above functions directly, since tables were supplied that enabled us to use them without performing any mathematical manipulations. The same holds for our discussion of beta distributions. First, we will give the mathematical form for the beta probability distribution function; then we will present tables that will enable us to use the beta distribution in our Bayesian analysis.

The beta distribution function is

$$Y = \frac{\phi^{a-1}(1 - \phi)^{b-1}}{\beta(a, b)} \qquad (0 \le \phi \le 1; a, b > 0) \qquad (16.6)$$

Table 16.2 Percentile Points for Selected Beta Distributions

$P(\phi \le \phi_1)$	Beta Distribution (8, 2)	(15, 5)	(21, 6)	(27.5, 22.5)
.005	.4150	.4729	.5450	.3701
.010	.4560	.5017	.5703	.3872
.025	.5175	.5443	.6064	.4121
.050	.5708	.5809	.6375	.4340
.100	.6316	.6225	.6722	.4597
.125	.6531	.6373	.6846	.4690
.166⅔	.6825	.6577	.7015	.4819
.200	.7022	.6715	.7130	.4910
.250	.7277	.6895	.7279	.5028
.300	.7479	.7055	.7410	.5135
.333⅓	.7633	.7152	.7490	.5200
.400	.7877	.7334	.7640	.5327
.500	.8203	.7585	.7847	.5507
.600	.8502	.7824	.8044	.5685
.666⅔	.8692	.7984	.8177	.5810
.700	.8786	.8066	.8244	.5875
.750	.8928	.8194	.8350	.5979
.800	.9074	.8330	.8464	.6095
.833⅓	.9174	.8429	.8546	.6181
.875	.9307	.8567	.8662	.6306
.900	.9392	.8661	.8740	.6394
.950	.9590	.8901	.8944	.6636
.975	.9719	.9085	.9102	.6840
.990	.9829	.9272	.9268	.7070
.995	.9879	.9383	.9365	.7227

where $\beta(a, b)$ is a constant that depends on the values a and b. The exact value of the constant $\beta(a, b)$ will not be important to us since we will be getting the probability values we need from a table.

For our purposes, mere selection of a and b defines a specific beta distribution. For example, if $a = 2$ and $b = 2$, the beta distribution has the form shown in Figure 16.1 as Distribution S. Thus, selecting a prior distribution to characterize our beliefs about ϕ means selecting appropriate values for a and b.

Before discussing procedures that will aid in the selection of these a- and b-values, we will examine some of the characteristics of beta distributions. A specific beta distribution will be identified as $\beta(a, b)$.[10]

---

[10] The use of $\beta(a, b)$ to identify a specific distribution and also to identify the constant in equation (16.6) should not cause any confusion. It will always be clear from the context whether $\beta(a, b)$ refers to a beta probability distribution or just to a specific constant.

Table 16.2 (Continued)

$P(\phi \leq \phi_1)$	Beta Distribution			
	(25, 25)	(31, 21)	(55, 45)	(57.5, 42.5)
.005	.3229	.4188	.4218	.4466
.010	.3391	.4360	.4341	.4590
.025	.3634	.4612	.4521	.4774
.050	.3847	.4830	.4680	.4932
.100	.4097	.5084	.4861	.5114
.125	.4188	.5176	.4927	.5180
$.166\frac{2}{3}$	.4316	.5303	.5019	.5272
.200	.4404	.5392	.5082	.5335
.250	.4522	.5508	.5166	.5419
.300	.4628	.5613	.5241	.5494
$.333\frac{1}{3}$	.4694	.5677	.5287	.5541
.400	.4820	.5800	.5377	.5629
.500	.5000	.5974	.5503	.5755
.600	.5182	.6146	.5629	.5880
$.666\frac{2}{3}$	.5306	.6265	.5717	.5967
.700	.5372	.6328	.5764	.6013
.750	.5478	.6428	.5838	.6086
.800	.5596	.6538	.5920	.6168
$.833\frac{1}{3}$	.5684	.6620	.5981	.6228
.875	.5812	.6738	.6071	.6316
.900	.5903	.6823	.6134	.6379
.950	.6153	.7050	.6309	.6551
.975	.6366	.7241	.6459	.6698
.990	.6609	.7456	.6631	.6866
.995	.6771	.7598	.6748	.6978

The mean, median, mode, and variance of a beta distribution are functions of the a- and b-values. The formulas for these characteristics of the distribution are given in Table 16.1 on p. 393.

While the summary statistics shown in Table 16.1 are useful, perhaps a more meaningful way to describe a particular beta distribution is to identify selected percentile points of the distribution (e.g., P_{25}, P_{50}, P_{75}). A very abbreviated table of selected percentile points for a few selected values of a and b is given as Table 16.2. The first column in Table 16.2 shows the probability that $\phi \leq \phi_1$, where ϕ_1 is a specific ϕ-value in a beta distribution. For example, consider $\beta(8, 2)$. Specific ϕ-values from this distribution are shown in the column headed (8, 2) of Table 16.2. For $\beta(8, 2)$, if $\phi_1 = .7022$, then $P(\phi \leq .7022) = .200$. Or if $\phi_1 = .8928$, then $P(\phi \leq .8928) = .750$.

In Table 16.2, the values under each of the beta distributions are actually percentile points. They can be used to describe a given beta distribution. The specific percentile of interest is found by locating the appropriate probability in column 1 and then identifying the ϕ-value in the beta distribution under consideration. For example, suppose we want to find the 50th percentile (P_{50} or the median) of $\beta(21, 6)$. We first locate .500 in column 1 and then look in the column headed (21, 6) to find the median. In this instance the median is .7847, a value that agrees quite well with the approximate one we computed in Table 16.1. Similarly, if we are interested in the first quartile point (P_{25}) for $\beta(21, 6)$, we first find .250 in column 1, and then move to the (21, 6) column to find the appropriate value, .7279. [That is, $P(\phi \leq .7279) = .25$.] The third quartile point for $\beta(21, 6)$ is .8350 [i.e., $P(\phi \leq .8350) = .75$].The three quartile points .728, .785, and .835 provide a reasonably good description of the beta distribution for $a = 21$ and $b = 6$.

The data in Table 16.2 also enable us to make the type of probability statement about ϕ that we have previously hinted will be helpful in our Bayesian analysis. For example, in the mastery testing situation, if we decide to label the student a "master" if $\phi \geq .80$, we may want to find $P(\phi \geq .80)$. If the $\beta(21, 6)$ distribution represents our beliefs about a student's ability parameter (ϕ), we can see in Table 16.2 that this probability is slightly greater than .40.[11]

16.9   Describing Beta Distributions: Credibility Intervals

The use of percentile values makes it possible for us to make statements that describe a beta distribution and thus identify our "beliefs" about the parameter. For example, if $\beta(21, 6)$ represents our beliefs about ϕ, we could say, "The probability that the student's ability parameter (ϕ) is less than .835 is .75." Such statements are typically very useful ones to make; however, other useful kinds of statements can also be made using these same tables. Such statements refer to limits *between* which the quantity of interest lies with a stated probability. For example, the two quartile values obtained above enable us to state: "The probability that the student's ability parameter ϕ lies between .728 (i.e., P_{25}) and .835 (i.e., P_{75}) is .50." The interval .728–.835 is called a *50 percent credibility interval* for the ability parameter ϕ because 50 percent is the measure of the strength of our belief that the student's ability parameter lies in that interval.

There is, of course, nothing unique about the particular 50 percent credibility interval we have chosen. There are many 50 percent credibility intervals for ϕ. We might have chosen the interval from $\phi = 0$ up to the median, or the interval between P_{20} and P_{70}. However, the 50 percent interval between P_{25} and P_{75} is often a very useful one in

[11] In Table 16.2, $P(\phi \leq .8044) = .60$. Therefore, $P(\phi \geq .80) \approx .40$.

describing a beta distribution. In general, the interval that contains the central C percent of the posterior probability, leaving an amount $\frac{1}{2}[(100 - C)\%]$ on each side, is called a *central C percent credibility interval*. If, in any context, it is necessary to draw attention to the fact that we have chosen such an interval, we will call it a *central*, or *equal-tailed* (because equal areas are left under the two tails of the distribution), *credibility interval*.

Central credibility intervals may not be very useful if the distribution is very skewed, as will be the case if the values of a and b are quite different. For example, when $a = 2$ and $b = 12$, the central 50 percent credibility interval is (.074, .196) and the mode is .083.[12] Thus, the mode is very close to one end of the central interval, and the picture conveyed by that interval alone may be misleading. This motivates us to consider another method for obtaining credibility intervals.

In these circumstances, it may be preferable to compute a C percent highest density interval or *highest density region*—in brief, a $C\%$ *HDR*. This is the C percent credibility interval that has the property that the value of the beta distribution function (16.6) is greater at all points inside the interval than at any point outside it. Speaking very loosely, we could say that points inside the *HDR* correspond to more probable values of ϕ than points outside it. The *HDR* is most easily visualized in terms of the graph of the probability distribution. This curve is higher at points inside the interval than at points outside.

Figure 16.2 displays the beta distribution $\beta(21, 6)$. The 50 percent, 75 percent, 90 percent, and 95 percent *HDR* credibility intervals are the segments of the ϕ-scale contained within the indicated vertical lines. If $\beta(21, 6)$ adequately represents our beliefs about ϕ, we can see from Figure 16.2 that the 50 percent *HDR* is approximately (.75, .85). Therefore, if $\beta(21, 6)$ characterizes our beliefs about ϕ, we should be willing to bet at even odds (1 to 1) that ϕ is between .75 and .85. Figure 16.2 suggests some more general properties of the *HDR*, as well. The ordinates [values from equation (16.6)] at the ends of the interval must be equal. Any C percent *HDR* contains the mode. It is also true that for a given C percent the *HDR* is the shortest possible C percent credibility interval. This last property gives the *HDR* a certain uniqueness that might also be considered a reason for preferring it to the somewhat arbitrarily chosen central interval. If the distribution is symmetric and unimodal, the central C percent interval and the C percent *HDR* coincide.

A drawback to the use of *HDR*'s is that they cannot be calculated from standard tables of percentile points such as Table 16.2. However, for the important families of distributions used in Bayesian inference,

---

[12] The interval limits cannot be found in Table 16.2, since $\beta(2, 12)$ is not included in this highly abridged table.

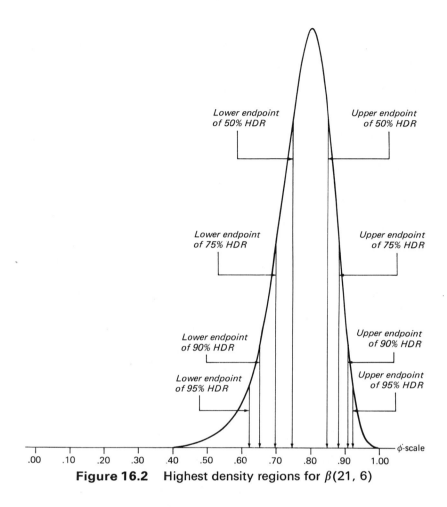

Figure 16.2   Highest density regions for $\beta(21, 6)$

formulas exist that generate *HDR*'s, and a simple iterative procedure enables the particular *HDR* containing the specified *C* percent probability to be determined using an electronic computer. Some *HDR*-values for selected beta distributions have been computed and are readily available to practitioners.[13] A sampling of such values for selected beta distributions is given in Table 16.3.[14]

[13] G. Isaacs, D. Christ, M. Novick, and P. Jackson, *Tables for Bayesian Statisticians*, Iowa Testing Programs, Iowa City, Iowa, 1974.

[14] The student will no doubt wonder what relationship exists between the credibility intervals of Bayesian statistics and the confidence intervals of classical statistics. Generally, these intervals do not agree numerically. They also have different meanings. The credibility interval involves a direct probability statement about the parameter, while the confidence interval makes a probability statement about a random interval.

Table 16.3   Highest Density Regions for Selected Beta Distributions

C%	(8, 2)	(15, 5)	(21, 6)	(27.5, 22.5)
	Beta Distribution			
25	(.836, .908)	(.747, .807)	(.774, .824)	(.529, .575)
50	(.786, .938)	(.710, .837)	(.744, .849)	(.504, .599)
75	(.711, .966)	(.658, .873)	(.701, .879)	(.470, .632)
90	(.624, .985)	(.601, .905)	(.654, .906)	(.435, .665)
95	(.567, .991)	(.564, .922)	(.622, .921)	(.414, .685)

C%	(25, 25)	(31, 21)	(55, 45)	(57.5, 42.5)
	Beta Distribution			
25	(.477, .523)	(.578, .622)	(.535, .567)	(.561, .592)
50	(.452, .548)	(.553, .645)	(.517, .585)	(.543, .610)
75	(.419, .581)	(.520, .677)	(.493, .608)	(.519, .633)
90	(.385, .615)	(.486, .708)	(.469, .632)	(.494, .656)
95	(.363, .637)	(.464, .726)	(.452, .647)	(.478, .671)

We note from Table 16.3 that a 50 percent *HDR* for $\beta(21, 6)$ is (.744, .849). Thus, if our beliefs about ϕ are represented by $\beta(21, 6)$, we should be willing to bet at even odds (1 to 1) that ϕ is between .744 and .849.

16.10 Selecting a Prior Distribution

Finally, we come to the selection of a beta distribution that will characterize our beliefs about ϕ for a given student. Sophisticated selection methods are available that require the use of an electronic computer.[15] The method we will show here, however, is a simple one. Nonetheless, it is sufficient to provide the student with some insights into the process of selecting this prior distribution.

Propensities, of course, are never strictly known, and therefore a judgmental process must always be relied on. The task that we face is to quantify our prior beliefs about ϕ in a coherent way. This is accomplished by selecting from the class of beta distributions a single distribution having characteristics that match our beliefs. Essentially, the procedure consists of selecting a pair of (a, b) values and examining the beta distribution to see if it adequately quantifies our beliefs. If it

[15] M. R. Novick, "A Course in Bayesian Statistics," *The American Statistician*, 29 (1975), 94–98; and M. R. Novick, "High School Attainment: An Example of a Computer-assisted Bayesian Approach to Data Analysis," *International Statistical Review*, 41 (1973), 264–271.

does not, new (a, b) values are selected. This procedure is continued until a satisfactory distribution is found.

Two questions naturally arise: (1) How do we select the first set of (a, b) values? (2) What procedures do we use to examine the selected beta distribution? The second question is easier to answer, and we will answer it first. Once a particular beta distribution has been selected, tables similar to Tables 16.2 and 16.3 can be used to ascertain if the particular beta distribution adequately characterizes our beliefs about ϕ. From these tables we can extract probability statements about ϕ that we then examine to see if they adequately reflect our beliefs. A specific illustration of this procedure will be given after we consider the first question noted above.

The selection of the first set of (a, b) values to identify a beta distribution that will adequately describe our beliefs about ϕ is not a trivial task, but it is manageable. The various beta distributions identified in Figure 16.1 may help in a general way. However, we must be much more specific than these illustrative curves permit. The procedure we shall use requires two initial decisions. First, we must make a judgment about the expected value or mean of the beta distribution that will represent our prior beliefs. Second, we must indicate how much "weight" our prior beliefs are worth. This weight can be thought of as the number of observations we feel our prior information is worth. For example, we might feel that our prior information is worth as many observations as we will gather when the new data are collected.

Now, while it is not intuitively obvious, there is theory to support the notion that the number of observations we feel our prior information is worth can be set equal to $a + b$. Thus, if the mean of the prior distribution is specified and if the weight of the prior information is given, we have the following two equations:

$$\text{Mean} = \mu = \frac{a}{a + b} \qquad \text{(see Table 16.1)}$$

Sample size equivalence of prior information $= m = a + b$.

These equations can easily be solved for a and b. The solutions are:

$$a = m\mu \qquad \text{and} \qquad b = m(1 - \mu)$$

If we judge the mean of our prior distribution of ϕ to be $\mu = .80$ and the sample equivalence number to be $m = 10$, then $a = 10(.8) = 8$ and $b = 10(.2) = 2$ and our prior distribution is $\beta(8, 2)$. Thus, as a first estimate of our "belief distribution" we have the beta distribution with $a = 8$ and $b = 2$. We know this distribution has a mean value that agrees with our specified mean of .80 and gives a weight of ten observations to our prior information. But can we rely on this distribution?

In choosing a prior distribution it would seem reasonable to take a good look at various characteristics of the distribution to be sure that we feel comfortable in working with them. For example, in the mastery testing situation, assume we had decided to advance a student to the next unit of instruction if $\phi \geq .80$. In this situation we might wish to ascertain $P(\phi \geq .80)$ in our prior distribution. If this value was found to be .99, we might feel that this probability is too high. Or, if $P(\phi \geq .80) = .10$, we might feel that this probability is too low. Our prior beliefs imply in the first case that the odds are 99 to 1 in favor of the student's being a "master" and in the second that they are 9 to 1 in favor of the student's being a "nonmaster." If such extreme odds seem unreasonable, we will have to select a new distribution. Remember, when we assert a particular prior distribution for a parameter, we must be willing to live with all of the possible bets it implies.

Actually, from Table 16.2, we note that if $\beta(8, 2)$ represents our prior beliefs, then $P(\phi \geq .80) \approx .55$ (i.e., $1 - .45$). Thus, if we use $\beta(8, 2)$ as the prior distribution for our testing problem, for all practical purposes we are saying that it is almost as likely for a student to be a "master" as it is for him to be a "nonmaster." (The actual odds in favor of a master are .55 to .45, or 1.22 to 1.)

Credibility intervals provide an additional way to examine our prior distribution. For example, from Table 16.2 the 50 percent central density interval for $\beta(8, 2)$ is (.7277, .8928) and from Table 16.3 the 50 percent HDR is (.786, .938). Thus for either of these intervals we should be willing to bet at even odds (i.e., 1 to 1) that ϕ is in the interval. If we feel that the intervals are too wide or too narrow for an even-odds bet, we would have to choose another beta distribution to represent our prior beliefs about ϕ.

If, on the basis of analyses similar to these, we decide that the beta distribution selected is not adequate, then we must either select a different mean value or allow our prior information to be weighted differently. These new values would then lead to a new beta distribution and this new distribution would also be examined as indicated above. This cycle would continue until an appropriate beta distribution is found. It should be obvious that this is a tedious process. In fact, to employ this procedure adequately would require the use of an electronic computer. As we noted in footnote 15, a computer program exists that will implement the procedure we have only hinted at here. However, in this chapter, since our purpose is merely to illustrate the fundamental concepts of a Bayesian data analysis, we will forego this more complex procedure. We will assume that once the mean (μ) and the sample size equivalence (m) are specified, the beta distribution so identified will serve as an adequate representation of our prior beliefs about ϕ.

16.11 Describing Posterior Beliefs: Combining Prior and New Information Using Bayes' Theorem

The basic process of Bayesian inference requires that a prior set of beliefs about a parameter be combined with new information to yield a posterior set of beliefs about the parameter. In the preceding section, we examined how our prior information about one specific parameter, ϕ, could be quantified. In this section, we describe how the sample data (new pieces of information) are characterized and then combined with the prior distribution to yield a posterior distribution of beliefs. The combining process is accomplished through the use of Bayes' theorem. We shall illustrate the procedure using the mastery testing situation discussed in Section 16.7.

The number of correct responses r on the posttest is a binomial variable (see Section 9.7). Then, if ϕ is known (which of course it is not) the probability distribution of r for a student whose propensity is ϕ can be written as follows:

$$P(r \mid \phi) = \binom{n}{r} \phi^r (1 - \phi)^{n-r} \qquad \text{[see (9.1)]}$$

where $n = $ the number of items in the test—i.e., the number of "new" observations made. As noted in Section 9.7, this distribution is called the binomial distribution. Examples of the application of this formula were given in Section 9.7. In the language we have been developing, we can be more precise and say that $P(r \mid \phi)$ is the conditional distribution of r given ϕ. If ϕ is known, we can make probability statements about r. Such statements, however, are not typically of great interest. Rather, what is of interest is the parameter ϕ, whose value is unknown.

We want to be able to make probability statements about ϕ given our prior belief and the sample data (r). Symbolically, we might represent this as $P(\phi \mid r)$. What we need is a formula to get us from $P(r \mid \phi)$ to $P(\phi \mid r)$. Bayes' theorem is the formula.

$$P(\phi \mid r) = \frac{P(r \mid \phi)P(\phi)}{P(r)} \qquad (16.7)$$

where

$$P(\phi \mid r) = \text{the probability distribution of } \phi \text{ given } r$$
$$P(r \mid \phi) = \text{the probability distribution of } r \text{ given } \phi$$
$$P(\phi) = \text{our prior probability distribution for } \phi$$
$$P(r) = \text{a constant that will not need to be defined}$$

Equation (16.7) is completely analogous to equation (16.5).[16]
  Now, by our previous work we know that

$$P(r \mid \phi) = \binom{n}{r} \phi^r (1 - \phi)^{n-r} \tag{a}$$

and

$$P(\phi) = \frac{\phi^{a-1}(1 - \phi)^{b-1}}{\beta(a, b)} \tag{b}$$

Substituting these quantities into equation (16.7) we have

$$P(\phi \mid r) = \frac{\binom{n}{r} \phi^r (1 - \phi)^{n-r} \phi^{a-1}(1 - \phi)^{b-1}}{P(r)\beta(a, b)} \tag{c}$$

Combining terms in the numerator we have[17]

$$P(\phi \mid r) = \frac{\binom{n}{r} \phi^{r+a-1}(1 - \phi)^{n-r+b-1}}{P(r)\beta(a, b)} \tag{d}$$

Now we note that part of equation (d) is analogous to the beta probability distribution function (16.6). You may recall that the beta distribution function is of the form

$$\frac{\phi^{a-1}(1 - \phi)^{b-1}}{\beta(a, b)}$$

The right-hand side of equation (d) is of the form

$$\frac{\binom{n}{r}}{P(r)} \cdot \frac{\phi^{r+a-1}(1 - \phi)^{n-r+b-1}}{\beta(a, b)} \tag{e}$$

We also note that $\binom{n}{r}$, $P(r)$, and $\beta(a, b)$ are all constants. If by chance these constants were to combine to yield a constant of the form

---

[16] Note that the expression in the denominator of (16.5) is a constant.

[17] Recall that $x^c x^d = x^{c+d}$. For example, $x^3 x^2 = x^{3+2} = x^5$.

$\beta(r + a, n - r + b)$, expression (e) would become

$$P(\phi \mid r) = \frac{\phi^{r+a-1}(1 - \phi)^{n-r+b-1}}{\beta(r + a, n - r + b)} \qquad (16.8)$$

which is a beta distribution with $a' = r + a$ and $b' = n - r + b$. If the constants did combine in this fashion, then our posterior distribution of beliefs about ϕ would be represented by a beta distribution with $a' = r + a$ and $b' = n - r + b$. Since the family of beta distributions is an extremely useful family for describing degrees of belief about ϕ, it would be nice if these constants did combine to form $\beta(r + a, n - r + b)$. As you probably guessed, the three constants do indeed combine in this fashion. Therefore, our posterior distribution of beliefs can be represented by a beta distribution.

It can be seen that equation (16.8) is identical to equation (b) except that a has been replaced by $r + a$ and b has been replaced by $n - r + b$. The prior distribution has been updated, so to speak, from $\beta(a, b)$ to $\beta(a + r, b + n - r)$. This means that we are in a sense just adding prior information (a, b) and sample information $(r, n - r)$ to express our posterior information. The convenient way in which prior information and sample information combine when a prior beta distribution is used with a binomial model is a major reason for choosing this class of prior distributions.

We shall now illustrate the above procedure using the mastery testing example. Recall from Section 16.10 that our prior set of beliefs is to be represented by the beta distribution with $a = 8$ and $b = 2$:

$$P(\phi) = \frac{\phi^{8-1}(1 - \phi)^{2-1}}{\beta(8, 2)}$$

Assume that for the sample information $n = 10$ (i.e., ten items) and $r = 7$ (i.e., seven correct answers).[18] Then

$$P(r \mid \phi) = \binom{7}{3}\phi^{7}(1 - \phi)^{10-7}$$

According to Equation (16.8), our posterior distribution of beliefs is

$$P(\phi \mid r) = \frac{\phi^{8+7-1}(1 - \phi)^{10-7+2-1}}{\beta(8 + 7, 10 - 7 + 2)}$$

which is $\beta(15, 5)$.[19]

---

[18] The use of $n = 10$ is consistent with our previous decision to give equal weight to our prior beliefs and our new data.

[19] It is unnecessary to write these formulas to identify the posterior beta, which is simply $\beta(a + r, b + n - r)$.

From the information given in Table 16.2 we can now make various probability statements about ϕ. For example, the following facts about our posterior degree of belief can be found:

1 $P(\phi \leq .80) \approx .67$ or $P(\phi \geq .80) \approx .33$

2 $P(\phi \leq .70) \approx .30$ or $P(\phi \geq .70) \approx .70$

3 $P(.6895 \leq \phi \leq .8194) \approx .50$ (the central 50 percent credibility interval)

Also from Table 16.3, we have

$$P(.710 \leq \phi \leq .837) = .50 \text{ (the 50 percent highest density region)}$$

Remarks:

1. In this section we have shown how prior information about ϕ can be combined with new information to yield a posterior distribution of beliefs about ϕ. This posterior distribution is the full probabilistic expression of our "old" and "new" knowledge (beliefs) about ϕ. In the mastery testing situation, our beta posterior distribution represents our degree of belief about a student's ability parameter ϕ. For example, if the criterion for mastery is set at $\phi \geq .80$, and our posterior distribution is $\beta(15, 5)$, then $P(\phi \geq .80) \approx .33$. In this situation, it would seem best to declare the student a nonmaster and recommend remedial work. On the other hand, if the mastery criterion is set at $\phi \geq .70$, then for $\beta(15, 5)$ the $P(\phi \geq .70) \approx .70$, and we might feel that we should label the student a master.

The procedure as developed above does not specify any rules for deciding what evidence will be accepted as indicating mastery or nonmastery. Such rules would seem to be necessary if the Bayesian analysis is to be useful. The specification of such rules requires a consideration of the importance of the types of errors that can be made. For example, in the mastery testing situation, it may be considered a more crucial error to designate a student a master when the student is a nonmaster (a false positive) than to designate a student a nonmaster when the student is a master (a false negative). This additional piece of our Bayesian analysis is discussed in the next section.

2. As we have seen, the beta distribution has two parameters, a and b. By giving various positive values to these, we obtain a *family* of probability distributions of the form (16.6), each of which when used as a prior density combines in a very convenient way with the probability function for the observation r—the binomial distribution. When the prior distribution combines with the model distribution to give a posterior distribution from the same family as the prior distribution, we refer to the family of prior distributions as the family of *natural conjugate distributions* for the model distribution. In this situation a beta prior distribution is a natural conjugate distribution since it

combines with the binomial model distribution to give a beta posterior distribution.

   3. In Section 16.10 we noted that the sample size equivalence of our prior information was equal to $a + b$, where the a and b were for the prior distribution. For the mastery testing example our prior was $\beta(8, 2)$ and the sample size equivalence was 10. Our posterior distribution for this example was based on ten additional pieces of information (i.e., the responses to the ten items). Thus, in effect, our posterior distribution, $\beta(15, 5)$, has a sample size equivalence of 20, which is $a + b + n$.

   4. This type of analysis, which uses a beta distribution as the prior distribution and the binomial distribution as the distribution for the data, is sometimes referred to as a beta-binomial analysis.

16.12 A Decision Problem in Mastery Testing

Assume that in the mastery testing situation introduced in Section 16.7 we have established a criterion level of .80. This means that if a student has a ϕ-value of .80 or higher, he is considered a master, and if the student's ϕ-value is less than .80, he is considered a nonmaster.

   We must therefore decide if the student should be treated as a master and allowed to go on to the next unit of instruction or be treated as a nonmaster and given more work on the present assignment. Since we do not know the student's ϕ-value for certain, the quantity of interest is the probability that the student's ϕ-value is equal to or greater than .80. Our question then is: "How large must this probability be before the teacher allows the student to go on to the next assignment?"

   The answer to this question depends on the losses associated with the two possible decisions. Let us suppose that there is no loss associated with allowing a master to go on to the next assignment, and no loss associated with giving a nonmaster more work on the present assign-ment. However, assume there is a loss $K > 0$ associated with treating a student as a master when he is a nonmaster. Similarly, assume there is a loss L in treating a student as a nonmaster when he is a master. The losses involved are shown in the following diagram.

Act as if Student is a

		Nonmaster	Master
Student is a	Master ($\phi \geq .80$)	L	0
	Nonmaster ($\phi < .80$)	0	K

   Our desire might be to minimize our loss, but we cannot do this with imperfect information. The best we can do is to minimize our *expected loss.* If we declare a student to be a master, then we define the expected loss to be

$$EL_M = 0 \cdot P(\phi \geq .80) + K \cdot P(\phi < .80) = K \cdot P(\phi < .80)$$

This expression is the weighted average of the two possible losses 0 and K given the decision *master*, each weighted by the appropriate posterior probability. Similarly, the expected loss given the decision *nonmaster* is

$$EL_{NM} = L \cdot P(\phi \geq .80) + 0 \cdot P(\phi < .80) = L \cdot P(\phi \geq .80)$$

Based on the available information, the better decision will be determined by choosing the decision that yields the lesser expected loss. In general, $EL_M > EL_{NM}$ if and only if

$$K \cdot P(\phi < \phi_0) > L \cdot P(\phi \geq \phi_0) \qquad \text{(a)}$$

where ϕ_0 is our criterion level ($\phi_0 = .80$ in the above example). We have this simple form because in each case one of the terms in the expected loss is zero. Thus, if $K \cdot P(\phi < \phi_0) > L \cdot P(\phi \geq \phi_0)$ we should act as though the student is a nonmaster. Likewise, if $K \cdot P(\phi < \phi_0) < L \cdot P(\phi \geq \phi_0)$ we should act as though the student is a master.

The inequality (a) can be written as follows:

$$\frac{P(\phi < \phi_0)}{P(\phi \geq \phi_0)} > \frac{L}{K} \qquad \text{(b)}$$

This form of the inequality spotlights the fact that we need not stipulate K and L in any absolute scale. We need only stipulate the ratio L/K. For example, in the mastery testing situation $P(\phi < .80) \approx .67$ and $P(\phi \geq .80) \approx .33$ in our posterior distribution for ϕ. Therefore, if $.67/.33 > L/K$, or $2/1 > L/K$, we should act as though the student is a nonmaster, since $EL_M > EL_{NM}$.[20] Likewise, if $2/1 < L/K$, we should act as though the student is a master, since then $EL_{NM} > EL_M$. Putting this another way, we shall act as if the student is a master if the loss involved in incorrectly identifying the student as a nonmaster is two (or more) times the loss involved in incorrectly identifying him as a master.

---

[20] Read "since the expected loss if we declare him a master when he is a nonmaster is greater than the expected loss if we declare him a nonmaster when he is a master."

16.13   Summary Statement

In this chapter we have attempted to provide a sufficient introduction to Bayesian methods to give the student a taste of the complexity and power of these methods. At this point it should be useful to summarize the points we have been making and to indicate how we feel Bayesian statistics should fit into the repertoire of standard statistical methods. At the same time we shall indicate the limitations in the application of Bayesian methods given the present "state of the art." Let us begin with a review of the essentials of the Bayesian approach.

In Bayesian statistics the posterior distribution of the parameter (in our example a beta distribution for the binomial proportion ϕ) is the complete probabilistic statement of knowledge and beliefs about the parameter. When I say to you that my posterior distribution for Diane's ability ϕ is $\beta(15, 5)$, then I have conveyed to you a mathematical summarization of everything I know about her ability on this task.

The statement that my beliefs correspond to $\beta(15, 5)$ is, of course, in itself not a directly informative statement. Few people can translate such a statement into anything very meaningful without a computer, or at least without paper and pencil and some statistical tables. The point, however, is that all information is contained in that probability distribution and indeed you can get out of it whatever you need without too much effort.

If I tell you that my beliefs correspond to $\beta(15, 5)$ you may wish to use this information for one of several possible purposes. The first thing you might want to do is to summarize the information contained in this distribution so that it will be easier to think about. The problem here is similar to that faced in the early chapters of this text where it was pointed out that the first objective of a statistical analysis is to provide useful summarizations of the data.

In these chapters such summarizations took the form of point and interval estimates. Useful point estimates were discussed, specifically the mean, median, and mode. Interval estimates were also discussed and both one- and two-sided intervals were proposed for use. These same ideas can now be used to summarize the information in a posterior distribution. Again point estimates (mean, median, and mode) are available, as are various kinds of credibility intervals. The latter include one- and two-sided intervals; and among useful two-sided intervals are central intervals and highest density intervals.

Hypothesis testing of the two-tailed sort as it is usually developed in classical statistics plays no part in Bayesian methods. Consider the binomial model we have been studying and the example in Section 16.7. Assume our posterior distribution for ϕ is $\beta(15, 5)$. Following the thinking of classical statistics we might be tempted to test the null hypothesis H_0: $\phi = .70$ against the alternative H_1: $\phi \neq .70$.[21] However, from a Bayesian point of view this makes no sense, since the probability that $\phi = .70$ is zero (the area under the curve for the null hypothesis set is zero). A one-sided test of H_0: $\phi \leq .70$ against the alternative $\phi > .70$ does make sense; and since for $\beta(15, 5)$, $P(\phi > .70) \approx .70$,[22] we might want to act as if ϕ was bigger than .70 though formally this can be done only by considering losses as indicated in Section 16.12.

The important point about Bayesian inference is that the method is always the same and that to do a Bayesian analysis one need only follow five clearly defined steps. Without formally carrying out such an analysis, let us consider step by step the Bayesian approach to comparing the difference in the mean effects of a treatment and control group. The steps are as follows.

1 *State the model for the experiment and in doing so identify the unknown parameter(s).* In this case the model will be a normal distribution for both treatment and control groups. A common variance will be assumed.

2 *Determine your prior distribution for this parameter.* A prior distribution on three parameters will be required in this case.

3 *Gather your data and use Bayes' theorem to give you a posterior distribution for your parameter: When more than one parameter is present in a problem, use only the posterior distribution on the parameter of interest to the decision you face.* In this case the parameter of interest is the difference between the two means.

4 *Describe your posterior distribution using point and interval estimates.* This step will be described in more detail below.

5 *Make your decision, considering the losses involved in the various possible incorrect decisions.*

We can denote the parameters of our model as μ_T and μ_C (the unknown means for the treatment and control groups) and σ^2 (the common variance). If we assume a convenient quantification of prior information, one using a natural conjugate distribution, the posterior distribution of μ_T will be a normal distribution as will be the distribution of μ_C. If we define a difference parameter $\Delta = \mu_T - \mu_C$, it too will have a posterior normal distribution. This posterior distribution of this difference parameter contains all the information we need for rational decision making.

---

[21] Previously, $\phi_0 = .70$ was suggested along with .80 as a possible criterion level for mastery.

[22] See Table 16.2.

Suppose, for example, that the posterior normal distribution for Δ has mean of 2 and standard deviation of 1. We would, of course, begin our presentation by giving a point estimate that surely would have the value 2, since the mean, median, and mode of this distribution are all equal to 2. Since the normal distribution is symmetric, central and highest density intervals coincide and therefore the two-tailed intervals we might choose to report might be[23]

$$P(.04 \leq \Delta \leq 3.96) = .95 \quad \text{and} \quad P(-.58 \leq \Delta \leq 4.58) = .99$$

In each case the subject of the probability sentence is the unknown parameter Δ. We can also state probabilities that Δ is in any interval of interest and thus we can easily and precisely describe various subintervals of each of the above credibility intervals. We can, for example, determine precisely the odds ratio for the interval $1.5 \leq \Delta \leq 2.0$ as against the interval $1.0 \leq \Delta \leq 1.5$. This cannot be done in classical statistics. We can determine $P(\Delta > 0)$. That this probability is about .98 may not be of great interest, despite the emphasis put on a parallel calculation in classical statistics.

In Bayesian statistics we are led by the nature of the system to ask ourselves how much of a difference makes a difference. Perhaps you would seriously consider abandoning the old method (control) in favor of the new method (treatment) if you were reasonably sure that the gain would be *enough*. This forces you to ask the question, "How much is enough?" Perhaps, for you, a value of $\Delta = 1$ is enough. You would then take as the crucial statement in your analysis

$$P(\Delta > 1) \approx .84$$

This for you may be enough evidence to suggest the use of the new treatment. Again, that decision would depend on the relative losses of the two possible incorrect decisions.

It should not surprise students at this point to learn that the author of this chapter believes that all serious statistical work should ideally be Bayesian. Several practical reasons prevent the immediate realization of that ideal. First, Bayesian methods are substantially more complex than classical methods. One must quantify prior beliefs and explicitly state a loss function. These tasks are not easy, although new methods of computer-assisted data analysis do help substantially. Even now it is possible for an investigator to sit at a computer terminal and be led through a complex Bayesian analysis merely by responding to simple

[23] The equation on the left is arrived at as follows. In the standard normal distribution $P(-1.96 \leq z \leq +1.96) = .95$ (see Table II, Appendix C). Hence, in a *ND* with $\mu_\Delta = 2$ and $\sigma_\Delta = 1$, $P(.04 \leq \Delta \leq 3.96) = .95$.

questions put by the computer. Second, although at present it is possible to investigate all of the problems discussed in this book using Bayesian methods, Bayesian methods are not available for a wide variety of complex problems for which classical methods are available. Many people are reluctant to invest the time necessary for mastering Bayesian thinking when the repertoire of available techniques is so limited. However, new Bayesian techniques are being made available regularly and it may well be that within a decade Bayesian methods may be available for the analysis of most educational and psychological data sets. If you are to decide how much time you ought to invest now in learning Bayesian methods, you will have to assess your personal probability that Bayesian methods will be important a decade from now or even sooner and also the relative losses involved with incorrect judgments at this point. If you decide that at this crucial point in your educational career you want to get the instruction you will need for a professional career spanning 30 to 40 years, you may wish to investigate the present offerings in Bayesian statistics. Study of a recent text may be useful.[24]

Without in any way retreating from the position that Bayesian methods are the preferred methods of statistical decision making, it must be acknowledged that many data analyses are simply not worth the effort required by a Bayesian analysis. Sometimes one wants just a quick summarization of the data and a quick judgment of whether there is anything in the data worth thinking about. The methods of this book, particularly when given a Fisherian rather than a Neyman-Pearson interpretation, are very useful in such situations. Furthermore, we must all learn to walk before we can run. Perhaps the discussion of the limitations of the classical method given here will help us all to walk a straight line when using these methods.

[24] See, for example, M. R. Novick and P. H. Jackson, *Statistical Methods for Educational and Psychological Research*, McGraw-Hill, New York, 1974.

17

Correlation

17.1 Introduction to the Concept of Correlation

Frequently in educational and psychological research measures of two or more characteristics (scores on two or more dimensions) are obtained for each of a number of individuals or objects. Most of our previous work in this book has been related to the analysis of a single measure. In this chapter we extend our analysis procedures to the two-variable (or bivariate) situation.[1] Assume, for example, that we have measures of height and weight for each of a number of 12-year-old boys; or measures of high school achievement and freshman-year college achievement; or measures of the perimeter and side for each of a number of squares. We shall be concerned here with the tendency for the pairs of measures to correspond in relative magnitude—that is, to have the same relative position in their respective distributions. In other words, we shall be concerned with the extent to which individuals or objects that are average, above average, or below average in one dimension tend also to be average, above average, or below average, respectively, in the other dimension. We shall refer to such correspondence as *correlation*.

Clearly, the correlation between the perimeters and sides of squares is an example of *perfect* correlation. Since the perimeter of any square is four times the length of its side ($P = 4S$) it obviously follows that in any collection of squares, the one with the largest side will have the largest perimeter, the one with the second largest side will have the second largest perimeter, and so on. The correlation between heights

---

[1] Analysis procedures for situations where more than two measures are obtained on each individual are available, but they are not considered in this book.

and weights of 12-year-old boys, by contrast, is not perfect. It is a matter of common observation that 12-year-old boys who are average, above average, or below average in height *tend* to be average, above average, or below average, respectively, in weight. Yet exceptions to this tendency are not uncommon, and it would not be at all unusual to discover in a given collection of 12-year-old boys that the tallest was not also the heaviest. The situation is, of course, similar in the case of measures of high school achievement and freshman-year college achievement.

And then there are dimensions or characteristics between which no perceptible correlation can be found to exist. This is the case, for example, with a measure of intelligence such as IQ and a measure of some physical dimension such as height for a population of fifth-grade boys. Such variables are sometimes said to be *uncorrelated*. Uncorrelated dimensions or variables are characterized by the fact that large, small, or average values of one occur with the same relative frequency with all values of the other.

Though still other situations exist,[2] we shall at this point refer to only one, namely, the tendency for individuals who are above average in one dimension to be below average in the other, while those who are below average in the first tend to be above average in the second. Such dimensions are still said to be correlated, but correlated *inversely*, rather than *directly* as in the situations first described. For the children in the seventh grade of almost any elementary school, for example, chronological age and scholastic ability are likely to be correlated inversely; the over-age children in the grade are usually among the dullest, while the youngest children are usually among the brightest. This follows from the fact that dull children have been retarded and bright children accelerated in their school progress. For a reason that will become apparent later, statisticians refer to variables that are correlated inversely as being *negatively correlated* and to variables that are correlated directly as being *positively correlated*.

Suppose that the "objects" under consideration are a number of trips between two cities, A and B, which are 100 miles apart, and that the two dimensions involved are time required and rate (miles per hour) traveled. Again we have an example of perfect correlation. Here, however, the correlation is negative instead of positive as in the case of perimeters and sides of squares. Since the time of any trip is 100 divided by the rate ($t = 100/r$), it follows that the trip for which the time was greatest is that for which the rate was least, that the trip for which the time was second greatest is that for which the rate was second least, and so on. Thus, a perfect negative as well as a perfect positive correlation may exist.

---

[2] An example of another will be presented later (see Figure 17.11).

In statistical work we actually have no concern at all with perfectly correlated dimensions or variables. Instead, our concern is entirely with variables that only tend to correspond (either positively or negatively) in relative magnitude. Fundamentally, the correlation problem in statistics is one of assessing the *degree* to which imperfectly correlated variables are correlated. We need some means of answering such questions as the following.

1 Is the correlation between height and weight for 12-year-old boys greater than that for adult males?
2 Which of the following variables is most closely correlated with first-year college grade-point average?
  a High school grade-point average
  b Rank in high school graduating class
  c Intelligence as measured by an individual test such as Wechsler's
  d Scholastic aptitude as measured by some group test such as the *Cognitive Abilities Test*[3]
  e Performance on high school tests of general educational development such as the ITED battery[4]
3 To what extent is success as an office secretary correlated with performance on some test of English grammar?
4 To what extent are the weekly sales at a grocery store correlated with weekly expenditures for newspaper advertisements? for radio advertisements?

The situations represented in these questions are, of course, only a few of the many that call for assessment of the *degree* to which imperfectly correlated variables are correlated. Some quantitative index of degree of correlation would clearly be most useful. This chapter is primarily concerned with the development and interpretation of one such index.

17.2   The Scatter Diagram

Before we present a quantitative index of correlation, we shall consider a scheme for displaying graphically the degree of correlation between two variables. This device, known as the *scatter diagram* or dot chart, does not provide the needed quantitative index referred to in the foregoing section. It does, however, provide for a simple pictorial presentation of a given correlational situation that may be readily understood, even by a person not trained in statistics.

[3] *Cognitive Abilities Test*, Houghton Mifflin Company, Boston, Mass.

[4] *Iowa Tests of Educational Development*, Iowa Testing Programs, University of Iowa, Iowa City, Iowa.

Table 17.1   Perimeters (*P*) and Sides (*S*) of Ten Squares

P	S	P	S
12	3.0	10	2.5
4	1.0	14	3.5
20	5.0	6	1.5
16	4.0	8	2.0
2	0.5	18	4.5

Table 17.1 gives the perimeters and sides of a collection of ten squares. Figure 17.1 shows the scatter diagram for these ten pairs of values. Figure 17.1 was constructed by marking off *P*- and *S*-scales along rectangular coordinate axes and locating a point corresponding to each pair of values at the intersection of lines drawn perpendicularly from the individual values on their respective scales. It is customary to show only the points; the perpendiculars are shown in Figure 17.1 only for the pair of dimensions of the first square of Table 17.1. It is clear that in this case involving perfectly correlated variables the points representing the pairs of values are arranged in a straight line. Not all perfectly correlated dimensions follow this straight-line pattern (curved-line arrangements are possible). But whenever pairs of dimensions do follow this pattern, they must be perfectly correlated. That is, the largest value of one will always be associated with the largest value of the other, and the second largest of the one associated with the second largest of the other, and so on.

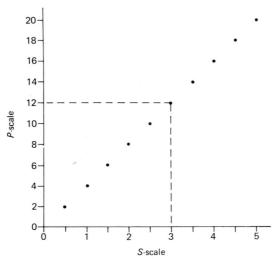

Figure 17.1   Scatter diagram of perimeters and sides of ten squares

Table 17.2   Heights (*H*) and Weights (*W*) of 50 Randomly Selected 12-Year-Old Boys

H	W	H	W	H	W	H	W	H	W
67	138	62	89	59	94	57	89	56	77
66	109	61	122	59	67	57	85	56	66
63	105	61	110	59	66	57	80	55	75
63	101	61	103	58	109	57	78	55	71
63	81	61	89	58	102	57	77	55	70
62	125	61	88	58	85	57	76	55	67
62	121	60	85	58	81	57	72	55	61
62	118	60	70	58	73	57	69	54	64
62	104	59	101	58	70	57	68	53	78
62	99	59	98	57	95	56	79	52	58

Consider next Table 17.2, which contains pairs of height and weight scores for 50 randomly selected 12-year-old boys. The heights and weights are given to the nearest inch and pound. The pairs of values have been arranged in order of height and, within a given height, in order of weight. The scatter diagram for these pairs of heights and weights is shown in Figure 17.2. There is clearly a *tendency* for the height and weight scores to be positively correlated. However, the

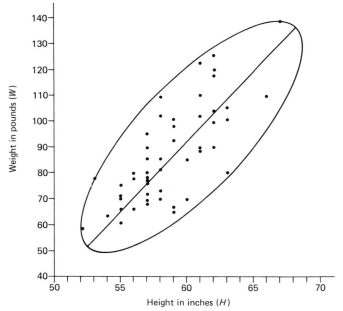

Figure 17.2   Scatter diagram of heights and weights of 50 twelve-year-old boys

Table 17.3 Scores on Tests of General Mathematical Ability (*M*) and Reading Rate (*R*) Made by 50 College Freshmen

M	R	M	R	M	R	M	R	M	R
59	52	54	56	51	26	49	53	47	49
58	49	53	66	50	57	49	49	47	41
58	38	53	60	50	53	49	48	47	37
57	60	53	58	50	50	49	42	47	36
56	62	53	54	50	49	49	33	47	35
56	61	53	36	50	46	48	53	47	33
56	55	52	53	50	45	48	45	46	55
56	48	52	51	50	42	48	39	46	52
55	51	52	48	50	36	47	62	44	41
54	58	52	46	49	59	47	55	41	39

correlation is not perfect, and the points corresponding to the pairs of values no longer fall on a straight line. Yet the points do tend to scatter about such a line in a sort of elliptical pattern. The more nearly the arrangement of the points in such a scatter diagram follows a straight-line pattern—that is, the narrower the elliptical field—the higher is the degree of correlation between the variables involved.

The scatter diagram for scores made on tests of general mathematical ability and reading rate by 50 college freshmen (see Table 17.3) is shown in Figure 17.3. Comparison of Figures 17.2 and 17.3 clearly shows that these mathematical ability and reading rate scores are not as highly correlated as are height and weight scores for 12-year-old boys. The elliptical pattern of dots is much wider in Figure 17.3 than in Figure 17.2. This implies that at least in some instances large *M*-scores must be paired with relatively small *R*-scores and small *M*-scores with relatively large *R*-scores.

Figure 17.4 shows the scatter diagram for reading comprehension test scores (*R*) and heights (*H*) in centimeters of 50 fourth-grade pupils (see Table 17.4). It is clear that for these pupils there is virtually no correlation between these variables. Large, medium, and small height measures are associated with reading scores of any magnitude. Far from being arranged along a line in an elliptical field, the dots are scattered about in an area bounded by a circle.

Our observations from Figures 17.1–17.4 should now allow us to state in a general way what we can learn from scatter diagrams about the degree of correlation between pairs of variables. Variables for which the correlation is high result in scatter diagrams in which the field of points is a narrow ellipse. As the correlation decreases, these elliptical fields widen, becoming circular when there is a complete lack of correlation.

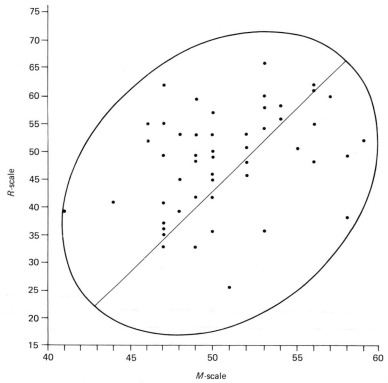

Figure 17.3   Scatter diagram of scores on tests of
general mathematical ability (*M*) and reading rate (*R*)
for 50 college freshmen

In all the foregoing examples, save the last, the variables involved
were positively correlated. It should be obvious that the scatter diagram
functions equally well when the variables are negatively correlated. The
only difference is that the line about which the points scatter will slope
downward to the right instead of upward to the right. This, of course,
results from the fact that when variables are negatively correlated large
values of one variable tend to be associated with small values of the
other.

We shall present here only one example of a scatter diagram involving
negatively correlated variates. Suppose we have two pairs of objects.
Let the objects of the first pair be designated A and B and those of the
second pair C and D. Now suppose that the task is to decide whether
A and B or C and D are the more similar. Psychologists have demonstrated that the actual degree of difference in similarity (i.e., dis-

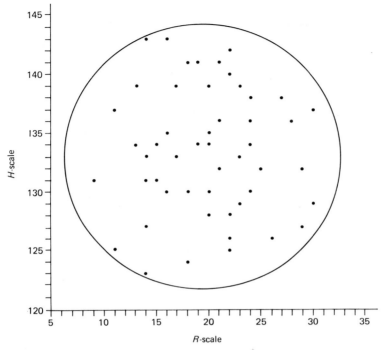

Figure 17.4 Scatter diagram of scores on a reading comprehension test (*R*) and heights (*H*) in centimeters for 50 fourth-grade pupils

Table 17.4 Scores on a Reading Comprehension Test (*R*) and Height (*H*) in Centimeters of 50 Fourth-Grade Pupils

R	H	R	H	R	H	R	H	R	H
30	137	24	134	21	141	18	141	14	143
30	129	24	130	21	136	18	130	14	133
29	132	23	139	21	132	18	124	14	131
29	127	23	133	20	139	17	139	14	127
28	136	23	129	20	135	17	133	14	123
27	138	22	142	20	134	16	143	13	139
26	126	22	140	20	130	16	135	13	134
25	132	22	128	20	128	16	130	11	137
24	138	22	126	19	141	15	134	11	125
24	136	22	125	19	134	15	131	9	131

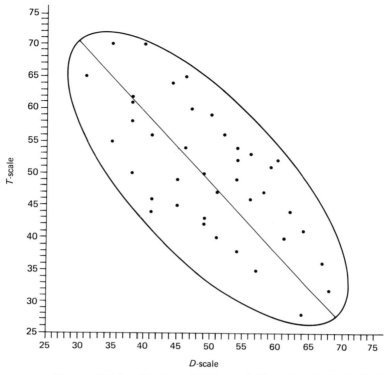

Figure 17.5   Scatter diagram of 40 pairs of dissimilarity and decision-time scores

similarity), physically assessed, is negatively correlated with the time required for a subject to make a decision, that is, perform the task.[5] Table 17.5 contains physically assessed dissimilarity scores and decision-time scores for 40 independent performances of the decision task by a single subject. The objects involved were patches of gray of varying degrees of luminosity, and decision times were measured to the nearest hundredth of a second. All measurements were converted to standard scores with a mean of 50 and an S of 10 (see Section 8.5). The scatter diagram for these data is given in Figure 17.5. The degree of deviation from a straight line appears about the same as for the pairs of height and weight scores for 12-year-old boys plotted in Figure 17.2. Here, however, the elliptical field slopes downward to the right, indicating that the correlation is negative.

---

[5] For example, see William N. Dember, "The Relation of Decision-Time to Stimulus Similarity," *Journal of Experimental Psychology*, 53 (January 1957), 68–72.

Table 17.5 Physically Assessed Dissimilarity Scores (*D*)
and Decision-Time Scores (*T*) for 40 Decisions by a Single
Subject

D	T	D	T	D	T	D	T
68	32	56	53	49	50	41	46
67	36	56	46	49	43	41	44
64	41	54	54	49	42	40	70
64	28	54	52	47	60	38	62
62	44	54	49	46	65	38	61
61	40	54	38	46	54	38	58
60	52	52	56	45	49	38	50
59	51	51	47	45	45	35	70
58	47	51	40	44	64	35	55
57	35	50	59	41	56	31	65

17.3   The Bivariate Frequency Distribution

It is not unusual, particularly with large collections of data, to find a
pair of scores both members of which have the same magnitude as the
corresponding scores of one or more other pairs in the collection. This
gives rise to a difficulty in the preparation of a scatter diagram because
of the fact that only one dot can occupy any given position. This
difficulty may be circumvented by the use of a *bivariate frequency
distribution* or table.

> **DN 17.1**   A bivariate frequency distribution is a scheme for the joint
> presentation of pairs of scores made by the same individuals on two
> variates that shows the frequencies with which the individuals are
> distributed among all possible pairings of the score values for the two
> variates.

Let us consider a simple hypothetical example. Suppose that one of
the variates (*X*) involves the values 1, 2, 3, 4, and 5 and that the other
variate (*Y*) involves the values 4, 5, 6, and 7. There are, in all, 20
(i.e., 5 × 4) possible ways these *X*- and *Y*-values may be paired. The
simplest and most compact method of displaying these 20 possible
different pairings is provided by a two-way or double-entry table, the
columns of which correspond to the different values of one variate (*X*)
and the rows to the different values of the other variate (*Y*). Any given
pairing is then associated with that cell of the table formed by the
intersection of the column and row corresponding to the values
involved, and the frequency with which this pairing occurs in the
collection is entered in the cell. Table 17.6 contains 30 pairs of hypothetical *X*- and *Y*-values. The bivariate frequency distribution for these
30 pairs is shown in Figure 17.6. In classifying the pairs it is convenient
to make a tally mark in the cell for each pair falling in it, and then

Table 17.6 Thirty Pairs of Hypothetical Scores on Variates *X* and *Y*

X	Y	X	Y	X	Y
4	7	5	7	5	6
2	6	3	5	2	5
2	4	4	5	3	6
5	6	3	5	4	5
4	6	3	6	5	7
3	5	3	5	4	6
3	5	1	5	4	6
4	6	3	5	2	5
1	4	2	5	1	4
2	5	4	6	3	6

simply count the marks to determine the frequency for each cell. Ordinarily, of course, only the frequencies are shown.[6] It is clear from inspection of Figure 17.6 that a bivariate frequency distribution may be interpreted as a scatter diagram. It should also be noted that if the cell frequencies are summed by columns and rows, we obtain the two ordinary single-variate frequency distributions for the *X*- and *Y*-scores (see lower and right margins of the figure). In a bivariate table these single-variate distributions are sometimes referred to as *marginal distributions*.

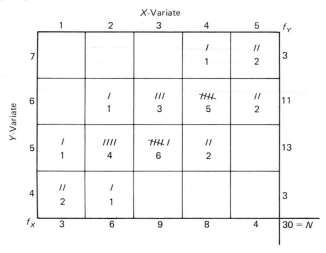

Figure 17.6 Bivariate frequency distribution of 30 pairs of scores of Table 17.6

[6] It is suggested that students set up for themselves a four-row by five-column table and independently classify the pairs of scores given in Table 17.6. The result may be checked against Figure 17.6.

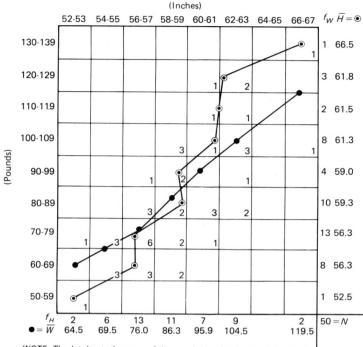

(NOTE: The dots locate the means of the pounds in each column and the circles the means of the inches in each row. These means are the subject of subsequent comment and may be ignored at this point.)

Figure 17.7   Grouped bivariate frequency distribution for height and weight scores of Table 17.2

If the range of values of either or both variates is large, it may be desirable to let the columns and rows of the double-entry table correspond to intervals along the score scales. This results in a "grouped" bivariate frequency distribution analogous to the grouped frequency distributions described in Chapter 3. Figure 17.7 presents a bivariate frequency distribution of this type. The pairs of scores involved are the height and weight scores given in Table 17.2. The height scores have been grouped into intervals of 2 units and the weight scores into intervals of 10 units.

17.4   An Index of Correlation

Although it is possible to obtain some notion of the degree of correlation between two sets of measures by inspection of a scatter diagram, the information thus obtained is not usually precise enough for comparative

Table 17.7   Sums of Products of Pairs of Hypothetical Scores

A	B	AB	C	AC	D	AD	E	AE	F	AF
13	13	169	9	117	5	65	5	65	1	13
9	9	81	13	117	9	81	1	9	5	45
7	7	49	7	49	13	91	7	49	7	49
5	5	25	1	5	1	5	13	65	9	45
1	1	1	5	5	7	7	9	9	13	13
	$\Sigma = 325$			293		249		197		165

purposes. In this section, therefore, we shall consider the problem of defining a particular quantitative index of the degree of correlation between two sets of measures for the same individuals.

Table 17.7 shows how the sums of the products of two sets of hypothetical measures vary with changes in the order of some of the sets. The B-values are exactly the same as the A-values so that A and B are obviously perfectly correlated. The C-, D-, E-, and F-values are the same as the B-values except that they are arranged in different order and, hence, bear differing degrees of correlation with the A-values. The C-values clearly tend to be positively correlated with the A-values, whereas it is difficult to detect any systematic correlation whatever between A- and D-values. The E-values tend to be negatively correlated with the A-values, and the F-values are perfectly correlated negatively with the A-values. It will be observed that the sums of products of the AB, AC, AD, AE, and AF pairs decrease as the correlation shifts by degrees from perfect and positive to perfect and negative. This suggests that a useful quantitative index of correlation may be based on the sum of the products of the pairs of values involved.

However, we cannot use such a sum directly. There are two reasons why. In the first place, the magnitude of this sum is affected by the unit of measurement involved. Consider, for example, a set of D'-values that measure the same characteristic as the D-values but in terms of a different unit. Let this unit be one-tenth that of the D-unit; then $D' = 10D$. The D'-values corresponding to the D-values of Table 17.7 are 50, 90, 130, 10, and 70, respectively; and the sum of the products of AD' pairs is 2,490, a value far larger than any sum shown in Table 17.7 in spite of the fact that there is no clear indication of any correlation between the pairs of A- and D'-values. This sum is clearly not comparable to the sums of Table 17.7 because of the difference in units involved. Hence, if an index of correlation based on the sum of the products of the pair values is to be useful for the purpose of comparing the degree of correlation between different sets of variates, some way must be found to express the pair values of the different sets in terms of comparable units. This is accomplished by simply expressing all original

Table 17.8 z-Scores for the A- and D-Values of Table 17.7 and for D'-Values where $D' = 10D$

z_A	z_D	$z_A z_D$	$z_{D'}$	$z_A z_{D'}$
+1.5	− .5	−.75	− .5	−.75
+ .5	+ .5	+.25	+ .5	+.25
.0	+1.5	.0	+1.5	.0
− .5	−1.5	+.75	−1.5	+.75
−1.5	.0	.0	.0	.0
		$\Sigma = +.25$		$\Sigma = +.25$

or raw-score values as z-scores by application of (8.13). For example, the mean and standard deviation of both the A- and D-scores of Table 17.7 are 7 and 4, respectively, and the mean and standard deviation of the D'-scores are 70 and 40. Applying (8.13), we obtain the A, D, and D' z-scores shown in Table 17.8. The D and D' z-values are seen to be identical. Obviously the AD and AD' z-score products must also be identical.

This brings us to the second reason why sums of products cannot always be used directly as an index of correlation: the magnitudes of such sums depend in part on the number of pairs on which they are based. Direct comparison of sums of products requires that the sums compared be based on the same number of pairs—a completely

Table 17.9 z-Scores, Products, Sums, and r-Values for Sets of Score Values Given in Table 17.7

A	B	AB	C	AC
+1.5	+1.5	+2.25	+ .5	+.75
+ .5	+ .5	+ .25	+1.5	+.75
.0	.0	.0	.0	.0
− .5	− .5	+ .25	−1.5	+.75
−1.5	−1.5	+2.25	− .5	+.75
		$\Sigma = +5$		$\Sigma = +3$
		$r = +1$		$r = +.6$

D	AD	E	AE	F	AF
− .5	−.75	− .5	−.75	−1.5	−2.25
+ .5	+.25	−1.5	−.75	− .5	− .25
+1.5	.0	.0	.0	.0	.0
−1.5	+.75	+1.5	−.75	+ .5	− .25
.0	.0	+ .5	−.75	+1.5	−2.25
	$\Sigma = +.25$		$\Sigma = -3$		$\Sigma = -5$
	$r = +.05$		$r = -.6$		$r = -1$

impractical restriction. This difficulty is easily overcome. It is necessary only to use the product *per pair*, or mean product, instead of the total product. Thus we arrive at the following definition of an index of the correlation (r) between pairs of measures X and Y, for the same individuals or objects.

$$r = \frac{\sum z_{X_i} z_{Y_i}}{N} \tag{17.1}$$

This index was created by an English statistician, Karl Pearson, and is known as the Pearson product-moment correlation coefficient. It is also variously referred to as a Pearson r, a simple r, or an ordinary r.

Table 17.9 shows the pairs of z-values, their products, the sums of their products, and the values of r for each of the hypothetical sets of scores of Table 17.7.

17.5   Some Properties of r

If in each pair of X's and Y's the z-score values are the same, the correlation is obviously perfect and positive. What is the value of r in this instance? When the z-values are the same in each pair, the sum of the z-score products becomes the sum of the squares of a complete set of z-scores. Symbolically, $\sum z_{X_i} z_{Y_i} = \sum z_{X_i}^2 = \sum z_{Y_i}^2$. Thus, if we can find the value of $\sum z_{X_i}^2$ or $\sum z_{Y_i}^2$, we will know the value of r for a perfect positive correlation. You may remember that the standard deviation of z-scores is 1 (see Section 8.5). Therefore, the variance of the z-scores is 1. Since z-scores have a mean of zero (see Section 8.5), each z-score can be considered a deviation score. By the definition of the variance (7.4), $S_z^2 = \sum z_i^2/N$. But $S_z^2 = 1$. Therefore, $1 = \sum z_i^2/N$ and $\sum z^2 = N$. Hence, when there is a perfect and positive relationship, the correlation coefficient r assumes the value of $+1$ (see r for A and B in Table 17.9). That is, if $z_{X_i} = z_{Y_i}$ for each i, then

$$r = \frac{\sum z_i^2}{N} = \frac{N}{N} = 1$$

Moreover, if in each pair of X's and Y's the z-scores have the same absolute values but are opposite in sign, the correlation is perfect and negative. In this situation r assumes the value -1 (see r for A and F in Table 17.9). That is, if $z_{X_i} = -z_{Y_i}$, then

$$r = \frac{-\sum z_i^2}{N} = \frac{-N}{N} = -1$$

Now consider a collection of pairs of measures for which the correlation is positive and high but not perfect. This is equivalent to saying that *most* individuals (pairs) that are above the mean on one measure are also above the mean on the other, whereas only a *relatively few* are above the mean on one measure and below the mean on the other (see scatter diagram for $r = .9$, Figure 17.8). In this situation most of the pairs will consist of either two positive or two negative z-scores, so

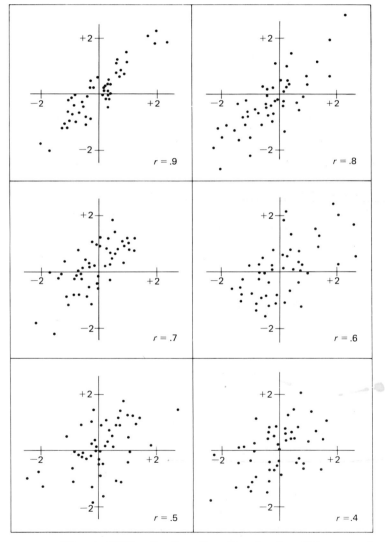

Figure 17.8 Scatter diagram of pairs of z-scores for selected values of *r*

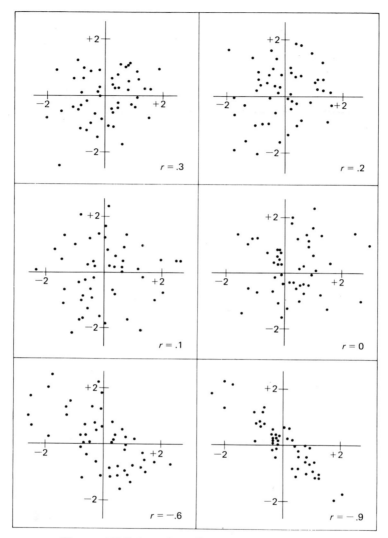

Figure 17.8 (continued)

that most of the products will be positive. Moreover, since the correlation is high, many of these positive products will be quite large,
because high z-scores for one variate tend to be paired with high z-scores
for the other, and low z-scores for one variate paired with low
z-scores for the other. For the entire collection the sum of the positive
products will greatly exceed the sum of the negative products. Hence,
the overall algebraic sum of products will be positive. Of course, since
the correlation is not perfect this sum will necessarily be some value less

than N so that r, the mean z-score product, will be some positive value less than 1.

Next, suppose the correlation is positive but low. This means that, while again most individuals above average in one measure are above average in the other, and vice versa, there will now be a larger number of instances in which individuals above average on one measure are below average on the other (see scatter diagram for $r = .3$, Figure 17.8). There will also be fewer large products, since individuals with extreme z-scores (either high or low) on one measure will seldom also have extreme z-scores on the other. Hence, while the sum of the positive z-score products will still exceed that of the negative z-score products, we would not expect the net sum to be as large as when the correlation is high. In other words, the mean z-score product will be smaller for low than for high degrees of relationship.

Next, consider the case of unrelated measures. To say that two sets of measures are entirely uncorrelated for a given collection is to say that individuals above (or below) average on one measure are equally likely to be above average, average, or below average on the other (see scatter diagram for $r = 0$, Figure 17.8). For the entire collection, then, the number of positive z-score products will be approximately equal to the number of negative z-score products. Also, the individual products will tend to be small, since two extreme z-scores will seldom be found in the same pair. Moreover, the sum of the negative products will tend to be approximately the same size as that of the positive products, so that the algebraic sum for the entire collection will approximate zero. Hence, in this situation the value of r will be close to zero.

Finally, it should be apparent that if the correlation is negative—that is, if most individuals above average on one measure are below average on the other—then the z-score product for most pairs will be negative in sign (see scatter diagrams for $r = -.6$ or $r = -.9$, Figure 17.8). The algebraic sum of products, and hence the mean z-score product, r, will now be negative, and the absolute magnitude of this mean product will depend on the degree of relationship.

We may now summarize as follows.

1 When the correlation is positive, r will be positive. When the correlation is negative, r will be negative.[7]
2 When the relationship is positive and perfect, $r = +1$, and $r = -1$ when the relationship is negative and perfect.
3 When there is a complete lack of relationship, $r = 0$. (Note: This is not to say that if $r = 0$ a complete lack of correlation

[7] It is this characteristic of r that has resulted in the use of the terms *positive* and *negative* to describe the type of correlation in statistics rather than the terms *direct* and *inverse*, which are commonly used in the mathematics of variation.

must always exist. We shall later show that under certain circumstances, r may be zero even if the relationship is perfect. Thus, $r = 0$ is a necessary but not a sufficient condition for a complete lack of correlation. We will discuss this fact in more detail in Section 17.7.)

4 For intermediate degrees of correlation, r will assume values between -1 and $+1$. The larger the absolute value of r, the higher or closer the correlation.

We shall later demonstrate that r is not *directly proportional* to the degree of correlation. That is, $r = .3$ does not imply "half" as close a correlation as $r = .6$. That this is true is obvious from a comparison of the scatter diagrams of Figure 17.8. These scatter diagrams were developed to help the student gain a sort of visual conception of the degree of correlation indicated by r-values of various magnitudes. It is clear from this figure, for example, that the change in the closeness of the correlation is much greater from $r = .7$ to $r = .9$ than from $r = .1$ to $r = .3$.

17.6   Linear and Curvilinear Types of Correlation

Up to this point in our discussion we have ignored the possibility of curvilinear types of correlation. We have concerned ourselves solely with pairs of variables that *tended* to be directly proportional, that is, to be linearly related. All the scatter diagrams or bivariate frequency distributions thus far presented reveal this tendency by the elliptical configuration of their respective fields of points. Before considering curvilinearly correlated variables we shall indicate more precisely what is meant by a linear or rectilinear type of relationship.

Figure 17.9 shows the scatter diagram for a set of 37 pairs of hypothetical score values. The dots fall into a roughly elliptical pattern.[8] The solid line is the major axis of the ellipse formed by the dots; it

[8] In this section we are concerned only with establishing a rough notion of the general nature of the scatter diagrams that would arise in the case of samples from populations for which the relationship is linear as compared with those arising from samples taken from populations for which the relationship is curvilinear. The elliptical pattern to which we refer has to do with the character of the contour lines formed by connecting cells of equal frequency in a bivariate frequency table. If a bivariate frequency table were somehow set up for a large sample from a population in which the relationship between two variables is linear, the contour lines connecting points (cells) of equal frequency would tend to be elliptical. (Perhaps we might think of these contour lines as "isofrequencies," just as isobars on a weather map are lines connecting points at which the barometric pressure is the same.) When we speak of an elliptical pattern, it is really these contour lines we are referring to.

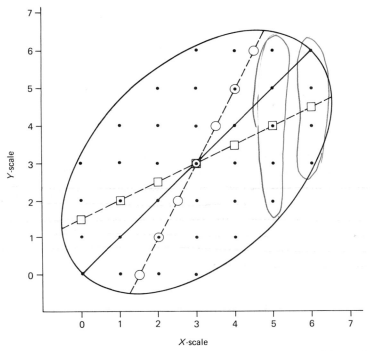

Figure 17.9 Scatter diagram of 37 pairs of hypothetical X- and Y-values

corresponds to the lines shown in Figures 17.2, 17.3, and 17.5. In our previous discussion we have implied that this is the straight line about which the points tend to be scattered. Actually, this implication is incorrect—or, at most, it is true only in a very crude sense. Consider, for example, the four Y-scores associated with the largest X-value ($X = 6$). Of these four scores three are below this line. Similarly, three of the five Y-scores associated with $X = 5$ are below this line. The Y-scores associated with small X-values, on the other hand, tend to lie above this line. In fact, the only subset of Y-scores that is symmetrically distributed about this line is the subset associated with $X = 3$.

Obviously there must be some line that fits the Y-scores better than does this major axis. If we are to describe the Y-scores as tending to be scattered about a straight line, it would appear that a better line to use would be the one that, if it exists, passes through the means of the subsets of Y-scores associated with the same X-score. For the subsets of such scores in the collection of Figure 17.9, these means have been indicated by open squares. The "better" line we have been talking about is the line determined by these squares.

While this line obviously fits the Y-scores better than the major axis does, it does not fit the X-scores as well. Consider, for example, the subset of X-scores associated with a Y-score of 4. Two of these six scores are to the right of the major axis but only one is to the right of the line determined by the means of subsets of Y-scores. This suggests that the trend of the X-scores can best be represented by a still *different* line. For this purpose we shall use the straight line that, if it exists, passes through the means of the subsets of X-scores associated with the same Y-score. In Figure 17.9 these subset X-score means have been indicated by the open circles, and the line about which the X-values tend to scatter is taken to be the one determined by these means.

We shall refer to the straight line determined by the subset Y-means (squares in Figure 17.9) as the Y *trend line* and to the straight line determined by the subset X-means (circles in Figure 17.9) as the X *trend line*. If, for a given collection of pairs of imperfectly correlated scores, two such trend lines do, in fact, exist, the scores are said to be *linearly* or *rectilinearly* correlated. Of course, if the relationship is perfect as well as linear, only one Y-score value will be associated with any given X-score value and all points will lie on a *single* straight line.

To summarize we shall state two conditions that must be satisfied before the relationship between a given set of pairs of variables can be said to be perfectly linear.

1 The graphically plotted means of the Y-scores corresponding to a given X-score must lie on a straight line.
2 The graphically plotted means of the X-scores corresponding to a given Y-score must lie on a straight line.

There are two very important points to note with regard to these conditions. First, it should be clear from Figure 17.9 that *perfect linearity does not imply perfect correlation. Variables that exhibit perfect linearity may exhibit any degree of correlation.* Second, perfect linearity is an ideal condition rarely, if ever, satisfied in real collections of data. In studying relationships, as in studying averages or proportions, we are usually seeking population facts. For example, we are not ordinarily interested so much in the correlation between height and weight for a particular group of 12-year-old boys as in the correlation between height and weight for the entire population of 12-year-old boys. It may be that the condition of perfect linearity does not hold in the case of these variables for this population. Even if it did, it is not likely that perfect linearity would be found in a sample taken from it. Even if a large number of pairs is selected, the number of weight scores associated with a particular height score may be relatively small, so that their mean will be relatively unstable—that is, subject to a rather large sampling error. Moreover, if the sampling is random, these errors are as likely to be in one direction as in the other, with the result that the means of the subsamples of weights associated with fixed heights may deviate rather markedly from a straight line.

Actually, then, the practical issue is not whether the condition of perfect linearity holds for a given collection of pairs, but rather whether the collection exhibits a sufficient tendency toward linearity to warrant the assumption that the linearity condition holds for the population represented. While a statistical test of the significance of departure from linearity is available,[9] consideration of it is beyond the scope of this text. We shall simply resort to a visual inspection of the scatter diagram or bivariate frequency distribution. If the field of points appears to be roughly elliptical, it is not unreasonable to assume that the condition of linearity holds for the population represented. If there is doubt, it may be advisable to compute the means of the Y (columns in a bivariate table) and X (rows in a bivariate table) subsamples and to locate them on the diagram or table. If linearity holds for the population, these Y- and X-means will tend to fall along straight lines. These lines will intersect, with the angle between them becoming smaller as the degree of correlation increases, and will merge into a single line as r approaches unity. Since the subsample means for a given collection of data are usually based on relatively small numbers of cases, they may fluctuate quite markedly from a true straight-line arrangement without vitiating the underlying assumption of linearity for the population. The critical point is that they appear to be arranged along a straight rather than a curved line.

While it may be that heights and weights for a population of a given sex and age are not perfectly linearly related, scatter diagrams of height-weight data for samples from such populations do not indicate any marked departure from linearity.[10] The subsample weight means (●) and subsample height means (○) for a sample of 50 twelve-year-old boys are shown in the bivariate frequency distribution of Figure 17.7. The subsample weight means exhibit a very clear fit to a straight-line pattern. The fit of the subsample height means is far less precise, but it appears, nevertheless, that there is a tendency for these means also to fall along a straight line. The heights and weights of this particular collection would, therefore, be regarded as being linearly related, though not perfectly so.

[9] That is, a test of the hypothesis that in the population the means of the subsets of Y-scores (or X-scores) associated with the same X-score (or Y-score) fall on a straight line. For a description of this statistical test, see F. N. Kerlinger and E. J. Pedhazur, *Multiple Regression in Behavioral Research*, Holt, Rinehart and Winston, New York, 1973, pp. 199–205.

[10] Height-weight scatter diagrams are definitely curvilinear for samples from populations of boys (or girls) when the age of the individuals constituting the population is allowed to vary, say, from 4 to 17. For samples from populations consisting of individuals of the same age, this curvilinearity is not apparent.

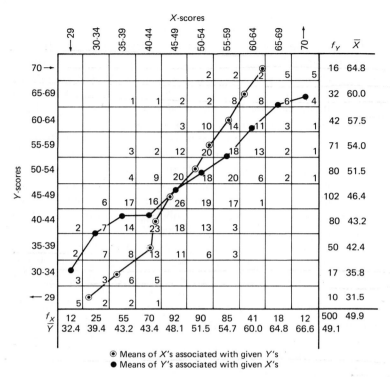

Figure 17.10 Bivariate frequency distribution for a random sample of 500 from a population having a correlation coefficient of .7 and satisfying perfectly the condition of linearity

Figure 17.10 is a bivariate table for a random sample of 500 pairs selected from a population of pairs of X- and Y-values that is known to have a correlation coefficient of .7 and to satisfy perfectly the condition of linearity. The subsample Y-means (the solid black dots) and X-means (the open circles with dots inside) have been located in this table with reference to the score scales. Even with a sample this large, considerable fluctuation from a true straight-line pattern remains.

Figure 17.11 shows the bivariate frequency distribution for a hypothetical set of 100 pairs of ages and memory scores on a test on motion picture film plots.[11] The means (●) of subsamples of memory scores

---

[11] Although these particular 100 scores were fabricated for the purpose of illustration, they nevertheless were made to conform to data reported by H. E. Jones, in "Psychological Studies of Motion Pictures: II, Observation and Recall as a Function of Age," *University of California Publications in Psychology*, 3 (1928), 225–243

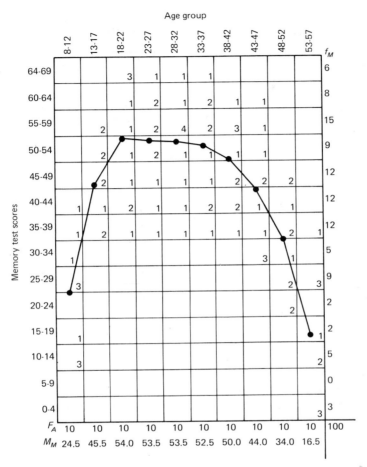

Figure 17.11 Hypothetical bivariate frequency distribution of age and memory scores on a test on motion picture film plots

have been located in this table with reference to the score scales. Clearly, neither the individual scores nor the means of subsamples of memory scores follow a straight-line pattern. Instead of falling into an elliptical pattern, the individual pairs of scores appear to be scattered in a curved field; and the subsample means tend to fall along a curved line. The correlation appears to be positive for ages 8 to 22, to be zero from ages 22 to 37, and to be negative for ages above 37. Relationships such as this, which do not exhibit linearity, are said to be *curvilinear*.

Many variations of curvilinearity are possible. For a few examples, see Figure 17.12, which presents boundaries of hypothetical fields of

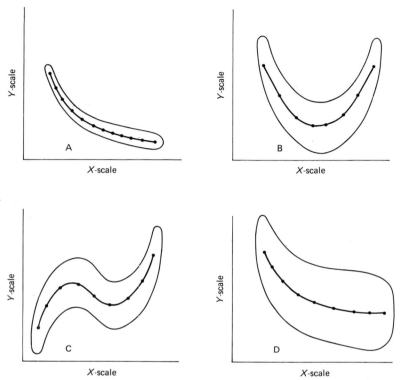

Figure 17.12   Boundaries of hypothetical field of scatter-diagram points and Y-trend curves for various types of curvilinear relationships

scatter-diagram points. In each of these examples, the points are scattered about a curved line determined by the means of subgroups of Y-scores (see Figure 17.9). The shapes of these curved lines characterize the underlying nature of a particular type of curvilinear relationship, just as the straight line characterizes a linear relationship. But whereas there is only one type of linear relationship—a relationship is either linear or it is not—there are innumerable types of curvilinear relationships. Curvilinear relationships are much more difficult to describe than are linear relationships. Not only must the type of relationship—i.e., type of trend curve—be described, but also the degree of relationship must be indicated. The situation is complicated by the fact that both type and degree may be one thing when the data are considered with reference to the Y trend curve and quite another when the data are considered with reference to the X trend curve. As in linear correlation, the degree of relationship may vary considerably for the same curve type. In Figure 17.12, A and D are identical in type, but the relationship is much closer in A, as is indicated by the lesser width of its point field. That is, the pair points do not deviate as widely from the trend curve in A as they do in D. Just as in linear correlation, the degree of relationship in curvilinear correlation is perfect if all individual pair points fall directly on the trend curve, and the greater the tendency for the points to deviate from this curve, the lower the degree of relationship.

17.7 Effect of Curvilinearity on the Mean z-Score Product, r

Assume a projectile to be fired at an angle of 30° from the earth's surface with a forward velocity of 1,600 feet per second. Then the relationship between time (T) in flight in seconds and height (H) above ground in feet is a perfect curvilinear relationship which, if air resistance is neglected and the constant of gravity taken to be 32, is described by the formula

$$H = 800T - 16T^2$$

Table 17.10 gives corresponding pairs of T- and H-values. For example, the table shows that after an elapsed time of 5 seconds the height of the projectile is 3,600 feet. The means and standard deviations of these time and height scores were obtained and used in converting them into z-score units, which are also given in Table 17.10. Figures 17.13 and 17.14 show the scatter diagrams for the pairs of measures in original and z-score units, respectively. It is obvious that the correlation is perfect with all points falling precisely on the trend curve. The pairs

Table 17.10 Heights of a Particular Projectile after a Given Lapse of Time

T	H	z_T	z_H	$z_H z_T$
0	0	−1.6	−1.7	+2.72
5	3,600	−1.3	− .7	+ .91
10	6,400	− .9	+ .1	− .09
15	8,400	− .6	+ .7	− .42
20	9,600	− .3	+1.0	− .30
25	10,000	.0	+1.1	.00
30	9,600	+ .3	+1.0	+ .30
35	8,400	+ .6	+ .7	+ .42
40	6,400	+ .9	+ .1	+ .09
45	3,600	+1.3	− .7	− .91
50	0	+1.6	−1.7	−2.72
				$\Sigma = .00$

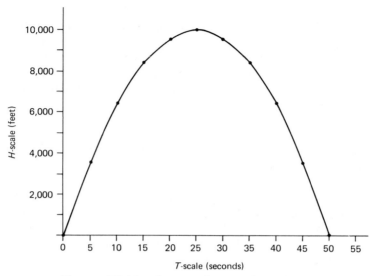

Figure 17.13   Scatter diagram for pairs of original time and height measures for a particular projectile in flight

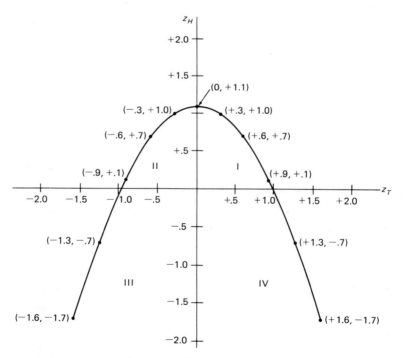

Figure 17.14   Scatter diagram for pairs of projectile time and height measures in z-score units

of z-score values have also been entered in Figure 17.14 in parentheses adjacent to the point represented, the first value in each instance being the z-score for T and the second the z-score for H. Note that for each pair of scores in Quadrant I of Figure 17.14, there is a pair in Quadrant II having the same corresponding absolute values. The same is true of the pairs of scores in Quadrants III and IV. Now the signs of the scores of the Quadrant I pairs are alike (both positive), whereas the signs of the scores of the Quadrant II pairs differ. Consequently, the sum of the products of pairs of z-scores in Quadrant I has the same absolute value but differs in sign from that of the pairs in Quadrant II. The net z-score product for these two quadrants is, therefore, zero. The same is true of the corresponding net for Quadrants III and IV. Hence, it follows that the value of the mean z-score product, r, is *zero*— a value we have learned to interpret as indicative of a complete absence of relationship!

Obviously, the index r is not appropriate for describing degree of correlation between curvilinearly related variables; some index based on a more general definition of relationship is required. While such indexes are available, their consideration is beyond the scope of this text. Here, we will simply stress the point that *the applicability of r is limited to linear types of relationships*. This implies that a required first step in any correlation analysis is the preparation of either a scatter diagram or a bivariate table for the purpose of determining whether the pairs of values conform sufficiently to a linear (elliptical) pattern to justify the use of r as a descriptive index.

17.8 The Calculation of r from the Original Score Values

In addition to the definitional formula (17.1) for r, there are a number of other formulas that can be used to compute this correlation coefficient. Most computer programs use one of these alternate formulas rather than (17.1). In this section we present some of these formulas. We first present the formulas, then apply all the formulas to a single set of data.

Formulas using deviation scores

$$r = \frac{\sum x_i y_i}{N S_X S_Y} \tag{17.2}$$

Proof* Let X and Y represent the original score values. Then,

* Optional.

for pair i

$$z_{x_i} = \frac{X_i - \bar{X}}{S_X} = \frac{x_i}{S_X} \quad \text{and} \quad z_{y_i} = \frac{Y_i - \bar{Y}}{S_Y} = \frac{y_i}{S_Y}$$

Now substituting into (17.1) we have

$$r = \frac{\sum (1/S_X)x_i(1/S_Y)y_i}{N}$$

$$= \frac{\sum x_i y_i}{N S_X S_Y} \quad \text{(see Rule 5.1)}$$

$$r = \frac{\sum x_i y_i}{\sqrt{(\sum x_i^2)(\sum y_i^2)}} \tag{17.3}$$

Proof* By (17.2),

$$r = \frac{\sum x_i y_i}{N S_X S_Y}$$

Substituting (7.5) for S_X and S_Y we have

$$r = \frac{\sum x_i y_i}{N \sqrt{\left(\dfrac{\sum x_i^2}{N}\right)\left(\dfrac{\sum y_i^2}{N}\right)}}$$

$$= \frac{\sum x_i y_i}{\sqrt{(\sum x_i^2)(\sum y_i^2)}}$$

A formula using the covariance of X and Y

DN 17.2   Given a collection of pairs of scores (X, Y). Then the mean of the products of the deviations of the scores constituting the pairs from their respective means is known as the *covariance* of the collection of pairs of scores.

Stated symbolically, the covariance of a collection of pairs of X- and Y-scores is

$$Cov(XY) = \frac{\sum x_i y_i}{N} \tag{17.4}$$

* Optional.

Remark: $Cov(XY)$ is an index of the extent to which the members of the pairs of X- and Y-scores tend to vary in the same way, i.e., to "co-vary." If the scores of the pairs tend to be positively related, a large X is likely to be paired with a large Y so that both vary from the other X- and Y-scores in the collection in the same way (both will be above their respective means). The corresponding deviation scores (x and y) will both be large in absolute value and have positive signs so that their product (xy) will make a substantial positive contribution to the sum of deviation products, i.e., to $\sum x_i y_i$. Similarly, a pair of scores consisting of a small X and a small Y co-vary in that both will fall below their respective means. Their deviation scores will tend to be large in absolute value and have negative signs so that their product will be positive and again the contribution to $\sum x_i y_i$ is substantial and positive. Scores that do not co-vary in the same way may have deviation scores that are opposite in sign so that their product is negative and its contribution to $\sum x_i y_i$ is negative.

Table 17.11 shows the deviations, the deviation sums of products, the covariances, and the correlations for the hypothetical sets of scores given in Table 17.7. Like the correlations (r-values), the deviation sums of products and the covariances are negative when the relationship is negative. It follows that there ought to be a relationship between the index of covariance and the correlation coefficient that is itself the covariance of pairs of scores in standard form [compare (17.1) and (17.4)]. Direct substitution of $Cov(XY)$ as defined in (17.4) into (17.2) gives this relationship.

$$r = \frac{Cov(XY)}{S_X S_Y} \tag{17.5}$$

Each hypothetical set of scores in Table 17.7 has a standard deviation of 4. Hence, by dividing the covariances given in Table 17.11 by $4 \times 4 = 16$, we may obtain the correlations. (Compare the correlations thus obtained with those given in Table 17.9.)

A formula using original score values[12]

$$r = \frac{\sum X_i Y_i - \frac{(\sum X_i)(\sum Y_i)}{N}}{\sqrt{\left(\sum X_i^2 - \frac{(\sum X_i)^2}{N}\right)\left(\sum Y_i^2 - \frac{(\sum Y_i)^2}{N}\right)}} \tag{17.6}$$

[12] Formula (17.6) applies to raw scores prior to any grouping. Each individual pair of scores is used in the formula. A technique for calculating r from a bivariate table is available but is not presented here. See the first edition of this book, pp. 391–395.

Table 17.11   Deviation Scores and Products for the Hypothetical Data of Table 17.7

A	B	AB	C	AC	D	AD	E	AE	F	AF
+6	+6	+36	+2	+12	−2	−12	−2	−12	−6	−36
+2	+2	+4	+6	+12	+2	+4	−6	−12	−2	−4
0	0	0	0	0	+6	0	0	0	0	0
−2	−2	+4	−6	+12	−6	+12	+6	−12	+2	−4
−6	−6	+36	−2	+12	0	0	+2	−12	+6	−36
Σ		+80		+48		+4		−48		−80
Cov		+16		+9.6		+.8		−9.6		−16
r		+1		+.60		+.05		−.60		−1

Proof* By (17.3),

$$r = \frac{\sum x_i y_i}{\sqrt{(\sum x_i^2)(\sum y_i^2)}}$$

By (7.6),

$$\sum x_i^2 = \sum X_i^2 - \frac{(\sum X_i)^2}{N} \quad \text{and} \quad \sum y_i^2 = \sum Y_i^2 - \frac{(\sum Y_i)^2}{N}$$

Also

$$\begin{aligned}
\sum x_i y_i &= \sum (X_i - \bar{X})(Y_i - \bar{Y}) \\
&= \sum (X_i Y_i - X_i \bar{Y} - \bar{X} Y_i + \bar{X}\bar{Y}) \\
&= \sum X_i Y_i - \bar{Y} \sum X_i - \bar{X} \sum Y_i + N\bar{X}\bar{Y}
\end{aligned}$$

[See (5.21), (5.22), and (5.23).] Now substituting from (6.2) for $\bar{X}$ and $\bar{Y}$, we have

$$\begin{aligned}
\sum x_i y_i &= \sum X_i Y_i - \frac{(\sum X_i)(\sum Y_i)}{N} - \frac{(\sum X_i)(\sum Y_i)}{N} + \frac{(\sum X_i)(\sum Y_i)}{N} \\
&= \sum X_i Y_i - \frac{(\sum X_i)(\sum Y_i)}{N}
\end{aligned} \tag{17.7}$$

Finally, substituting these raw-score equivalents of deviation scores into (17.3) gives (17.6).

An example using (17.2), (17.3), (17.5), and (17.6) Hypothetical pairs of scores for five subjects on two variables (X and Y) and the quantities derived from these scores that are necessary for using formulas (17.2), (17.3), (17.5), and (17.6) are given in Table 17.12.

* Optional.

Table 17.12 Hypothetical Pairs of Scores for Five Subjects

Subject	X-Score	Y-Score	XY	$x = X - \bar{X}$	$y = Y - \bar{Y}$	xy
1	20	4	80	8	1	8
2	4	1	4	-8	-2	16
3	8	2	16	-4	-1	4
4	12	5	60	0	2	0
5	16	3	48	4	0	0

$\Sigma X = 60 \quad \Sigma Y = 15 \quad \Sigma XY = 208 \quad \Sigma x = 0 \quad \Sigma y = 0 \quad \Sigma xy = 28$

$\Sigma X^2 = 880 \quad \Sigma Y^2 = 55 \qquad\qquad \Sigma x^2 = 160 \quad \Sigma y^2 = 10$

$$S_X^2 = \frac{880}{5} - \left(\frac{60}{5}\right)^2 = 32$$

$$S_Y^2 = \frac{55}{5} - \left(\frac{15}{5}\right)^2 = 2$$

$$\text{Cov}(XY) = \frac{\Sigma xy}{N} = \frac{28}{5} = 5.6$$

Now by (17.2),

$$r = \frac{\sum x_i y_i}{N S_X S_Y}$$

$$= \frac{28}{5\sqrt{2}\sqrt{32}} = \frac{28}{5\sqrt{64}} = \frac{28}{(5)(8)} = \frac{28}{40} = .70$$

or by (17.3)

$$r = \frac{\sum x_i y_i}{\sqrt{(\sum x_i^2)(\sum y_i^2)}}$$

$$= \frac{28}{\sqrt{(160)(10)}} = \frac{28}{\sqrt{1,600}} = \frac{28}{40} = .70$$

or by (17.5)

$$r = \frac{\text{Cov}(XY)}{S_X S_Y} = \frac{5.6}{\sqrt{2}\sqrt{32}} = \frac{5.6}{\sqrt{64}} = \frac{5.6}{8} = .70$$

or by (17.6)

$$r = \frac{\sum X_i Y_i - \frac{(\sum X_i)(\sum Y_i)}{N}}{\sqrt{\left(\sum X_i^2 - \frac{(\sum X_i)^2}{N}\right)\left(\sum Y_i^2 - \frac{(\sum Y_i)^2}{N}\right)}}$$

$$= \frac{208 - \frac{(60)(15)}{5}}{\sqrt{\left(880 - \frac{(60)^2}{5}\right)\left(55 - \frac{(15)^2}{5}\right)}} = \frac{28}{\sqrt{(160)(10)}} = .70$$

To conclude this section we discuss how a linear transformation (see Chapter 8) of the X- or Y-values affects the magnitude of the correlation coefficient.

> **RULE 17.1**   Given N pairs of X- and Y-scores. Let $L_X = CX + A$, where C and A are constants. Also, let $L_Y = DY + B$, where D and B are constants. Then,
>
> $$|r_{L_X L_Y}| = |r_{(CX+A)(DY+B)}| = |r_{XY}|$$
>
> provided neither C nor D is zero.

Verbally, Rule 17.1 states that the absolute value of the correlation between X and Y is not changed by a linear transformation of either or both the X- and Y-scores.[13]

For example, consider the five pairs of scores given in Table 17.12. Recall that for these scores the correlation between X and Y was .70. Assume the following linear transformations of the X- and Y-scores:

$$L_X = 2X + 1 \quad \text{and} \quad L_Y = -3Y + 3$$

According to Rule 17.1, the absolute value of the correlation between L_X and L_Y will be .70. The algebraic value for r will be $-.70$. [You may wish to verify this by actually forming the new sets of scores and then applying either (17.1), (17.2), (17.3), (17.5), or (17.6).]

17.9   Remarks Regarding the Meaning of a Given Value of r

We have already noted that while the coefficient of correlation, r, is a convenient quantitative *index* of relationship, it may not be considered as directly proportional to the *degree* of relationship (see Section 17.5, and also Figure 17.8). An r of .80, for example, may not be said to represent twice as close a relationship as one of .40. In order to make such a statement we would have to be able to describe, *independently of r*, precisely what we mean by closeness or degree of relationship, and no such description or definition that is generally acceptable has as yet been proposed. Lacking a definition of "degree of relationship," we are unable to state in general how r changes in value for given changes in that degree.

The computation of r, after all, is only one of a number of possible arbitrary mathematical procedures that, when applied to a set of

---

[13] If D and C are both positive or both negative, the value of $r_{L_X L_Y}$ and the value of r_{XY} will be identical. However, if C and D are of opposite signs, then $r_{L_X L_Y}$ and r_{XY} will also be opposite in sign.

related measures, will yield a single numerical value somehow indicative of the degree of relationship. The coefficient r is based on z-score products. Other indexes could be derived from z-score *differences* for the pairs concerned, or from their z-score *ratios*, or from the *squared differences* between pairs of z-scores, or from similar measures based on percentile ranks instead of z-scores. For the most part these possibilities do not possess the characteristics that would make them as convenient to use and interpret as r.[14] Which of them is most nearly directly proportional to the "degree of relationship" we cannot say, since this would depend on how we defined degree of relationship. For precisely the same reason, we cannot say in general that r is any better than other possible indexes *in this particular respect*.

Various schemes have, nevertheless, been suggested to assist the student of statistics to appreciate the significance of a given value of r. Some of these are quite helpful in certain restricted types of situations; but in other situations or in general they may be seriously misleading and hence must be used with extreme caution.

One of the most common and most misleading of these practices has been that of classifying certain r-values as "high," "medium," or "low." For example, an r of .30 or less has been said to be "low," one between .30 and .70 "medium," one from .70 to .90 "high," and one above .90 "very high." The numerical values of r corresponding to each of these verbal categories has, of course, differed for various classifiers. The point is that such classifications are invariably misleading, since what constitutes a "high" or a "low" correlation is a *relative* matter, and differs markedly for different types of variates. Coefficients of correlation as high as .5 between measures of a physical and a mental trait are *extremely rare*, and a correlation of .6 between two such traits would be considered *phenomenal*. On the other hand, correlations of this magnitude between reliable measures of two mental traits are quite common, and would be considered as only "medium" for most groups in which we are interested. Again, a correlation of .9 between two independent measures of the same trait—for example, between the scores on two equivalent tests of spelling ability—might be considered as only "medium" or even "low," particularly if the tests were long and comprehensive. In this latter situation, an r of .6 would certainly be regarded as extremely low. There is no single classification, then, that is applicable in *all* situations. Because of the danger that they will be applied in situations in which they are not valid, it is best that any and all such classifications be disregarded entirely by the beginning student.

---

[14] As will be shown in the following chapter, the index r does arise in a mathematical solution to a somewhat different problem and, hence, possesses mathematical properties which make it preferable to the other possibilities suggested.

The fact remains, nevertheless, that the adjectives "high", "low," and "medium" are convenient to use with reference to correlation coefficients and degrees of correlation. We have, in fact, used them in this chapter and shall continue to do so. This may appear inconsistent with what has just been said. We shall try for the most part, however, to use these adjectives to refer only to the absolute mathematical magnitude of r. The adjective "high" as we shall apply it with regard to a correlation coefficient refers to a value of r high up along the scale of possible values (near 1.00), the adjective "low" to a value of r near .00, and the adjective "medium" to a value of r near .50. Used in this sense, "high" does not imply "important" or "consequential," nor does "low" mean "of no importance" or "of no consequence." It is important to distinguish between this use of the adjectives "low" and "high" and their use as names of categories in some classification scheme for interpreting or evaluating r as an index of degree of relationship.

Another scheme that has been used to aid in interpreting a given value of r involves the use of the concept of variance. As we will show in a later chapter, when the correlation coefficient is squared and multiplied by 100, the resulting value represents the percent of the variance of one of the variables that can, in a noncausal sense, be accounted for by variation in the other. That is, the square of the Pearson correlation coefficient[15] indicates the proportion of variance in Y (or X) that can be accounted for by or associated with the variance in X (or Y).[16] Thus, for example, if the correlation between scores on a reading achievement test and an arithmetic test is .50, we know that 25 percent of the variance in reading achievement scores can be accounted for by the variation in the arithmetic scores. Likewise, 25 percent of the variance in arithmetic scores can be accounted for by the variation in the reading scores. Table 17.13 provides selected r- and $100r^2$-values.

The final scheme that we will consider for interpreting the value of a given r involves the use of the concept of prediction. Although the prediction problem is relatively complicated, the basic ideas can be grasped fairly easily.

In many situations, the measurement of two variables is separated by some time span. When this occurs—as it would in the case of High School GPA and College GPA, for example—it is often desired to use the measures obtained at time 1 (the predictors) to *predict* the measures at time 2 (the criteria). Since two measures are or ultimately become available for each individual, it is possible to compute a correlation between them. As one might suspect, the degree of correlation between

[15] The index r^2 is sometimes referred to as the coefficient of determination.

[16] This is not meant to imply that the variance in Y (or X) is caused by X (or Y). More will be said about this issue in Section 17.11.

Table 17.13   Selected Values of r and $100r^2$

r	$100r^2$	r	$100r^2$
.00	0	.55	30+
.05	0+	.60	36
.10	1	.65	42+
.15	2+	.70	49
.20	4	.75	56+
.25	6+	.80	64
.30	9	.85	72+
.35	12+	.90	81
.40	16	.95	90+
.45	20+	.98	96+
.50	25	.99	98+

the predictor and the criterion is related to the accuracy of the prediction process. This relationship makes it possible to examine the meaning of a given correlation coefficient by examining the degree of accuracy in our predictions.

Perhaps the easiest method for illustrating different degrees of accuracy (and hence different values of r) is to use a bivariate frequency table. Table 17.14 contains six bivariate frequency distributions that represent the accuracy of prediction for six different values of the Pearson correlation coefficient. As an aid in interpreting this table, you may want to think of the criterion variable as College Freshman GPA and the predictor variable as High School GPA. If $r = .50$, then of the top 1,000 (out of 4,000) students on the HSGPA scale, 480 will be in the top 1,000 (out of 4,000) on the College GPA scale, 279 in the next 1,000, 168 in the next 1,000, and 73 in the bottom 1,000.

The various subsets of data in Table 17.14 represent nothing more than bivariate frequency distributions for selected values of r. Thus, the data in the table are really not much different (except for the number of cases) from the data supplied by the scatter plots of Figure 17.8.

In summary, the above schemes may help you gain a better feel for what a given value of r means. However, we recommend that the beginning student make no attempt to arrive at an absolute interpretation of r. Look upon it simply as an index value that is indicative of, but not linearly related to, the degree of relationship. When comparing r-values of different magnitudes, you should avoid trying to estimate "how much" closer the relationship is in one case than in another, but should be content instead with the knowledge that there *is* a difference of some indeterminate amount. You should be careful, also, never to compare r-values even in this way except when the relationships are known to be linear. If you wish to secure a more definite notion of what an r of a given magnitude really means, you can do no better

Table 17.14   Accuracy of Prediction for Different Values of the Correlation Coefficient (1,000 Cases in Each Row or Column)

A. $r = .00$

Quarter on Predictor	Quarter on Criterion			
	4th	3d	2d	1st
1st	250	250	250	250
2d	250	250	250	250
3d	250	250	250	250
4th	250	250	250	250

D. $r = .60$

Quarter on Predictor	Quarter on Criterion			
	4th	3d	2d	1st
1st	45	141	277	537
2d	141	264	318	277
3d	277	318	264	141
4th	537	277	141	45

B. $r = .40$

Quarter on Predictor	Quarter on Criterion			
	4th	3d	2d	1st
1st	104	191	277	428
2d	191	255	277	277
3d	277	277	255	191
4th	428	277	191	104

E. $r = .70$

Quarter on Predictor	Quarter on Criterion			
	4th	3d	2d	1st
1st	22	107	270	601
2d	107	270	353	270
3d	270	353	270	107
4th	601	270	107	22

C. $r = .50$

Quarter on Predictor	Quarter on Criterion			
	4th	3d	2d	1st
1st	73	168	279	480
2d	168	258	295	279
3d	279	295	258	168
4th	480	279	168	73

F. $r = .80$

Quarter on Predictor	Quarter on Criterion			
	4th	3d	2d	1st
1st	6	66	253	675
2d	66	271	410	253
3d	253	410	271	66
4th	675	253	66	6

From Robert L. Thorndike and Elizabeth Hagen, Measurement and Evaluation in Psychology and Education, *3d ed., John Wiley and Sons, New York, 1969, p. 173. Reprinted by permission of the publisher.*

than to study the scatter diagram or the distribution of tally marks in the cells of the bivariate table from which it was computed.

17.10 Cautions in Interpreting Correlation Coefficients: The Influence of the Variability of the Measures on the Magnitude of *r*

If, in a study of the relationship between measures of two traits, we selected two groups of individuals or objects and found that one group showed greater variability in these measures than the other, we would find, too, that the coefficient of correlation *r* between the measures would be greater for the more variable than for the more homogeneous group. This fact may easily be inferred from a comparison of scatter

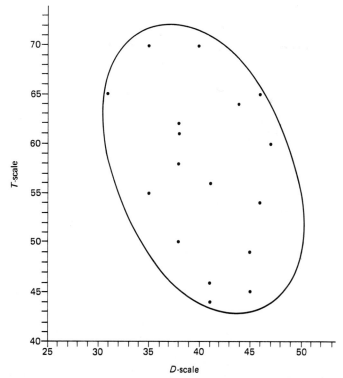

Figure 17.15   Scatter diagram for 17 pairs of time-dissimilarity scores with no dissimilarity score exceeding 47

diagrams of pairs of scores for homogeneous and heterogeneous groups.

For example, suppose in the study of the correlation between discrimination decision time and physically assessed dissimilarity of objects to be discriminated (see Section 17.2) that only highly similar objects were used. Let us assume that for no set of objects was the dissimilarity score greater than 47. Figure 17.15 shows the scatter diagram for time versus dissimilarity for the 17 sets of objects of Table 17.5 for which the dissimilarity scores do not exceed 47. Clearly, this elliptical field of points is much broader in relation to the length of its major axis than is that of Figure 17.5, in which the dissimilarity scores involved ranged from 31 to 68.[17] The correlation between the 40 pairs of time-dissimilarity scores of Table 17.5 and Figure 17.5 is −.70, a rather substantial negative correlation. The correlation between the 17

[17] In comparing Figures 17.15 and 17.5 the student should take into account differences in the physical distances representing the scale units.

pairs of scores pictured in the scatter diagram of Figure 17.15, by contrast, is only $-.30$.

As a second example, consider the correlation between scores on a reading comprehension test (R) and heights in centimeters (H) for a group of fourth-grade pupils. Since it is known that there is an almost complete lack of relationship between these variates for a group of such individuals, the boundary of the scatter diagram point field will be approximately circular. Now consider the same measurements for a group of third-grade children. An approximately equal lack of correlation will again be observed. However, while there will be some overlapping of the height and reading score distributions for these two groups, we would expect that, on the average, the third-grade group would be lower both in height and reading comprehension than the fourth-grade group. Hence, the circle prescribing the boundary of the point field for the third-grade scatter diagram would lie below and to the left of the circle for the fourth-grade scatter diagram. Similarly, for a fifth-grade group we would expect the boundary circle—again indicating an almost complete lack of relationship—to lie above and to the right of the fourth-grade circle, and for a sixth-grade group we would expect the circle to lie above and to the right of that for the fifth grade. The placement of these various boundary circles is shown in Figure 17.16.

Now suppose we consider the boundary of the point field for the scatter diagram of such reading comprehension and height scores for a mixed group of third-, fourth-, fifth-, and sixth-graders. Obviously, points from each of the circular fields of Figure 17.16 are included within the new boundary, and the resulting point field has the shape of a long, narrow ellipse, indicating a substantial degree of correlation. Although the correlation between reading comprehension and height was virtually nil for the relatively homogeneous groups consisting of pupils at the same grade level, the correlation between these same variables now has become substantial when determined for a heterogeneous group consisting of pupils at various grade levels.

These examples show the marked effect on the magnitude of r resulting from either a curtailment or an increase in variability of the measures involved. The magnitude of the coefficient of correlation between measures of two traits for a given set of individuals or objects depends, then, on the variability of these measures for the given set— or, as the same idea is frequently expressed, it depends on the "range of talent" of the set. Actually, the magnitude of the coefficient of correlation is, therefore, subject to at least a degree of willful manipulation. It follows that it is not meaningful to speak of *the* correlation between any two traits or characteristics, apart from any description of the particular collection of individuals or objects involved. Statements such as, "the correlation between height and weight is .70," or "there

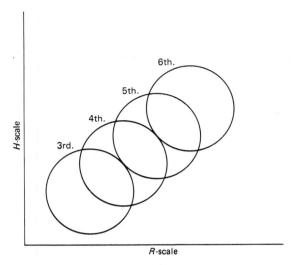

Figure 17.16 Hypothetical circular boundaries of scatter-diagram point fields of reading comprehension (*R*) and height (*H*) scores for separate groups of third-, fourth-, fifth-, and sixth-grade pupils

is only a low correlation between intelligence and spelling ability," are indicative of loose thinking. *Such statements can be made only with reference to a specific group and, hence, should always be accompanied by a description of the particular group involved, including a description of its variability in the measures concerned.* Comparisons of degree of relationship should, therefore, not be based on comparisons of *r*-values unless these values are established for groups that are at least approximately alike in "range of talent."

17.11 Cautions in Interpreting Correlation Coefficients: Causal versus Casual or Concomitant Relationship

One other very important admonition remains to be made. No more serious blunder in the interpretation of correlation coefficients can be committed than that of assuming that the correlation between two traits is a measure of the extent to which an individual's status in one trait is *caused by* his status in the other. It is indefensible, for example, to argue that, *because* a high correlation exists between measures of reading comprehension and arithmetic problem-solving ability for the individuals in a given group, problem-solving ability is therefore dependent on reading comprehension, or vice versa. Does a given student really do well in reading *because* he is a good problem-solver? Maybe so, but this does not follow from the statistical evidence of correlation.

The observed correlation between measures of two traits is *sometimes* due to a cause-and-effect relationship between them, but there is nothing in the statistical evidence to indicate which, if either, is the cause and which the effect. For example, there is a fairly high correlation between age and grade status of elementary school children. In this case, of course, we know that we cannot increase a pupil's age simply by promoting him from one grade to the next—age is not due to or *caused by* grade status—but we know this because of logical considerations that are quite independent of the statistical correlation.

Correlations are *sometimes* observed between traits that have no cause-and-effect connection whatever, the observed correlation being due entirely to a third factor (or to several factors) that happens to be related to each of the traits in question. The correlation between reading comprehension and height scores for a mixed group of third-, fourth-, fifth-, and sixth-grade children (see Figure 17.16 and Section 17.10) results from the effect of age and training as reflected by grade status. Since reading comprehension is related to training and to some extent to age, and since height is related to age, and since age and training as reflected by grade status are in turn related, it follows that a relationship between reading comprehension and height will be present in any group whose members differ in grade status. Obviously, this is not to say that an individual understands what he reads *because* he is tall in stature.

Or consider the positive correlation in the general population between ages of mothers at parturition and the intelligence of their offspring. This phenomenon has been observed because women of high intellectual standards and ability tend, for economic and cultural reasons, to be married later in life, and not *because* middle age is the best time to bear intelligent children. Again, in both these examples, we reached our conclusions on the basis of logical considerations that were quite independent of the direction or magnitude of any observed correlation.

Finally, the observed correlation between two traits may *sometimes* be in just the *opposite* direction from a cause-and-effect relationship that really exists. In almost any high school or college course there is a *negative* correlation (of usually about −.30) between quality of grades earned and number of hours spent in study. The students who make the highest grades tend to be those who spend the least time in studying, while those who make low grades tend to spend more than the average amount of time in study. It would be absurd, however, to contend on the basis of such evidence that anyone can make higher grades by studying less. The negative correlation is largely due to the fact that intelligence is positively related to quality of grades and negatively related to time spent in studying—that the less able students *must* study more even to approach, let alone equal, the achievement of their more able classmates. The *causal connection* between quality of grades earned and time spent in study is *positive*, even though the observed correlation is negative.

Whenever a substantial correlation is observed between two sets of measures, one of several possibilities may apply: (1) there is no cause-and-effect connection; (2) a cause-and-effect connection is present in the same direction as the observed correlation; (3) there is a cause-and-effect connection, but in the opposite direction from the observed correlation. Which of these possibilities exists, and what is the strength of the cause-and-effect connection (if any), *cannot* be determined from the observed correlation. Any interpretations concerning cause-and-effect must be based on logical considerations and not on the observed correlation. The observed correlation may *suggest* a cause-and-effect relationship, but can never *prove* that it exists, or show in what degree it exists.

17.12 Inferential Procedures Related to Correlation Coefficients: An Introduction

Frequently in educational and psychological research a correlation coefficient between variables X and Y is computed for a sample selected from a larger population. Since the r-value for the sample will probably not be exactly equal to the population coefficient of correlation between these two variables (the obtained r probably contains some sampling error), some inferential procedures are needed to help assess the potential magnitude of the sampling error in r. It should not be surprising that hypothesis testing procedures and procedures for establishing confidence interval estimates have been developed for use with correlation coefficients. In the remaining sections of this chapter we examine one set of inferential procedures that has been developed for use with Pearson correlation coefficients.

17.13 The Normal Bivariate Model

The appropriateness of the inferential procedures we present depends on one major assumption. For the subsequent procedures to be valid, it must be assumed that the pairs of X- and Y-values have been selected from a *normal bivariate population*. Since this normal bivariate population assumption is difficult to describe in precise mathematical terms, we shall attempt only a verbal description of the concept.

The bivariate frequency distribution was defined in Section 17.3. Consider such a distribution in the case of an infinite population of individuals for each of whom there exists a pair of scores, say X and Y. Now suppose that the X-scores considered alone are normally distributed for the population and suppose the same to be true of the Y-scores. Further suppose that the classes or intervals of both X- and Y-scales in this bivariate frequency distribution are infinitesimal. Then the bivariate table (for examples of such tables, see Figures 17.6 and 17.7) would contain an infinity of cells formed by the intersections of the vertical columns extending from the X-scale intervals and the horizontal rows extending from the Y-scale intervals. Corresponding to each of these cells there is some joint relative frequency—that is, the proportion of individuals whose X- and Y-scores fall simultaneously, or jointly, in the X- and Y-intervals associated with the particular cell. Now if for *any* vertical, horizontal, or diagonal array of cells these joint relative frequencies are those of a normal distribution, the population is said to be a normal bivariate population. An investigation of the sampling distribution of values of a statistic such as r—values derived from samples selected at random from a normal bivariate population— is said to involve the normal bivariate model.

17.14 Fisher's Logarithmic Transformation of r

If for a normal bivariate population the value of the population correlation (ρ, *rho*) is in the neighborhood of zero, and if the number of pairs in a random sample from such a population is large, the sampling distribution of the sample correlation (r) *tends* toward a normal distribution. However, if the population correlation differs from zero, the sampling distribution departs from normality in form unless the sample is *extremely* large. This departure becomes more and more marked as the value of ρ approaches plus or minus one. That such is the case is readily seen to be intuitively reasonable when one considers that the maximum value any r can assume is unity and that if ρ is large, say $+.80$ or $+.90$, the r-values have much more room to vary to the lower side of ρ than to the higher side. In such situations, therefore, the sampling distribution of r will be negatively skewed. On the other hand, if ρ is in the neighborhood of $-.80$ or $-.90$, the sampling distribution of r will be positively skewed. If ρ is near zero, the sampling distribution will tend to be normal for large samples, but it will still not be normal for small samples. Consequently, if hypotheses about ρ (particularly hypotheses other than $\rho = 0$) or hypotheses regarding the equality of the ρ-values of two populations are to be tested, then normal-distribution sampling theory is not appropriate; to test such hypotheses, special methods must be employed if reliable results are to be obtained.

In 1915 R. A. Fisher introduced a new statistic that was a function of r.[18] Suppose we have given an infinity of r-values each based on a random sample of N pairs of values selected from a normal bivariate population for which the correlation coefficient has the value ρ. These r-values, of course, constitute the sampling distribution of r for random samples of N cases from this population. Fisher showed that if each of these r-values were transformed into this new statistic, the resulting values would be *approximately* normally distributed, with a mean corresponding to the transformed value of ρ and variance of $1/(N - 3)$. He demonstrated that this would be true regardless of the value of ρ even for samples that are quite small. Since this new statistic is a function of, or a transformation of, a value on the r-scale, it is possible, by expressing any ρ- or r-value in terms of this new statistic, to use its sampling distribution indirectly to test hypotheses about ρ.

Fisher called this new statistic z. We shall designate it by z_r to prevent confusion with previous meanings we have associated with z. This statistic is defined as follows:

$$z_r = \tfrac{1}{2} \log_e \frac{1 + r}{1 - r}$$

The z_r-value corresponding to any r-value may be obtained by computing $(1 + r)/(1 - r)$ and by using a table of natural logarithms to find one-half the logarithm of the result of this computation. It is unnecessary, however, for the student to master the use of a table of natural logarithms in order to effect this transformation. Values of z_r corresponding to values of r from .000 to .995 by increments of .005 have been determined and are given in Table V, Appendix C. To find the z_r-value corresponding to any of these r-values, it is necessary only to refer to this table.

The foregoing theory may be summarized in the form of a rule.

RULE 17.2 For random samples of N from a normal bivariate population for which the correlation between the variables is ρ, the sampling distribution of

$$z_r = \tfrac{1}{2} \log_e \frac{1 + r}{1 - r.} \tag{17.8}$$

is a normal distribution with mean

$$z_\rho = \tfrac{1}{2} \log_e \frac{1 + \rho}{1 - \rho} \tag{17.9}$$

and with variance

$$\sigma_{z_r}^2 = \frac{1}{N - 3} \tag{17.10}$$

[18] R. A. Fisher, "Frequency Distribution of the Values of the Correlation Coefficient in Samples from an Indefinitely Large Population," *Biometrika*, 10 (1915), 507–521.

Examples of the application of Fisher's z_r statistic to tests of hypotheses about population correlation coefficients and to the determination of interval estimates for such coefficients are given in the following sections.

17.15 Testing the Hypothesis $\rho = 0$ Using Fisher's z-Transformation

A researcher was interested in studying the relationship between a personality measure (X) and reading achievement (Y) for junior high school girls. She selected 103 girls at random from a large junior high school and obtained scores for all the girls selected on both measures. The observed correlation between these measures was .25. Assume the researcher wished to test the $H_0: \rho = 0$. The procedure is outlined below.[19]

$Step\ 1.$ $H_0: \rho = 0$; $H_1: \rho > 0$; $H_2: \rho < 0$

$Comment:$ For purposes of this example we have assumed that the actual value of the population correlation may differ in either direction from the value hypothesized.

$Step\ 2.$ $\alpha = .05$

$Comment:$ This represents an arbitrary selection for illustrative purposes.

$Step\ 3.$ $R: z \leq -1.96$ and $z \geq +1.96$; or $|z| \geq 1.96$

$Comment:$ The Fisher transformation of r is normally distributed. Hence, the standard normal deviate, z, may be used as the test statistic.

$Step\ 4.$ Calculation of test statistic, z, for data at hand.

To compute the value of the test statistic, we proceed as follows. From Table V, Appendix C:

$$z_\rho = z_{.00} = .0000 \quad \text{and} \quad z_r = z_{.25} = .2554$$

Also

$$\sigma_{z_r} = \frac{1}{\sqrt{103 - 3}} = \frac{1}{10} = .1$$

---

[19] This procedure is the same regardless of the hypothesized value of ρ. Thus, for example, the procedure would be applicable for testing $H_0: \rho = .80$.

Hence, applying the sampling theory summarized in Rule 17.2, we have

$$z = \frac{z_r - z_\rho}{\sigma_{z_r}} = \frac{.2554 - .0000}{.1} = \frac{.2554}{.1} = 2.554$$

Step 5. Decision. Reject *H*. (Why?)

Comment: This decision also implies rejection of the alternative $\rho < 0$. (Why?) Hence, the only remaining possibility is that $\rho > 0$.

17.16 Establishing a Confidence Interval for ρ

In some experimental situations, no relevant hypothesis for ρ exists. In these instances the experimenter is more likely simply to want an estimate of the value of the population correlation. In this section we shall illustrate the use of the Fisher transformation to establish an interval estimate of ρ.

Since for a normal bivariate population with correlation ρ the statistic z_r is approximately normally distributed with mean z_ρ and standard error $1/\sqrt{N-3}$, it is possible to apply the reasoning of Section 14.4 to the problem of approximating a 100γ percent confidence interval for the population value of z_ρ (i.e., the value of the Fisher z corresponding to ρ). The formulas for these limits are:

$$z_{\rho_1}, z_{\bar{\rho}_1} = z_{r_1} \mp z_{\gamma/2} \frac{1}{\sqrt{N-3}} \tag{17.11}$$

Once z_ρ and $z_{\bar{\rho}}$ are determined, it is possible to determine ρ and $\bar{\rho}$ by entering Table V, Appendix C, with the z_ρ and $z_{\bar{\rho}}$ values and by reading the corresponding values of *r*.

To illustrate we shall establish the 95 percent confidence interval for ρ given $r = .25$ for a sample of 103. Here $z_{\gamma/2} = z_{.475} = 1.96$ and

$$\sigma_{z_r} = \frac{1}{\sqrt{N-3}} = \frac{1}{\sqrt{103-3}} = .1$$

Also from Table V, Appendix C, $z_{.25} = .2554$. Now applying (17.11) we have

$$z_{\rho_1}, z_{\bar{\rho}_1} = .2554 \mp (1.96)(.1) = .0594, .4514$$

Now in Table V, Appendix C, consider successive *r*-values ending with a 5 in the thousandths position as the real limits of a unit interval on the *r*-scale where the unit is .01. To find the *r*-value to the nearest hundredth that corresponds to a given z_r-value, first locate the interval on the r-scale in which the z_r-value falls. Then the unit point (midpoint) of this interval is the required r-value. The z_r-value of .0594 is between the z_r-values .055056 and .065092, which correspond to the interval limits .055 and .065. Hence, the nearest two-decimal r-value corresponding to $z_r = .0594$ is .06. Similarly, $z_r = .4514$ corresponds to a point in the r-scale interval bounded by .415 and .425, so that the nearest two-decimal r-value is .42. Hence, the values of ρ_1 and $\bar{\rho}_1$ are, respectively, .06 and .42. That is, $C(.06 \le \rho \le .42) = 95\%$. Note that, unlike in all previous illustrations of confidence intervals, the limits of this interval are different distances from the sample r of .25. This result is, of course, consistent with the skewness of the r sampling distribution.

17.17 Test of the Hypothesis that Two Normal Bivariate Populations Have the Same ρ-Value

The question often arises whether the degree of relationship between one pair of variables is different from that for another pair. This question may be encountered in a variety of ways.

(1) It may involve the correlation between variates X and Y for one population as compared with that between these same variates for another population. For example, is the correlation between height and weight for 15-year-old boys the same as for adult males? Or is the correlation between performance on the Wechsler Intelligence Scale for Children (WISC) and performance on an arithmetic achievement test the same for sixth-grade boys as for sixth-grade girls?

(2) It may involve the correlation between variates X and Y for one population as compared with that between variates A and B for either the same or different populations. For example, is the correlation between performance on a dental aptitude test and success as a dental student for a population of dental students the same as the correlation between performance on an engineering aptitude test and success as an engineering student for a population of engineering students?[20] Or is the correlation between pitch discrimination ability and tonal memory for a population of high-school-age girls the same as that between sense of time and rhythm for the same population?

(3) It may involve the correlation between variates X and Y for one population as compared with that between variates X and A for either the same or another population. For example, is the correlation between college achievement and performance on a scholastic aptitude test for a population of college men equal to the correlation between

[20] This amounts to asking whether success in one area can be predicted with more or less accuracy than success in another.

college achievement and some measure of high school achievement for this same (or some different) population?[21]

Even though the same individuals or objects are involved, each of the foregoing situations can be viewed as pertaining to two bivariate populations. For instance, in the last example cited the population objects are college men. Nevertheless, for these objects two bivariate populations of scores exist, namely, one involving measures of college achievement and scholastic aptitude, and the other involving measures of college achievement and high school achievement. Now if both of these bivariate populations can be reasonably assumed to be normal, the hypothesis that the correlation (ρ) for one of them is of the same magnitude as that for the other can be tested by using the Fisher transformation. The procedure is identical for all situations, *requiring only that the sample r-values be based on independent random samples of population objects.* In the case of the population of college men, the random sample of such men for which the correlation between college achievement and scholastic aptitude is obtained must be selected independently from the random sample of such men for which the correlation between college and high school achievement is obtained.[22]

Since the test procedure is the same for all the situations described so long as independent random samples are employed, a single illustrative example will suffice. Suppose that the correlation between IQ (as measured by the Stanford-Binet Intelligence Scale) and performance on a particular group test of mental ability is found to be .56 for a random sample of 60 school children at the third-grade level and that the correlation between these same variates is found to be .74 for a random sample of 40 school children at the fifth-grade level. The question is: How do the population correlations compare? Are they equal in magnitude, or is one or the other larger? This question may be answered by a test of a statistical hypothesis. Designate the third- and fifth-grade populations as 1 and 2, respectively. Then:

Step 1. $H_0: \rho_1 - \rho_2 = 0; \quad H_1: \rho_1 - \rho_2 < 0; \quad H_2: \rho_1 - \rho_2 > 0$

Comment: Since either population may have the larger ρ-value, both of the above alternatives to H_0 have been considered.

Step 2. $\alpha = .05$

[21] This amounts to asking whether success in a given area is better predicted by one variable than by another.

[22] Procedures for testing the hypothesis that $\rho_{xy} = \rho_{ab}$ or that $\rho_{xy} = \rho_{xa}$ that use the same sample of individuals to obtain the sample r-values are available but are beyond the scope of this text. See I. Olkin, "Correlations Revisited," in *Improving Experimental Design and Statistical Analysis,* ed. J. Stanley, Rand McNally, Chicago, 1967.

Comment: This value was arbitrarily selected for purposes of illustration since the terms of the example provide no basis for choosing a particular α-value.

Step 3. $R: z \leq -1.96$ and $z \geq +1.96$

Comment: We know from Rule 17.2 that if the two bivariate populations are normal, the Fisher transformations of r_1 and r_2 will be approximately normally distributed. Hence, by Rule 13.1 the $z_{r_1} - z_{r_2}$ differences will be normally distributed and the standard normal deviate is, then, appropriate as a test statistic.

Step 4. Computation of test statistic, z, for the sample.

Comment: In the comment under Step 3, it was pointed out that since z_{r_1} and z_{r_2} are normally distributed, it follows from Rule 13.1 that the difference $z_{r_1} - z_{r_2}$ is normally distributed. Rule 13.1 further indicates that this sampling distribution of differences will have a mean value of $z_{p_1} - z_{p_2}$ and a variance of $\sigma_{z_{r_1}}^2 + \sigma_{z_{r_2}}^2$. Hence, the test statistic z is given by

$$z = \frac{(z_{r_1} - z_{r_2}) - (z_{p_1} - z_{p_2})}{\sqrt{\sigma_{z_{r_1}}^2 + \sigma_{z_{r_2}}^2}}$$

Since if p_1 does in fact equal p_2, $z_{p_1} - z_{p_2} = 0$, and, since

$$\sigma_{z_{r_1}}^2 = \frac{1}{n_1 - 3} \quad \text{and} \quad \sigma_{z_{r_2}}^2 = \frac{1}{n_2 - 3}$$

we know that the formula for the test statistic z may also be written

$$z = \frac{z_{r_1} - z_{r_2}}{\sqrt{\dfrac{1}{n_1 - 3} + \dfrac{1}{n_2 - 3}}} \tag{17.12}$$

In the example at hand,

$$r_1 = .56, \quad \text{and so} \quad z_{r_1} = .632822$$
$$r_2 = .74, \quad \text{and so} \quad z_{r_2} = .950477$$
$$n_1 = 60, \quad \text{and so} \quad \frac{1}{n_1 - 3} = .017544$$
$$n_2 = 40, \quad \text{and so} \quad \frac{1}{n_2 - 3} = .027027$$

Hence,

$$z = \frac{.632822 - .950477}{\sqrt{.017544 + .027027}} \approx \frac{-.318}{.211} = -1.51$$

Step 5. Decision: Retain H_0. (Why?)

17.18 Effects of Violations of the Bivariate Normal Assumption

The inferential procedures presented in Sections 17.14 through 17.17 were valid if the X- and Y-variables followed a bivariate normal distribution. As was noted in Section 10.2, no *real* collection of real outcomes can be truly normally distributed. Likewise, no real collection of bivariate data can truly follow a bivariate normal distribution.

How do departures from bivariate normality affect the adequacy of the inferential procedures described in the previous sections? Unfortunately, the consequences of violating the bivariate normal assumption have not been extensively investigated. Unlike in the situation related to the effects of violations of the normality and equal variability conditions on the validity of t-distribution theory for testing $H_0 : \mu_1 = \mu_2$ (Section 15.9), relatively few investigations have been conducted to study the effects of violating the bivariate normal assumption. The investigations that have been done have used the Monte Carlo approach, which was discussed in some detail in Section 15.9. On the basis of the findings of such studies, the following conclusions seem justified.[23]

1 When the true correlation is low (say, $\rho < .25$), the sampling distribution of z_r conforms closely to the theoretical distribution described by Rule 17.2 even if the bivariate normality condition is violated. Therefore, under this circumstance, the z-test for a hypothesis about ρ is robust. That is, the probability statements made about z using the standard normal curve are accurate for most practical purposes.

2 When the true correlation is high (say, $\rho > .80$), the empirical sampling distribution of z_r differs markedly from the theoretical distribution described by Rule 17.2 when the bivariate normal-

---

[23] These conclusions are based on the results of the following two studies: (1) R. Norris and Howard F. Hjelm, *An Empirical Investigation of the Effects of Nonnormality upon the Sampling Distribution of the Product Moment Correlation Coefficient*, Final Report of Cooperative Research Project No. 637, Office of Education, 1960; and (2) B. Brown, *An Empirical Investigation of the Effects of Violations of Assumptions upon Certain Tests of the Product Moment Correlation Coefficient*, doctoral dissertation, Pennsylvania State University, 1969.

ity condition does not hold.[24] Therefore, the z-test of a hypothesis about ρ is not robust under such conditions.

The above conclusions apply to the validity of the use of the z_r-transformation in testing a hypothesis about ρ. Since the procedure used to test the significance of the difference between two observed correlations (Section 17.17) is a function of the difference between two z_r-transformations, it follows that the validity of this second procedure is dependent on the validity of each of the z_r-transformations. If both z_{r_1} and z_{r_2} conform closely to the distribution described by Rule 17.2, then the probability statement applied to the z-statistic used to test $H_0: \rho_1 - \rho_2 = 0$ will be accurate. Thus, the conclusions noted above for the test of a hypothesis about ρ also apply to the test of the hypothesis that two population correlation coefficients are equal.

17.19 Summary Statement

Research studies in psychology and education are frequently concerned with the degree of relationship that exists between pairs of scores for two different variables or dimensions. The most widely used index that is appropriate when the relationship is linear is the Pearson product moment correlation coefficient, r. In this chapter we have defined r, examined its characteristics, and discussed factors that must be considered in interpreting it. We also presented some sampling-error theory that made it possible for us to test hypotheses about population correlation coefficients (ρ), to establish confidence interval estimates of ρ, and to test the hypothesis that two population correlation coefficients are equal.

The Pearson r also plays an important role in the next chapter, which treats the prediction or estimation of an individual's score on one variable, say Y, given his score on a second variable, say X. (Several examples of situations where such predictions would be useful are given in Section 18.1.) It will be seen that the accuracy with which we can make these predictions is related to the degree of relationship between X and Y—that is, to the magnitude of r.

---

[24] For example, if the two marginal distributions are markedly skewed, the bivariate distribution would differ substantially from bivariate normal.

18

The Prediction Problem

18.1 Statement of the Problem

Suppose that for each of a number (N) of individuals or objects we have measures of two characteristics that are not perfectly correlated. For individual i we shall represent these two scores as X_i and Y_i. Now suppose that for some individual, not included among the N, we have available only an X-score. The problem is to use the information or experience embodied in the N pairs of scores we do have to make an estimate of the Y-score for this individual.

For example, suppose that for a large number of individuals we have some measure (X), such as grade-point average, of high school achievement, and a similar measure (Y) of achievement in college. Now suppose we are confronted with the problem of advising a recent high school graduate who is considering attending college. We know little about this individual other than what his high school achievement record tells us. Our problem is to use our knowledge of, or past experience regarding, the relationship between high school and college achievement to estimate for this individual what his college achievement record (Y) would be were he to attend college, given only information regarding his high school achievement (X).

Other situations involving the same problem are numerous. The Wechsler Intelligence Scale for Children (WISC) must be individually administered by a specially trained expert who would have difficulty in averaging more than four such testings per school day. The Henmon-Nelson Tests of Mental Ability, on the other hand, may be given to large groups of children in about 30 minutes. Here the problem is to use past experience with children who have taken both these tests to estimate a particular child's WISC score given his or her Henmon-Nelson score. Or the problem may be to estimate on the basis of past experience with the performance of a large number of individuals on some test (sometimes several tests are used) and their subsequent success on some job or task (e.g., selling a certain product, learning to fly a plane, practicing medicine, surviving a certain surgical operation), the success on this job or task of another individual, given only a record of his performance on the test.

Because in so many of the situations in which this problem arises the required estimates pertain to some future status, it is customary to refer to these estimates as *predictions* and to the general problem as the prediction problem. In this chapter we shall present a solution for this problem and give some attention to the accuracy of the predictions it provides.

18.2   A Possible Solution to the Prediction Problem, and Its Weaknesses

Suppose we let the individual whose Y-score we wish to predict be designated as d and let his known X-score be designated X_d. Now we wish to apply our past experience with individuals whose X- and Y-scores are both known to us to predict d's Y-score. One rather obvious approach would involve sorting out, from among all the individuals with whom we have had past experience, those whose X-scores are the same as d's, that is, of magnitude X_d. The individuals constituting this specially selected subgroup are all like one another—and like d—in terms of performance or status on the X-test or X-characteristic. We do not, of course, expect every member of this subgroup to make precisely the same Y-score, since we have not required, in setting up the problem situation, that the relationship between X and Y be perfect. There will be more or less variation among the Y-scores for this subgroup depending on whether the correlation between X and Y is low or high.

We shall view the collection of Y-scores for this subgroup as though it were a random sample from a subpopulation of individuals whose scores on the X-trait are all of magnitude X_d. We shall also regard the individual d, who is a member of this subpopulation, as having been selected at random from it. Since d's Y-score is unknown, we do not know just where along the scale of values of the various Y-scores of this subpopulation the particular Y-score for d falls. As a guess (estimate or prediction), however, we shall use an estimate of the mean of this subpopulation, since the expected value of a score selected at random from a population is the mean of the population (see Section 9.6). This, of course, is to say that we shall simply use the mean of the sub-sample.

For example, suppose that we are informed that the height of a randomly selected 12-year-old boy is 63 inches and are asked to estimate or "predict" his weight. Suppose further that our past experience with the heights and weights of 12-year-old boys is as shown in Table 17.2. From the 50 pairs of height and weight scores given in this table, we select those pairs in which the height score is 63, the same as that of the particular 12-year-old whose weight is to be estimated. There are three such pairs of scores: (63, 105), (63, 101), and (63, 81). The weight scores of these three pairs are now regarded as a random sample from the subpopulation of weight scores for 12-year-old boys who are 63 inches tall. We shall use the mean of this sample, that is, $(105 + 101 + 81)/3 = 95.7$, as an estimate of the mean of this subpopulation of weights, and this population estimate in turn as the predicted weight of the particular boy in question.

Now, there are certain rather obvious weaknesses in this approach. We shall simply mention two that are particularly critical. In the first place, even if our overall experience with the two characteristics involved related to a large number of individuals, it is not likely that our experience with individuals whose X-scores are of magnitude X_d will be very extensive. That is, among all the individuals for whom we have information about X and Y performance or status, there may be only a few whose X-scores are the same as that of d. It follows that our estimate of the mean of the particular subpopulation of Y-scores involved is likely to be based on a rather small sample and, hence, is likely to involve a large sampling error. In the height-weight problem, for example, our estimate of the mean of the particular subpopulation of weights involved had to be based on a sample of only *three* cases.

In the second place, the approach suggested is highly inefficient in the sense that it makes so little use of the sum total of the available experience with the characteristics involved. Attention is given only to the single subgroup of Y-scores paired with the score X_d. The subgroups of Y-scores paired with $X_d + 1$, or $X_d + 2$, or $X_d - 1$ are completely ignored. *It is quite probable that these subgroups contain information regarding trends in the general level of the Y-scores associated with different X-scores that would, if taken into account, make possible more accurate estimation or prediction.*

For these reasons we shall abandon the solution here suggested in favor of one less subject to the weaknesses just cited.

18.3   A Preferable Solution to the Prediction Problem in a Special Case: Linear Prediction

Suppose that the characteristics with which we are concerned are linearly related for the population involved. This means, theoretically, that for the entire population the means of the subpopulations consisting of Y-scores that are paired with the same X-score lie on a straight line (see Section 17.6). In this *special case* of linear correlation we can

Table 18.1   A Random Sample of 20 Pairs of X- and Y-Values Selected from a Population for Which X and Y Are Linearly Related

X	Y	X	Y	X	Y	X	Y
10	11	8	7	6	6	4	5
9	10	8	6	6	4	4	3
9	8	7	9	5	6	3	4
9	6	7	7	5	4	3	3
8	9	7	5	5	3	3	2

improve our method of estimating the mean of any such subpopulation over that previously suggested by using all the data to determine the line that best fits the subsample means. The ordinates (Y-values) of the points on this line corresponding to the different X-values may then be used as estimates of the means of the subpopulations of Y-scores associated with given X-score values.

By way of illustrating this scheme of attacking the prediction problem, assume the 20 pairs of X- and Y- scores given in Table 18.1 to be a random sample from a population of linearly correlated pairs. Table 18.2 gives the means of the subsamples of Y-values associated with like X-values. For example, three Y-values, 10, 8, and 6, having the mean 8, are associated with an X-value of 9. Table 18.2 gives the means of this and the other similar subsamples of Y-values. The scatter diagram for the 20 pairs of Table 18.1 is shown in Figure 18.1. The open circles in this figure locate the means of the subsamples of Y-scores associated with like X-scores. Clearly, these subsample Y-means do not fall on a straight line. However, they do exhibit a *tendency* to do so. Since the particular pairs of scores involved were selected at random from a population of pairs for which the relationship between X and Y is known to be linear, it follows that the deviations of these Y subsample means

Table 18.2   Means of Subsamples of the Y-Values of Table 18.1 That Are Associated with Same X-Value

X-Value	Subsample Y-Mean
10	11
9	8
8	7.33
7	7
6	5
5	4.33
4	4
3	3

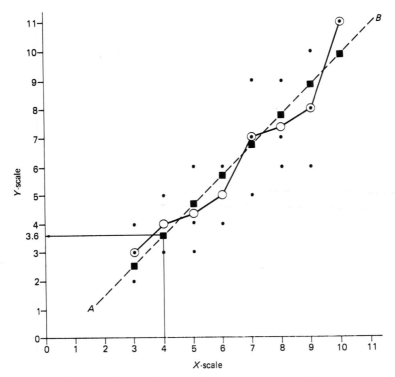

Figure 18.1 Scatter diagram for pairs of X- and Y-values of Table 18.1

from a straight-line pattern must be due to sampling error. In fact, we would expect the sampling errors involved in these means to be considerable, since the subsamples on which they are based are extremely small (one to three cases). A straight line fitted to these subsample means provides us with estimates of the subpopulation means that are more precise than those provided by the individual subsample means because the placement of the line is based on the simultaneous consideration of all the subsample means, and, therefore, not only takes into account more of the information available in the data but also smoothes out the sampling errors in these subsample means.

In Figure 18.1 the line AB was fitted to the subsample means by the simple device of sliding a transparent straightedge into the position that would appear to the eye to represent the line of "best fit" to these subsample means. A square has been placed at each point on this line that corresponds to a particular integral value of X. The Y-values corresponding to these squares become our estimates of the subpopulation means. We read from the figure, for example, that for the subpopulation of individuals whose X-scores are 4, the mean of their Y-scores, thus estimated, is 3.6.

Although the procedure just described provides estimates of the subpopulation means that are superior to those provided by the individual subsample means, it still involves several weaknesses. We shall cite two. First, the estimates it provides are not unique. This obviously results from the fact that in visually fitting a line to a given set of subsample means, different individuals would be likely to select somewhat different placements of the line; consequently, they would obtain different estimates of the subpopulation means, in spite of the fact that the same data were involved in each instance. Second, the procedure gives each subsample mean equal importance in spite of the fact that some means are based on larger subsamples than others. For example, when the position of line AB in Figure 18.1 was determined, the Y-mean of the subsample for $X = 10$ was given as much attention as the Y-mean of the subsample for $X = 9$ in spite of the fact that the former is based on only a single case while the latter is based on three cases. Obviously, the accuracy of the fitting procedure could be greatly improved if some way could be found to weight each subsample mean in accordance with the size of the subsample involved. Actually this is not difficult to accomplish. All we need do is to fit the line to the individual Y-values (i.e., to the dots of the scatter diagram) rather than to the subsample Y-means. Of course, this requires giving attention to many more points. And giving attention to more points increases the difficulty of establishing an optimum placement visually, which increases the likelihood that different individuals working with the same data will establish different lines.

If, then, lines are to be fitted with reference to individual values, some method that is more precise than this crude visual one must be found. A method for determining a unique "best-fitting" line has been provided by the mathematicians. This method is described in the following section.

18.4   Fitting a Prediction Line by the Method of Least Squares

The general formula for *any* straight line located with reference to a set of rectangular coordinate axes is

$$Y = bX + c \tag{18.1}$$

Points plotted to correspond to pairs of X- and Y-values that satisfy this equation all fall on a straight line. The placement of a *particular* line depends on the values assigned the constants b and c. The value assigned

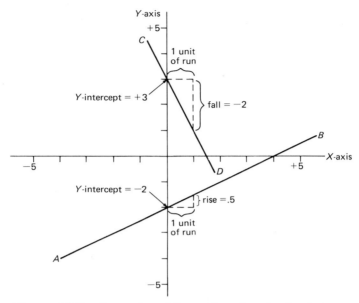

Figure 18.2   Examples of lines placed on basis of slope and Y-intercept information

c obviously indicates the point at which the line intercepts the Y-axis, since $Y = c$ when $X = 0$. The value assigned b indicates the slope of the line, that is, the vertical distance the line rises (b positive) or falls (b negative) per unit of horizontal distance. These two pieces of information—slope and Y-intercept—are all that is necessary to place a particular line with reference to a set of rectangular coordinate axes.

For example, consider the particular line

$$Y = .5X - 2$$

Here b, the slope, is .5 and c, the Y-intercept, is -2. The location of this line with reference to a set of rectangular coordinate axes is shown in Figure 18.2 as line AB. The line

$$Y = -2X + 3$$

which has a slope of -2 and a Y-intercept at $+3$, is shown in Figure 18.2 as line CD.

Now for a given set of imperfectly correlated X- and Y-pairs, the problem of obtaining the "best-fitting" line for predicting Y can be reduced to the determination of appropriate values for b (the slope) and c (the Y-intercept). Before a procedure for determining these values

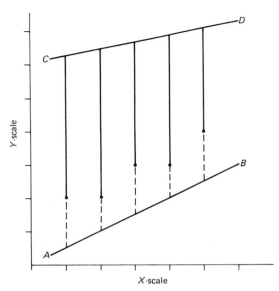

Figure 18.3   Scatter diagram of five hypothetical X- and Y-pairs with two lines of differing closeness of fit

can be established, however, it is first necessary to specify precisely what is meant by "best-fitting." Various definitions are possible. We shall consider only one.

Figure 18.3 shows a scatter diagram for five imaginary pairs of X- and Y-values. Two lines, AB and CD, have been drawn in this figure. Neither of these lines provides anything even approaching a close fit to the points of this scatter diagram. Of the two lines, however, AB clearly fits better. If we measure the vertical (i.e., vertical with reference to the X-axis) distances of the points from AB (see broken lines from points to AB in Figure 18.3) it is clear that in the aggregate they are less than the distances of the points from CD (see solid lines from points to CD in Figure 18.3). Clearly, it would be no problem to draw some third line in Figure 18.3 that would provide a far better fit to the points than AB. If such a line were drawn, the distances of the points from it would total less than those of the points from AB. This suggests the use of the aggregate distance of the points from a line as an index of the "goodness-of-fit" of the line to the points. The smaller this total distance, the better the fit.

Unfortunately, however, the use of the absolute values of these distances results in an index that is awkward to handle mathematically. The situation is much like the one that led us to adopt the variance or standard deviation in preference to the mean deviation as an index of variability (see Section 7.3). Here we shall discard the total of the absolute deviations of the points from the line as an index of goodness-of-fit and use instead *the total of the squares of these algebraic deviations.* We are now in a position to set up a precise definition of the phrase "best-fitting" as it applies to a straight line placed in the point field of a scatter diagram. We shall simply define the best-fitting line as the line for which the value of our goodness-of-fit index is least. This definition states what is generally known in statistics as the *least-squares criterion* of fit. We shall now consider a somewhat more formal statement of this criterion as it specifically applies to the prediction problem.

Let the prediction equation be represented by[1]

$$\hat{Y} = bX + c \tag{18.2}$$

For a specific X_i-value we have[2]

$$\hat{Y}_i = bX_i + c \tag{18.2a}$$

Then for a given pair of values, X_i and Y_i, the vertical distance of the corresponding point from this line is given by

$$Y_i - \hat{Y}_i = Y_i - (bX_i + c)$$

where $\hat{Y}_i$ is the point on the line corresponding to X_i (see Figure 18.4). We shall refer to this distance as the deviation of the point from the line. Now suppose we have N pairs of X- and Y-values. Then our index (G) of the goodness-of-fit of the line to these particular points is, by definition

$$G = \sum(Y_i - \hat{Y}_i)^2 = \sum(Y_i - [bX_i + c])^2 \tag{18.3}$$

and the best-fitting line according to the least-squares criterion is that line for which the value of G is least.

Mathematical statisticians have proved that the values of b and c that result in a minimum value of G for a particular set of N points are those given by the following formulas.

$$b = \frac{\sum x_i y_i}{\sum x_i^2} \quad (x_i = X_i - \overline{X}; y_i = Y_i - \overline{Y}) \tag{18.4}$$

$$c = \overline{Y} - b\overline{X} \tag{18.5}$$

[1] The caret above the Y is to remind the reader that the value of $bX + c$, while in units of the Y-scale, is actually an estimate of a subpopulation *mean*. The caret was used instead of the bar since the latter is reserved to indicate the actual obtained mean of some specific set of scores.

[2] Note that $\hat{Y}_i$ is a linear transformation of X_i. See Section 8.3.

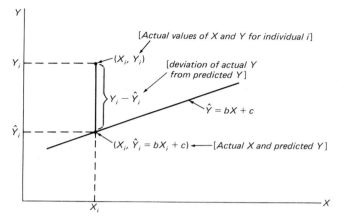

Figure 18.4   Distance of point X_i, Y_i from the line as measured along a perpendicular to the X-axis

In these formulas $\overline{Y}$ and $\overline{X}$ represent, respectively, the means of all Y-scores and all X-scores, of which there are N each. To use (18.5) it is, of course, first necessary to obtain the value of b by (18.4). We shall illustrate the application of these formulas in the next section.

18.5   The Problem of the High School Counselor

In her capacity as a high school counselor, Ms. Jones is frequently called upon to advise graduating students on their potential for success in college. In the past, she has given a certain college aptitude test to graduating students planning to attend college and then, after the lapse of a year, has obtained from each college involved a report on their success in college in the form of their freshman-year grade-point averages. She uses this experience, together with other information about the student, as a basis for predicting college success. We shall illustrate here how Ms. Jones, using only her past experience with this aptitude test and freshman-year grade-point averages, might predict the freshman-year grade-point average for one of her current advisees.

First, Ms. Jones will use her past experience with the two variables involved to derive a prediction equation of the type described in the preceding section. Table 18.3 shows the record of this past experience.[3] Below this table are the computations leading to the determination of $\overline{X}$, $\overline{Y}$, $\sum x_i^2$, and $\sum x_i y_i$. These are the values needed to determine b and c

---

[3] No sensible counselor would, under ordinary circumstances, be satisfied with the limited amount ($N = 50$) of experience recorded in Table 18.3. We have greatly reduced the number of cases that would usually be used simply for convenience of illustration.

Table 18.3 Scores on a Scholastic Aptitude Test (X) and Freshman-Year Grade-Point Averages (Y) for 50 Randomly Selected College Students

X	Y	X	Y	X	Y	X	Y	X	Y
14	4.0	11	2.9	10	2.9	10	1.4	8	2.6
14	3.4	11	2.8	10	2.8	9	2.8	8	2.4
14	3.2	11	2.7	10	2.7	9	2.7	8	2.3
13	3.7	11	2.6	10	2.6	9	2.6	8	1.8
13	2.7	11	2.5	10	2.2	9	2.4	8	1.4
12	2.7	11	2.4	10	2.1	9	2.1	8	1.1
12	2.4	11	2.2	10	1.9	9	1.7	8	0.9
12	2.2	11	2.0	10	1.8	9	1.5	8	0.8
12	2.1	11	1.9	10	1.7	9	1.1	7	1.7
11	3.5	10	3.2	10	1.6	9	0.9	7	0.8

$$\Sigma X = 505 \qquad \Sigma Y = 112.4 \qquad \Sigma XY = 1{,}178$$
$$\bar{X} = 10.1 \qquad \bar{Y} = 2.248 \qquad (\Sigma X)(\Sigma Y)/N = 1{,}135.24$$
$$\Sigma X^2 = 5{,}251 \qquad \Sigma Y^2 = 280.56 \qquad \Sigma xy = \overline{42.76}$$
$$(\Sigma X)^2/N = 5{,}100.5 \qquad (\Sigma Y)^2/N = 252.6752$$
$$\Sigma x^2 = \overline{150.5} \qquad \Sigma y^2 = \overline{27.8848}$$

by means of (18.4) and (18.5). (The computation of Σy_i^2 is also shown since we shall have need for this value later.) Though the work is arranged in columns instead of on a line, the student will recognize that Σx_i^2 and Σy_i^2 were computed by application of (7.6) and that $\Sigma x_i y_i$ was computed by (17.7). Now using (18.4) and 18.5), Ms. Jones finds

$$b = \frac{42.76}{150.5} = .284$$

$$c = 2.248 - (.284)(10.1) = -.620$$

Substituting these results into (18.2), she obtains the following prediction equation:

$$\hat{Y}_i = .284X_i - .620$$

Next Ms. Jones will administer the college aptitude test to the advisee involved to obtain his X-score. Assume this score turns out to be 13. Ms. Jones then substitutes 13 for X in the prediction equation to determine an estimate of the particular advisee's expected freshman-year grade-point average.

$$\hat{Y} = (.284)(13) - .620 = 3.07 \approx 3.1$$

Since the expected value is well above the mean ($2.248 \approx 2.25$) for the entire group, the counselor advises the student that his chances of a

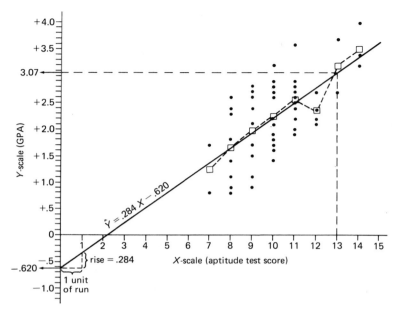

Figure 18.5   Scatter diagram, subsample means (□), and prediction line for 50 pairs of aptitude-test scores and college freshmen grade-point averages of Table 18.3

successful college career appear to be very good. She will encourage such an advisee to make every effort to attend college.

It will be observed that it is quite unnecessary for Ms. Jones actually to locate the line corresponding to the prediction equation with reference to a set of coordinate axes in order to effect the predictions. In fact, the only reason for ever plotting the scatter diagram is to ascertain whether or not the assumption of linearity is justifiable. *This, of course, is reason enough.* The scatter diagram for the 50 pairs of values given in Table 18.3 is shown in Figure 18.5. It is clear that for these data an assumption of linearity is justifiable. To illustrate further the theory involved, the means of the subgroups of Y-values corresponding to the different X-values are shown as open squares (□) in Figure 18.5. The prediction line is also shown. Of course, for purposes of the practical application of this prediction process, it is not necessary to show on the scatter diagram either these subgroup Y-means or the prediction line. The importance of plotting the scatter diagram, however, cannot be over-emphasized, since it affords one very good check on the appropriateness of the straight-line solution to the particular prediction problem.[4]

---

[4] Other methods of testing departure from linearity are available but are beyond the scope of this text. See footnote 9 on page 433.

It is also important that the student fully appreciate just what an estimate yielded by this solution to the prediction problem is. It represents an estimate of the mean of the Y-scores made by a sub- population of individuals all of whom make the same X-score. Even if the estimate obtained is an accurate one (i.e., of approximately the same magnitude as the subpopulation mean), it still may or may not be a good estimate of a particular individual's Y-score, since this score may or may not be located near the subpopulation mean. Moreover, the particular method of estimation involved is based on the assumption that the particular subpopulation mean is one of a family of such means all of which fall on the same straight line. The estimation of the particular subpopulation mean is actually effected by first estimating the position of this line. This makes it possible to take into account past experience with individuals who do not belong to the particular subpopulation in question at the moment. If Ms. Jones had had to limit her estimate of the particular advisee's college success to her past experience with individuals belonging only to the particular subpopulation involved, she would have had only two cases with which to work, since only two of the 50 in her experience pool had X-scores of 13. Instead, she was able to use her entire pool of past experience to estimate the placement of the line, which, in turn, provided the value of the particular subpopulation estimate required.

A full understanding of the fundamental nature of this solution to the prediction problem is essential to an intelligent application of it. Particularly, it should serve to stress how crucial the validity of the assumption of linearity is to the success of the process.[5]

18.6   Other Forms of the Prediction Equation

If we substitute the expression for c given in (18.5) into (18.1) we obtain

$$\hat{Y} = bX + \bar{Y} - b\bar{X}$$

or

$$\hat{Y} = b(X - \bar{X}) + \bar{Y} \qquad (18.6)$$

Equation (18.6) tells us that if the X-score is expressed as a deviation from the mean ($\bar{X}$) of all N of the X-scores, the predicted value (Y) is the product of the line's slope (b) times the X-score deviation (x) plus

[5] When the relationship is curvilinear the prediction problem may be solved by fitting an appropriate curve to the data. Consideration of the curvilinear problem is beyond the scope of this text.

the mean ($\overline{Y}$) of all N of the Y-scores. That is,

$$\hat{Y} = bx + \overline{Y} \tag{18.6a}$$

Subtraction of $\overline{Y}$ from both members of (18.6a) gives

$$\hat{Y} - \overline{Y} = bx$$

or

$$\hat{y} = bx \quad (\hat{y} = \hat{Y} - \overline{Y}) \tag{18.7}$$

That is, the predicted value expressed as a deviation from the overall Y-mean is simply the product of the slope (b) times the deviation of the X-score from the overall X-mean.

We shall next consider a different form of expressing the slope (b) of the prediction line. From (18.4) we may write

$$b = \frac{\sum x_i y_i}{\sum x_i^2} = \frac{\sum x_i y_i}{\sqrt{\sum x_i^2}\,\sqrt{\sum x_i^2}} \cdot \frac{\sqrt{\sum y_i^2}}{\sqrt{\sum y_i^2}}$$

Here, b as given in (18.4) has simply been multiplied by an expression equal to unity and, hence, has not been changed in value. Now, if we rearrange the factors in the denominator we obtain

$$b = \frac{\sum x_i y_i}{\sqrt{\sum x_i^2}\,\sqrt{\sum y_i^2}} \cdot \frac{\sqrt{\sum y_i^2}}{\sqrt{\sum x_i^2}}$$

The value of the first factor in this result is r [see (17.3)]; and if we divide numerator and denominator of the second factor by $\sqrt{N}$, these terms become the Y and X standard deviations [see (7.5)]. Hence,

$$b = r\,\frac{S_Y}{S_X} \tag{18.8}$$

Now substituting this result into (18.6) and (18.7) we obtain

$$\hat{Y} = r\,\frac{S_Y}{S_X}(X - \overline{X}) + \overline{Y} \tag{18.9}$$

or

$$\hat{Y} = r\,\frac{S_Y}{S_X}x + \overline{Y} \tag{18.9a}$$

and

$$\hat{y} = r\,\frac{S_Y}{S_X}x \quad (\hat{y} = \hat{Y} - \overline{Y}) \tag{18.10}$$

A particularly common form of the prediction equation is that given in (18.10). Dividing through both members of (18.10) by S_Y we obtain

$$\frac{\hat{y}}{S_Y} = r \frac{x}{S_X}$$

or

$$\hat{z}_{\hat{y}} = r z_X \tag{18.11}$$

Thus we see that the deviation of the predicted value from the overall Y-mean in units of the overall Y standard deviation is simply the product of r times the X-value expressed in z-score units. In other words, if we were to take the trouble to convert all Y- and X-scores into z-units by application of

$$z_Y = \frac{Y - \overline{Y}}{S_Y} \quad \text{and} \quad z_X = \frac{X - \overline{X}}{S_X}$$

and if we then were to fit a line to the points of the scatter diagram of these z-values using the least-squares criterion of goodness-of-fit, we would obtain a line whose slope (b-value) was r and whose intercept (c-value) was zero.

Except for the fact that the predicted value as given by 18.11 is expressed in terms of a different scale, there is no difference in its meaning or interpretation. It still represents an estimate of a sub-population mean. Now, however, the subpopulation scores involved are in terms of z-units, and the predicted score may itself be interpreted as a type of standard score, that is, as a deviation from a mean ($\overline{Y}$) in units of a standard deviation (S_Y). Strictly speaking, however, it is not a z-score. And because certain aspects of the argument are useful in another connection it will be instructive to note specifically why it is not.

Suppose that for each of the N individuals in the sample we obtained a predicted score by means of (18.6a). The sum of these N scores may be expressed as follows:

$$\sum \hat{Y}_i = b \sum x_i + \sum \overline{Y}$$

or

$$\sum \hat{Y}_i = N\overline{Y} \qquad \qquad \text{[see (6.7) and (5.23)]}$$

Dividing both members by N we obtain

$$M_{\hat{Y}} = \overline{Y} \tag{18.12}$$

That is, the mean of the N predicted scores (i.e., the $\hat{Y}$'s) is the same as the mean of the N actual Y-scores. Hence, the fact that the deviations of the $\hat{Y}$-values were measured from $\overline{Y}$ instead of $M_{\hat{Y}}$ does *not* violate the definition of a z-score. Now suppose that for each of the N individuals in the sample we obtain a predicted score in deviation form by application of (18.10) and that we square each such score. The sum of the squares of these deviation scores may be written.

$$\sum \hat{y}_i^2 = r^2 \frac{S_Y^2}{S_X^2} \sum x_i^2 \qquad \text{[see (5.21)]}$$

and dividing both members by N we obtain

$$S_{\hat{Y}}^2 = r^2 \frac{S_Y^2}{S_X^2} \cdot S_X^2$$

or

$$S_{\hat{Y}}^2 = r^2 S_Y^2 \qquad (18.13)$$

That is, the variance of the N predicted scores for the sample is the product of the square of r times the variance of the N actual Y-scores. Since r is some value less than one (unless, of course, the relationship is perfect), r^2 is less than one, and it follows that the variance of the predicted scores for the sample is some fraction (i.e., r^2) of the variance of the actual Y-scores.[6] Now to express the predicted scores in terms of a true z-scale, we should divide the deviations (the $\hat{y}$'s) by $S_{\hat{Y}}$. But to obtain our $\hat{z}_Y$—see (18.11)—we divided these deviations by a different value, namely, S_Y. It is for this reason that the values yielded by (18.11) are not expressed in terms of a true z-scale. As a reminder of this fact, we placed the caret over both the z and its Y subscript in writing the left-hand member of (18.11).

In spite of the fact that the $\hat{z}_{\hat{Y}}$-values are not true z-scores, they do represent a distance from a mean in units of a standard deviation and, consequently, may be interpreted in much the same manner as ordinary z-scores.[7] Since the mean and standard deviation used are those of the actual Y-scores, the $\hat{z}_{\hat{Y}}$-values may, in fact, be interpreted as points on a z-score scale established with reference to the actual Y-scores.

---

[6] This is the relationship that was used in Section 17.9 to provide one basis for interpreting a given value of r. At that time we noted that r^2 equals the proportion of the Y-variance that can be accounted for by variation in X—i.e., that is predictable from X. Or, $r^2 = S_{\hat{Y}}^2/S_Y^2$.

[7] The standard values of the mean and standard deviation used with a true or ordinary distribution of z-scores are zero and unity, respectively. The corresponding standard values of the distribution of z-scores defined by (18.11) are clearly zero and r.

For the data of Table 18.3 (the problem of the high school counselor) the values of the Y and X standard deviations and of r are .747, 1.735, and .660, respectively. For these data, then, (18.9) is

$$\hat{Y} = (.660)\frac{0.747}{1.735}(X - \bar{X}) + \bar{Y}$$

$$= .284(X - 10.1) + 2.248$$

$$= .284X - 2.868 + 2.248$$

$$= .284X - .620$$

as before.

Also for these data, (18.11) is simply

$$\hat{z}_Y = .660z_X$$

And for the advisee whose X-score was 13,

$$z_X = \frac{13 - 10.1}{1.735} = +1.67$$

and

$$\hat{z}_Y = (.660)(1.67) = 1.10$$

That is the estimated mean of a subpopulation of individuals whose z_X-scores are all $+1.67$ is above the obtained Y-mean by an amount equal to 1.1 times the obtained Y standard deviation. This, of course, is the value used by the counselor as an indication of the expected freshman-year performance of this particular advisee.

18.7 The Accuracy of Prediction: The Correlation Coefficient as an Index

In this section, we present a rationale for the use of the Pearson correlation coefficient as an index of the accuracy of our predictions. We investigate the validity of r as an index of accuracy from three slightly different viewpoints. These different viewpoints should provide additional insights into the meaning of a given value of r and into some of the more subtle aspects of the prediction problem.[8]

---

[8] You may remember that earlier (in Section 17.9) we used this relationship between r and the degree of accuracy of our predictions to help us interpret the meaning of a given value of r.

Rationale I Clearly, the successful application of the prediction procedure to an individual depends on the likelihood that the individual's actual Y-status is somewhere near the Y-mean of the subpopulation of which this individual is a member (the subpopulation of individuals with the same X-score). The likelihood of an individual's Y-score being near the mean of the subpopulation to which he belongs is in turn a function of the variability of the Y-scores constituting the subpopulation. If these scores do not vary markedly, the Y-score for a particular individual cannot differ markedly from the subpopulation mean even if it is one of the more extreme scores of the subpopulation. On the other hand, if the Y-scores constituting the subpopulation vary widely in magnitude, the likelihood that the Y-score for a particular individual will deviate substantially from the subpopulation mean becomes much greater.

Now the tendency of the Y-scores constituting the subpopulations to be concentrated about their respective means is reflected by the width of the elliptical boundary of the scatter diagram. When this boundary is narrow, the points for a subsample must lie close to the prediction line and the Y-values for these points cannot differ very markedly from $\hat{Y}$. If the boundary is wide, then at least some of the subsample points must deviate rather markedly from the prediction line, and the use of $\hat{Y}$ (the point on the line that provides the estimate of the subpopulation mean) as a predicted score will result in rather gross errors in the case of at least some members of the subpopulation. We have previously seen that the width of the elliptical boundary of the scatter diagram is a function of the degree of correlation between the X- and Y-variates. It follows, therefore, that the correlation coefficient may also be interpreted as an index of the accuracy with which our solution to the prediction problem may be applied. The larger the absolute value of r between X and Y—that is, the closer the relationship, be it positive or negative—the more accurate our predictions will be.

Rationale II The validity of r as an index of accuracy of prediction can be approached in another way. If the prediction of Y given X can be effected with perfect accuracy, then, of course, the predicted Y-score for any individual will be the same as his actual Y-score, and hence, for a given group of individuals the variance of the predicted Y-scores ($S_{\hat{Y}}^2$) will be the same as the variance of the actual Y-scores ($S_{\hat{Y}}^2$). If, on the other hand, knowledge of X is of no help whatever in predicting Y, then the best prediction we can make regarding any individual's Y-score is simply $\overline{Y}$, the mean Y-score for all the individuals in our experience pool.[9] Since in this situation the

---

[9] While not proven here, it is true that if X is of no help whatever in predicting Y, then $G = \Sigma (Y_i - \hat{Y}_i)^2$ is a minimum when Y_i equals $\overline{Y}$ for all i (all individuals).

predicted score will be the same for any individual, the variance of the predicted scores for a given group of individuals will be zero. As knowledge of X provides a basis for some differentiation in predicting Y, the variance of the predicted scores becomes some value greater than zero; it approaches the variance of the actual Y-scores as a limit, as the accuracy of prediction approaches perfection. This suggests the following definition of an index of accuracy of prediction.

> **DN 18.1** An index of the accuracy with which the prediction process may be applied to the individuals of a given group is provided by the ratio of the variance of their predicted Y-scores to the variance of their actual Y-scores:

$$\text{Index of accuracy of prediction} = \frac{S_{\hat{Y}}^2}{S_Y^2} \tag{18.14}$$

But from (18.13) we see that the value of this ratio is r^2, or that

$$r = \frac{S_{\hat{Y}}}{S_Y} \tag{18.15}$$

Thus, again we find that the magnitude of the correlation coefficient is indicative of the accuracy of the prediction process. It is not surprising, then, that the placement of the prediction line is in part a function of r [see (18.8), (18.9), and (18.11)].[10]

Rationale III There is still a third way in which the validity of r as an index of the accuracy of prediction can be demonstrated. Consider the correlation between the actual Y-scores of the individuals of the experiment pool and their respective predicted scores ($\hat{Y}$-scores). Such an r is clearly an index of the accuracy of prediction, for the closer the agreement between the actual and predicted Y-values is, the larger the magnitude of this r becomes. If the prediction is perfect, that is, if every predicted score equals the corresponding actual score, then the value of this r must be unity. Similarly, if there is no relationship whatever between actual and predicted scores—that is, if the prediction process fails completely to yield accurate predictions—then the value of this r becomes zero. Intermediate values of this r are, of course, indicative of various degrees of relationship (agreement) between predicted and actual scores.

Now since the $\hat{Y}$-values are obtained from the X-values by multiplying by a constant (b) and adding a constant (c)—see (18.2)—it follows from Rule 17.1 that the absolute value of the correlation between Y

---

[10] When the Y- and X-scores involved are expressed in standard-score form, the value of r alone determines the slope of the line.

and $\hat{Y}$ is the same as the absolute value of the correlation between X and Y. That is,

$$|r_{\hat{Y}Y}| = |r_{(bX+c)Y}| = |r_{XY}|$$

Hence, the remarks made regarding $r_{\hat{Y}Y}$ as an index of the accuracy of prediction apply to r_{XY}. That is, r_{XY} is indicative of agreement between actual and predicted values in precisely the sense of $r_{\hat{Y}Y}$.

18.8   The Accuracy of Prediction: The Standard Error of Estimate as an Index

We have seen how the likelihood of gross errors in the application of the prediction process to individuals depends on the variability of the actual scores making up the subpopulations to which these individuals belong (i.e., the individuals with the same X-score). This suggests the use of an estimate of the variance or the standard deviation of the actual Y-scores of a subpopulation as an index of the accuracy of the prediction process applied to its members: the smaller this variance, the more accurate the prediction process.

For example, consider the data in Table 18.3, which are related to the problem of the school counselor. Four individuals have an X-score of 12. The corresponding Y-scores are 2.7, 2.4, 2.2, and 2.1. The mean of these four scores is 2.35 and the estimated variance is [see (11.12)]:

$$\frac{\sum (Y_i - \overline{Y})^2}{N - 1}$$

$$= \frac{(2.7 - 2.35)^2 + (2.4 - 2.35)^2 + (2.2 - 2.35)^2 + (2.1 - 2.35)^2}{3}$$

$$\approx .07$$

The smaller this variance (or standard deviation), the better the prediction. Likewise, it should be possible to estimate the variances of the subpopulations of Y-scores corresponding to each of the other X-values.

However, there are at least three weaknesses associated with the procedure as here illustrated. First, instead of a single index, a multiplicity of indexes is implied, one for each subpopulation of Y-scores—a situation as inconvenient as it is bountiful. Second, the variance estimates are computed using the observed means of the subsamples of Y-values. In our example above, the variance of the four scores was computed to be around 2.35, the actual mean of the four scores in this particular subsample. However, in the earlier sections of this chapter we attempted to develop a rationale for using the $\hat{Y}$-values obtained from the best-fitting line (in a least-squares sense) as "better" (or more accurate) estimates of the subpopulation means. Therefore, we can improve upon our procedure by using these more accurate estimates of the subpopulation means from which to measure the Y-score deviations.

The third weakness related to the use of the estimated Y-score variance at each X-score as an index of accuracy is that our experience pool may contain only a relatively few individuals from any given subpopulation, so that estimates of the variances of the Y-scores of subpopulations made by this procedure will often be based on very small samples and may consequently involve large sampling errors. For example, only four individuals had an X-score of 12. This is the same problem that led us to abandon the actual mean of the sub-sample of Y-scores corresponding to a given X as the "best" estimate of the subpopulation Y-mean and, under the assumption of linearity, to adopt instead the best-fitting line to estimate subpopulation means.

Both the first and third weaknesses cited can be eliminated if one additional assumption can be made, namely, that the Y-scores of any subpopulation of individuals making a given X-score have the same degree of variability as those of any other such subpopulation. This assumption is technically known as the *homoscedasticity* (equal scatter) assumption. Figure 18.6 illustrates a set of homoscedastic subpopula-tions when there are only three different X-values. The distribution of Y-scores for all subpopulations combined is also shown in Figure 18.6.

If the homoscedasticity assumption is reasonable (we will discuss later a method of examining whether it is), then mathematical statisti-cians have shown that an appropriate estimate of the common sub-population variance is given by

↓ based on larger sample size as opposed to $\bar{Y}$.

$$\tilde{\sigma}^2_{y \cdot x} = \frac{\sum (Y_i - \hat{Y}_i)^2}{N - 2} \qquad (18.16)$$

where $\hat{Y}_i$ is the predicted Y-score for the ith individual and Y_i is the actual Y-score.[11] The corresponding standard deviation is given by

$$\tilde{\sigma}_{y \cdot x} = \sqrt{\frac{\sum (Y_i - \hat{Y}_i)^2}{N - 2}} \qquad (18.17)$$

The value of $\tilde{\sigma}_{y \cdot x}$ given by (18.17) may be thought of as an estimate of the standard deviation of the actual Y-scores for any subpopulation

---

[11] The numerator of the variance of (18.16) is the index G as defined in (18.3). The subscript $y \cdot x$ indicates y for a fixed or given x. The term $\tilde{\sigma}^2_{y \cdot x}$ is an estimate of the assumed common variance of the Y-scores of subpopulations of individuals making the same X-score.

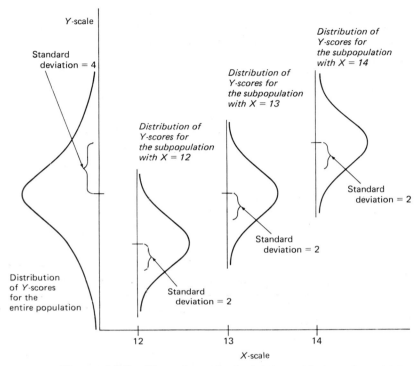

Figure 18.6 Three hypothetical subpopulations for which the homoscedastic assumption holds

of individuals whose X-scores are all of the same magnitude. Of course, to interpret it in this way requires that we assume the variability of the Y-scores of any subpopulation to be the same as that of any other.

When $\tilde{\sigma}_{y \cdot x}$ is interpreted as an estimate of the standard deviation of a subpopulation of Y-scores each of which is paired with the same X-score, it may be regarded as an index of the accuracy with which the prediction process may be applied to individuals. Since the "estimate" or "prediction" we make for any member of a particular subpopulation is the $\hat{Y}$-value for that subpopulation, the $Y - \hat{Y}$ deviations represent differences between actual and estimated values and hence are measures of the *error* in our estimation. In fact, (18.17) is sometimes presented using a notation related to this error concept. If we let $e_i = Y_i - \hat{Y}_i$ then (18.16) becomes

$$\tilde{\sigma}_{y \cdot x}^2 = \frac{\sum e_i^2}{N - 2} \tag{18.18}$$

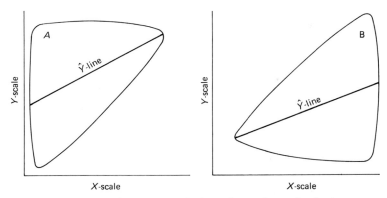

Figure 18.7   Boundaries of two hypothetical scatter-diagram point fields (*A* and *B*) for which condition of homoscedasticity does not hold

And (18.17) becomes

$$\tilde{\sigma}_{y \cdot x} = \sqrt{\frac{\sum e_i^2}{N - 2}} \qquad\qquad (18.19)$$

Thus, the value of $\tilde{\sigma}_{y \cdot x}$ is the square root of a sort of mean value of the squares of these errors for the individuals in the experience pool. The larger these errors, on the average, the larger the value of $\tilde{\sigma}_{y \cdot x}$. It is for this reason that the value $\tilde{\sigma}_{y \cdot x}$ is known as a *standard error of estimate* or more fully as *the standard error of estimating Y for a given X.*

It is possible to use an estimate of the standard deviation of a sub-population of *Y*-scores as an index of the accuracy of individual estimates—that is, as a standard error of estimate—even if the condition of homoscedasticity does not hold. In this case, however, the use of (18.18) is not appropriate and the estimate of the subpopulation standard deviation will necessarily be based on only those values constituting the subsample from that subpopulation.[12] The magnitude of such a standard error of estimate will, of course, be meaningful only with reference to the particular subpopulation; and a separate determination must be made for each subpopulation. *If the point field of the scatter diagram is elliptical, it is generally safe to assume that the condition of homoscedasticity holds*. Figure 18.7 shows the boundaries of two hypothetical point fields, *A* and *B*, for which the condition of

---

[12] If the populations are not homoscedastic, $\tilde{\sigma}_{y \cdot x}$ represents a sort of average standard error of estimate. As such, its value would be too high for some sub-populations and too low for others. Therefore, it would be best when dealing with heteroscedastic data to compute the standard error of estimate using only the *Y*-values for a given *X*-score, or perhaps for a given interval along the *X*-scale.

homoscedasticity does not hold. In the case of the A-plot, the standard errors of estimate will obviously be much greater for the subpopulations of Y-values associated with small X-values than for the subpopulations associated with large X-values. Predictions made for individuals having small X-scores are likely to involve gross errors, whereas those made for individuals having large X-scores will, on the whole, be quite accurate. The situation is reversed in the case of plot B.

18.9 Computation of $\tilde{\sigma}_{y \cdot x}$

To find a value for $\tilde{\sigma}_{y \cdot x}$ using (18.18), an error score must be computed for each individual. However, it is possible to obtain $\tilde{\sigma}_{y \cdot x}^2$ without computing each error score. Only r and S_Y^2 are really needed. Equation (18.20) shows the relationship.

$$\tilde{\sigma}_{y \cdot x}^2 = \frac{N}{N-2} S_Y^2 (1 - r^2) \tag{18.20}$$

Or, taking the square root

$$\tilde{\sigma}_{y \cdot x} = \sqrt{\frac{N}{N-2}} S_Y \sqrt{1 - r^2} \tag{18.21}$$

Proof* For any individual in the experience pool, say individual i,

$$
\begin{aligned}
e_i &= Y_i - \hat{Y}_i \\
&= Y_i - bX_i - c && \text{[substituting for } \hat{Y}_i \text{ from (18.2a)]} \\
&= Y_i - bX_i - \bar{Y} + b\bar{X} && \text{[substituting for } c \text{ from (18.5)]} \\
&= (Y_i - \bar{Y}) - b(X_i - \bar{X}) \\
&= y_i - bx_i
\end{aligned}
$$

Therefore,

$$e_i^2 = y_i^2 + b^2 x_i^2 - 2bx_i y_i$$

An expression like this can be obtained for each of the N individuals; and summing these N expressions, we obtain

$$\sum e_i^2 = \sum y_i^2 + b^2 \sum x_i^2 - 2b \sum x_i y_i \qquad \text{[see (5.21)]}$$

But from (18.4) we see that

$$\sum x_i y_i = b \sum x_i^2$$

---

* Optional. However, the student should make note of formulas (18.22) and (18.26), since these are used later.

Hence, substituting for $\sum x_i y_i$ we obtain

$$\sum e_i^2 = \sum y_i^2 + b^2 \sum x_i^2 - 2b^2 \sum x_i^2$$

or

$$\sum e_i^2 = \sum y_i^2 - b^2 \sum x_i^2 \tag{18.22}$$

Or if we substitute from (18.4) for b we have

$$\sum e_i^2 = \sum y_i^2 - \frac{(\sum x_i y_i)^2}{\sum x_i^2} \tag{18.23}$$

Or if we multiply numerator and denominator of the last term of the rightmost member of (18.23) by $\sum y_i^2$ we obtain

$$\sum e_i^2 = \sum y_i^2 - r^2 \sum y_i^2 \qquad [\text{see } (17.3)]$$

or

$$\sum e_i^2 = \sum y_i^2 (1 - r^2) \tag{18.24}$$

If we divide both sides of (18.24) by N we obtain

$$S_{y \cdot x}^2 = S_Y^2 (1 - r^2) \tag{18.25}$$

or

$$S_{y \cdot x} = S_Y \sqrt{1 - r^2} \tag{18.26}$$

where $S_{y \cdot x}$ is the standard error of estimate for the given experience pool of N individuals. Some writers refer to $S_{y \cdot x}$ as *the* standard error of estimate and advocate its use as an index of accuracy of the prediction process. This process, however, is not needed for use with members of the experience pool but rather for use with members of the subpopulations whose actual *Y*-scores are unknown. It would appear, therefore, that the population estimate of the standard error of estimate given by (18.19) provides a more realistic assessment of error in the prediction process than does the sample value of (18.26). If we divide both members of (18.24) by $N - 2$ instead of N we obtain

$$\tilde{\sigma}_{y \cdot x}^2 = \frac{\sum y_i^2}{N - 2} (1 - r^2)$$

$$= \frac{N \sum y_i^2}{(N - 2)N} (1 - r^2)$$

$$= \frac{N}{N - 2} S_Y^2 (1 - r^2)$$

That is,

$$\tilde{\sigma}_{y \cdot x}^2 = \frac{N}{N-2} S_Y^2 (1 - r^2) = \frac{N}{N-2} S_{y \cdot x}^2 \qquad (18.27)$$

or

$$\tilde{\sigma}_{y \cdot x} = \sqrt{\frac{N}{N-2}} S_{y \cdot x} = \sqrt{\frac{N}{N-2}} S_Y \sqrt{1 - r^2} \qquad (18.28)$$

Comment: Since $\sqrt{N/(N-2)}$ will always be some value greater than unity it follows that the population estimate of the standard error of estimate will be larger than the corresponding sample value. Of course, as N becomes large, $\sqrt{N/(N-2)}$ approaches unity and the need for distinguishing between $\tilde{\sigma}_{y \cdot x}$ and $S_{y \cdot x}$ becomes of less practical importance.

As an example of the computation of $\tilde{\sigma}_{y \cdot x}$, consider the data of the problem of the high school counselor (see Table 18.3). For these data:

$$S_Y^2 = \frac{\sum y^2}{N} = \frac{27.8848}{50} = .5577$$

$$r^2 = \left(\frac{\sum xy}{\sqrt{\sum x^2} \sqrt{\sum y^2}} \right)^2 = \frac{(\sum xy)^2}{(\sum x^2)(\sum y^2)} = \frac{42.76^2}{(150.5)(27.8848)}$$

$$= .4357$$

By (18.20)

$$\tilde{\sigma}_{y \cdot x}^2 = \left(\frac{50}{50-2} \right) (.5577)(1 - .4357)$$

$$= \left(\frac{50}{48} \right) (.3147) \approx .3278$$

and

$$\tilde{\sigma}_{y \cdot x} \approx .5725$$

Thus, the estimated standard error of predicting Y for a given X is approximately one-half of a letter grade unit. The magnitude of $\tilde{\sigma}_{y \cdot x}$ provides some indication of the magnitude of errors in future prediction. Thus, in our example, the "average"[13] error was approximately .57. In the next chapter we will use $\tilde{\sigma}_{y \cdot x}$ to establish confidence intervals for a given predicted value.

---

[13] Average in the sense that a standard deviation is a sort of average.

In concluding this section attention is directed to the relationship between the variance of the Y-scores constituting the experience pool and the variances of the errors of estimate and of the predicted scores. From (18.8) we see that

$$b^2 = r^2 \frac{S_Y^2}{S_X^2} = r^2 \frac{\sum y_i^2}{\sum x_i^2}$$

or

$$b^2 \sum x_i^2 = r^2 \sum y_i^2$$
$$= \sum \hat{y}_i^2 \qquad\qquad \text{[see (18.13)]}$$

Now substituting in (18.22) we obtain

$$\sum e_i^2 = \sum y_i^2 - \sum \hat{y}_i^2$$

or

$$\sum y_i^2 = \sum \hat{y}_i^2 + \sum e_i^2 \qquad\qquad (18.29)$$

If we divide both members of (18.29) by N, we obtain

$$S_Y^2 = S_{\hat{Y}}^2 + S_{y \cdot x}^2 \qquad\qquad (18.30)$$

That is, the variance of all the Y-scores in the experience pool is made up of two component variances: (1) the variance of the corresponding estimated Y-values ($\hat{Y}$'s), and (2) the variance of the errors in these estimated values ($e = Y - \hat{Y}$).

18.10 Some Comparisons between r and $\tilde{\sigma}_{y \cdot x}$

We have already shown (see Section 18.7) how the accuracy of the prediction process is a function of the degree of correlation between the two variates involved. Hence, it is not surprising to find that the standard error of estimate is also a function of this correlation. However, the standard error of estimate is also a function of the overall Y standard deviation (S_Y) and varies with S_Y in such a way as to have an advantage not possessed by the index r.

We have seen (Section 17.10) how r is affected by the "range-of-talent" encompassed by the collection of individuals involved. If the use of $S_{y \cdot x}$ or $\tilde{\sigma}_{y \cdot x}$ is appropriate at all—that is, if the condition of homoscedasticity holds—its value is by contrast independent of the range of talent in the experience pool. If the range of talent is increased, r tends to increase, making $\sqrt{1 - r^2}$ decrease. In this case, however,

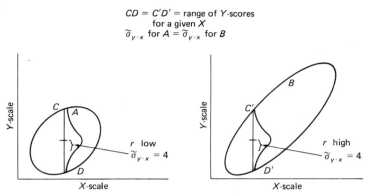

Figure 18.8   Boundaries of two hypothetical scatter-diagram point fields of same width but differing in length

the value of S_Y will also increase so that the standard error of estimate is the product of an increasing and a decreasing value [see (18.21) and (18.26)] and hence tends to remain constant for a given pair of variates. The student can perhaps better visualize this property of the standard error of estimate by recalling that r increases as the point field of the scatter diagram becomes elongated in relation to its width, whereas the magnitude of $\tilde{\sigma}_{y \cdot x}$ reflects only the width of this point field without regard to its length. Figure 18.8, for example, shows the boundaries of the scatter-diagram point fields for two imaginary experience pools involving the same variates. Boundary A applies to a collection limited in range of talent, whereas Boundary B applies to a collection involving a much more extensive range of talent. The value of r will be much greater for the B than for the A collection. However, the variation among Y-scores for given values of X tends to be the same for both plots as is shown in the diagram by the ranges CD and $C'D'$. It is this variation that is reflected by $\tilde{\sigma}_{y \cdot x}$, and the value of $\tilde{\sigma}_{y \cdot x}$ will consequently be the same for both plots.

The fact that $\tilde{\sigma}_{y \cdot x}$ is relatively independent of range of talent has led some writers to advocate its use in preference to r as an index both of degree of relationship and of accuracy of prediction. However, it, too, has a disadvantage as an index in that it is expressed in terms of Y-scale units. This makes it impossible to use $\tilde{\sigma}_{y \cdot x}$ to compare the relative effectiveness of two or more prediction situations unless the Y-scales are comparable. The correlation coefficient, r, on the other hand, has the advantage of being an abstract number independent of the units of measurement. It may be used as a basis for comparing the accuracy of different prediction situations even though the units involved are not comparable.

It will be instructive to study the relationship between r and $S_{y \cdot x}$ for a given range of talent, that is, for a given value of S_Y. It is clear from (18.26) that $\sqrt{1 - r^2}$ is the proportion or fraction that the sample standard error of estimate $S_{y \cdot x}$ is of the Y standard deviation (S_Y). When r is zero, this proportion is one (the standard error of estimate equals the Y standard deviation), and there is no improvement in the accuracy of prediction resulting from knowledge of an individual's X-score. As r increases, this proportion gradually decreases, becoming zero when $r = 1$. A standard error of estimate of zero, of course, is indicative of errorless predictions. Values of this proportion between one and zero are indicative of the extent to which errors of estimate or prediction are reduced from their possible maximum as indicated by S_Y to a possible minimum of zero as a result of taking into account information about the individuals' X-scores. For example, if the correlation between Y and X is .80, this proportion ($\sqrt{1 - .80^2}$) is .6, indicating that $S_{y \cdot x}$ is 60 percent of the maximum value it would have been were r equal to 0 instead of .80. That is, as a result of taking into account information about X when $r = .80$, we *reduce* the "average"[14] magnitude of the prediction errors by 40 percent ($100 - 60 = 40$) over what they would be were we to ignore this information. Figure 18.9 shows graphically the percentage of reduction in the "average" magnitude of the estimation or prediction error that is associated with various values of r. Inspection of this figure clearly shows that r must become quite large before an appreciable percentage of reduction is achieved. An r of .50, for example, reduces the "average" error of estimate by only about 13.4 percent, and an r of almost .98 is necessary to bring about an 80 percent reduction. It is for this reason that some writers have advocated that the prediction or estimation process under consideration should be employed only when the correlation between X and Y is very high—say .90 or higher. It may indeed be advisable to avoid making such predictions when r is low if it is possible to do so. Frequently, however, a prediction cannot be avoided. If this is the case, it is better to make use of the information about X than to ignore it, regardless of how slight the gain in accuracy may be, that is, regardless of the fact that the correlation between X and Y may be quite low.[15]

[14] Average in the sense that a standard deviation is a sort of average.

[15] In situations involving the selection of a relatively small group of individuals from a large number of individuals (e.g., in selecting from among GI personnel individuals to attend a service academy), a considerable gain may be made through the use of a selection test even though the correlation between success and the selection test is quite low (say .30 or even .20), *if* the number of potentially successful individuals is small in relation to the total group. The interested student will find a presentation of this point in: Anne Anastasi, *Psychological Testing*, 3d ed., The Macmillan Company, New York, 1968, pp. 131 ff.; and Lee J. Cronbach, *Essentials of Psychological Testing*, 3d ed., Harper & Brothers, New York, 1970, pp. 429 ff.

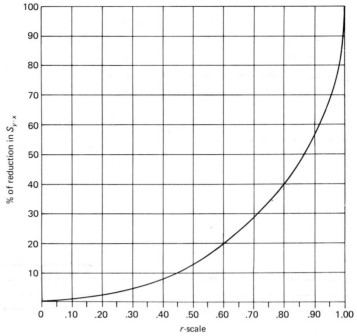

Figure 18.9   Percentage of reduction in "average" magnitude of prediction errors for various values of r

It is of utmost importance, especially in such circumstances, that the predictor be fully cognizant of the fallibility of the procedure and interpret his results accordingly.

18.11 The Concept of Regression

The prediction equation in standard-score form [see (18.11)] indicates clearly that for any situation in which r is less than one, an estimated or predicted value deviates by a lesser amount from the overall Y-mean in units of the Y standard deviation than does the corresponding X-value. from the overall X-mean in units of the X standard deviation. By way of illustration, Figure 18.10 shows the boundary of the point field of a hypothetical scatter diagram in which the variates are expressed in z-score form and in which r is assumed to be about .75. Points falling in the heavy black column have z_X-score values of $+2.0$. The estimated z_Y-mean of this subpopulation is the corresponding point on the prediction line ($\hat{z}_Y = rz_X = .75 \times 2.0 = 1.5$). Since r is less than one, this point will necessarily be nearer the origin (the intersection of the

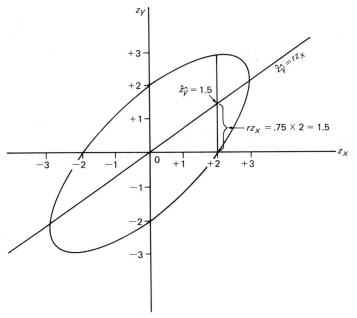

Figure 18.10   Diagram showing how estimated z_y-mean for subgroups of individuals whose z_x-scores are 2.0 is necessarily less than 2.0

axes) than the z_X-value of $+2.0$. The origin, or point at which z_X and z_Y both equal zero, locates the means of the z_X- and z_Y-scales, and the unit values of these scales are 1 standard deviation. Hence, it follows that the mean of the Y-scores of any subgroup of individuals making the same X-score lies closer in terms of standard deviation units to the general Y-mean than does the particular X-score value to the X-mean. This tendency for the subgroup Y-means to *regress* toward the general or overall Y-mean is known as the *regression effect* or the *phenomenon of regression*.

   While regression effect is mathematically inherent in our solution to the prediction problem, it is in no sense an artifact of that solution. The phenomenon is one that we have all observed in the "real world," but that we have seldom attempted to describe in quantitative terms. Suppose, for example, that we consider a group of adults all of whom are 6 feet 6 inches tall. We would also expect to find these individuals to be above average in weight, but we would hardly expect them on the average to be as extreme in weight as in height. Or suppose that tests in general mathematical ability and in knowledge of contemporary affairs are administered to all freshmen in a large university. Now, if from the total group we were to select a number of individuals because they were very outstanding in their performance on the math test, we would find that, while most of these individuals would be above average in knowledge of contemporary affairs, only a few of them would be as far above average in this knowledge as in mathematical ability. That is, the mean score for these selected individuals on the contemporary affairs test would be lower (when the scores are expressed in comparable terms, such as z-scores) than their scores on the math test. *This phenomenon of regression is characteristic of any two linearly correlated variates.*

A further graphic representation of this phenomenon will be helpful in arriving at a more exact understanding of its character. The two frequency curves in Figure 18.11 represent the distributions of measures of performance on a scholastic aptitude test and of subsequent success in college for the same large group of individuals. Both distributions are plotted along comparable (z-score) scales. The X-distribution represents the distribution of aptitude test scores, and the Y-distribution that of success in college. We have assumed a correlation of .66 between these two variates since this was the value previously used in the problem of the high school counselor. Now consider a subgroup of individuals, all of whom make scores of +2.0 on the aptitude test. The estimated mean of the college-success scores for this subgroup is (.66)(2), or +1.32. A heavy line has been drawn from +2.0 on the aptitude scale to +1.32 on the success scale. Note that this line points inward toward the middle of the success distribution. That is, the mean of the success scores for the members of this subgroup lies closer to (has regressed toward) the general mean of the success distribution than does their aptitude score (+2.0) to the general mean of the aptitude distribution. Of course, there will be considerable variation in the success scores of the members of this subgroup. In fact, the standard deviation (standard error of estimate) of their success scores will be only about 25 percent smaller than that of the total success distribution (see Figure 18.9). This implies that the standard deviation of the subgroup success scores will be .75 [see also formula (18.26)]. A hypothetical distribution curve for these subgroup success scores having a mean of 1.32 and a standard deviation of .75 has been sketched into Figure 18.11.[16] The large dots are spaced at a distance of 1 standard deviation (.75) and the lines fanning out from the aptitude score of 2.0 are intended to help the student picture how different individuals making this particular aptitude score make different success scores. While a few individuals make success scores above the level of their aptitude score, most achieve success scores of

[16] This distribution curve has been highly magnified in relation to the rest of the figure. Theoretically its total area should be the same percentage of the area of the whole Y-distribution that the number of individuals having z_X-scores of 2 is of the whole X-distribution. If these distributions are assumed to be normal and if the z-values are determined to the nearest tenth, this is approximately only one-half of one percent.

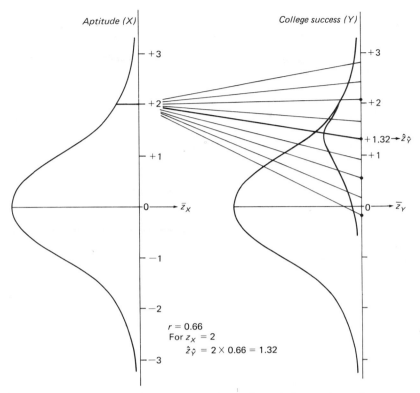

Aptitude (X)   *College success (Y)*

$r = 0.66$
For $z_X = 2$
$\hat{z}_{\hat{y}} = 2 \times 0.66 = 1.32$

Figure 18.11   Diagram illustrating phenomenon of
regression of Y-scores for a subgroup of individuals making
the same X-score

less than 2, that is, success scores below the level of their aptitude score.[17]
In other words, there is an overall regression effect when the subgroup
is considered as a whole.

   This picture suggests what would be found in the distributions of any
two positively and linearly related traits for any group. If the relationship between the traits is perfect (i.e., if $r = 1$), then, for a subgroup of
individuals, the lines that join their common X-trait standard score to
their Y-trait standard scores will merge into a single horizontal line,
since in this case each individual's Y-trait standard score will be the
same as his X-trait standard score. If the relationship is high but not
perfect, these lines will spread apart forming a relatively narrow fan,

---

[17] If we assume the subgroup success scores to be normally distributed,

$$z = \frac{2 - 1.32}{.75} = .91 \quad \text{and} \quad P(z \leq .91) = .82$$

That is, the success scores of some 82 percent of the members of this subgroup will
be below the level of their aptitude scores.

and the heavy line (i.e., the line to the Y-trait mean for the subgroup) will be deflected (will regress) only slightly toward the middle (general mean) of the Y-distribution. If the relationship is very low but positive, these lines will fan out to nearly all parts of the Y-distribution, and the heavy line will point more sharply into the middle of that distribution. If the traits are wholly unrelated (i.e., if $r = 0$), the lines will fan out through the whole of the Y-distribution, and the Y-mean for the subgroup will coincide with the general Y-mean. For example, if for a population of sixth-grade boys the X-trait is height and the Y-trait intelligence[18] and lines are drawn from a score interval near the lower end of the height distribution to the positions of the corresponding intelligence scores, these lines would spread throughout the entire intelligence distribution around a subgroup mean, which would coincide with the general mean in intelligence. This is the same as saying that short persons are just as variable in intelligence and have the same average intelligence as tall persons, or, for that matter, as the population in general, regardless of differences in height.

If the relationship between the two variables is negative, most of the lines from any one score interval in the X-distribution will go to the *opposite* half of the Y-distribution, as will the heavy line extending to the subgroup Y-mean. This subgroup mean will, nevertheless, still be nearer the general Y-mean than the X-score interval is to the general X-mean.

In general, then, the higher the degree of correlation is, the narrower will be the fan-shaped pattern of lines drawn from score intervals in the X-distribution to the corresponding scores in the Y-distribution, and the more nearly horizontal will be the heavy line drawn to the subgroup Y-mean—that is, the less will be the regression. Nevertheless, as long as the relationship is not perfect, this heavy line will point inward, however slightly. In other words, for individuals selected from a given group because they are alike in one trait, the *mean* value of a second related trait will *regress* toward the general mean of the second trait. The amount of this regression is inversely related to the coefficient of correlation between the two measures. With perfect correlation there is no regression. With zero correlation the regression is complete, that is, the subgroup Y-means coincide with the general Y-mean.

18.12 Regression Terminology

We have seen that if the variates are expressed in z-score form, the prediction line provides estimates of the means of z_Y-scores for subpopulations of individuals making the same z_X-score. Clearly, then, in

---

[18] The correlation between these traits is approximately zero.

this situation the prediction line indicates the degree of regression along the z_Y-scale that is associated with a given z_X-value. This being the case it would seem reasonable to call such a line a regression line. In fact, it has become customary in statistical literature to refer to all prediction lines as *regression lines* and to all prediction equations as *regression equations*. This terminology is used even in situations involving curvi-linearly related variables—situations in which the concept of regression as developed in the preceding section is not meaningful. In conjunction with the use of this terminology there has evolved a related terminology applicable to other aspects of the prediction problem. Because this regression terminology is so widely used, it is important that the student be familiar with it.

To start at the beginning, it is customary to refer to the topic of this chapter as the *regression problem* instead of the prediction problem. Then, as we have already indicated, equation (18.2) and other forms of it such as are given by (18.6), (18.6a), (18.7), (18.9), (18.9a), (18.10), and (18.11) are known as *regression equations* instead of prediction equations, and the lines represented by these equations are known as *regression lines* rather than prediction lines.[19] Since it is the slope of the line that indicates regression, and since the slope is given by the value of b, it has become customary to refer to b as a *regression coefficient* or a *regression weight*. The predicted values are sometimes called *regressed values*, though they are also commonly referred to as estimates or predictions.

The sum of squares of the deviations of the regressed (predicted) values from the general Y-mean for all members of the experience pool is known as the *regression sum of squares* or the *sum of squares due to regression*. This sum of squares is often denoted symbolically by ss_{reg}.

$$ss_{reg} = \sum \hat{y}_i^2 \qquad (\hat{y}_i = \hat{Y}_i - \bar{Y}) \qquad (18.31)$$

The sum of squares of the deviations of the actual Y-scores from the general Y-mean for all members of the experience pool is known as the *total sum of squares*, and is often denoted by ss_T:

$$ss_T = \sum y_i^2 \qquad (y_i = Y_i - \bar{Y}) \qquad (18.32)$$

The deviations of the actual (Y) from the regressed $(\hat{Y})$ values are sometimes called *residuals* instead of errors of estimate,[20] since they represent that part of the total $Y - \bar{Y}$ deviation that would remain

---

[19] Except for a change in metric, the same line is specified by each of these equations.

[20] The term "error," which we have previously employed, is also used by many writers.

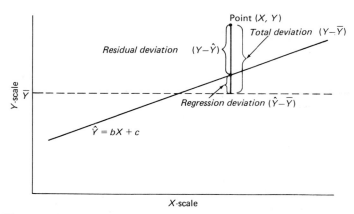

Figure 18.12   Diagram showing total deviation as
consisting of regression deviation and residual deviation

were the regression deviation $\hat{Y} - \overline{Y}$ to be subtracted from it. (For an
example, see Figure 18.12.) The sum of the squares of the residual
deviations is sometimes called the *residual sum of squares* and is denoted
by ss_{res}[21]

$$ss_{res} = \sum e_i^2 \qquad (e_i = Y_i - \hat{Y}_i) \tag{18.33}$$

Translating (18.29) into terms of this notation we have

$$ss_T = ss_{reg} + ss_{res} \tag{18.34}$$

It is a common practice to compute ss_{res} as a residual, that is, as the
difference between ss_T and ss_{reg}.
  From (18.18) we see that

$$\tilde{\sigma}_{y \cdot x}^2 = \frac{ss_{res}}{N - 2} \tag{18.35}$$

Or for just the individuals constituting the experience pool at hand
we have

$$S_{y \cdot x}^2 = \frac{ss_{res}}{N} \tag{18.36}$$

Also, since

$$S_Y^2 = \frac{ss_T}{N}$$

---

[21] It is also often called the *error sum of squares*.

and

$$S_{\hat{Y}}^2 = \frac{ss_{reg}}{N},$$

it follows from (18.13) that

$$\frac{ss_{reg}}{N} = r^2 \frac{ss_T}{N}$$

or

$$r^2 = \frac{ss_{reg}}{ss_T} \tag{18.37}$$

Note also that the G-value of (18.3) is ss_{res}. That is, in regression terminology, our criterion for the placement of the regression line is that placement which minimimizes the residual (error) sum of squares. Since ss_T is a constant for a given experience pool, and since ss_T is the sum of ss_{res} and ss_{reg}, it follows that our method of placing the line is one that maximizes the regression sum of squares.

18.13 Summary Statement

In this chapter we examined the problem of estimating (predicting) a score on one dimension (Y) given a score on another (X) in the special case in which previous experience with the two variables (dimensions) indicates that they are linearly related. Using past experience (data) pertaining to both variables, we obtained a linear equation of the form $\hat{Y}_i = bX_i + c$ by fitting a line to the individual pairs of X- and Y-scores in such a way as to minimize the error ($e_i = Y_i - \hat{Y}_i$) sum of squares. Specific X-values could then be substituted into this equation to obtain estimated $\hat{Y}$-values.

Two indexes of the accuracy of the prediction process were examined: namely, the product-moment correlation coefficient (r), and the standard error of estimate ($S_{y \cdot x}$ or $\tilde{\sigma}_{y \cdot x}$), which is based on the error sum of squares ($\sum e_i^2$). The latter index might be more appropriately described as an index of inaccuracy inasmuch as large values of it are indicative of inaccuracy.

In the next chapter we examine certain inferential procedures related to the prediction (regression) problem. As you will see, $\tilde{\sigma}_{y \cdot x}$ is a basic component of these inferential procedures.

19

Sampling-Error Theory for Simple Linear Regression

19.1 Introduction: The Regression Model

In the preceding chapter, we developed the concept of using a best-fitting straight line (in a least-squares sense) to predict scores on one variable from the scores on another. Our major illustrative example was the problem of the high school counselor, which involved the prediction of college grade-point average using aptitude test scores. In this chapter we shall treat briefly some simple sampling-error theory regarding b, the slope of the best-fitting line, and show how this theory may be applied to the testing of certain statistical hypotheses and to the determination of certain interval estimates. In this section we describe the model to which this sampling-error theory applies. The remaining sections present the specific sampling-error theory and illustrate applications of this theory. The major illustrative example will again be the problem of the high school counselor.

We shall begin with a review of the nature of the data at hand. We presumably have an experience pool of N individuals for each of whom two scores, X and Y, are available. The X-score is the independent or predictor variable and the Y-score the dependent or "to-be-predicted" variable. Not all N of the X-scores are different in magnitude. Assume that there are k different X-values, where k is some integer less than N. Let these values be designated $X_1, X_2, \ldots, X_j, \ldots, X_k$, and let the number of X_1-scores be represented by n_1, the number of X_2-scores by n_2, and so on. Then

$$\sum_{j=1}^{k} n_j = N \tag{19.1}$$

Now the n_1 individuals making X-scores of magnitude X_1 do not all make the same Y-score. We shall regard the n_1 scores that constitute the subset of Y-scores made by these individuals as having been selected at random from a subpopulation of Y-scores for individuals whose X-scores are all of magnitude X_1. Similarly, we shall regard the n_2 scores constituting the second subset of Y-scores as a random sample from a subpopulation of Y-scores for individuals whose X-scores are all of magnitude X_2. We shall regard all the remaining subsets of Y-scores associated with like X-scores in a similar fashion. Thus, we consider our experience pool as consisting of k random subsamples of Y-scores, each having been selected from a different population characterized by the fact that all its members have the same X-score.

In solving the prediction problem we made one further assumption regarding the nature of these subpopulations: we assumed their means to fall on a straight line. The form of the equation of this line that we shall consider here is that given by (18.6). That is,

$$\hat{Y} = b(X - \overline{X}) + \overline{Y} = bx + \overline{Y} \qquad (19.2)$$

In this form of the equation, the independent variable X is expressed as a deviation from $\overline{X}$, b is the slope, and $\overline{Y}$ the Y-intercept. To obtain this equation it is necessary only to apply (18.4) and (6.2) to the data in the sample experience pool to determine the values of b, $\overline{X}$, and $\overline{Y}$.

Suppose now that we repeat the procedure with a second sample experience pool selected by choosing at random n_1 Y-scores from the subpopulation of individuals whose X-scores are of magnitude X_1, n_2 Y-scores from the subpopulation of individuals whose X-scores are of magnitude X_2, and so on. The X-scores for the N individuals constituting this new experience pool will be the same as before, and consequently the value of $\overline{X}$ will remain the same. Owing to the operation of chance, however, the Y-scores constituting the subsamples will differ somewhat from those of the original experience pool. Hence, the new values of b and $\overline{Y}$ may be expected to differ from those previously determined.

Now assume this particular sampling procedure to be repeated indefinitely. Each repetition will, of course, result in the same $\overline{X}$-value. The values of b and $\overline{Y}$, however, will vary from sample to sample. The relative frequency distributions of these b- and $\overline{Y}$-values are the sampling distributions of the statistics b and $\overline{Y}$ (DN 11.6, p. 216). These sampling distributions represent the theoretical totality of experience with variation in the values of b and $\overline{Y}$ for sample experience pools selected in the manner described from the subpopulations involved. By imposing two additional conditions on the nature of the subpopulations of Y-scores, it is possible to derive mathematical curves that serve as models of the sampling distributions of b and $\overline{Y}$. These conditions are: (1) homoscedasticity—equal variability of Y-scores from subpopulation to subpopulation;[1] and (2) normality of the subpopulation Y-score distributions.

We shall now summarize the foregoing description using a different order of presentation. That is, we shall begin with a statement about the population. The total population consists of k subpopulations of individuals for each of whom there is an X-score and a Y-score. The X-scores differ in magnitude from subpopulation to subpopulation but are of the same magnitude for all individual members of any given subpopulation. The Y-scores differ in magnitude from individual to individual within the same subpopulation. All the subpopulation Y-scores (1) are normally distributed, (2) are equally variable, and (3) have means falling on a straight line. This third condition may be stated symbolically as follows. Let $\mu_{y \cdot x}$ represent the Y-mean of a subpopulation. Then

$$\mu_{y \cdot x} = \beta x + \mu_Y \tag{19.3}$$

where β is the slope and μ_Y the intercept of the population regression line.

The sample experience pool is formed by selecting at random n_1 individuals from the first subpopulation, n_2 individuals from the second, and so on. The theoretical repetitions of this sampling procedure all involve the random selection of *these same numbers* of individuals from the same subpopulations. It follows that the overall X-score distributions are the same for all repetitions of the sampling routine. Only the Y-scores vary from sample to sample and, hence, only those statistical indexes (b and $\overline{Y}$) that involve Y-score values are subject to sampling error. This implies that any tests of statistical hypotheses, or any statistical estimates, based on a sample experience pool properly apply only to the total population composed of the particular k subpopulations from which the subsamples are presumed to have been selected.

It may appear that this method of sampling is not generally appropriate, because in most practical applications the individuals that make up a sample experience pool are selected as a simple random sample from the total population, thus making the X-characteristic as well as the Y-characteristic subject to random sampling fluctuation. Actually, however, in the prediction (regression) problem, our concern is with the estimation of subpopulation Y-means. If, as assumed, these means do lie on a straight line, the placement of this line is independent of the particular subpopulations involved. In fact, samples from any

---

[1] This condition is that previously imposed in connection with the use of the standard error of estimate as an index of the accuracy of the prediction process. (See Section 18.8; note particularly the definition on p. 483.)

two of them provide us with a basis for estimating the placement of the line. How the particular subpopulations to be studied are selected is, then, not a matter of practical concern. If the condition of linearity is met, they may be selected at random—as, in effect, is the case when individuals constituting the sample pool are selected at random from the total population.

19.2   The Sampling Distributions of b and $\overline{Y}$

In this section we shall simply present, without mathematical—or, for that matter, intuitive—justification, the descriptions of the theoretical sampling distributions of b and $\overline{Y}$ as they have been determined by mathematical statisticians. Students will be able to apply this theory in testing hypotheses and in making interval estimates even though they are not prepared to understand its mathematical basis.

Given: an infinity of sample experience pools selected from a set of subpopulations of the type described and in the manner described in the preceding section. Then:

> **RULE 19.1**   The sampling distribution of b is a normal distribution with mean β [see (19.3)] and variance

$$\sigma^2{}_b = \frac{\sigma^2_{y \cdot x}}{\sum x_i{}^2} \qquad (i = 1, 2, \dots, N) \tag{19.4}$$

> **RULE 19.1a**   The standard error of the sampling distribution of Rule 19.1 is

$$\sigma_b = \frac{\sigma_{y \cdot x}}{\sqrt{\sum x_i{}^2}} \tag{19.5}$$

The standard error of b may be estimated by using $\tilde{\sigma}_{y \cdot x}$ as given by (18.21) in place of $\sigma_{y \cdot x}$ in (19.5). That is,

$$\tilde{\sigma}_b = \frac{\tilde{\sigma}_{y \cdot x}}{\sqrt{\sum x_i{}^2}} \tag{19.6}$$

or[2]

$$\tilde{\sigma}_b = \frac{\sqrt{\dfrac{N}{N-2}} \; S_Y \sqrt{1 - r^2}}{\sqrt{\sum x_i{}^2}} \tag{19.6a}$$

[2] Of course, other formulas could be given for $\tilde{\sigma}_b$ that are functions of the X- and Y-scores directly. For example, if we incorporate instructions for finding $\tilde{\sigma}_{y \cdot x}$ as given by (18.19) and (18.23), we have

$$\tilde{\sigma}_b = \sqrt{\frac{(\sum x_i{}^2)(\sum y_i{}^2) - (\sum x_i y_i)^2}{(N-2)(\sum x_i{}^2)^2}}$$

For example, in the problem of the high school counselor (see Section 18.5) $\sum x_i^2 = 150.5$ (see Table 18.3) and $\tilde{\sigma}_{y \cdot x} \approx .5725$ (see p. 488). Hence, application of (19.6) gives

$$\tilde{\sigma}_b = \frac{.5725}{\sqrt{150.5}} \approx .047$$

The estimated standard error of the sampling distribution of b as given by (19.6) is appropriate for use in computing the t-statistic as defined by (15.1). That is, if β is the population value of the slope of the prediction (regression) line, then under the conditions noted above

$$t = \frac{b - \beta}{\tilde{\sigma}_b} \qquad (df = N - 2) \tag{19.7}$$

To see that the number of degrees of freedom for $\tilde{\sigma}_b$ and consequently for the t of (19.7) is $N - 2$, refer to (19.6). Note that $\tilde{\sigma}_b$ as given by (19.6) is a function of $\tilde{\sigma}_{y \cdot x}$, which in turn is based on the deviations of the N Y-scores from the sample prediction line. The measurement of these deviations, of course, required the determination of the slope b and intercept c of this line as auxiliary values derived from the observations. Hence, by the rule for determining df (see p. 340), we have $df = N - 2$.

Formula (19.7) is of considerable practical importance, since it indicates that t may be used as a test statistic in testing any specific hypothesis about the value of β, or in establishing an interval estimate of β. Before illustrating such applications of (19.7), we shall consider the sampling distribution of $\overline{Y}$.

Again we have given an infinity of sample experience pools selected from a set of subpopulations of the type described and in the manner described in Section 19.1. Then:

RULE 19.2   The sampling distribution of $\overline{Y}$ is a normal distribution with mean μ_Y [see (19.3)] and variance

$$\sigma_{\overline{Y}}^2 = \frac{\sigma_{y \cdot x}^2}{N} \tag{19.8}$$

RULE 19.2a   The standard error of the sampling distribution of Rule 19.2 is

$$\sigma_{\overline{Y}} = \frac{\sigma_{y \cdot x}}{\sqrt{N}} \tag{19.9}$$

The standard error of $\overline{Y}$ may be estimated by using $\tilde{\sigma}_{y \cdot x}$ as given by (18.21) in place of $\sigma_{y \cdot x}$ in (19.9). That is,

$$\tilde{\sigma}_{\overline{Y}} = \frac{\tilde{\sigma}_{y \cdot x}}{\sqrt{N}} \tag{19.10}$$

For example, using the data of the problem of the high school counselor we have

$$\tilde{\sigma}_{\bar{Y}} = \frac{.5725}{\sqrt{50}} \approx .081$$

As was true of the estimated standard error of b, this estimated standard error of $\bar{Y}$ has $N - 2$ degrees of freedom and is appropriate for use in computing the t-statistic as defined by (15.1). That is, if μ_Y is the population value of the Y-intercept of the prediction line, then

$$t = \frac{\bar{Y} - \mu_Y}{\tilde{\sigma}_{\bar{Y}}} \qquad (df = N - 2) \tag{19.11}$$

This t may be used in testing any hypothesis about the value of μ_Y, or in establishing an interval estimate of μ_Y.

19.3 Testing Hypotheses about β: An Example

We shall use the situation and data of the problem of the high school counselor to illustrate tests of statistical hypothesis about the value of β. This parameter is actually more important than μ_Y because of the effect of its magnitude on the accuracy of the prediction process. From (18.8) we see that

$$r = b \frac{S_X}{S_Y} \tag{19.12}$$

or, for the total population

$$\rho = \beta \frac{\sigma_X}{\sigma_Y} \tag{19.13}$$

That is, the population correlation, ρ (*rho*), is in part a function of the population slope, β. We have previously learned how the correlation coefficient may be interpreted as an index of the accuracy of the prediction process (see Section 18.7 and Figure 18.9), If β has the value zero, then ρ is zero, and information about X is of no assistance whatever in predicting the value of Y. Consequently, a test of the hypothesis that $\beta = 0$ is of considerable interest, for unless this hypothesis can be rejected the use of the prediction equation is completely fruitless.[3]

---

[3] The test of the hypothesis that $\beta = 0$ is often referred to as a test of the significance of b.

Hence, we shall show how the high school counselor would test the hypothesis that $\beta = 0$.

Step 1. $H_0: \beta = 0$; $H_1: \beta > 0$.

Comment: It is not plausible that the scholastic aptitude test could correlate negatively with college achievement. Consequently, β cannot be negative[4] and the counselor appropriately tests the hypothesis against the single alternative cited.

Step 2. $\alpha = .01$

Comment: The counselor reasons that it would be far more costly to misadvise on the basis of a worthless prediction equation (to make a Type I error) than not to use an equation capable of improving, to some extent at least, the soundness of her advice (to make a Type II error). Reasoning thus, she elects a small level of significance.

Step 3. $R: t \geq +2.42$

Comment: The counselor's experience pool contained 50 pairs of scores: $N = 50$. Hence, the number of degrees of freedom for the test statistic t involved is 48 (i.e., $N - 2$). Table IV, Appendix C, does not include data for the distribution of t for $df = 48$. We have previously intimated (see page 338) that when $df > 30$ the t-values may be interpreted as unit normal deviates (i.e., as z-values). In this example, however, we have had the counselor use the t-distribution for $df = 40$, that is, that tabled t-distribution having the largest df that is smaller than the actual df involved. This amounts to using a level of significance slightly smaller than .01.

Step 4. Calculation of t for data at hand.

We have already calculated (in Sections 18.5 and 19.2) the values we need for solving for t in (19.7):

$$b = +.284 \quad \text{and} \quad \tilde{\sigma}_b = .047$$

Therefore,

$$t = \frac{.284 - 0}{.047} = 6.04$$

Step 5. Reject. (Why?)

---

[4] The signs of ρ and β must be the same since σ_X and σ_Y are positive [see (19.13)].

Comment: Rejection of the hypothesis $\beta = 0$ implies acceptance of the only alternative $\beta > 0$. This means that some improvement in accuracy of prediction may be expected through use of the prediction equation.

19.4 Establishing Confidence Intervals for β and μ_Y

The formulas for the limits of the 100γ percent confidence interval for the population slope (regression coefficient) β can be written by application of (15.11). Here the T_1 is, of course, the particular value of the slope (b_1) for the sample at hand, and $\tilde{\sigma}_T$ is $\tilde{\sigma}_b$ as given by (19.6).[5]

$$\underline{\beta}_1, \bar{\beta}_1 = b_1 \mp t_{\gamma/2}\, \tilde{\sigma}_b \qquad (19.14)$$

where $df = N - 2$.

Example Using the data of the problem of the high school counselor (see Table 18.3), establish the 95 percent confidence interval for the slope, β, of the prediction line for the population involved.

Here $N = 50$ so that $df = 48$. As in the preceding sections we shall use the t-distribution for $df = 40$. Now $t_{\gamma/2} = t_{.475}$. Hence, we enter the t-table of Appendix C in the column headed $P = .500 - \gamma/2 = .025$. Here we find that for $df = 40$, $t = 2.02$. Since for the data at hand, $b_1 = +.284$ and $\tilde{\sigma}_b = .047$, application of (19.14) gives

$$\underline{\beta}_1, \bar{\beta}_1 = .284 \mp (2.02)(.047) = .189, .379$$

Then the confidence interval is

$$C(.189 \leq \beta \leq .379) = 95\%$$

Similarly, by application of (15.11), we can write formulas for the limits of the 100γ percent confidence interval for the population value, μ_Y, of the Y-intercept of the prediction line. Here the T_1 is the value of the Y-intercept ($\bar{Y}_1$) for the experience pool at hand, and $\tilde{\sigma}_T$ is $\tilde{\sigma}_{\bar{Y}}$ as

---

[5] To conserve space we have written the two formulas involved in one line by using the double minus or plus sign. The lower limit $\underline{\beta}$ is given by application of the formula with the minus sign and the upper limit $\bar{\beta}$ by application of the formula with the plus sign. This form will be used in writing all subsequent formulas for interval limits.

given by (19.10). Thus, we have

$$\mu_{Y_1}, \bar{\mu}_{Y_1} = \bar{Y}_1 \mp t_{\gamma/2}\,\tilde{\sigma}_{\bar{Y}} \qquad (19.15)$$

where $df = N - 2$.

Example Using the data of the problem of the high school counselor (see Table 18.3), establish the 95 percent confidence interval for the Y-intercept, μ_Y, of the prediction line for the population involved.

Here $\bar{Y}_1 = 2.248$ and $\tilde{\sigma}_{\bar{Y}} = .081$ (see p. 505). Hence, application of (19.15) gives

$$\mu_{Y_1}, \bar{\mu}_{Y_1} = 2.248 \mp (2.02)(.081) = 2.084, 2.412$$

The confidence interval we want is

$$C(2.084 \le \mu_Y \le 2.412) = 95\%$$

19.5   The Sampling Distribution of $\hat{Y}$

As indicated in (19.3), $\mu_{y \cdot x}$ is the symbol we have used to represent the mean Y-score for a subpopulation of individuals making the same X-score. Its estimator, $\hat{Y}$, is the point on the prediction line corresponding to the particular value of X involved. If this value of X is expressed as a deviation from $\bar{X}$, then (19.2) gives the estimated value of $\mu_{y \cdot x}$. That is,

$$\tilde{\mu}_{y \cdot x} = \hat{Y} = bx + \bar{Y} \qquad (x = X - \bar{X}) \qquad (19.16)$$

Now the variance of the sampling distribution of $\hat{Y}$ for a given value of x has been shown to be the sum of the variances of the bx and $\bar{Y}$ sampling distributions. Since we are concerned only with a particular subpopulation, the value of x is a constant. Hence, by (8.6) it follows that

$$\sigma_{bx}{}^2 = x^2\sigma_b{}^2$$

Therefore

$$\sigma_{\hat{Y}}{}^2 = x^2\sigma_b{}^2 + \sigma_{\bar{Y}}{}^2$$

It has also been shown that for the situation or model described in Section 19.1, the sampling distribution of $\hat{Y}$-values for a given subpopulation (i.e., for a given x) is a normal distribution with a mean corresponding to that of the subpopulation (i.e., $\mu_{y \cdot x}$). These facts are summarized in the following rule

> **RULE 19.3** Given an infinity of sample experience pools selected from a set of subpopulations of the type described and in the manner described in Section 19.1. Then for any particular subpopulation the sampling distribution of $\hat{Y}$ is a normal distribution with mean $\mu_{y \cdot x}$ and variance

$$\sigma_{\hat{y}}^2 = x^2 \sigma_b^2 + \sigma_{\bar{y}}^2 \tag{19.17}$$

> where $x = X - \bar{X}$, with X representing the particular X-score made by all members of this subpopulation.

> **RULE 19.3a** The standard error of the sampling distribution of Rule 19.3 is

$$\sigma_{\hat{y}} = \sqrt{x^2 \sigma_b^2 + \sigma_{\bar{y}}^2} \tag{19.18}$$

This standard error may be estimated by putting $\tilde{\sigma}_b$ as given by (19.6) and $\tilde{\sigma}_{\bar{y}}$ as given by (19.10) in place of σ_b and σ_Y. That is

$$\tilde{\sigma}_Y = \sqrt{x^2 \frac{\tilde{\sigma}_{y \cdot x}^2}{\sum x_i^2} + \frac{\tilde{\sigma}_{y \cdot x}^2}{N}}$$

or

$$\tilde{\sigma}_Y = \tilde{\sigma}_{y \cdot x} \sqrt{\frac{x^2}{\sum x_i^2} + \frac{1}{N}} \tag{19.19}$$

The estimated standard error of the sampling distribution of $\hat{Y}$ for a given x-value as given by (19.19) is appropriate for use in computing the t-statistic as defined by (15.1). This estimate, like $\tilde{\sigma}_b$ and $\tilde{\sigma}_{\bar{y}}$, is a function of $\tilde{\sigma}_{y \cdot x}$ and hence has $N - 2$ degrees of freedom [see remarks following (19.7)].

In most practical situations, no relevant hypothesis regarding $\mu_{y \cdot x}$ exists. Instead the principal concern is with the accuracy with which $\mu_{y \cdot x}$ is estimated. As will be shown in the following section, the foregoing sampling theory makes it possible to establish confidence intervals for the various subpopulation $\mu_{y \cdot x}$-values.

It is important to note that $\tilde{\sigma}_Y$ depends on the X-score made by the individuals of the subpopulation involved. This is reflected in (19.19) by the presence of the x-value. Inspection of (19.19) shows that $\tilde{\sigma}_Y$ is least for that subpopulation of individuals whose X-scores are at the X-mean, for in this special case $x = \bar{X} - \bar{X} = 0$, and $\tilde{\sigma}_Y$ takes the same value as $\tilde{\sigma}_{\bar{y}}$ [see (19.10)]. The farther the subpopulation X-score from $\bar{X}$, the larger the value of σ_Y. From this it follows that the use of the prediction line to estimate $\mu_{y \cdot x}$-values is much less accurate for extreme subpopulations than for subpopulations more centrally located with reference to the X-scale. In general, *it is not wise to use prediction lines to estimate $\mu_{y \cdot x}$-values for extreme subpopulations—particularly if these subpopulations are not well represented in the experience pool.*

19.6   Confidence Intervals for the $\mu_{y \cdot x}$-Values

Formulas for the limits of the 100γ percent confidence intervals for the values of the subpopulation Y-means can be written by application of (15.11). In this instance, T_1 is the particular value of the estimated subpopulation mean $(\hat{Y}_1)$ for the experience pool at hand, and $\tilde{\sigma}_T$ is $\tilde{\sigma}_Y$ as given by (19.19). Thus, we have

$$\mu_{y \cdot x_1}, \bar{\mu}_{y \cdot x_1} = \hat{Y}_1 \mp t_{\gamma/2}\tilde{\sigma}_{y \cdot x} \sqrt{\frac{x^2}{\sum x_i^2} + \frac{1}{N}} \qquad (19.20)$$

where $df = N - 2$.

Example Using the data of the problem of the high school counselor (see Table 18.3), establish the 95 percent confidence interval for the Y-mean $(\mu_{y \cdot x})$ of the subpopulation of individuals whose X-scores are 9.

Here $N = 50$ so that $df = 48$. However, as in preceding examples we shall use the t-distribution for $df = 40$. Since $t_{\gamma/2} = t_{.475}$ we enter the t-table of Appendix C in the column headed $P = .500 - \gamma/2 = .025$. Here we find that for $df = 40$, $t = 2.02$. Moreover, since $\bar{X} = 10.1$, we have for the data at hand

$$\hat{Y}_1 = (+.284)(9 - 10.1) + 2.248 = 1.936$$

Also $\sum x_i^2 = 150.5$ and $\tilde{\sigma}_{y \cdot x} = .5725$. Hence application of (19.20)

Table 19.1   Limits $\mu_{y \cdot x}$ and $\bar{\mu}_{y \cdot x}$ of the 95 Percent Confidence Intervals for the Y-Means of the Subpopulations in the High School Counselor's Experience Pool of Table 18.3

X	$\hat{Y}$	$\tilde{\sigma}_Y$	$\mu_{y \cdot x}$	$\bar{\mu}_{y \cdot x}$
7	1.368	.166	1.033	1.703
8	1.652	.127	1.395	1.909
9	1.936	.096	1.742	2.130
10	2.220	.081+	2.056	2.384
$10.1 = \bar{X}$	$2.248 = \bar{Y}$	$.081- = \tilde{\sigma}_{\bar{y}}$	2.084	2.412
11	2.504	.091	2.320	2.688
12	2.788	.120	2.546	3.030
13	3.072	.158	2.753	3.391
14	3.356	.199	2.954	3.758

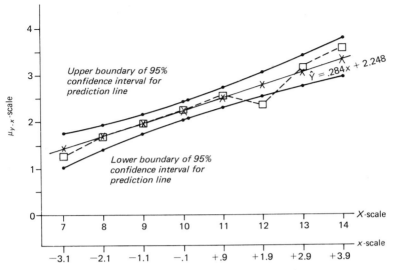

Figure 19.1 Boundaries of 95 percent confidence interval for the prediction line of the problem of the high school counselor

gives

$$\mu_{y \cdot x_1}, \bar{\mu}_{y \cdot x_1} = 1.936 \mp 2.02 \left(.5725 \sqrt{\frac{(9 - 10.1)^2}{150.5} + \frac{1}{50}}\right)$$

$$= 1.936 \mp (2.02)(.096) = 1.742, 2.130$$

The confidence interval we are looking for is

$$C(1.742 \le \mu_{y \cdot x} \le 2.130) = 95\%$$

Table 19.1 gives the limits of the 95 percent confidence intervals for the Y-means of all the subpopulations represented in the high school counselor's experience pool, that is, for X-values of 7, 8, 9, 10, 11, 12, 13, and 14. Also included are the values for $\mu_{y \cdot x_1}$ and $\bar{\mu}_{y \cdot x_1}$ for the hypothetical subpopulation of individuals whose X-scores have the value 10.1.[6] These values are identical with those previously determined for μ_{Y_1} and $\bar{\mu}_{Y_1}$. This follows from the fact that when $X = 10.1$, $x = 0$, and in this situation $\hat{Y} = \bar{Y}$ [see (19.2)] and $\tilde{\sigma}_Y = \tilde{\sigma}_{\bar{Y}}$ [compare (19.19) and (19.10)].

Figure 19.1 shows a plot of the subsample Y-means (represented by squares), the prediction line ($\hat{Y} = .284x + 2.248$), the estimated sub-

[6] Hypothetical in the sense that, although the X-trait is assumed to be continuous, the X-scores are integers—i.e., consist of measurements reported to the nearest whole number.

population Y-means (i.e., $\hat{Y}$-values, represented by crosses), and the values for $\mu_{y \cdot x}$ and $\bar{\mu}_{y \cdot x}$ (represented by dots) given in Table 19.1. These latter points (dots) have been connected by two curved lines, which may be interpreted as the boundaries of the 95 percent confidence interval for the entire population prediction line.

19.7   Confidence Intervals for Individual Predictions

Prediction or regression equations provide values that are estimates of subpopulation means. But usually we are not particularly interested in interpreting these values as estimates of subpopulation means. Rather, we interpret them as estimates or predictions of individual status. As has been previously explained (see Section 18.7), the accuracy of individual estimates depends not only on the accuracy with which the subpopulation mean is estimated but also on where within the subpopulation the individual's actual Y-score happens to fall.

Suppose that for each of an infinity of sample experience pools of the type described in Section 19.1 we determine a prediction equation. Suppose further that in each instance we use the equation determined to predict a Y-score for an individual selected at random from a particular subpopulation. The differences between the actual and predicted Y-scores (the $Y - \hat{Y}$ values) may be thought of as constituting a distribution of errors of individual estimates. The variability of this distribution of errors depends on (1) the variation in the placement of the prediction line itself, and (2) the variation of the actual Y-scores for the particular subpopulation. We have already learned that the magnitude of the first source of variation is indicated by $\sigma_{\hat{Y}}^2$ [see (19.17)]. The corresponding index for the second source of variation is simply $\sigma_{y \cdot x}^2$, that is, the variance of the Y-scores for the particular subpopulation. It has been shown that the variance of the distribution of errors of individual estimates is simply the sum of these two variances.

$$
\begin{aligned}
\sigma_e^2 &= \sigma_Y^2 + \sigma_{y \cdot x}^2 \\
&= x^2 \sigma_b^2 + \sigma_{\bar{Y}}^2 + \sigma_{y \cdot x}^2 \qquad \text{[see (19.17)]} \\
&= \frac{x^2 \sigma_{y \cdot x}^2}{\sum x_i^2} + \frac{\sigma_{y \cdot x}^2}{N} + \sigma_{y \cdot x}^2 \qquad \text{[see (19.4) and (19.8)]}
\end{aligned}
$$

Hence,

$$
\sigma_e^2 = \sigma_{y \cdot x}^2 \left(\frac{x^2}{\sum x_i^2} + \frac{1}{N} + 1 \right) \tag{19.21}
$$

Or in terms of standard error

$$
\sigma_e = \sigma_{y \cdot x} \sqrt{ \frac{x^2}{\sum x_i^2} + \frac{1}{N} + 1 } \tag{19.22}
$$

It will be observed that this standard error, like that of $\hat{Y}$ (i.e., like that of the line itself), depends on x. This is to say that the error distribution associated with one subpopulation differs in variability from that associated with another. As was true of the $\hat{Y}$ sampling distributions, those error distributions associated with subpopulations that are centrally located with regard to X are less variable than those associated with subpopulations that are farther removed from the X-mean.

It is also known that for the model under consideration (i.e., for the situation described in Section 19.1), these error distributions are normal distributions with means of zero. Their standard errors may be estimated by using $\tilde{\sigma}_{y \cdot x}$ as given by (18.21) in place of $\sigma_{y \cdot x}$ in (19.22). This estimated standard error, being, like those previously considered, a function of $\tilde{\sigma}_{y \cdot x}$, has $N - 2$ degrees of freedom and is appropriate for use in computing the t-statistic as defined in (15.1).

The formula for the estimated standard error of the error distribution, associated with the subpopulation of individuals whose X-scores expressed as deviations from the X-mean are represented by x, is

$$\tilde{\sigma}_e = \tilde{\sigma}_{y \cdot x} \sqrt{\frac{x^2}{\sum x_i^2} + \frac{1}{N} + 1} \qquad (19.23)$$

We can now use the t-distribution for $N - 2$ degrees of freedom to establish the error that would be exceeded regardless of direction $100(1 - \gamma)$ percent of the time in the long run. Let e represent the error. Then

$$t = \frac{e - \mu_e}{\tilde{\sigma}_e} = \frac{e - 0}{\tilde{\sigma}_e} = \frac{e}{\tilde{\sigma}_e} \qquad (df = N - 2)$$

Hence,

$$e = t\tilde{\sigma}_e \qquad (df = N - 2)$$

and the error that will be exceeded $100(1 - \gamma)$ percent of the time regardless of direction in the long run is

$$e_{1 - \gamma} = t_{\gamma/2}\tilde{\sigma}_e \qquad (df = N - 2) \qquad (19.24)$$

It is now possible to establish the limits of the 100γ percent confidence interval for a prediction or regression estimate interpreted as an estimate of an individual score. Let Υ represent the actual value of the Y-score of an individual selected at random from the subpopulation involved. Then the limits of the 100γ percent confidence interval for Υ are given by

$$\underline{\Upsilon}_1, \overline{\Upsilon}_1 = \hat{Y}_1 \mp t_{\gamma/2}\tilde{\sigma}_e \qquad (19.25)$$

where $df = N - 2$ and $\tilde{\sigma}_e$ is as given by (19.23).

Example Using the data of the high school counselor's experience pool, establish the 95 percent confidence interval for the Y-score (Υ) of an individual whose X-score is 9.

Here $N = 50$ so that $df = 48$. However, as in preceding examples, we shall use the t-distribution for $df = 40$. Since $t_{\gamma/2} = t_{.475}$, we enter the t-table of Appendix C in the column headed $P = .500 - \gamma/2 = .025$. Here we find that for $df = 40$, $t = 2.02$. Since $\overline{X} = 10.1$, we have for the data at hand

$$\hat{Y}_1 = (+.284)(9 - 10.1) + 2.248 = 1.936$$

Also for the data at hand

$$\tilde{\sigma}_e = (.5725)\sqrt{\frac{(9 - 10.1)^2}{150.5} + \frac{1}{50} + 1} = .580 \qquad [\text{see } (19.23)]$$

Hence, application of (19.25) gives

$$\underline{\Upsilon}_1, \overline{\Upsilon}_1 = 1.936 \mp (2.02)(.580) = .764, 3.11$$

And the confidence interval is

$$C(.764 \leq \Upsilon \leq 3.11) = 95\%$$

Comment: This result will undoubtedly give rise to some amusement on the part of the discerning student. For an individual whose aptitude (X) score is somewhat below average $[(9 - 10.1)/1.73 \approx -.64$ standard deviations], we have, using a confidence coefficient of .95, predicted a freshman-year grade-point average anywhere from roughly .8 (less than a D average) to 3.1 (slightly better than a B average). Such a prediction scarcely seems specific enough to be of much value. This result further emphasizes the importance of basing predictions not only on large experience pools but also, and what is more important, on information about a variable that is closely related to the variable to be predicted. The closer this relationship, the greater the reduction in $\tilde{\sigma}_{y \cdot x}$ and also in $\tilde{\sigma}_e$; and the smaller $\tilde{\sigma}_e$, the narrower the confidence interval—that is, the more accurate the prediction of the individual Y-score. While predictions based on low relationships ought always to be avoided if possible, the fact remains that, if they cannot be avoided, it is better to take knowledge of the predictor variable into account than not to consider it at all.

Of course, if we are willing to use a smaller confidence coefficient, the interval may be narrowed. It is not uncommon in making individual predictions to determine the error that would be exceeded 50 percent of the time in the long run.[7] This amounts to using $\gamma = .5$. That is, the long-run probability that intervals determined by using (19.25) with $\gamma/2 = .25$ will contain the actual individual Y-score is .5. In our example, the value of t for $\gamma/2 = .25$ is .68. Hence, the limits of the 50 percent confidence interval would be

$$\underline{Y}_1, \overline{Y}_1 = 1.936 + (.68)(.581) = 1.541, 2.331$$

And the confidence interval would be

$$C(1.541 \leq Y \leq 2.331) = 50\%$$

19.8   Testing the Hypothesis $\rho = 0$ Using a t-Statistic

You may recall that a procedure for testing the hypothesis that $\rho = 0$ was developed in Section 17.15. At that point, we assumed a bivariate normal distribution and used a test statistic based on Fisher's z-transformation of r.

In Section 19.3 we developed a procedure for testing the hypothesis that $\beta = 0$. This procedure assumed the regression model described in Section 19.1 and used a test statistic that followed a t-distribution with $N - 2$ degrees of freedom. Also, in Section 19.3 we noted the following relationship [see (19.13)]:

$$\rho = \beta \frac{\sigma_X}{\sigma_Y}$$

It should be clear from this equation that testing the hypothesis that $\beta = 0$ is the equivalent of testing the hypothesis that $\rho = 0$.[8] If β is assumed to be zero, then (19.7) is simply

$$t = \frac{b}{\tilde{\sigma}_b} \qquad (df = N - 2) \tag{19.26}$$

If the experimental situation is primarily concerned with relationships and not predictions, it is useful to put (19.26) in a more convenient form involving the statistic r rather than the statistic b. This form is

$$t(df = N - 2) = \frac{r}{\sqrt{1 - r^2}} \sqrt{N - 2} \tag{19.27}$$

---

[7] This error is referred to as the *probable error*.

[8] This is true since both σ_X and σ_Y are assumed to be greater than zero. Otherwise, the prediction problem is trivial.

Proof * We begin with equation (19.26):

$$t = \frac{b}{\tilde{\sigma}_b}$$

But

$$b = r\frac{S_Y}{S_X} \qquad\qquad [\text{see } (18.8)]$$

and

$$\tilde{\sigma}_b = \frac{\tilde{\sigma}_{y \cdot x}}{\sqrt{\sum x_i^2}} = \frac{\tilde{\sigma}_{y \cdot x}}{S_X\sqrt{N}} \qquad\qquad [\text{see } (19.6) \text{ and } (7.5)]$$

However,

$$\tilde{\sigma}_{y \cdot x} = \sqrt{\frac{N}{N-2}}\, S_{y \cdot x} \qquad\qquad [\text{see } (18.28)]$$

$$= \sqrt{\frac{N}{N-2}}\, S_Y\sqrt{1 - r^2} \qquad\qquad [\text{see } (18.26)]$$

Hence,

$$\tilde{\sigma}_b = \frac{\sqrt{\dfrac{N}{N-2}}\, S_Y\sqrt{1 - r^2}}{S_X\sqrt{N}} = \frac{S_Y}{S_X} \cdot \frac{\sqrt{1 - r^2}}{\sqrt{N-2}}$$

Therefore,

$$t = \frac{r\dfrac{S_Y}{S_X}}{\dfrac{S_Y}{S_X} \cdot \dfrac{\sqrt{1 - r^2}}{\sqrt{N-2}}} = \frac{r}{\dfrac{\sqrt{1 - r^2}}{\sqrt{N-2}}}$$

or

$$t = \frac{r}{\sqrt{1 - r^2}}\sqrt{N-2}$$

for $df = N - 2$. This ends the proof.

Formula (19.27) is clearly more convenient for testing the hypothesis $\rho = 0$ in studies of relationship not involving prediction, for in such studies r rather than b is the more useful statistic.

* Optional.

To illustrate the use of this statistic to test $H_0: \rho = 0$, we shall use the example given in Section 17.15. In that section we gave the following information:

X = personality measure
Y = reading achievement
N = 103 (junior high school girls)
r = .25

The statistical procedure that the researcher could have used to test $H_0: \rho = 0$ using a t-statistic is outlined below

Step 1. $H_0: \rho = 0$; $H_1: \rho > 0$; $H_2: \rho < 0$

Comment: As before, we have assumed that the actual value of the population correlation may be either positive or negative.

Step 2. $\alpha = .05$

Comment: This simply represents an arbitrary selection for illustrative purposes.

Step 3. $R: t \geq 1.99$ and $t \leq -1.99$

Comment: Table IV does not contain the appropriate *df*-value for this experiment $(df = N - 2 = 103 - 2 = 101)$. However, the t-value for $df = 60$ is 2.00, and the appropriate t-value for $df = 120$ is 1.98. Thus, 1.99 is a reasonable estimate of an appropriate t-value for $df = 101$. In Section 17.15, the critical region was established on the z-scale ($z \geq 1.96$ and $z \leq -1.96$).

Step 4. Calculation of the particular t for the observed data.

$$t = \frac{r}{\sqrt{1 - r^2}} \sqrt{N - 2} \qquad (df = N - 2)$$

$$= \frac{.25}{\sqrt{1 - .25^2}} \sqrt{101}$$

$$\approx 2.59$$

Comment: For the same data, the z-statistic computed in Section 17.15 was 2.55.

Step 5. Decision: Reject H_0. (Why?)

Comment: As the above example indicates, the two procedures for testing $H_0: \rho = 0$ lead to very similar results. Even though the two procedures were derived under the different conditions of the normal bivariate model and the regression model, from a practical viewpoint there is little difference in the outcome. However, it should be remembered that the procedure developed in this section is valid only for testing $H_0: \rho = 0$, whereas the procedure developed in Section 17.15 was valid for any hypothesized value of ρ.

19.9   Summary Statement

In this chapter we presented the regression model for one dependent variable ("predicted" variable) and one independent variable (predictor variable). We also examined the most frequently used inferential procedures for this situation.

It is not uncommon to find research studies in which an investigator has used scores on two or more variables to predict the scores on a criterion variable. Such a situation would have occurred, for example, in the problem of the high school counselor (Section 18.5) had the counselor used both scores on the college aptitude test and high school grade-point averages to predict college grade-point averages. While we did not examine such multiple prediction (or multiple regression) situations, the basic concepts developed in this chapter should provide an excellent foundation for a study of the more complicated procedures associated with the multiple prediction problem.

Appendix A
Glossary of Symbols

Symbols that are unique to the discussion in which they are used and defined are not included in this glossary. The numbers in parentheses following the definition indicate the page on which the symbol is first used.

The glossary is divided into three parts: (1) nonalphabetical symbols, (2) English-letter symbols, and (3) Greek-letter symbols. The symbols in part 1 are arranged alphabetically according to the name of the symbol. The symbols in parts 2 and 3 are arranged alphabetically according to the particular alphabet involved.

1. Nonalphabetical Symbols

$\approx$	"Is approximately equal to." (85)
$\wedge$	"Caret." The caret, placed above the symbol representing a score, represents an estimate of that score. If the score is represented by Y, then $\hat{Y}$ represents an estimate of its value. (471)
$>$, $<$	"Greater than" and "less than" signs. Used to indicate that one quantity is greater than (or less than) another: $a > b$ indicates that the quantity represented by a is greater than the quantity represented by b, and $a < b$ indicates that the quantity represented by a is less than the quantity represented by b. (147)
$\geq$, $\leq$	"Greater than or equal to" and "less than or equal to" signs. A combination of the "greater than" sign ($>$) or "less than" sign ($<$) with the "equals" sign ($=$). $a \geq b$ indicates that the quantity represented by a is either greater than or equal to the quantity represented by b. (150)

∞	"Infinity." (181)
$\mp$	"Minus and plus sign" indicating both the difference and sum of two quantities: $a \mp b$ indicates both $a - b$ and $a + b$. (330)
$\sqrt{}$	"Square root" sign. $\sqrt{a}$ indicates the square root of the quantity represented by a. (112)
$\sim$	"Tilde." The tilde, placed above the symbol representing a population parameter, indicates an *estimate* of this parameter. If a population standard deviation is represented by σ, then $\tilde{\sigma}$ represents an estimate of its value. (236)

2. English-Letter Symbols

A	Value of an arbitrary reference point on a score scale. (95)
a, b	Magnitudes of constants. (78)
a, b	Parameters of a beta distribution, $\beta(a, b)$. (393)
b	Slope of a linear prediction (or regression) equation for a real collection of data. (471)
A, B	Designate events in a probability statement. (382)
BD	Binomial distribution. (200)
BPD	Binomial probability distribution. (172)
c	Number of classes in a frequency distribution. Also, magnitude of a constant. (71, 128)
c	Y-intercept of a linear prediction (or regression) equation for a real collection of data. (471)
C	Magnitude of a constant. Also, indicates confidence interval. (75, 326)
c and d	Distances that, marked off below and above the population parameter on the scale of values of the statistic, establish an interval such that the probability of the statistic in this interval is some arbitrarily selected value. (321)
$C\% \ HDR$	A C percent highest density region credibility interval. (397)
cf	Cumulative frequency of a class in a frequency distribution. (53)
C_1, C_2, etc.	First centile, second centile, etc. (52)
$Cov(XY)$	Covariance of X- and Y-scores. (440)
D	Magnitude of a constant. (444)
D	Difference between a pair of scores. (285)
$\bar{D}$	Mean of a real collection of differences between pairs of scores. (307)

df	Number of degrees of freedom of a statistic. (337)
D_1, D_2, etc.	First decile, second decile, etc. (52)
e	Limiting value of $(1 + x)^{1/x}$ as x approaches zero. Approximately 2.7183. Used as the base in the natural system of logarithms. (182)
e	Difference between an individual's actual Y-score and predicted (regressed) Y-score; that is, the error in a predicted score. (484)
E	Event. (148)
EA	Extreme area. The probability of a value of a statistic being equal to or greater than a particular observed value if the hypothesis is true. (303)
$E(X)$	Expected value of a score (X) selected at random from a collection of scores. (159)
f	Magnitude of a class (interval) frequency in a frequency distribution. (21)
f_X, f_Y	Frequency of a column (f_X) or row (f_Y) in a bivariate frequency table. (422)
G	Sum of squares of the deviations of a given collection of points from the least-squares line of best fit. The deviations involved are measured along the Y-scale (axis). (471)
H_0	A statistical hypothesis to be tested. (245)
H_1, H_2	Alternative hypotheses. (245)
i	Used as a subscript to designate individuals in a collection. (69)
j	Used as a subscript to designate classes in a frequency distribution. (71)
$\log_e N$	Natural logarithm (base e) of the number represented by N. (455)
M	Overall mean of a real collection of scores made up of a number of subcollections (subgroups). (92)
m	Sample size equivalence of prior information in a Bayesian analysis. (400)
M_Z	Mean of a linearly transformed collection of scores; the standard value adopted as the mean of a system of standard scores. (138)
MD	Mean deviation. (109)
Mdn	Median. (52)
Mo	Mode. (87)
M_Y	Mean of a complete real collection of predicted (regressed) scores. (477)
$\mathcal{N}$	Represents a "large" number of repetitions in a Monte Carlo experiment. (153)
N	Number of scores in a collection. (42)

n	Number of trials in a binomial experiment. (164)
n	Number of scores in a subgroup. (92)
ND	Normal distribution. (192)
NPD	Normal probability distribution. (180)
p	Magnitude of a relative frequency. (74)
p	Proportion of objects of a certain type in a collection. (167)
P	Power of a test of a statistical hypothesis. (268)
P_x	The xth percentile: P_5 = the fifth percentile. (51)
PD	Probability distribution. (156)
PR	Percentile rank. (51)
$P(s_j)$	Probability of sample point j. (149)
$P(A \mid B)$	Probability of event A given that event B has occurred. (384)
Q	Semi-interquartile range. (107)
Q_1, Q_2, Q_3	First, second, and third quartiles, respectively. (52)
r	Number of A types in n trials of a binomial experiment. (165)
r, r_{XY}	Product-moment correlation coefficient for a real collection of pairs of scores, i.e., pairs of X- and Y-values. (426)
R	Range of a collection of scores—the difference between the least and greatest score values. (106)
R	Critical region or region of rejection used in testing a statistical hypothesis. (249)
R	Affixed as a subscript to the symbol for a statistic to represent a boundary point of a critical region. (249)
rcf	Relative cumulative frequency of a class in a frequency distribution. (54)
$rcf(\%)$	Relative cumulative frequency expressed as a percent. (54)
rf	Relative frequency of a class in a frequency distribution. (41)
s_j	Sample point j. (149)
S, S^2	Standard deviation (S) and variance (S^2) of a real collection of scores. (111)
$S_Y, S_Y{}^2$	Standard deviation (S_Y) and variance $(S_Y{}^2)$ of a real collection of predicted (regressed) scores. (478)
$S_{\hat{y} \cdot x}, S_{\hat{y} \cdot x}^2$	Standard error of estimate $(S_{y \cdot x})$ for a real collection of predicted (regressed) scores and the corresponding variance $(S_{y \cdot x}^2)$. (487)
S_Z	Standard deviation of a linearly transformed collection of scores; the standard value adopted as the standard deviation of a system of standard scores. (138)

$\mathscr{S}$	Sample space. (147)
ss_{reg}	Sum of squares of deviations of predicted (regressed) Y-values from the overall mean of the actual Y-values. (497)
ss_{res}	Sum of squares of deviations of actual Y-values from predicted (regressed) Y-values. (498)
ss_T	Sum of squares of deviations of actual Y-values from the overall mean of these values. (497)
t	A test statistic the sampling distribution of which is "Student's" distribution. (337)
T	Any statistic. (215)
$t_{\gamma/2}$	A distance on the scale of the t-distribution which, if marked off in one direction from center (zero), establishes a segment of the t-scale such that the probability of a t-value in this segment is one-half of an arbitrarily selected probability value represented by γ. (361)
X	Random variable. (159)
X, Y	Magnitude of a raw score. Also the value of a class (interval) midpoint in a frequency distribution. (21)
$x, X - \overline{X}$	Algebraic (signed) deviation of a score from the mean ($\overline{X}$) of the collection to which it belongs. (93)
$\lvert x \rvert, \lvert X - \overline{X} \rvert$	Absolute value of the deviation of a score from the mean of the collection to which it belongs. (109)
$\overline{X}, \overline{Y}$	Mean of a real collection of scores that are represented by X (or Y). (88)
y	Ordinate of the normal curve in standard-score (z) form. (184)
Y	Ordinate of a normal curve. Also, a linear transformation. (181, 128)
$\hat{y}$	Deviation of a predicted (regressed) score from the overall mean of the actual scores for a real collection of data. (476)
$\hat{Y}$	Predicted (regressed) score. Actually an estimate of a subpopulation mean obtained by use of the least-squares line of best fit. (471)
z	Standard score derived from a raw score by a linear transformation that fixes zero and unity as the mean and standard deviation of the transformed collection. (137)
z	Used to designate a normally distributed variate having mean and variance of zero and unity. (184)
Z	Standard score derived from a raw score by a linear transformation that fixes M_Z ($M \neq 0$) and S_Z ($S \neq 1$) as the mean and standard deviation of the transformed

collection (M and S are arbitrarily selected standard values other than zero and unity). (138)

$z_{\gamma/2}$ A distance on the scale of the unit normal distribution (i.e., mean $= 0$, variance $= 1$) which, if marked off in one direction from center (zero), establishes a segment of the scale such that the probability of z in this segment is one-half of an arbitrarily selected probability value represented by γ. (324)

z_r Fisher logarithmic transformation of a product-moment correlation coefficient for a sample from a normal bivariate population. (455)

z_ρ Fisher logarithmic transformation of the product-moment correlation coefficient for a normal bivariate population. (455)

$\hat{z}_Y$ Predicted (regressed) score when the given pairs of score values are expressed in standard form (i.e., as z-scores). (477)

3. Greek-Letter Symbols

α (Lower-case *alpha*) Level of significance used in testing a statistical hypothesis. (245)

β (Lower-case *beta*) Probability of a Type II error in testing a statistical hypothesis. (263)

β Slope of the population prediction (regression) line. (502)

$\beta(a, b)$ A beta distribution with parameters a and b. (393)

$\beta(a, b)$ The constant in a beta distribution. (393)

γ (Lower-case *gamma*) Confidence coefficient associated with an interval estimate. The proportion of intervals that contain the parameter in the theoretical universe of such intervals. (320)

Δ (Upper-case *delta*) Difference between the means of two populations. (331)

θ_0 (Lower-case *theta*) A specific value hypothesized for the parameter θ. E.g., μ_0 is a value hypothesized for the population mean μ. (264)

$\underline{\theta}_1, \bar{\theta}_1$ Lower and upper limits of an interval estimate of the population parameter represented by θ. E.g., $\underline{\mu}_1, \bar{\mu}_1$ represent the limits of an interval estimate of the population mean μ. (321)

μ (Lower-case *mu*) Mean of a population or of a hypothetical collection of scores. (88)

μ_D	Mean of a population of differences between pairs of scores. (285)
μ_D	Difference between the means of two populations. (308)
μ_e	Mean of the error distribution of predicted (regressed) scores for a given X-value. (513)
μ_Y	Overall Y-mean for all subpopulations in a regression situation. (502)
$\mu_{y \cdot x}$	Mean of Y-scores for a subpopulation of individuals making the same X-score. (502)
ξ	(Lower-case *xi*) Median of a population. (232)
π	(Lower-case *pi*) Ratio of the circumference of a circle to its diameter; approximately 3.1416. (182)
ρ	(Lower-case *rho*) Product-moment correlation coefficient for a population. (454)
σ, σ^2	(Lower-case *sigma*) Standard deviation (σ) and variance (σ^2) of a probability distribution or a population of scores. (161)
$\sigma_b, \sigma_b{}^2$	Standard error (σ_b) and variance ($\sigma_b{}^2$) of the sampling distribution of the slope of a prediction (regression) line. (503)
$\sigma_D, \sigma_D{}^2$	Standard deviation (σ_D) and variance ($\sigma_D{}^2$) of a population of differences between pairs of scores. (286)
$\sigma_e, \sigma_e{}^2$	Standard error (σ_e) and variance ($\sigma_e{}^2$) of the error distribution of predicted (regressed) scores for a given X-value. (512)
$\sigma_{Mdn}, \sigma^2_{Mdn}$	Standard error (σ_{Mdn}) and variance (σ^2_{Mdn}) of the sampling distribution of the median. (232)
$\sigma_p, \sigma_p{}^2$	Standard error (σ_p) and variance ($\sigma_p{}^2$) of the sampling distribution of a proportion. (230)
$\sigma_{p_1-p_2}, \sigma^2_{p_1-p_2}$	Standard error ($\sigma_{p_1-p_2}$) and variance ($\sigma^2_{p_1-p_2}$) of the sampling distribution of differences between two proportions. (289)
$\sigma_{\overline{X}}, \sigma_{\overline{X}}{}^2$	Standard error ($\sigma_{\overline{X}}$) and variance ($\sigma_{\overline{X}}{}^2$) of the sampling distribution of the mean. (225)
$\sigma_{\overline{X}_1-\overline{X}_2}, \sigma^2_{\overline{X}_1-\overline{X}_2}$	Standard error ($\sigma_{\overline{X}_1-\overline{X}_2}$) and variance ($\sigma^2_{\overline{X}_1-\overline{X}_2}$) of the sampling distribution of differences between two means. (288)
$\sigma_{\overline{Y}}, \sigma_{\overline{Y}}{}^2$	Standard error ($\sigma_{\overline{Y}}$) and variance ($\sigma_{\overline{Y}}{}^2$) of the sampling distribution of the overall Y-mean for all subpopulations in a prediction (regression) situation. (504)
$\sigma_Y, \sigma_Y{}^2$	Standard error (σ_Y) and variance ($\sigma_Y{}^2$) of the sampling distribution of a predicted (regressed) subpopulation mean. (509)

$\sigma_{y \cdot x},\ \sigma_{y \cdot x}^2$ Standard deviation $(\sigma_{y \cdot x})$ and variance $(\sigma_{y \cdot x}^2)$ of Y-scores for a subpopulation of individuals making the same X-score. $\sigma_{y \cdot x}$ is the population value of the standard error of estimate. (483)

$\sigma_{z_r},\ \sigma_{z_r}^2$ Standard error (σ_{z_r}) and variance $(\sigma_{z_r}^2)$ of the sampling distribution of the Fisher logarithmic transformation of the product-moment correlation coefficient for samples from a normal bivariate population. (455)

Σ (Upper-case *sigma*) Summation sign. Indicates "the sum of." (69)

Υ (Upper-case *upsilon*) Actual or true value of the dependent variable (Y) for a given individual in a prediction (regression) situation. (513)

ϕ (Lower-case *phi*) Proportion of objects or individuals of a certain type on a population. (165)

Appendix B
Selected Formulas and Rules

Page	Formula	Number
71	$\sum f_j = N$	(5.10)
74	$p_j = f_j/N$	(5.17)
75	$\sum f_j X_j = N \sum p_j X_j$	(5.19)
75	$\sum f_j X_j^2 = N \sum p_j X_j^2$	(5.20)
75	$\sum CX_i = C \sum X_i$	(5.21)
76	$\sum (X_i + Y_i - Z_i) = \sum X_i + \sum Y_i - \sum Z_i$	(5.22)
78	$\sum C = NC$	(5.23)
84	$Mdn = L_{50} + \dfrac{.5N - cf_{L_{50}}}{f_{50}} (U_{50} - L_{50})$	(6.1)
88	$\overline{X} = \dfrac{\sum X_i}{N}$	(6.2)
89	$\sum X_i = N\overline{X}$	(6.2a)
90	$\overline{X} = \dfrac{\sum f_j X_j}{N}$	(6.3)
91	$\overline{X} = \sum p_j X_j$	(6.3a)
92	$M = \dfrac{n_1 \overline{X}_1 + n_2 \overline{X}_2}{n_1 + n_2}$	(6.4)
93	$\sum (X_i - \overline{X}) = \sum x_i = 0$	(6.5),(6.7)
95	$\sum |X_i - A|$ is least when $A = Mdn$	(6.8)

527

Page	Formula	Number
106	$R = H - L$	(7.1)
107	$Q = \dfrac{Q_3 - Q_1}{2}$	(7.2)
109	$MD = \dfrac{\sum \lvert x_i \rvert}{N}, \qquad \lvert x_i \rvert = \lvert X_i - \bar{X} \rvert$	(7.3)
111	$S^2 = \dfrac{\sum x_i^2}{N}, \qquad x_i = X_i - \bar{X}$	(7.4)
112	$S = \sqrt{\dfrac{\sum x_i^2}{N}}, \qquad x_i = X_i - \bar{X}$	(7.5)
113	$\sum x_i^2 = \sum X_i^2 - \dfrac{(\sum X_i)^2}{N}, \qquad x_i = X_i - \bar{X}$	(7.6)
116	$S^2 = \dfrac{\sum X_i^2}{N} - \left(\dfrac{\sum X_i}{N}\right)^2 = \dfrac{\sum X_i^2}{N} - \bar{X}^2$	(7.7), (7.8)
117	$S^2 = \dfrac{\sum f_j X_j^2}{N} - \left(\dfrac{\sum f_j X_j}{N}\right)^2 = \dfrac{\sum f_j X_j^2}{N} - \bar{X}^2$	(7.9), (7.10)
118	$S^2 = \sum p_j X_j^2 - (\sum p_j X_j)^2$	(7.9a)
130	$M_{X+c} = \bar{X} + c$	(8.2)
131	$S_{X+c}^2 = S_X^2$	(8.3)
133	$M_{bX} = b\bar{X}$	(8.5)
134	$S_{bX}^2 = b^2 S_X^2$	(8.6)
136	$M_{bX+c} = b\bar{X} + c$	(8.8)
136	$S_{bX+c}^2 = b^2 S_X^2$	(8.9)
137	$z_i = \dfrac{X_i - \bar{X}}{S_X}$	(8.13)
138	$Z_i = S_Z z_i + M_Z$	(8.14)
165	$P(r \mid n, \phi) = \dbinom{n}{r} \phi^r (1 - \phi)^{n-r}$	(9.1)
181	$Y = \dfrac{1}{\sigma\sqrt{2\pi}}\, e^{-(X-\mu)^2/2\sigma^2}$	(10.1)
184	$y = \dfrac{1}{\sqrt{2\pi}}\, e^{-z^2/2}$	(10.2)

Page	Formula	Number
190	$z = \dfrac{X - \mu}{\sigma}$	(10.3)
190	$X = \sigma z + \mu$	(10.4)
191	$Y = \dfrac{y}{\sigma}$	(10.5)
215	$E = T - \theta$	(11.1)
225	$\sigma_{\overline{X}}^2 = \dfrac{\sigma^2}{N}$	(11.2)
225	$\sigma_{\overline{X}} = \dfrac{\sigma}{\sqrt{N}}$	(11.3)
230	$\sigma_p^2 = \dfrac{\phi(1 - \phi)}{N}$	(11.5)
230	$\sigma_p = \sqrt{\dfrac{\phi(1 - \phi)}{N}}$	(11.6)
232	$\sigma_{Mdn} \approx 1.25 \sigma_{\overline{X}}$ (for ND population only)	(11.9)
235	$E(S^2) = \dfrac{N - 1}{N}\, \sigma^2$	(11.10)
236	$\sigma^2 \approx \tilde{\sigma}^2 = \dfrac{NS^2}{N - 1}$	(11.11)
237	$\tilde{\sigma}^2 = \dfrac{\sum x_i^2}{N - 1}, \quad x_i = X_i - \overline{X}$	(11.12)
237	$\tilde{\sigma}^2 = \dfrac{Np(1 - p)}{N - 1}$ (for a dichotomous population)	(11.13)
237	$\tilde{\sigma}_{\overline{X}}^2 = \dfrac{\tilde{\sigma}^2}{N} = \dfrac{S^2}{N - 1}$	(11.14)
237	$\tilde{\sigma}_{Mdn}^2 \approx \dfrac{1.57 S^2}{N - 1}$ (for a ND population only)	(11.15)
238	$\tilde{\sigma}_p^2 = \dfrac{p(1 - p)}{N - 1}$	(11.16)
238	$\tilde{\sigma} = S\sqrt{\dfrac{N}{N - 1}}$	(11.17)

Page	Formula		Number

(also see formula in footnote 4, p. 330)

Page	Formula	Number

331 $\Delta_1, \bar{\Delta}_1 = (\bar{X}_1 - \bar{X}_2)_1 \mp z_{\gamma/2} \sqrt{\dfrac{S_1^{\,2}}{n_1 - 1} + \dfrac{S_2^{\,2}}{n_2 - 1}}$ (14.8a), (14.8b)

342 $t(df = N - 1) = \dfrac{\bar{X} - \mu}{\tilde{\sigma}_{\bar{X}}} = \dfrac{\bar{X} - \mu}{S/\sqrt{N - 1}}$

$= \dfrac{\bar{X} - \mu}{S} \sqrt{N - 1}$ (15.3)

347 $\tilde{\sigma}^2 = \dfrac{n_1 S_1^{\,2} + n_2 S_2^{\,2}}{n_1 + n_2 - 2}$ (15.5)

348 $t(df = n_1 + n_2 - 2) = \dfrac{\bar{X}_1 - \bar{X}_2}{\sqrt{\dfrac{n_1 S_1^{\,2} + n_2 S_2^{\,2}}{n_1 + n_2 - 2}\left(\dfrac{1}{n_1} + \dfrac{1}{n_2}\right)}}$ (15.8)

350 $t(df = N - 1) = \dfrac{\bar{D} - \mu_D}{\tilde{\sigma}_{\bar{D}}} = \dfrac{\bar{D} - \mu_D}{S_D/\sqrt{N - 1}}$ (15.9)

350 $t(df = N - 1) = \dfrac{\bar{D}\sqrt{N - 1}}{S_D}$ (15.10)

361 $\mu_1, \bar{\mu}_1 = \bar{X}_1 \mp t_{\gamma/2} \dfrac{S}{\sqrt{N - 1}}, \qquad df = N - 1$ (15.12a), (15.12b)

362 $\underline{\Delta}_1, \bar{\Delta}_1 = (\bar{X}_1 - \bar{X}_2)_1$ (15.13a), (15.13b)

$\mp t_{\gamma/2} \sqrt{\dfrac{n_1 S_1^{\,2} + n_2 S_2^{\,2}}{n_1 + n_2 - 2}\left(\dfrac{1}{n_1} + \dfrac{1}{n_2}\right)},$

where $df = n_1 + n_2 - 2$

363 $\mu_{D_1}, \bar{\mu}_{D_1} = \bar{D}_1 \mp t_{\gamma/2} \dfrac{S_D}{\sqrt{N - 1}}, \qquad df = N - 1$ (15.14a), (15.14b)

385 $P(A|B) = \dfrac{P(A \text{ and } B)}{P(B)}$ (16.1)

386 $P(A|B) = \dfrac{P(B|A)P(A)}{P(B)}$ (16.4)

388 $P(A_1|B) = \dfrac{P(B|A_1)P(A_1)}{P(B)} = \dfrac{P(B|A_1)P(A_1)}{\sum P(B|A_i)P(A_i)}$ (16.5)

393 $Y = \dfrac{\phi^{a-1}(1 - \phi)^{b-1}}{\beta(a, b)}, \qquad 0 \le \phi \le 1; a, b > 0$ (16.6)

Page	Formula	Number
402	$P(\phi \mid r) = \dfrac{P(r \mid \phi)P(\phi)}{P(r)}$	(16.7)
404	$P(\phi \mid r) = \dfrac{\phi^{r+a-1}(1 - \phi)^{n-r+b-1}}{\beta(r + a, n - r + b)}$	(16.8)
426	$r = \dfrac{\sum z_{X_i} z_{Y_i}}{N}$	(17.1)
439	$r = \dfrac{\sum x_i y_i}{N S_X S_Y}, \quad x_i = X_i - \bar{X}; y_i = Y_i - \bar{Y}$	(17.2)
440	$r = \dfrac{\sum x_i y_i}{\sqrt{(\sum x_i{}^2)(\sum y_i{}^2)}}, \quad \begin{array}{l} x_i = X_i - \bar{X}; \\ y_i = Y_i - \bar{Y} \end{array}$	(17.3)
440	$Cov(XY) = \dfrac{\sum x_i y_i}{N}$	(17.4)
441	$r = \dfrac{Cov(XY)}{S_X S_Y}$	(17.5)
441	$r = \dfrac{\sum X_i Y_i - \dfrac{(\sum X_i)(\sum Y_i)}{N}}{\sqrt{\left(\sum X_i{}^2 - \dfrac{(\sum X_i)^2}{N}\right)\left(\sum Y_i{}^2 - \dfrac{(\sum Y_i)^2}{N}\right)}}$	(17.6)
455	$z_r = \tfrac{1}{2} \log_e \dfrac{1 + r}{1 - r}$	(17.8)
455	$z_p = \tfrac{1}{2} \log_e \dfrac{1 + \rho}{1 - \rho}$	(17.9)
455	$\sigma_{z_r}{}^2 = \dfrac{1}{N - 3}$	(17.10)
457	$\underline{z}_\rho, \bar{z}_\rho = z_r \mp z_{\gamma/2} \dfrac{1}{\sqrt{N - 3}}$	(17.11)
460	$z = \dfrac{z_{r_1} - z_{r_2}}{\sqrt{\dfrac{1}{n_1 - 3} + \dfrac{1}{n_2 - 3}}}$	(17.12)
471	$\hat{Y} = bX + c$	(18.2)
471	$\hat{Y}_i = bX_i + c$	(18.2a)
471	$G = \sum (Y_i - \hat{Y}_i)^2 = \sum (Y_i - [bX_i + c])^2$	(18.3)

Page	Formula	Number
471	$b = \dfrac{\sum x_i y_i}{\sum x_i{}^2}, \qquad x_i = X_i - \overline{X}; y_i = Y_i - \overline{Y}$	(18.4)
471	$c = \overline{Y} - b\overline{X}$	(18.5)
475	$\hat{Y} = b(X - \overline{X}) + \overline{Y} = bx + \overline{Y}$	(18.6), (18.6a)
476	$\hat{y} = bx$	(18.7)
476	$b = r\dfrac{S_Y}{S_X}$	(18.8)
476	$\hat{Y} = r\dfrac{S_Y}{S_X}(X - \overline{X}) + \overline{Y} = r\dfrac{S_Y}{S_X}x + \overline{Y}$	(18.9), (18.9a)
476	$\hat{y} = r\dfrac{S_Y}{S_X}x, \qquad \hat{y} = (\hat{Y} - \overline{Y})$	(18.10)
477	$\hat{z}_{\hat{Y}} = rz_X$	(18.11)
477	$M_{\hat{Y}} = \overline{Y}$	(18.12)
478	$S_{\hat{Y}}{}^2 = r^2 S_Y{}^2$	(18.13)
481	$r = \dfrac{S_Y}{S_Y}$	(18.15)
483	$\tilde{\sigma}_{y \cdot x}^2 = \dfrac{\sum (Y_i - \hat{Y}_i)^2}{N - 2}$	(18.16)
484	$\tilde{\sigma}_{y \cdot x}^2 = \dfrac{\sum e_i{}^2}{N - 2}, \qquad e_i = (Y_i - \hat{Y}_i)$	(18.18)
485	$\tilde{\sigma}_{y \cdot x} = \sqrt{\dfrac{\sum e_i{}^2}{N - 2}}, \qquad e_i = Y_i - \hat{Y}_i$	(18.19)
486	$\tilde{\sigma}_{y \cdot x}^2 = \dfrac{N S_Y{}^2}{N - 2}(1 - r^2)$	(18.20)
487	$S_{y \cdot x}^2 = S_Y{}^2(1 - r^2)$	(18.25)
487	$S_{y \cdot x} = S_Y\sqrt{1 - r^2}$	(18.26)
488	$\tilde{\sigma}_{y \cdot x} = S_{y \cdot x}\sqrt{\dfrac{N}{N - 2}}$	(18.28)
489	$\sum y_i{}^2 = \sum \hat{y}_i{}^2 + \sum e_i{}^2,$ $y_i = Y_i - \overline{Y}; \hat{y}_i = \hat{Y}_i - \overline{Y}; e_i = Y_i - \hat{Y}_i$	(18.29)
489	$S_Y{}^2 = S_Y{}^2 + S_{y \cdot x}^2$	(18.30)
497	$ss_{\text{reg}} = \sum \hat{y}_i{}^2, \qquad \hat{y}_i = \hat{Y}_i - \overline{Y}$	(18.31)

Page	Formula	Number
497	$ss_T = \sum y_i^2, \qquad y_i = Y_i - \bar{Y}$	(18.32)
498	$ss_{res} = \sum e_i^2, \qquad e_i = Y_i - \hat{Y}_i$	(18.33)
498	$ss_T = ss_{reg} + ss_{res}$	(18.34)
498	$\tilde{\sigma}_{y \cdot x}^2 = \dfrac{ss_{res}}{N - 2}$	(18.35)
498	$S_{y \cdot x}^2 = \dfrac{ss_{res}}{N}$	(18.36)
499	$r^2 = \dfrac{ss_{reg}}{ss_T}$	(18.37)
502	$\mu_{y \cdot x} = \beta x + \mu_Y$	(19.3)
503	$\sigma_b^2 = \dfrac{\sigma_{y \cdot x}^2}{\sum x_i^2}, \qquad i = 1, 2, \ldots, N$	(19.4)
503	$\sigma_b = \dfrac{\sigma_{y \cdot x}}{\sqrt{\sum x_i^2}}$	(19.5)
503	$\tilde{\sigma}_b = \dfrac{\tilde{\sigma}_{y \cdot x}}{\sqrt{\sum x_i^2}}$	(19.6)
504	$t = \dfrac{b - \beta}{\tilde{\sigma}_b}, \qquad df = N - 2$	(19.7)
504	$\sigma_{\bar{Y}}^2 = \dfrac{\sigma_{y \cdot x}^2}{N}$	(19.8)
504	$\sigma_{\bar{Y}} = \dfrac{\sigma_{y \cdot x}}{\sqrt{N}}$	(19.9)
504	$\tilde{\sigma}_{\bar{Y}} = \dfrac{\tilde{\sigma}_{y \cdot x}}{\sqrt{N}}$	(19.10)
505	$t = \dfrac{\bar{Y} - \mu_Y}{\tilde{\sigma}_{\bar{Y}}}, \qquad df = N - 2$	(19.11)
505	$\rho = \beta \dfrac{\sigma_X}{\sigma_Y}$	(19.13)
507	$\underline{\beta}_1, \bar{\beta}_1 = b_1 \mp t_{\gamma/2} \tilde{\sigma}_b, \qquad df = N - 2$	(19.14)
508	$\mu_{Y_1}, \bar{\mu}_{Y_1} = \bar{Y}_1 \mp t_{\gamma/2} \tilde{\sigma}_{\bar{Y}}$	(19.15)
508	$\tilde{\mu}_{y \cdot x} = \hat{Y} = bx + \bar{Y}$	(19.16)

Page	Formula	Number
509	$\sigma_Y^2 = x^2\sigma_b^2 + \sigma_{\bar{Y}}^2$	(19.17)
509	$\sigma_Y = \sqrt{x^2\sigma_b^2 + \sigma_{\bar{Y}}^2}$	(19.18)
509	$\tilde{\sigma}_Y = \tilde{\sigma}_{y \cdot x}\sqrt{\dfrac{x^2}{\sum x_i^2} + \dfrac{1}{N}}$	(19.19)
510	$\mu_{x \cdot y_1}, \bar{\mu}_{x \cdot y_1} = \hat{Y}_1 \mp t_{\gamma/2}\tilde{\sigma}_{y \cdot x}\sqrt{\dfrac{x^2}{\sum x_i^2} + \dfrac{1}{N}}$	(19.20)
512	$\sigma_e^2 = \sigma_{y \cdot x}^2\left(\dfrac{x^2}{\sum x_i^2} + \dfrac{1}{N} + 1\right)$	(19.21)
512	$\sigma_e = \sigma_{y \cdot x}\sqrt{\dfrac{x^2}{\sum x_i^2} + \dfrac{1}{N} + 1}$	(19.22)
513	$\tilde{\sigma}_e = \tilde{\sigma}_{y \cdot x}\sqrt{\dfrac{x^2}{\sum x_i^2} + \dfrac{1}{N} + 1}$	(19.23)
513	$\underline{\Upsilon}_1, \overline{\Upsilon}_1 = \hat{Y}_1 \mp t_{\gamma/2}\tilde{\sigma}_e$	(19.25)
515	$t(df = N - 2) = \dfrac{r}{\sqrt{1 - r^2}}\sqrt{N - 2}$	(19.27)

Appendix C
Tables

Table I Squares and Square Roots of the Numbers from
1 to 1,000

Number	Square	Square Root	Number	Square	Square Root
1	1	1.000	51	26 01	7.141
2	4	1.414	52	27 04	7.211
3	9	1.732	53	28 09	7.280
4	16	2.000	54	29 16	7.348
5	25	2.236	55	30 25	7.416
6	36	2.449	56	31 36	7.483
7	49	2.646	57	32 49	7.550
8	64	2.828	58	33 64	7.616
9	81	3.000	59	34 81	7.681
10	1 00	3.162	60	36 00	7.746
11	1 21	3.317	61	37 21	7.810
12	1 44	3.464	62	38 44	7.874
13	1 69	3.606	63	39 69	7.937
14	1 96	3.742	64	40 96	8.000
15	2 25	3.873	65	42 25	8.062
16	2 56	4.000	66	43 56	8.124
17	2 89	4.123	67	44 89	8.185
18	3 24	4.243	68	46 24	8.246
19	3 61	4.359	69	47 61	8.307
20	4 00	4.472	70	49 00	8.367
21	4 41	4.583	71	50 41	8.426
22	4 84	4.690	72	51 84	8.485
23	5 29	4.796	73	53 29	8.544
24	5 76	4.899	74	54 76	8.602
25	6 25	5.000	75	56 25	8.660
26	6 76	5.099	76	57 76	8.718
27	7 29	5.196	77	59 29	8.775
28	7 84	5.292	78	60 84	8.832
29	8 41	5.385	79	62 41	8.888
30	9 00	5.477	80	64 00	8.944
31	9 61	5.568	81	65 61	9.000
32	10 24	5.657	82	67 24	9.055
33	10 89	5.745	83	68 89	9.110
34	11 56	5.831	84	70 56	9.165
35	12 25	5.916	85	72 25	9.220
36	12 96	6.000	86	73 96	9.274
37	13 69	6.083	87	75 69	9.327
38	14 44	6.164	88	77 44	9.381
39	15 21	6.245	89	79 21	9.434
40	16 00	6.325	90	81 00	9.487
41	16 81	6.403	91	82 81	9.539
42	17 64	6.481	92	84 64	9.592
43	18 49	6.557	93	86 49	9.644
44	19 36	6.633	94	88 36	9.695
45	20 25	6.708	95	90 25	9.747
46	21 16	6.782	96	92 16	9.798
47	22 09	6.856	97	94 09	9.849
48	23 04	6.928	98	96 04	9.899
49	24 01	7.000	99	98 01	9.950
50	25 00	7.071	100	1 00 00	10.000

Number	Square	Square Root	Number	Square	Square Root
101	1 02 01	10.050	151	2 28 01	12.288
102	1 04 04	10.100	152	2 31 04	12.329
103	1 06 09	10.149	153	2 34 09	12.369
104	1 08 16	10.198	154	2 37 16	12.410
105	1 10 25	10.247	155	2 40 25	12.450
106	1 12 36	10.296	156	2 43 36	12.490
107	1 14 49	10.344	157	2 46 49	12.530
108	1 16 64	10.392	158	2 49 64	12.570
109	1 18 81	10.440	159	2 52 81	12.610
110	1 21 00	10.488	160	2 56 00	12.649
111	1 23 21	10.536	161	2 59 21	12.689
112	1 25 44	10.583	162	2 62 44	12.728
113	1 27 69	10.630	163	2 65 69	12.767
114	1 29 96	10.677	164	2 68 96	12.806
115	1 32 25	10.724	165	2 72 25	12.845
116	1 34 56	10.770	166	2 75 56	12.884
117	1 36 89	10.817	167	2 78 89	12.923
118	1 39 24	10.863	168	2 82 24	12.961
119	1 41 61	10.909	169	2 85 61	13.000
120	1 44 00	10.954	170	2 89 00	13.038
121	1 46 41	11.000	171	2 92 41	13.077
122	1 48 84	11.045	172	2 95 84	13.115
123	1 51 29	11.091	173	2 99 29	13.153
124	1 53 76	11.136	174	3 02 76	13.191
125	1 56 25	11.180	175	3 06 25	13.229
126	1 58 76	11.225	176	3 09 76	13.266
127	1 61 29	11.269	177	3 13 29	13.304
128	1 63 84	11.314	178	3 16 84	13.342
129	1 66 41	11.358	179	3 20 41	13.379
130	1 69 00	11.402	180	3 24 00	13.416
131	1 71 61	11.446	181	3 27 61	13.454
132	1 74 24	11.489	182	3 31 24	13.491
133	1 76 89	11.533	183	3 34 89	13.528
134	1 79 56	11.576	184	3 38 56	13.565
135	1 82 25	11.619	185	3 42 25	13.601
136	1 84 96	11.662	186	3 45 96	13.638
137	1 87 69	11.705	187	3 49 69	13.675
138	1 90 44	11.747	188	3 53 44	13.711
139	1 93 21	11.790	189	3 57 21	13.748
140	1 96 00	11.832	190	3 61 00	13.784
141	1 98 81	11.874	191	3 64 81	13.820
142	2 01 64	11.916	192	3 68 64	13.856
143	2 04 49	11.958	193	3 72 49	13.892
144	2 07 36	12.000	194	3 76 36	13.928
145	2 10 25	12.042	195	3 80 25	13.964
146	2 13 16	12.083	196	3 84 16	14.000
147	2 16 09	12.124	197	3 88 09	14.036
148	2 19 04	12.166	198	3 92 04	14.071
149	2 22 01	12.207	199	3 96 01	14.107
150	2 25 00	12.247	200	4 00 00	14.142

Table I Squares and Square Roots of the Numbers from 1 to 1,000 (Continued)

Number	Square	Square Root	Number	Square	Square Root
201	4 04 01	14.177	251	6 30 01	15.843
202	4 08 04	14.213	252	6 35 04	15.875
203	4 12 09	14.248	253	6 40 09	15.906
204	4 16 16	14.283	254	6 45 16	15.937
205	4 20 25	14.318	255	6 50 25	15.969
206	4 24 36	14.353	256	6 55 36	16.000
207	4 28 49	14.387	257	6 60 49	16.031
208	4 32 64	14.422	258	6 65 64	16.062
209	4 36 81	14.457	259	6 70 81	16.093
210	4 41 00	14.491	260	6 76 00	16.125
211	4 45 21	14.526	261	6 81 21	16.155
212	4 49 44	14.560	262	6 86 44	16.186
213	4 53 69	14.595	263	6 91 69	16.217
214	4 57 96	14.629	264	6 96 96	16.248
215	4 62 25	14.663	265	7 02 25	16.279
216	4 66 56	14.697	266	7 07 56	16.310
217	4 70 89	14.731	267	7 12 89	16.340
218	4 75 24	14.765	268	7 18 24	16.371
219	4 79 61	14.799	269	7 23 61	16.401
220	4 84 00	14.832	270	7 29 00	16.432
221	4 88 41	14.866	271	7 34 41	16.462
222	4 92 84	14.900	272	7 39 84	16.492
223	4 97 29	14.933	273	7 45 29	16.523
224	5 01 76	14.967	274	7 50 76	16.553
225	5 06 25	15.000	275	7 56 25	16.583
226	5 10 76	15.033	276	7 61 76	16.613
227	5 15 29	15.067	277	7 67 29	16.643
228	5 19 84	15.100	278	7 72 84	16.673
229	5 24 41	15.133	279	7 78 41	16.703
230	5 29 00	15.166	280	7 84 00	16.733
231	5 33 61	15.199	281	7 89 61	16.763
232	5 38 24	15.232	282	7 95 24	16.793
233	5 42 89	15.264	283	8 00 89	16.823
234	5 47 56	15.297	284	8 06 56	16.852
235	5 52 25	15.330	285	8 12 25	16.882
236	5 56 96	15.362	286	8 17 96	16.912
237	5 61 69	15.395	287	8 23 69	16.941
238	5 66 44	15.427	288	8 29 44	16.971
239	5 71 21	15.460	289	8 35 21	17.000
240	5 76 00	15.492	290	8 41 00	17.029
241	5 80 81	15.524	291	8 46 81	17.059
242	5 85 64	15.556	292	8 52 64	17.088
243	5 90 49	15.588	293	8 58 49	17.117
244	5 95 36	15.620	294	8 64 36	17.146
245	6 00 25	15.652	295	8 70 25	17.176
246	6 05 16	15.684	296	8 76 16	17.205
247	6 10 09	15.716	297	8 82 09	17.234
248	6 15 04	15.748	298	8 88 04	17.263
249	6 20 01	15.780	299	8 94 01	17.292
250	6 25 00	15.811	300	9 00 00	17.321

Number	Square	Square Root	Number	Square	Square Root
301	9 06 01	17.349	351	12 32 01	18.735
302	9 12 04	17.378	352	12 39 04	18.762
303	9 18 09	17.407	353	12 46 09	18.788
304	9 24 16	17.436	354	12 53 16	18.815
305	9 30 25	17.464	355	12 60 25	18.841
306	9 36 36	17.493	356	12 67 36	18.868
307	9 42 49	17.521	357	12 74 49	18.894
308	9 48 64	17.550	358	12 81 64	18.921
309	9 54 81	17.578	359	12 88 81	18.947
310	9 61 00	17.607	360	12 96 00	18.974
311	9 67 21	17.635	361	13 03 21	19.000
312	9 73 44	17.664	362	13 10 44	19.026
313	9 79 69	17.692	363	13 17 69	19.053
314	9 85 96	17.720	364	13 24 96	19.079
315	9 92 25	17.748	365	13 32 25	19.105
316	9 98 56	17.776	366	13 39 56	19.131
317	10 04 89	17.804	367	13 46 89	19.157
318	10 11 24	17.833	368	13 54 24	19.183
319	10 17 61	17.861	369	13 61 61	19.209
320	10 24 00	17.889	370	13 69 00	19.235
321	10 30 41	17.916	371	13 76 41	19.261
322	10 36 84	17.944	372	13 83 84	19.287
323	10 43 29	17.972	373	13 91 29	19.313
324	10 49 76	18.000	374	13 98 76	19.339
325	10 56 25	18.028	375	14 06 25	19.363
326	10 62 76	18.055	376	14 13 76	19.391
327	10 69 29	18.083	377	14 21 29	19.416
328	10 75 84	18.111	378	14 28 84	19.442
329	10 82 41	18.138	379	14 36 41	19.468
330	10 89 00	18.166	380	14 44 00	19.494
331	10 95 61	18.193	381	14 51 61	19.519
332	11 02 24	18.221	382	14 59 24	19.545
333	11 08 89	18.248	383	14 66 89	19.570
334	11 15 56	18.276	384	14 74 56	19.596
335	11 22 25	18.303	385	14 82 25	19.621
336	11 28 96	18.330	386	14 89 96	19.647
337	11 35 69	18.358	387	14 97 69	19.672
338	11 42 44	18.385	388	15 05 44	19.698
339	11 49 21	18.412	389	15 13 21	19.723
340	11 56 00	18.439	390	15 21 00	19.748
341	11 62 81	18.466	391	15 28 81	19.774
342	11 69 64	18.493	392	15 36 64	19.799
343	11 76 49	18.520	393	15 44 49	19.824
344	11 83 36	18.547	394	15 52 36	19.849
345	11 90 25	18.574	395	15 60 25	19.875
346	11 97 16	18.601	396	15 68 16	19.900
347	12 04 09	18.628	397	15 76 09	19.925
348	12 11 04	18.655	398	15 84 04	19.950
349	12 18 01	18.682	399	15 92 01	19.975
350	12 25 00	18.708	400	16 00 00	20.000

Number	Square	Square Root	Number	Square	Square Root
401	16 08 01	20.025	451	20 34 01	21.237
402	16 16 04	20.050	452	20 43 04	21.260
403	16 24 09	20.075	453	20 52 09	21.284
404	16 32 16	20.100	454	20 61 16	21.307
405	16 40 25	20.125	455	20 70 25	21.331
406	16 48 36	20.149	456	20 79 36	21.354
407	16 56 49	20.174	457	20 88 49	21.378
408	16 64 64	20.199	458	20 97 64	21.401
409	16 72 81	20.224	459	21 06 81	21.424
410	16 81 00	20.248	460	21 16 00	21.448
411	16 89 21	20.273	461	21 25 21	21.471
412	16 97 44	20.298	462	21 34 44	21.494
413	17 05 69	20.322	463	21 43 69	21.517
414	17 13 96	20.347	464	21 52 96	21.541
415	17 22 25	20.372	465	21 62 25	21.564
416	17 30 56	20.396	466	21 71 56	21.587
417	17 38 89	20.421	467	21 80 89	21.610
418	17 47 24	20.445	468	21 90 24	21.633
419	17 55 61	20.469	469	21 99 61	21.656
420	17 64 00	20.494	470	22 09 00	21.679
421	17 72 41	20.518	471	22 18 41	21.703
422	17 80 84	20.543	472	22 27 84	21.726
423	17 89 29	20.567	473	22 37 29	21.749
424	17 97 76	20.591	474	22 46 76	21.772
425	18 06 25	20.616	475	22 56 25	21.794
426	18 14 76	20.640	476	22 65 76	21.817
427	18 23 29	20.664	477	22 75 29	21.840
428	18 31 84	20.688	478	22 84 84	21.863
429	18 40 41	20.712	479	22 94 41	21.886
430	18 49 00	20.736	480	23 04 00	21.909
431	18 57 61	20.761	481	23 13 61	21.932
432	18 66 24	20.785	482	23 23 24	21.954
433	18 74 89	20.809	483	23 32 89	21.977
434	18 83 56	20.833	484	23 42 56	22.000
435	18 92 25	20.857	485	23 52 25	22.023
436	19 00 96	20.881	486	23 61 96	22.045
437	19 09 69	20.905	487	23 71 69	22.068
438	19 18 44	20.928	488	23 81 44	22.091
439	19 27 21	20.952	489	23 91 21	22.113
440	19 36 00	20.976	490	24 01 00	22.136
441	19 44 81	21.000	491	24 10 81	22.159
442	19 53 64	21.024	492	24 20 64	22.181
443	19 62 49	21.048	493	24 30 49	22.204
444	19 71 36	21.071	494	24 40 36	22.226
445	19 80 25	21.095	495	24 50 25	22.249
446	19 89 16	21.119	496	24 60 16	22.271
447	19 98 09	21.142	497	24 70 09	22.293
448	20 07 04	21.166	498	24 80 04	22.316
449	20 16 01	21.190	499	24 90 01	22.338
450	20 25 00	21.213	500	25 00 00	22.361

Table I Squares and Square Roots of the Numbers from 1 to 1,000 (Continued)

Number	Square	Square Root	Number	Square	Square Root
501	25 10 01	22.383	551	30 36 01	23.473
502	25 20 04	22.405	552	30 47 04	23.495
503	25 30 09	22.428	553	30 58 09	23.516
504	25 40 16	22.450	554	30 69 16	23.537
505	25 50 25	22.472	555	30 80 25	23.558
506	25 60 36	22.494	556	30 91 36	23.580
507	25 70 49	22.517	557	31 02 49	23.601
508	25 80 64	22.539	558	31 13 64	23.622
509	25 90 81	22.561	559	31 24 81	23.643
510	26 01 00	22.583	560	31 36 00	23.664
511	26 11 21	22.605	561	31 47 21	23.685
512	26 21 44	22.627	562	31 58 44	23.707
513	26 31 69	22.650	563	31 69 69	23.728
514	26 41 96	22.672	564	31 80 96	23.749
515	26 52 25	22.694	565	31 92 25	23.770
516	26 62 56	22.716	566	32 03 56	23.791
517	26 72 89	22.738	567	32 14 89	23.812
518	26 83 24	22.760	568	32 26 24	23.833
519	26 93 61	22.782	569	32 37 61	23.854
520	27 04 00	22.804	570	32 49 00	23.875
521	27 14 41	22.825	571	32 60 41	23.896
522	27 24 84	22.847	572	32 71 84	23.917
523	27 35 29	22.869	573	32 83 29	23.937
524	27 45 76	22.891	574	32 94 76	23.958
525	27 56 25	22.913	575	33 06 25	23.979
526	27 66 76	22.935	576	33 17 76	24.000
527	27 77 29	22.956	577	33 29 29	24.021
528	27 87 84	22.978	578	33 40 84	24.042
529	27 98 41	23.000	579	33 52 41	24.062
530	28 09 00	23.022	580	33 64 00	24.083
531	28 19 61	23.043	581	33 75 61	24.104
532	28 30 24	23.065	582	33 87 24	24.125
533	28 40 89	23.087	583	33 98 89	24.145
534	28 51 56	23.108	584	34 10 56	24.166
535	28 62 25	23.130	585	34 22 25	24.187
536	28 72 96	23.152	586	34 33 96	24.207
537	28 83 69	23.173	587	34 45 69	24.228
538	28 94 44	23.195	588	34 57 44	24.249
539	29 05 21	23.216	589	34 69 21	24.269
540	29 16 00	23.238	590	34 81 00	24.290
541	29 26 81	23.259	591	34 92 81	24.310
542	29 37 64	23.281	592	35 04 64	24.331
543	29 48 49	23.302	593	35 16 49	24.352
544	29 59 36	23.324	594	35 28 36	24.372
545	29 70 25	23.345	595	35 40 25	24.393
546	29 81 16	23.367	596	35 52 16	24.413
547	29 92 09	23.388	597	35 64 09	24.434
548	30 03 04	23.409	598	35 76 04	24.454
549	30 14 01	23.431	599	35 88 01	24.474
550	30 25 00	23.452	600	36 00 00	24.495

Number	Square	Square Root	Number	Square	Square Root
601	36 12 01	24.515	651	42 38 01	25.515
602	36 24 04	24.536	652	42 51 04	25.534
603	36 36 09	24.556	653	42 64 09	25.554
604	36 48 16	24.576	654	42 77 16	25.573
605	36 60 25	24.597	655	42 90 25	25.593
606	36 72 36	24.617	656	43 03 36	25.612
607	36 84 49	24.637	657	43 16 49	25.632
608	36 96 64	24.658	658	43 29 64	25.652
609	37 08 81	24.678	659	43 42 81	25.671
610	37 21 00	24.698	660	43 56 00	25.690
611	37 33 21	24.718	661	43 69 21	25.710
612	37 45 44	24.739	662	43 82 44	25.729
613	37 57 69	24.759	663	43 95 69	25.749
614	37 69 96	24.779	664	44 08 96	25.768
615	37 82 25	24.799	665	44 22 25	25.788
616	37 94 56	24.819	666	44 35 56	25.807
617	38 06 89	24.839	667	44 48 89	25.826
618	38 19 24	24.860	668	44 62 24	25.846
619	38 31 61	24.880	669	44 75 61	25.865
620	38 44 00	24.900	670	44 89 00	25.884
621	38 56 41	24.920	671	45 02 41	25.904
622	38 68 84	24.940	672	45 15 84	25.923
623	38 81 29	24.960	673	45 29 29	25.942
624	38 93 76	24.980	674	45 42 76	25.962
625	39 06 25	25.000	675	45 56 25	25.981
626	39 18 76	25.020	676	45 69 76	26.000
627	39 31 29	25.040	677	45 83 29	26.019
628	39 43 84	25.060	678	45 96 84	26.038
629	39 56 41	25.080	679	46 10 41	26.058
630	39 69 00	25.100	680	46 24 00	26.077
631	39 81 61	25.120	681	46 37 61	26.096
632	39 94 24	25.140	682	46 51 24	26.115
633	40 06 89	25.159	683	46 64 89	26.134
634	40 19 56	25.179	684	46 78 56	26.153
635	40 32 25	25.199	685	46 92 25	26.173
636	40 44 96	25.219	686	47 05 96	26.192
637	40 57 69	25.239	687	47 19 69	26.211
638	40 70 44	25.259	688	47 33 44	26.230
639	40 83 21	25.278	689	47 47 21	26.249
640	40 96 00	25.298	690	47 61 00	26.268
641	41 08 81	25.318	691	47 74 81	26.287
642	41 21 64	25.338	692	47 88 64	26.306
643	41 34 49	25.357	693	48 02 49	26.325
644	41 47 36	25.377	694	48 16 36	26.344
645	41 60 25	25.397	695	48 30 25	26.363
646	41 73 16	25.417	696	48 44 16	26.382
647	41 86 09	25.436	697	48 58 09	26.401
648	41 99 04	25.456	698	48 72 04	26.420
649	42 12 01	25.475	699	48 86 01	26.439
650	42 25 00	25.495	700	49 00 00	26.458

Number	Square	Square Root	Number	Square	Square Root
701	49 14 01	26.476	751	56 40 01	27.404
702	49 28 04	26.495	752	56 55 04	27.423
703	49 42 09	26.514	753	56 70 09	27.441
704	49 56 16	26.533	754	56 85 16	27.459
705	49 70 25	26.552	755	57 00 25	27.477
706	49 84 36	26.571	756	57 15 36	27.495
707	49 98 49	26.589	757	57 30 49	27.514
708	50 12 64	26.608	758	57 45 64	27.532
709	50 26 81	26.627	759	57 60 81	27.550
710	50 41 00	26.646	760	57 76 00	27.568
711	50 55 21	26.665	761	57 91 21	27.586
712	50 69 44	26.683	762	58 06 44	27.604
713	50 83 69	26.702	763	58 21 69	27.622
714	50 97 96	26.721	764	58 36 96	27.641
715	51 12 25	26.739	765	58 52 25	27.659
716	51 26 56	26.758	766	58 67 56	27.677
717	51 40 89	26.777	767	58 82 89	27.695
718	51 55 24	26.796	768	58 98 24	27.713
719	51 69 61	26.814	769	59 13 61	27.731
720	51 84 00	26.833	770	59 29 00	27.749
721	51 98 41	26.851	771	59 44 41	27.767
722	52 12 84	26.870	772	59 59 84	27.785
723	52 27 29	26.889	773	59 75 29	27.803
724	52 41 76	26.907	774	59 90 76	27.821
725	52 56 25	26.926	775	60 06 25	27.839
726	52 70 76	26.944	776	60 21 76	27.857
727	52 85 29	26.963	777	60 37 29	27.875
728	52 99 84	26.981	778	60 52 84	27.893
729	53 14 41	27.000	779	60 68 41	27.911
730	53 29 00	27.019	780	60 84 00	27.928
731	53 43 61	27.037	781	60 99 61	27.946
732	53 58 24	27.055	782	61 15 24	27.964
733	53 72 89	27.074	783	61 30 89	27.982
734	53 87 56	27.092	784	61 46 56	28.000
735	54 02 25	27.111	785	61 62 25	28.018
736	54 16 96	27.129	786	61 77 96	28.036
737	54 31 69	27.148	787	61 93 69	28.054
738	54 46 44	27.166	788	62 09 44	28.071
739	54 61 21	27.185	789	62 25 21	28.089
740	54 76 00	27.203	790	62 41 00	28.107
741	54 90 81	27.221	791	62 56 81	28.125
742	55 05 64	27.240	792	62 72 64	28.142
743	55 20 49	27.258	793	62 88 49	28.160
744	55 35 36	27.276	794	63 04 36	28.178
745	55 50 25	27.295	795	63 20 25	28.196
746	55 65 16	27.313	796	63 36 16	28.213
747	55 80 09	27.331	797	63 52 09	28.231
748	55 95 04	27.350	798	63 68 04	28.249
749	56 10 01	27.368	799	63 84 01	28.267
750	56 25 00	27.386	800	64 00 00	28.284

Number	Square	Square Root	Number	Square	Square Root
801	64 16 01	28.302	851	72 42 01	29.172
802	64 32 04	28.320	852	72 59 04	29.189
803	64 48 09	28.337	853	72 76 09	29.206
804	64 64 16	28.355	854	72 93 16	29.223
805	64 80 25	28.373	855	73 10 25	29.240
806	64 96 36	28.390	856	73 27 36	29.257
807	65 12 49	28.408	857	73 44 49	29.275
808	65 28 64	28.425	858	73 61 64	29.292
809	65 44 81	28.443	859	73 78 81	29.309
810	65 61 00	28.460	860	73 96 00	29.326
811	65 77 21	28.478	861	74 13 21	29.343
812	65 93 44	28.496	862	74 30 44	29.360
813	66 09 69	28.513	863	74 47 69	29.377
814	66 25 96	28.531	864	74 64 96	29.394
815	66 42 25	28.548	865	74 82 25	29.411
816	66 58 56	28.566	866	74 99 56	29.428
817	66 74 89	28.583	867	75 16 89	29.445
818	66 91 24	28.601	868	75 34 24	29.462
819	67 07 61	28.618	869	75 51 61	29.479
820	67 24 00	28.636	870	75 69 00	29.496
821	67 40 41	28.653	871	75 86 41	29.513
822	67 56 84	28.671	872	76 03 84	29.530
823	67 73 29	28.688	873	76 21 29	29.547
824	67 89 76	28.705	874	76 38 76	29.563
825	68 06 25	28.723	875	76 56 25	29.580
826	68 22 76	28.740	876	76 73 76	29.597
827	68 39 29	28.758	877	76 91 29	29.614
828	68 55 84	28.775	878	77 08 84	29.631
829	68 72 41	28.792	879	77 26 41	29.648
830	68 89 00	28.810	880	77 44 00	29.665
831	69 05 61	28.827	881	77 61 61	29.682
832	69 22 24	28.844	882	77 79 24	29.698
833	69 38 89	28.862	883	77 96 89	29.715
834	69 55 56	28.879	884	78 14 56	29.732
835	69 72 25	28.896	885	78 32 25	29.749
836	69 88 96	28.914	886	78 49 96	29.766
837	70 05 69	28.931	887	78 67 69	29.783
838	70 22 44	28.948	888	78 85 44	29.799
839	70 39 21	28.965	889	79 03 21	29.816
840	70 56 00	28.983	890	79 21 00	29.833
841	70 72 81	29.000	891	79 38 81	29.850
842	70 89 64	29.017	892	79 56 64	29.866
843	71 06 49	29.034	893	79 74 49	29.883
844	71 23 36	29.052	894	79 92 36	29.900
845	71 40 25	29.069	895	80 10 25	29.916
846	71 57 16	29.086	896	80 28 16	29.933
847	71 74 09	29.103	897	80 46 09	29.950
848	71 91 04	29.120	898	80 64 04	29.967
849	72 08 01	29.138	899	80 82 01	29.983
850	72 25 00	29.155	900	81 00 00	30.000

Number	Square	Square Root	Number	Square	Square Root
901	81 18 01	30.017	951	90 44 01	30.838
902	81 36 04	30.033	952	90 63 04	30.854
903	81 54 09	30.050	953	90 82 09	30.871
904	81 72 16	30.067	954	91 01 16	30.887
905	81 90 25	30.083	955	91 20 25	30.903
906	82 08 36	30.100	956	91 39 36	30.919
907	82 26 49	30.116	957	91 58 49	30.935
908	82 44 64	30.133	958	91 77 64	30.952
909	82 62 81	30.150	959	91 96 81	30.968
910	82 81 00	30.166	960	92 16 00	30.984
911	82 99 21	30.183	961	92 35 21	31.000
912	83 17 44	30.199	962	92 54 44	31.016
913	83 35 69	30.216	963	92 73 69	31.032
914	83 53 96	30.232	964	92 92 96	31.048
915	83 72 25	30.249	965	93 12 25	31.064
916	83 90 56	30.265	966	93 31 56	31.081
917	84 08 89	30.282	967	93 50 89	31.097
918	84 27 24	30.299	968	93 70 24	31.113
919	84 45 61	30.315	969	93 89 61	31.129
920	84 64 00	30.332	970	94 09 00	31.145
921	84 82 41	30.348	971	94 28 41	31.161
922	85 00 84	30.364	972	94 47 84	31.177
923	85 19 29	30.381	973	94 67 29	31.193
924	85 37 76	30.397	974	94 86 76	31.209
925	85 56 25	30.414	975	95 06 25	31.225
926	85 74 76	30.430	976	95 25 76	31.241
927	85 93 29	30.447	977	95 45 29	31.257
928	86 11 84	30.463	978	95 64 84	31.273
929	86 30 41	30.480	979	95 84 41	31.289
930	86 49 00	30.496	980	96 04 00	31.305
931	86 67 61	30.512	981	96 23 61	31.321
932	86 86 24	30.529	982	96 43 24	31.337
933	87 04 89	30.545	983	96 62 89	31.353
934	87 23 56	30.561	984	96 82 56	31.369
935	87 42 25	30.578	985	97 02 25	31.385
936	87 60 96	30.594	986	97 21 96	31.401
937	87 79 69	30.610	987	97 41 69	31.417
938	87 98 44	30.627	988	97 61 44	31.432
939	88 17 21	30.643	989	97 81 21	31.448
940	88 36 00	30.659	990	98 01 00	31.464
941	88 54 81	30.676	991	98 20 81	31.480
942	88 73 64	30.692	992	98 40 64	31.496
943	88 92 49	30.708	993	98 60 49	31.512
944	89 11 36	30.725	994	98 80 36	31.528
945	89 30 25	30.741	995	99 00 25	31.544
946	89 49 16	30.757	996	99 20 16	31.559
947	89 68 09	30.773	997	99 40 09	31.575
948	89 87 04	30.790	998	99 60 04	31.591
949	90 06 01	30.806	999	99 80 01	31.607
950	90 25 00	30.822	1000	100 00 00	31.623

Table II Normal Curve Areas and Ordinates[1]

Col. 1	Col. 2	Col. 3	Col. 4	Col. 5	Col. 6	Col. 7	Col. 8
$+z_1$	$P(0 \leq z \leq z_1)$	$P(|z| \geq z_1)$	y	y as a % of y at μ	$P(z \leq +z_1)$	$P(z \leq -z_1)$	$-z_1$
0.00	.0000	1.0000	.3989	100.00	.5000	.5000	0.00
+0.01	.0040	.9920	.3989	99.99	.5040	.4960	−0.01
+0.02	.0080	.9840	.3989	99.98	.5080	.4920	−0.02
+0.03	.0120	.9761	.3988	99.95	.5120	.4880	−0.03
+0.04	.0160	.9681	.3986	99.92	.5160	.4840	−0.04
+0.05	.0199	.9601	.3984	99.87	.5199	.4801	−0.05
+0.06	.0239	.9522	.3982	99.82	.5239	.4761	−0.06
+0.07	.0279	.9442	.3980	99.76	.5279	.4721	−0.07
+0.08	.0319	.9382	.3977	99.68	.5319	.4681	−0.08
+0.09	.0359	.9283	.3973	99.60	.5359	.4641	−0.09
+0.10	.0398	.9203	.3970	99.50	.5398	.4602	−0.10
+0.11	.0438	.9124	.3965	99.40	.5438	.4562	−0.11
+0.12	.0478	.9045	.3961	99.28	.5478	.4522	−0.12
+0.13	.0517	.8966	.3956	99.16	.5517	.4483	−0.13
+0.14	.0557	.8887	.3951	99.02	.5557	.4443	−0.14
+0.15	.0596	.8808	.3945	98.88	.5596	.4404	−0.15
+0.16	.0636	.8729	.3939	98.73	.5636	.4364	−0.16
+0.17	.0675	.8650	.3932	98.57	.5675	.4325	−0.17
+0.18	.0714	.8572	.3925	98.39	.5714	.4286	−0.18
+0.19	.0753	.8493	.3918	98.21	.5753	.4247	−0.19
+0.20	.0793	.8415	.3910	98.02	.5793	.4207	−0.20
+0.21	.0832	.8337	.3902	97.82	.5832	.4168	−0.21
+0.22	.0871	.8259	.3894	97.61	.5871	.4129	−0.22
+0.23	.0910	.8181	.3885	97.39	.5910	.4090	−0.23
+0.24	.0948	.8103	.3876	97.16	.5948	.4052	−0.24
+0.25	.0987	.8026	.3867	96.92	.5987	.4013	−0.25
+0.26	.1026	.7949	.3857	96.68	.6026	.3974	−0.26
+0.27	.1064	.7872	.3847	96.42	.6064	.3936	−0.27
+0.28	.1103	.7795	.3836	96.16	.6103	.3897	−0.28
+0.29	.1141	.7718	.3825	95.88	.6141	.3859	−0.29
+0.30	.1179	.7642	.3814	95.60	.6179	.3821	−0.30
+0.31	.1217	.7566	.3802	95.31	.6217	.3783	−0.31
+0.32	.1255	.7490	.3790	95.01	.6255	.3745	−0.32
+0.33	.1293	.7414	.3778	94.70	.6293	.3707	−0.33
+0.34	.1331	.7339	.3765	94.38	.6331	.3669	−0.34
+0.35	.1368	.7263	.3752	94.06	.6368	.3632	−0.35

[1]Note: *The values in the various columns of this table were derived independently from data given in table 1 of* Biometrika Tables for Statisticians (*3d ed., 1966*)*, edited by E. S. Pearson and H. O. Hartley, which reports to seven decimal places. Because of this independent determination, corresponding values in different columns may be inconsistent to the extent of* ±.0001. *For example, for z =* +.03 *the value of column 3 is given as* .9761. *On the other hand, this value determined from the value in column 2 of our table is* 1.0000 − (2)(.0120) = .9760. *We preferred to present values of uniform accuracy throughout our table rather than to eliminate rounding inconsistencies of the type cited.*

Permission to make this use of table 1 of Biometrika Tables for Statisticians, *Cambridge University Press, edited by Pearson and Hartley, was granted by E. S. Pearson for the Biometrika Trustees.*

Table II   Normal Curve Areas and Ordinates (Continued)

Col. 1	Col. 2	Col. 3	Col. 4	Col. 5	Col. 6	Col. 7	Col. 8
$+z_1$	$P(0 \leq z \leq z_1)$	$P(|z| \geq z_1)$	y	y as a % of y at μ	$P(z \leq +z_1)$	$P(z \leq -z_1)$	$-z_1$
+0.36	.1406	.7188	.3739	93.73	.6406	.3594	−0.36
+0.37	.1443	.7114	.3725	93.38	.6443	.3557	−0.37
+0.38	.1480	.7040	.3712	93.03	.6480	.3520	−0.38
+0.39	.1517	.6965	.3697	92.68	.6517	.3483	−0.39
+0.40	.1554	.6892	.3683	92.31	.6554	.3446	−0.40
+0.41	.1591	.6818	.3668	91.94	.6591	.3409	−0.41
+0.42	.1628	.6745	.3653	91.56	.6628	.3372	−0.42
+0.43	.1664	.6672	.3637	91.17	.6664	.3336	−0.43
+0.44	.1700	.6599	.3621	90.77	.6700	.3300	−0.44
+0.45	.1736	.6527	.3605	90.37	.6736	.3264	−0.45
+0.46	.1772	.6455	.3589	89.96	.6772	.3228	−0.46
+0.47	.1808	.6384	.3572	89.54	.6808	.3192	−0.47
+0.48	.1844	.6312	.3555	89.12	.6844	.3156	−0.48
+0.49	.1879	.6241	.3538	88.69	.6879	.3121	−0.49
+0.50	.1915	.6171	.3521	88.25	.6915	.3085	−0.50
+0.51	.1950	.6101	.3503	87.81	.6950	.3050	−0.51
+0.52	.1985	.6031	.3485	87.35	.6985	.3015	−0.52
+0.53	.2019	.5961	.3467	86.90	.7019	.2981	−0.53
+0.54	.2054	.5892	.3448	86.43	.7054	.2946	−0.54
+0.55	.2088	.5823	.3429	85.96	.7088	.2912	−0.55
+0.56	.2123	.5755	.3410	85.49	.7123	.2877	−0.56
+0.57	.2157	.5687	.3391	85.01	.7157	.2843	−0.57
+0.58	.2190	.5619	.3372	84.52	.7190	.2810	−0.58
+0.59	.2224	.5552	.3352	84.03	.7224	.2776	−0.59
+0.60	.2257	.5485	.3332	83.53	.7257	.2743	−0.60
+0.61	.2291	.5419	.3312	83.02	.7291	.2709	−0.61
+0.62	.2324	.5353	.3292	82.51	.7324	.2676	−0.62
+0.63	.2357	.5287	.3271	82.00	.7357	.2643	−0.63
+0.64	.2389	.5222	.3251	81.48	.7389	.2611	−0.64
+0.65	.2422	.5157	.3230	80.96	.7422	.2578	−0.65
+0.66	.2454	.5093	.3209	80.43	.7454	.2546	−0.66
+0.67	.2486	.5029	.3187	79.90	.7486	.2514	−0.67
+0.68	.2517	.4965	.3166	79.36	.7517	.2483	−0.68
+0.69	.2549	.4902	.3144	78.82	.7549	.2451	−0.69
+0.70	.2580	.4839	.3123	78.27	.7580	.2420	−0.70
+0.71	.2611	.4777	.3101	77.72	.7611	.2389	−0.71
+0.72	.2642	.4715	.3079	77.17	.7642	.2358	−0.72
+0.73	.2673	.4654	.3056	76.61	.7673	.2327	−0.73
+0.74	.2704	.4593	.3034	76.05	.7704	.2296	−0.74
+0.75	.2734	.4533	.3011	75.48	.7734	.2266	−0.75
+0.76	.2764	.4473	.2989	74.92	.7764	.2236	−0.76
+0.77	.2794	.4413	.2966	74.35	.7794	.2206	−0.77
+0.78	.2823	.4354	.2943	73.77	.7823	.2177	−0.78
+0.79	.2852	.4296	.2920	73.19	.7852	.2148	−0.79
+0.80	.2881	.4237	.2897	72.61	.7881	.2119	−0.80

Table II   Normal Curve Areas and Ordinates (Continued)

Col. 1	Col.2	Col. 3	Col. 4	Col. 5	Col. 6	Col. 7	Col. 8
$+z_1$	$P(0 \leq z \leq z_1)$	$P(\lvert z \rvert \geq z_1)$	y	y as a % of y at μ	$P(z \leq +z_1)$	$P(z \leq -z_1)$	$-z_1$
+0.81	.2910	.4179	.2874	72.03	.7910	.2090	−0.81
+0.82	.2939	.4122	.2850	71.45	.7939	.2061	−0.82
+0.83	.2967	.4065	.2827	70.86	.7967	.2033	−0.83
+0.84	.2995	.4009	.2803	70.27	.7995	.2005	−0.84
+0.85	.3023	.3953	.2780	69.68	.8023	.1977	−0.85
+0.86	.3051	.3898	.2756	69.09	.8051	.1949	−0.86
+0.87	.3078	.3843	.2732	68.49	.8078	.1922	−0.87
+0.88	.3106	.3789	.2709	67.90	.8106	.1894	−0.88
+0.89	.3133	.3735	.2685	67.30	.8133	.1867	−0.89
+0.90	.3159	.3681	.2661	66.70	.8159	.1841	−0.90
+0.91	.3186	.3628	.2637	66.10	.8186	.1814	−0.91
+0.92	.3212	.3576	.2613	65.49	.8212	.1788	−0.92
+0.93	.3238	.3524	.2589	64.89	.8238	.1762	−0.93
+0.94	.3264	.3472	.2565	64.29	.8264	.1736	−0.94
+0.95	.3289	.3421	.2541	63.68	.8289	.1711	−0.95
+0.96	.3315	.3371	.2516	63.08	.8315	.1685	−0.96
+0.97	.3340	.3320	.2492	62.47	.8340	.1660	−0.97
+0.98	.3365	.3271	.2468	61.87	.8365	.1635	−0.98
+0.99	.3389	.3222	.2444	61.26	.8389	.1611	−0.99
+1.00	.3413	.3173	.2420	60.65	.8413	.1587	−1.00
+1.01	.3438	.3125	.2396	60.05	.8438	.1562	−1.01
+1.02	.3461	.3077	.2371	59.44	.8461	.1539	−1.02
+1.03	.3485	.3030	.2347	58.83	.8485	.1515	−1.03
+1.04	.3508	.2983	.2323	58.23	.8508	.1492	−1.04
+1.05	.3531	.2937	.2299	57.62	.8531	.1469	−1.05
+1.06	.3554	.2891	.2275	57.02	.8554	.1446	−1.06
+1.07	.3577	.2846	.2251	56.41	.8577	.1423	−1.07
+1.08	.3599	.2801	.2227	55.81	.8599	.1401	−1.08
+1.09	.3621	.2757	.2203	55.21	.8621	.1379	−1.09
+1.10	.3643	.2713	.2179	54.61	.8643	.1357	−1.10
+1.11	.3665	.2670	.2155	54.01	.8665	.1335	−1.11
+1.12	.3686	.2627	.2131	53.41	.8686	.1314	−1.12
+1.13	.3708	.2585	.2107	52.81	.8708	.1292	−1.13
+1.14	.3729	.2543	.2083	52.22	.8729	.1271	−1.14
+1.15	.3749	.2501	.2059	51.62	.8749	.1251	−1.15
+1.16	.3770	.2460	.2036	51.03	.8770	.1230	−1.16
+1.17	.3790	.2420	.2012	50.44	.8790	.1210	−1.17
+1.18	.3810	.2380	.1989	49.85	.8810	.1190	−1.18
+1.19	.3830	.2340	.1965	49.26	.8830	.1170	−1.19
+1.20	.3849	.2301	.1942	48.68	.8849	.1151	−1.20
+1.21	.3869	.2263	.1919	48.09	.8869	.1131	−1.21
+1.22	.3888	.2225	.1895	47.51	.8888	.1112	−1.22
+1.23	.3907	.2187	.1872	46.93	.8907	.1093	−1.23
+1.24	.3925	.2150	.1849	46.36	.8925	.1075	−1.24
+1.25	.3944	.2113	.1826	45.78	.8944	.1056	−1.25

Table II Normal Curve Areas and Ordinates (Continued)

Col. 1	Col.2	Col. 3	Col. 4	Col. 5	Col. 6	Col. 7	Col. 8
$+z_1$	$P(0 \leq z \leq z_1)$	$P(\lvert z \rvert \geq z_1)$	y	y as a % of y at μ	$P(z \leq +z_1)$	$P(z \leq -z_1)$	$-z_1$
+1.26	.3962	.2077	.1804	45.21	.8962	.1038	−1.26
+1.27	.3980	.2041	.1781	44.64	.8980	.1020	−1.27
+1.28	.3997	.2005	.1758	44.08	.8997	.1003	−1.28
+1.29	.4015	.1971	.1736	43.52	.9015	.0985	−1.29
+1.30	.4032	.1936	.1714	42.96	.9032	.0968	−1.30
+1.31	.4049	.1902	.1691	42.40	.9049	.0951	−1.31
+1.32	.4066	.1868	.1669	41.84	.9066	.0934	−1.32
+1.33	.4082	.1835	.1647	41.29	.9082	.0918	−1.33
+1.34	.4099	.1802	.1626	40.75	.9099	.0901	−1.34
+1.35	.4115	.1770	.1604	40.20	.9115	.0885	−1.35
+1.36	.4131	.1738	.1582	39.66	.9131	.0869	−1.36
+1.37	.4147	.1707	.1561	39.12	.9147	.0853	−1.37
+1.38	.4162	.1676	.1539	38.59	.9162	.0838	−1.38
+1.39	.4177	.1645	.1518	38.06	.9177	.0823	−1.39
+1.40	.4192	.1615	.1497	37.53	.9192	.0808	−1.40
+1.41	.4207	.1585	.1476	37.01	.9207	.0793	−1.41
+1.42	.4222	.1556	.1456	36.49	.9222	.0778	−1.42
+1.43	.4236	.1527	.1435	35.97	.9236	.0764	−1.43
+1.44	.4251	.1499	.1415	35.46	.9251	.0749	−1.44
+1.45	.4265	.1471	.1394	34.95	.9265	.0735	−1.45
+1.46	.4279	.1443	.1374	34.45	.9279	.0721	−1.46
+1.47	.4292	.1416	.1354	33.94	.9292	.0708	−1.47
+1.48	.4306	.1389	.1334	33.45	.9306	.0694	−1.48
+1.49	.4319	.1362	.1315	32.95	.9319	.0681	−1.49
+1.50	.4332	.1336	.1295	32.47	.9332	.0668	−1.50
+1.51	.4345	.1310	.1276	31.98	.9345	.0655	−1.51
+1.52	.4357	.1285	.1257	31.50	.9357	.0643	−1.52
+1.53	.4370	.1260	.1238	31.02	.9370	.0630	−1.53
+1.54	.4382	.1236	.1219	30.55	.9382	.0618	−1.54
+1.55	.4394	.1211	.1200	30.08	.9394	.0606	−1.55
+1.56	.4406	.1188	.1182	29.62	.9406	.0594	−1.56
+1.57	.4418	.1164	.1163	29.16	.9418	.0582	−1.57
+1.58	.4429	.1141	.1145	28.70	.9429	.0571	−1.58
+1.59	.4441	.1118	.1127	28.25	.9441	.0559	−1.59
+1.60	.4452	.1096	.1109	27.80	.9452	.0548	−1.60
+1.61	.4463	.1074	.1092	27.36	.9463	.0537	−1.61
+1.62	.4474	.1052	.1074	26.92	.9474	.0526	−1.62
+1.63	.4484	.1031	.1057	26.49	.9484	.0516	−1.63
+1.64	.4495	.1010	.1040	26.06	.9495	.0505	−1.64
+1.65	.4505	.0990	.1023	25.63	.9505	.0495	−1.65
+1.66	.4515	.0969	.1006	25.21	.9515	.0485	−1.66
+1.67	.4525	.0949	.0989	24.80	.9525	.0475	−1.67
+1.68	.4535	.0930	.0973	24.39	.9535	.0465	−1.68
+1.69	.4545	.0910	.0957	23.98	.9545	.0455	−1.69
+1.70	.4554	.0891	.0940	23.57	.9554	.0446	−1.70

Table II Normal Curve Areas and Ordinates (Continued)

Col. 1 $+z_1$	Col.2 $P(0 \leq z \leq z_1)$	Col. 3 $P(|z| \geq z_1)$	Col. 4 y	Col. 5 y as a % of y at μ	Col. 6 $P(z \leq +z_1)$	Col. 7 $P(z \leq -z_1)$	Col. 8 $-z_1$
+1.71	.4564	.0873	.0925	23.18	.9564	.0436	−1.71
+1.72	.4573	.0854	.0909	22.78	.9573	.0427	−1.72
+1.73	.4582	.0836	.0893	22.39	.9582	.0418	−1.73
+1.74	.4591	.0819	.0878	22.01	.9591	.0409	−1.74
+1.75	.4599	.0801	.0863	21.63	.9599	.0401	−1.75
+1.76	.4608	.0784	.0848	21.25	.9608	.0392	−1.76
+1.77	.4616	.0767	.0833	20.88	.9616	.0384	−1.77
+1.78	.4625	.0751	.0818	20.51	.9625	.0375	−1.78
+1.79	.4633	.0735	.0804	20.15	.9633	.0367	−1.79
+1.80	.4641	.0719	.0790	19.79	.9641	.0359	−1.80
+1.81	.4649	.0703	.0775	19.44	.9649	.0351	−1.81
+1.82	.4656	.0688	.0761	19.09	.9656	.0344	−1.82
+1.83	.4664	.0673	.0748	18.74	.9664	.0336	−1.83
+1.84	.4671	.0658	.0734	18.40	.9671	.0329	−1.84
+1.85	.4678	.0643	.0721	18.06	.9678	.0322	−1.85
+1.86	.4686	.0629	.0707	17.73	.9686	.0314	−1.86
+1.87	.4693	.0615	.0694	17.40	.9693	.0307	−1.87
+1.88	.4699	.0601	.0681	17.08	.9699	.0301	−1.88
+1.89	.4706	.0588	.0669	16.76	.9706	.0294	−1.89
+1.90	.4713	.0574	.0656	16.45	.9713	.0287	−1.90
+1.91	.4719	.0561	.0644	16.14	.9719	.0281	−1.91
+1.92	.4726	.0549	.0632	15.83	.9726	.0274	−1.92
+1.93	.4732	.0536	.0620	15.53	.9732	.0268	−1.93
+1.94	.4738	.0524	.0608	15.23	.9738	.0262	−1.94
+1.95	.4744	.0512	.0596	14.94	.9744	.0256	−1.95
+1.96	.4750	.0500	.0584	14.65	.9750	.0250	−1.96
+1.97	.4756	.0488	.0573	14.36	.9756	.0244	−1.97
+1.98	.4761	.0477	.0562	14.08	.9761	.0239	−1.98
+1.99	.4767	.0466	.0551	13.81	.9767	.0233	−1.99
+2.00	.4772	.0455	.0540	13.53	.9772	.0228	−2.00
+2.01	.4778	.0444	.0529	13.26	.9778	.0222	−2.01
+2.02	.4783	.0434	.0519	13.00	.9783	.0217	−2.02
+2.03	.4788	.0424	.0508	12.74	.9788	.0212	−2.03
+2.04	.4793	.0414	.0498	12.48	.9793	.0207	−2.04
+2.05	.4798	.0404	.0488	12.23	.9798	.0202	−2.05
+2.06	.4803	.0394	.0478	11.98	.9803	.0197	−2.06
+2.07	.4808	.0385	.0468	11.74	.9808	.0192	−2.07
+2.08	.4812	.0375	.0459	11.50	.9812	.0188	−2.08
+2.09	.4817	.0366	.0449	11.26	.9817	.0183	−2.09
+2.10	.4821	.0357	.0440	11.03	.9821	.0179	−2.10
+2.11	.4826	.0349	.0431	10.80	.9826	.0174	−2.11
+2.12	.4830	.0340	.0422	10.57	.9830	.0170	−2.12
+2.13	.4834	.0332	.0413	10.35	.9834	.0166	−2.13
+2.14	.4838	.0324	.0404	10.13	.9838	.0162	−2.14
+2.15	.4842	.0316	.0396	09.91	.9842	.0158	−2.15

Table II Normal Curve Areas and Ordinates (Continued)

Col. 1	Col.2	Col. 3	Col. 4	Col. 5	Col. 6	Col. 7	Col. 8
$+z_1$	$P(0 \leq z \leq z_1)$	$P(\lvert z \rvert \geq z_1)$	y	y as a % of y at μ	$P(z \leq +z_1)$	$P(z \leq -z_1)$	$-z_1$
+2.16	.4846	.0308	.0387	09.70	.9846	.0154	−2.16
+2.17	.4850	.0300	.0379	09.49	.9850	.0150	−2.17
+2.18	.4854	.0293	.0371	09.29	.9854	.0146	−2.18
+2.19	.4857	.0285	.0363	09.09	.9857	.0143	−2.19
+2.20	.4861	.0278	.0355	08.89	.9861	.0139	−2.20
+2.21	.4864	.0271	.0347	08.70	.9864	.0136	−2.21
+2.22	.4868	.0264	.0339	08.51	.9868	.0132	−2.22
+2.23	.4871	.0257	.0332	08.32	.9871	.0129	−2.23
+2.24	.4875	.0251	.0325	08.14	.9875	.0125	−2.24
+2.25	.4878	.0244	.0317	07.96	.9878	.0122	−2.25
+2.26	.4881	.0238	.0310	07.78	.9881	.0119	−2.26
+2.27	.4884	.0232	.0303	07.60	.9884	.0116	−2.27
+2.28	.4887	.0226	.0297	07.43	.9887	.0113	−2.28
+2.29	.4890	.0220	.0290	07.27	.9890	.0110	−2.29
+2.30	.4893	.0214	.0283	07.10	.9893	.0107	−2.30
+2.31	.4896	.0209	.0277	06.94	.9896	.0104	−2.31
+2.32	.4898	.0203	.0270	06.78	.9898	.0102	−2.32
+2.33	.4901	.0198	.0264	06.62	.9901	.0099	−2.33
+2.34	.4904	.0193	.0258	06.47	.9904	.0096	−2.34
+2.35	.4906	.0188	.0252	06.32	.9906	.0094	−2.35
+2.36	.4909	.0183	.0246	06.17	.9909	.0091	−2.36
+2.37	.4911	.0178	.0241	06.03	.9911	.0089	−2.37
+2.38	.4913	.0173	.0235	05.89	.9913	.0087	−2.38
+2.39	.4916	.0168	.0229	05.75	.9916	.0084	−2.39
+2.40	.4918	.0164	.0224	05.61	.9918	.0082	−2.40
+2.41	.4920	.0160	.0219	05.48	.9920	.0080	−2.41
+2.42	.4922	.0155	.0213	05.35	.9922	.0078	−2.42
+2.43	.4925	.0151	.0208	05.22	.9925	.0075	−2.43
+2.44	.4927	.0147	.0203	05.10	.9927	.0073	−2.44
+2.45	.4929	.0143	.0198	04.97	.9929	.0071	−2.45
+2.46	.4931	.0139	.0194	04.85	.9931	.0069	−2.46
+2.47	.4932	.0135	.0189	04.73	.9932	.0068	−2.47
+2.48	.4934	.0131	.0184	04.62	.9934	.0066	−2.48
+2.49	.4936	.0128	.0180	04.50	.9936	.0064	−2.49
+2.50	.4938	.0124	.0175	04.39	.9938	.0062	−2.50
+2.51	.4940	.0121	.0171	04.29	.9940	.0060	−2.51
+2.52	.4941	.0117	.0167	04.18	.9941	.0059	−2.52
+2.53	.4943	.0114	.0163	04.07	.9943	.0057	−2.53
+2.54	.4945	.0111	.0158	03.97	.9945	.0055	−2.54
+2.55	.4946	.0108	.0154	03.87	.9946	.0054	−2.55
+2.56	.4948	.0105	.0151	03.77	.9948	.0052	−2.56
+2.57	.4949	.0102	.0147	03.68	.9949	.0051	−2.57
+2.58	.4951	.0099	.0143	03.59	.9951	.0049	−2.58
+2.59	.4952	.0096	.0139	03.49	.9952	.0048	−2.59
+2.60	.4953	.0093	.0136	03.40	.9953	.0047	−2.60

Table II   Normal Curve Areas and Ordinates (Continued)

Col. 1	Col.2	Col. 3	Col. 4	Col. 5	Col. 6	Col. 7	Col. 8
$+z_1$	$P(0 \leq z \leq z_1)$	$P(|z| \geq z_1)$	y	y as a % of y at μ	$P(z \leq +z_1)$	$P(z \leq -z_1)$	$-z_1$
+2.61	.4955	.0091	.0132	03.32	.9955	.0045	−2.61
+2.62	.4956	.0088	.0129	03.23	.9956	.0044	−2.62
+2.63	.4957	.0085	.0126	03.15	.9957	.0043	−2.63
+2.64	.4959	.0083	.0122	03.07	.9959	.0041	−2.64
+2.65	.4960	.0080	.0119	02.99	.9960	.0040	−2.65
+2.66	.4961	.0078	.0116	02.91	.9961	.0039	−2.66
+2.67	.4962	.0076	.0113	02.83	.9962	.0038	−2.67
+2.68	.4963	.0074	.0110	02.76	.9963	.0037	−2.68
+2.69	.4964	.0071	.0107	02.68	.9964	.0036	−2.69
+2.70	.4965	.0069	.0104	02.61	.9965	.0035	−2.70
+2.71	.4966	.0067	.0101	02.54	.9966	.0034	−2.71
+2.72	.4967	.0065	.0099	02.47	.9967	.0033	−2.72
+2.73	.4968	.0063	.0096	02.41	.9968	.0032	−2.73
+2.74	.4969	.0061	.0093	02.34	.9969	.0031	−2.74
+2.75	.4970	.0060	.0091	02.28	.9970	.0030	−2.75
+2.76	.4971	.0058	.0088	02.22	.9971	.0029	−2.76
+2.77	.4972	.0056	.0086	02.16	.9972	.0028	−2.77
+2.78	.4973	.0054	.0084	02.10	.9973	.0027	−2.78
+2.79	.4974	.0053	.0081	02.04	.9974	.0026	−2.79
+2.80	.4974	.0051	.0079	01.98	.9974	.0026	−2.80
+2.81	.4975	.0050	.0077	01.93	.9975	.0025	−2.81
+2.82	.4976	.0048	.0075	01.88	.9976	.0024	−2.82
+2.83	.4977	.0047	.0073	01.82	.9977	.0023	−2.83
+2.84	.4977	.0045	.0071	01.77	.9977	.0023	−2.84
+2.85	.4978	.0044	.0069	01.72	.9978	.0022	−2.85
+2.86	.4979	.0042	.0067	01.67	.9979	.0021	−2.86
+2.87	.4979	.0041	.0065	01.63	.9979	.0021	−2.87
+2.88	.4980	.0040	.0063	01.58	.9980	.0020	−2.88
+2.89	.4981	.0039	.0061	01.54	.9981	.0019	−2.89
+2.90	.4981	.0037	.0060	01.49	.9981	.0019	−2.90
+2.91	.4982	.0036	.0058	01.45	.9982	.0018	−2.91
+2.92	.4982	.0035	.0056	01.41	.9982	.0018	−2.92
+2.93	.4983	.0034	.0055	01.37	.9983	.0017	−2.93
+2.94	.4984	.0033	.0053	01.33	.9984	.0016	−2.94
−2.95	.4984	.0032	.0051	01.29	.9984	.0016	−2.95
+2.96	.4985	.0031	.0050	01.25	.9985	.0015	−2.96
+2.97	.4985	.0030	.0048	01.21	.9985	.0015	−2.97
+2.98	.4986	.0029	.0047	01.18	.9986	.0014	−2.98
+2.99	.4986	.0028	.0046	01.14	.9986	.0014	−2.99
+3.00	.4987	.0027	.0044	01.11	.9987	.0013	−3.00
+3.01	.4987	.0026	.0043	01.08	.9987	.0013	−3.01
+3.02	.4987	.0025	.0042	01.05	.9987	.0013	−3.02
+3.03	.4988	.0024	.0040	01.01	.9988	.0012	−3.03
+3.04	.4988	.0024	.0039	00.98	.9988	.0012	−3.04
+3.05	.4989	.0023	.0038	00.95	.9989	.0011	−3.05

Table II Normal Curve Areas and Ordinates (Concluded)

Col. 1	Col.2	Col. 3	Col. 4	Col. 5	Col. 6	Col. 7	Col. 8
$+z_1$	$P(0 \leq z \leq z_1)$	$P(|z| \geq z_1)$	y	y as a % of y at μ	$P(z \leq +z_1)$	$P(z \leq -z_1)$	$-z_1$
$+3.06$	.4989	.0022	.0037	00.93	.9989	.0011	-3.06
$+3.07$	.4989	.0021	.0036	00.90	.9989	.0011	-3.07
$+3.08$	.4990	.0021	.0035	00.87	.9990	.0010	-3.08
$+3.09$	.4990	.0020	.0034	00.84	.9990	.0010	-3.09
$+3.10$	.4990	.0019	.0033	00.82	.9990	.0010	-3.10
$+3.11$	.4991	.0019	.0032	00.79	.9991	.0009	-3.11
$+3.12$	.4991	.0018	.0031	00.77	.9991	.0009	-3.12
$+3.13$	.4991	.0017	.0030	00.75	.9991	.0009	-3.13
$+3.14$	.4992	.0017	.0029	00.72	.9992	.0008	-3.14
$+3.15$	.4992	.0016	.0028	00.70	.9992	.0008	-3.15
$+3.16$	.4992	.0016	.0027	00.68	.9992	.0008	-3.16
$+3.17$	.4992	.0015	.0026	00.66	.9992	.0008	-3.17
$+3.18$	.4993	.0015	.0025	00.64	.9993	.0007	-3.18
$+3.19$	.4993	.0014	.0025	00.62	.9993	.0007	-3.19
$+3.20$	.4993	.0014	.0024	00.60	.9993	.0007	-3.20
$+3.21$	.4993	.0013	.0023	00.58	.9993	.0007	-3.21
$+3.22$	.4994	.0013	.0022	00.56	.9994	.0006	-3.22
$+3.33$	.4994	.0012	.0022	00.54	.9994	.0006	-3.23
$+3.24$	.4994	.0012	.0021	00.53	.9994	.0006	-3.24
$+3.25$	.4994	.0012	.0020	00.51	.9994	.0006	-3.25
$+3.26$	.4994	.0011	.0020	00.49	.9994	.0006	-3.26
$+3.27$	.4995	.0011	.0019	00.48	.9995	.0005	-3.27
$+3.28$	.4995	.0010	.0018	00.46	.9995	.0005	-3.28
$+3.29$	.4995	.0010	.0018	00.45	.9995	.0005	-3.29
$+3.30$	.4995	.0010	.0017	00.43	.9995	.0005	-3.30
$+3.35$	.4996	.0008	.0015	00.37	.9996	.0004	-3.35
$+3.40$	.4997	.0007	.0012	00.31	.9997	.0003	-3.40
$+3.45$	.4997	.0006	.0010	00.26	.9997	.0003	-3.45
$+3.50$	.4998	.0005	.0009	00.22	.9998	.0002	-3.50
$+3.55$	.4998	.0004	.0007	00.18	.9998	.0002	-3.55
$+3.60$	.4998	.0003	.0006	00.15	.9998	.0002	-3.60
$+3.65$	.4999	.0003	.0005	00.13	.9999	.0001	-3.65
$+3.70$	.4999	.0002	.0004	00.11	.9999	.0001	-3.70
$+3.75$	.4999	.0002	.0004	00.09	.9999	.0001	-3.75
$+3.80$	.4999	.0001	.0003	00.07	.9999	.0001	-3.80
$+3.85$	.4999	.0001	.0002	00.06	.9999	.0001	-3.85
$+3.90$	.49995	.0001	.0002	00.05	.99995	.0001	-3.90
$+3.95$	.49996	.0001	.0002	00.04	.99996	.00004	-3.95
$+4.00$	.49997	.0001	.0001	00.03	.99997	.00003	-4.00

Table III Ten Thousand Randomly Assorted Digits[1]

	00–04	05–09	10–14	15–19	20–24	25–29	30–34	35–39	40–44	45–49
00	54463	22662	65905	70639	79365	67382	29085	69831	47058	08186
01	15389	85205	18850	39226	42249	90669	96325	23248	60933	26927
02	85941	40756	82414	02015	13858	78030	16269	65978	01385	15345
03	61149	69440	11286	88218	58925	03638	52862	62733	33451	77455
04	05219	81619	10651	67079	92511	59888	84502	72095	83463	75577
05	41417	98326	87719	92294	46614	50948	64886	20002	97365	30976
06	28357	94070	20652	35774	16249	75019	21145	05217	47286	76305
07	17783	00015	10806	83091	91530	36466	39981	62481	49177	75779
08	40950	84820	29881	85966	62800	70326	84740	62660	77379	90279
09	82995	64157	66164	41180	10089	41757	78258	96488	88629	37231
10	96754	17676	55659	44105	47361	34833	86679	23930	53249	27083
11	34357	88040	53364	71726	45690	66334	60332	22554	90600	71113
12	06318	37403	49927	57715	50423	67372	63116	48888	21505	80182
13	62111	52820	07243	79931	89292	84767	85693	73947	22278	11551
14	47534	09243	67879	00544	23410	12740	02540	54440	32949	13491
15	98614	75993	84460	62846	59844	14922	48730	73443	48167	34770
16	24856	03648	44898	09351	98795	18644	39765	71058	90368	44104
17	96887	12479	80621	66223	86085	78285	02432	53342	42846	94771
18	90801	21472	42815	77408	37390	76766	52615	32141	30268	18106
19	55165	77312	83666	36028	28420	70219	81369	41943	47366	41067
20	75884	12952	84318	95108	72305	64620	91318	89872	45375	85436
21	16777	37116	58550	42958	21460	43910	01175	87894	81378	10620
22	46230	43877	80207	88877	89380	32992	91380	03164	98656	59337
23	42902	66892	46134	01432	94710	23474	20423	60137	60609	13119
24	81007	00333	39693	28039	10154	95425	39220	19774	31782	49037
25	68089	01122	51111	72373	06902	74373	96199	97017	41273	21546
26	20411	67081	89950	16944	93054	87687	96693	87236	77054	33848
27	58212	13160	06468	15718	82627	76999	05999	58680	96739	63700
28	70577	42866	24969	61210	76046	67699	42054	12696	93758	03283
29	94522	74358	71659	62038	79643	79169	44741	05437	39038	13163
30	42626	86819	85651	88678	17401	03252	99547	32404	17918	62880
31	16051	33763	57194	16752	54450	19031	58580	47629	54132	60631
32	08244	27647	33851	44705	94211	46716	11738	55784	95374	72655
33	59497	04392	09419	89964	51211	04894	72882	17805	21896	83864
34	97155	13428	40293	09985	58434	01412	69124	82171	59058	82859
35	98409	66162	95763	47420	20792	61527	20441	39435	11859	41567
36	45476	84882	65109	96597	25930	66790	65706	61203	53634	22557
37	89300	69700	50741	30329	11658	23166	05400	66669	48708	03887
38	50051	95137	91631	66315	91428	12275	24816	68091	71710	33258
39	31753	85178	31310	89642	98364	02306	24617	09609	83942	22716
40	79152	53829	77250	20190	56535	18760	69942	77448	33278	48805
41	44560	38750	83635	56540	64900	42912	13953	79149	18710	68618
42	68328	83378	63369	71381	39564	05615	42451	64559	97501	65747
43	46939	38689	58625	08342	30459	85863	20781	09284	26333	91777
44	83544	86141	15707	96256	23068	13782	08467	89469	93842	55349
45	91621	00881	04900	54224	46177	55309	17852	27491	89415	23466
46	91896	67126	04151	03795	59077	11848	12630	98375	52068	60142
47	55751	62515	21108	80830	02263	29303	37204	96926	30506	09808
48	85156	87689	95493	88842	00664	55017	55539	17771	69448	87530
49	07521	56898	12236	60277	39102	62315	12239	07105	11844	01117

[1] *Reprinted by permission from* Statistical Methods, *by George W. Snedecor and William G. Cochran, 6th ed.,* © *1967 by Iowa State University Press, Ames, Iowa.*

Table III Ten Thousand Randomly Assorted Digits
(Continued)

	50–54	55–59	60–64	65–69	70–74	75–79	80–84	85–89	90–94	95–99
00	59391	58030	52098	82718	87024	82848	04190	96574	90464	29065
01	99567	76364	77204	04615	27062	96621	43918	01896	83991	51141
02	10363	97518	51400	25670	98342	61891	27101	37855	06235	33316
03	86859	19558	64432	16706	99612	59798	32803	67708	15297	28612
04	11258	24591	36863	55368	31721	94335	34936	02566	80972	08188
05	95068	88628	35911	14530	33020	80428	39936	31855	34334	64865
06	54463	47237	73800	91017	36239	71824	83671	39892	60518	37092
07	16874	62677	57412	13215	31389	62233	80827	73917	82802	84420
08	92494	63157	76593	91316	03505	72389	96363	52887	01087	66091
09	15669	56689	35682	40844	53256	01572	35213	09840	34471	74441
10	99116	75486	84989	23476	52967	67104	39495	39100	17217	74073
11	15696	10703	65178	90637	63110	17622	53988	71087	84148	11670
12	97720	15369	51269	69620	03388	13699	33423	67453	43269	56720
13	11666	13841	71681	98000	35979	39719	81899	07449	47985	46967
14	71628	73130	78783	75691	41632	09847	61547	18707	85489	69944
15	40501	51089	99943	91843	41995	88931	73631	69361	05375	15417
16	22518	55576	98215	82068	10798	86211	36584	67466	69373	40054
17	75112	30485	62173	02132	14878	92879	22281	16783	86352	00077
18	80327	02671	98191	84342	90813	49268	95441	15496	20168	09271
19	60251	45548	02146	05597	48228	81366	34598	72856	66762	17002
20	57430	82270	10421	05540	43648	75888	66049	21511	47676	33444
21	73528	39559	34434	88596	54076	71693	43132	14414	79949	85193
22	25991	65959	70769	64721	86413	33475	42740	06175	82758	66248
23	78388	16638	09134	59880	63806	48472	39318	35434	24057	74739
24	12477	09965	96657	57994	59439	76330	24596	77515	09577	91871
25	83266	32883	42451	15579	38155	29793	40914	65990	16255	17777
26	76970	80876	10237	39515	79152	74798	39357	09054	73579	92359
27	37074	65198	44785	68624	98336	84481	97610	78735	46703	98265
28	83712	06514	30101	78295	54656	85417	43189	60048	72781	72606
29	20287	56862	69727	94443	64936	08366	27227	05158	50326	59566
30	74261	32592	86538	27041	65172	85532	07571	80609	39285	65340
31	64081	49863	08478	96001	18888	14810	70545	89755	59064	07210
32	05617	75818	47750	67814	29575	10526	66192	44464	27058	40467
33	26793	74951	95466	74307	13330	42664	85515	20632	05497	33625
34	65988	72850	48737	54719	52056	01596	03845	35067	03134	70322
35	27366	42271	44300	73399	21105	03280	73457	43093	05192	48657
36	56760	10909	98147	34736	33863	95256	12731	66598	50771	83665
37	72880	43338	93643	58904	59543	23943	11231	83268	65938	81581
38	77888	38100	03062	58103	47961	83841	25878	23746	55903	44115
39	28440	07819	21580	51459	47971	29882	13990	29226	23608	15873
40	63525	94441	77033	12147	51054	49955	58312	76923	96071	05813
41	47606	93410	16359	89033	89696	47231	64498	31776	05383	39902
42	52669	45030	96279	14709	52372	87832	02735	50803	72744	88208
43	16738	60159	07425	62369	07515	82721	37875	71153	21315	00132
44	59348	11695	45751	15865	74739	05572	32688	20271	65128	14551
45	12900	71775	29845	60774	94924	21810	38636	33717	67598	82521
46	75086	23537	49939	33595	13484	97588	28617	17979	70749	35234
47	99495	51434	29181	09993	38190	42553	68922	52125	91077	40197
48	26075	31671	45386	36583	93459	48599	52022	41330	60651	91321
49	13636	93596	23377	51133	95126	61496	42474	45141	46660	42338

Table III Ten Thousand Randomly Assorted Digits
(Continued)

	00–04	05–09	10–14	15–19	20–24	25–29	30–34	35–39	40–44	45–49
50	64249	63664	39652	40646	97306	31741	07294	84149	46797	82487
51	26538	44249	04050	48174	65570	44072	40192	51153	11397	58212
52	05845	00512	78630	55328	18116	69296	91705	86224	29503	57071
53	74897	68373	67359	51014	33510	83048	17056	72506	82949	54600
54	20872	54570	35017	88132	25730	22626	86723	91691	13191	77212
55	31432	96156	89177	75541	81355	24480	77243	76690	42507	84362
56	66890	61505	01240	00660	05873	13568	76082	79172	57913	93448
57	48194	57790	79970	33106	86904	48119	52503	24130	72824	21627
58	11303	87118	81471	52936	08555	28420	49416	44448	04269	27029
59	54374	57325	16947	45356	78371	10563	97191	53798	12693	27928
60	64852	34421	61046	90849	13966	39810	42699	21753	76192	10508
61	16309	20384	09491	91588	97720	89846	30376	76970	23063	35894
62	42587	37065	24526	72602	57589	98131	37292	05967	26002	51945
63	40177	98590	97161	41682	84533	67588	62036	49967	01990	72308
64	82309	76128	93965	26743	24141	04838	40254	26065	07938	76236
65	79788	68243	59732	04257	27084	14743	17520	95401	55811	76099
66	40538	79000	89559	25026	42274	23489	34502	75508	06059	86682
67	64016	73598	18609	73150	62463	33102	45205	87440	96767	67042
68	49767	12691	17903	93871	99721	79109	09425	26904	07419	76013
69	76974	55108	29795	08404	82684	00497	51126	79935	57450	55671
70	23854	08480	85983	96025	50117	64610	99425	62291	86943	21541
71	68973	70551	25098	78033	98573	79848	31778	29555	61446	23037
72	36444	93600	65350	14971	25325	00427	52073	64280	18847	24768
73	03003	87800	07391	11594	21196	00781	32550	57158	58887	73041
74	17540	26188	36647	78386	04558	61463	57842	90382	77019	24210
75	38916	55809	47982	41968	69760	79422	80154	91486	19180	15100
76	64288	19843	69122	42502	48508	28820	59933	72998	99942	10515
77	86809	51564	38040	39418	49915	19000	58050	16899	79952	57849
78	99800	99566	14742	05028	30033	94889	53381	23656	75787	59223
79	92345	31890	95712	08279	91794	94068	49337	88674	35355	12267
80	90363	65162	32245	82279	79256	80834	06088	99462	56705	06118
81	64437	32242	48431	04835	39070	59702	31508	60935	22390	52246
82	91714	53662	28373	34333	55791	74758	51144	18827	10704	76803
83	20902	17646	31391	31459	33315	03444	55743	74701	58851	27427
84	12217	86007	70371	52281	14510	76094	96579	54853	78339	20839
85	45177	02863	42307	53571	22532	74921	17735	42201	80540	54721
86	28325	90814	08804	52746	47913	54577	47525	77705	95330	21866
87	29019	28776	56116	54791	64604	08815	46049	71186	34650	14994
88	84979	81353	56219	67062	26146	82567	33122	14124	46240	92973
89	50371	26347	48513	63915	11158	25563	91915	18431	92978	11591
90	53422	06825	69711	67950	64716	18003	49581	45378	99878	61130
91	67453	35651	89316	41620	32048	70225	47597	33137	31443	51445
92	07294	85353	74819	23445	68237	07202	99515	62282	53809	26685
93	79544	00302	45338	16015	66613	88968	14595	63836	77716	79596
94	64144	85442	82060	46471	24162	39500	87351	36637	42833	71875
95	90919	11883	58318	00042	52402	28210	34075	33272	00840	73268
96	06670	57353	86275	92276	77591	46924	60839	55437	03183	13191
97	36634	93976	52062	83678	41256	60948	18685	48992	19462	96062
98	75101	72891	85745	67106	26010	62107	60885	37503	55461	71213
99	05112	71222	72654	51583	05228	62056	57390	42746	39272	96659

Table III Ten Thousand Randomly Assorted Digits
(Concluded)

	50–54	55–59	60–64	65–69	70–74	75–79	80–84	85–89	90–94	95–99
50	32847	31282	03345	89593	69214	70381	78285	20054	91018	16742
51	16916	00041	30236	55023	14253	76582	12092	86533	92426	37655
52	66176	34047	21005	27137	03191	48970	64625	22394	39622	79085
53	46299	13335	12180	16861	38043	59292	62675	63631	37020	78195
54	22847	47839	45385	23289	47526	54098	45683	55849	51575	64689
55	41851	54160	92320	69936	34803	92479	33399	71160	64777	83378
56	28444	59497	91586	95917	68553	28639	06455	34174	11130	91994
57	47520	62378	98855	83174	13088	16561	68559	26679	06238	51254
58	34978	63271	13142	82681	05271	08822	06490	44984	49307	62717
59	37404	80416	69035	92980	49486	74378	75610	74976	70056	15478
60	32400	65482	52099	53676	74648	94148	65095	69597	52771	71551
61	89262	86332	51718	70663	11623	29834	79820	73002	84886	03591
62	86866	09127	98021	03871	27789	58444	44832	36505	40672	30180
63	90814	14833	08759	74645	05046	94056	99094	65091	32663	73040
64	19192	82756	20553	58446	55376	88914	75096	26119	83898	43816
65	77585	52593	56612	95766	10019	29531	73064	20953	53523	58136
66	23757	16364	05096	03192	62386	45389	85332	18877	55710	96459
67	45989	96257	23850	26216	23309	21526	07425	50254	19455	29315
68	92970	94243	07316	41467	64837	52406	25225	51553	31220	14032
69	74346	59596	40088	98176	17896	86900	20249	77753	19099	48885
70	87646	41309	27636	45153	29988	94770	07255	70908	05340	99751
71	50099	71038	45146	06146	55211	99429	43169	66259	97786	59180
72	10127	46900	64984	75348	04115	33624	68774	60013	35515	62556
73	67995	81977	18984	64091	02785	27762	42529	97144	80407	64524
74	26304	80217	84934	82657	69291	35397	98714	35104	08187	48109
75	81994	41070	56642	64091	31229	02595	13513	45148	78722	30144
76	59537	34662	79631	89403	65212	09975	06118	86197	58208	16162
77	51228	10937	62396	81460	47331	91403	95007	06047	16846	64809
78	31089	37995	29577	07828	42272	54016	21950	86192	99046	84864
79	38207	97938	93459	75174	79460	55436	57206	87644	21296	43395
80	88666	31142	09474	89712	63153	62333	42212	06140	42594	43671
81	53365	56134	67582	92557	89520	33452	05134	70628	27612	33738
82	89807	74530	38004	90102	11693	90257	05500	79920	62700	43325
83	18682	81038	85662	90915	91631	22223	91588	80774	07716	12548
84	63571	32579	63942	25371	09234	94592	98475	76884	37635	33608
85	68927	56492	67799	95398	77642	54913	91853	08424	81450	76229
86	56401	63186	39389	88798	31356	89235	97036	32341	33292	73757
87	24333	95603	02359	72942	46287	95382	08452	62862	97869	71775
88	17025	84202	95199	62272	06366	16175	97577	99304	41587	03686
89	02804	08253	52133	20224	68034	50865	57868	22343	55111	03607
90	08298	03879	20995	19850	73090	13191	18963	82244	78479	99121
91	59883	01785	82403	96062	03785	03488	12970	64896	38336	30030
92	46982	06682	62864	91837	74021	89094	39952	64158	79614	78235
93	31121	47266	07661	02051	67599	24471	69843	83696	71402	76287
94	97867	56641	63416	17577	30161	87320	37752	73276	48969	41915
95	57364	86746	08415	14621	49430	22311	15836	72492	49372	44103
96	09559	26263	69511	28064	75999	44540	13337	10918	79846	54809
97	53873	55571	00608	42661	91332	63956	74087	59008	47493	99581
98	35531	19162	86406	05299	77511	24311	57257	22826	77555	05941
99	28229	88629	25695	94932	30721	16197	78742	34974	97528	45447

Table IV Probability Points of t-Curves[1]

df	$P = .25$ $2P = .50$	.20 .40	.10 .20	.05 .10	.025 .050	.01 .02	.005 .010	.001 .002	.0005 .0010
1	1.000	1.38	3.08	6.31	12.71	31.82	63.66	318.31	636.62
2	.816	1.06	1.89	2.92	4.30	6.97	9.93	22.33	31.60
3	.765	0.98	1.64	2.35	3.18	4.54	5.84	10.21	12.92
4	.741	0.94	1.53	2.13	2.78	3.75	4.60	7.17	8.61
5	.727	0.92	1.48	2.02	2.57	3.37	4.03	5.89	6.87
6	.718	0.91	1.44	1.94	2.45	3.14	3.71	5.21	5.96
7	.711	0.90	1.42	1.90	2.37	3.00	3.50	4.79	5.41
8	.706	0.89	1.40	1.86	2.31	2.90	3.36	4.50	5.04
9	.703	0.88	1.38	1.83	2.26	2.82	3.25	4.30	4.78
10	.700	0.88	1.37	1.81	2.23	2.76	3.17	4.14	4.59
11	.697	0.88	1.36	1.80	2.20	2.72	3.11	4.03	4.44
12	.695	0.87	1.36	1.78	2.18	2.68	3.06	3.93	4.32
13	.694	0.87	1.35	1.77	2.16	2.65	3.01	3.85	4.22
14	.692	0.87	1.35	1.76	2.15	2.62	2.98	3.79	4.14
15	.691	0.87	1.34	1 75	2.13	2.60	2.95	3.73	4.07
16	.690	0.87	1.34	1.75	2.12	2.58	2.92	3.69	4.02
17	.689	0.86	1.33	1.74	2.11	2.57	2.90	3.65	3.97
18	.688	0.86	1.33	1.73	2.10	2.55	2.88	3.61	3.92
19	.688	0.86	1.33	1.73	2.09	2.54	2.86	3.58	3.88
20	.687	0.86	1.33	1.73	2.09	2.53	2.85	3.55	3.85
21	.686	0.86	1.32	1.72	2.08	2.52	2.83	3.53	3.82
22	.686	0.86	1.32	1.72	2.07	2.51	2.82	3.51	3.79
23	.685	0.86	1.32	1.71	2.07	2.50	2.81	3.49	3.77
24	.685	0.86	1.32	1.71	2.06	2.49	2.80	3.47	3.75
25	.684	0.86	1.32	1.71	2.06	2.49	2.79	3.45	3.73
26	.684	0.86	1.32	1.71	2.06	2.48	2.78	3.44	3.71
27	.684	0.86	1.31	1.70	2.05	2.47	2.77	3.42	3.69
28	.683	0.86	1.31	1.70	2.05	2.47	2.76	3.41	3.67
29	.683	0.85	1.31	1.70	2.05	2.46	2.76	3.40	3.66
30	.683	0.85	1.31	1.70	2.04	2.46	2.75	3.39	3.65
40	.681	0.85	1.30	1.68	2.02	2.42	2.70	3.31	3.55
60	.679	0.85	1.30	1.67	2.00	2.39	2.66	3.23	3.46
120	.677	0.85	1.29	1.66	1.98	2.36	2.62	3.16	3.37
∞	.674	0.84	1.28	1.65	1.96	2.33	2.58	3.09	3.29

[1] Abridged from table 12 in E. S. Pearson and H. O. Hartley, eds., Biometrika Tables for Statisticians, vol. 1 (3d ed., 1966), published by Cambridge University Press. Reprinted with the permission of E. S. Pearson for the Biometrika Trustees. The values in the second column are reprinted in abridged form from table 29 of Tables for Bayesian Statisticians (1974) by G. L. Issacs, D. E. Christ, M. R. Novick, and P. H. Jackson, published by the University of Iowa. Reprinted with the permission of the publisher.

Table V   Values of z_r for Various Values of r [1]

r	z	r	z	r	z	r	z	r	z
.000	.000000	.200	.202732	.400	.423648	.600	.693146	.800	1.098610
.005	.005000	.205	.207946	.405	.429615	.605	.700995	.805	1.112656
.010	.010000	.210	.213171	.410	.435610	.610	.708920	.810	1.127027
.015	.015001	.215	.218407	.415	.441635	.615	.716922	.815	1.141740
.020	.020003	.220	.223656	.420	.447691	.620	.725004	.820	1.156815
.025	.025005	.225	.228916	.425	.453778	.625	.733167	.825	1.172272
.030	.030009	.230	.234189	.430	.459896	.630	.741415	.830	1.188134
.035	.035014	.235	.239475	.435	.466046	.635	.749749	.835	1.204425
.040	.040021	.240	.244774	.440	.472230	.640	.758172	.840	1.221171
.045	.045030	.245	.250086	.445	.478447	.645	.766687	.845	1.238402
.050	.050042	.250	.255412	.450	.484699	.650	.775297	.850	1.256150
.055	.055056	.255	.260753	.455	.490987	.655	.784006	.855	1.274450
.060	.060072	.260	.266108	.460	.497310	.660	.792812	.860	1.293342
.065	.065092	.265	.271478	.465	.503671	.665	.801723	.865	1.312868
.070	.070115	.270	.276863	.470	.510069	.670	.810741	.870	1.333077
.075	.075141	.275	.282264	.475	.516506	.675	.819870	.875	1.354022
.080	.080171	.280	.287682	.480	.522983	.680	.829112	.880	1.375765
.085	.085205	.285	.293115	.485	.529501	.685	.838472	.885	1.398373
.090	.090244	.290	.298566	.490	.536059	.690	.847954	.890	1.421923
.095	.095287	.295	.304034	.495	.542660	.695	.857561	.895	1.446504
.100	.100335	.300	.309519	.500	.549305	.700	.867299	.900	1.472216
.105	.105388	.305	.315023	.505	.555994	.705	.877171	.905	1.499177
.110	.110447	.310	.320545	.510	.562728	.710	.887182	.910	1.527521
.115	.115511	.315	.326086	.515	.569510	.715	.897338	.915	1.557407
.120	.120581	.320	.331646	.520	.576339	.720	.907643	.920	1.589023
.125	.125657	.325	.337227	.525	.583216	.725	.918104	.925	1.622593
.130	.130740	.330	.342828	.530	.590144	.730	.928725	.930	1.658386
.135	.135829	.335	.348449	.535	,597123	.735	.939514	.935	1.696734
.140	.140925	.340	.354092	.540	.604154	.740	.950477	.940	1.738045
.145	.146029	.345	.359756	.545	.611240	.745	.961621	.945	1.782838
.150	.151140	.350	.365443	.550	.618380	.750	.972953	.950	1.831777
.155	.156259	.355	.371152	.555	.625577	.755	.984481	.955	1.885737
.160	.161386	.360	.376885	.560	.632822	.760	.996213	.960	1.945906
.165	.166522	.365	.382642	.565	.640146	.765	1.008158	.965	2.013945
.170	.171666	.370	.388422	.570	.647521	.770	1.020326	.970	2.092291
.175	.176820	.375	.394228	.575	.654959	.775	1.032725	.975	2.184719
.180	.181982	.380	.400059	.580	.662461	.780	1.045368	.980	2.297555
.185	.187155	.385	.405916	.585	.670029	.785	1.058265	.985	2.442657
.190	.192337	.390	.411799	.590	.677665	.790	1.071429	.990	2.646647
.195	.197529	.395	.417710	.595	.685370	.795	1.084873	.995	2.994474

[1] Taken from E. F. Lindquist, Statistical Analysis in Educational Research, Boston, Houghton Mifflin, 1940.

Index

Absolute value, 109
  of deviations from mean, 109
  of deviations from median, 110
Accuracy of prediction, 479–486
Addition law for mutually exclusive events, 384
Aggregate proximity
  and fitting prediction lines, 469–471
  and median, 94–95
American Institute of Public Opinion, 210
Anastasi, A., 174
Area
  and binomial distribution, 200–201
  and normal distribution, 183, 185, 190–198
  and probability distribution, 156, 176–179
  and t-distribution, 339
  see also Extreme area
Arithmetic mean. *See* Mean, arithmetic
Average deviation, 109–110
Averages. *See* Location indexes
Axes
  of histogram, 27–28
  and ogive, 55–56
  of relative frequency distribution, 41
  and scatter diagram, 415

Bakan, D., 313
Bayesian inference
  and Bayes theorem, 386–390, 402–406
  and beta distribution, 391–406
  and binomial distribution, 402–406
  and classical inference, 377–378
  and expected loss, 406–407
  and interpretation of probability in, 377–378, 379–382
  and posterior probabilities, 385, 405–407
  need for prior information in, 378, 399–401
  and prior probabilities, 385, 399–401
  need for probability statements about parameters in, 377–378
  see also Bayesian statistics
Bayesian statistics
  contrasted with Fisherian statistics, 377–378
  contrasted with Neyman-Pearson statistics, 377–378
  see also Bayesian inference
Bayes theorem
  use in Bayesian inference, 402–404
  for continuous random variables, 389–390, 402–404
  for events, 386–388
Beta-binomial analysis, 406
Beta probability distributions
  credibility intervals for, 396–399
  defined, 393
  parameters of, 393

  use as a posterior probability model, 403–405
  use as a prior probability model, 399–401
  table of highest density regions, 399
  table of percentile points, 394–395
Betting odds, 379–380
Bias in sampling, 122, 217–218, 220–221
  defined, 217–218
  and sampling error, 217
  see also Unbiased estimates
Bimodal distributions, 31–32, 86
Binomial experiment
  characteristics of, 164–165
  rule for assigning probability values to outcomes of, 165
Binomial probability distribution
  approximation of, by normal probability distribution, 198–203
  rule for assigning probability values to outcomes from a binomial experiment, 165
  and Bayesian inference, 402–404
  defined, 165
  derivation of probability rule, 170–172
  mean of, 172
  tables for, 169
  and testing hypotheses about a population proportion, 364–371
  variance of, 172
Bivariate frequency distribution, 421–423
  defined, 421
  grouped, 423
  marginal distributions in, 422
  and scatter plots, 421
  see also Normal bivariate model
Bracht, G. H., 208
Bradley, J., 358
Brown, B., 461

Cahalan, J. D., 220
Centiles, 52
Central-limit theorem, 227
Central tendency, indexes of. *See* Location indexes
Christ, D. E., xviii, 358, 398, 559
Class interval, midpoint of, 26–27
Class interval, size of. *See* Class selection in frequency distributions
Class limits
  and continuous and discrete data, 25–27
  and integral limits, 26
  and measurement to last unit, 26
  and measurement to nearest unit, 25–26
  and midpoint or index value, 26
  and real limits, 26
Class selection in frequency distributions, 24–25, 32–39
  and computation of statistical indexes, 32, 72